Linux Programming Tools Unveiled

Linux Programming Tools Unveiled

Edited by :

N. B. Venkateswarlu, Ph.D

Director, RITCH CENTER
GVP College of Engineering
Visakhapatnam
&
Visiting Professor
GIET, Gunupur, Orissa
Email: venkat_ritch@yahoo.com
Web Site:www.ritchcenter.com

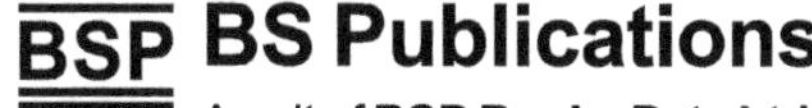

BS Publications
A unit of **BSP Books Pvt., Ltd.**

4-4-309, Giriraj Lane, Sultan Bazar,
Hyderabad - 500 095
Phone : 040 - 23445605, 23445688

Published by

A unit of **BSP Books Pvt., Ltd.**

4-4-309, Giriraj Lane, Sultan Bazar,
Hyderabad - 500 095
Phone : 040 - 23445605, 23445688
e-mail : info@bspbooks.net

ISBN : 978-93-52300-20-4 (HB)

Dedicated to

Dr. A.P.J. Abdul Kalam, (1931-2015)
Former President of India
who fostered the Free/Open SW
activity in Indian subcontinent

Sri Venkateswara University

Tirupati - 517 502, Andhra Pradesh, India

Prof. Dr. S. Jayarama Reddy
Ph.D
Vice Chancellor

Foreword

It gives me immense pleasure to be associated with the publication of this book titled "LINUX Programming Tools Unveiled' which explores the collaborative spirit of Free Open Source Software Movement (FOSS) and especially the important facets of Linux Operating System with Computer Science point of view.

The author gave nice outline of the FOSS movement along with Linux success stories in SW industry. Industry needed aspects such as mixed/hybrid programming is described in an illustrative manner with examples such as combining C and C++, C and Java and C and FORTRAN. Also, how command line arguments can be handled by C/C++ programs, how environment can be managed, how system limits can be used to improve a program performance etc., are dealt in a lucid manner. How assembly programming can be done under Linux, how to mix C and assembly is discussed in detail. Most important aspects of the book is that the author gave a practical example to write a bare boot (OS) program creation from the scratch.

How static and dynamic libraries are developed and commissioned in Linux is explained. Memory management, memory errors, Linux memory management, etc., are described with good illustrative examples. A popularly used tool for detecting memory errors, Valgrind and Electric Fence, are explained with concept oriented examples. The chapter on gcov and gprof explains about profiling of a C program to improve its performance. Chapters on make, rcs, SW tools explain how they can be used for SW development in practice.

I strongly feel that almost 500 ready to run programming examples is the main attraction in this book.

I found that this book will be very useful for Computer Science undergraduate courses such as Operating Systems, Language Processors, and systems programming. This book will also very much useful for practicing SW Engineers related to device drivers, embedded systems. I am certain that this would serve as an excellent textbook for introducing FOSS courses in the Engineering Eduction Programmes in India as well as elsewhere.

I shall congratulate the author who incidentally happens to be our alumnus. I wish him to bring many more books and contribute to scientific development in India.

S. JAYARAMA REDDY

Preface

Since early 1970, Unix operating system has gone through many metamorphosis. As of now many variants of Unix systems are available and some of them are commercial and where as the others are freely available. In the recent years, Linux, a public domain, freely available Unix variant has attracted the people very much. Till today, Unix is believed to be bread and butter of Computer Science intern's. However, because of this freely available Unix variant, many people are becoming Unix enthusiasts especially in India.

Hundreds of books had been written in the past, which explores various facets of Unix such as user commands, shell programming, Unix internals, device drivers, and kernel development. This book is an attempt to explain SW development tools in a lucid and problem oriented manner. The examples, which are discussed, are raised from the author's lectures at RITCH center and also from the suggestions (answers) made by thousands of Linux enthusiasts in USENET groups on Linux and personnel web pages of many Linux enthusiasts.

This book assumes that the reader has good exposure to theoretical aspects of operating systems design, C programming, data structures and good hands on experience in Unix/Linux environment.

Today's complex production environments demands superior application performance. Linux is having extraordinary advantages such as: complete source code access, availability of exceptional optimization, testing tools (of course that are scattered across the Internet and poorly documented). Only few experts know how to use them together to solve real problems. This book is aimed at bringing up more number of experts to meet ever increasing demand of system SW testing.

First chapter starts with Linux success stories and explains about general aspects of Operating Systems to Linux specific. It explores about the facilities and tools available in Linux for SW development.

Second chapter explains about gcc (GNU) toolchain in detail. The step by step illustrative examples make the reader to get practical exposure to assembler, pre-processor, and linker. Also, it deals with how really a C program is executed, how Linux OS is involved, shell is involved. How to combine C and C++, C and Java, and C and Fortran also described in a lucid manner.

Third chapter deals with how command line arguments can be handled by C/C++ programs. How getopt library, argp library can be used to design command line interface is discussed. Fourth chapter discusses about environment variables and their management. Also, how they can be manipulated from a C program is emphasized. System limits are explored in fifth chapter. How to set a resource's system limits from shell and from a C program is emphasized. Moreover, what is the implication of resource limits on programs is explained with easy examples.

Sixth chapter explains about how assembly programming can be done under Linux. Both AT&T and Intel style assembly coding is explained with elementary examples. How to mix C and assembly is discussed in detail. Also, how system calls can be called from assembly, how modules can be developed in assembly are high-lighted. A bare boot (OS) program creation is discussed at the end.

In seventh chapter how static and dynamic libraries are developed and commissioned in Linux is explained in a step by step fashion. How Libtool can be used for library development is discussed at the end. Eighth chapter deals with Lex/Yacc tools which are essential for a Computer Science intern to engage in compiler development. This chapter explains the concepts of lex and yacc specification files in detail. Almost, fifty lucid examples are given to make a novice to be comfortable with Lex and Yacc.

Memory management, memory errors, Linux memory management, etc., are described in ninth chapter with illustrative examples. A popularly used tool for detecting memory errors, Electric Fence, is explained with concept oriented examples. Tenth chapter describes memory mapping of files. It emphasizes the need for memory mapping; especially for large files and the impact on program's performance.

Gnu debugger (gdb) is detailed in chapter 11 with numerous concept oriented examples. How a C programs can be debugged is explained in a step by step fashion. Setting break points, watch points etc are explained. How to observe the contents of processor registers, stack contents, variable values are explained in a easy manner. The chapters on gcov and gprof explains about profiling of a C program to improve its performance.

A chapter on Valgrind is another main attraction with this book. How memory can be checked for memory leaks, segment violations etc., is described with numerous examples. Also, how the same can be used to analyze the cache performance is dealt in an illustrative manner.

Chapters on make, rcs, SW tools explains about how they can be used for SW development in practice. The examples used in them makes the reader to comfortably transform to a practicing SW professional.

- Author

Acknowledgments

There are many people, to whom I profoundly indebted while bringing out this book. Especially, those thousands of Linux enthusiasts, who actively participate in mailing lists, USENET groups are the ones who should be thanked by me first.

I shall also thank my wife Dr. Sarada and the little Appu, my daughter for bearing me while preparing this manuscript and sacrificing their marvelous Sunday evenings also.

I would like to express my sincere thanks to Prof BR Gandhi, Prof P Soma Raju, Secretary, and the Computer Science & IT Departments staff and students of GVP Engg College, Visakhapatnam. Also, I shall express my sincere thanks to staff and students of RITCH center, Visakhapatnam.

Prof PSVSK Raju, KLC, Vijayawada, Prof N Patel, BIT Ranchi, Dr. MN Reddy, APPU, Hyderabad deserves to recollect them for their consistent and constant encouragement. Also, I am very grateful to Dr. S.P. Panda, Chairman, Dr. C.D. Panda, Secretary, Mr. Rao, AO, Mr. Govindarajulu, Mr. Prasad of GIET, Gunupr. The encouragement given by Dr Surya Rao, Director, Mrs. Jaya S Rao, Director, Prof Jena of Roland Institute of Technology is very much appreciated.

Lastly, I would like to express my thanks to the publisher Mr. Nikhil Shah for bringing this book.

- Author

Contents

4. Environment

5. System Limits

6. Assembly in Linux

7. Libraries

8. Lex & Yacc

9. Unix Memory Management

10. Memory Mapped Files

11. GNU DEBUGGER

12. GCOV: A coverage Testing Tool

13. PROFILING

14. Valgrind and Alleyoop

1 Programmers View of Linux

"First, they ignore you.
Then they laugh at you.
Then they fight you.
Then you win."

The above quotation by Mahatma Gandhi best suits to none other than Linux. Initially, Linux is conceived as a hobby and a tool for learning Intel[1] 80386 microprocessor and was smuggled into organizations through the back door by rebellious engineers, as their bosses are ignoring the Linux. As the young SW engineers fiddling with Linux and spoiling their marvelous nights their bosses continued to laugh at them. Now, Linux has grown into a multi-billion dollar wave that is sweeping the server, ERP and IT markets. In fact, in a Giga Information Group report on Linux, analysts Stacey Quandt and Bob Zimmerman estimate that Linux distribution providers accounted for a US$2.5 billion market in 2002, based on server revenues.

It all started when **Linus Torvalds**, a student at the University of Helsinki, created the first version of Linux almost 14 years ago in August 1991. Released as open-source software under the Free Software Foundation's GNU General Public License (GPL), it quickly grew into a complete operating-system package, with the contributions of hundreds of programmers. Since 1994, when version 1.0 was released, organizations have been able to download free copies or purchase commercial distributions from companies such as **Slackware**, **Red Hat.** Some of these Linux suppliers also provide consulting services, and maintenance.

Many people raise a question about Linux "if it's released under the Free Software Foundation's GPL, shouldn't it be free?". In a word, **no**. Any company can charge money for products that include Linux, as long as the source code remains available. The GPL allows people to distribute (and charge for) their own versions of free software. In fact, according to the Free Software Foundation, the "free" in free software refers to ***liberty*, *not price***. In the foundation's definition, free software provides organizations the freedom to run software for any purpose, study how it works, modify it, and improve or re-release it.

Another common misconception about Linux is that it's a complete operating system. In reality Linux refers to the " kernel or core " of the operating system. Combining Linux with a set of open-source GNU programs from the Free Software Foundation turns it into what most people know as Linux forming both the full operating system and the core of most Linux distributions. Distributions are the versions of Linux, GNU programs, and other tools that are offered by different companies, organizations, or individuals. Popular distributions include **Red Hat, United Linux, SuSE, Caldera**, and others. Each distribution might be based on a different version of the Linux kernel, but all migrate forward over time, picking up core changes that are made to the kernel and keeping everything in synchronous (in some what loosely).

[1] Intel Corporation

Eric S. Raymond's famous essay, "The Cathedral and the Bazaar" argues that most commercial software is built like cathedrals by small groups of artisans working in isolation. Open-source software, like Linux, is developed collectively over the Internet, which serves as an electronic bazaar for innovative ideas. "It's subversive," says Raymond of open-source software, "because it takes all of the thirty-year verities that we understand about software engineering and stands them upon their head."

The first of the two programming styles is closed source - the traditional factory-production model of proprietary software, in which customers get a sealed block of computer binary bits that they cannot examine, modify, or evolve. Microsoft is the most famous practitioner of this approach. The other style is open-source, the Internet engineering tradition in which software source code is generally available for inspection, independent peer review, and rapid evolution. The standard-bearer of this approach is the Linux operating environment.

With Linux, new changes come through an open development model, meaning that all new versions are available to the public, regardless of their quality. Linux's versioning scheme is designed to let users understand whether they're using a stable version or a development version. Even decimal-numbered releases [such as 2.0, 2.2, and 2.4] are considered stable versions, while odd-numbered releases [such as 2.3 and 2.5] are beta-quality releases intended for developers only.

1.1 A Glance At Success Stories of Linux

For much of the 1990s, Linux was primarily an experiment "something that developers fiddled with and used on local servers to see how well it worked and how secure it was". Then, with the Internet boom of the late 1990s, many companies started using Linux for their Web servers, fueling the first wave of corporate Linux adoption. In fact, by 2002, Linux servers represented 30 percent of the Web server market. But even as Linux achieved greater penetration in the Web server market, something else was needed in order for it to reach the next level for organizations to start using it for enterprise application servers, database servers, and application servers. Many break through's took place during the last 10 years which made Linux as an attractive competitor for many commercial OS's.

Oracle Goes Linux

"We'll be running our whole business on Linux" stated Larry Ellison[2] in June 2002. What might have been a hollow statement if said by some CEOs, Ellison's stake-in-the-ground pronouncement for Linux has turned into a corporate wide crusade. In fact, Oracle's commitment to Linux in the enterprise entails migrating many of its key internal and external systems to Linux, including Oracle.com, Oracle Files Online, Oracle Outsourcing, Oracle Financials, and more. For example, Oracle Files Online is a huge internal file-sharing system "with more than 12.5 million documents" built on top of Oracle Database. It s 4TB of data is used by more than 40,000 employees, and the entire system runs on Linux.

Although Oracle can't support all the hundreds of Linux distributions, it does support a variety from around the world, including selected Red Hat and UnitedLinux versions from Conectiva, SCO, SuSE, and TurboLinux. "It's very important that we make sure our open-source contributions are focused," says Enright. "We work with Red Hat and the UnitedLinux distributors and make open-source contributions into their threads, which are then combined in the Linux Common Kernel and redistributed to all the Linux providers."

---

[2] CEO, Oracle Inc

TV Voting

Linux servers at Mobliss, Inc., (USA) powered the cell phone "voting for American Idol" the first major wireless interactive TV voting ever seen in the U.S. For Mobliss, the choice to use Linux was an easy one to make. "Linux has a proven track record of driving some of the most highly trafficked sites on the internet," says Brian Hill, chief operating officer at Seattle-based Mobliss. The bottom line is that it gives us the ability to deploy high-powered services very inexpensively with all the features and software that we need to be in the position to set the pace in our industry.

Linux Network Cluster Used to Investigate Iceland's Weather and Geothermal Energy Sources

The Icelandic Energy Authority (IEA) in conjunction with Iceland's Institute for Meteorological Research (IMR) needed a supercomputing solution that could produce 3D simulations of geothermal reservoirs and weather events. The IEA and IMR were limited in the types of problems they could solve unless a powerful, cost-effective computing solution was found. After investigating several supercomputing options, the Icelandic agencies decided to deploy a Linux Network cluster solution because of its powerful computing capabilities, significant price to performance ratio, and ICE cluster management tools for ease of use and improved system reliability. With its new supercomputing solution in place, the IEA and IMR can complete 3D simulations and make important decisions concerning Iceland's energy resources and weather predictions that were not previously possible.

Olafur RÃgnvaldsson, CEO, Institute for Meteorological Research quotes that "A powerful supercomputing solution was needed that could produce high-quality simulations quickly, be easy-to-manage and cost effective. Compared to more traditional supercomputers, the price-to-performance ratio of Linux Network clusters is unbeatable and the performance increase allows us to complete simulations and make important decisions that were previously impossible."

Online Wind Speed Monitoring System (United Kingdom)

Brighton based electronics supplier Amplicon has been actively supporting and contributing to one of the city's latest projects in its collaboration with Piertopier, an experimental project team that provides wireless Internet access on Brighton beach. Users can connect to the Internet free of charge, when in the range of any of the nodes on the seafront.

Amplicon donated weather monitoring equipment for real time wind speed and direction logging in the form of a wind sensor and the NPort 4511 programmable communication gateway starter kit, which allows systems to be controlled without the use of a PC. NPort 4511 is a very flexible, cost effective device with greater reliability than a typical PC. It can monitor and control serial instruments independently, as well as perform front-end data processing functions such as serial device addressing, data trimming, data tagging, encryption, and character case conversion.

An SNMP agent, which constantly listens for queries, is also used as part of this particular application, allowing information to be retrieved from the NPort 4511 device via its Ethernet port. Piertopier's web server is running software that can produce graphs, and every 5 minutes it sends an SNMP query to the Ethernet port on NPort 4511 to request wind direction, speed, and gust readings. The query makes its way over the Internet to Piertopier node 1, and then to NPort 4511 via the wireless link between nodes 1 and 2. NPort 4511 sends back a reply, and then the process is repeated.

After receiving the SNMP reply, the software updates the graphs, which are then made available on the Piertopier web server.

In addition, an XML feed is produced which can be downloaded by any user. Water/wind sports enthusiasts, such as wind surfers, sailing club members, and others who are part of Brighton's sports community, find this information invaluable, as it directly impacts on their daily leisure activities.

David Evans, Amplicon's Data Communications Product Manager commented that "Amplicon is always very keen to help out in the local community, and especially where a project can benefit from our area of expertise. We are pleased to have collaborated with Piertopier and hope to see Brighton's wireless network expand over the coming months."

Linux in Hollywood

It may not be getting as much hoopla as **Spiderman** or the latest Star Wars flick, but Linux is making a dramatic entrance this summer in movie theaters across the country. The animated film "**Spirit, Stallion of the Cimarron**," released recently, marks a milestone in movie making: It is the first movie created entirely on Linux systems.

It won't be the last, either. Recent announcement that the Walt Disney Company will be shifting to the Linux platform for their movie-making is just the latest in a long line of Linux success stories in Hollywood.

The digital animation industry has been experimenting with Linux for several years–parts of the 1997 film **Titanic**, for example, were done on Linux. But now, Hollywood's animation studios are in the midst of a wholesale migration to the open source operating system. At Dreamworks Animation, the studio responsible for Spirit, as well as films like Shrek and Antz, almost all film production work is now done on Linux. The move has slashed the company's computing infrastructure costs in half.

Like most of the digital animation industry, Dreamwork has relied for years on high-powered graphics workstations from Silicon Graphics. Two years ago, with the lease coming up on its existing SGI machines, the company decided to switch to Linux on Intel. "We wanted to get faster machines to our animators," says Ed Leonard, Dreamwork's Head of Animation Technology. "And the performance of Intel-based systems was growing more quickly than that of proprietary hardware."

Dreamworks replaced $25,000 SGI systems with machines that cost well under $5,000, and provided more performance to boot. "We're getting machines that are four or five times faster at 20% of the cost," says Leonard. "That's pretty compelling."

The company's animators now do their work on more than 500 Linux workstations, primarily dual-processor Hewlett-Packard systems running Red Hat Linux. In Dreamwork's render farm, a similar number of rack mounted Linux servers are used to turn the single frame drawings created by the animators into lifelike movies.

While Dreamworks is further along the Linux path than most other Hollywood animation studios, the rest of the industry is not far behind. Linux is already being used to make movies at studios including Digital Domain, which used it to render some images of the ill-fated Titanic at Weta Digital.

The movement towards Linux among animation studios is nothing short of a "**tidal wave**," says Mike Balma, Linux Solutions Strategist at HP, which is making a major effort to supply the Linux systems to film industry. At least two major studios, Pixar and George Lucas' Industrial Light and Magic, are reported to be on the verge of major deployments of Linux.

Getting to this point, however, required an unprecedented level of cooperation among competing studios. Many studio executives were growing increasingly concerned about relying solely on one vendor, SGI, which dominated the high-end graphics industry. Their technical staff saw the advantages of being able to run Linux on inexpensive commodity hardware, and wanted the flexibility that access to the operating system's source code allowed. But while some of the studios internally produced packages, such as Pixar's PRMan image renderer, ran on Linux, much of the key third-party software required to produce animated films didn't.

That changed with a summer 2000 meeting of the Visual Effects Society, the industry group for the film animation industry. Dubbed the "VES Linux Summit," the studios used the occasion to make the case for Linux to their software vendors. Software producers such as Alias Wavefront, of Toronto, Canada, paid attention. Shortly after the meeting, Alias Wavefront announced a Linux port of Maya, its well-known special effects package. "Customer demand for a Linux version of Maya has driven this development," said Bob Bennett, General Manager of the Entertainment Business Unit for Alias Wavefront. Today, there are Linux versions of most of the industry's key software packages.

Support for the new systems was also a concern for studio executives. When Dreamworks bought its systems from SGI, says Leonard, "We had one company supplying an integrated system: CPU, graphics cards, operating system and software. Now that those pieces come from different places, trying to synchronize them can be a challenge."

Dreamworks tackled this by signing a support contract with HP, which is also supplying many of its machines. But not running proprietary hardware also gives the studio flexibility. "Since these are commodity components," says Leonard, "if a computer breaks, we can just go to Fry's[3] and pick up the parts we need."

Other film studios have been impressed with the techie-to-techie help available online from other Linux users. "The quality of technical support in the Linux community," says Steve Rosenbluth, control systems designer at Jim Henson's Creature Shop studio, "is equal to or better than the technical support from commercial companies."

New South Wales OSR

As CIO for the New South Wales Office of State Revenue (OSR), Mike Kennedy is responsible for the IT systems that monitor and collect taxes, for example on regulated transactions such as land purchases, security and stock sales, and duties on goods sold.

Over the past three years the OSR has been able to automate 30 percent of its business duties by using Oracle9i Application Server (running on Linux) for its e-commerce implementation. The OSR has also lowered its cost for collecting money to less than 6 cents per AUS$100, which is the most efficient of all state offices. Transaction times have also been cut to less than 10 seconds for approximately 96 percent of its transactions.

Perhaps it's the heady feeling of handling all that money that makes one bold, but when the OSR decided to migrate to Linux, it didn't waste any time doing departmental or pilot applications. "We went straight in for a core business application that's critical to our business "e-commerce" and now Oracle9iAS is supporting the system that collects AUS$11 billion," says Kennedy. "We're not just stomping around on the edges." With the new system, e-commerce transactions have gone from zero to 30 percent in two years and have doubled in the last six months. Originally OSR was running its Oracle8i

[3] Electronic's of San Jose, California,USA.

database and some PHP on Linux, and then about two years ago it installed the Oracle9i Application Server running on Linux along with J2EE programs and XML e-commerce connections. It's all been remarkably stable. "We've been running all that Web infrastructure very successfully," says Kennedy. "**We run five operating systems" everything from Linux to NT to Solaris to NetWare" and Linux has probably been more stable than the other four**." And, OSR is currently implementing Oracle9i RAC on Red Hat Linux to further improve the reliability of its services.

Not only has moving to Linux dramatically cut the OSR's processing time and cost, but it's also a considerably cheaper platform than traditional alternatives. "The capital cost savings are significant. The big capital item is the hardware itself, and the ability to buy Dell boxes or any old Intel boxes compared to buying high-end UNIX boxes is the real benefit," says Kennedy. "They're basically about a quarter of the price."

Hays Medical Center

You might not expect doctors to be the target market for Linux, but Hays Medical Center (HMC), in Hays, Kansas, does. That's because HMC has recently migrated a series of applications from its AS/400, Lotus Notes, and Windows systems to a variety of Oracle products running on Linux servers. "We want the system to be an integral part of everyone's daily life," says Alan Wamser, a systems analyst at HMC. "That's how they will do business through our Oracle Portal, including calendar, e-mail, scheduling, and many HR applications." Overall, approximately 1,000 people" everyone from doctors to maintenance staff" will be using the portal. Although implementation is still in process, HMC deployed its Web site and the Oracle database on Linux in January and is currently migrating its Lotus Notes applications to Oracle Collaboration Suite.

By using Oracle's Collaboration Suite; Oracle9i Database; Oracle9iAS; and, in the future, Oracle9i RAC (all running on Linux), HMC is able to meet the hospital's needs for information sharing, internal communications, and healthcare patient-information support without having to spend additional money on legacy systems and managing multiple platforms. Its previous IT architecture had a variety of systems and operating systems: Web applications running on Lotus Notes, NT servers doing ASP, and more. "One of our goals was to consolidate this into one platform and one architecture so we didn't have to manage multiple development environments and maintain different types of systems," says Wamser.

HMC needed a system that would be very scalable and reliable. Being a core system in a healthcare environment means no downtime. "With Red Hat and Oracle's initiative with Unbreakable Linux and its scalability, we don't have to purchase more expensive hardware," says Wamser. "We can just plug in more boxes with Oracle9i RAC. Because of Oracle's clustering technology, it made a great deal of sense to us that Linux was probably the way to go for scalability."

To start off its migration, HMC replaced some of the DNS servers around the hospital with Linux, adding more Linux servers as they went along. To take the next step, though, HMC needs to work with the CFO to justify all the costs and compare them to HMC's existing RS6000 systems and Lotus Notes system on the AS/400. For example, the difference in yearly maintenance costs on an RS6000 or AS/400 versus an enterprise Linux box is considerable. "Part of the justification we've made is that Intel is cheaper than our existing systems. But we also needed high availability, which is why we felt that Linux, rather than NT, was the way to go," says Wamser.

Golden Gate University

Like many organizations migrating to Linux, the differential in the cost of hardware was an important factor for Golden Gate University (GGU), in San Francisco. The 100-year-old accredited university specializes in business and law education for professionals who live remotely or attend school part-time. When it came time to develop a new intranet to support GGU's 1,000 faculty distributed throughout the U.S., money caused the university to seriously consider migrating to Linux. "The total cost of acquisition and support and everything else was about 30 to 40 percent lower with Linux on Dell than it was for used high-end UNIX boxes," says Sanjeev Mohan, enterprise database architect at GGU. "Comparing Dell and Linux to top-of-the-line UNIX boxes, it was closer to 60 percent cheaper for the Dell hardware."

Originally, GGU's applications were running on Sun boxes. But, as Mohan's team evaluated technology needs going forward and looked at what it needed to support application growth and data-center needs, it decided to start testing existing applications on Red Hat Linux on Dell hardware. "From that point forward, we came to the realization that the cost of deploying Dell and Red Hat Linux was significantly lower than running the similar configurations on Sun," says Keith Rajecki, GGU's IT infrastructure manager.

The decision to move forward with Linux took time, though. After considering it on and off for a year, it was Oracle's announcement of Unbreakable Linux that clinched the decision. "When Red Hat and Dell came out with their partnership where they provided integrated support for Linux on the Dell platform, and then when Oracle joined Red Hat and Dell and provided three-way integrated support servers and certified all of its Oracle9i products on Linux, that's really the industry support we were looking for to move ahead with it," says Anthony Hill, GGU's CTO. The university is now running Oracle9i Database on a highly available Linux cluster, as well as Oracle E-Business Suite 11i and the Oracle9i technology stack on Linux servers.

Although GGU could have used Oracle9i RAC or advanced replication in order to ensure high availability, GGU decided that a logical Data Guard would be the best solution. It set up a primary database that the applications point to, as well as a logical database running on a second Linux server. In the case of failure of the primary database, GGU can switch or fail over to the standby database, with minimal downtime. GGU has configured Oracle Data Guard so that no data is lost. The whole system is monitored through Oracle Enterprise Manager, which can page people on a cell phone in the case of an error.

Although the current Oracle on Linux systems support GGU's intranet, the university is also actively building a new Web site with Oracle and Linux that will support between 50,000 and 100,000 registered users. Based on GGU's experience, Oracle on Linux is a solid and reliable choice. "Compared to Oracle9 on Windows, our Oracle on Linux implementation is much more reliable," says Mohan. "We've closely monitored things such as block corruption, and hardware failure, and find that the combination of Dell hardware and Red Hat Linux makes Oracle very reliable" which is a major testament to the ability of the platform."

IBM Initiatives

In the recent years, support of IBM in Linux related HW/SW are note worthy. Some of them includes:

Linux on eServer

Linux on Mainframes

Linux on personal systems

Linux on POWER PC

Linux on TotalStorage

Linux on workstation

Indian Ventures

In the recent years, many Indian MNC giants such as Wipro, TCS, InfoSys shifted their preferences to Linux. LIC has its operations functioning on Oracle under Linux. A popular technological university, JNTU, Hyderabad, A.P with almost 250 Technical colleges under it started on-line testing using Linux and MySQL.

1.2 So What Makes Linux So Popular?

Here are a few of the reasons - though obviously every Linux user will have his/her own reasons.

It's Free

Linux is free. Really and truly free. We can browse to any of the distributors of Linux (there's a list at the end of this document), find the "download" link and download a complete copy of the entire operating system plus extra software without paying a cent. We can also buy a boxed version of course. For a few dollars you get the CDs, manuals etc delivered to our door, plus telephone or online support. By comparison, "home" versions of Windows are priced at around $200.

With Linux we also don't have to worry about paying again every time we upgrade the operating system - the upgrades are obviously free too. Again, with Windows we can expect to pay close to $100 every time a new version of the operating system is released if we want to keep up to date.

Finally, due to the way that Linux's license is written up, it guarantees that Linux always will remain free.

It's Open Source

This means two things: First, that your CDs (or the download site) contain an entire copy of the source code for Linux. Secondly, we may legally make modifications to improve it.

While this might not mean much to people who are not programmers, it makes a vital difference: There are thousands of people who possess the source code and are capable of improving the code or fixing any problem which may be noticed, sometimes within hours of it first being reported. When such a problem is found, it is sent off to the coordinating team in charge of the module in question, who will update the software and issue a patch. ***What all this boils down to is that bugs in Linux get fixed much faster than any other operating system.***

It's Modular

When we install Windows, we install one large operating system as a complete unit. We cannot, for example, install Windows without its Graphical User Interface, or without its printing support. We install everything or nothing.

Linux, on the other hand, is a very modular operating system. We can install or run exactly the bits and pieces of Linux that we want. In most cases we will choose one of the predefined setups from the installation menu, but we are not forced to. In some cases this makes a lot of sense. For example, if we are setting up a server, we might want to disable the graphical user interface once it is set up correctly, thus freeing up memory and the processor for the more important task at hand.

It also allows us to upgrade parts of the operating system without affecting the rest. For example, we might want to get the latest version of Gnome or KDE without changing the kernel.

More Choice's

Also due to its modularity, we get more choice of components to use. One example is the user interface. Many people choose KDE, which is very easy for Windows users to learn. Others choose Gnome, which is more powerful but less similar to Windows. There are also several simple alternatives for less-powerful computers, which make less demands on the hardware available.

Portable

Linux runs on practically every piece of equipment which qualifies as a computer. We can run Linux on huge multiprocessor servers or a PDA. Apart from Pentiums of various flavors, there are versions of Linux (called "ports") on Atari, Amiga, Macintosh, PowerMac, PowerPC, NeXT, Alpha, Motorola, MIPS, HP, PowerPC, Sun Sparc, Silicon Graphics, VAX/MicroVax, VME, Psion 5, Sun UltraSparc.... the list is endless.

In fact, Sony is currently experimenting with a port of Linux for its Playstation 2, while another guy apparently started a project to port it to Nintendo-64. At **Sandia computer labs, US**: On the left is a wrist watch developed by IBM. On the right is one of the corridors within the CPLANT supercomputer at Sandia National Labs in the US. Nice thing is that they're both running Linux!!!!.

Lots of Extras

When we get your Linux CD we normally get quite a lot of software thrown in which is not usually included with operating systems. Using only the applications that come with Linux, we can set up a full web, ftp, database and email server for example. We have a firewall built into the kernel of the operating system, one or more office suites, graphics programs (powerful ones that is), music players, and lots more. Different distributions of Linux offer different "extra programs". Slackware, for example, is quite simple (though it still provides all the commonly needed programs), while SuSE Linux comes with seven CDs and a DVD-ROM!

Stability

All applications can crash, but in Windows any one of those can bring down the entire operating system - our only recourse could be to switch off (and with some new "soft-switch" PCs, even that doesn't work - we have to pull out the power cable). Ofcourse, Windows NT is much more stable but costs more than Win9x.

In comparison, Linux is rock-solid. Every application runs independently of all others - if one crashes, it crashes alone. Most Linux servers run for months on end, never shutting down or rebooting. Even the GUI is independent of the kernel of the operating system.

A system crash under Linux is so rare that someone created a screensaver made out of crash-screens from other operating systems, just to show Linux users what they look like!!.

Networking

The networking facilities offered by Linux are positively awe-inspiring. Any box with a modem can browse the web, but with Linux (as with most Unix's), that's child's play. We can use terminal sessions, secure shells, share drives from across the world, run a wide variety of servers and much more.

We can, for example, connect XWindows to another Linux PC across a network. If we have more than one computer, we don't have to physically use the screen, keyboard and mouse connected to each computer - from any computer we can connect to any other computer, running applications etc. as if they were on our own PC. Many people use this facility very frequently at work if they have several Linux servers in different parts of the building.

We can have dual or triple OS's on a PC

Very often, new Linux enthusiasts will have the following queries.

Do I have to remove Windows to try Linux?

No. We can install Linux on a computer which already has Windows running, and keep them both. We can then select which one of them to load every time you switch on.

Can Linux and Windows read each others' files?

Yes. Linux can read Windows' files - it supports the FAT and FAT32 file system's, and sometimes NTFS, so it's quite easy to transfer files from one operating system to the other. The opposite, however, is not possible.

Can I use Microsoft Office (or other Windows Applications) in Linux?

No. Linux is a totally different operating system. Generally, Windows applications cannot run under Linux. Actually there is a module called WINE which allows us to run various small Windows programs in Linux, but MS-Office is beyond its abilities. However there are alternatives under Linux for most Windows applications. For an office suite, we have the choice of StarOffice (which can read and write MS-Office files), KOffice, GnomeOffice, WordPerfect Office, etc.

Can Windows and Linux machines interact via network?

Definitely. We can use SAMBA to share files or connect to shared directories or printers. With SAMBA we can set up our Linux computer to function as a full NT server - complete with authentication, file/printer sharing and so on. Apart from that, Linux comes with excellent FTP, Web and similar services which are accessible to all computers.

Linux Configuration Tool

LinuxConf is a popular utility which allows the configuration of most parts of Linux and its applications from one place.

Linux Distributions

Here are some of the more popular distributions of Linux. A more complete list can be found here.

- **Knoppix** **www.knoper.net**
- **Red Hat** **www.redhat.com**
- **SuSE** **www.suse.com**
- **Yoper** **ww.yoper.com**
- **MEPIS** **www.mepis.org**
- **Debian** **www.debian.org**
- **Slackware** **www.slackware.com**
- **TurboLinux** **www.turbolinux.com**

1.3 Salient Features of Linux

Here are some of the benefits and features that Linux provides over single-user operating systems (such as MS-DOS) and other versions of UNIX for the PC.

Full multitasking and 32-bit support: Linux, like all other versions of UNIX, is a real multitasking system, allowing multiple users to run many programs on the same system at once. The performance of a 50 MHz 486 system running Linux is comparable to many low- to medium-end workstations, such as those from Sun Microsystems and DEC, running proprietary versions of UNIX. Linux is also a full 32-bit operating system, utilizing the special protected-mode features of the Intel 80386 and 80486 processors.

GNU software support: Linux supports a wide range of free software written by the GNU Project, including utilities such as the GNU C and C++ compiler, gawk, groff, and so on. Many of the essential system utilities used by Linux are GNU software.

The X Window System: The X Window System is the de facto industry standard graphics system for UNIX machines. A free version of The X Window System (known as ``Xfree86") is available for Linux. The X Window System is a very powerful graphics interface, supporting many applications. For example, we can have multiple login sessions in different windows on the screen at once. Other examples of X Windows applications are Seyon, a powerful telecommunications program; Ghostscript, a PostScript language processor; and XTetris, an X Windows version of the popular game.

TCP/IP networking support: TCP/IP (``Transmission Control Protocol/Internet Protocol") is the set of protocols which links millions of university and business computers into a worldwide network known as the Internet. With an Ethernet connection, we can have access to the Internet or to a local area network from our Linux system. Or, using SLIP (``Serial Line Internet Protocol"), we can access the Internet over the phone lines with a modem.

Virtual memory and shared libraries: Linux can use a portion of our hard drive as virtual memory, expanding our total amount of available RAM. Linux also implements shared libraries, allowing programs which use standard subroutines to find the code for these subroutines in the libraries at runtime. This saves a large amount of space on our system, as each application doesn't store its own copy of these common routines.

1.4 Simple View of An Operating System: Linux an Example

An Operating System is the SW layer between the hardware and user as shown in the following Figure 1.1 and gives clean and easy interface to the user.

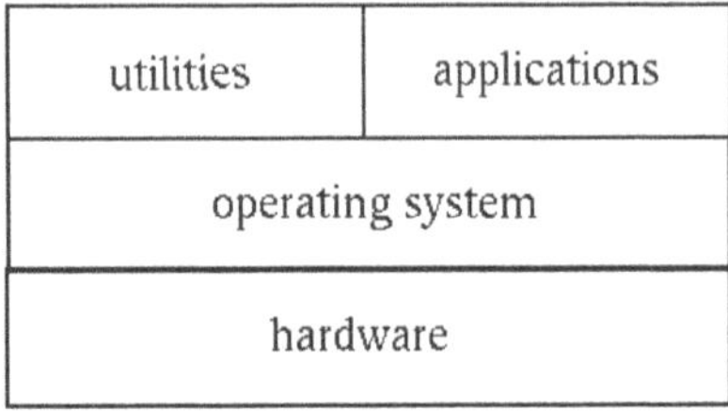

Figure 1.1 A Typical Operating System.

An Operating System is responsible for the following functions

- Device management using device drivers
- Process management using processes and threads
- Inter-process communication
- Memory management
- File systems

In addition, all operating systems come with a set of standard utilities. The utilities allow common tasks to be performed such as

- being able to start and stop processes
- being able to organize the set of available applications
- organize files into sets such as directories
- view files and sets of files
- edit files
- rename, copy, delete files
- communicate between processes

The Linux or Unix kernel looks like (Figure 1.2)

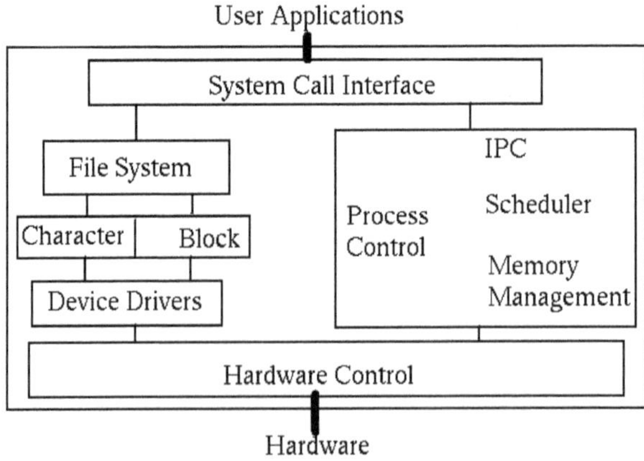

Figure 1.2 Unix Kernel.

Kernel

The *kernel* of an operating system is the part responsible for all other operations. When a computer boots up, it goes through some initialization functions, such as checking memory. It then loads the kernel and switches control to it. The kernel then starts up all the processes needed to communicate with the user and the rest of the environment (e.g. the LAN). The kernel is always loaded into memory, and kernel functions always run, handling processes, memory, files and devices. The traditional structure of a kernel is a *layered* system, such as Unix. In this, all layers are part of the kernel, and each layer can talk to only a few other layers. Application programs and utilities live above the kernel.

Most of the Operating Systems being built now use instead a *micro kernel*, which minimizes the size of the kernel. Many traditional services are made into user level services. Communication being services is often by an explicit *message passing* mechanism.

The major micro-kernel Operating System is Mach. Many others use the concepts of Mach (see Figure 1.3).

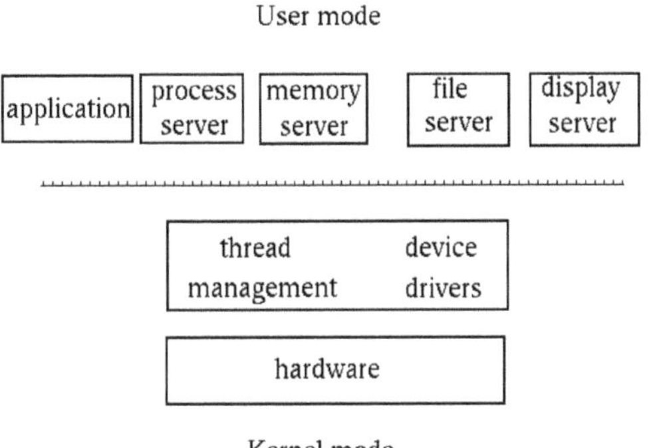

Figure 1.3 Micro Kernel Architecture.

Command Interpreter

When a user interacts with an Operating System they always do so through the intermediary of a command interpreter. This responds to user input in the following ways

- It starts applications
- It stops applications
- It allows the user to switch control between applications

It may allow control over communication between an application and other applications or the user

The command interpreter may be character-based, as in the MSDOS COMMAND.COM or the Unix shells. It may be a GUI shell, such as the Windows 3.1 Program Manager. The interpreter may be simple, or can have the power of a full programming language. It may be imperative (as in the Unix shells), use message passing (as in AppleScript) or use visual programming metaphors such as drag-and-drop for object embedding (as in Microsoft's OLE). It is important to distinguish between the command interpreter and the underlying Operating System. The command interpreter may only use a subset of the capabilities offered by the Operating System; it may offer them in a clumsy or sophisticated way; it may require complex skills or be intended for novices

1.5 The x86 Linux boot process

The most fundamental and obvious difference between x86 boards and systems based on PPC, ARM, and others is that the x86 board will ship with one or more layers of manufacturer-supplied "black box" firmware that helps you with power-on initialization and the task of loading the operating system out of secondary storage. This firmware takes the system from a cold start to a known, friendly software environment ready to run your operating system. Figure 1.4 is a diagram of the typical PC boot process, with considerably more detail than you tend to find in PC-centric literature:

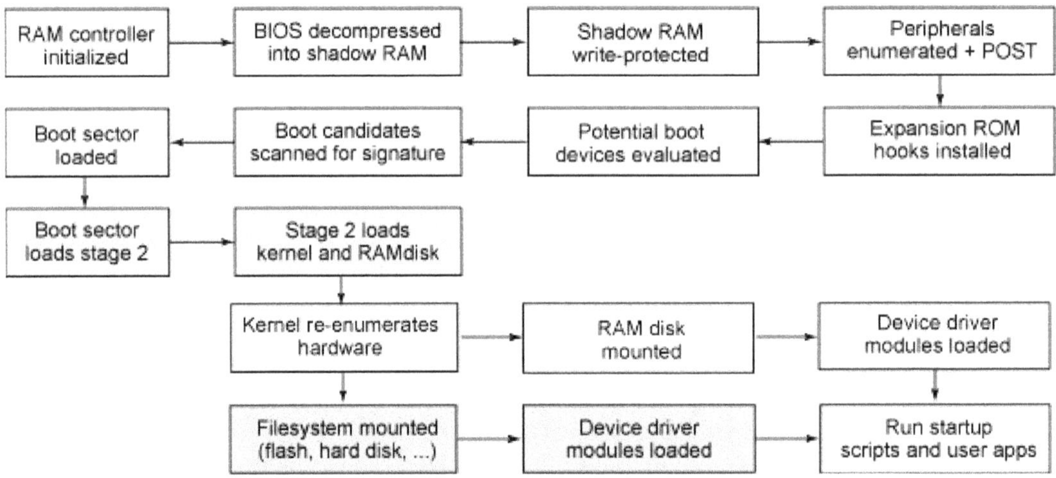

Figure 1.4 Typical start-up process for x86 Linux.

Typical start-up process for x86 Linux

For cost reasons, modern PC mainboard BIOS code is always stored compressed in flash. The only directly executable code in that chip is a tiny boot stub. Therefore, the first task on power-up is to initialize the mainboard chipset enough to get the DRAM controller working so that the main BIOS code can be decompressed out of flash into a mirror area in RAM, referred to as shadow RAM. This area is then write-protected and control is passed to the RAM-resident code. Shadow RAM is permanently stolen by the mainboard chipset; it cannot later be reclaimed by the operating system. For legacy reasons, special hardware mappings are set up so that the shadow RAM areas appear in the CPU's real-mode memory map at the locations where old operating systems like MS-DOS would expect to find them.

Keep in mind that the PC is an open architecture. This openness even extends down to firmware modules within the BIOS itself. Once the power-on initialization (POI) code has run, the next step it takes is to enumerate peripherals, and optionally install hooks provided by expansion ROMs in those peripherals. (Some of those expansion ROMs – for instance, the video BIOS in a system that has onboard integrated video hardware – will physically reside in the main BIOS image, but conceptually they are separate entities). The reasons the BIOS has to do this redundant initialization are:

1. The main BIOS itself needs basic console services to announce messages and allow the user to override default start-up behavior and configure system-specific parameters.
2. Historical issues limit the size of a user-supplied bootloader program to slightly less than 512 bytes. Since this isn't enough space to implement all the possible device drivers that might be required to access different displays and storage devices, it's necessary for the BIOS to install standardized software interfaces for all installed, recognized hardware that might be required by the bootloader.

Once all the BIOS-supported system peripherals are initialized, the main BIOS code will run through candidate boot devices (in accordance with a user-configurable preference list) looking for a magic signature word. Storage devices for IBM-compatible PCs have historically used a sector size of 512 bytes, and therefore the BIOS only loads the first 512 bytes from the selected boot device. The operating system's installation program is responsible for storing sufficient code in that zone to bootstrap the remainder of the IPL process.

Although it would be possible to write a minimalist Linux bootloader that would fit into such a space, practical Linux bootloaders for the PC consist of two stages: a small stub that lives in the boot sector, and a larger segment that lives somewhere else on the boot medium, usually inside the partition that contains the root file system. LILO and Grub are the best-known boot loaders for mainstream Linux installations, and SYSLINUX is a popular choice for embedded distributions.

Using a RAMdisk

The primary purpose of the boot loader is to load the operating system kernel from secondary storage into RAM. In a Linux system (x86 or otherwise), the boot loader can also optionally load an initial RAMdisk image. This is a small file system that resides entirely in RAM. It contains a minimal set of modules to get the operating system off the ground before mounting the primary root file system. The original design purpose for initial RAMdisk support in the kernel was to provide a means whereby numerous optional device drivers could be made available at boot time (potentially drivers that needed to be loaded before the root file system could be mounted).

We can get an idea of the original usage scenario for the RAMdisk by considering a bootable Linux installation CD-ROM. The disk needs to contain drivers for many different hardware types, so that it can boot properly on a wide variety of different systems. However, it's desirable to avoid building an enormous kernel with every single option statically linked (partly for memory space reasons, but also to a lesser degree because some drivers "fight" and shouldn't be loaded simultaneously). The solution to this problem is to link the bare minimum of drivers statically in the kernel, and to build all the remaining drivers as separately loadable modules, which are then placed in the RAMdisk. When the unknown target system is booted, the kernel (or start-up script) mounts the RAMdisk, probes the hardware, and loads only those modules appropriate for the system's current configuration.

We can compress the boot copy of the root file system, and there is no run time performance hit. Although it's possible to run directly out of a compressed file system, there's obviously an overhead every time your software needs to access that file system. Compressed file systems also have other annoyances, such as the inability to report free space accurately (since the estimated free space is a function of the anticipated compression ratio of whatever data we plan to write into that space).

1.6 Programming for Linux using GNU Tools[4]

Linux has a rich programming environment, all the more so due to its adoption of the entire GNU tool set. In this section we explain the complete GNU environment for beginning or intermediate programmers on Linux.

Some people say there is nothing but the GNU way to develop software. While there is a wide set of tools a typical Linux/UNIX software developer uses in his everyday work, the GNU development tools are a complete framework. It's absolutely free and powerful. There is no problem to see their source code. And it's not worse than any other commercial "killer-apps" widely used on other platforms. Newbie Linux programmers may be scared of new kinds of development process, but the GNU tools are friendly.

Modeling

We use the modeling tool every time we cannot imagine the complete architecture of a system or a separate module after a quick look at the task description. We run it, sit back and start finding the best way to implement the task ahead. We can drag and drop use-case units, draw diagrams, database tables, relations, sequences of actions, packages structure and other stuff. A good and free program named **Dia** distributed under the terms of the GNU Public License that does much the same thing. It enables us to unleash all of our brain power and explain everything we think about future system's internals using the Unified Modeling Language. It's just a simple and incredibly powerful tool. Having all the diagrams we can easily remember what, when and why the system does what it does. We can even easily pass our task to a person who doesn't speak our language, but is familiar with the magic solution - UML.

Writing source code

After the modeling step is done we may get into coding. Here in the GNU world we can find a wide variety of different programs for text editing. We can find text editors that differ not only in their feature sets but even by the user interface concept. We can use visual editors such as mcedit and joe, text-command oriented editors like vi and vim. There are even script-driven ones like emacs that is very extensible with scripts in lisp. People who have only recently gotten involved in Linux and UNIX programming prefer visual editors rather than command-based. The only thing we should notice is that we can choose any kind of editor for our programming and documentation writing. We can even write poems using any of those great pieces of software in any way we like.

---

[4] Konstantin "konst" Klyagin, lives in Kharkov, Ukraine.

Version control

When a project is pretty big and we have been developing it for a while releasing new versions, bug fixes and stuff, we probably need to track all the changes we make to the source. The GNU development framework has a tool named CVS that can help us.

CVS is a version control system. Every time we want to record modifications it asks us for a comment. Then we can check out an old version of our project from the repository and view the log of changes. It's extremely useful if, say, one of our recent modifications caused a bug.

Also we can develop several branches of a project separately. Let them be, say, "devel" and "stable". Using the CVS branching facility we can create a branch, add a feature or make a major change and then merge it with the main line of the source, leaving our free to experiment without the danger of damaging our existing work.

The modifications are held in a repository which can be accessed locally or from a remote workstation with TCP/IP. We can even use SSL for secure communications. This requires some extra setup. In order to do that, the CVS server software must be run via the SSL wrapper program, and the client must have a patch applied. It can be downloaded at http://konst.org.ua/cvss/

Let's focus on the CVS's ability to work via TCP/IP. It makes the software very useful. For example, it enables developers to collaborate physically being located anywhere in the world. Every developer has their own local copy of the source. When a part of a work is ready he checks in the modifications and optionally comments them. Also there is a common practice to have a repository remotely available to the public in read-only mode, so testers can check out the most recent versions.

Compiling

The GNU compilers are the things we cannot imagine the world without. We need the GNU C compiler to compile your Linux kernel, various programs and it is even used to build itself. GNU compilers are the one's without which we cannot imagine good cross-platform activities to be taken place.

There are also C++, Fortran, Ada, Effel, and even GNU Java compilers which we can use for development.

Dependencies Tracking

The situation with a project that has only one source file seems to be quite clear. We just have to execute the compiler every time we make a change to the code and then have a new executable. If we have a set of source files and headers, Compiling all the source files every time to make a minor modification can be annoying. Here the GNU make program comes to help us. This example Makefile demonstrates how to define dependencies and rules to build this project.

```
all: hello
hello: hello.o sayhi.o misc.o ui.o gcc hello.o sayhi.o misc.o ui.o -o hello
```

This Makefile uses implicit rules to make *.o from *.c. But what about headers? They don't seem to be in the dependency tracking. We can include them into the Makefile in the following way:

```
all      : hello
hello    : hello.o sayhi.o misc.o ui.o gcc hello.o sayhi.o misc.o ui.o -o hello
hello.o : hello.c hello.h sayhi.o: sayhi.c sayhi.h misc.o: misc.c misc.h ui.o:
          ui.c ui.h
```

Now it's better, but we will have to update the dependencies stuff every time we add "#include" statements to our sources. Here a useful option of GNU C compiler comes to help you.

```
gcc -MM hello.c
```

Options such as -I specify additional directories to search for headers can be used also. Upon execution it prints the dependencies string for hello.o ready to include into our Makefile.

Now the final step. How can combine common make rules with dependencies auto-generated with the GNU C compiler?

```
all: hello
hello: dep hello.o sayhi.o misc.o ui.o gcc hello.o sayhi.o misc.o ui.o -o hello
clean: rm -f *.o hello .deps
dep: echo >.deps for i in hello.c sayhi.c misc.c ui.c; do gcc -MM $$i
>>.deps; done
-include .deps
```

The dep target creates a file .deps that contains all the dependencies between source and header files. Also, we have added the standard clean target. It's a common practice to include it into Makefiles so it could be easy to clean up all the generated stuff.

autoconf/automake

Aside from using the previously described methods there is a way to pay less attention to the Makefiles and build rules and concentrate on code we write. This is possible with the magic suite named autoconf/automake. It's really an amazing beast doing all of filthy work for us. Apart from taking care of Makefiles with all dependencies and other stuff for our projects, it has a mechanism to detect our system specific parameters before the compilation and building steps are performed. Start with writing the Makefile.am to define what exactly we want to build.

```
bin_PROGRAMS = hello hello_SOURCES = hello.c sayhi.c misc.c ui.c
AUTOMAKE_OPTIONS = foreign
```

The last line tells automake it's not the GNU package, e.g. it does not contain standard files named NEWS, README, AUTHORS and ChangeLog that are necessary if we want our package to be GNU compliant.

After we have Makefile.am in the project directory, there is another input file for the suite named configure.in. It's responsible for the system specific parameters checking we have mentioned before. The minimalist configure.in is below.

```
AC_INIT(hello.c) # Initializes the configure script. On start it will check for the main source file specified here first.

AM_INIT_AUTOMAKE(hello, 1.0) # Tells automake we have project named "hello" version 1.0

AC_PROG_CC # Adds a check for C compiler

AC_OUTPUT(Makefile) # The output file is Makefile. All the build stuff will be put there
```

Now we are done with the autoconf/automake input specification. Run the following programs in the order given.

```
aclocal autoconf automake -a -c
```

This will finally create the configure script, Makefile.in and add some default documentation to our project. Now it's finally ready to compile, debug and even to distribute.

Everyone who wants to build our program on his or her Linux computer needs to run ./configure make

We run ./configure so Makefile is created from Makefile.in. This is how the autoconf/automake is organized. It generates Makefile.in from our Makefile.am. Then Makefile.in is processed by ./configure script so all the system specific things would be considered and included into the final Makefile. It will also have a default install and uninstall targets which are extremely useful for our program users.

Debugging

Not a difficult thing to do in Linux: Let me introduce the GNU Debugger or gdb. It allows us to look inside our programs to see what's going on there. We can see the code executing, inspect variables and stack, set breakpoints, etc. C, C++, Modula-2, Chill, Pascal and Fortran languages are supported by gdb.

Programmers who came to Linux from desktop OS's such as MS-DOS, OS/2 or Windows may find the gdb command line interface less than useful. They often prefer visual debugging, but the gdb approach to user interface does have its advantages. For example, we can have a log of debugging a program, debug programs on remote in a telnet session on a slow link, etc. Whatever, there are a whole bunch of text mode and graphical visual front-end to gdb, so it's up to everybody to use what he or she likes.

But let's have a quick look at what gdb can do itself. Let's start with running our program. Small hint: In order to debug a program it should be compiled with debug info and without optimization. Usually the last isn't paid much attention, but sometimes it interferes with debugging a lot. It sometimes happens that we cannot see some variables and whole lines of code in the debugger because of optimization. So it's our enemy if we want to debug comfortably.

To turn of the optimization and tell the compiler to put debug info into the binary add the following line to our Makefile.am.

```
CXXFLAGS = -g3 -O0
```

Those parameters, passed to a compiler, enable maximum debug info and turn off the optimization respectively.

To run a program in debugger issue the following command.

```
gdb ./hello
```

For watching its execution line-by-line use the "next" command that abbreviates to "n". Note, first we have to set a breakpoint at the first line of the main() function and run the program.

```
(gdb) break main Breakpoint 1 at 0x8048462: file hello.c, line 9. (gdb) run
Starting program: /home/konst/cuj/./hello

Breakpoint 1, main () at hello.c:9 9 printf("hello, world!\n"); (gdb)
```

This was probably the most simple debugging session we will ever see. Nevertheless it has a lot of facilities such as attaching to an already running program, watching variables, conditional breakpoints, examining the stack, trace points and much more. It can also inspect "core" files that are generated by programs before they crush to see what the crush was caused by.

Profiling

Linux programmers usually use the GNU profiler (gprof) to find out where a program spends its time. It allows us to learn which functions were used and how long it takes to execute each of them. This way we can track routines that work slower than we expected. Whereas gdb allows us to see the program execution as it goes, gprof provides us with overall execution statistics.

GNU profiling is easy. In order to profile a program we should compile and link it with -pg parameter. Then we simply execute it and get the gmon.out file containing all the statistics collected. The file can be analyzed with the gprof program so we can see a complete graph and appropriate explanations on its output.

Distributing

Say, we have a complete program we are going to distribute - ship it to our customers or release it under the GPL and spread the word. There are various formats Linux programs are distributed in.

The most widely used one is a source archive, usually it's a gzipped tar file (package-version.tar.gz for example). If we use the autoconf/automake suite generating such an archive is not a problem at all. It creates a "dist" Makefile target which can generate a package ready for distributing. The resulting tar.gz includes the configure script and all the autoconf/automake stuff the end user needs to build and install the program on their system.

The tar.gz format is distribution independent. As it usually contains a program source, we should compile it every time we want it to be installed on a new computer. But it's not always necessary. Popular Linux distributions to distribute binaries and sources also.

RedHat Linux, as well as some others use RPM format for packaging. A program named rpm (RedHat package manager) that enables we to generate such packages of our own programs. All we need in order to make an RPM distribution is just write so called specification file and feed rpm with it. The spec file includes a brief description, dependency list, application group, changelog, and a list of files to be installed. After we run the manager we have two packages, they are source and binary RPMs. Using rpm, user can query its database for the list of files that belong to a package, remove the whole package, see what packages depend on it, etc.

Debian package format is almost the same as RPM and almost as popular. To make a package we should fill up the debian/ directory in our project root directory with several specification files and run the package generation tool called dpkg-buildpackage.

Both Debian and RedHat distribution package formats allow the package maintainer to add scripts executed before the installation, after the installation, and before and after removing the package files. As they can generate source packages, binary packages from them can be built easily both with RPM and Debian tools.

Integrated Development Environments

What if we prefer complete environments rather than building our development process with separate brick-like tools? Linux has such software. Usually integrated development environment software has an internal source editor module and front-ends for the GNU tools such as gdb, autoconf/automake and optionally cvs, rpm and others. There are GUI and console text-mode IDEs.

The most famous of X-windows based IDEs for Linux is KDevelop. Being a part of the KDE project it's widely used for developing KDE applications. It has everything a KDE programmer dreams about including the reference on the Qt library which KDE uses for GUI.

People who prefer console may remember RHIDE, a text-mode programming IDE available for Linux. It had been ported to Linux from DOS where it had been a part of DJGPP tools, looks more like a DOS program. Having an internal editor and gdb front-end it lacked vital support for cvs, automake and stuff. Mmotor, a complete IDE that includes powerful editor with configurable syntax highlight feature. It includes support for gdb, cvs, automake/autoconf, RPM and templates for C, C++ and Java programs.

1.7 Conclusions

This chapter discusses about success stories of Linux since its inception. It explains how Linux kernel boots in an illustrative manner. Also, it gives an overall picture of programming under Linux.

2 Compiling C and C++ Programs Under Linux

2.1 Introduction To C Compiler

The easiest case of compilation is when we have all our source code set in a single file. Lets assume there is a file named 'x.c' that we want to compile. We will do so using a commands similar to:

cc x.c (In most of the flavors of Unix's)

gcc x.c (In Gnu C compiler)

acc x.c (In Solaris)

Every compiler might show its messages (errors, warnings, etc.) differently, but in all cases, we will get a file 'a.out' as a result, if the compilation completed successfully. Note that some older systems (e.g. SunOs) come with a C compiler that does not understand ANSI-C, but rather the older 'K&R' C style. In such a case, we need to use gcc (hopefully it is installed), or learn the differences between ANSI-C and K&R C (not recommended if we don't *really* have to), or move to a different system.

Compilation in general is split into roughly 5 stages (as shown in Figure 2.1) to name: Preprocessing, Parsing, Translation, Assembling, and Linking

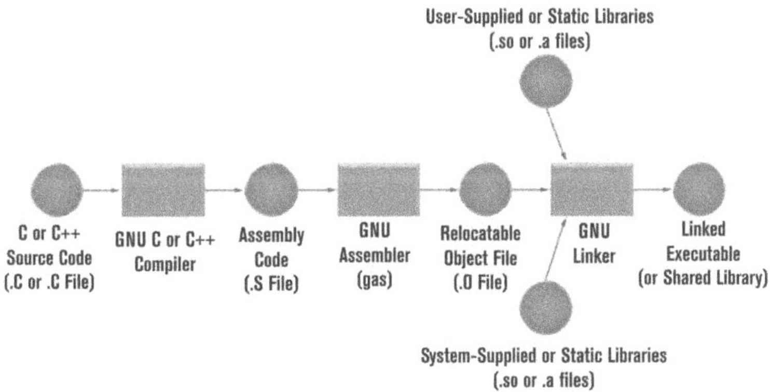

Figure 2.1 Stages in C Program Compilation.

2.1.1 Understanding Of Compilation Steps

Now that we've learned that compilation is not just a simple process, lets try to see what is the complete list of steps taken by the compiler in order to compile a C program.

1. Driver - what we invoked as "cc" or "gcc". This is actually the "engine", that drives the whole set of tools the compiler is made of. We invoke it, and it begins to invoke the other tools one by one, passing the output of each tool as an input to the next tool.

2. C Pre-Processor - normally called "cpp". It takes a C source file, and handles all the pre-processor definitions (#include files, #define macros, conditional source code inclusion with #ifdef, etc.)
3. The C Compiler - normally called "cc1". This is the actual compiler, that translates the input file into assembly language.
4. Optimizer - sometimes comes as a separate module and sometimes as the found inside the compiler module. This one handles the optimization on a representation of the code that is language-neutral. This way, we can use the same optimizer for compilers of different programming languages.
5. Assembler - sometimes called "as". This takes the assembly code generated by the compiler, and translates it into machine language code (object files).
6. Link - Loader - This is the tool that takes all the object files (and C libraries), and links them together, to form one executable file, in a format the operating system supports. A Common format these days is known as "ELF". On SunOs systems, and other older systems, a format named "a.out" was used. This format defines the internal structure of the executable file - location of data segment, location of source code segment, location of debug information and so on.

If we run the following commands we get the executable files of the above programs namingly cpp (don't confuse cpp as c plus plus!!), cc1, as and collect2.

```
gcc –print-prog-name=cpp
gcc –print-prog-name=cc1
gcc –print-prog-name=as
gcc –print-prog-name=collect2
```

As explained above, the compilation is split in to many different phases; not all compiler's employs exactly the same phases, and sometimes (e.g. for C++ compilers) the situation is even more complex. But the basic idea is quite similar - split the compiler into many different parts, to give the programmer more flexibility, and to allow the compiler developers to re-use as many modules as possible in different compilers for different languages (by replacing the preprocessor and compiler modules), or for different architectures (by replacing the assembly and linker-loader parts).

2.2 Detailed Analysis of Compilation Process

The compilation command

"gcc sourcetile name" gives executable file with name "a.out".

Suppose that we want the resulting program to be called with another name other than "a.out" then we can use the following lines to compile.

```
cc –o executable_filename  x.c
gcc –o executable_filename  x.c
```

2.2.1 Running The Resulting Program

Once we created the program, we wish to run it. This is usually done by simply typing its name at the command prompt.

```
executable_filename
```

However, this requires that the current directory be in our PATH (which is a environment variable informing our Unix shell where it has to look for programs we're trying to run. See chapter on environment variables). In many cases, this directory is not placed in our PATH. Thus in order to run our program we can try:

```
./executable_filename
```

This time we explicitly told our Unix shell that we want to run the program which is in the current directory. If we're lucky enough, this will be suffice. However, yet one more obstacle could block our path - file permission flags!!!.

When a file is created in the system, it is immediately given some access permission flags. These flags tell the system who should be given access to the file, and what kind of access will be given to them. Traditional Unix systems use 3 kinds of entities to which they grant (or deny) access: The user which owns the file, the group which owns the file, and everybody else. Each of these entities may be given access to read the file ('r'), write to the file ('w') and execute the file ('x').

Now, when the compiler created the program file for us, we became owners of the file. Normally, the compiler would make sure that we get all permissions to the file - read, write and execute. If not set, we can set the permissions of the file properly (the owner of a file can normally change the permission flags of the file) using a command.

```
chmod u+rwx executable_filename
```

This means "the user ('u') should be given ('+') permissions read ('r'), write ('w') and execute ('x') to the file 'executable_filename'. Now, we'll surely be able to run our program. Again, normally we'll have no problem running the file, but if we copy it to a different directory, or transfer it to a different computer over the network, it might loose its original permissions, and thus we'll need to set them properly, as shown above. Note too that we cannot just move the file to a different computer and expect it to run - it has to be a computer with a matching operating system (to understand the executable file format), and matching CPU architecture (to understand the machine-language code that the executable file contains).

Finally, the run-time environment has to match. For example, if we compiled the program on an operating system with one version of the standard C library, and we try to run it on a version with an incompatible standard C library, the program might crush, or complain that it cannot find the relevant C library. This is especially true for systems that evolve quickly (e.g. Linux with libc5 vs. Linux with libc6), so be careful!!.

2.2.2 The C Preprocessor

The preprocessor is what handles the logic behind all the # directives in C. It runs in a single pass, and essentially is just a substitution engine.

Consider the following simple program with the definitions of a symbolic constants (also called as manifest constants) and a macro. In the following program NUM is defined and during the pre-processing stage where ever NUM is written in the program, there 3 will be replaced. In many production programs, we prefer to use a macro in place of a fixed constant such that in future if we want to change the fixed constant, we change this macro line only. This makes programmer life easy.

```
#define NUM 3
#define NORM(a,b)  sqrt(a*a+b*b)
int main()
{
int i;
float val;

for(i=0;i<NUM;i++)
printf("Hello  %d \n", i);

val=NORM(2,3);

return 0;
}
```

To only preprocess the C language program:

gcc –E filename.c

The following is the output after preprocessing. For the simplicity sake we did not include any header file such as "stdio.h". The bold text matter in the following text is the result after preprocessing.

```
int main()
{
int i;
float val;

for(i=0;i<3;i++)
printf("Hello  %d \n", i);

val=sqrt(2*2 +3*3);

return 0;
}
```

The **gcc -E** runs only the preprocessor stage. This places all include files into your .c file, and also translates all macros into inline C code and replaces all the occurrences of symbolic constants with their values or definitions. We can add **-o file** to redirect result of preprocessing in to a file. That is, using command like the following.

```
gcc –E filename.c –o outputfilename
```

#undef

#undef fulfills the inverse functionality of **#define**. It eliminates to the list of defined constants the one that has the name passed as a parameter to **#undef.**

```
#define MAX_WIDTH 100
char str1[MAX_WIDTH];
#undef MAX_WIDTH
#define MAX_WIDTH 200
char str2[MAX_WIDTH];
```

#ifdef, #ifndef, #if, #endif, #else and #elif

These directives allow to discard part of the code of a program if a certain condition is not fulfilled.

#ifdef allows that a section of a program is compiled only if the *defined constant* that is specified as the parameter has been defined, independently of its value. Its operation is:

```
#ifdef name
// code here
#endif
```

For example

```
#include<stdio.h>
int main()
{
int i=0;

#ifdef DEBUG
for(i=0;i<NUM;i++)
#endif

printf("Hello  %d \n", i);

return 0;
}
```

If we compile the above program with "**gcc -D DEBUG filename.c**" and run, we can find that the for loop is executed. We can check the same from the output of preprocessing stage with -E option.

If we compile the above program with "**gcc filename.c**" and run, we can find that loop is executed. That is if DEBUG is defined then for loop is included in the program and compiled otherwise it is not included.

Similarly, execute the following program

```
#include<stdio.h>
int main()
{
int i=0;

#if DEBUG==1
for(i=0;i<NUM;i++)
#endif

printf("Hello  %d \n", i);

return 0;
}
```

If we compile the above program with "**gcc -D DEBUG=1 filename.c**" or "**gcc -D DEBUG filename.c**" and run we will find for loop is executed. We can check the same from the output of preprocessing stage with -E option.

If we compile the above program with "gcc filename.c" and run then we will find that no for loop is executed.

#ifndef serves for the opposite for **#ifdef**. The code between the **#ifndef** directive and the **#endif** directive is only compiled if the constant name that is specified has not been defined previously. For example:

```
#ifndef MAX_WIDTH
#define MAX_WIDTH 100
#endif
char str[MAX_WIDTH];
```

For example:

```
#include<stdio.h>

#ifndef N
#define N 100
#endif

int main()
{
int i=0;
```

```
for(i=0;i<N;i++)

printf("Hello  %d \n", i);

return 0;
}
```

Compile the above program with the following commands and check how the program behaves by running the resulting executable program.

gcc filename.c
gcc -D N=5 filename.c

In the first case, the *defined constant N* has not yet been defined it would be defined with a value of 100. Thus for loop runs 100 times. Where as in the second case, we are giving constant N value as 5 along with gcc command. Thus, it will be considered as 5 and thus for loop runs five times.

Also, the **#if**, **#else** and **#elif** (*elif = else if*) directives serve (see the above example) so that the portion of code that follows is compiled only if the specified condition is met. The condition can only serve to evaluate constant expressions. For example:

```
#if MAX_WIDTH>200
#undef MAX_WIDTH
#define MAX_WIDTH 200

#elsif MAX_WIDTH<50
#undef MAX_WIDTH
#define MAX_WIDTH 50

#else
#undef MAX_WIDTH
#define MAX_WIDTH 100
#endif

char str[MAX_WIDTH];
```

Notice how the structure of chained directives **#if**, **#elsif** and **#else** finishes with **#endif**.

These conditional compilation statements enable the programmer to control the execution of preprocessor directives, and the compilation of program code. Each of the conditional preprocessor directives evaluates a constant integer expression. Cast expressions, sizeof() expressions, and enumeration constants cannot be evaluated in preprocessor directives. The conditional preprocessor construct is much like the if selection structure.

Consider the following code:

```
#if !defined(NULL)
#define NULL 0
#endif
```

These directives determine if NULL is defined or not. The expression, defined(NULL) evaluates to 1 if NULL is defined; 0 otherwise. If the result is 0, !defined(NULL) evaluates to 1, and NULL is defined.

We can also use logical AND and OR operators of C language like :

```
#if (SIMVAL != 2 && SIMVAL != 3)
#error SIMVAL must be defined to either 2 or 3
#endif
```

#line

When we compile a program the compiler shows the error that happened preceded by the name of the file and the line within the file where it has taken place. The **#line** directive allows us to control both things, the line numbers within the code files as well as the file name that we want to appear when an error takes place. For example, the following directive:

#line *number* **"***filename***"**

Where *number* is the new line number that will be assigned to the next code line. The line number of successive lines will be increased one by one from this. *The filename* is an optional parameter that serves to replace the file name that will be shown in case of error from this directive until another one changes it again or the end of the file is reached. For example:

```
#line 1 "assigning variable"
int a?;
```

This code will generate an error that will be shown as error in file "assigning variable", line 1.

This #line preprocessor directive causes the subsequent source code lines to be renumbered starting with the specified constant integer value. The directive

```
#line 100
```

Starts line numbering from 100 beginning with the next source code line.

The directive normally is used to help make the messages produced by syntax errors and compiler warnings more meaningful. Don't be wary the line numbers do not appear in the source file.

#error

This directive aborts the compilation process when it encounters the error which is specified as the parameter.

```
#ifndef __cplusplus
#error A C++ compiler is required
#endif
```

This example aborts the compilation process if the *defined constant* **__cplusplus** is not defined.

#warning

This directive does not aborts the compilation process when it is found returning the error that is specified as the parameter.

```
#ifndef __cplusplus
#warning A C++ compiler is required
#endif
```

If the *defined constant* **__cplusplus** is not defined this example gives warning message and continues the compilation process

#include

This directive has also been used assiduously in other sections of this tutorial. When the preprocessor finds an **#include** directive it replaces it by the whole content of the specified file. There are two ways to specify a file to be included:

#include "*file*"
#include <*file*>

The only difference between both expressions is the directories in which the compiler is going to look for the file. In the first case where the file is specified between quotes, the file is looked for in the same directory that includes the file containing the directive. In case that it is not there, the compiler looks for the file in the default directories where it is configured to look for the standard header files.

If the file name is enclosed between angle-brackets **<>** the file is looked for directly where the compiler is configured to look for the standard header files.

The # And ## Operators

The # and ## preprocessor operators are available in ANSI C. The # operator causes a replacement text token to be converted to a string surrounded by double quotes.

Consider the following macro definition.

```
#define HELLO(x) printf("Hello, " #x "\n");
```

When HELLO(John) appears in a program file, it is expanded to

```
printf("Hello, " "John" "\n");
```

The string "John" replaces #x in the replacement text. Strings separated by white space are concatenated during preprocessing, so the above statement is equivalent to :

```
printf("Hello, John\n");
```

Note that the # operator **must** be used in a macro with arguments because the operand of # refers to an argument of the macro.

The ## operator concatenates two tokens. Consider the following macro definition.

```
#define CAT(p,q) p ## q
```

When CAT appears in the program, its arguments are concatenated and used to replace the macro. For example, CAT(O,K) is replaced by OK in the program. The ## operator must have two operands.

Program example:

```
#include <stdio.h>
#include <stdlib.h>
#define HELLO(x) printf("Hello, " #x "\n");
#define SHOWFUNC(x) Use ## Func ## x
int main(void)
{
//new concatenated identifier, UseFuncOne
char * SHOWFUNC(One);
char * SHOWFUNC(Two);
SHOWFUNC(One) = "New name, UseFuncOne";
SHOWFUNC(Two) = "New name, UseFuncTwo";
HELLO(Birch);
printf("SHOWFUNC(One) -> %s \n",SHOWFUNC(One));
printf("SHOWFUNC(One) -> %s \n",SHOWFUNC(Two));
system("pause");
return 0;
}
```

There are standard predefined macros as shown in Table 2.1. The identifiers for each of the predefined macros begin and end with two underscores. These identifiers and the defined identifier cannot be used in #define or #undef directive.

There are a lot more predefined macros extensions that are compilers specific, please check our compiler documentation. The standard macros are available with the same meanings regardless of the machine or operating system our compiler installed on.

```
#include<stdio.h>
int main()
{
printf("%d %s %s %s %s\n", __LINE__, __DATE__, __TIME__, __FILE__);

}
```

Table 2.1 The predefined macros.

Symbolic Constant	Explanation
__DATE__	The date the source file is **compiled** (a string of the form "mmm dd yyyy" such as "Jan 19 1999").
__LINE__	The line number of the current source code line (an integer constant).
__FILE__	The presumed names of the source file (a string).
__TIME__	The time the source file is **compiled** (a string literal of the form :hh:mm:ss).
__STDC__	The integer constant 1. This is intended to indicate that the implementation is ANSI C compliant.

#pragma

This directive is used to specify diverse options to the compiler. These options are specific for the platform and the compiler we use. Consult the manual or the reference of our compiler for more information on the possible parameters that we can define with

```
#pragma
```

If we use –save-temps option with gcc compiler, it saves the temporary files which it creates while machine language file is created.

For example:

```
gcc –save-temps a.c
```

The above command creates files "a.i", "a.s", "a.o" and "a.out" (in the order). That is "a.i" is created after preprocessing and is text file. The file "a.s" is created by assembler from the file "a.i". The file "a.o" is object file created from "a.s" and finally "a.out" is created after linking.

The –M option displays dependencies among the files needed for make command. For example, if we have a file "a.h" which another file "b.h" and "a.h" is included in "a.c" and if we execute the following command

```
gcc -M a.c
```

We get the following output.

a.o: a.c /usr/include/stdio.h <other system defined header files> a.h b.h

This knowledge is needed to make files which we may explain in detail in the forthcoming chapters.

Similarly, -H option with gcc produce output how the files are included during preprocessing stage. That first which file is included and then which file is included, etc. Try the following command.

gcc –H a.c

Also, try both the options and observe the output.

gcc –M -H a.c

2.2.3 The Assembler

The gcc compiler has options to generate assembly code also from the C source. To achive this we have to use -s .

Consider the following program.

```
#include<stdio.h>
int main()
{
int i=3;
printf("Hello  %d \n", i*2);

return 0;
}
```

gcc -S will take .c files as input and generates .s assembly files in AT&T syntax. If we wish to have Intel syntax, add the option -masm=intel. To gain some association between variables and stack usage, use add -fverbose-asm to the flags.

For example:

gcc –S b.c

Assembly code generated by gcc.

```
    .file    "b.c"
    .section .rodata

.LC0:
    .string  "Hello  %d \n"
    .text
```

```
.globl main
    .type   main,@function

main:
    pushl   %ebp
    movl    %esp, %ebp
    subl    $8, %esp
    andl    $-16, %esp
    movl    $0, %eax
    subl    %eax, %esp
    movl    $3, -4(%ebp)
    subl    $8, %esp
    movl    -4(%ebp), %eax
    sall    $1, %eax
    pushl   %eax
    pushl   $.LC0
    call    printf
    addl    $16, %esp
    movl    $0, %eax
    leave
    ret
.Lfe1:
    .size   main,.Lfe1-main
    .ident  "GCC: (GNU) 3.2.2 20030222 (Red Hat Linux 3.2.2-5)"
```

The program gcc itself is actually just a front end that executes various other programs corresponding to each stage in the compilation process. To get it to print out the commands it executes at each step, use **gcc -v**

In addition, gcc can be called with various optimization options that can do interesting things to the assembly code output. There are between 4 and 7 general optimization classes that can be specified with a -ON, where 0 <= N <= 6. 0 is no optimization (default), and 6 is usually maximum, although often no optimizations are done past 4, depending on architecture and gcc version.

There are also several fine-grained assembly options that are specified with the -f flag. The most interesting are -funroll-loops, -finline-functions, and -fomit-frame-pointer. Loop unrolling means to expand a loop so that there are n copies of the code for n iterations of the loop (i.e. no jmp statements to the top of the loop). On modern processors, this optimization is negligible. Inlining functions means to effectively convert all functions in a file to macros, and place copies of their code directly in line in the calling function (like the C++ inline keyword). This only applies for functions called in the same C file as their definition. It is also a relatively small optimization. Omitting the frame pointer (aka the base pointer) frees up an extra register for use in our program. If we have more than 4 heavily used local variables, this may be rather large advantage, otherwise it is just a nuisance (and makes debugging much more difficult).

2.2.4 Creating Object Files but not linked files

If we need to create only object files from the C or C++ source files –c option can be used. Usually this option is used with individual C files to create their object files; further, these object files can be used in creating libraries (explained in next chapters) and SW system.

gcc –c filename.c

We will get file with the name "filename.o".

Let's suppose we have files `a.c', `b.c' and `c.c'. We can execute the following command.

gcc -c a.c b.c c.c

This creates files `a.o', `b.o' and `c.o'. Next we link them into one file called `myprog'. Please make sure that one of the file contains main() function!!!.

gcc -o myprog a.o b.o c.o

2.2.5 Creating Debug-Ready Code

Normally, when we write a program, we want to be able to debug it - that is, test it using a debugger that allows running it step by step, setting a break point before a given command is executed, looking at contents of variables during program execution, and so on. In order for the debugger to be able to relate between the executable program and the original source code, we need to tell the compiler to insert information to the resulting executable program that'll help the debugger. This information is called "debug information". In order to add that to our program, we have to compile with –g flag.

gcc -g file.c -o executable_filename

The '-g' flag tells the compiler to use debug info, and is recognized by mostly any compiler out there. We have to note that the resulting file is much larger than that created without usage of the '-g' flag. The difference in size is due to the debug information. We may still remove this debug information using the strip command, like this:

strip executable_filename

We may note that the size of the file now is even smaller than if we didn't use the '-g' flag in the first place. This is because even a program compiled without the '-g' flag contains some symbol information (function names, for instance), that the strip command removes. We may read the subsequent sections to know more about strip command.

2.2.6 Creating Optimized Code

After we created a program and debugged it properly, we normally want it to compile into an efficient code, and the resulting file to be as small as possible. The compiler can help us by optimizing the code, either for speed (to run faster), or for space (to occupy a smaller space), or some combination of the two. The basic way to create an optimized program would be like this:

```
gcc -O file.c -o  executable_filename
```

The '-O' flag tells the compiler to optimize the code. This also means the compilation will take longer, as the compiler tries to apply various optimization algorithms to the code. This optimization is supposed to be conservative, in that it ensures us the code will still perform the same functionality as it did when compiled without optimization (well, unless there are bugs in our compiler). Usually we can define an optimization level by adding a number to the '-O' flag. The higher the number - the better optimized the resulting program will be, and the slower the compiler will complete the compilation. One should note that because optimization alters the code in various ways, as we increase the optimization level of the code, the chances are higher that an improper optimization will actually alter our code, as some of them tend to be non-conservative, or are simply rather complex, and contain bugs. For example, for a long time it was known that using a compilation level higher than 2 (or was it higher than 3?) with gcc results bugs in the executable program. After being warned, if we still want to use a different optimization level (lets say 4), we can do it this way:

```
gcc -O4 single_compile.c -o single_compile
```

GCC supports an almost infinite number of command line options dealing with optimization. Using them properly requires thorough understanding of compilation theory and source code optimization theory, or we might damage your resulting code. Aho, Sethi and Ulm.

Also, some other options such as –floop-optimize, -finline-functions, or f-no-inline-functions etc can be used depending upon the requirement.

2.2.7 Getting Extra Compiler Warnings

Normally the compiler only generates error messages about erroneous code that does not comply with the C standard, and warnings about things that usually tend to cause errors during runtime. However, we can usually instruct the compiler to give us even more warnings, which is useful to improve the quality of our source code, and to expose bugs that will really bug us later. With gcc, this is done using the '-W' flag. For example, to let the compiler to use all types of warnings it is familiar with; we'll use a command line like:

```
cc -Wall filename.c –o filename
```

This will first annoy us - we'll get all sorts of warnings that might seem irrelevant. However, it is better to eliminate the warnings than to eliminate the usage of this flag. Usually, this option will save us more time than it will cause us to waste, and if used consistently; we will get used to coding proper code without thinking too much about it. One should also note that some code that works on some architecture with one compiler might break if we use a different compiler, or a different system, to compile the code on. When developing on the first system, we'll never see these bugs, but when moving the code to a different platform, the bug will suddenly appear. Also, in many cases we eventually will want to move the code to a new system, even if we had no such intentions initially.

Note that sometimes '-Wall' will give us too many errors, and then we could try to use some less verbose warning level. Read the compiler's manual to learn about the various '-W' options, and use those that would give we the greatest benefit. Initially they might sound too strange to make any sense, but if we are a more experienced programmer, we will learn which could be of good use to us.

2.2.8 Linking Libraries

Whenever we use library functions other than standard libc functions, we have to include appropriate header file and at the same time during compilation we have to use –l option to inform the compiler that it has to link with the specified library. For example, if we use any mathematical functions such as sqrt(), pow(), log10() etc., in our program aa.c then we have to compile the same with –lm option. That is:

```
gcc –o aa aa.c –lm
```

In the above command, -lm informs the gcc that it has to search for a library file " libm.so.*" in standard directories. Similarly, if we use any X windows library functions we may have to give –lx11 or –lxt along the command line with gcc command which makes it to search for library files "libx11.so.* " and "libxt.so.*" in standard directories.

If we want to instruct the gcc that it has to search for some other directories for the required library files, we have to use –L option with it. In the chapter on "Libraries" we have described about this in detail.

It is also common that functions are developed as separate files and use them and create final executable file. Whether we are using the standard library function or the one's developed by us, the compiler toolchain (the ones explained in Figure 2.1) has to be able to build the executable according to specifications that the kernel understands and expects.

The part of the toolchain that makes sure that our program meets the kernel's expectations is the linker, ld. Actually, the linker performs several functions that are crucial to the process of building a working executable, and so it's worth taking a deeper look at this little-known portion of the compiler toolchain.

What the Linker Does[1]

Any time you run an executable, the kernel must create a new virtual address space for the process to run in and then load (or copy) the executable into that newly created space.

As discussed earlier, each process is given its own virtual address space, which is partitioned into identical large sections (as depicted in Figure 2.5 such as text, data, stack, and heap). The kernel expects that the start of these large sections of a process will always be located at the same virtual address.

---

[1] Benjamin Chelf,chelf@codesourcery.com.

In order for that to be possible, every program must be set up according to the specifications that the kernel expects at the time that it's compiled, and that's one of the linker's jobs. The linker and the kernel share an understanding of how the virtual address space should be laid out, and the linker knows how to put all the pieces of a program that we're compiling into the proper sections of the virtual address space. It also adjusts things so that all of the different addresses that are used by the program point where they should. (We'll talk more about this little later).

One section of the virtual address space contains the actual machine code instructions that make up the program -- the section labeled "Other Program Data," which contains the code (or text) segment. Let's see how the linker builds this part of the executable.

Object Files

As discussed earlier, after the compiler (gcc) and the assembler (as) finish their respective jobs, they hand off a set of relocatable object modules to the linker, which must then make a functioning executable out of them.

We might be wondering what "relocatable" means in this particular context. In this case, it doesn't mean "may be relocated," but rather "must be relocated." The linker builds the code segment by placing the code from each object module -- one after another -- in the code segment portion of the virtual address space as though it were placing different sized books in a bookshelf.

When the assembler builds each object module, there's absolutely no way that it can know exactly where that module will reside in the virtual address space, so it doesn't bother to try to figure it out. Instead, it lets the linker adjust the addresses in every module. This adjustment process is known as "relocation" (and this is where the term "relocatable object module" comes from).

Disassembling Object Files

In order to appreciate what the linker has to do in order to make all of this work, let's take a closer look at an object file and see just what it contains. Since they contain assembly code that's been run through the assembler, we can "disassemble" the object file in order to recover the original assembly code.

Listing of the three files: a.c, b.c, and main.c are as follows..

File a.c

```
int a ()
{
  int i = 0;
i++;
 foo:
i--;
  goto foo;
}
```

File b.c

```
int b()
{
 b();
}
```

File main.c

```
main()
{
a();
b();
}
```

Compile these functions separately. That is,

```
gcc –c a.c
gcc –c b.c
gcc –c main.c
gcc –o a m.o a.o b.o
```

Once they've been compiled into the object modules a.o, b.o, and main.o, we can run the command **objdump -d** on each of them in order to see what their assembly code looks like (see Figure 2.2).

```
a.o:    file format elf32-i386
00000000 <a>:
   0:  push   %ebp
   1:  mov    %esp,%ebp
   3:  sub    $0x4,%esp
   6:  movl   $0x0,0xfffffffc(%ebp)
   d:  lea    0xfffffffc(%ebp),%eax
  10:  incl   (%eax)
  12:  lea    0xfffffffc(%ebp),%eax
  15:  decl   (%eax)
  17:  jmp    12 <a+0x12>

b.o:    file format elf32-i386
00000000 <b>:
   0:  push   %ebp
   1:  mov    %esp,%ebp
   3:  sub    $0x8,%esp
   6:  call   7 <b+0x7>
   b:  mov    %ebp,%esp
   d:  pop    %ebp
   e:  ret

main.o:  file format elf32-i386
00000000 <main>:
   0:  push   %ebp
   1:  mov    %esp,%ebp
   3:  sub    $0x8,%esp
   6:  call   7 <main+0x7>
   b:  call   c <main+0xc>
  10:  mov    %ebp,%esp
  12:  pop    %ebp
  13:  ret
```

Figure 2.2 Disassembly for a.o, b.o, and main.o.

In each listing, the first column starts at 0 and increases. This is the location (or address) of the assembly language instruction which is listed in the subsequent columns.

The assembler always starts building an object module at address 0. The linker must relocate all of these instructions to their new virtual addresses.

There are two other areas of importance in the address to the linker: the jumps (or branches) made by the code, and calls to functions.

Relative Jumps

In the assembly code for a.o, notice that the instruction at address 17 reads "jmp 12 <a+0x12>" (and corresponds to the goto in a.c). Indicating that the program should jump to the instruction at address 12 (which is "lea 0x fffffffc(%ebp),%eax").

However, the destination address 12 was specified as being relative to the start of the a() function. That's what the "<a+0x12>" means: jump to the instruction that's 12 bytes after the start of the a() function. This means that no matter where the a() function is placed in the virtual address space, the jump always knows where to go. This is called a relative jump, and nearly every compiler creates code that uses them.

The use of relative jumps is one characteristic of what's known as "position-independent code" (PIC). In addition to being relocatable, modules compiled in PIC mode can be turned into shared libraries, which can also be used simultaneously by multiple processes, reducing the memory use of the entire system. We'll talk more about shared libraries in next chapters.

Because the compiler generated the relative jump, the linker only needs to relocate the jump instruction to its new place in the virtual address space. The actual instruction itself doesn't need to be changed. However, the linker does need to change an instruction whenever functions are being called.

Calling Functions in Other Modules

Let's look at disassembly for b.o, specifically the instruction at address 6: "call 7 <b+0x7>". This means we should call a function. However, it looks like the call is to a function at address 7, which is right in the middle of an instruction. What's going on here?

It turns out that 7 is not an actual address, but rather an offset or index into a table. As b.c is compiled, a table of functions that are called from within b.c is created. This table contains "relocation records" and can be listed by running "objdump -x" on b.o.

The relocation records for b.o and main.o are shown in Figure 2.3 (note that they have been slightly edited because of space constraints). We can see that the value of the offset for "a" is 7 , which corresponds to the call to the function a() in b.c.

```
b.o:
RELOCATION RECORDS FOR [.text]:
OFFSET   VALUE
00000007 a

main.o:
RELOCATION RECORDS FOR [.text]:
OFFSET   VALUE
00000007 a
0000000c b
```

Figure 2.3 Relocation Records for b.o and main.o.

When the linker processes b.o, it takes a look at the relocation records and sees if the function a() is present in any of the other object modules (or system libraries). If the relocation record were not found, an "unsatisfied reference" error would be generated.

However, as the function a() does exist (in a.o), the call instruction is then rewritten -- or patched -- in order to be able to use the virtual address of the a() function within a.o.

We can examine the two call instructions in main.o and how that generates two relocation records (to the functions a() and b()).

The Finished Product

Let's take a look at what the three modules look like once the linker has finished its task. Figure 2.4 contains a dump of the final executable (obtained by running **"objdump -d"** on the executable). That is :

Objdump –d a

```
08048430 <a>:
 8048430:  push   %ebp
 8048431:  mov    %esp,%ebp
 8048433:  sub    $0x4,%esp
 8048436:  movl   $0x0,0xfffffffc(%ebp)
 804843d:  lea    0xfffffffc(%ebp),%eax
 8048440:  incl   (%eax)
 8048442:  lea    0xfffffffc(%ebp),%eax
 8048445:  decl   (%eax)
 8048447:  jmp    8048442 <a+0x12>
...
08048450 <b>:
 8048450:  push   %ebp
 8048451:  mov    %esp,%ebp
 8048453:  sub    $0x8,%esp
 8048456:  call   8048430 <a>
 804845b:  mov    %ebp,%esp
 804845d:  pop    %ebp
...

08048460 <main>:
 8048460:  push   %ebp
 8048461:  mov    %esp,%ebp
 8048463:  sub    $0x8,%esp
 8048466:  call   8048430 <a>
 804846b:  call   8048450 <b>
 8048470:  mov    %ebp,%esp
 8048472:  pop    %ebp
```

Figure 2.4 How a(), b(), and main() Appear in the Final Executable. ("a")

Also note that the jmp instruction at 0x 8048447 in the a() function is the same as it was in the a.o file. Although the "12" has been replaced in the output with the correct virtual address, it's still really "<a+0x12>". The call instructions to a() and b() have also had the correct addresses inserted.

2.2.9 Monitoring Compilation Times

It is possible with –time option to know the actual CPU time taken by preprocessor, cc1, and linker etc. The –Q option gives detail information about the compilation.

gcc -time b1.c a.c

```
# cc1 0.02 0.01
# as 0.00 0.00
# cc1 0.01 0.01
# as 0.00 0.00
# collect2 0.02 0.01
```

gcc –Q b1.c a.c

```
main
   Execution times (seconds)
   life analysis    :  0.01 (33%) usr  0.00 ( 0%) sys   0.01 (14%) wall
   preprocessing    :  0.01 (33%) usr  0.01 (100%) sys 0.00 ( 0%)  wall
   parser           :  0.00 ( 0%) usr  0.00 ( 0%) sys   0.03 (43%) wall
   final            :  0.00 ( 0%) usr  0.00 ( 0%) sys   0.01 (14%) wall
   TOTAL            :  0.03            0.01             0.07
   LCM

Execution times (seconds)
   Parser           :  0.00 ( 0%) usr    0.00 ( 0%) sys  0.01 (33%) wall
   global alloc     :  0.01 (100%) usr   0.00 ( 0%) sys  0.01 (33%) wall
   TOTAL            :  0.01              0.00            0.03
```

Architecture Specific Optimizations

Some of the features of compiler are very specific to computer architecture. It is wise to specify the architecture type along the command line to gcc command such that the resultant executable file is created which exploits the available architectural features of the processor. For this we use option –march. For example:

```
gcc  -march=pentium4 a.c
gcc –march=athlon-xp  a.c
gcc  -march=i386  a.c
gcc  -march=i686  a.c
```

2.2.10 Specifying Include Directories Along The Command Line

With the help of -I option we can specify a set of directory names along with gcc command to search for include files (header files). Directories named by -I are searched before the standard system include directories. It is dangerous to specify a standard system include directory with -I option.

Example:

```
gcc -o aa  aa.c -I /home/venkat/lib
```

To know which directories are searched by the gcc from find include files, run the following command.

```
gcc -print-search-dirs
```

Output is as follows:

```
install: /usr/lib/gcc-lib/i386-redhat-linux/3.2.2/
programs: =/usr/lib/gcc-lib/i386-redhat-linux/3.2.2/:/usr/lib/gcc-lib/i386-redhat-linux/3.2.2/:/usr/lib/gcc-lib/i386-redhat-linux/:/usr/lib/gcc/i386-redhat-linux/3.2.2/:/usr/lib/gcc/i386-redhat-linux/:/usr/lib/gcc-lib/i386-redhat-linux/3.2.2/../../../../i386-redhat-linux/bin/i386-redhat-linux/3.2.2/:/usr/lib/gcc-lib/i386-redhat-linux/3.2.2/../../../../i386-redhat-linux/bin/
libraries: =/usr/lib/gcc-lib/i386-redhat-linux/3.2.2/:/usr/lib/gcc/i386-redhat-linux/3.2.2/:/usr/lib/gcc-lib/i386-redhat-linux/3.2.2/../../../../i386-redhat-linux/lib/i386-redhat-linux/3.2.2/:/usr/lib/gcc-lib/i386-redhat-linux/3.2.2/../../../../i386-redhat-linux/lib/:/usr/lib/gcc-lib/i386-redhat-linux/3.2.2/../../../i386-redhat-linux/3.2.2/:/usr/lib/gcc-lib/i386-redhat-linux/3.2.2/../../../:/lib/i386-redhat-linux/3.2.2/:/lib/:/usr/lib/i386-redhat-linux/3.2.2/:/usr/lib/
```

2.2.11 Size Command

The size program prints out the size in bytes of each of the text, data, and BSS sections, along with the total size in decimal and hexadecimal.

size a.out

```
 text    data    bss    dec    hex filename
 1458     276      8   1742    6ce a.out
```

An executable file contains code, data and BSS (block started by symbol). However, when a program is loaded and a process is created then it will have five conceptually different areas of memory allocated to it (More details can be discussed in next chapters):

Code

Also referred as the ***text segment*** (The respective portion in the executable file is called as the *text section)*, this is the area in which the executable instructions reside. Linux and Unix arrange things so that multiple running instances of the same program share their code if possible; only one copy of the instructions for the same program resides in memory at any time.

Initialized data

Statically allocated and global data that are initialized with nonzero values live in the *data segment*. Each process running the same program has its own data segment. The portion of the executable file containing the data segment is the ***data section***.

Zero-initialized data

Global and statically allocated data that are initialized to zero by default are kept in what is colloquially called the *BSS* area of the process. Each process running the same program has its own BSS area. When running, the BSS data are placed in the data segment. In the executable file, they are stored in the *BSS section*.

In order to support above statements, the following programs are compiled and on their executable file's, size command is executed.

```
#include <stdio.h>
main()
{

static int a[2048]={9,9,0,0};

}
```

Result of the size command on the executable file of the above program.

```
text  data  bss  dec  hex    filename
702   8464         4  9170   23d2   a.out
```

```
#include <stdio.h>
int a[2048]={9,9,0,0};
main()
{
}
```

Result of the size command on the executable file of the above program.

```
text  data   bss   dec    hex    filename
702   8464   4     9170   23d2   a.out
```

The above two programs results suggests that both initialized static and global variables occupies data segment.

```
#include <stdio.h>
int a[2048];
main()
{
}
```

Result of the size command on the executable file of the above program.

text	data	bss	dec	hex	filename
702	252	8224	9178	23da	a.out

```
#include <stdio.h>
main()
{
static int a[2048];
}
```

Result of the size command on the executable file of the above program.

text	data	bss	dec	hex	filename
702	252	8224	9178	23da	a.out

The above two programs results suggests that both un initialized static and global variables occupies BSS segment.

```
#include <stdio.h>
main()
{

int a[2048];

}
```

Result of the size of command the executable file of the above program.(same results will be observed if the array is initialized to some values)

text	data	bss	dec	hex	filename
706	252	4	962	3c2	a.out

The above program's results suggests that the automatic arrays will not occupy either data or BSS segments.

Heap

The *heap* is where dynamic memory (obtained by malloc() and friends) comes from. As memory is allocated on the heap, the process's address space grows. It is also typical for the heap to start immediately after the BSS area of the data segment.

Stack

The *stack segment* is where local variables are allocated. Local variables are all variables declared inside the opening left brace of a function body (or other left brace) that aren't defined as static. Also stack is used for storing function parameters, as well as for "invisible" bookkeeping information generated by the compiler, for function return value and for storing return address representing the return from a function to its caller. Variables stored on the stack "disappear" when the function containing them returns; the space on the stack is reused for subsequent function calls.

When a program is running, the initialized data, BSS, and heap areas are usually placed into a single contiguous area: the data segment. The stack and code segments are separate from the data segment.

2.2.12 The strip command

This command discards all symbols from object files. It modifies the object files themselves instead of writing the modified copies with different names. It can work on archive files also. This may reduce the executable file size substantially with simple programs. Ofcourse, after executing strip command the resulting executable file can be executed without any difficulty.

```
strip a.out
```

If we want the resulting file to be written in another file with -o option.

```
strip a.out –o a        #here file "a" is executable file after stripping
strip –s a.out –o a # removes all symbols from executable file
strip –g a.out –o a # removes debugging information from the executable file
```

Checkup the size of the executable file (using ls –l command) after and before the strip command to see the change in file size.

The strip program removes the symbols such as the program's variables and function names from the object (executable) file. (The symbols are not loaded into memory when the program runs.) This can save significant disk space for a large program, which make it impossible to debug a core dump if it occur (On modern systems this isn't worth the trouble; don't use strip). Even after removing the symbols, the file is still larger than what gets loaded into memory since the object file format maintains additional data about the program, such as what shared libraries it may use, if any.

2.2.13 The as command

It is also possible to first create an assembly code (from C source), and then object code and then finally executable code.

```
gcc –S  file.c              #creates file.s
as   file.s  -o file.o      # object file aa.o is created
gcc  file.o                 # executable file a.out is created
```

By simply typing a.out at the command prompt we can execute the program.

It is also possible to add some assembly programs if needed to the generated assembly program (Next chapter's talks about this in detail).

2.2.14 The ldd command

This command prints the shared libraries required by each of the programs given along the command line. Also, if we specify the shared library name along the command line it displays what other shared libraries it uses.

For example

ldd /usr/lib/lynx gives the following output

```
libncurses.so.5 => /usr/lib/libncurses.so.5 (0x40033000)
libssl.so.4 => /lib/libssl.so.4 (0x40072000)
libcrypto.so.4 => /lib/libcrypto.so.4 (0x400a7000)
libc.so.6 => /lib/tls/libc.so.6 (0x42000000)
libz.so.1 => /usr/lib/libz.so.1 (0x40198000)
libresolv.so.2 => /lib/libresolv.so.2 (0x401a6000)
libgssapi_krb5.so.2 => /usr/kerberos/lib/libgssapi_krb5.so.2 (0x401b9000)
libkrb5.so.3 => /usr/kerberos/lib/libkrb5.so.3 (0x401cc000)
libk5crypto.so.3 => /usr/kerberos/lib/libk5crypto.so.3 (0x4022a000)
libcom_err.so.3 => /usr/kerberos/lib/libcom_err.so.3 (0x4023a000)
libdl.so.2 => /lib/libdl.so.2 (0x4023c000)
/lib/ld-linux.so.2 => /lib/ld-linux.so.2 (0x40000000)
```

ldd /usr/lib/libncurses.so.5 gives the following output

```
libc.so.6 => /lib/tls/libc.so.6 (0x42000000)
/lib/ld-linux.so.2 => /lib/ld-linux.so.2 (0x40000000)
```

2.2.15 Creating Dynamic Executable and Static Executable

By default, gcc creates dynamic executable files. Usually, the resulting file size will be smaller than the statically linked executable file.

gcc aa.c

ls –l a.out command displays the size as:

```
-rwxr-xr-x 1  root          root     11531 Nov 30 01:32    a.out
```

gcc -static aa.c

ls –l a.out command displays the size as:

```
-rwxr-xr-x 1  root          root     423439 Nov 30 01:34   a.out
```

To check whether the executable file is statically linked or dynamically linked, we can use:

file objectfilename

For example:

gcc aa.c
file a.out

The above command gives the following results.

a.out: ELF 32-bit LSB executable, Intel 80386, version 1 (SYSV), for GNU/Linux 2.2.5, dynamically linked (uses shared libs), not stripped

gcc –static aa.c
file a.out

The above command gives the following results.

a.out: ELF 32-bit LSB executable, Intel 80386, version 1 (SYSV), for GNU/Linux 2.2.5, statically linked, not stripped

The above commands can work on stripped executable files also.

2.2.16 Indent Command

With the help of this command, we can change the appearance of a C program by inserting or deleting whitespaces.

Example

indent C_source_filename

2.2.17 splint command

With the help of this command we can check C programs for security vulnerabilities, common programming mistakes, certain language constructs that may cause portability problems, syntax and data type errors. In fact, this identifies syntactical errors better than the compiler and produces errors in better human understandable form.

```
#include <stdio.h>
int main ()
{
int a,*x;
a=1.656;
x=1009;
scanf("%d",a);
x=(char *)malloc(10);
free(x);
printf("%d", *x);
return 0;
}
```

Result of splint command on the above file:

```
aa.c: (in function main)
aa.c:5:1: Assignment of double to int: a = 1.656
  To allow all numeric types to match, use +relaxtypes.
aa.c:6:1: Assignment of int to int *: x = 1009
  Types are incompatible. (Use -type to inhibit warning)
aa.c:7:12: Format argument 1 to scanf (%d) expects int * gets int: a
  Type of parameter is not consistent with corresponding code in format
string.
  (Use -formattype to inhibit warning)
   aa.c:7:9: Corresponding format code
aa.c:7:1: Return value (type int) ignored: scanf("%d", a)
```

Result returned by function call is not used. If this is intended, can cast result to (void) to eliminate message. (Use -retvalint to inhibit warning)

aa.c:8:1: Assignment of char * to int *: x = (char *)malloc(10)

To make char and int types equivalent, use +charint.

aa.c:10:15: Variable x used after being released

Memory is used after it has been released (either by passing as an only param or assigning to an only global). (Use -usereleased to inhibit warning)

aa.c:9:6: Storage x released

aa.c:10:15: Dereference of possibly null pointer x: *x

A possibly null pointer is dereferenced. Value is either the result of a function which may return null (in which case, code should check it is not null), or a global, parameter or structure field declared with the null qualifier. (Use -nullderef to inhibit warning) aa.c:8:3: Storage x may become null

Now run splint command on the following program.

```
#include<stdio.h>
void ff()
{
int *p=(int *) malloc(10);
}
int main()
{
char *p="rama";
free(p);
printf("%s\n", p);
}
```

Output of splint:

```
nul.c: (in function ff)
nul.c:5:2: Fresh storage p not released before return
A memory leak has been detected. Storage allocated locally is not released
before the last reference to it is lost. (Use -mustfreefresh to inhibit warning)
nul.c:4:27: Fresh storage p created
nul.c:4:6: Variable p declared but not used
A variable is declared but never used. Use /*@unused@*/ in front of
declaration to suppress message. (Use -varuse to inhibit warning)
nul.c: (in function main)
```

nul.c:9:6: Function call may modify observer p: p
Storage declared with observer is possibly modified. Observer storage may not be modified. (Use -modobserver to inhibit warning)
nul.c:8:9: Storage p becomes observer
nul.c:9:6: Observer storage p passed as only param: free (p)
Observer storage is transferred to a non-observer reference. (Use -observertrans to inhibit warning)
nul.c:8:9: Storage p becomes observer
nul.c:10:16: Variable p used after being released
Memory is used after it has been released (either by passing as an only param or assigning to an only global). (Use -usereleased to inhibit warning)
nul.c:9:6: Storage p released
nul.c:11:2: Path with no return in function declared to return int
There is a path through a function declared to return a value on which there is no return statement. This means the execution may fall through without returning a meaningful result to the caller. (Use -noret to inhibit warning)

2.2.18 Use of cc1 command

We can execute cc1 command directly. However, it needs "a.i" file, i.e the file after which is created preprocessing the source. It gives statistics such as the following.

/usr/lib/gcc-lib/i386-redhat-linux/cc1 a.i

Output

main

Execution times (seconds)

Preprocessing	:	0.01 (6%) usr	0.00 (0%) sys	0.01 (6%) wall
parser	:	0.01 (6%) usr	0.00 (0%) sys	0.01 (6%) wall
flow analysis	:	0.01 (6%) usr	0.00 (0%) sys	0.01 (6%) wall
mode switching	:	0.01 (6%) usr	0.00 (0%) sys	0.01 (6%) wall
global alloc	:	0.01 (6%) usr	0.00 (0%) sys	0.01 (6%) wall
reg stack	:	0.01 (6%) usr	0.00 (0%) sys	0.01 (6%) wall
rest of compilation	:	0.01 (6%) usr	0.00 (0%) sys	0.01 (6%) wall
TOTAL	:	0.16	0.01	0.17

2.3 Functions with Variable Number of Arguments

Most of the young C programmers wonders how it became possible for C standard library developers to write functions such as printf(), scanf() to take variable number of arguments. Also, it is often desirable to implement a function where the number of arguments is not known, or is not constant, when the function is written.

```
int f(int, ... ) {
        .     .
        .
}
```

In order to achieve this, the functions declared in the <stdarg.h> header file must be included. This introduces a new type, called a va_list, and three functions that operate on objects of this type, called va_start, va_arg, and va_end.

Before manipulating variable argument list, va_start must be called whose prototype is:

```
void va_start(valist ap, parmN);
```

The va_start macro initializes ap for subsequent use by the functions va_arg and va_end. The second argument to va_start, parmN is the identifier naming the rightmost parameter in the variable parameter list in the function definition (the one just before the , ...). The identifier parmN must not be declared with register storage class or as a function or array type.

The arguments supplied can be accessed by calling va_arg() macro repeatedly. This is peculiar because the type returned is determined by an argument to the macro. Note that this is impossible to implement as a true function, only as a macro. It is defined as

```
type va_arg(va_list ap, type);
```

Each call to this macro will extract the next argument from the argument list as a value of the specified type (If the next argument is not of the specified type, the behavior is undefined). Take care here to avoid problems which could be caused by arithmetic conversions. Use of char or short as the second argument to va_arg is invariably an error: these types always promote up to one of signed int or unsigned int, and float converts to double. Note that it is implementation defined whether objects declared to have the types char, unsigned char, unsigned short and unsigned bitfields will promote to unsigned int, rather complicating the use of va_arg.

The behavior is also undefined if va_arg is called when there were no further arguments.

When all the arguments have been processed, the va_end function should be called. This will prevent the va_list supplied from being used any further. If va_end is not used, the behavior is undefined.

The entire argument list can be re-traversed by calling va_start again, after calling va_end. The va_end function is declared as

```
void va_end(va list ap);
```

The following example shows the use of va_start, va_arg, and va_end to implement a function that returns the average of its integer arguments.

```
#include <stdlib.h>
#include <stdarg.h>
#include <stdio.h>

int AVG(int nargs, ...){
        register int i;
        int avg;
        va_list ap;

        va_start(ap, nargs);
    avg=0;
        for(i = 1; i <= nargs; i++)
                avg+= va_arg(ap, int);

        va_end(ap);
        return (avg/nargs);
}

void f(void) {
        printf("%d\n",AVG(3, 33,44,55));
}


main(){
        f();
        exit(0);
}
```

2.4 Compiling a Multi-Source "C" Programs

We have learned how to compile a single-source program properly (hopefully by now you played a little with the compiler and tried out a few examples of your own). Yet, sooner or later we'll see that having all the source in a single file is rather limiting, for several reasons:

- As the file grows, compilation time tends to grow, and for each little change, the whole program has to be re-compiled.
- It is very hard, if not impossible, that several people will work on the same project together in this manner.
- Managing our code becomes harder. Backing out erroneous changes becomes nearly impossible.
- Also, developing programs as a single file limits code sharing or reusing.

The solution to this would be to split the source code into multiple files, each containing a set of closely-related functions (or, in C++, all the source code for a single class).

There are two possible ways to compile a multi-source C program. The first is to use a single command line to compile all the files. Suppose that we have a program whose source is found in files "main.c", "a.c", and "b.c". We could compile it this way:

```
gcc main.c a.c b.c -o hello_world
```

This will cause the compiler to compile each of the given files separately, and then link them all together to one executable file named "hello_world". Two comments about this program:

1. If we define a function (or a variable) in one file, and try to access them from the second file, we need to declare them as external symbols in the second file. This is done using the C "extern" keyword.
2. The order of presenting the source files on the command line may be altered. The compiler (actually, the linker) will know how to take the relevant code from each file into the final program, even if the first source file tries to use a function defined in the second or third source file.

The problem with this way of compilation is that even if we only make a change in one of the source files, all of them will be re-compiled when we run the compiler again. In order to overcome this limitation, we can divide the compilation process into two phases - compiling, and linking. Let us first see how this is done, and then we will explain.

```
cc -c main.cc
cc -c a.c
cc -c b.c
cc main.o a.o b.o -o hello_world
```

Each of the first 3 commands takes one source file, each compiles it into "object file", (as explained above) with the same names, but with a ".o" suffix. It is the "-c" flag that tells the compiler only to create an object file, and not to generate a final executable file just yet. The object file contains the code for the source file in machine language, but with some unresolved symbols. For example, the "main.o" file refers to a symbol named "func_a", which is a function defined in file "a.c". Thus, after creating the 3 object files, we use the 4th command to link the 3 object files into one program. The linker (which is invoked by the compiler now) takes all the symbols from the 3 object files, and links them together - it makes sure that when "func_a" is invoked from the code in object file "main.o", the function code in object file "a.o" gets executed. Further more, the linker also links the standard C library into the program, in this case, to resolve the "printf" symbol properly.

To see why this complexity actually helps us, we should note that normally the link phase is much faster than the compilation phase. This is especially true when doing optimizations, since that step is done before linking. Now, lets assume we change the source file "a.c", and we want to re-compile the program. We'll only need now two commands:

```
cc -c a.c
cc main.o a.o b.o -o hello_world
```

In our small example, it's hard to notice the speed-up, but in a case of having few tens of files each containing a few hundred lines of source-code, the time saving is significant; not to mention about even larger projects.

2.5 How main() is executed on Linux[2]

In the previous sections, we have explained how to compile C language programs in addition to other tools usage. In the following paragraphs, we try to answer the question how does Linux execute main()? On Linux, our C main() function is executed by the cooperative work of GCC, libc and Linux's binary loader. Preferably read chapter on "Assembly Programming under Linux" also. We will use the following simple C program ("simple.c") to illustrate how it works.

```
include<stdio.h>
int main()
{
  return(0);
}
```

gcc -o simple simple.c

To see what's in the executable, let's use a tool "objdump". More about this command will be discussed in the next chapters.

objdump -f simple

```
simple:     file format elf32-i386
architecture: i386, flags 0x00000112:
EXEC_P, HAS_SYMS, D_PAGED
start address 0x080482d0
```

From the output we can understand that the the file is "ELF32" format and the start address is "0x080482d0".

ELF is acronym for **Executable and Linking Format**. It's one of the several object and executable file formats used on Unix systems. For our discussion, the interesting thing about ELF is its header format. Every ELF executable has ELF header, which is the following.

```
typedef struct
{
unsigned char    e_ident[EI_NIDENT];  /* Magic number and other info */
Elf32_Half       e_type;              /* Object file type */
```

[2] **http://www.linuxgazette.com/**

```
Elf32_Half      e_machine;      /* Architecture */
Elf32_Word      e_version;      /* Object file version */
Elf32_Addr      e_entry;        /* Entry point virtual address */
Elf32_Off       e_phoff;        * Program header table file offset */
Elf32_Off       e_shoff;        /* Section header table file offset */
Elf32_Word      e_flags;        /* Processor-specific flags *
Elf32_Half      e_ehsize;       /* ELF header size in bytes */
Elf32_Half      e_phentsize;    /* Program header table entry size */
Elf32_Half      e_phnum;        /* Program header table entry count */
Elf32_Half      e_shentsize;    /* Section header table entry size */
Elf32_Half      e_shnum;        /* Section header table entry count */
Elf32_Half      e_shstrndx;     /* Section header string table index */
} Elf32_Ehdr;
```

In the above structure, there is "e_entry" field, which is starting address of an executable.

What's starting address "0x080482d0"?

For this question, let's disassemble the machine language file "simple". There are several tools to disassemble an executable. We will use objdump for this purpose also.

objdump --disassemble simple

The output is a little bit long, so we will not show entire output from objdump. Our intention is see what's at address 0x080482d0. Here is the output.

```
080482d0 <_start>:
80482d0:    31 ed             xor     %ebp,%ebp
80482d2:    5e                pop     %esi
80482d3:    89 e1             mov     %esp,%ecx
80482d5:    83 e4 f0          and     $0xfffffff0,%esp
80482d8:    50                push    %eax
80482d9:    54                push    %esp
80482da:    52                push    %edx
80482db:    68 20 84 04 08    push    $0x8048420
80482e0:    68 74 82 04 08    push    $0x8048274
80482e5:    51                push    %ecx
80482e6:    56                push    %esi
80482e7:    68 d0 83 04 08    push    $0x80483d0
80482ec:    e8 cb ff ff ff    call    80482bc <_init+0x48>
80482f1:    f4                hlt
80482f2:    89 f6             mov     %esi,%esi
```

Those people who knows assembly language can understand that the executable file contains some kind of starting routine called "_start" at the starting address. It clears a register, push some values into stack and call a function. According to this instruction, the stack frame should look like this.

```
Stack Top   -------------------
            0x80483d0
            -------------------
            jesi
            -------------------
            ecx
            -------------------
            0x8048274
            -------------------
            0x8048420
            -------------------
            edx
            -------------------
            esp
            -------------------
            eax
            -------------------
```

If we look at disassembled output from objdump carefully, we can see that the addresses pushed into stack are addresses of functions. To summarize:

0x80483d0 : This is the address of our main() function.

0x8048274 : _init function.

0x8048420 : _fini function _init and _fini is initialization/finalization functions of GCC.

Let us look for address 80482bc from the disassembly output.

```
80482bc:    ff 25 48 95 04 08        jmp    *0x8049548
```

Here *0x8049548 is a pointer operation.

It just jumps to an address stored at address 0x8049548.

As we know that this object file "simple" is dynamically linked, the address may be filled during run time. As explained earlier, if we issue the command "ldd simple" we get the following result.

```
libc.so.6               =>    /lib/i686/libc.so.6     (0x42000000)
/lib/ld-linux.so.2      =>    /lib/ld-linux.so.2      (0x40000000)
```

We can see all the libraries dynamically linked with simple. And all the dynamically linked data and functions have "dynamic relocation entry" in executable file i.e in ELF records.

We can see all dynamic link entries with objdump command.

```
objdump -R simple

simple:     file format elf32-i386

DYNAMIC RELOCATION RECORDS
OFFSET   TYPE              VALUE
0804954c    R_386_GLOB_DAT     __gmon_start__
08049540    R_386_JUMP_SLOT    __register_frame_info
08049544    R_386_JUMP_SLOT    __deregister_frame_info
08049548    R_386_JUMP_SLOT    __libc_start_main
```

Here address 0x8049548 is called "jump slot", which perfectly makes sense. And according to the table, actually we want to call __libc_start_main.

The __libc_start_main is a function in libc.so.6. If we look for __libc_start_main in glibc source code, the prototype looks like this.

```
extern int BP_SYM (__libc_start_main)(int *main)(int, char **, char**),
                        int argc,
                        char *__unbounded *__unbounded ubp_av,
                        void (*init) (void),
                        void (*fini) (void),
                        void (*rtld_fini) (void),
                        void *__unbounded stack_end)
__attribute__ ((noreturn));
```

And all the assembly instructions is to set up argument stack and call __libc_start_main.

What this function does is setup/initialize some data structures/environments and call our main().

Let's look at the stack frame with this function prototype.

```
Stack Top  ------------------
           0x80483d0          main
           -------------------
           esi                argc
           -------------------
           ecx                argv
           -------------------
           0x8048274          _init
           -------------------
           0x8048420          _fini
           -------------------
           edx                _rtlf_fini
           -------------------
```

```
esp                 stack_end
-------------------
eax                 this is 0
-------------------
```

According to this stack frame, esi, ecx, edx, esp, eax registers should be filled with appropriate values before __libc_start_main() is executed. And clearly this registers are not set by the startup assembly instructions shown before. Instead kernel involves in between.

Really, when we execute a program by entering a name at the shell prompt, this is what happens on Linux machine.

1. The shell calls the kernel system call "execve" with argc/argv.
2. The kernel system call handler gets control and start handling the system call. In kernel code, the handler is "sys_execve". On x86, the user-mode application passes all required parameters to kernel with the following registers.
   - ebx : pointer to program name string
   - ecx : argv array pointer
   - edx : environment variable array pointer.
3. The generic execve kernel system call handler, which is do_execve, is called. What it does is set up a data structure and copy some data from user space to kernel space and finally calls search_binary_handler(). Linux can support more than one executable file format such as a.out and ELF at the same time. For this functionality, there is a data structure "struct linux_binfmt", which has a function pointer for each binary format loader. And search_binary_handler() just looks up an appropriate handler and calls it. In our case, load_elf_binary() is the handler. Here is the bottom line of the function. It first sets up kernel data structures for file operation to read the ELF executable image in. Then it sets up a kernel data structure: code size, data segment start, stack segment start, etc. And it allocates user mode pages for this process and copies the argv and environment variables to those allocated page addresses. Finally, argc, the argv pointer, and the environment variable array pointer are pushed to user mode stack by create_elf_tables(), and start_thread() starts the process execution rolling.

   Layout of segment created can be represented with *Figure 2.5* Yellow parts represent correspondent program sections. Shared libraries are not shown here; their layout duplicates layout of program.

code	.text section
data	.data section
bss	.bss section
... ...	free space
stack	stack (described later)
arguments	program arguments
environment	program environment
program name	filename of program (duplicated in arguments section)
Null (dword)	final dword of zero

Figure 2.5 Segment layout of an ELF binary.

Stack layout

Initial stack layout is very important, because it provides access to command line and environment of a program. Here is a picture (Figure 2.6) of what is on the stack when program is launched:

argc	[dword] argument counter (integer)
Argv[0]	[dword] program name (pointer)
argv[1] **...** **argv[argc-1]**	[dword] program args (pointers)
NULL	[dword] end of args (integer)
env[0] **env[1]** **...** **env[n]**	[dword] environment variables (pointers)
NULL	[dword] end of environment (integer)

Figure 2.6 Stack layout of an ELF binary.

By the time, when the _start assembly instruction gets control of execution, the stack frame contain

```
Stack Top        -------------
                 argc
```

```
-------------
argv pointer
-------------
env pointer
-------------
```

To Summarize

1. GCC build your program with crtbegin.o/crtend.o/gcrt1.o And the other default libraries are dynamically linked by default. Starting address of the executable is set to that of _start.
2. Kernel loads the executable and setup text/data/bss/stack, especially, kernel allocate page(s) for arguments and environment variables and pushes all necessary information on stack.
3. Control is passed to _start. _start gets all information from stack setup by kernel, sets up argument stack for __libc_start_main, and calls it.
4. The __libc_start_main initializes necessary stuffs, especially C library(such as malloc) and environment and calls our main.
5. Our main is called with main(argv, argv) Actually, here one interesting point is the signature of main. The __libc_start_main thinks main's signature as main(int, char **, char **).

The same procedure can be explained in Figure 2.7 along with the names of the functions.

Function	Kernel file	Comments
shell	...	on user side one types in program name and strikes enter
execve()	...	shell calls libc function
Sys_execve()	...	libc calls kernel...
Sys_execve()	arch/i386/kernel/process.c	arrive to kernel side
Do_execve()	fs/exec.c	open file and do some preparation
search_binary_handler()	fs/exec.c	find out type of executable
load_elf_binary()	fs/binfmt_elf.c	load ELF (and needed libraries) and create user segment
start_thread()	include/asm-i386/processor.h	and finally pass control to program code

Figure 2.7 Startup process of an ELF binary[3].

2.6 What Linux Does for Executable File

When we execute a program (say a.out), after checking for shell functions or aliases (and finding none for this command), the shell calls fork() so that now two copies of the shell are running (for more on the fork() system call, see Stevens, Venkateswarlu). After the fork() returns, the resulting child shell process calls the exec() system call, which causes

[3] source for figures 2,3 and 4 is linuxassembly.com

the operating system to load and run the a.out program in place of the child shell, effectively killing the shell (but not the process). The parent (shell process) waits for a.out to finish, then issues another command.

Once the child shell calls exec() to start running a.out, the kernel has to do some work before the program can begin execution. Linux kernel when it ran through the exec() functions, it would eventually lead to a function in the kernel called load_elf_binary() (located in the kernel source file fs/binfmt_elf.c) that copies the data from the .bss section of the executable into the bss segment in the new process's virtual address space. It also copies the .data section into the new data segment, and the .text section into the new text segment.

After the segments are set up and the arguments to the program and its environment are copied into the address space, load_elf_binary() calls the start_thread() function, and the program begins executing the code in its text segment.

Each new library that is dynamically loaded gets its own text, bss, and data segments in the process address space. The operating system stacks them up as they are loaded. We can see this best by looking at a process while it's running.

We can get a map of a running process's virtual address space by looking in the file /proc/pid/maps, where pid is the process ID of the one we're interested in. To see the process's virtual address map, run:

more /proc/23098/maps

Here, 23098 is the PID of the process.

Figure 2.8 shows the map of the process space of the executable. The numbers in the first column show the virtual address ranges for each of the segments. The first two are for the text and data segments of a.out. There's no bss segment in the process map since there was no data in the bss section of a.out.

```
08048000-08049000 r-xp 00000000 /home/chelf/linuxmag/0202/a.out
08049000-0804a000 rw-p 00000000 /home/chelf/linuxmag/0202/a.out
40000000-40015000 r-xp 00000000 /lib/ld-2.2.4.so
40015000-40016000 rw-p 00014000 /lib/ld-2.2.4.so
40016000-40017000 rw-p 00000000
40017000-4001b000 r-xp 00000000 /lib/libsafe.so.1.3
4001b000-4001c000 rw-p 00003000 /lib/libsafe.so.1.3
4001c000-4001d000 r-xp 00000000 /home/chelf/linuxmag/0202/b.so
4001d000-4001e000 rw-p 00000000 /home/chelf/linuxmag/0202/b.so
4001e000-4001f000 rw-p 00000000
40025000-40027000 r-xp 00000000 /lib/libdl-2.2.4.so
40027000-40029000 rw-p 00001000 /lib/libdl-2.2.4.so
40029000-40155000 r-xp 00000000 /lib/libc-2.2.4.so
40155000-4015a000 rw-p 0012b000 /lib/libc-2.2.4.so
4015a000-4015f000 rw-p 00000000
bfffe000-c0000000 rwxp fffff000
```

Figure 2.8 A map of the address space of a.out.

We can identify the text segment by the "x" in the second column (it stands for "executable," just like in the output from ls -l). The "w" means the segment is writable and identifies the data segment. Executable segments cannot be written on because Linux doesn't allow self-modifying code. All segments must be readable (the "r" in the second column).

The lower segments for our executable are the segments for the "ld" library. In this case, "ld" doesn't stand for the ld linker, but rather what's called the program interpreter (yes, that's a very poor name for it). The program interpreter analyzes the executable, figures out which shared libraries are necessary for it to run, and locates and loads them into the virtual address space for the executable. In this case, it brought in libc, libdl, and libsafe.

The libsafe library (along with libc) is always linked into executables by the ld linker. It ensures that you don't overflow your stack or try to write past what you are currently allowed (For more on libsafe, see http://www.gnu.org/directory/libsafe.html).

Also in the map, we can see the shared library we built, b.so. However, this library wasn't loaded into the virtual address space by the program interpreter.

2.7 Compiling A Single-Source "C++" Program

Now that we saw how to compile C programs, the transition to C++ programs is rather simple. All we need to do is use a C++ compiler, in place of the C compiler we used so far. So, if our program source is in a file named; 'executable_filename.cc' ('cc' to denote C++ code. Some programmers prefer a suffix of 'C' for C++ code), we will use a command such as the following:

g++ file.cc -o executable_filename

Or on some systems we'll use "CC" instead of "g++" (for example, with Sun's compiler for Solaris), or "aCC" (HP's compiler), and so on. We would note that with C++ compilers there is less uniformity regarding command line options, partially because until recently the language was evolving and had no agreed standard. But still, at least with g++, we will use "-g" for debug information in the code, and "-O" for optimization.

2.8 Combining C and C++ programs

While developing practical SW systems, we may encounter the need for mixed language programming. That is, we may be required to use some C programs and some other C++ programs while building the SW system. This can be achieved in many ways. In the chapter on Assembly Language, we will discuss about how to mix assembly with C.

In the case of C and C++ mixed programming, we can compile C programs using gcc compiler and create object files and using g++ compiler we can compile C++ programs and create object files. All the object files can be used to create final executable file.

For example, consider the following C function in a file a.c. We can use the same in C++ program (g1.C) by specifying that "a.c" file is external file and contains C code as shown in the program "g1.C".

File a.c:

```
int LCM(int x, int y)
{
 int a=x<y?y:x;

while(a<=(x*y))
{
 if( (a%x==0)&&(a%y==0)) return a;
a++;
}
}
```

File g1.C

```
#include<iostream.h>
extern "C" {
#include "a.c"
}

int main()
{

int x,y;

cout<<"Enter Two Integers"<<endl;

cin>>x>>y;

cout<<"LCM="<<LCM(x,y)<<endl;

}
```

To compile and run this C++ program, we can enter the following commands.

```
g++ -o g1 g1.C
./g1
```

Note: Please note that we can directly use the C file which is having a function code as there is no difference exists between functions of C and C++. That is, we can as well modify the g1.C to have the following code.

```
#include<iostream.h>

int LCM(int,int);
int main()
{

int x,y;

cout<<"Enter Two Integers"<<endl;

cin>>x>>y;

cout<<"LCM="<<LCM(x,y)<<endl;

}
```

To compile and run the g1.C, execute the following commands.

```
g++ -o g11 g1.C a.c
./g11
```

In the following example, we have explained how a C function (the one defined in the above a.c file) can be used in C++ and specifically from a member function of a class. A header file "a.h" is used in C++ program "RAT.C". This header file contains preprocessor directives to indicate the C++ compiler that LCM is an external "C" function. Compile "RAT.C" to object file. Then both the object files are linked to get the finally executable file (Note: this "RAT.C" defines a class to represent rational number and overloads + operator between rational number type of objects).

File a.h

```
#ifdef __cplusplus
extern "C" {
#endif
extern int LCM(int, int);
#ifdef __cplusplus
}
#endif
```

File RAT.C

```
#include<iostream.h>

#include "a.h"

class RAT
```

```
{
int p,q;

public:
void INP()
{
cin>>p>>q;
TRIM();
}
void OUT()
{
cout <<p<<"/"<<q<<endl;
}
RAT operator+(RAT X)
{
 RAT T;
 int lcm=LCM(q,X.q);
 T.p=p*lcm/q+X.p*lcm/X.q;
 T.q=lcm;
T.TRIM();
return T;
}
void TRIM()
{
 int a=p>q?q:p;

/* Finding GCF */
while(a)
{
 if( (p%a==0)&&(q%a==0)) break;

a--;
}
/* Divide both numerator and denominator with GCF*/

p=p/a; q=q/a;


}
};

int main()
{
RAT A,B,C;
A.INP();
B.INP();
```

```
C=A+B;
C.OUT();
}
```

To compile and Test

```
gcc –c a.c
g++ -c RAT.C
g++ RAT.o a.o

./a.out
1 2
2 3
7/6
```

Similarly, if we want a C++ function to be used in a C program, first we have to mention that C++ function is having external linkage for C language.

An example C++ file "y.C"

```
extern "C" int abs(int x)
{
 return (x<0?-x:x);
}
```

Header file "y.h"

```
#ifdef __cplusplus
extern "C"
#endif
int abs(int x);
```

C file "z.c"

```
#include<stdio.h>
#include "y.h"
int main()
{
 int p=-19;

printf("%d\n", abs(p) );
}
```

To create executable file, continue the following manner.

```
gcc –c z.c
g++ -c y.C
g++ -o aa z.o y.o
./aa
```

We can declare at most one function of an overloaded set as extern "C" because only one C function can have a given name. If we need to access overloaded functions from C, we can write C++ wrapper functions with different names as the following example demonstrates.

File having C++ overloaded functions (yy.C)

```
 int abs(int x)
{
 return (x<0?-x:x);
}
 float abs(float x)
{
 return (x<0?-x:x);
}
 double abs(double x)
{
 return (x<0?-x:x);
}

extern "C" int abs_int(int x){ return abs(x); }
extern "C" float abs_float(float x){ return abs(x); }
extern "C" double abs_double(double x){ return abs(x); }
```

Header file "yy.h" contains

```
#ifdef __cplusplus
extern "C"
#endif
int abs_int(int x);
double abs_float(float x);
float abs_double(double x);
```

The c program which calls the functions in C++ program contains the following.

```
#include<stdio.h>
#include "yy.h"
int main()
{
 int p=-19;
float x=1.212;
double y=-1.222222;

printf("%d %f %lf\n", abs_int(p), abs_float(x), abs_double(y) );
}
```

To create executable file, continue the following manner.

```
gcc –c zz.c
g++ -c yy.C
g++ -o aaa zz.o yy.o
./aaa
```

We may also need wrapper functions to call template functions because template functions cannot be declared as extern "C". The above "yy.C" C++ program can be changed as follows to achieve this.

```
template<class A>
 A abs(A x)
{
 return (x<0?-x:x);
}

extern "C" int abs_int(int x){ return abs(x); }
extern "C" float abs_float(float x){ return abs(x); }
extern "C" double abs_double(double x){ return abs(x); }
```

As usual, compile this C++ program separately and C program separately and link using g++.

The following examples, explains how to pass C++ class type of objects/addresses to C functions.

The following header file "RAT.h" has to be included in both C and C++ programs. In C++ program if this header is included, class RAT will be defined and at the same time function f() will declared as external. Similarly, if this header file is included in a C program, then class RAT will not get defined. Rather, an incomplete declaration of structure with the same name RAT gets defined. In addition, declarations of the functions f(), XYZ() are included.

We did write extern "C" functions in C++ that access class RAT objects and call them from C code. This became possible as unlike C++, C will not distinguish pointers whether they are of class RAT type or struct RAT type. Thus, it became possible to send class RAT type of object to C function. However, this is not a good programming practice though.

```
#ifndef RAT_H
 #define RAT_H

 #ifdef __cplusplus

class RAT
{
 int p,q;
public:
void INP(){ cin>>p>>q;}
void OUT(){ cout<<p<<"\t"<<q<<endl;}
};

 #else
   typedef
     struct RAT
       RAT;
 #endif

 #ifdef __cplusplus
 extern "C" {
 #endif

 #if defined(__STDC__) || defined(__cplusplus)
   extern void f(RAT *);
   extern void XYZ(RAT *);
 #else
   extern void f();        /* K&R style */
   extern void XYZ();
 #endif

 #ifdef __cplusplus
 }
 #endif

 #endif /*RAT_H*/
```

```
The C++ program file (pp.C)
#include<iostream.h>
#include "RAT.h"

void XYZ(RAT *P)
{
P->INP();
P->OUT();
}

int main()
{
 RAT A;
f(&A);
}

The C program file (pq.c)
#include "RAT.h"
void f( RAT *A)
{
 XYZ(A);
}
```

To compile and run the program, do execute the following commands.

```
g++ -c pp.C
gcc –c pq.c
g++ -o pp  pp.o pq.o
./pp
```

2.9 How to use C/C++ functions in Java

Some times, we may need to use C programs in a Java program. To achieve this, we may need to use JNI (Java Native Interface). The following steps are needed to achieve this.

1. Begin by writing the Java program. Create a Java class that declares the native method; this class contains the declaration or signature for the native method. It also includes a main method which calls the native method.

   Consider the following Java program file HelloWorld.java which prints "Hello World!". Here, the native method displayHelloWorld() is declared which is supposed to print the above message. Its implementation is explained later.

```
class HelloWorld {
   public native void displayHelloWorld();
```

```
    static {
        System.loadLibrary("hello");
    }

    public static void main(String[] args) {
        new HelloWorld().displayHelloWorld();
    }
}
```

2. Compile the Java class that declares the native method and the main method. That is, enter the following command at command prompt.

   javac HelloWorld.java

   This creates HelloWorld.class file.

3. Generate a header file for the native method using javah with the native interface flag -jni. Once we've generated the header file, we have the formal signature for our native method.

   javah -jni HelloWorld

   The javah utility program generates a header file (.h file) from the HelloWorld class. The header file provides a C function signature for the implementation of the native method displayHelloWorld defined in that class.

   The name of the header file is the Java class name with a .h appended to the end. For example, the command shown above will generate a file named HelloWorld.h.

   By default, javah places the new .h file in the same directory as the .class file. Use the -d option to instruct javah to place the header files in a different directory.

   Content of the generated .h file is as follows:

```
/* DO NOT EDIT THIS FILE - it is machine generated */

#ifndef __HelloWorld__
#define __HelloWorld__

#include <jni.h>

#ifdef __cplusplus
extern "C"
{
#endif
extern JNIEXPORT void JNICALL Java_HelloWorld_displayHelloWorld (JNIEnv
*env, jobject);
```

```
#ifdef __cplusplus
}
#endif

#endif /* __HelloWorld__ */
```

Notice that the implementation of the native function, as it appears in the header file, accepts two parameters even though, in its definition on the Java side, it accepts no parameters. The JNI requires every native method to have these two parameters. The first parameter for every native method is a JNIEnv interface pointer. It is through this pointer that our native code accesses parameters and objects passed to it from the Java application. The second parameter is jobject, which references the current object itself. In a sense, we can think of the jobject parameter as the "this" variable in Java. For a native instance method, such as the displayHelloWorld method in our example, the jobject argument is a reference to the current instance of the object. For native class methods, this argument would be a reference to the method's Java class. Our example ignores both parameters.

4. Write the implementation of the native method in the programming language of our choice, such as C or C++. In the following, the file HelloWorldImp.c content is displayed which shows implementation of the native method declared in .java file.

```
#include <jni.h>
#include "HelloWorld.h"
#include <stdio.h>

JNIEXPORT void JNICALL
Java_HelloWorld_displayHelloWorld(JNIEnv *env, jobject obj)
{
   printf("Hello world!\n");
   return;
}
```

5. Compile the header and implementation files into a shared library file.

```
gcc -fpic -c HelloWorldImp.c
gcc -shared -Wl,-soname,libhello.so -o libhello.so HelloWorldImp.c
```

6. Run the Java program.

```
java HelloWorld
```

If there is any problem with the loading the shared library, libhello.so then change environment variable LD_LIBRARY_PATH to include current directory or the directory where libhello.so is located.

For example, run the following command at the dollar prompt.

```
LD_LIBRARY_PATH=$LD_LIBRARY_PATH:.
export LD_LIBRARY_PATH
```

2.10 Using Fortran in C/C++

Sometimes it may be also needed to mix Fortran and C/C++ programs. In the following paragraphs, we will explain how a Fortran subroutine can be called from C/C++ functions and also a C/C++ function from Fortran routine.

1. First prepare C/C++ function which is supposed to be called from a Fortran routine (say a1.C). Make sure that function name should have underscore at the end and is in lower case. Fortran passes all the arguments in passing by reference fashion thus make sure that our C/C++ function follows the same convention. That is, if we are really planning to pass an integer from Fortran to a C function, then in the C/C++ function definition we have to declare the argument as long * type (Remember that long is equivalent variable type in C/C++ for Fortran's INTEGER). Also, remember to declare that the function is external type as explained in the previous sections.

```
#include<iostream.h>
extern "C"
{
void lcm_(long *p, long *q, long *r)

{
 long x=*p,y=*q;
 long a=x<y?y:x;

while(a<=(x*y))
{
 if( (a%x==0)&&(a%y==0)) break;

a++;
}

*r=a;
}
}
```

Compile the above program with the following command such that we will get an object file a1.o.

```
g++ -c a1.C
```

2. Similarly, if we want to call a Fortran routine from a C/C++ program include its declaration also. For example, see the following file bb.C how it will be done.

```
extern "C" int mymain_();
int main()
{
   return mymain_();
}
```

Compile this file also using the following command which gives an object file bb.o .

g++ -c bb.C

3. Write a Fortran program in a file (say a.f) which calls the function (lcm) defined in the file a1.C.

```
SUBROUTINE MYMAIN
write(*,*)'Enter Two Integers'
read(*,*) M,N
CALL LCM(M,N,K)
write(*,*) 'LCM=', K
RETURN
END
```

Compile this Fortran program using the following command which gives the object file a.o.

f77 -c a.f

4. Link all the above object files using g++ using an option -lg2c (In old versions of GCC you may have to use -lf2c).

g++ -o bb bb.o a1.o a.o -lg2c

5. Test the above program by typing its name at the command prompt.

./bb

2.11 Conclusions

This chapter explains about the compiling C program's in Linux Unix environment. The compilation stages and their objectives are explained in a step by step fashion. Also, multi file programming is also explained. At the end, how a "c++" program can be compiled under Unix is also explained. Also, how C, C++, Java, Fortran programs can be mixed also explained in a step by step fashion. Moreover, we have explained how actually main() is initiated and how Linux OS coordinates the same is explained.

3 Command Line Arguments

3.1 Introduction

The previous chapter explained how the Unix/Linux system starts a C program by calling the function `main'. In ISO C, we can define `main' either to take no arguments, or to take two arguments that represent the command line arguments to the program, like this:

```
int main (int ARGC, char *ARGV[])
int main (int ARGC, char **ARGV)
```

The command line arguments are the whitespace-separated tokens given in the shell prompt along with the program; thus, in `cat foo bar', the arguments are `foo' and `bar'. The only way a program can look at its command line arguments is via the arguments of `main'. If `main' doesn't take arguments, then we cannot get at the command line. Rather, we can say that this is another way of giving input to the program while it is running.

The value of the ARGC argument is set to the number of command line arguments. The ARGV argument is a vector of C strings; its elements are the individual command line argument strings or tokens given along with the command. The file name of the program being run is also included in the vector as the first element; the value of ARGC counts this element. A null pointer always follows the last element: `ARGV[ARGC]' is this null pointer. To be specifically, all the strings given along the command line are stored in the programs address space and their addresses are stored in this character pointer array. At the same time, ARGC value is initialised to the number of command line arguments including the program name (This may differ in some languages such as Java). **See stack layout in Chapter 2 for more details.**

For the command `cat foo bar', ARGC is 3 and ARGV has three elements, `"cat"', `"foo"' and `"bar"'.

Example 1

The following example prints all the command line arguments including the program name.

```
#include <stdio.h>
int main(int argc, char *argv[])
{
  int i;
for(i=0;i<argc; i++) printf("%s\n", argv[i]);

return 0;
}
```

Let the above program name is a.c. Compile with the following command.

gcc –o a a.c

Fro example, run the same in the following manner.

a rao raj 123 abhi 1233

The result what we get is:

```
a
rao
raj
123
abhi
1233
```

Please note that even if numbers which are given along the command line, they will be stored like strings in the memory and their addresses are available in argv pointer array.

Example 2

Write a program which takes a string along the command line and prints "Yes" if it is a palindrome; otherwise prints "No".

```
#include <stdio.h>
#include<stdlib.h>
#include<string.h>
int main(int argc, char *argv[])
{
 int i, j, n;

 n=strlen(argv[1]);
                /* length of the string (argv[1] ) given along the command line
*/

/* compares first character with last character and vice versa*/

for(i=0, j=n-1;  i<j; i++, j--)
if(argv[1][i]!=argv[1][j]) break;

if(i>=j) printf("Yes\n");
else
   printf("No\n");

return 0;
}
```

Example 3

Write a program which takes a set of numbers (integers) along the command line and prints their average.

```
#include <stdio.h>
#include<stdlib.h>
int main(int argc, char *argv[])
{
 int i;
float s=0;

for(i=1;i<argc; i++) s += atoi(argv[i]);

/* Mind that first argument is program name itself. Thus, i is taken from 1.
Also mind that the numbers are stored as strings. Thus, atoi() function is
called to get value of the integer from the string
*/

printf("Average=%f\n",  s/(float) (argc-1) );

return 0;
}
```

Example 4

Write a program which takes room dimensions length, breadth and height along command line and calculates volume and surface area to be white washed(I guess, you are not going to white wash floor!!!). The program should have the following command line interface; that is after the string "-l", length value can be given. Similarly, after "-b" and "-h" strings we have to give breadth and height values. However, user is free to give data in any order they like. That is, the program should work similarly for all the following styles (Assuming VSA is the machine language file name).

```
VSA -l 10 -b 3 -h 2
VSA -l 10 -h 2 -b 3
VSA -b 3 -l 10 -h 2
VSA -b 3 -h 2 -l 10
VSA -h 2 -b 3 -l 10
VSA -h 2 -l 10 -b 3
```

```
#include <stdio.h>
#include<stdlib.h>
#include<string.h>

int main(int argc, char *argv[])
{
 int i, L,B,H,VOL,SA;
```

```
for(i=1;i<argc; i=i+2)
{
if(strcmp(argv[i],"-l")==0)  L=atoi(argv[i+1]);
if(strcmp(argv[i],"-b")==0)  B=atoi(argv[i+1]);
if(strcmp(argv[i],"-h")==0)  H=atoi(argv[i+1]);

}

VOL=L*B*H;
SA=2*(L+B)*H + L*B;

printf("Volume=%d\n Surface Area=%d\n", VOL, SA);

return 0;
}
```

In Unix systems you can define `main' a third way, using three arguments:

```
int main (int ARGC, char *ARGV[], char *ENVP[])
int main (int ARGC, char **ARGV, char **ENVP)
```

The first two arguments are just the same as explained above. The third argument ENVP gives the program's environment; it is the same as the value of `environ'. More about environment is discussed in fourth chapter.

3.2 Program Argument Syntax Conventions

POSIX recommends these conventions for command line arguments.

- Arguments are options if they begin with a hyphen delimiter (`-').
- Multiple options may follow a hyphen delimiter in a single token if the options do not take arguments. Thus, `-abc' is equivalent to `-a -b -c'.
- Option names are single alphanumeric characters.
- Certain options require an argument. For example, the `-o' command of the `gcc' command requires an argument -- an output file name.
- An option and its argument may or may not appear as separate tokens. (In other words, the whitespace separating them is optional.) Thus, `-o foo' and `-ofoo' are equivalent.
- Options typically precede other non-option arguments.

The implementations of `getopt' and `argp_parse' in the GNUC library normally make it appear as if all the option arguments were specified before all the non-option arguments for the purposes of parsing, even if the user of your program intermixed option and non-option arguments. They do this by reordering the elements of the ARGV array. This behavior is nonstandard; if we want to suppress it, define the `_POSIX_OPTION_ORDER' environment variable.

Note on Standard Environment

The argument `--' terminates all options; any following arguments are treated as non-option arguments, even if they begin with a hyphen.

A token consisting of a single hyphen character is interpreted as an ordinary non-option argument. By convention, it is used to specify input from or output to the standard input and output streams.

Options may be supplied in any order, or appear multiple times. The interpretation is left up to the particular application program.

GNU adds "long options" to these conventions. Long options consist of `--' followed by a name made of alphanumeric characters and dashes. Option names are typically one to three words long, with hyphens to separate words. Users can abbreviate the option names as long as the abbreviations are unique.

To specify an argument for a long option, write `--NAME=VALUE'. This syntax enables a long option to accept an argument that is itself optional.

Eventually, the GNU system will provide completion for long option names in the shell.

3.3 Parsing Program Arguments

If the syntax for the command line arguments to our program is simple enough, we can simply pick the arguments off from ARGV by hand. But unless our program takes a fixed number of arguments, or all of the arguments are interpreted in the same way (as file names, for example), we are usually better off using `getopt' or `argp_parse' to do the parsing.

The function 'getopt' is more standard (the short-option only version of it is a part of the POSIX standard), but using `argp_parse' is often easier, both for very simple and very complex option strutures, because it does more of the dirty work for us.

3.3.1 Parsing program options using `getopt'

The `getopt' and `getopt_long' functions automate some of the chore involved in parsing typical Unix command line options.

Using the `getopt' function

Here are the details about how to call the `getopt' function. To use this facility, our program must include the header file `unistd.h'.

- Variable: int opterr

If the value of this variable is nonzero, then `getopt' prints an error message to the standard error stream if it encounters an unknown option character or an option with a missing required argument. This is the default behavior. If we set this variable to zero, `getopt' does not print any messages, but it still returns the character `?' to indicate an error.

- Variable: int optopt

When `getopt' encounters an unknown option character or an option with a missing required argument, it stores that option character in this variable. We can use this for providing your own diagnostic messages.

- Variable: int optind

This variable is set by `getopt' to the index of the next element of the ARGV array to be processed. Once `getopt' has found all of the option arguments, we can use this variable to determine where the remaining non-option arguments begin. The initial value of this variable is `1'.

- Variable: char * optarg

This variable is set by `getopt' to point at the value of the option argument, for those options that accept arguments.

Prototype of the function getopt() as follows.

int getopt (int ARGC, char **ARGV, const char *OPTIONS)

The `getopt' function gets the next option argument from the argument list specified by the ARGV and ARGC arguments. Normally these values come directly from the arguments received by `main'.

The OPTIONS argument is a string that specifies the option characters that are valid for this program. An option character in this string can be followed by a colon (`:') to indicate that it takes a required argument. If an option character is followed by two colons (`::'), its argument is optional; this is a GNU extension.

The function `getopt' has three ways to deal with options that follow non-options ARGV elements. The special argument `--' forces in all cases the end of option scanning.

The default is to permute the contents of ARGV while scanning it so that eventually all the non-options are at the end. This allows options to be given in any order, even with programs that were not written to expect this.

If the OPTIONS argument string begins with a hyphen (`-'), this is treated specially. It permits arguments that are not options to be returned as if they were associated with option character `\1'.

POSIX demands the following behavior: The first non-option stops option processing. This mode is selected by either setting the environment variable `POSIXLY_CORRECT' or beginning the OPTIONS argument string with a plus sign (`+').

The `getopt' function returns the option character for the next command line option. When no more option arguments are available, it returns `-1'. There may still be more non-option arguments; you must compare the external variable `optind' against the ARGC parameter to check this.

If the option has an argument, `getopt' returns the argument by storing it in the variable OPTARG. We don't ordinarily need to copy the `optarg' string, since it is a pointer into the original ARGV array, not into a static area that might be overwritten.

If `getopt' finds an option character in ARGV that was not included in OPTIONS, or a missing option argument, it returns `?' and sets the external variable `optopt' to the actual option character. If the first character of OPTIONS is a colon (`:'), then `getopt' returns `:' instead of `?' to indicate a missing option argument. In addition, if the external variable `opterr' is nonzero (which is the default), `getopt' prints an error message.

Example 5

Here is an example showing how `getopt' is typically used. The key points to notice are: Normally, `getopt' is called in a loop. When `getopt' returns `-1', indicating no more options are present, the loop terminates. A `switch' statement is used to dispatch on the return value from `getopt'. In typical use, each case just sets a variable that is used later in the program.

A second loop is used to process the remaining non-option arguments.

```
#include <unistd.h>
#include <stdio.h>

int     main (int argc, char **argv)
{
  int aflag = 0;
  int bflag = 0;
  char *cvalue = NULL;
  int index;
  int c;

  opterr = 0;

  while ((c = getopt (argc, argv, "abc:")) != -1)
    switch (c)
      {

      case 'a':
        aflag = 1;
        break;

      case 'b':
        bflag = 1;
        break;

      case 'c':
        cvalue = optarg;
        break;
```

```
        case '?':
          if (isprint (optopt))
            fprintf (stderr, "Unknown option `-%c'.\n", optopt);
          else
            fprintf (stderr, "Unknown option character `\\x%x'.\n",    optopt);
          return 1;

        default:
          abort ();
        }

    printf ("aflag = %d, bflag = %d, cvalue = %s\n", aflag, bflag, cvalue);

    for (index = optind; index < argc; index++)
      printf ("Non-option argument %s\n", argv[index]);

    return 0;
  }
```

Here are some examples showing what this program (assuming **testopt** is the name of the executable file) prints with different combinations of arguments:

testopt
aflag = 0, bflag = 0, cvalue = (null)

testopt -a -b
aflag = 1, bflag = 1, cvalue = (null)

testopt -ab
aflag = 1, bflag = 1, cvalue = (null)

testopt -c foo
aflag = 0, bflag = 0, cvalue = foo

testopt -cfoo
aflag = 0, bflag = 0, cvalue = foo

testopt arg1
aflag = 0, bflag = 0, cvalue = (null)
Non-option argument arg1

testopt -a arg1
aflag = 1, bflag = 0, cvalue = (null)
Non-option argument arg1

testopt -c foo arg1

aflag = 0, bflag = 0, cvalue = foo

Non-option argument arg1

testopt -a -- -b

aflag = 1, bflag = 0, cvalue = (null)

Non-option argument -b

testopt -a -

aflag = 1, bflag = 0, cvalue = (null)

Non-option argument -

Example 6

The following program (is used to realize Example 4) to calculate volume and surface area using the function getopt().

```
#include<stdio.h>
#include<stdlib.h>
#include<unistd.h>

int main(int N, char **a)
{
 int L,B,H,VOL,SA; char V;

while((V=getopt(N,a,"l:b:h:"))!=-1)
{
  switch(V)
{
 case 'l':L=atoi(optarg);break;
 case 'b':B=atoi(optarg);break;
 case 'h':H=atoi(optarg);break;
}
}

VOL=L*B*H;
SA=2*H*(L+B)+L*B;

printf("Volume=%d\nSurface Area=%d\n", VOL,SA);
}
```

This program also works in the same as that of Example 4. In addition, the following command line interface is also acceptable. Note that here also the executable file name is assumed as VSA. That is, for each option and its value, we do not required to give any space.

VSA -l10 -b3 -h2
VSA -l10 -h2 -b3
VSA -b3 -l10 -h2
VSA -b3 -h2 -l10
VSA -h2 -b3 -l10
VSA -h2 -l10 -b3

Also, check the above program by giving the options repeatedly. Most recent option value is considered. For example, if we execute the following command, length, breadth and heights becomes 13, 3 and 2 respectively.

VSA -l10 -b3 -h2 -l13

Similarly, if we execute the following command, breadth and height values becomes different as the option – indicates that after that any following arguments are treated as non-option arguments, even if they begin with a hyphen.

VSA -l 10 -- -b 2 -h 3

Example 7

The following program takes a filename along the command line and displays its content on the screen there are no arguments are given. If -l option is given then the file content is displayed in lower case. If -h option is given then the file content will be displayed in upper case. If both -l and -h options are given then upper case characters are displayed in lower case and lower case one's are displayed in upper case. Also, we can give arguments in any order you like, i.e if we assume program (executable file name) is CAT then the following styles are acceptable.

CAT filename

CAT filename -l
CAT -l filename

CAT filename -h
CAT -h filename

CAT -h filename -l
CAT -l filename -h
CAT -lh filename
CAT -hl filename

CAT filename -lh
CAT filename -hl
CAT -h -l filename
CAT -l -h filename
CAT filename -l -h
CAT filename -h -l

```
#include<stdio.h>
#include<stdlib.h>
#include<unistd.h>

int main(int N, char **a)
{
int L=1,H=2; char V, S[20];
FILE *ip;

while((V=getopt(N,a,"lh"))!=-1)
{
 switch(V)
{
 case 'l':
    L=0;
    break;
 case 'h':
    H=0;
    break;
}

}

printf("%d\n", optind);

ip=fopen(a[optind],"r");
if(ip==0)
 {
printf("Unable to open file\n");
 exit(-1);
 }

while(!feof(ip))
{
 V=fgetc(ip);
switch(L+H)
{
```

```
case 3:
   fputc(V,stdout);
   break;
case 2:
   fputc(tolower(V),stdout);
   break;
case 1:
   fputc(toupper(V),stdout);
   break;
case 0:
   if(isupper(V)) fputc(tolower(V),stdout);
   else     fputc(toupper(V),stdout);
   break;
}
}

return 0;
}
```

3.3.2 Parsing Long Options with `getopt_long'

To accept GNU-style long options as well as single-character options, use `getopt_long' instead of `getopt'. This function is declared in `getopt.h', not `unistd.h'. We should make every program accept long options if it uses any options.

- Data Type: struct option

This structure describes a single long option name for the sake of `getopt_long'. The argument LONGOPTS must be an array of these structures, one for each long option. Terminate the array with an element containing all zeros.

The `struct option' structure has these fields:

char *name

This field is the name of the option. It is a string.

int has_arg

This field says whether the option takes an argument. It is an integer, and there are three legitimate values: `no_argument', `required_argument' and `optional_argument'.

int *flag

int val

These fields control how to report or act on the option when it occurs.

If `flag' is a null pointer, then the `val' is a value which identifies this option. Often these values are chosen to uniquely identify particular long options.

If `flag' is not a null pointer, it should be the address of an `int' variable which is the flag for this option. The value in `val' is the value to store in the flag to indicate that the option was seen.

Prototype of the function getopt_long() is as follows.

int getopt_long (int ARGC, char *const *ARGV, const char *SHORTOPTS, const struct option *LONGOPTS, int *INDEXPTR)

Decode options from the vector ARGV (whose length is ARGC). The argument SHORTOPTS describes the short options to accept, just as it does in `getopt'. The argument LONGOPTS describes the long options to accept (see above).

When `getopt_long' encounters a short option, it does the same thing that `getopt' would do: it returns the character code for the option, and stores the options argument (if it has one) in `optarg'.

When `getopt_long' encounters a long option, it takes actions based on the `flag' and `val' fields of the definition of that option.

If `flag' is a null pointer, then `getopt_long' returns the contents of `val' to indicate which option it found. We should arrange distinct values in the `val' field for options with different meanings, so we can decode these values after `getopt_long' returns. If the long option is equivalent to a short option, we can use the short option's character code in `val'.

If `flag' is not a null pointer, that means this option should just set a flag in the program. The flag is a variable of type `int' that we define. Put the address of the flag in the `flag' field. Put in the `val' field the value we would like this option to store in the flag. In this case, `getopt_long' returns `0'.

For any long option, `getopt_long' tells us the index in the array LONGOPTS of the options definition, by storing it into `*INDEXPTR'. We can get the name of the option with `LONGOPTS[*INDEXPTR].name'. So we can distinguish among long options either by the values in their `val' fields or by their indices. We can also distinguish in this way among long options that set flags.

When a long option has an argument, `getopt_long' puts the argument value in the variable `optarg' before returning. When the option has no argument, the value in `optarg' is a null pointer. This is how we can tell whether an optional argument was supplied.

When `getopt_long' has no more options to handle, it returns `-1', and leaves in the variable `optind' the index in ARGV of the next remaining argument.

Since long option names were used before the `getopt_long' options was invented there are program interfaces which require programs to recognize options like `-option value' instead of `--option value'.

To enable programs to use the GNU getopt functionality there is one more function available known as getopt_long_only() whose prototype is give as follows.

int getopt_long_only (int ARGC, char *const *ARGV, const char *SHORTOPTS, const struct option *LONGOPTS, int *INDEXPTR)

The `getopt_long_only' function is equivalent to the `getopt_long' function but it allows to specify the user of the application to pass long options with only `-' instead of `--'. The `--' prefix is still recognized but instead of looking through the short options if a `-' is seen it is first tried whether this parameter names a long option. If not, it is parsed as a short option.

Assuming `getopt_long_only' is used starting an application with

app -foo

The `getopt_long_only' will first look for a long option named `foo'. If this is not found, the short options `f', `o', and again `o' are recognized.

Example 8

The following program is an example to explain Parsing Long Options with `getopt_long' function.

```
#include <stdio.h>
#include <stdlib.h>
#include <getopt.h>

/* Flag set by `--verbose'. */

static int verbose_flag;

int    main (int argc, char **argv)
    {
  int c;

  while (1)
    {
      static struct option long_options[] =
        {
          /* These options set a flag. */
          {"verbose", no_argument,      &verbose_flag, 1},
          {"brief",   no_argument,      &verbose_flag, 0},
      /* These options don't set a flag.  We distinguish them by their indices.
*/

          {"add",     no_argument,      0, 'a'},
          {"append",  no_argument,      0, 'b'},
          {"delete",  required_argument, 0, 'd'},
          {"create",  required_argument, 0, 'c'},
          {"file",    required_argument, 0, 'f'},
          {0, 0, 0, 0}
        };

  /* `getopt_long' stores the option index here. */

      int option_index = 0;

      c = getopt_long (argc, argv, "abc:d:f:",  long_options, &option_index);
```

```
        /* Detect the end of the options. */

        if (c == -1)            break;

        switch (c)
         {
         case 0:
          /* If this option set a flag, do nothing else now. */

          if (long_options[option_index].flag != 0) break;

          printf ("option %s", long_options[option_index].name);
          if (optarg)        printf (" with arg %s", optarg);
          printf ("\n");

    break;

         case 'a':
                  puts ("option -a\n");
                  break;

         case 'b':
                 puts ("option -b\n");
                 break;

         case 'c':
                 printf ("option -c with value `%s'\n", optarg);
                 break;

         case 'd':
                   printf ("option -d with value `%s'\n", optarg);
                   break;

         case 'f':
                 printf ("option -f with value `%s'\n", optarg);
                 break;

         case '?':
          /* `getopt_long' already printed an error message. */
          break;

         default:
          abort ();
         }
```

```
  }

/* Instead of reporting `--verbose' and `--brief' as they are encountered,
   we report the final status resulting from them. */

if (verbose_flag)
  puts ("verbose flag is set");

/* Print any remaining command line arguments (not options). */

if (optind < argc)
  {
    printf ("non-option ARGV-elements: ");
    while (optind < argc)
      printf ("%s ", argv[optind++]);
    putchar ('\n');
  }

 exit (0);
}
```

If we assume the executable file of the above program is "arg6" , then the following lines explains how command line options can be given (bold) and corresponding output from the program.

arg6 --verbose
verbose flag is set

arg6 –a
option –a

arg6 --add
option –a

As we have defined that option –a does not take any argument, the following command line argument considers "-add" option as "-a" option and "-d" option and the value of "-d" option as 'd'. Please note that in above program we have defined "-d" option that its takes some value.

arg6 -add
opton –a
option –d with value 'd'

As we have defined that option –f as having value either of the following are equivalent.

arg6 -f aaa
option –f with value 'aaa'

arg6 -faaa
option –f with value 'aaa'

arg6 --f aaa
option –f with value 'aaa'

arg6 --file aaa
option –f with value 'aaa'

arg6 --file=aaa
option –f with value 'aaa'

Example 9

The example for volume and surface area calculation of Example 4 can be modified to use the getopt_long() as follows. If we assume that VSA is the executable file, the following style of command line interface also is acceptable in addition to the ones specified in previous examples 4 and 7.

VSA --length 10 --breadth 3 --height 2
VSA --length=10 --breadth=3 --height=2
VSA --l=10 --h=2 --b=3
VSA --l 10 --h 2 --b 3

```
#include <stdio.h>
#include <stdlib.h>
#include <getopt.h>

int
main (int argc, char **argv)
{
 int c,V,SA,L,B,H;

 while (1)
  {
   static struct option long_options[] =
    {
     {"length", required_argument,      0, 'l'},
     {"height",  required_argument, 0, 'h'},
     {"breadth",  required_argument, 0, 'b'},
     {0, 0, 0, 0}
```

```
      };
     int option_index = 0;

     c = getopt_long (argc, argv, "l:h:b:",
                  long_options, &option_index);

     if (c == -1) break;

     switch (c)
      {
      case 'b':
     B=atoi(optarg);
       break;

      case 'l':
     L=atoi(optarg);
       break;

      case 'h':
     H=atoi(optarg);
       break;



      default:
       abort ();
      }
    }

 V=L*B*H;
 SA=2*H*(L+B)+L*B;
 printf("Volume=%d\nSurface Area=%d\n", V,SA);

   exit (0);
  }
```

3.3.3 Parsing Program Options with Argp

Argp is an interface for parsing Unix-style argument vectors. Argp provides features unavailable in the more commonly used `getopt' interface. These features include automatically producing output in response to the `--help' and `--version' options, as described in the GNU coding standards. Using argp makes it less likely that programmers will neglect to implement these additional options or keep them up to date.

Argp also provides the ability to merge several independently defined option parsers into one, mediating conflicts between them and making the result appear seamless. A library can export an argp option parser that user programs might employ in conjunction with their own option parsers, resulting in less work for the user programs. Some programs may use only argument parsers exported by libraries, thereby achieving consistent and efficient option-parsing for abstractions implemented by the libraries.

The header file `<argp.h>' should be included to use argp.

The `argp_parse' Function

The main interface to argp is the `argp_parse' function. In many cases, calling `argp_parse' is the only argument-parsing code needed in `main'.

The prototype of this function is given as:

error_t argp_parse (const struct argp *ARGP, int ARGC, char **ARGV, unsigned FLAGS, int *ARG_INDEX, void *INPUT)

The `argp_parse' function parses the arguments in ARGV, of length ARGC, using the argp parser ARGP.

A value of zero is the same as a `struct argp' containing all zeros. FLAGS is a set of flag bits that modify the parsing behavior. INPUT is passed through to the argp parser ARGP, and has meaning defined by ARGP. A typical usage is to pass a pointer to a structure which is used for specifying parameters to the parser and passing back the results.

Unless the `ARGP_NO_EXIT' or `ARGP_NO_HELP' flags are included in FLAGS, calling `argp_parse' may result in the program exiting. This behavior is true if an error is detected, or when an unknown option is encountered.

If ARG_INDEX is non-null, the index of the first unparsed option in ARGV is returned as a value.

The return value is zero for successful parsing, or an error code if an error is detected. Different argp parsers may return arbitrary error codes, but the standard error codes are: `ENOMEM' if a memory allocation error occurred, or `EINVAL' if an unknown option or option argument is encountered.

Argp Global Variables

These variables make it easy for user programs to implement the `--version' option and provide a bug-reporting address in the `--help' output. These are implemented in argp by default.

- Variable: const char * argp_program_version

If defined or set by the user program to a non-zero value, then a `--version' option is added when parsing with `argp_parse', which will print the `--version' string followed by a newline and exit. The exception to this is if the `ARGP_NO_EXIT' flag is used.

- Variable: const char * argp_program_bug_address

If defined or set by the user program to a non-zero value, `argp_program_bug_address' should point to a string that will be printed at the end of the standard output for the `--help' option, embedded in a sentence that says `Report bugs to ADDRESS.'.

- Variable: argp_program_version_hook

If defined or set by the user program to a non-zero value, a `--version' option is added when parsing with `arg_parse', which prints the program version and exits with a status of zero. This is not the case if the `ARGP_NO_HELP' flag is used. If the `ARGP_NO_EXIT' flag is set, the exit behavior of the program is suppressed or modified, as when the argp parser is going to be used by other programs.

It should point to a function with this type of signature:

void PRINT-VERSION (FILE *STREAM, struct argp_state *STATE)

This variable takes precedence over `argp_program_version', and is useful if a program has version information not easily expressed in a simple string.

- Variable: error_t argp_err_exit_status

This is the exit status used when argp exits due to a parsing error. If not defined or set by the user program, this defaults to: `EX_USAGE' from `<sysexits.h>'.

Specifying Argp Parsers

The first argument to the `argp_parse' function is a pointer to a `struct argp', which is known as an "argp parser":

- Data Type: struct argp

This structure specifies how to parse a given set of options and arguments, perhaps in conjunction with other argp parsers. It has the following fields:

`const struct argp_option *options'

A pointer to a vector of `argp_option' structures specifying which options this argp parser understands; it may be zero if there are no options at all.

`argp_parser_t parser'

A pointer to a function that defines actions for this parser; it is called for each option parsed, and at other well-defined points in the parsing process. A value of zero is the same as a pointer to a function that always returns `ARGP_ERR_UNKNOWN'.

`const char *args_doc'

If non-zero, a string describing what non-option arguments are called by this parser. This is only used to print the `Usage:' message. If it contains newline's, the strings separated by them are considered alternative usage patterns and printed on separate lines. Lines after the first are prefixed by ` or: ' instead of `Usage:'.

`const char *doc'

If non-zero, a string containing extra text to be printed before and after the options in a long help message, with the two sections separated by a vertical tab (`'\v'', `'\013'') character. By convention, the documentation before the options is just a short string explaining what the program does. Documentation printed after the options describe behavior in more detail.

`const struct argp_child *children'

A pointer to a vector of `argp_children' structures. This pointer specifies which additional argp parsers should be combined with this one.

`char *(*help_filter)(int KEY, const char *TEXT, void *INPUT)'

If non-zero, a pointer to a function that filters the output of help messages.

`const char *argp_domain'

If non-zero, the strings used in the argp library are translated using the domain described by this string. If zero, the current default domain is used.

Of the above group, `options', `parser', `args_doc', and the `doc' fields are usually all that are needed. If an argp parser is defined as an initialized C variable, only the fields used need be specified in the initializer. The rest will default to zero due to the way C structure initialization works. This design is exploited in most argp structures; the most-used fields are grouped near the beginning, the unused fields left unspecified.

Specifying Options in an Argp Parser

The `options' field in a `struct argp' points to a vector of `struct argp_option' structures, each of which specifies an option that the argp parser supports. Multiple entries may be used for a single option provided it has multiple names. This should be terminated by an entry with zero in all fields. Note that when using an initialized C array for options, writing `{ 0 }' is enough to achieve this.

- Data Type: struct argp_option

This structure specifies a single option that an argp parser understands, as well as how to parse and document that option. It has the following fields:

`const char *name'

The long name for this option, corresponding to the long option `--NAME'; this field may be zero if this option _only_ has a short name. To specify multiple names for an option, additional entries may follow this one, with the `OPTION_ALIAS' flag set.

`int key'

The integer key provided by the current option to the option parser. If KEY has a value that is a printable ASCII character (i.e., `isascii (KEY)' is true), it _also_ specifies a short option `-CHAR', where CHAR is the ASCII character with the code KEY.

`const char *arg'

If non-zero, this is the name of an argument associated with this option, which must be provided (e.g., with the `--NAME=VALUE' or `-CHAR VALUE' syntaxes), unless the `OPTION_ARG_OPTIONAL' flag is set, in which case it _may_ be provided.

`int flags'

Flags associated with this option, some of which are referred to above. *Note Argp Option Flags::.

`const char *doc'

A documentation string for this option, for printing in help messages.

If both the `name' and `key' fields are zero, this string will be printed tabbed left from the normal option column, making it useful as a group header. This will be the first thing printed in its group. In this usage, it's conventional to end the string with a `:' character.

`int group'

Group identity for this option.

In a long help message, options are sorted alphabetically within each group, and the groups presented in the order 0, 1, 2, ..., N, -M, ..., -2, -1.

Every entry in an options array with this field 0 will inherit the group number of the previous entry, or zero if it's the first one. If it's a group header with `name' and `key' fields both zero, the previous entry + 1 is the default. Automagic options such as `--help' are put into group -1.

Note that because of C structure initialization rules, this field often need not be specified, because 0 is the correct value.

Flags for Argp Options

The following flags may be or'd together in the `flags' field of a `struct argp_option'. These flags control various aspects of how that option is parsed or displayed in help messages:

`OPTION_ARG_OPTIONAL'

The argument associated with this option is optional.

`OPTION_HIDDEN'

This option isn't displayed in any help messages.

`OPTION_ALIAS'

This option is an alias for the closest previous non-alias option. This means that it will be displayed in the same help entry, and will inherit fields other than `name' and `key' from the option being aliased.

`OPTION_DOC'

This option isn't actually an option and should be ignored by the actual option parser. It is an arbitrary section of documentation that should be displayed in much the same manner as the options. This is known as a "documentation option".

If this flag is set, then the option `name' field is displayed unmodified (e.g., no `--' prefix is added) at the left-margin where a _short_ option would normally be displayed, and this documentation string is left in it's usual place. For purposes of sorting, any leading whitespace and punctuation is ignored, unless the first non-whitespace character is `-'. This entry is displayed after all options, after `OPTION_DOC' entries with a leading `-', in the same group.

`OPTION_NO_USAGE'

This option shouldn't be included in `long' usage messages, but should still be included in other help messages. This is intended for options that are completely documented in an argp's `args_doc' field. Including this option in the generic usage list would be redundant, and should be avoided.

For instance, if `args_doc' is `"FOO BAR\n-x BLAH"', and the `-x' option's purpose is to distinguish these two cases, `-x' should probably be marked `OPTION_NO_USAGE'.

Argp Parser Functions

The function pointed to by the `parser' field in a `struct argp' defines what actions take place in response to each option or argument parsed. It is also used as a hook, allowing a parser to perform tasks at certain other points during parsing.

Argp parser functions have the following type signature:

error_t PARSER (int KEY, char *ARG, struct argp_state *STATE)

where the arguments are as follows:

KEY

For each option that is parsed, PARSER is called with a value of KEY from that option's `key' field in the option vector. PARSER is also called at other times with special reserved keys, such as `ARGP_KEY_ARG' for non-option arguments. *Note Argp Special Keys::.

ARG

If KEY is an option, ARG is its given value. This defaults to zero if no value is specified. Only options that have a non-zero `arg' field can ever have a value. These must _always_ have a value unless the `OPTION_ARG_OPTIONAL' flag is specified. If the input being parsed specifies a value for an option that doesn't allow one, an error results before PARSER ever gets called.

If KEY is `ARGP_KEY_ARG', ARG is a non-option argument. Other special keys always have a zero ARG.

STATE

STATE points to a `struct argp_state', containing useful information about the current parsing state for use by PARSER.

When PARSER is called, it should perform whatever action is appropriate for KEY, and return `0' for success, `ARGP_ERR_UNKNOWN' if the value of KEY is not handled by this parser function, or a Unix error code if a real error occurred.

- Macro: int ARGP_ERR_UNKNOWN

Argp parser functions should return `ARGP_ERR_UNKNOWN' for any KEY value they do not recognize, or for non-option arguments (`KEY == ARGP_KEY_ARG') that they are not equipped to handle.

A typical parser function uses a switch statement on KEY:

```
error_t
parse_opt (int key, char *arg, struct argp_state *state)
{
switch (key)
   {
case OPTION_KEY:
    ACTION
     break;
    ...
    default:
    return ARGP_ERR_UNKNOWN;
     }
   return 0;
    }
```

Special Keys for Argp Parser Functions

In addition to key values corresponding to user options, the KEY argument to argp parser functions may have a number of other special values. In the following example ARG and STATE refer to parser function arguments.

`ARGP_KEY_ARG'

This is not an option at all, but rather a command line argument, whose value is pointed to by ARG.

When there are multiple parser functions in play due to argp parsers being combined, it's impossible to know which one will handle a specific argument. Each is called until one returns 0 or an error other than `ARGP_ERR_UNKNOWN'; if an argument is not handled, `argp_parse' immediately returns success, without parsing any more arguments.

Once a parser function returns success for this key, that fact is recorded, and the `ARGP_KEY_NO_ARGS' case won't be used. However, if while processing the argument a parser function decrements the `next' field of its STATE argument, the option won't be considered processed; this is to allow you to actually modify the argument, perhaps into an option, and have it processed again.

`ARGP_KEY_ARGS'

If a parser function returns `ARGP_ERR_UNKNOWN' for `ARGP_KEY_ARG', it is immediately called again with the key `ARGP_KEY_ARGS', which has a similar meaning, but is slightly more convenient for consuming all remaining arguments. ARG is 0, and the tail of the argument vector may be found at `STATE->argv + STATE->next'. If success is returned for this key, and `STATE->next' is unchanged, all remaining arguments are considered to have been consumed. Otherwise, the amount by which `STATE->next' has been adjusted indicates how many were used. Here's an example that uses both, for different args:

```
...
case ARGP_KEY_ARG:
  if (STATE->arg_num == 0)
    /* First argument */
    first_arg = ARG;
  else
    /* Let the next case parse it. */
    return ARGP_KEY_UNKNOWN;
  break;
case ARGP_KEY_ARGS:
  remaining_args = STATE->argv + STATE->next;
  num_remaining_args = STATE->argc - STATE->next;
  break;
```

`ARGP_KEY_END'

This indicates that there are no more command line arguments. Parser functions are called in a different order, children first. This allows each parser to clean up its state for the parent.

`ARGP_KEY_NO_ARGS'

Because it's common to do some special processing if there aren't any non-option args, parser functions are called with this key if they didn't successfully process any non-option arguments. This is called just before `ARGP_KEY_END', where more general validity checks on previously parsed arguments take place.

`ARGP_KEY_INIT'

This is passed in before any parsing is done. Afterwards, the values of each element of the `child_input' field of STATE, if any, are copied to each child's state to be the initial value of the `input' when _their_ parsers are called.

`ARGP_KEY_SUCCESS'

Passed in when parsing has successfully been completed, even if arguments remain.

`ARGP_KEY_ERROR'

Passed in if an error has occurred and parsing is terminated. In this case a call with a key of `ARGP_KEY_SUCCESS' is never made.

`ARGP_KEY_FINI'

The final key ever seen by any parser, even after `ARGP_KEY_SUCCESS' and `ARGP_KEY_ERROR'. Any resources allocated by `ARGP_KEY_INIT' may be freed here. At times, certain resources allocated are to be returned to the caller after a successful parse. In that case, those particular resources can be freed in the `ARGP_KEY_ERROR' case.

In all cases, `ARGP_KEY_INIT' is the first key seen by parser functions, and `ARGP_KEY_FINI' the last, unless an error was returned by the parser for `ARGP_KEY_INIT'. Other keys can occur in one the following orders. OPT refers to an arbitrary option key:

OPT... `ARGP_KEY_NO_ARGS' `ARGP_KEY_END' `ARGP_KEY_SUCCESS'

The arguments being parsed did not contain any non-option arguments.

(OPT | `ARGP_KEY_ARG')... `ARGP_KEY_END' `ARGP_KEY_SUCCESS'

All non-option arguments were successfully handled by a parser function. There may be multiple parser functions if multiple argp parsers were combined.

(OPT | `ARGP_KEY_ARG' )... `ARGP_KEY_SUCCESS'

Some non-option argument went unrecognized.

This occurs when every parser function returns `ARGP_KEY_UNKNOWN' for an argument, in which case parsing stops at that argument if ARG_INDEX is a null pointer. Otherwise an error occurs.

In all cases, if a non-null value for ARG_INDEX gets passed to `argp_parse', the index of the first unparsed command-line argument is passed back in that value.

If an error occurs and is either detected by argp or because a parser function returned an error value, each parser is called with `ARGP_KEY_ERROR'. No further calls are made, except the final call with `ARGP_KEY_FINI'.

Functions For Use in Argp Parsers

Argp provides a number of functions available to the user of argp (*note Argp Parser Functions::), mostly for producing error messages. These take as their first argument the STATE argument to the parser function.

- Function: void argp_usage (const struct argp_state *STATE)

Outputs the standard usage message for the argp parser referred to by STATE to `STATE->err_stream' and terminate the program with `exit (argp_err_exit_status)'.

- Function: void argp_error (const struct argp_state *STATE, const char *FMT, ...)

Prints the printf format string FMT and following args, preceded by the program name and `:', and followed by a `Try ... --help' message, and terminates the program with an exit status of `argp_err_exit_status'.

- Function: void argp_failure (const struct argp_state *STATE, int STATUS, int ERRNUM, const char *FMT, ...)

Similar to the standard gnu error-reporting function `error', this prints the program name and `:', the printf format string FMT, and the appropriate following args. If it is non-zero, the standard Unix error text for ERRNUM is printed. If STATUS is non-zero, it terminates the program with that value as its exit status.

The difference between `argp_failure' and `argp_error' is that `argp_error' is for _parsing errors_, whereas `argp_failure' is for other problems that occur during parsing but don't reflect a syntactic problem with the input, such as illegal values for options, bad phase of the moon, etc.

- Function: void argp_state_help (const struct argp_state *STATE, FILE *STREAM, unsigned FLAGS)

Outputs a help message for the argp parser referred to by STATE, to STREAM. The FLAGS argument determines what sort of help message is produced.

Error output is sent to `STATE->err_stream', and the program name printed is STATE->name'.

The output or program termination behavior of these functions may be suppressed if the `ARGP_NO_EXIT' or `ARGP_NO_ERRS' flags are passed to `argp_parse'.

This behavior is useful if an argp parser is exported for use by other programs (e.g., by a library), and may be used in a context where it is not desirable to terminate the program in response to parsing errors. In argp parsers intended for such general use, and for the case where the program _doesn't_ terminate, calls to any of these functions should be followed by code that returns the appropriate error code:

```
if (BAD ARGUMENT SYNTAX)
{
argp_usage (STATE);
return EINVAL;
}
```

If a parser function will _only_ be used when `ARGP_NO_EXIT' is not set, the return may be omitted.

Argp Parsing State

The third argument to argp parser functions is a pointer to a `struct argp_state', which contains information about the state of the option parsing.

- Data Type: struct argp_state

This structure has the following fields, which may be modified as noted:

`const struct argp *const root_argp'

The top level argp parser being parsed. Note that this is often _not_ the same `struct argp' passed into `argp_parse' by the invoking program. It is an internal argp parser that contains options implemented by `argp_parse' itself, such as `--help'.

`int argc'
`char **argv'

The argument vector being parsed. This may be modified.

`int next'

The index in `argv' of the next argument to be parsed. This may be modified.

One way to consume all remaining arguments in the input is to set `STATE->next = STATE->argc', perhaps after recording the value of the `next' field to find the consumed arguments. The current option can be re-parsed immediately by decrementing this field, then modifying `STATE->argv[STATE->next]' to reflect the option that should be reexamined.

`unsigned flags'

The flags supplied to `argp_parse'. These may be modified, although some flags may only take effect when `argp_parse' is first invoked.

`unsigned arg_num'

While calling a parsing function with the KEY argument `ARGP_KEY_ARG', this represents the number of the current arg, starting at 0. It is incremented after each `ARGP_KEY_ARG' call returns. At all other times, this is the number of `ARGP_KEY_ARG' arguments that have been processed.

`int quoted'

If non-zero, the index in `argv' of the first argument following a special `--' argument. This prevents anything that follows from being interpreted as an option. It is only set after argument parsing has proceeded past this point.

`void *input'

An arbitrary pointer passed in from the caller of `argp_parse', in the INPUT argument.

`void **child_inputs'

These are values that will be passed to child parsers. This vector will be the same length as the number of children in the current parser. Each child parser will be given the value of `STATE->child_inputs[I]' as _its_ `STATE->input' field, where I is the index of the child in the this parser's `children' field.

`void *hook'

For the parser function's use. Initialized to 0, but otherwise ignored by argp.

`char *name'

The name used when printing messages. This is initialized to `argv[0]', or `program_invocation_name' if `argv[0]' is unavailable.

`FILE *err_stream'

`FILE *out_stream'

The stdio streams used when argp prints. Error messages are printed to `err_stream', all other output, such as `--help' output) to `out_stream'. These are initialized to `stderr' and `stdout' respectively.

`void *pstate'

Private, for use by the argp implementation.

Combining Multiple Argp Parsers

The `children' field in a `struct argp' enables other argp parsers to be combined with the referencing one for the parsing of a single set of arguments. This field should point to a vector of `struct argp_child', which is terminated by an entry having a value of zero in the `argp' field.

Where conflicts between combined parsers arise, as when two specify an option with the same name, the parser conflicts are resolved in favor of the parent argp parser(s), or the earlier of the argp parsers in the list of children.

- Data Type: struct argp_child

An entry in the list of subsidiary argp parsers pointed to by the `children' field in a `struct argp'. The fields are as follows:

`const struct argp *argp'

The child argp parser, or zero to end of the list.

`int flags'

Flags for this child.

`const char *header'

If non-zero, this is an optional header to be printed within help output before the child options. As a side-effect, a non-zero value forces the child options to be grouped together. To achieve this effect without actually printing a header string, use a value of `""'. As with header strings specified in an option entry, the conventional value of the last character is `:'.

`int group'

This is where the child options are grouped relative to the other `consolidated' options in the parent argp parser. The values are the same as the `group' field in `struct argp_option'. All child-groupings follow parent options at a particular group level. If both this field and `header' are zero, then the child's options aren't grouped together, they are merged with parent options at the parent option group level.

Flags for `argp_parse'

The default behavior of `argp_parse' is designed to be convenient for the most common case of parsing program command line argument. To modify these defaults, the following flags may be or'd together in the FLAGS argument to `argp_parse':

`ARGP_PARSE_ARGV0'

Don't ignore the first element of the ARGV argument to `argp_parse'. Unless `ARGP_NO_ERRS' is set, the first element of the argument vector is skipped for option parsing purposes, as it corresponds to the program name in a command line.

`ARGP_NO_ERRS'

Don't print error messages for unknown options to `stderr'; unless this flag is set, `ARGP_PARSE_ARGV0' is ignored, as `argv[0]' is used as the program name in the error messages. This flag implies `ARGP_NO_EXIT'. This is based on the assumption that silent exiting upon errors is bad behavior.

`ARGP_NO_ARGS'

Don't parse any non-option args. Normally these are parsed by calling the parse functions with a key of `ARGP_KEY_ARG', the actual argument being the value. This flag needn't normally be set, as the default behavior is to stop parsing as soon as an argument fails to be parsed.

`ARGP_IN_ORDER'

Parse options and arguments in the same order they occur on the command line. Normally they're rearranged so that all options come first.

`ARGP_NO_HELP'

Don't provide the standard long option `--help', which ordinarily causes usage and option help information to be output to `stdout' and `exit (0)'.

\`ARGP_NO_EXIT'

Don't exit on errors, although they may still result in error messages.

\`ARGP_LONG_ONLY'

Use the gnu getopt \`long-only' rules for parsing arguments. This allows long-options to be recognized with only a single \`-' (i.e. \`-help'). This results in a less useful interface, and its use is discouraged as it conflicts with the way most GNU programs work as well as the GNU coding standards.

\`ARGP_SILENT'

Turns off any message-printing/exiting options, specifically \`ARGP_NO_EXIT', \`ARGP_NO_ERRS', and \`ARGP_NO_HELP'.

Customizing Argp Help Output

The \`help_filter' field in a \`struct argp' is a pointer to a function that filters the text of help messages before displaying them. They have a function signature like:

```
char *HELP-FILTER (int KEY, const char *TEXT, void *INPUT)
```

Where KEY is either a key from an option, in which case TEXT is that option's help text.. Alternately, one of the special keys with names beginning with \`ARGP_KEY_HELP_' might be used, describing which other help text TEXT will contain.

The function should return either TEXT if it remains as-is, or a replacement string allocated using \`malloc'. This will be either be freed by argp or zero, which prints nothing. The value of TEXT is supplied _after_ any translation has been done, so if any of the replacement text needs translation, it will be done by the filter function. INPUT is either the input supplied to \`argp_parse' or it is zero, if \`argp_help' was called directly by the user.

Special Keys for Argp Help Filter Functions

The following special values may be passed to an argp help filter function as the first argument in addition to key values for user options. They specify which help text the TEXT argument contains:

\`ARGP_KEY_HELP_PRE_DOC'

The help text preceding options.

\`ARGP_KEY_HELP_POST_DOC'

The help text following options.

\`ARGP_KEY_HELP_HEADER'

The option header string.

\`ARGP_KEY_HELP_EXTRA'

This is used after all other documentation; TEXT is zero for this key.

\`ARGP_KEY_HELP_DUP_ARGS_NOTE'

The explanatory note printed when duplicate option arguments ha been suppressed.

\`ARGP_KEY_HELP_ARGS_DOC'

The argument doc string; formally the \`args_doc' field from the argp parser.

The `argp_help' Function

Normally programs using argp need not be written with particular printing argument-usage-type help messages in mind as the standard `--help' option is handled automatically by argp. Typical error cases can be handled using `argp_usage' and `argp_error'. However, if it's desirable to print a help message in some context other than parsing the program options, argp offers the `argp_help' interface.

- Function: void argp_help (const struct argp *ARGP, FILE *STREAM, unsigned FLAGS, char *NAME)

This outputs a help message for the argp parser ARGP to STREAM. The type of messages printed will be determined by FLAGS.

Any options such as `--help' that are implemented automatically by argp itself will _not_ be present in the help output; for this reason it is best to use `argp_state_help' if calling from within an argp parser function.

Flags for the `argp_help' Function

When calling `argp_help' or `argp_state_help' the exact output is determined by the FLAGS argument. This should consist of any of the following flags, or'd together:

`ARGP_HELP_USAGE'

A Unix `Usage:' message that explicitly lists all options.

`ARGP_HELP_SHORT_USAGE'

A Unix `Usage:' message that displays an appropriate placeholder to indicate where the options go; useful for showing the non-option argument syntax.

`ARGP_HELP_SEE'

A `Try ... for more help' message; `...' contains the program name and `--help'.

`ARGP_HELP_LONG'

A verbose option help message that gives each option available along with its documentation string.

`ARGP_HELP_PRE_DOC'

The part of the argp parser doc string preceding the verbose option help.

`ARGP_HELP_POST_DOC'

The part of the argp parser doc string that following the verbose option help.

`ARGP_HELP_DOC'

`(ARGP_HELP_PRE_DOC | ARGP_HELP_POST_DOC)'

`ARGP_HELP_BUG_ADDR'

A message that prints where to report bugs for this program, if the `argp_program_bug_address' variable contains this information.

`ARGP_HELP_LONG_ONLY'

This will modify any output to reflect the `ARGP_LONG_ONLY' mode.

The following flags are only understood when used with `argp_state_help'. They control whether the function returns after printing its output, or terminates the program:

`ARGP_HELP_EXIT_ERR'

This will terminate the program with `exit (argp_err_exit_status)'.

`ARGP_HELP_EXIT_OK'

This will terminate the program with `exit (0)'.

The following flags are combinations of the basic flags for printing standard messages:

`ARGP_HELP_STD_ERR'

Assuming that an error message for a parsing error has printed, this prints a message on how to get help, and terminates the program with an error.

`ARGP_HELP_STD_USAGE'

This prints a standard usage message and terminates the program with an error. This is used when no other specific error messages are appropriate or available.

`ARGP_HELP_STD_HELP'

This prints the standard response for a `--help' option, and terminates the program successfully.

Argp Examples

These example programs demonstrate the basic usage of argp.

A Minimal Program Using Argp

This is perhaps the smallest program possible that uses argp. It won't do much except give an error messages and exit when there are any arguments, and prints a rather pointless message for `--help'.

Example 10

This is (probably) the smallest possible program that uses argp. It won't do much except give an error messages and exit when there are any arguments, and print a (rather pointless) messages for – help.

```
#include <argp.h>

int main (int argc, char **argv)
{
 argp_parse (0, argc, argv, 0, 0, 0);
 exit (0);
}
```

Assuming that "arg1" is the executable file, the following options such as "—help" and "—usage" gives the output as shown below.

```
arg1 -help
arg1 -?
Usage: arg1 [OPTIONS...]
-?, --help                    Give this help list
    --usage                   Give a short message

arg1 --usage
Usage:  arg1 [-?][--help] [--usage]
```

Example 11

A Program to explain how to use Argp with Only Default Options

This program doesn't use any options or arguments, it uses argp to be compliant with the GNU standard command line format.

In addition to giving no arguments and implementing a `--help' option, this example has a `--version' option, which will put the given documentation string and bug address in the `--help' output, as per GNU standards.

The variable `argp' contains the argument parser specification. Adding fields to this structure is the way most parameters are passed to `argp_parse'. The first three fields are normally used, but they are not use a in this small program. There are also two global variables that argp uses to name, `argp_program_version' and `argp_program_bug_address'. They are considered global variables because they will almost always be constant for a given program, even if they use different argument parsers for various tasks.

In addition to making sure no arguments are given, and implementing a -help option, this example will have a-version option, and will put the given documentation string and bug address in the -help output, as per GNU standards.

The variable ARGP contains the argument parser specification; adding fields to this structure is the way most parameters are passed to argp_parse (the first three fields are usually used, but not in this small program).

```
#include <argp.h>

const char *argp_program_version = "arg2 1.0";
const char *argp_program_bug_address =   "<bug-gnu-utils@gnu.org>";

/* Program documentation. */

static char doc[] = "Arg2- a pretty minimal program using argp";
```

/* Our argument parser. The `options', `parser', and `args_doc' fields are zero because we have neither options or arguments; `doc' and `argp_program_bug_address' will be used in the output for `--help', and the `--version' option will print out `argp_program_version'. */

```
static struct argp argp = { 0, 0, 0, doc };

int main (int argc, char **argv)
{
  argp_parse (&argp, argc, argv, 0, 0, 0);
  exit (0);
}
```

Assuming that "arg2" is the executable file, the following options such as "—help", "—usage", "-V", and "-?" gives the output as shown below.

arg2 --help
arg2 -?

```
Usage: arg2 [OPTIONS...]
-?, --help                  Give this help list
    --usage                 Give a short message
 -V, --version              Print Program version
```

arg2 --usage

```
Usage:  arg2 [-?V][--help] [--usage] [--version]
```

arg2 -V

```
arg2 1.0
```

Example 12

This Program is to explain how Argp is made to deal with user options. We now use the first four fields in `argp' and specify `parse_opt' as the parser function.

Note that in this example, `main' uses a structure to communicate with the `parse_opt' function, a pointer to which it passes in the `input' argument to `argp_parse'. It is retrieved by `parse_opt' through the `input' field in its `state' argument. It is also possible to use global variables instead, but using a structure like this is somewhat more flexible and clean.

/* This program uses the same features as example 2, and uses options and arguments.

We now use the first four fields in ARGP, so here's a description of them:

OPTIONS	-	A pointer to a vector of struct argp_option (see below)
PARSER	-	A function to parse a single option, called by argp
ARGS_DOC	-	A string describing how the non-option arguments should look
DOC	-	A descriptive string about this program; if it contains a vertical tab character (\v), the part after it will be printed *following* the options

The function PARSER takes the following arguments:

KEY - An integer specifying which option this is (taken from the KEY field in each struct argp_option), or a special key specifying something else; the only special keys we use here are ARGP_KEY_ARG, meaning a non-option argument, and ARGP_KEY_END, meaning that all arguments have been parsed

ARG - For an option KEY, the string value of its argument, or NULL if it has none

STATE- A pointer to a struct argp_state, containing various useful information about the parsing state; used here are the INPUT field, which reflects the INPUT argument to argp_parse, and the ARG_NUM field, which is the number of the current non-option argument being parsed.

It should return either 0, meaning success, ARGP_ERR_UNKNOWN, meaning the given KEY wasn't recognized, or an errno value indicating some other error.

Note that in this example, main uses a structure to communicate with the parse_opt function, a pointer to which it passes in the INPUT argument to argp_parse. Of course, it's also possible to use global variables instead, but this is somewhat more flexible.

The OPTIONS field contains a pointer to a vector of struct argp_option's; that structure has the following fields (if you assign your option structures using array initialization like this example, unspecified fields will be defaulted to 0, and need not be specified):

NAME - The name of this option's long option (may be zero)

KEY - The KEY to pass to the PARSER function when parsing this option, and the name of this option's short option, if it is a printable ascii character

ARG - The name of this option's argument, if any

FLAGS - Flags describing this option; some of them are:

OPTION_ARG_OPTIONAL - The argument to this option is optional

OPTION_ALIAS - This option is an alias for the previous option

OPTION_HIDDEN - Don't show this option in -help output

DOC - A documentation string for this option, shown in -help output

An options vector should be terminated by an option with all fields zero. */

```
#include <argp.h>

const char *argp_program_version =  "argp3 1.0";
const char *argp_program_bug_address =  "<bug-gnu-utils@gnu.org>";

/* Program documentation. */
static char doc[] =  "Argp3 -- a program with options and arguments using
argp";
```

```
/* A description of the arguments we accept. */

static char args_doc[] = "ARG1 ARG2";

/* The options we understand. */
static struct argp_option options[] = {
  {"verbose",  'v', 0,      0,  "Produce verbose output" },
  {"quiet",    'q', 0,      0,  "Don't produce any output" },
  {"silent",   's', 0,      OPTION_ALIAS },
  {"output",   'o', "FILE", 0,  "Output to FILE instead of standard output" },
  { 0 }
};

/* Used by `main' to communicate with `parse_opt'. */

struct arguments
{
  char *args[2];                /* ARG1 & ARG2 */
  int silent, verbose;
  char *output_file;
};

/* Parse a single option. */
static error_t    parse_opt (int key, char *arg, struct argp_state *state)
{

  /* Get the INPUT argument from `argp_parse', which we
     know is a pointer to our arguments structure. */

  struct arguments *arguments = state->input;

  switch (key)
    {
    case 'q':
    case 's':
                   arguments->silent = 1;
                  break;
    case 'v':
      arguments->verbose = 1;
      break;
    case 'o':
```

```
      arguments->output_file = arg;
      break;

    case ARGP_KEY_ARG:
      if (state->arg_num >= 2)
        /* Too many arguments. */
        argp_usage (state);

      arguments->args[state->arg_num] = arg;

      break;

    case ARGP_KEY_END:
      if (state->arg_num < 2)
        /* Not enough arguments. */
        argp_usage (state);
      break;

    default:
      return ARGP_ERR_UNKNOWN;
    }
  return 0;
}

/* Our argp parser. */
static struct argp argp = { options, parse_opt, args_doc, doc };

int main (int argc, char **argv)
{
  struct arguments arguments;

  /* Default values. */
  arguments.silent = 0;
  arguments.verbose = 0;
  arguments.output_file = "-";

  /* Parse our arguments; every option seen by `parse_opt' will
     be reflected in `arguments'. */

  argp_parse (&argp, argc, argv, 0, 0, &arguments);
```

```
  printf ("ARG1 = %s\nARG2 = %s\nOUTPUT_FILE = %s\n"
      "VERBOSE = %s\nSILENT = %s\n",
      arguments.args[0], arguments.args[1],
      arguments.output_file,
      arguments.verbose ? "yes" : "no",
      arguments.silent ? "yes" : "no");

  exit (0);
}
```

Example 13

This example is used to explain how argp can be used with the Example 4. If we assume executable file name for this program also VSA, the following style of command line interface is acceptable.

```
VSA --length=21 --breadth=22   --height=32
VSA --length 21 --breadth 22   --height 32
VSA -l 21 –b 22   -h 32
VSA -l21 –b22   -h32

#include <argp.h>

    const char *argp_program_version =
      "VSA 1.0";
    const char *argp_program_bug_address =
      "<venkat_ritch@yahoo.com>";

    /* Program documentation. */
    static char doc[] ="VSA using argp";


    /* The options we understand. */
    static struct argp_option options[] = {
      {"verbose",  'v', 0,      0,  "Produce verbose output" },
      {"length",   'l', "LENGTH", 0, "Length of the Room" },
      {"breadth",   'b', "BREADTH", 0, "Breadth of the Room" },
      {"height",   'h', "HEIGHT", 0, "Height of the Room" },
      { 0 }
    };

    struct arguments
    {
      int  verbose;
```

```
  int LL;
  int BB;
  int HH;
};

static error_t parse_opt (int key, char *arg, struct argp_state *state)
{
  struct arguments *arguments = state->input;

  switch (key)
    {
    case 'v':
      arguments->verbose = 1;
      break;
    case 'b':
      arguments->BB =atoi( arg);
      break;
    case 'l':
      arguments->LL =atoi( arg);
      break;
    case 'h':
      arguments->HH =atoi( arg);
      break;

    default:
      return ARGP_ERR_UNKNOWN;
    }
  return 0;
}

/* Our argp parser. */
static struct argp argp = { options, parse_opt, 0, doc };

int main (int argc, char **argv)
{
  struct arguments arguments;
int L,B,H,V,SA;

  /* Default values. */
  arguments.verbose = 0;
  arguments.LL = 0;
  arguments.BB = 0;
  arguments.HH = 0;
```

```
        argp_parse (&argp, argc, argv, 0, 0, &arguments);

    printf("Length=%d\n", arguments.LL);
    printf("Breadth=%d\n", arguments.BB);
    printf("Height=%d\n", arguments.HH);

      L=arguments.LL;
      H=arguments.HH;
      B=arguments.BB;

      V=L*B*H;
      SA=2*H*(L+B) + L*B;
      printf("Volume=%d\nSurface Area=%d\n", V, SA);

        exit (0);
    }
```

VSA --usage displays

```
Usage: VSA [-v?V] [-b BREADTH] [-h HEIGHT] [-l LENGTH]
   [-breadth=BREADTH] [-height=HEIGHT] [-length=LENGTH]
   [--verbose] [--help] [--usage]
   [--version]
```

3.3.4 A Program Using Multiple Combined Argp Parsers

This program uses the same features as example 12, but has more options, and presents more structure in the `--help' output. It also illustrates how you can `steal' the remainder of the input arguments past a certain point for programs that accept a list of items. It also illustrates the KEY value `ARGP_KEY_NO_ARGS', which is only given if no non-option arguments were supplied to the program.

For structuring help output, two features are used: _headers_ and a two part option string. The _headers_ are entries in the options vector. The first four fields are zero. The two part documentation string are in the variable `doc', which allows documentation both before and after the options. The two parts of `doc' are separated by a vertical-tab character (`'\v'', or `'\013''). By convention, the documentation before the options is a short string stating what the program does, and after any options it is longer, describing the behavior in more detail. All documentation strings are automatically filled for output, although newlines may be included to force a line break at a particular point. In addition, documentation strings are passed to the `gettext' function, for possible translation into the current locale.

Example 14

/* This program uses the same features as example 12, but has more options, and somewhat more structure in the -help output. It also shows how you can `steal' the remainder of the input arguments past a certain point, for programs that accept a list of items. It also shows the special argp KEY value ARGP_KEY_NO_ARGS, which is only given if no non-option arguments were supplied to the program.

For structuring the help output, two features are used, *headers* which are entries in the options vector with the first four fields being zero, and a two part documentation string (in the variable DOC), which allows documentation both before and after the options; the two parts of DOC are separated by a vertical-tab character ('\v', or '\013'). By convention, the documentation before the options is just a short string saying what the program does, and that afterwards is longer, describing the behavior in more detail. All documentation strings are automatically filled for output, although newlines may be included to force a line break at a particular point. All documentation strings are also passed to the `gettext' function, for possible translation into the current locale. */

```
#include <stdlib.h>
#include <error.h>
#include <argp.h>

const char *argp_program_version =
  "argp-ex4 1.0";
const char *argp_program_bug_address =
  "<bug-gnu-utils@prep.ai.mit.edu>";

/* Program documentation. */
static char doc[] =
  "Argp example #4 -- a program with somewhat more complicated\
options\
\vThis part of the documentation comes *after* the options;\
 note that the text is automatically filled, but it's possible\
 to force a line-break, e.g.\n<-- here.";

/* A description of the arguments we accept. */
static char args_doc[] = "ARG1 [STRING...]";

/* Keys for options without short-options. */
#define OPT_ABORT  1            /* -abort */

/* The options we understand. */
static struct argp_option options[] = {
  {"verbose",  'v', 0,       0, "Produce verbose output" },
  {"quiet",    'q', 0,       0, "Don't produce any output" },
  {"silent",   's', 0,       OPTION_ALIAS },
  {"output",   'o', "FILE",  0,
   "Output to FILE instead of standard output" },

  {0,0,0,0, "The following options should be grouped together:" },
  {"repeat",   'r', "COUNT", OPTION_ARG_OPTIONAL,
   "Repeat the output COUNT (default 10) times"},
```

```
  {"abort",   OPT_ABORT, 0, 0, "Abort before showing any output"},

  { 0 }
};

/* Used by `main' to communicate with `parse_opt'. */
struct arguments
{
  char *arg1;                 /* ARG1 */
  char **strings;             /* [STRING...] */
  int silent, verbose, abort; /* `-s', `-v', `--abort' */
  char *output_file;          /* FILE arg to `--output' */
  int repeat_count;           /* COUNT arg to `--repeat' */
};

/* Parse a single option. */
static error_t
parse_opt (int key, char *arg, struct argp_state *state)
{
  /* Get the `input' argument from `argp_parse', which we
     know is a pointer to our arguments structure. */
  struct arguments *arguments = state->input;

  switch (key)
    {
    case 'q': case 's':
      arguments->silent = 1;
      break;
    case 'v':
      arguments->verbose = 1;
      break;
    case 'o':
      arguments->output_file = arg;
      break;
    case 'r':
      arguments->repeat_count = arg ? atoi (arg) : 10;
      break;
    case OPT_ABORT:
      arguments->abort = 1;
      break;
      case ARGP_KEY_NO_ARGS:
      argp_usage (state);

    case ARGP_KEY_ARG:
```

```
      /* Here we know that `state->arg_num == 0', since we
         force argument parsing to end before any more arguments can
         get here. */
      arguments->arg1 = arg;

      /* Now we consume all the rest of the arguments.
         `state->next' is the index in `state->argv' of the
         next argument to be parsed, which is the first STRING
         we're interested in, so we can just use
         `&state->argv[state->next]' as the value for
         arguments->strings.

         In addition, by setting `state->next' to the end
         of the arguments, we can force argp to stop parsing here and
         return. */
      arguments->strings = &state->argv[state->next];
      state->next = state->argc;

      break;

    default:
      return ARGP_ERR_UNKNOWN;
    }
  return 0;
}

/* Our argp parser. */
static struct argp argp = { options, parse_opt, args_doc, doc };

int main (int argc, char **argv)
{
  int i, j;
  struct arguments arguments;

  /* Default values. */
  arguments.silent = 0;
  arguments.verbose = 0;
  arguments.output_file = "-";
  arguments.repeat_count = 1;
  arguments.abort = 0;

  /* Parse our arguments; every option seen by `parse_opt' will be
     reflected in `arguments'. */
  argp_parse (&argp, argc, argv, 0, 0, &arguments);
```

```
    if (arguments.abort)
  error (10, 0, "ABORTED");

 for (i = 0; i < arguments.repeat_count; i++)
  {
   printf ("ARG1 = %s\n", arguments.arg1);
   printf ("STRINGS = ");
   for (j = 0; arguments.strings[j]; j++)
    printf (j == 0 ? "%s" : ", %s", arguments.strings[j]);
   printf ("\n");
   printf ("OUTPUT_FILE = %s\nVERBOSE = %s\nSILENT = %s\n",
         arguments.output_file,
         arguments.verbose ? "yes" : "no",
         arguments.silent ? "yes" : "no");
  }

 exit (0);
}
```

Argp User Customization

The formatting of argp `--help' output may be controlled to some extent by a program's users, by setting the `ARGP_HELP_FMT' environment variable to a comma-separated list of tokens. Whitespace is ignored:

`dup-args'
`no-dup-args'

These turn "duplicate-argument-mode" on or off. In duplicate argument mode, if an option that accepts an argument has multiple names, the argument is shown for each name. Otherwise, it is only shown for the first long option. A note is subsequently printed so the user knows that it applies to other names as well. The default is `no-dup-args', which is less consistent, but prettier.

`dup-args-note'

`no-dup-args-note'

These will enable or disable the note informing the user of suppressed option argument duplication. The default is `dup-args-note'.

`short-opt-col=N'

This prints the first short option in column N. The default is 2.

`long-opt-col=N'

This prints the first long option in column N. The default is 6.

`doc-opt-col=N'

This prints `documentation options' in column N. The default is 2.

`opt-doc-col=N'

This prints the documentation for options starting in column N. The default is 29.

`header-col=N'

This will indent the group headers that document groups of options to column N. The default is 1.

`usage-indent=N'

This will indent continuation lines in `Usage:' messages to column N. The default is 12.

`rmargin=N'

This will word wrap help output at or before column N. The default is 79.

Parsing of Suboptions

Having a single level of options is sometimes not enough. There might be too many options which have to be available or a set of options is closely related.

For this case some programs use suboptions. One of the most prominent programs is certainly `mount'(8). The `-o' option take one argument which itself is a comma separated list of options. To ease the programming of code like this the function `getsubopt' is available.

- Function: int getsubopt (char **OPTIONP, const char* const *TOKENS, char **VALUEP)

The OPTIONP parameter must be a pointer to a variable containing the address of the string to process. When the function returns the reference is updated to point to the next suboption or to the terminating `\0' character if there is no more suboption available.

The TOKENS parameter references an array of strings containing the known suboptions. All strings must be `\0' terminated and to mark the end a null pointer must be stored. When `getsubopt' finds a possible legal suboption it compares it with all strings available in the TOKENS array and returns the index in the string as the indicator.

In case the suboption has an associated value introduced by a `=' character, a pointer to the value is returned in VALUEP. The string is `\0' terminated. If no argument is available VALUEP is set to the null pointer. By doing this the caller can check whether a necessary value is given or whether no unexpected value is present.

In case the next suboption in the string is not mentioned in the TOKENS array the starting address of the suboption including a possible value is returned in VALUEP and the return value of the function is `-1'.

Example 15

The following example is used to explain how parsing of suboptions cab be done.

The code which might appear in the `mount'(8) program is a perfect example of the use of `getsubopt':

```
#include <stdio.h>
#include <stdlib.h>
```

```
#include <unistd.h>
int do_all;
const char *type;
int read_size;
int write_size;
int read_only;

enum
{
  RO_OPTION = 0,
  RW_OPTION,
  READ_SIZE_OPTION,
  WRITE_SIZE_OPTION,
  THE_END
};

const char *mount_opts[] =
{
  [RO_OPTION] = "ro",
  [RW_OPTION] = "rw",
  [READ_SIZE_OPTION] = "rsize",
  [WRITE_SIZE_OPTION] = "wsize",
  [THE_END] = NULL
};

int
main (int argc, char *argv[])
{
  char *subopts, *value;
  int opt;

  while ((opt = getopt (argc, argv, "at:o:")) != -1)
    switch (opt)
      {
      case 'a':
        do_all = 1;
        break;
      case 't':
        type = optarg;
        break;
      case 'o':
        subopts = optarg;
        while (*subopts != '\0')
          switch (getsubopt (&subopts, mount_opts, &value))
```

```
          {
          case RO_OPTION:
            read_only = 1;
            break;
          case RW_OPTION:
            read_only = 0;
            break;
          case READ_SIZE_OPTION:
            if (value == NULL)
              abort ();
            read_size = atoi (value);
            break;
          case WRITE_SIZE_OPTION:
            if (value == NULL)
              abort ();
            write_size = atoi (value);
            break;
          default:
            /* Unknown suboption. */
            printf ("Unknown suboption `%s'\n", value);
            break;
          }
        break;
      default:
        abort ();
      }

  /* Do the real work. */

  return 0;
}
```

3.3.5 Use of POPT[1] Library

The popt library is also essentially used for parsing command-line options.The popt library is highly portable and should work on any POSIX platform. It is found superior in many ways when compared to parsing the argv array by hand or using the getopt functions getopt() and getopt_long(). Some specific advantages of popt are:

- it does not utilize global variables, thus enabling multiple passes in parsing argv.
- it can parse an arbitrary array of argv-style elements, allowing parsing of command-line-strings from any source.
- it provides a standard method of option aliasing (to be discussed at length below).
- it can exec external option filters.
- finally, it can automatically generate help and usage messages for the application.

---

[1] ftp://ftp.rpm.org/pub/rpm/dist.

Like getopt_long(), the popt library supports short and long style options. Recall that a short option consists of a - character followed by a single alphanumeric character. A long option, common in GNU utilities, consists of two - characters followed by a string made up of letters, numbers and hyphens. Long options are optionally allowed to begin with a single -, primarily to allow command-line compatibility between popt applications and X toolkit applications. Either type of option may be followed by an argument. A space separates a short option from its arguments; either a space or an = separates a long option from an argument.

RPM, a popular Linux package management program, makes heavy use of popt's features. Many of its command-line arguments are implemented through popt aliases, which makes RPM an excellent example of how to take advantage of the popt library.

The set of functions available in this library are:

poptContext poptGetContext(const char * name, int argc, const char ** argv,
const struct poptOption * options, int flags);

void poptFreeContext(poptContext con);

void poptResetContext(poptContext con);

int poptGetNextOpt(poptContext con);

const char * poptGetOptArg(poptContext con);

const char * poptGetArg(poptContext con);

const char * poptPeekArg(poptContext con);

const char ** poptGetArgs(poptContext con);

const char *const poptStrerror(const int error);

const char * poptBadOption(poptContext con, int flags);

int poptReadDefaultConfig(poptContext con, int flags);

int poptReadConfigFile(poptContext con, char * fn);

int poptAddAlias(poptContext con, struct poptAlias alias, int flags);

int poptParseArgvString(char * s, int * argcPtr, const char * argvPtr);**

```
int poptDupArgv(int argc, const char ** argv, int * argcPtr,
                                const char *** argvPtr);

int poptStuffArgs(poptContext con, const char ** argv);
```

1. THE OPTION TABLE

   Applications provide popt with information on their command-line options by means of an "option table," i.e., an array of struct poptOption structures:

```
#include <popt.h>

struct poptOption {
   const char * longName; /* may be NULL */
   char shortName;       /* may be '\0' */
   int argInfo;
   void * arg;          /* depends on argInfo */
   int val;            /* 0 means don't return, just update flag */
   char * descrip;       /* description for autohelp -- may be NULL */
   char * argDescrip;     /* argument description for autohelp */
};
```

Each member of the table defines a single option that may be passed to the program. Long and short options are considered a single option that may occur in two different forms. The first two members, longName and shortName, define the names of the option; the first is a long name, while the latter is a single character.

The argInfo member tells popt what type of argument is expected after the argument. If no option is expected, POPT_ARG_NONE should be used.

For numeric values, if the argInfo value is bitwise or'd with one of POPT_ARGFLAG_OR, POPT_ARGFLAG_AND, or POPT_ARGFLAG_XOR, specified, -longopt is accepted as well. Otherwise it should point to a variable of the type indicated in the right-most column of the table above. will perhaps not escape the attention of hunt-and-peck typists that an argument, the variable that error returned if the conversion fails.

POPT_ARG_VAL causes arg to be set to the (integer) value of val when the argument is found. This is most often useful for mutually-exclusive arguments in cases where it is not an error for multiple arguments to occur and where we want the last argument specified to win; for example, "rm -i -f". POPT_ARG_VAL causes the parsing function not to return a value, since the value of val has already been used.

If the argInfo value is bitwise or'd with POPT_ARGFLAG_OPTIONAL, the argument to the long option may be omitted. If the long option is used without an argument, a default value of zero or NULL will be saved (if the arg pointer is present), otherwise behavior will be identical to a long option with argument. should return when the option is encountered. If it is 0, the parsing function does not return a value, instead parsing the next command-line argument. if automatic help messages are desired (automatic usage messages can arguments. see below) in the main one which provides the table entries for these use popt's automatical help, popt displays the appropriate message on stderr as soon as it finds the option, and exits the program with a return code of 0. If we want to use popt's automatic help generation in a different way, we need to explicitly add the option entries to your programs. If the argInfo value is bitwise or'd with POPT_ARGFLAG_DOC_HIDDEN, the argument will not be shown in help output. If the argInfo value is bitwise or'd with POPT_ARGFLAG_SHOW_DEFAULT, the initial value of the arg will be shown in help output.

The final structure in the table should have all the pointer values set. There are two types of option table entries which do not specify command line options. When either of these types of entries are used, the longName element must be NULL and the shortName element must be '\0'.The first of these special entry types allows the application to nest another option table in the current one; such nesting may extend quite deeply (the actual depth is limited by the program's stack). Including other option tables allows a library to provide a standard set of command-line options to every program which uses it (this is often done in graphical programming toolkits, for example). To do this, set the argInfo field to POPT_ARG_INCLUDE_TABLE and the arg field to point to the table which is being included. If automatic help generation is being used, the descrip field should contain a overall description of the option table being included. The other special option table entry type tells popt to call a function (a callback) when any option in that table is found. This is especially useful when included option tables are being used, as the program which provides the top-level option table doesn't need to be aware of the other options which are provided by the included table. When a callback is set for a table, the parsing function never returns information on an option in the table. Instead, options information must be retained via the callback or by having popt set a variable through the option's arg field.

Option callbacks should match the following prototype:

The first parameter is the context which is being parsed (see the next section for information on contexts), opt points to the option which triggered this callback, and arg is the option's argument. If the option does not take an argument, arg is NULL. The final parameter, data is taken from the descrip field of the option table entry which defined the callback. As descrip is a pointer, this allows callback functions to be passed an arbitrary set of data (though a typecast will have to be used). The option table entry which defines a callback has an argInfo of POPT_ARG_CALLBACK, an arg which points to the callback function, and a descrip field which specifies an arbitrary pointer to be passed to the callback. popt can interleave the parsing of multiple command-line sets. It allows this by keeping all the state information for a particular set of command-line arguments in a modified outside the popt library.

The first parameter, should be the name of the application whose options are being parsed, two arguments specify the command-line arguments to parse. These are which was described in the previous section. The final parameter, can take one of three values:

IfB IfB

IfB IfR.

Value

POPT_CONTEXT_NO_EXEC

POPT_CONTEXT_KEEP_FIRST

POPT_CONTEXT_POSIXMEHARDER

A poptContext keeps track of which options have already been parsed and which remain, among other things. If a program wishes to restart option processing of a set of arguments, it can reset the poptContext by passing the context as the sole argument to poptResetContext().

When argument processing is complete, the process should free the poptContext as it contains dynamically allocated components. The poptFreeContext() function takes a poptContext as its sole argument and frees the resources the context is using.

Here are the prototypes of both poptResetContext() and poptFreeContext():

```
#include <popt.h>
void poptFreeContext(poptContext con);
void poptResetContext(poptContext con);
```

After an application has created a poptContext, it may begin parsing arguments. poptGetNextOpt() performs the actual argument parsing.

```
#include <popt.h>
int poptGetNextOpt(poptContext con);
```

Taking the context as its sole argument, this function parses the next command-line argument found. After finding the next argument in the option table, the function fills in the object pointed to by the option table entry's arg pointer if it is not NULL. If the val entry for the option is non-0, the function then returns that value. Otherwise, poptGetNextOpt() continues on to the next argument.

poptGetNextOpt() returns -1 when the final argument has been parsed, and other negative values when errors occur. This makes it a good idea to keep the val elements in the options table greater than 0.

If all of the command-line options are handled through arg pointers, command-line parsing is reduced to the following line of code:

```
rc = poptGetNextOpt(poptcon);
```

Many applications require more complex command-line parsing than this, however, and use the following structure:

```
while ((rc = poptGetNextOpt(poptcon)) > 0) {
    switch (rc) {
        /* specific arguments are handled here */
    }
}
```

When returned options are handled, the application needs to know the value of any arguments that were specified after the option. There are two ways to discover them. One is to ask popt to fill in a variable with the value of the option through the option table's arg elements. The other is to use poptGetOptArg():

```
#include <popt.h>
const char * poptGetOptArg(poptContext con);
```

This function returns the argument given for the final option returned by poptGetNextOpt(), or it returns NULL if no argument was specified.

Many applications take an arbitrary number of command-line arguments, such as a list of file names. When popt encounters an argument that does not begin with a -, it assumes it is such an argument and adds it to a list of leftover arguments. Three functions allow applications to access such arguments:

```
const char * poptGetArg(poptContext con);
```

This function returns the next leftover argument and marks it as processed.

```
const char * poptPeekArg(poptContext con);
```

The next leftover argument is returned but not marked as processed. This allows an application to look ahead into the argument list, without modifying the list.

```
const char ** poptGetArgs(poptContext con);
```

All the leftover arguments are returned in a manner identical to argv. The final element in the returned array points to NULL, indicating the end of the arguments.

The popt library can automatically generate help messages which describe the options a program accepts. There are two types of help messages which can be generated. Usage messages are a short messages which lists valid options, but does not describe them. Help messages describe each option on one (or more) lines, resulting in a longer, but more useful, message. Whenever automatic help messages are used, the descrip and argDescrip fields struct poptOption members should be filled in for each option.

The POPT_AUTOHELP macro makes it easy to add --usage and --help messages to your program, and is described in part 1 of this man page. If more control is needed over your help messages, the following two functions are available:

```
#include <popt.h>
void poptPrintHelp(poptContext con, FILE * f, int flags);
void poptPrintUsage(poptContext con, FILE * f, int flags);
```

poptPrintHelp() displays the standard help message to the stdio file descriptor f, while poptPrintUsage() displays the shorter usage message. Both functions currently ignore the flags argument; it is there to allow future changes.

ERROR HANDLING

All of the popt functions that can return errors return integers. When an error occurs, a negative error code is returned. The following table summarizes the error codes that occur:

Error	Description
POPT_ERROR_NOARG	Argument missing for an option.
POPT_ERROR_BADOPT	Option's argument couldn't be parsed.
POPT_ERROR_OPTSTOODEEP	Option aliasing nested too deeply.
POPT_ERROR_BADQUOTE	Quotations do not match.
POPT_ERROR_BADNUMBER	Option couldn't be converted to number.
POPT_ERROR_OVERFLOW	A given number was too big or small.

Here is a more detailed discussion of each error:

POPT_ERROR_NOARG

An option that requires an argument was specified on the command line, but no argument was given. This can be returned only by poptGetNextOpt().

POPT_ERROR_BADOPT

An option was specified in argv but is not in the option table. This error can be returned only from poptGetNextOpt().

POPT_ERROR_OPTSTOODEEP

A set of option aliases is nested too deeply. Currently, popt follows options only 10 levels to prevent infinite recursion. Only poptGetNextOpt() can return this error.

POPT_ERROR_BADQUOTE

A parsed string has a quotation mismatch (such as a single quotation mark). poptParseArgvString(), poptReadConfigFile(), or poptReadDefaultConfig() can return this error.

POPT_ERROR_BADNUMBER

A conversion from a string to a number (int or long) failed due to the string containing nonnumeric characters. This occurs when poptGetNextOpt() is processing an argument of type POPT_ARG_INT, POPT_ARG_LONG, POPT_ARG_FLOAT, or POPT_ARG_DOUBLE.

POPT_ERROR_OVERFLOW

A string-to-number conversion failed because the number was too large or too small. Like POPT_ERROR_BADNUMBER, this error can occur only when poptGetNextOpt() is processing an argument of type POPT_ARG_INT, POPT_ARG_LONG, POPT_ARG_FLOAT, or POPT_ARG_DOUBLE.

POPT_ERROR_ERRNO

A system call returned with an error, and errno still contains the error from the system call. Both poptReadConfigFile() and poptReadDefaultConfig() can return this error.

Two functions are available to make it easy for applications to provide good error messages.

```
const char *const poptStrerror(const int error);
```

This function takes a popt error code and returns a string describing the error, just as with the standard strerror() function.

```
const char * poptBadOption(poptContext con, int flags);
```

If an error occurred during poptGetNextOpt(), this function returns the option that caused the error. If the flags argument is set to POPT_BADOPTION_NOALIAS, the outermost option is returned. Otherwise, flags should be 0, and the option that is returned may have been specified through an alias.

These two functions make popt error handling trivial for most applications. When an error is detected from most of the functions, an error message is printed along with the error string from poptStrerror(). When an error occurs during argument parsing, code similar to the following displays a useful error message:

```
fprintf(stderr, "%s: %s\n",
        poptBadOption(optCon, POPT_BADOPTION_NOALIAS),
        poptStrerror(rc));
```

OPTION ALIASING

One of the primary benefits of using popt over getopt() is the ability to use option aliasing. This lets the user specify options that popt expands into other options when they are specified. If the standard grep program made use of popt, users could add a --text option that expanded to -i -n -E -2 to let them more easily find information in text files.

SPECIFYING ALIASES

Aliases are normally specified in two places: /etc/popt and the .popt file in the user's home directory (found through the HOME environment variable). Both files have the same format, an arbitrary number of lines formatted like this:

```
appname alias newoption expansion
```

The appname is the name of the application, which must be the same as the name parameter passed to poptGetContext(). This allows each file to specify aliases for multiple programs. The alias keyword specifies that an alias is being defined; currently popt configuration files support only aliases, but other abilities may be added in the future. The next option is the option that should be aliased, and it may be either a short or a long option. The rest of the line specifies the expansion for the alias. It is parsed similarly to a shell command, which allows \, ", and ' to be used for quoting. If a backslash is the final character on a line, the next line in the file is assumed to be a logical continuation of the line containing the backslash, just as in shell.

The following entry would add a --text option to the grep command, as suggested at the beginning of this section.

```
grep alias --text -i -n -E -2
```

ENABLING ALIASES

An application must enable alias expansion for a poptContext before calling poptGetNextArg() for the first time. There are three functions that define aliases for a context:

```
int poptReadDefaultConfig(poptContext con, int flags);
```

This function reads aliases from /etc/popt and the .popt file in the user's home directory. Currently, flags should be NULL, as it is provided only for future expansion.

```
int poptReadConfigFile(poptContext con, char * fn);
```

The file specified by fn is opened and parsed as a popt configuration file. This allows programs to use program-specific configuration files.

```
int poptAddAlias(poptContext con, struct poptAlias alias, int flags);
```

Occasionally, processes want to specify aliases without having to read them from a configuration file. This function adds a new alias to a context. The flags argument should be 0, as it is currently reserved for future expansion. The new alias is specified as a struct poptAlias, which is defined as:

```
struct poptAlias {
    const char * longName; /* may be NULL */
    char shortName; /* may be '\0' */
    int argc;
    const char ** argv; /* must be free()able */
};
```

The first two elements, longName and shortName, specify the option that is aliased. The final two, argc and argv, define the expansion to use when the aliases option is encountered.

PARSING ARGUMENT STRINGS

Although popt is usually used for parsing arguments already divided into an argv-style array, some programs need to parse strings that are formatted identically to command lines. To facilitate this, popt provides a function that parses a string into an array of strings, using rules similar to normal shell parsing.

```
#include <popt.h>
int poptParseArgvString(char * s, int * argcPtr,
                char *** argvPtr);
int poptDupArgv(int argc, const char ** argv, int * argcPtr,
                const char *** argvPtr);
```

The string s is parsed into an argv-style array. The integer pointed to by the argcPtr parameter contains the number of elements parsed, and the final argvPtr parameter contains the address of the newly created array. The routine poptDupArgv() can be used to make a copy of an existing argument array.

The argvPtr created by poptParseArgvString() or poptDupArgv() is suitable to pass directly to poptGetContext(). Both routines return a single dynamically allocated contiguous block of storage and should be free()'d when the application is finished with the storage.

HANDLING EXTRA ARGUMENTS

Some applications implement the equivalent of option aliasing but need to do so through special logic. The poptStuffArgs() function allows an application to insert new arguments into the current poptContext.

```
#include <popt.h>
int poptStuffArgs(poptContext con, const char ** argv);
```

The passed argv must have a NULL pointer as its final element. When poptGetNextOpt() is next called, the "stuffed" arguments are the first to be parsed. popt returns to the normal arguments once all the stuffed arguments have been exhausted.

Example 16

The following example is a simple program illustrating at least some of the features of the extremely rich popt library.

```
#include <popt.h>
#include <stdio.h>

void usage(poptContext optCon, int exitcode, char *error, char *addl) {
   poptPrintUsage(optCon, stderr, 0);
   if (error) fprintf(stderr, "%s: %s, error, addl);
   exit(exitcode);
}

int main(int argc, char *argv[]) {
  char   c;          /* used for argument parsing */
  int    i = 0;      /* used for tracking options */
  char   *portname;
  int    speed = 0;   /* used in argument parsing to set speed */
  int    raw = 0;     /* raw mode? */
  int    j;
  char   buf[BUFSIZ+1];
  poptContext optCon;   /* context for parsing command-line options */

  struct poptOption optionsTable[] = {
        { "bps", 'b', POPT_ARG_INT, &speed, 0,
           "signaling rate in bits-per-second", "BPS" },
        { "crnl", 'c', 0, 0, 'c',
           "expand cr characters to cr/lf sequences" },
        { "hwflow", 'h', 0, 0, 'h',
           "use hardware (RTS/CTS) flow control" },
```

```
        { "noflow", 'n', 0, 0, 'n',
           "use no flow control" },
        { "raw", 'r', 0, &raw, 0,
           "don't perform any character conversions" },
        { "swflow", 's', 0, 0, 's',
           "use software (XON/XOF) flow control" } ,
        POPT_AUTOHELP
        { NULL, 0, 0, NULL, 0 }
};

optCon = poptGetContext(NULL, argc, argv, optionsTable, 0);
poptSetOtherOptionHelp(optCon, "[OPTIONS]* <port>");

if (argc < 2) {
    poptPrintUsage(optCon, stderr, 0);
    exit(1);
}

/* Now do options processing, get portname */
while ((c = poptGetNextOpt(optCon)) >= 0) {
  switch (c) {
    case 'c':
      buf[i++] = 'c';
      break;
    case 'h':
      buf[i++] = 'h';
      break;
    case 's':
      buf[i++] = 's';
      break;
    case 'n':
      buf[i++] = 'n';
      break;
  }
}
portname = poptGetArg(optCon);
if((portname == NULL) || !(poptPeekArg(optCon) == NULL))
  usage(optCon, 1, "Specify a single port", ".e.g., /dev/cua0");

if (c < -1) {
  /* an error occurred during option processing */
  fprintf(stderr, "%s: %s\n",
        poptBadOption(optCon, POPT_BADOPTION_NOALIAS),
        poptStrerror(c));
  return 1;
```

```
    }

    /* Print out options, portname chosen */
    printf("Options  chosen: ");
    for(j = 0; j < i ; j++)
      printf("-%c ", buf[j]);
    if(raw) printf("-r ");
    if(speed) printf("-b %d ", speed);
    printf("\nPortname chosen: %s\n", portname);

    poptFreeContext(optCon);
    exit(0);
}
```

Example 17

This example shows how to use popt handle command-line options.

```
#include <popt.h>
#include <stdio.h>

int main(int argc, char *argv[])
{
   /* option parsing variables */
   char ch;
   poptContext opt_con;   /* context for parsing command-line options */
   char *extra_arg;

static struct poptOption options_table[] = {
{ "add",    'a', POPT_ARG_NONE, NULL, 'a', "perform add opration", "ADD" },
{ "block",  'b', POPT_ARG_NONE, NULL, 'b', "block something", "BLOCK" },
{ "catch",  'c', POPT_ARG_NONE, NULL, 'c', "catch something", "CATCH" },
{ "delete", 'd', POPT_ARG_NONE, NULL, 'd', "delete a number of things",
"DELETE" },
   POPT_AUTOHELP
   { NULL, 0, 0, NULL, 0 } /* end-of-list terminator */
   };

   opt_con = poptGetContext(NULL, argc, (const char **)argv,
options_table, 0);

   /* Now do options processing */
   while ((ch = poptGetNextOpt(opt_con)) >= 0) {
   printf("between while & switch: ch = %c\n", ch);
   switch (ch) {
```

```
            case 'a':
    printf("handling 'a' option.\n");
                    break;
            case 'b':
    printf("handling 'b' option.\n");
                    break;
            case 'c':
    printf("handling 'c' option.\n");
                    break;
            case 'd':
    printf("handling 'd' option.\n");
                    break;
    }
    }

    if (ch < -1) {
    // the user specified an invalid option, tell them
    poptPrintHelp(opt_con, stderr, 0);
    }

    /* non-option args */
    while (extra_arg = (char *)poptGetArg(opt_con)) {
    printf("extra arg: %s\n", extra_arg);
    exit(1);
    }


    /* cleanup */
    poptFreeContext(opt_con);

    return 0;
}
```

Example 18

This example shows how to use popt to set the value of some static vars.

```
#include <popt.h>
#include <stdio.h>

int main(int argc, char *argv[])
{
    /* option parsing variables */
    char ch;
    poptContext opt_con;   /* context for parsing command-line options */
```

```
/* flags that get set */
static char *blockstr = "";
static char *catchstr = "";
static int num_dels = 0;

static struct poptOption options_table[] = {
{ "add",    'a', POPT_ARG_NONE,   NULL,      'a', "perform add opration",
NULL },
{ "block",  'b', POPT_ARG_STRING, &blockstr, 'b', "block something",
"BLOCKME" },
{ "catch",  'c', POPT_ARG_STRING, &catchstr, 'c', "catch something",
"CATCHME" },
{ "delete", 'd', POPT_ARG_INT,    &num_dels, 'd', "delete", "#DELETES"
},
POPT_AUTOHELP
{ NULL, 0, 0, NULL, 0 } /* end-of-list terminator */
};

opt_con = poptGetContext(NULL, argc, (const char **)argv,
options_table, 0);
//poptSetOtherOptionHelp(opt_con, "[OPTIONS]");

/* Now do options processing */
while ((ch = poptGetNextOpt(opt_con)) >= 0) {
printf("between while & switch: ch = %c\n", ch);
switch (ch) {
        case 'a':
                printf("handling 'a' option.\n");
                break;
        case 'b':
                printf("handling 'b' option, argument is '%s'.\n",
                poptGetArg(opt_con));
                break;
        case 'c':
                printf("handling 'c' option, argument is '%s'.\n",
                poptGetArg(opt_con));
                break;
        case 'd':
                printf("handling 'd' option, argument is '%i'.\n",
                poptGetArg(opt_con));
                break;
}
}
if (ch < -1) {
// the user specified an invalid option, tell them
poptPrintHelp(opt_con, stderr, 0);
```

```
    exit(1);
    }

    printf("\n\nPost-option processing:\n");
    printf("  blockstr = %s\n", blockstr);
    printf("  catchstr = %s\n", catchstr);
    printf("  num_dels = %i\n", num_dels);


    /* cleanup */
    poptFreeContext(opt_con);

    return 0;
}
```

Example 19

This program is written to explain how popt library can be used to handle command line arguments of a program which calculates room volume and surface area (same as Example 4). This program will have same command line interface as that of examples 6, 9 and 13.

```
#include <popt.h>
#include <stdio.h>

int main(int argc, char *argv[])
{
    /* option parsing variables */
    char ch;
    poptContext opt_con;

  /* context for parsing command-line options */

    static int num_h= 0, num_l=0, num_b=0,V,SA;

    static struct poptOption options_table[] = {
    { "length", 'l', POPT_ARG_INT,    &num_l, 'l', "length", "Length" },
    { "breadth", 'b', POPT_ARG_INT,    &num_b, 'b', "breadth", "Breadth" },
    { "height", 'h', POPT_ARG_INT,    &num_h, 'h', "height", "Height" },
    POPT_AUTOHELP
    { NULL, 0, 0, NULL, 0 } /* end-of-list terminator */
    };
    opt_con = poptGetContext(NULL, argc, (const char **)argv,
    options_table, 0);
```

```
while ((ch = poptGetNextOpt(opt_con)) >= 0) ;

    if (ch < -1) {
    // the user specified an invalid option, tell them
    poptPrintHelp(opt_con, stderr, 0);
    exit(1);
    }

    printf("\nPost-option processing:\n");
    printf("  Length= %i\n", num_l);
    printf("  Breadth= %i\n", num_b);
    printf("  Breadth= %i\n", num_h);
    V=num_l*num_b*num_h;
    SA=2*(num_l+num_b)*num_h  + num_l*num_b;
    printf("Volume=%d\nSurface Area=%d\n", V,SA);


    /* cleanup */
    poptFreeContext(opt_con);

    return 0;
}
```

3.3.6 CLIG Package

This program is a command line interface generator. Essentially it requires a specification file like lex/yacc to specify the command line interface. (How to write this specification file is discussed in the subsequent pages). Once this specification file is written, by running 'clig' command on this file, we can generate C language program to process command line arguments, header file having functions prototypes and also a manual page. The clig command can be used at the command prompt as follows. Here, command line specification is assumed be given in the file "clifile".

clig clifile [-o outprefix] [-m manpage] [-d]

-o Clig generates a .c and a .h files with outprefix as their primary name. By default the name is clifile without suffix.

-m is used to define the name of the manual page to generate or edit. The default is equal to the string specified with the Name-command in clifile suffixed with .1

-d in addition to the command-line parser, the generated .c-file contains the function

```
showOptionValues(void)
```

Which, when called after calling parseCmdline(), will print all parameters defined by default or found on the command line. ShowOptionValues() is mainly used for debugging purposes.

The generated source code file contains a command line parser with the prototype

```
mdline *parseCmdline(int argc, char **argv)
```

which returns its result in a structure of type Cmdline.

Also, the function

```
void usage(void)
```

is generated and will be called by the command-line parser, if the command line contains obvious errors.

Specification File

The description-file or specification file is a line-oriented ascii-file. Each line contains a command which either describes an option or specifies additional information necessary to generate parseCmdline(), usage(), showOptionValues() and the manual page. A command starts with the command-name followed by mandatory parameters and possibly followed by optional parameters. If a command does not fit on a line, it may be continued on the next line if the previous line is terminated by a backslash (\).

For example, consider a flag option named -v which is meant to instruct the program to operate verbosely: (Note the backslash on the next line!)

```
Flag -v verbose \
   {verbose operation generating blurb}
```

Here, the command's name is Flag. It has three parameters: The first, -v, is the string to be detected by the command line parser. The second, verbose, is the name of a variable in the structure Cmdline which will be set by the parser, if -v is on the command line. The third parameter, i.e. everything between the braces, is a string which will be printed by usage().

In general, every parameter of a description-command should be enclosed in braces, as soon as it contains white space.

Currently, options of type **flag, string, floating point, integer and files** are supported. Except for flag options, all option-descriptions allow to specify how many arguments are expected for the option and whether the option is mandatory or not. For non-mandatory options, default values can be specified and will be returned by parseCmdline() if necessary. In addition, for floating point and integer options, a range can be declared, and the parser will exit the program with an error message, if the option's argument lies outside the given range.

In some applications where files are created by programs with complicated command lines, it is often desirable to store the full command line in the generated file for documentation purposes. Therefore clig can generate code to concatenate the whole command line into one string before it is parsed and store it in a variable in the generated structure.

Clig necessitates that the used has to specify some MANDATORY COMMANDS such as the following two commands:

Name program-name

The Name-command specifies the name of the program. The string **program-name** is used in the generated manual page and also specifies the default name of the manual page. However the specified name is not used anywhere in the C-code, because use of argv[0] is preferred there.

Usage Command

The Usage command specifies a one line description of the program's intent and functionA typical example would be

```
Usage {program to delete your home directory}
```

STRING OPTIONS

String option variable usage [count=lo,hi] [mandatory | default=values]

The String command declares option to have zero or more string arguments. The structure Cmdline will contain the entries variable, variableP and variableC. The value of variableP will be set nonzero, if the option was found on the command line. If the optional parameter count= is not present, variable is of type char* and will point to the string found after the option. The parser will abort the program, if there is no string after the option.

The parameter usage specifies a string printed by usage() as a description of the option.

The optional parameter count=lo,hi declares, how many strings are expected as arguments to option. An example is

```
{count=3,7},
```

telling the parser that at least three and at most seven strings must be present after the option. As a special case, the upper bound may be oo, indicating that there is no upper limit for the number of strings expected after option. If the count allows more than one option argument (hi>1), the type of Cmdline.variable will be char**. If the count=-parameter allows at most one option argument, the type of Cmdline.variable will be char*. In both cases, the value of Cmdline.variableC will be set to the number of option arguments found.

The optional parameter mandatory tells the parser, that this option must be present. The parser will print an error message and terminate the program, if the option is not on the command line. The parameter mandatory cannot be use together with default=values.

The optional parameter default=values specifies one or more default values to be returned in Cmdline.variable if option is not on the command line. In main(), no difference can be detected between actual command line arguments and default values inserted by the parser.

Example use of String:

```
String -l labels {labels for x and y-axis} \
   {count = 2,2} \
   {default = {samples} {f in Hz} }
```

Please note how each default value is enclosed in braces. Actually samples need not be enclosed in braces here, since it contains no whitespace. The parameter {count = 2,2} specifies that -l must be followed by exactly two strings.

FLOAT OPTIONS

Float option variable usage [count=lo,hi] [mandatory | default=values] [range=lo,hi]

The Float command declares option to have zero or more floating point arguments. The description of variable, usage, count= and mandatory applies as for the String-command. The type of Cmdline.variable is float, if there is no count=-parameter or if it allows at most one option argument. It is float* otherwise.

The optional parameter range=lo,hi specifies a range for the option arguments. The special values -oo for lo and oo for hi are recognized. As an example,

```
{range = -oo,1.0}
```

specifies, that each option argument must be less or equal to 1.0. If the command line parser finds an argument of option which is not in the given range, it prints a suitable error messages and exits the program.

WARNING: The implementation of the default=-parameter is currently incomplete insofar, as the specified default values are not checked by clig, i.e. the following would go unnoticed:

```
{default = 1.0} {range = 500.0, 600.0}
```

In this case, if option is not on the command line, main() would find in Cmdline.variable the out-of-range value 1.0. (Maybe this is a feature?)

Example use of Float:

```
Float -p prob {list of probabilities adding up to one} \
   {range = 0.0, 1.0}  {default = 0.1 0.2 0.7} \
   {count = 1,oo}
```

Please note, that the additional constraint requiring the values summing to 1.0 cannot be checked by the parser, but must be checked by your main() function.

INT OPTIONS

Int option variable usage [count=lo,hi] [mandatory | default=values] [range=lo,hi]

The Int command declares option to have zero or more integer arguments. The description of variable, usage, count=, mandatory and range= applies as for the Float-command. Even the note about the unchecked default values applies. However, the type of Cmdline.variable is int or int* depending on the count=-parameter.

Example use of Int:

```
Int -b blocksize {size of internal buffer} \
   {range = 1024,oo} \
   {default = 1024}
```

FLAG OPTIONS

Flag option variable usage

The Flag command declares an option without any parameters. The command line parser merely checks for the existence of option on the command line. If it is found, the parser returns a nonzero value in Cmdline.variableP as for all other option types. However, there are no variables named Cmdline.variable and Cmdline.variableC in the structure returned to main().

Example use of Flag:

```
Flag -v verbose {verbose operation}
```

OTHER COMMANDS

Rest name usage [count=lo,hi]

The Rest command specifies, what the parser should do with command line arguments not associated with any option. If clifile does not contain a Rest command, the parser will generate an error message for those arguments and terminate the program. If Rest is present, non-option arguments are left in char** Cmdline.argv while their number is recorded in int Cmdline.argc. The parameters name and usage are printed by usage(). The optional count=-parameter works as described for the String command. It does not, however, influence the type of Cmdline.argv, because this is always set equal to argv+1, where argv is the value passed to parseCmdline().

Example use of Rest:

Rest infiles {input files} {count = 1,oo}

```
Commandline argvstr
```

If you want to record the whole command line of a program in one of its output files for documentation purposes, this command comes in handy. If clig finds it in the description file it generates code to concatenate all command line arguments in one string. The code is called automatically within the function parseCmdline() just before the command line is actually parsed. The result is stored in the structure returned by parseCmdline() in entry argvstr.

Example use of Commandline:

Commandline tool

In your main() you can access the whole command line as one string like this:

```
...
Cmdline *cmd = parseCmdline(argc, argv);
```

```
printf("Full command line is `%s'\n", cmd->tool);
...
```

Version version

The Version command specifies a string to be used as a version-identification of the generated parser. Currently it is merely printed as part of the usage-information. An example using my favorite type of version numbers would be

```
Version 1995-08-22
```

Description description

The Description command should not be used. Instead, the respective section in the generated manual page should be filled out. The main reason for this advice is, that clig copies description AS IS into the manual page, so it can be typed into the manual page file in the first place. Please remember that the generated manual page needs some hand-tuning anyway, because for example the `SEE ALSO'-section cannot be generated. Since this command should not be used, no example is given.

For example, we plan to develop the C program using clig for calculating volume and surface area of the room (Example 4). The configuration file as follows.

```
Name VSA

Usage {Used to calculate volume and surface areas of a room whose length,
breatdh and height is given}

Commandline tool
Int -l l {Specify the length} \
   mandatory
Int -b b {Specify the breadth} \
   mandatory
Int -h h {Specify the height} \
   mandatory
```

Example 20

Main program is as follows:

```
#include<stdio.h>
#include <stdlib.h>

#include "cmdline.h"

int
main(int argc, char **argv)
```

```
{

int V, SA, L, B, H;
  Cmdline *cmd = parseCmdline(argc, argv);
  showOptionValues();

  /*****
```

Normally you use cmd somewhere here instead of just calling showOptionValues. In this demo however, the c-compiler would complain without the following.

```
  *****/
  cmd->tool = cmd->tool;

L=cmd->l;
B=cmd->b;
H=cmd->h;
V=L*B*H;
SA=2*H*(L+B)+L*B;
printf("Volume =%d\n Surface Area=%d\n", V, SA);
  return EXIT_SUCCESS;
}
```

The make file (whose name can be makefile) is as folows:

```
CFLAGS = -W -Wall
SRC = main.c cmdline.c

OBJ = $(SRC:%.c=%.o)

VSA: $(OBJ)
    $(CC) -o $@ $(CFLAGS) $(OBJ)

cmdline.c cmdline.h: cmdline.cli
    clig -d cmdline.cli

main.o: main.c cmdline.h

clean:
    rm -f *.o cmdline.[ch] *~
```

In order to create the program VSA, simply type make at the command prompt. Then check the generated program by typing command in the following style or any other style described in previous sections.

```
./VSA -l 10 -b 12 -h 21
```

3.3.7 SuperGetOpt Library[2]

The supergetopt library makes it very easy to handle all kinds of command-line arguments in a printf() sort of way. All styles of command-line args are supported and all arguments are checked for type validity. We do not require to create header files, no argument order to worry about.

This package can be downloaded from www.ibiblio.org/pub/linux/devel. After extracting the files run make command which creates a static library names "libSuperGet.a". Move this library file to either /lib or /usr/lib. This library contains one function, supergetopt(), which we need for argc/argv handling. Also, a number of functions exist convert strings to argc/argv format in this library. This package comes with "supertget.h" header file which has to be included in our program.

The function **supergetopt()** has the following syntax:

```
supergetopt( int argc, char *argv[],
        "flagA:[*][formatA]", functionToBeCalledA,
        "flagB:[*][formatB]", functionToBeCalledB,
        ... /* arbitrarily long list of flag/function pairs */
        NULL);
```

If we observe the above function prototype, we may find some pairs of strings and function names are given after second argument, i.e argv. Here, the strings contains flags (or options) to be given along the command line and what type of value they expect. What value they expect is specified in C style format such as %d, %c, %s or %f. For example, in the above function call "flagX" is an arbitrary keyword like "--help" or "+debug" or "display" which can be given along the command line for the program which is calling this function, where as the "format" is a concatenation of printf()-like % formats, and the optional '*' implies an arbitrarily long list of values of the specified format are expected. The corresponding function will be called only if the flag is seen on the Commandline. The specified function will be called with pointers to the arguments (not the arguments themselves). In all cases, the ":" is required as a separator between options and format string.

NOTE: Supergetopt's string memory is not static, so we must make a copy of the string if we wish to use it later on in our program. The strdup() function is a good choice.

Fixed number of arguments to a flag

If '*' is not specified, the number arguments to a given flag is the number of "%X"s in the format (fixed). The specified function will be called with pointers to the arguments (not the arguments themselves). In the special case of strings, which are already char pointers, they will get passed as a 'char *' (not 'char **').

---

[2] apr@planet.net

Arbitrary number of arguments to a given flag

If '*' is specified, then only one '%' may appear in the format. In this case, our function can be designed to have two arguments, as in:

```
yourFunction( type x[], int numArgs )
```

where "type" is one of char, int, long, short, float, double, char, char *. Again, in the special case of strings, note that this means char *x[].

Flags without arguments

If the format is not specified, no arguments are expected to our flag (e.g. "--help"), and our function will be called with no arguments to it.

Arguments without flags

If we wish to specify arguments without flags, just use an empty flag, as in ":%f%d". This entry should be last on the list or arg pairs to supergetopt() and only one can exist, for obvious reasons.

Every flag must have a corresponding function irrespective of whether it takes argument or not.

For example, if we want to design command line interface to a program "XYZ" which is of the form:

XYZ -name string -age 12 -heightandweight 5.67 87.23

Then the supergetopt() function should be the following style.

```
supergetopt( int argc, char *argv[],
        "-name:%s", FuncA,
        "-age:%d", FunB,
        "-heightandweight:%d%d", FunC,
        ...        /* arbitrarily long list of flag/function pairs */
        NULL);
```

The FuncA has to be defined as taking address of a character pointer.

The FuncB has to be defined as taking address of an integer.

The FuncC has to be defined as taking addresses of two integers.

Example 21

The following program (VSA.c) is to design command line interface for problem defined in example 4.

```
#include<stdio.h>
#include"superget.h"
int L,B,H;
void LENGTH(int *f)
{
L=*f;
}
void BREADTH(int *f)
{
```

```
B=*f;
}
void HEIGHT(int *f)
{
H=*f;
}
int main( int argc, char *argv[] )
{
int V,SA;
long n;
n = supergetopt( argc, argv,"-l:%d", LENGTH, "-b:%d", BREADTH, "-h:%d",
HEIGHT, NULL );
V=L*B*H;
SA=2*H*(L+B) + L*B;
printf("Volume=%d\n Surface Area=%d\n", V, SA);
 return(1);
}
```

To compile the program:

gcc –o aa VSA.c libSuperGet.a

Here, we are assuming that the library libSuperGet.a is available in the current directory itself. If it is available in standard directories such as /lib or /usr/lib then the following command can be used to compile the same.

gcc –o aa VSA.c -lSuperGet.a

To run

./aa –l 10 –b 10 –h 12

3.3.8 argtable2 Library[3]

This is an ANSI C library for parsing GNU style command line options. The same can be downloaded from www.sourceforge.net and installed. When we extract the package and compile the sources available there in, we will get two libraries namingly libargtable2.a (static version) and libargtable2.so (dynamic version). They can be moved to standard directories such as /lib or /usr/lib. Also, it comes along with a header file "argtable2.h" which can be placed in standard directory such as /usr/include.

To parse the command line options, first we have to construct an arg_xxx struct for each command line option expected. These structures will hold the values that are extracted from the command line. There are various forms of the arg_xxx struts (which are explained in the following paragraphs), each one specialized for a particular type of

[3] Stewart Heitmann <sheitmann@users.sourceforge.net>

option (i.e.: literal, integer, double, string, filename). Each option may be given a short option tag (e.g.: -x) and/or a long option tag (e.g.: --verbose), or no tags at all in which case the argument is identified by its position on the command line. The latter are called untagged arguments.

Each arg_xxx struct can store multiple occurrences of a command line option. When an arg_xxx struct is constructed, we specify the minimum and maximum number of occurrences that we wish the option to handle. The arg_xxx constructor function will then allocate sufficient storage within the struct for the maximum number of occurrences. If we wish to handle an infinite number of occurrences of an option then we really only need specify the maximum number to be equal to argc as that is the maximum number of occurrences that is possible for any given command line invocation. Later on when the parsing is performed, the number of occurrences of the option on the command line is checked for legality. Too many or too few will be flagged accordingly.

Constructing an arg_xxx data structure

Each arg_xxx struct has it own unique set of constructor functions and while these may differ slightly between arg_xxx structures, they are generally of the form:

struct arg_xxx* arg_xxx0 (const char *shortopts, const char *longopts, const char *datatype, const char *glossary)

struct arg_xxx* arg_xxx1 (const char *shortopts, const char *longopts, const char *datatype, const char *glossary)

struct arg_xxx* arg_xxxn (const char *shortopts, const char *longopts, const char *datatype, int mincount, int maxcount, const char *glossary)

The arg_xxx0() and arg_xxx1() forms are merely abbreviated forms of arg_xxxn() and are provided as a convenience for the most common arrangements of command line options; to name that have zero-or-one occurrences (mincount=0,maxcount=1) and those that have one exactly one occurrence (mincount=1,maxcount=1) respectively.

The const char* shortopts parameter defines the options short form tag (eg: -x, -k3, -D"macro"). It can be left as NULL if a short option is not required, otherwise use it to specify the desired short option character in the string (without the leading "-" and without any whitespace). For example, the short option -v is defined simply as "v". In fact, a command line option may have multiple alternate short form tags defined for it by concatenating the desired characters into the shortopts string. For instance "abc" defines an option which will accept any of the three equivalent short forms -a, -b, -c interchangeably.

The const char* longopts parameter is similar to shortopts, except it defines the options long form tags (eg: --help, --depth=3, --name=myfile.txt). It too can be left as NULL if not required, and it too can have multiple equivalent tags defined but these must be separated by commas. For example, if we wish to define two equivalent long options --quiet and --silent then we would give longopts as "quiet,silent". Remember not to include any whitespace.

If both shortopts and longopts are given as NULL then the resulting option is an untagged argument.

The const char* datatype parameter is a descriptive string we can use to customize the appearance of the argument data type in error messages and so forth. It does not affect the actual data type definition as that is a fixed property of the arg_xxx struct. So for example, defining a datatype of "<int>" will result in the option being display something like "-x <int>" or "--foo=<int>" depending upon your option tags. If given as NULL, the datatype string will revert to the default value for the particular arg_xxx struct. We can effectively disable the default by specifying datatype as an empty string.

The int mincount parameter specifies the minimum number of occurrences that the option must appear on the command line. If the option does not appear at least that many times then the parser reports it as a syntax error. The mincount defaults to 0 for the arg_xxx0() functions and 1 for arg_xxx1() functions.

The int maxcount parameter specifies the maximum number of occurrences that the option may appear on the command line. Any occurrences beyond the maximum are discarded by the parser reported as syntax errors. The maxcount defaults to 1 for both the arg_xxx0() and arg_xxx1() functions.

The const char* glossary parameter is another descriptive string but this one appears in the glossary table summarizing the programs command line options. The glossary table is generated automatically by the arg_print_glossary function (see later). For example, a glossary string of "the foobar factor" would appear in the glossary table along side the option something like:

```
--foo=<int> the foobar factor
```

Specifying a NULL glossary string causes that option to be omitted from the glossary table.

Command Line options and related arg_xxx() functions

Literal Options

Examples

```
-x, -y, -z, --help, --verbose
```

Data Structure

```
struct arg_lit
  {
  struct arg_hdr hdr;
  int count;
  };
```

Constructor Functions

```
struct arg_lit* arg_lit0 (const char *shortopts, const char *longopts, const char *glossary)

struct arg_lit* arg_lit1 (const char *shortopts, const char *longopts, const char *glossary)

struct arg_lit* arg_litn (const char *shortopts, const char *longopts, int mincount, int maxcount, const char *glossary)
```

Description

Literal options take no argument values so all that is to be seen in the arg_lit struct is the count of the number of times the option was present on the command line. Upon a successful parse, count is guaranteed to be within the mincount and maxcount limits set for the option at construction.

Integer Options

Examples

-x2, -y 7, -z-3, --size=734, --count 124

Data Structure

```
struct arg_int
  {
  struct arg_hdr hdr;
  int count;
  int *ival;
  };
```

Constructor Functions

```
struct arg_int* arg_int0 (const char *shortopts, const char *longopts, const
char *datatype, const char *glossary)

struct arg_int* arg_int1 (const char *shortopts, const char *longopts, const
char *datatype, const char *glossary)

struct arg_int* arg_intn (const char *shortopts, const char *longopts, const
char *datatype, int mincount, int maxcount, const char *glossary)
```

Description

The arg_int struct contains the count of the number of times the option was present on the command line and a pointer (ival) to an array containing the integer values given with those particular options. The array is fixed at construction time to hold maxcount integers at most.

Upon a successful parse, count is guaranteed to be within the mincount and maxcount limits set for the option at construction with the appropriate values store in the ival array. The parser will not accept any values beyond that limit.

It is quite acceptable to set default values in the ival array prior to calling arg_parse if desired as the parser does alter ival entries for which no command line argument is received.

Double Options

Examples

-x2.234, -y 7e-03, -z-3.3E+6, --pi=3.1415, --tolerance 1.0E-6

Data Structure

```
struct arg_dbl
  {
  struct arg_hdr hdr;
  int count;
  double *dval;
  };
```

Constructor Functions

struct arg_dbl* arg_dbl0 (const char *shortopts, const char *longopts, const char *datatype, const char *glossary)

struct arg_dbl* arg_dbl1 (const char *shortopts, const char *longopts, const char *datatype, const char *glossary)

struct arg_dbl* arg_dbln (const char *shortopts, const char *longopts, const char *datatype, int mincount, int maxcount, const char *glossary)

Description

Like arg_int but the arguments values are stored as doubles in dval.

String Options

Examples

-Dmacro, -t mytitle, -m "my message string", --title="hello world"

Data Structure

```
struct arg_str
  {
  struct arg_hdr hdr;
  int count;
  const char **sval;
  };
```

Constructor Functions

```
struct arg_str* arg_str0 (const char *shortopts, const char *longopts, const char *datatype, const char *glossary)

struct arg_str* arg_str1 (const char *shortopts, const char *longopts, const char *datatype, const char *glossary)

struct arg_str* arg_strn (const char *shortopts, const char *longopts, const char *datatype, int mincount, int maxcount, const char *glossary)
```

Description

Like arg_int but the arguments values are pointers to strings. Note that the string pointers in sval[] actually refer to the original argv[] command line string buffers so you should not attempt to alter them.

Filename Options

Examples

-o myfile, -Ihome/foo/bar, --input=~/doc/letter.txt, --name a.out

Data Structure

```
struct arg_file
  {
  struct arg_hdr hdr;
  int count;
  const char **filename;
  const char **basename;
  const char **extension;
  };
```

Constructor Functions

```
struct arg_file* arg_file0 (const char *shortopts, const char *longopts, const char *datatype, const char *glossary)

struct arg_file* arg_file1 (const char *shortopts, const char *longopts, const char *datatype, const char *glossary)

struct arg_file* arg_filen (const char *shortopts, const char *longopts, const char *datatype, int mincount, int maxcount, const char *glossary)
```

Description

Like arg_str but the argument strings are presumed to have filename qualities so some additional pasring is done to separate out the filenames basename and extension (if they exist). The three arrays filename[], basename[], extension[] each store up to maxcount entries, and the ith entry of each of these arrays refer to different components of the same string buffer.

For instance, -o /home/heitmann/mydir/foo.txt would be parsed as:

```
filename[i]  = "/home/heitmann/mydir/foo.txt"
basename[i]  =                      "foo.txt"
extension[i] =                          "txt"
```

If the filename has no leading path then the basename is the same as the filename, and if no extension could be identified then it is given as NULL. Note that filename extensions are defined as all text following the last "." in the filename. Thus -o foo would be parsed as:

```
filename[i]  = "foo"
basename[i]  = "foo"
extension[i] = NULL
```

As with arg_str, the string pointers in filename[], basename[], and extension[] actually refer to the original argv[] command line string buffers so we should not attempt to alter them.

Note also that the parser only ever treats the filenames as strings and never attempts to open them as files or perform any directory lookups on them.

Remark Options

Data Structure

```
struct arg_rem
  {
  struct arg_hdr hdr;
  };
```

Constructor Function

```
struct arg_rem* arg_rem (const char* datatype, const char* glossary)
```

Description

The arg_rem struct is a dummy struct in the sense it does not represent a command line option to be parsed. Instead it provides a means to include additional datatype and glossary strings in the output of the arg_print_syntax, arg_print_syntaxv, and arg_print_glossary functions. As such, arg_rem structs may be used in the argument table to insert additional lines of text into the glossary descriptions or to insert additional text fields into the syntax description. It has no data members apart from the mandatory arg_hdr struct.

End of Table Options

Data Structure

```
struct arg_end
  {
  struct arg_hdr hdr;
  int count;
  int *error;
  void **parent;
  const char **argval;
  };
```

Constructor Function

```
struct arg_end* arg_end (int maxerrors)
```

Description

The arg_end struct is primarily used to mark the end of an argument table and doesn't represent any command line option. Every argument table must have an arg_end structure as its last entry.

Apart from terminating the argument table, the arg_end structure also stores the error codes generated by the arg_parse function as it attempts to parse the command line with the given argument table. The maxerrors parameter passed to the arg_end constructor specifies the maximum number of errors that the structure can store. Any further errors are discarded and replaced with the single error code ARG_ELIMIT which is later reported to the user by the message "too many errors". A maxerrors limit of 20 is quite reasonable.

The arg_print_errors function will print the errors stored in the arg_end struct in the same order as they occurred, so there is no need to understand the internals of the arg_end struct.

For those that are curious, the three arrays error[], parent[], and argval[] are each allocated maxerrors entries at construction. As usual, the count variable gives the number of entries actually stored in these arrays. The same value applies to all three arrays as the i'th entry of each all refer to different aspects of the same error condition.

The error[i] entry holds the error code returned by the hdr.scanfn function of the particular arg_xxx that is reporting the error. The meaning if the code is usually known only to the issuing arg_xxx struct. The predefined error codes that arg_end handles from the parser itself are the exceptions.

The parent[i] entry points to the parent arg_xxx structure that reported the error. That same arg_xxx structure is also responsible for displaying a pertinent error message when called on to do so by the arg_print_errors function. It calls the hdr.errorfn function of each parent arg_xxx struct listed in the arg_end structure.

Lastly, the argval[i] entry points to the command line argument at which the error occurred, although this may be NULL when there is no relevant command line value. For instance, if an error reports a missing option then there will be no matching command line argument value.

Defining the argument table

Once the arg_xxx structs are in hand they must be collated into an argument table. The argument table is merely an array of void pointers that point to the various arg_xxx structs constructed previously. The last entry of the argument table must always point to an arg_end struct. The arg_end struct is a special case in that it does not represent a command line option but instead serves to terminate the argument table. It also stores the errors encountered by the parser for that argument table. Thus when we construct the arg_end struct we specify the maximum number of errors we wish it to store, errors beyond that limit are discarded. An arbitrary number like 20 usually suffices.

The following example shows an argument table that defines the command line options: [-a] [-b] [-c] [--scalar=<n>] [-v|--verbose] [-o myfile] <file> [<file>]

```
struct arg_lit *a      =  arg_lit0("a", NULL, "the -a option");
struct arg_lit *b      =  arg_lit0("b", NULL, "the -b option");
struct arg_lit *c      =  arg_lit0("c", NULL, "the -c option");
struct arg_int *scal   =  arg_int0(NULL, "scalar","<n>", "foo value");
struct arg_lit *verb   =  arg_lit0("v", "verbose, "verbose output");
struct arg_file *o     =  arg_file0("o", NULL,"myfile", "output file");
struct arg_file *file  =  arg_filen(NULL,NULL,"<file>",1,2,"input files");
struct arg_end *end    =  arg_end(20);
void *argtable[]       =  {a,b,c,scal,verb,o,file,end};
```

Having constructed our arg_xxx structs we should ensure that all of them were successfully allocated by checking that none of them returned NULL. We could do that manually, but the arg_nullcheck function has been provided for just that purpose. It checks the argument table for NULL entries and returns non-zero if any were encountered.

```
if (arg_nullcheck(argtable) != 0)
   printf("error: insufficient memory");
```

Parsing the command line

With the argument table defined, it is simply a matter of passing it onto the arg_parse function along with argc and argv. The parser will extract the command line arguments according to the specifications within the argument table and store the results back in the arg_xxx data structures. Any errors that are encountered are recorded in the argument tables arg_end struct for reporting later and a count of those errors is returned by the function.

```
int nerrors = arg_parse(argc,argv,argtable);
```

If the number of errors returned is zero then we know that the command line arguments were all correctly parsed and their results are stored in the arg_xxx structs ready for use. Otherwise we can choose to retry parsing the command line with an alternative argument table if we have one, or just display the errors and exit.

Error Reporting

If the arg_parse function reported errors then we need to display them as arg_parse does not do so itself. As mentioned earlier, the arg_parse function stores the errors it encounters in the argument tables arg_end struct. We dont need to know the internal details of the arg_end struct, we simply call the arg_print_errors function to print those errors in the order they were encountered.

```
if (nerrors>0) arg_print_errors(stdout,end,"myprog");
```

Notice that we also pass it the program name, in this case "myprog", as the function prepends the name to each error message it prints as in myprog: invalid option "-x".

Displaying the command line syntax

The arg_print_syntax and arg_print_syntaxv functions display the command line syntax defined by an argument table. The latter is the verbose form (distinguished by the "v" suffix on the function name) and displays all alternative forms of each option verbatim, for example:

```
[-a] [-b] [-c] [--scalar=<n>] [-o myfile] [-v|--verbose] <file> [<file>]
```

Whereas the former displays the syntax in abbreviated GNU style wherein only the first form of each option is displayed. Furthermore all short options are concatenated into a single option string at the head of the display, so for example -a -b -c -v is displayed as -abcv.

```
[-abcv] [--scalar=<n>] [-o myfile] <file> [<file>]
```

Notice that optional command line arguments are automatically enclosed in square brackets whereas mandatory arguments are not.

Displaying the option glossary

The arg_print_glossary function displays a glossary table of all the command line options defined by an argument table in which the options syntax is shown beside the options glossary string.

```
arg_print_glossary(stdout, argtable, " %-25s %s\n");
```

The format string passed to the arg_print_glossary function is actually a printf format string. It must contain exactly two "%s" format parameters, the first is for the options syntax string and the second is for the arguments glossary string. Here is some example output:

```
-a                the -a option
-b                the -b option
-c                the -c option
--scalar=<n>      foo value
-v,--verbose      verbose option
-o myfile         output file
<file>            input files
```

List of Functions Available

int arg_nullcheck (void **argtable)

Returns non-zero if the argtable[] array contains any NULL entries up until the terminating arg_end* entry. Returns zero otherwise.

int arg_parse (int argc, char **argv, void **argtable)

Parse the command line arguments in argv[] using the command line syntax specified in argtable[], returning the number of errors encountered. Error details are recorded in the argument tables arg_end structure from where they can be displayed later with the arg_print_errors function. Upon a successful parse, the arg_xxx structures referenced in argtable[] will contain the argument values extracted from the command line.

void arg_print_option (FILE *fp, const char *shortopts, const char *longopts, const char *datatype, const char *suffix)

This function prints an options syntax, as in -K|--scalar=<int>, where the short options, long options, and datatype are all given as parameters of this function. It is primarily used within the arg_xxx structures errorfn functions as a way of displaying an options syntax inside of error messages. However, it can also be used in user code if desired. The suffix string is provided as a convenience for appending newlines and so forth to the end of the display and can be given as NULL if not required.]

void arg_print_syntax (FILE *fp, void **argtable, const char *suffix)

Prints the GNU style command line syntax for the given argument table, as in: [-abcv] [--scalar=<n>] [-o myfile] <file> [<file>]

The suffix string is provided as a convenience for appending newlines and so forth to the end of the display and can be given as NULL if not required.

void arg_print_syntaxv (FILE *fp, void **argtable, const char *suffix)

Prints the verbose form of the command line syntax for the given argument table, as in: [-a] [-b] [-c] [--scalar=<n>] [-o myfile] [-v|--verbose] <file> [<file>]

The suffix string is provided as a convenience for appending newlines and so forth to the end of the display and can be given as NULL if not required.

void arg_print_glossary (FILE *fp, void **argtable, const char *format)

Prints a glossary table describing each option in the given argument table. The format string is passed to printf to control the formatting of each entry in the glossary. It must have exactly two "%s" format parameters as in "%-25s %s\n", the first is for the options syntax and the second for its glossary string. If an options glossary string is NULL then that option in omitted from the glossary display.

void arg_print_errors (FILE *fp, struct arg_end *end, const char *progname)

Prints the details of all errors stored in the end data structure. The progname string is prepended to each error message.

void arg_freetable (void ** argtable, size_t n)

De-allocates the memory used by each arg_xxx struct referenced by argtable[]. It does this by calling free for each of the n pointers in the argtable array and then nullifying them for safety.

Example 22

```
#include "argtable2.h"
#include<stdio.h>


/* global arg_xxx structs */
struct arg_lit *a, *b, *c, *verb;
struct arg_int *scal;
struct arg_file *o, *file;
struct arg_end *end;


int main(int argc, char **argv)
{
/* the global arg_xxx structs are initialised within the argtable */

int nerrors;
void *argtable[] =
{
a=arg_lit0("a", NULL, "the -a option"),
b=arg_lit0("b", NULL, "the -b option"),
c=arg_lit0("c", NULL, "the -c option"),
scal=arg_int0(NULL,"scalar","<n>","foo value"),
verb=arg_lit0("v","verbose", "verbose output"),
o=arg_file0("o", NULL, "myfile", "outputfile"),
file=arg_filen(NULL, NULL, "<file>",1,2, "input files"),
end=arg_end(20),
};

nerrors=arg_parse(argc,argv,argtable);
printf("No of Errors %d\n", nerrors);

printf("%d \n", scal->ival[0]);
return 0;

}
```

To compile:

gcc -o aa test.c libargtable2.a

Here, I am assuming the library libargtable2.a is available in the current directory itself.

If it would have been kept in standard directories such as /lib or /usr/lib, then the following command can be used to compile the same.

gcc -o aa test.c –largtable2.a

To run:

./aa –a –b –c - -scalar=12 –o xyz file1 file2

or

./aa -abc - -scalar=12 –o xyz file1 file2

Check the above program by printing the value of nerrors. Only when we execute the above program with the above given styles it gives nerrors as zero; otherwise its value will be other than zero.

Example 23

This example is to explain how this library can be used for calculating volume and surface area of a room (example 4).

```
#include "argtable2.h"
#include<stdio.h>

/* global arg_xxx structs */
struct arg_int *L,*B,*H;
struct arg_end *end;

int main(int argc, char **argv)
{

int V, SA,length,breadth,height;

/* the global arg_xxx structs are initialised within the argtable */
int nerrors;
void *argtable[] =
{
```

```
L=arg_int0(NULL,"l","<n>","length value"),
B=arg_int0(NULL,"b","<n>","breadth value"),
H=arg_int0(NULL,"h","<n>","length value"),
end=arg_end(20),
};

nerrors=arg_parse(argc,argv,argtable);

length=L->ival[0];
breadth=B->ival[0];
height=H->ival[0];

V=length*breadth*height;
SA=2*height*(length+breadth)+length*breadth;

printf("Volume=%d\nSurface Area=%d\n", V,SA);
return 0;
```

To compile:

gcc -o VSA test1.c libargtable2.a

To run:

./VSA - -l=12 - -b=12 - -h=12

3.4 Conclusions

This chapter explores how a C program's command line arguments can be managed with the help of libraries such as getopt(), argp(). Many illustrative examples are given for each of the library. GNU command line interface style is also emphasized.

4 Environment

4.1 Introduction to Environmental Variables

These variables influence the behavior of the shell, user interfaces, application programs, compilers, etc. For example, Java compiler looks for an environment variable CLASSPATH and uses its value to locate for any readymade (default or standard) class files. Also, word processing SW such as LaTex, TeX uses environment variables such as TEXHOME, PKFONTS etc. We can change behavior of our shell by changing the environment variables values. For example, by executing the command "PS1=Hello" at the $ prompt, the prompt changes to Hello. Also, many application programs which are dynamically linked will be using the value of LD_LIBRARY_PATH to locate the machine language codes of any function needed for them while running (We have discussed more about this concept in chapter on Libraries).

Note, in a more general context, each process has an "environment", that is, a group of variables that hold information that the process may reference. In this sense, the shell behaves like any other process. Every time a shell starts, it creates shell variables that correspond to its own environmental variables. Updating or adding new shell variables causes the shell to update its environment, and all the shell's child processes (the commands it executes) inherit this environment. Caution!. The space allotted to the environment is limited. Creating too many environmental variables or ones that use up excessive space may cause problems.

If we execute "env" command at the command prompt, we may see the details of all the environment variables defined in our current shell. The output may look like

```
PATH=/bin:/sbin:/usr/local/bin
MANPATH=/usr/man:/usr/man/man1:/usr/man/man2
IFS=
TERM=VT100
HOST=darkstar
USER=guest
HOME=/usr/guest
MAIL=/var/spool/mail/guest
MAILCHECK=300
```

Environment variables are used by shell and other application programs. For example, the value of MAILCHECK, i.e 300 indicates that the mailer daemon will check for every 300 seconds for new mail arrivals and intimate the same to the user. A dynamic business user who may receive frequent emails can set this variable to a low value such that the mailer informs about new mail arrivals as soon as they arrive.

Similarly, PATH environment variable is used by shell in locating the executable file of the commands typed by the user at the $ prompt. System will check for the executable files in the directories of the PATH variable and if it finds the executable it will be loaded and executed. Otherwise, we may get error "bad command or file not found".

Let the following C language file name as "a.c".

```
#include<stdio.h>
main()
{
printf("Hello\n");
}
```

Compile the same using.

```
gcc -o aa  a.c
```

The file "a.c" is the C language source file and "aa" is executable file.

Assuming PATH is set properly, by simply typing "aa" at the $ prompt we can run the above program. If the value of PATH variable don't have dot (".") then we may get an error "bad command or file not found" as the system is not in a position to identify the file "aa". However, the same can executed by typing ./aa (this problem is very much seen with Redhat Linux distributions).

Sometimes, if we have created an executable file with name as "test" (normally, new users behavior is to create executable file with name "test") then if we type "test" at the dollar prompt, the above "test" may not run. This is because, there is a "test" Unix command!. And it's executable file is first found by shell while searching in the directories of PATH environment variable for executable file of "test" program. To solve such a problem, we can add . (dot) to PATH environment variable as following.

PATH=.:$PATH

If a script sets environmental variables, they need to be "exported", that is, reported to the environment local to the script. This is the function of the export command.

Main difference between shell variables and environment variables is that the latter are inheritable to sub-shell's [Venkateshwarlu]. Environment variables either defined in a shell or modified in a shell are visible in its sub-shells only. That is, parent shells do not see the environment variables defined in its sub-shell's or the modifications done to environment variables in the sub-shell's. Please note that $ prompt indicates that we are in bash shell.

```
X=Hello
Y=How
echo $PATH         // displays value of PATH environment variable
echo $X            // displays value of X shell variable
echo $Y            // displays value of X shell variable
export Y           // makes Y as environment variable

bash               // a sub-shell bash is created. Run ps -Al in other
terminal to see it.
echo $PATH         // displays value of PATH environment variable which is
same as above
echo $X            // displays nothing as X shell variable is not inherited
```

```
echo $Y          // displays how as Y is environment variable
Z=Raj
export Z
echo $Z          // displays Z variable value

csh              // another sub shell is initiated
echo $PATH       // displays value of PATH environment variable which is
same as above
echo $X          // displays nothing as X shell variable is not inherited
echo $Y          // displays how as Y is environment variable
Z=Raj
export Z
echo $Z          // displays Z variable value
exit  or ^c      // to come out from C shell

^d               // to come out from bash sub-shell

echo $PATH       // displays value of PATH environment variable which is
same as above
echo $X          // displays  X shell variable value
echo $Y          // displays how as Y is environment variable
Z=Raj
export Z
echo $Z          // displays nothing as Z is not visible
```

Note

A script can export variables only to child processes, that is, only to commands or processes that particular script initiates. A script invoked from the command line cannot export variables back to the command line environment. Child processes can not export variables back to the parent processes that spawned them.

4.1.1 How can I read the whole environment?

We have discussed about the environment variables in the previous section as a user point of view. The following discussion explains how we can know the environment variables from a C program. A global variable, **environ**, holds a pointer to an array of pointers to environment strings, each string in the form "NAME = value". A NULL pointer is used to mark the end of the array. Here's a program to print the current environment (like printenv or env command of Unix/Linux).

Example 1

```
#include <stdio.h>

extern char **environ;

int main()
{
   char **ep = environ;
```

```
    char *p;
    while ((p = *ep++))
        printf("%s\n", p);
    return 0;
}
```

In general, the environ variable is also passed as the third, optional, parameter to main(); that is, the above program could have been written as follows.

Example 2

```
#include <stdio.h>

int main(int argc, char **argv, char **envp)
{
    char *p;
    while ((p = *envp++))
        printf("%s\n", p);
    return 0;
}
```

However, while pretty universally supported, this method isn't actually defined by the POSIX standards.

4.1.2 How can I get/set an environment variable from a program?

Getting the value of an environment variable is done by using getenv().

```
#include <stdlib.h>

char *getenv(const char *name);
```

Setting the value of an environment variable is done by using putenv().

```
#include <stdlib.h>

int putenv(char *string);
```

The string passed to putenv must *not* be freed or made invalid, since a pointer to it is kept by putenv(). This means that it must either be a static buffer or allocated off the heap. The string can be freed if the environment variable is redefined or deleted via another call to putenv().

Remember that environment variables are inherited; each process has a separate copy of the environment. As a result, we can't change the value of an environment variable in another process, such as the shell. Suppose we want to get the value for the TERM environment variable. We would use this code:

```
char *envvar;

envvar=getenv("TERM");

printf("The value for the environment variable TERM is ");
if(envvar)
{
   printf("%s\n",envvar);
}
else
{
   printf("not set.\n");
}
```

Now suppose we want to create a new environment variable called MYVAR, with a value of MYVAL.

```
static char envbuf[256];

sprintf(envbuf,"MYVAR=%s","MYVAL");

if(putenv(envbuf))
{
   printf("Sorry, putenv() couldn't find the memory for %s\n",envbuf);
   /* Might exit() or something here if we can't live without it */
}
```

Example 3

The following example is to demonstrate that child inherits enviornmnet from parent. In the following example forK () is called to create a child process. In both the process envionment variables are printed. (When ever a process calls sleep it goes to waiting state next process will be picked by the scheduler).

```
#include<unistd.h>
#include<stdlib.h>

int main()
{
   char *p;
```

```
    putenv("XZ=Hello");
    if(fork()==0)
    {
     putenv("YZ=How are you");
     if(p = getenv("XZ")) printf("%s\n",p);
     if(p = getenv("YZ")) printf("%s\n",p);
    }
    else
    {
     sleep(5);
     if(p = getenv("XZ")) printf("%s\n",p);
     if(p = getenv("YZ")) printf("%s\n",p);
    }
    return 0;
}
```

Here, child process runs first always as sleep() is called in the parent first. If parent starts first, it immediately goes to sleeping state. Child gives output as:

```
Hello
How are You.
```

Then parent gives output as:

```
Hello
```

In the parent process, we can see the environment variable "YZ". As parent can not inherit properties from child process. That is whatever environment variables defined in child process or modified in child process are visible only its child processes but not in its parent.

Example 4

The following example is to show that the child process will inherit all the environment information from parent process. When you run this program, same environment variables are printed two times.

```
#include<unistd.h>
#include<stdio.h>
#include<fcntl.h>

extern char **environ;

int main(int n, char **a)
{
   int i;
   fork();
   for(i = 0; environ[i]; i++)
    printf("%s\n",environ[i]);
   return 0;
}
```

Example 5

Write a program which opens a file "xyz" in current working directory and writes "Hello" in it. If environment variable "TMP" is defined then the file "xyz" has to be created in the directory pointed by the value of this variable.

```
#include<stdio.h>

void main(int argc, char*argv[])
{
FILE *ip;
char s[40], *p;

if((p=getenv("TMP"))!=NULL)
        sprintf(s,"%s/%s", p, "xyz");
else
    sprintf(s,"xyz");

ip=fopen(s, "w");

if(ip==0) { printf("Error in opening file"); exit(-1); }

fprintf(ip,"Hello\n");


fclose(ip);

}
```

If the above program is compiled and the resultant executable file name is "xx" then the following commands at the shell prompt can be used to test the program.

```
xx
cat xyz
TMP=/tmp
export TMP
xx
cat  /tmp/xyz
```

Example 6

Write a program to emulate UNIX's cat command; however with a little different interface. If an environment variable UP is defined and its value is YES then the file content has to be converted to uppercase and then written into the destination file. If an environment variable LOW is defined and its value is YES then the file content has to be converted to lowercase and then written into the destination file. If both the environment variables are defined then uppercase characters has to be converted to lowercase and vice-versa. If both the environment variables are not defined or not having value YES then the program has to simply behave similar to normal UNIX cat command and copy the source file content as it is to destination.

```
#include<stdio.h>
#include<string.h>
#include<stdlib.h>
void main(int argc, char*argv[])
{
FILE *ip, *op;

int up=0,low=0;
char  V;

if(argc!=3) {printf("Two arguments are needed\n"); exit(-1); }
ip=fopen(argv[1], "r");

if(ip==0) { printf("Error in opening file"); exit(-1); }

op=fopen(argv[2],"w");

if(strcmp(getenv("UP"),"YES")==0) up=1;

if(strcmp(getenv("LOW"),"YES")==0)low=2;

while(!feof(ip))
{
V=fgetc(ip);
switch(up+low)
{
case 0:  fputc(V,op); break;
case 1:  fputc(toupper(V),op); break;
case 2:  fputc(tolower(V),op); break;
case 3:
        if(isupper(V))
  fputc(tolower(V),op);
    else
      fputc(toupper(V),op);
            break;
```

```
}
}

fclose(ip);
fclose(op);

}
```

If the above program is compiled and the resultant executable file name is "yy" then the following commands at the shell prompt can be used to test program.

```
yy rao raj
        #copies the content of file rao to raj without any modification.
        #Assuming UP, LOW are undefined.
cat raj


UP=YES
export UP
yy rao raj1     #  copies the content of file rao to raj1 and coverts all the
                   characters to uppercase

cat raj1


UP=
LOW=YES
export LOW
yy rao raj2     # copies the content of file rao to raj2 and coverts all the
                   characters to lowercase

cat raj2


UP=YES
export UP
yy rao raj3     #  copies the content of file rao to raj3 and coverts all
                   the lower case characters to uppercase and upper case to
                   lower case. Assuming all the above commands are
                   executed sequentially.
cat raj3
```

Example 7

Program reads a program name along the command line and prints from which directory it get executed. Here, PATH environment variable values is used and in each of its directory the availability of given file is searched using function find-dir ().

```
#include<stdio.h>
#include<dirent.h>
#include<unistd.h>
#include<string.h>

int find_dir(const char *file, const char *path)
{
   DIR *D;
   struct dirent *dir;
   if ((D = opendir(path)) == NULL)
   {
   perror("Opendir");
   return 0;
   }
   while((dir = readdir(D)))
   {
   if (strcmp(dir->d_name,file) == 0)
      return 1;
   }
   return 0;
}

int main(int argc, char **argv)
{
   char *p, *q;
   int k;
   if(argc == 1)
   {
   printf("Usage: %s  [FILE]\n",argv[0]);
   return -1;
   }
   p = getenv("PATH");
   while(1)
   {
```

```
        q = index(p, ':');
        p = strtok(p, ":");
        if ((k = find_dir(argv[1], p))) break;
        if (q == 0) break;
        p = q+1;
        }
        (k) ? printf("\n%s\n",p) : printf("File not found\n");
        return 0;
    }
```

4.2 Conclusions

This chapter deals with management of environment of a system. How a C program can be used to access environment variables, change them and how a new environment variable can be defined etc., concepts are explained with lucid examples.

5 System Limits

5.1 Introduction

User resource limits are important to the security and stability of a machine. If the machine that we wish to secure allows untrusted users to run programs, then there is risk for abuse. Abuse is not limited to users that have telnet shell access. If we allow users to run CGI scripts on our web-server, these are also untrusted programs. Our system can be abused just as easily from CGI scripts. The potential exists for a malicious user to run a program that would eat up resources on the machine and make it unstable or completely unusable for all the other users. This type of Denial of Service (DoS) Attack is preventable with appropriate resource limits. It is also possible that a well intentioned user who may make a simple programming error which could cause their program to use unnecessary amounts of system resources. Both of these situations can be prevented by the proper implementation of resource limits. This is necessary for the stability of any Linux machine.

Some errors such as "stack overflow", "Virtual memory exausted", "Unable to fork()", etc., are cryptic to normal users. They are controlled system resources limits. User by resource limits dictate the amount of resources that can be used for a particular session by a user. The resources that can be controlled are:

- Maximum size of core files
- Maximum size of a process's data segment
- Maximum size of files created
- Maximum size that may be locked into memory
- Maximum size of resident memory
- Maximum number of file descriptors open at one time
- Maximum size of the stack
- Maximum amount of cpu time used
- Maximum number of processes allowed
- Maximum size of virtual memory available

It is important to note that these settings are per-session (per terminal session). This means that they are only effective for the time that the user is logged in (and for any processes that they run during that period). They are not global settings. In other words, they are only active for the duration of the session and the settings are not cumulative. This is applicable for terminal sessions in GUI mode also. For example, if you set the maximum number of processes to 11, the user may only have 11 processes running per session. They are not limited to 11 total processes on the machine as m/c may initiate another session. Each of the settings is per process settings during the session, with the exception of the maximum number of processes.

There are two types of limits that can be set for each property (listed above) namingly hard and soft limits. A hard limit cannot be changed by the user once it is set. A soft limit, however, can be changed by the user but cannot exceed the hard limit. A normal user can not change hard limit of a resource. We can change a hard limit of a resource to be smaller than its current soft limit unless the soft limit is first reduced.

Very often some programs/SW systems demands limits to be adjusted to make them working. For example, Oracle 10i needs number of processes and number of files to be set 2047 and 4096 respectively[1]

---

[1] http://www.linux-services.org/oracle/

These example C programs illustrate why resource limits are so important. They are provided here for educational purposes only, do not run them on a machine unless you have explicit permission to do so. The following two examples are given to explain resource usage attacks.

The following C program, as simple as it is, has the potential to bring a machine to stand still without proper user resource limits.

Example 1

```
#include<stdio.h>
int main()
{
    while(1)
    fork();
    return 0;
}
```

This program runs as an infinite loop calling the fork() function. The system call fork() creates a child process that is virtually identical to the parent. In other words, it creates another instance of the program. As we can see, unrestrained this would create an incredible number of processes and as a result the system will eventually lock up and become unstable. If we are fortunate enough to catch someone doing this before it gets too bad, we might be able to kill some of the processes. However, this is not a viable solution to the problem.

A shell program with the following two lines also may make the system to come to stand still.

```
echo Hello
$0
```

Enter the above two lines in a file (say xyz) and give user executable permissions and run the same by typing the following at command prompt.

```
chmod u+x xyz
./xyz
```

Here is where user resource limits come in. It is possible to limit the number of processes that a user can launch in a single session. In other words, the user (probably who is logged in through telnet) who runs these program's can be limited to the number of times the fork() system call can create child processes. While these program's will still raise the system's load, a proper limit on processes will stop these from going out of control.

Memory Usage Attack

Some times a malicious user may attack your system by using all the available RAM. This may also happen by a rogue process that does not properly manage its RAM. The following is an example of a program whose only purpose is to allocate as much RAM as possible and never return it for re-use.

Example 2

```
#include<stdio.h>
int main()
{

        char *p;
        while(1)
                p = (char *)malloc(sizeof(char) * 4096);
    return 0;
}
```

Without any resource limits, this program will continue to allocate RAM until there is no more RAM or swap space available. This may take a while depending on the size of RAM and swap space available, but it will eventually render the system useless and require a reboot.

5.2 Setting user resource limits

There are two main methods of implementing user resource limits on a Linux machine. One involves using the properties of the login shell to set these limits, the other uses PAM (Pluggable Authentication Modules). Each have some advantages but in general they accomplish the same goal, i.e to limit the abuse that can occur on a machine.

5.2.1 Setting limits via the Shell

Most login shells provide a method of setting user resource limits (A login shell is a program such as bash that provides an interface to the user when they log into the machine via telnet or from console). The major advantage to using this method of setting resource limits is that all Linux machines have login shells such as bash. The primary disadvantage is that the limits will only apply to users that have shell access to the server and will only apply to programs that run from the shell.

Bash has a built-in command called ulimit that enables the user to set resource limits. The usage of this command is given as:

ulimit [-SHacdflmnpstuv [limit]]

This command provides control over the resources available to the shell and to processes started by it, on systems that allow such control. The value of limit can be a number in the unit specified for the resource, or the value unlimited. The -H and -S options specify that the hard or soft limit is set for the given resource. A hard limit cannot be increased once it is set; a soft limit may be increased up to the value of the hard limit. If neither -H nor -S is specified, both the soft and hard limits are set. If limit is omitted, the current value of the soft limit of the resource is printed, unless the -H option is given. When more than one resource is specified, the limit name and unit are printed before the value. Other options are interpreted as follows:

-a All current limits are reported

-c The maximum size of core files created

-d The maximum size of a process's data segment

-f The maximum size of files created by the shell

-l The maximum size that may be locked into memory

-m The maximum resident set size

-n The maximum number of open file descriptors (most systems do not allow this value to be set)

-p The pipe size in 512-byte blocks (this may not be set)

-s The maximum stack size

-t The maximum amount of cpu time in seconds

-u The maximum number of processes available to a single user

-v The maximum amount of virtual memory available to the shell

If limit is given, it is the new value of the specified resource (the -a option is for display only). If no option is given, then -f is assumed. Values are in 1024-byte increments, except for -t, which is in seconds, -p, which is in units of 512-byte blocks, and -n and -u, which are unscaled values. The return status is 0 unless an invalid option is encountered, a non-numeric argument other than unlimited is supplied as limit, or an error occurs while setting a new limit.

The following commands displays soft limits of all resources.

ulimit -a

ulimit -S -a

```
core file size          (blocks, -c) 0
data seg size           (kbytes, -d) unlimited
file size               (blocks, -f) unlimited
pending signals         (-i) 1024
max locked memory       (kbytes, -l) 32
max memory size         (kbytes, -m) unlimited
open files              (-n) 1024
pipe size               (512 bytes, -p) 8
POSIX message queues    (bytes, -q) 819200
stack size              (kbytes, -s) 10240
cpu time                (seconds, -t) unlimited
max user processes      (-u) 3967
virtual memory          (kbytes, -v) unlimited
file locks              (-x) unlimited
```

If we want to know individual resource's resource limit we can simply run ulimit command with the respective option without any value.

Similarly, the following command displays system wide hard limits of all resources.

ulimit -H -a

For example the following command displays soft limit for current core file size.

```
ulimit -c
0

ulimit -S -c
0
```

For example the following command displays hard limit of current core file size.

```
ulimit -H  -c
unlimited
```

For example the following command sets hard limit of current core file size to 10000.

ulimit -H -c 10000

For example the following command tries to set soft limit of current core file size to 100000. However, we will get an error message as we can set soft limit to be more than hard limit.

ulimit -S -c 100000

If we execute the following program when core size limit is zero no core file is created in the P.W.D. Where as if you set core file size limit as above and execute the same program, we will find a core file in the P.W.D. In this program, we are trying to store some integer at address pointed by the value of variable X, which is uninitialised. The memory pointed by the value of X might not have been allocated to this program. Thus, the scanf function is violating the OS rules. Thus, we will get memory segment violation error, leading to core dump. When core dump takes place the process state information is written in to a core file. This file can be used to analyze the why a program is crashed. However, if core file size limit is zero then core file will not be created. This example is to demonstrate this. The same example is discussed in a different context in chapter on GDB.

Example 3

```
#include<stdio.h>

int main()
{
int X;

scanf("%d", X);

}
```

In order to know the importance virtual memory the following exercise is carried out. By executing the following command we found that virtual memory's soft and hard limits are set as unlimited currently.

```
ulimit -v 100000
ls
a1.c a.out core.5565 info typescript
ulimit -v 10000
ls
a1.c a.out core.5565 info typescript
ulimit -v 1000
ls
ls: error while loading shared libraries: libc.so.6: failed to map segment from shared object: Cannot allocate memory
ls
Segmentation fault (core dumped)
```

From the above example, we can also identify that if the virtual memory is not sufficient, program gives segment violation. That is, the ls command gave segment violation when virtual memory limit is set at 1000 where as for limits of 10000 and 100000 etc., it worked nicely.

Similarly, to explain more about the limits, we have set the stack size as 3 using the following command and tried to open a file using vi editor. we got an error message out-of-stack error.

```
ulimit -S -s 3
vi aaa
```

Similarly, set CPU time limit as 1 second using "**ulimit -S -t 1**" and run the following program. We will find this program will be killed automatically after one second.

Example 4

```
#include<stdio.h>

int main()
{

while(1);

}
```

Example using limits set by the shell

As we can see, it is fairly straightforward to use the ulimit command. However, the question still remains as to how we enforce these commands every time a user logs in to the shell. Fortunately, the contents of /etc/profile are executed every time bash is launched as a login shell. It is then possible to place a series of ulimit commands to set a hard limit on various resources.

For example, the following line is seen in the file /etc/profile in Fedora CORE 3 of Redhat which makes the core size as zero. That is, on this machine even if memory segment violation takes place, core file will not be created.

```
ulimit -S -c 0 > /dev/null 2>&1
```

Similarly, if we want to limit all users except the user root. We only want to allow a maximum of 40 open files per process, a maximum resident set size of 16384 Kbytes (16MB), maximum data segment of 16384 Kbytes (16MB), a maximum stack size of 8192 Kbytes (8MB), and a maximum core size of 16384 Kbytes (16MB).

To accomplish this, we can place the following in the /etc/profile file.

```
if [ "$USER" != "root" ]; then
      ulimit -n 40 -u 16 -m 16384 -d 16384 -s 8192 -c 16384
fi
```

Now when all users except root log in, they will have the resource limits described above set for their session. The hard and soft limit will be set to the same number for each of the types that appear in the preceding ulimit code. These limits will stay no matter what programs they run in that session. We can verify that the limits are set by checking typing **ulimit -a** in the shell.

The actual values that we choose to limit will vary. The above limits are being used successfully on a machine that has many untrusted users that are allowed to run programs. It may be more appropriate to choose lower resource limits (especially those regarding memory usage) depending on the hardware you have. We can always raise the limits by editing the /etc/profile file if We find that the limits are too restrictive or not restrictive enough.

5.2.2 The system calls getrlimit() and setrlimit()

These functions are used to change resource limits and know the resource limits from a program. The prototypes of these functions are given as:

```
int getrlimit(int resource, struct rlimit *rlp);
int setrlimit(int resource, const struct rlimit *rlp);
```

The rlimit structure is defined as:

```
struct rlimit {
    rlim_t   rlim_cur;
    rlim_t   rlim_max;
    };
```

The names of the functions getrlimit() and setrlimit() sounds that the former is enquire about the current limits of the resources where as the latter is to set the resource limits.

Each call to either getrlimit() or setrlimit() identifies a specific resource to be operated upon as well as a resource limit. A resource limit is represented by an rlimit structure. The rlim_cur member specifies the current or soft limit and the rlim_max member specifies the maximum or hard limit. Soft limits may be changed by a process to any value that is less than or equal to the hard limit. A process may (irreversibly) lower its hard limit to any value that is greater than or equal to the soft limit. Only a process with appropriate privileges can raise a hard limit. Both hard and soft limits can be changed in a single call to setrlimit() subject to the constraints described above.

The value RLIM_INFINITY, defined in <sys/resource.h>, shall be considered to be larger than any other limit value. If a call to getrlimit() returns RLIM_INFINITY for a resource, it means the implementation shall not enforce limits on that resource. Specifying RLIM_INFINITY as any resource limit value on a successful call to setrlimit() shall inhibit enforcement of that resource limit.

The following resources are available in the system.

RLIMIT_CORE

This is the maximum size of a core file, in bytes, that may be created by a process. A limit of 0 shall prevent the creation of a core file. If this limit is exceeded, the writing of a core file shall terminate at this size.

RLIMIT_CPU

This is the maximum amount of CPU time, in seconds, used by a process. If this limit is exceeded, SIGXCPU shall be generated for the process. If the process is catching or ignoring SIGXCPU, or all threads belonging to that process are blocking SIGXCPU, the behavior is unspecified.

RLIMIT_DATA

This is the maximum size of a process' data segment, in bytes. If this limit is exceeded, the malloc() function will fail with errno set to [ENOMEM].

RLIMIT_FSIZE

This is the maximum size of a file, in bytes, that may be created by a process. If a write or truncate operation would cause this limit to be exceeded, SIGXFSZ shall be generated for the thread. If the thread is blocking, or the process is catching or ignoring SIGXFSZ, continued attempts to increase the size of a file from end-of-file to beyond the limit shall fail with errno set to [EFBIG].

RLIMIT_NOFILE

This is a number one greater than the maximum value that the system may assign to a newly-created descriptor. If this limit is exceeded, functions that allocate a file descriptor shall fail with errno set to [EMFILE]. This limit constrains the number of file descriptors that a process may allocate.

RLIMIT_STACK

This is the maximum size of the initial thread's (process) stack, in bytes. The implementation does not automatically grow the stack beyond this limit. If this limit is exceeded, SIGSEGV shall be generated for the thread. If the thread is blocking SIGSEGV, or the process is ignoring or catching SIGSEGV and has not made arrangements to use an alternate stack, the disposition of SIGSEGV shall be set to SIG_DFL before it is generated.

RLIMIT_AS

This is the maximum size of a process' total available memory, in bytes. If this limit is exceeded, the malloc() and mmap() functions shall fail with errno set to [ENOMEM]. In addition, the automatic stack growth fails with the effects outlined above.

When using the getrlimit() function, if a resource limit can be represented correctly in an object of type rlim_t, then its representation is returned; otherwise, if the value of the resource limit is equal to that of the corresponding saved hard limit, the value returned shall be RLIM_SAVED_MAX; otherwise, the value returned shall be RLIM_SAVED_CUR.

When using the setrlimit() function, if the requested new limit is RLIM_INFINITY, the new limit shall be "no limit"; otherwise, if the requested new limit is RLIM_SAVED_MAX, the new limit shall be the corresponding saved hard limit; otherwise, if the requested new limit is RLIM_SAVED_CUR, the new limit shall be the corresponding saved soft limit; otherwise, the new limit shall be the requested value. In addition, if the corresponding saved limit can be represented correctly in an object of type rlim_t then it shall be overwritten with the new limit.

The result of setting a limit to RLIM_SAVED_MAX or RLIM_SAVED_CUR is unspecified unless a previous call to getrlimit() returned that value as the soft or hard limit for the corresponding resource limit.

The determination of whether a limit can be correctly represented in an object of type rlim_t is implementation-defined. For example, some implementations permit a limit whose value is greater than RLIM_INFINITY and others do not.

The exec family of functions shall cause resource limits to be saved.

RETURN VALUE

Upon successful completion, getrlimit() and setrlimit() shall return 0. Otherwise, these functions shall return -1 and set errno to indicate the error.

ERRORS

The getrlimit() and setrlimit() functions shall fail if:

[EINVAL]

An invalid resource was specified; or in a setrlimit() call, the new rlim_cur exceeds the new rlim_max.

[EPERM]

The limit specified to setrlimit() would have raised the maximum limit value, and the calling process does not have appropriate privileges.

The setrlimit() function may fail if:

[EINVAL]

The limit specified cannot be lowered because current usage is already higher than the limit.

The following program gets terminated after expiry of its CPU time limit of one second though this is supposed to run for always. This gives a message CPU limit expired when it is completed.

Example 5

```
#include<sys/resource.h>
#include<time.h>
#include<unistd.h>

int main()
{

struct rlimit rt1;
getrlimit(RLIMIT_CPU, &rt1);
rt1.rlim_cur=1;
setrlimit(RLIMIT_CPU, &rt1);
while(1);
return 0;
}
```

Example 6

The following example displays both hard and soft limits for all the resources. Also, it tries to allocate memory by calling malloc() function. On some systems, this may be failed at 500MB. Where as on others it may be failed at 100MB itself. In order to compile this program, use -DLINUX option with gcc.

```
#include <sys/time.h>
#include <sys/resource.h>
#include <unistd.h>
#include <stdio.h>
#include <stdlib.h>

int main(int argc, char **argv)
{
struct rlimit rlim;
```

```
void *p;

getrlimit(RLIMIT_CPU, &rlim);
printf("CPU: cur - %ld max - %ld\n", rlim.rlim_cur, rlim.rlim_max);

getrlimit(RLIMIT_FSIZE, &rlim);
printf("FSIZE: cur - %ld max - %ld\n", rlim.rlim_cur, rlim.rlim_max);

getrlimit(RLIMIT_DATA, &rlim);
printf("DATA: cur - %ld max - %ld\n", rlim.rlim_cur, rlim.rlim_max);

getrlimit(RLIMIT_STACK, &rlim);
printf("STACK: cur - %ld max - %ld\n", rlim.rlim_cur, rlim.rlim_max);

getrlimit(RLIMIT_CORE, &rlim);
printf("CORE: cur - %ld max - %ld\n", rlim.rlim_cur, rlim.rlim_max);

#ifdef LINUX

getrlimit(RLIMIT_RSS, &rlim);
printf("RSS: cur - %ld max - %ld\n", rlim.rlim_cur, rlim.rlim_max);

getrlimit(RLIMIT_NPROC, &rlim);
printf("NPROC: cur - %ld max - %ld\n", rlim.rlim_cur, rlim.rlim_max);

#else
getrlimit(RLIMIT_VMEM, &rlim);
printf("VMEM: cur - %ld max - %ld\n", rlim.rlim_cur, rlim.rlim_max);

getrlimit(RLIMIT_AS, &rlim);
printf("AS: cur - %ld max - %ld\n", rlim.rlim_cur, rlim.rlim_max);

#endif
getrlimit(RLIMIT_NOFILE, &rlim);
printf("NOFILE: cur - %ld max - %ld\n", rlim.rlim_cur, rlim.rlim_max);

#ifdef LINUX
getrlimit(RLIMIT_MEMLOCK, &rlim);
printf("MEMLOCK: cur - %ld max - %ld\n", rlim.rlim_cur, rlim.rlim_max);
#endif

if((p = malloc(100000000)) == NULL)
{
printf("malloc 100M failed\n");
```

```
}
else
{
printf("malloc 100M succeeded\n");
}
if(p) free(p);
if((p = malloc(500000000)) == NULL)
{
printf("malloc 500M failed\n");
}
else
{
printf("malloc 500M succeeded\n");
}
if(p) free(p);
return 0;
}
```

Example 7

Execute the following program and identify we are able to open 512 files. However, if we take fd array as FILE * type and use fopen() instead of open(), will you be in a position to create 512 files?. If not guess why?.

```
#include <stdio.h>
#include <limits.h>
#include <fcntl.h>
#include <unistd.h>
#include <sys/resource.h>
#include <sys/stat.h>
#include <sys/types.h>

int main (int argc, char ** argv)
{
int rv = 0;
int i;
unsigned char data[1024] = {'\0'};
char tmp[128];
int fd[512];
struct rlimit mylim;

if ((rv = getrlimit(RLIMIT_NOFILE, &mylim)) == -1)
perror("1rst getrlimit");
else
{
```

```
printf("hardlimit: %ld softlimit: %ld\n", mylim.rlim_max, mylim.rlim_cur);
mylim.rlim_cur = 1024;

if ((rv = setrlimit(RLIMIT_NOFILE, &mylim)) == -1)
perror("setrlimit");
else if ((rv = getrlimit(RLIMIT_NOFILE, &mylim)) == -1)
perror("2nd getrlimit");
else
{
printf("hardlimit: %ld softlimit: %ld\n", mylim.rlim_max, mylim.rlim_cur);

for (i = 0; i < 512; i++)
{
sprintf(tmp, "%3d.dat", i);
if ((fd[i] = open(tmp, O_CREAT | O_TRUNC | O_WRONLY,
S_IRUSR | S_IWUSR | S_IRGRP | S_IROTH)) == -1)
{
perror("fileopen");
printf("open files: %d\n", i);
i++; break;
}
else
if (write(fd[i], (void*)&data, sizeof(data)) != sizeof(data))
perror("filewrite");
}
while(i--)
close(fd[i]);
}
}
return rv;
}
```

Example 8

The following example (ex.8.c) is used to demonstrate the importance of stack size limit on the program's execution. Here, a large array is declared and a element is stored and the same is attempted to print via printf() function. When we run this program we will get segment violation. The same program is tested after changing (increasing) the stack size. Now, we did not get segment violation error. The same is tested using gdb. See the following session output. **We recommand to come to this example after going through chapter on GDB.**

```
#include<stdio.h>
#include<string.h>
 CHR(int n)
{
```

```
char *p=(char*) malloc(n);
}

int main()
{
int a[10240000];
a[10240000-1]=10;
printf("%d\n", a[10240000-1]);
CHR(10);
CHR(10000000);
return 0;
}
```

gcc -g ex 8.c
gdb -q a.out

```
Using host libthread_db library "/lib/tls/libthread_db.so.1".
(gdb) b 11
Breakpoint 1 at 0x80483d8: file a5.c, line 11.
(gdb) b 12
Breakpoint 2 at 0x80483df: file a5.c, line 12.
(gdb) b 13
Breakpoint 3 at 0x80483f2: file a5.c, line 13.
(gdb) r
Starting program: /root/valgrind/mem/a.out

Breakpoint 1, main () at a5.c:11
11      a[10240000-1]=10;
(gdb) n
12      printf("%d\n", a[10240000-1]);
(gdb) n

Program received signal SIGSEGV, Segmentation fault.
0x080483e2 in main () at a5.c:12
12      printf("%d\n", a[10240000-1]);
```

(gdb) n

```
Program terminated with signal SIGSEGV, Segmentation fault.
The program no longer exists.
(gdb) q
ulimit -S -s 10240000
```

gdb -q a.out

```
Using host libthread_db library "/lib/tls/libthread_db.so.1".
(gdb) b 11
Breakpoint 1 at 0x80483d8: file a5.c, line 11.
```

```
(gdb) b 12
Breakpoint 2 at 0x80483df: file a5.c, line 12.
(gdb) b 13
Breakpoint 3 at 0x80483f2: file a5.c, line 13.
(gdb) r
Starting program: /root/valgrind/mem/a.out

Breakpoint 1, main () at a5.c:11
11      a[10240000-1]=10;
(gdb) n
12      printf("%d\n", a[10240000-1]);
(gdb) n
10

Breakpoint 3, main () at a5.c:13
13      CHR(10);
(gdb) n
14      CHR(10000000);
(gdb) n
15      return 0;
(gdb) n
16      }
(gdb) n
0x004fbe33 in __libc_start_main ()
  from /lib/tls/libc.so.6
(gdb)
Single stepping until exit from function __libc_start_main,
which has no line number information.

Program exited normally.
(gdb) q
```

5.2.3 Setting limits via PAM modules

If we have a system that uses PAM (Pluggable Authentication Modules) for authentication, we have another option for setting user resource limits. PAM comes with a resource limits module that is well documented here.

Authentication with PAM for various different applications are controlled by the files located in /etc/pam.d. To set limits for users that login via telnet (from a console), we need to first edit /etc/pam.d/login and add the following line at the end of the series of lines that begin with session:

```
session  required /lib/security/pam_limits.so
```

It is possible that this line may already be there depending on what distribution we are using, you should not add it again if it is already there.

The limits are then managed by editing the /etc/security/limits.conf file. See the documentation for the format of this file.

The major advantages of using PAM for resource limits is that different users can easily be assigned different limits as well as users that are a member of a group. PAM also allows us to limit the priority (see man nice for more information) that the processes will be assigned and to determine the maximum number of logins (to prevent the user from logging in many times to attempt to avoid the process limitations).

First, edit the /etc/pam.d/login and /etc/pam.d/sshd files and add the limits module as described here. This will make sure that both telnet and ssh connections are resource limited. We also may wish to do this for the /etc/pam.d/ftpd to limit ftpd resource usage as well.

```
@nbv        hard        nproc        10
```

Here, we are specifying that for user "nbv", hard limits for number of process's as 10.

There are some limitations with the current implementation of user resource limits. The largest is that we can only apply resource limits per session. There is no way at the moment to place a quota on the number of resources a certain user may use globally on the system.

5.3 Conclusions

This chapter high lights about system resources and their management. It explains about hard and soft limits and also how the same can be changed through Linux commands is emphasized. Moreover, what will be the implication of these resource limits are explained with illustrative examples. At the end, how a C program can change the system limits when it is running is explained. In addition, how PAM can be used to manage resources is explained.

6 Assembly in Linux

6.1 Introduction

Assembly language is widely used in SW system development from early days. SW systems ranging from simple application programs to complex OS's, compilers, linkers, daemons etc ., are written in Assembly. There is no doubt that in the high level languages are widely used for most of the problems. However, where ever performance is the criterion, assembly language or mixture of high level language and assembly is used un-opposesedly. For example, some Linux kernel modules are written in assembly, resulting in a fast, reliable, portable, maintainable OS. Even a successful game like DOOM which is almost massively written in C contains a tiny part written in asssembly for speed up.

Also, in applications such as embedded systems where code size limitations are very crucial, use of assembly language is very much encouraged.

We can not access BIOS functions from Linux as this OS uses protected mode; encourages use of OS services instead. Also, we can't use int 0x10, int 0x13, etc., Fortunately, almost everything can be implemented by means of system calls or library functions. In the worst case we may go through direct port access, or make a kernel patch to implement needed functionality, or use LRMI library to access BIOS functions.

6.1.1 The advantages of Assembly

Though programming using assembly language is considered to be time consuming mind blowing, assembly programming has the following noted advantages compared to high level languages.

- we can access machine-dependent registers and I/O.
- we can control the exact code behavior in critical sections that might otherwise involve deadlock between multiple software threads or hardware devices
- you can break the conventions of our usual compiler, which might allow some optimizations (like temporarily breaking rules about memory allocation, threading, calling conventions, etc).
- we can build interfaces between code fragments using incompatible conventions (e.g. produced by different compilers, or separated by a low-level interface)
- we can get access to unusual programming modes of your processor (e.g. 16 bit mode to interface startup, firmware, or legacy code on Intel PC's).
- we can produce reasonably fast code for tight loops to cope with a bad non-optimizing compiler (but then, there are free optimizing compilers available!).
- we can produce hand-optimized code perfectly tuned for our particular hardware setup, though not to someone else's.
- we can write some code for our new language's optimizing compiler (that is something what very few ones will ever do, and even they not often).
- we can be in complete control of our code

6.1.2 The disadvantages of Assembly

Assembly is a very low-level language (the lowest above hand-coding the binary instruction patterns). This means

- it is long and tedious to write initially.
- it is quite bug-prone.
- our bugs can be very difficult to chase.
- our code can be fairly difficult to understand and modify, i.e. to maintain
- the result is non-portable to other architectures, existing or upcoming.
- our code will be optimized only for a certain implementation of a same architecture: for instance, among Intel-compatible platforms each CPU design and its variations (relative latency, through-output, and capacity, of processing units, caches, RAM, bus, disks, presence of FPU, MMX, 3DNOW, SIMD extensions, etc) implies potentially completely different optimization techniques. New designs keep popping up, so don't expect either this listing and our code to be up-to-date.
- we spend more time on a few details and can't focus on small and large algorithmic design, that are known to bring the largest part of the speed up (e.g. you might spend some time building very fast list/array manipulation primitives in assembly; only a hash table would have sped up our program much more; or, in another context, a binary tree; or some high-level structure distributed over a cluster of CPUs).
- a small change in algorithmic design might completely invalidate all our existing assembly code. So that either we're ready (and able) to rewrite it all, or we tied to a particular algorithmic design.
- On code that ain't too far from what's in standard benchmarks, commercial optimizing compilers outperform hand-coded assembly (well, that's less true on the x86 architecture than on RISC architectures, and perhaps less true for widely available/free compilers; anyway, for typical C code, GCC is fairly good).
- And in any case, "compilers make it a lot easier to use complex data structures, and compilers don't get bored halfway through and generate reliably pretty good code".

They will also correctly propagate code transformations throughout the whole (huge) program when optimizing code between procedures and module boundaries.

Though we might find that using assembly is sometimes needed, and might even be useful in a few cases where it is not:

- minimize use of assembly code.
- encapsulate this code in well-defined interfaces.
- have your assembly code automatically generated from patterns expressed in a higher-level language than assembly (e.g. GCC inline assembly macros).
- have automatic tools translate these programs into assembly code.
- have this code be optimized if possible.
- All of the above, i.e. write (an extension to) an optimizing compiler back-end.

6.1.3 How to achieve efficient code

In order to speed up the code, we should do it only for parts of a program that a profiling tool has consistently identified as being a performance bottleneck.

Hence, if we identify some code portion as being too slow, we should

- first try to use a better algorithm,
- then try to compile it rather than interpret it,
- then try to enable and tweak optimization from your compiler,
- then give the compiler hints about how to optimize,
- then possibly fallback to assembly programming
- check whether assembly generated code can be obviously enhanced with hand-coded assembly (or by tweaking compiler switches).

- when that's the case, start from generated code and modify it instead of starting from scratch.
- more generally, use generated code as stubs to modify, which at least gets right the way our assembly routines interface to the external world.
- track down bugs in our compiler (hopefully the rarer)

Finally, before we end up writing assembly, we should inspect generated code, to check that the problem really is with bad code generation, as this might really not be the case: compiler-generated code might be better than what we would have written, particularly on modern multi-pipelined architectures! Slow parts of a program might be intrinsically so. The biggest problems on modern architectures with fast processors are due to delays from memory access, cache-misses, TLB-misses, and page-faults; register optimization becomes useless, and we'll more profitably re-think data structures and threading to achieve better locality in memory access. Perhaps a completely different approach to the problem might help, then.

The standard way to have assembly code be generated is to invoke our compiler with the -S flag. This works with most Unix compilers, including the GNU C Compiler (GCC), but YMMV. As for GCC, it will produce more understandable assembly code with the -fverbose-asm command-line option. Of course, if want to get good assembly code, don't forget our usual optimization options and hints!.

6.2 Writing Assembly Programs Under Linux

Intel x86 assembly is widely used in DOS/Windows platforms. GAS (Gnu assembler on which GCC depends) was invented to support a 32-bit Unix compiler, it uses standard AT&T syntax, which resembles a lot the syntax for standard m68k assemblers, and is standard in the UNIX world. This syntax is neither worse, nor better than the Intel syntax. Intel (IA-32) and AT&T syntax Assembly language are very different to each other in appearance, and this will lead to confusion when one first comes across AT&T syntax after having learnt Intel syntax first, or vice versa. In the following paragraphs, we would like to emphasize the conceptual differences between Intel style of assembly and AT&T style and how assembly programs can be run under Linux as our objective is not to teach complete assembly programming rather is to explain how assembly programs can be compiled and executed. For fuller details about assembly language one can read popular books on them such as [14].

Registers

Registers are like the local variables of the CPU, except there are a fixed number of them. For the x86 CPU, there are only 4 main registers for doing integer calculations: A, B, C, and D. Each of these 4 registers can be accessed 4 different ways: as a 32 bit value (eax), as a 16 bit value (ax), and as a low and a high 8 bit value (al and ah). There are five more registers that we will see used occasionally - namely SI, DI, SP and BP. SI and DI are around from the DOS days when people used 64k segmented addressing, and can be used as integer like normal registers now. SP and BP are two special registers used to handle an area of memory called the stack. There is one last register, the instruction pointer IP that we may not modify directly, but is changed through jmps and calls.

Prefixes

In Intel syntax there are no register prefixes or immediate prefixes. In AT&T however registers are prefixed with a '%' and immediate operands are prefixed with a '$'. Intel syntax hexadecimal or binary data are suffixed with 'h' and 'b' respectively. Also if the first hexadecimal digit is a letter then the value is prefixed by a '0'.

Example:

Intex Syntax	AT&T Syntax
mov eax,1	movl $1,%eax
mov ebx,0ffh	movl $0xff,%ebx
int 80h	int $0x80

Direction of Operands

The direction of the operands in Intel syntax is opposite to that of AT&T syntax. In Intel syntax the first operand is the destination, and the second operand is the source whereas in AT&T syntax the first operand is the source and the second operand is the destination. The advantage of AT&T syntax in this situation is obvious. We read to left to right, we write to left to right, so this way is only natural.

Example:

Intex Syntax	AT&T Syntax
instr dest,source	instr source,dest
mov eax,[ecx]	movl (%ecx),%eax

Memory Operands.

Memory operands as seen above are different also. In Intel syntax the base register is enclosed in '[' and ']' whereas in AT&T syntax it is enclosed in '(' and ')'.

Example:

Intex Syntax	AT&T Syntax
mov eax,[ebx]	movl (%ebx),%eax
mov eax,[ebx+3]	movl 3(%ebx),%eax

The AT&T form for instructions involving complex operations is very obscure compared to Intel syntax. The Intel syntax form of these is segreg:[base+index*scale+disp]. The AT&T syntax form is %segreg:disp(base,index,scale).

Index/scale/disp/segreg are all optional and can simply be left out. Scale, if not specified and index is specified, defaults to 1. Segreg depends on the instruction and whether the app is being run in real mode or pmode. In real mode it depends on the instruction whereas in pmode its unnecessary. Immediate data used should not '$' prefixed in AT&T when used for scale/disp.

Example:

Intel Syntax	AT&T Syntax
instr foo,segreg:[base+index*scale+disp]	instr %segreg:disp(base,index,scale),foo
mov eax,[ebx+20h]	movl 0x20(%ebx),%eax
add eax,[ebx+ecx*2h	addl (%ebx,%ecx,0x2),%eax
leaeax,[ebx+ecx]	leal (%ebx,%ecx),%eax
sub eax,[ebx+ecx*4h-20h]	subl -0x20(%ebx,%ecx,0x4),%eax

As we can see, AT&T is very obscure. [base+index*scale+disp] makes more sense at a glance than disp(base,index,scale).

Suffixes

As we may have noticed, the AT&T syntax mnemonics have a suffix. The significance of this suffix is that of operand size. 'l' is for long, 'w' is for word, and 'b' is for byte. Intel syntax has similar directives for use with memory operands, i.e. byte ptr, word ptr, dword ptr. "dword" of course corresponding to "long". This is similar to type casting in C but it doesn't seem to be necessary since the size of registers used is the assumed datatype.

Example:

Intel Syntax	AT&T Syntax
mov al,bl	movb %bl,%al
mov ax,bx	movw %bx,%ax
mov eax,ebx	movl %ebx,%eax
mov eax, dword ptr [ebx]	movl (%ebx),%eax

Example 1

The following program simply moves 28 to register eax and calls ret. When we call ret program exits normally and the value in the register eax will becomes exit status of the program.

```
.globl main
main:
    movl $28, %eax
    ret
```

Let the above program name is "ex1.s". Compile the above program with

gcc –o ex1 ex1.s

Run the same by typing

./ex1

The exit status will become 28 (execute echo $? command at dollar prompt).

Example 2

Now consider the following assembly code which is used to explain about use of AT&T style of instructions.

```
.data
.text
.globl    main
main:
    movl    $0x10, %eax
    movl    $0x20, %ebx
    addl    %eax,  %ebx
```

```
    movl   $1, %eax
    int    $0x80

    ret
```

Let the above program name is "ex1a.s". Compile the above program with

gcc –o ex1a ex1a.s

Run the same by typing

./ex1a

The exit status will become same as sum of 0x10 and 0x20, i.e decimal 48 (execute echo $? command at dollar prompt). Actually, we are moving 0x10 and 0x20 to eax and ebx registers and adding them. Their sum is available in ebx. Now, we are moving 1 to eax register (which is system call number of exit) and then int 0x80 is executed such that system call exit will be executed and then program exits. The exit status of this program becomes the value available in register ebx, i.e., 48.

Example 3

The following example is to explain how a string can be used in assembly. We are moving length of the string to register edx, address of string to ecx, 1 (file descriptor of stdout) to ebx and 4 (write system call number) to eax. Then int 0x80 is called such that write system call is executed and thus we may see the message on the screen. In order to run any system call, the arguments required has to be moved to registers ebx, ecx etc., and system call number has to be pushed into eax before calling int 0x80 (More discussion is made in the next sections). Thus, we did also move all the arguments required for write system call, that is, number of bytes, address and file descriptor number into registers in reverse order and then write system call number 4 is moved to eax register before calling int 0x80 instruction.

```
.data
msg:
    .ascii    "Hello How are you"

    len = . - msg
.text
.globl main

main:
    movl   $len, %edx
    movl   $msg, %ecx
    movl   $1, %ebx
    mov    $4, %eax
    int    $0x80

    ret
```

Let the above program name is "ex2a.s". Compile the above program with

gcc –o ex2a ex2a.s

Run the same by typing

./ex2a

Example 4

The following assembly program gives factorial value of 5.

```
.globl main
main:
    movl $5, %eax
    movl $1, %ebx
L1: cmpl $0, %eax
    je L2
    imull   %eax, %ebx
    decl    %eax
    jmp L1
L2: movl %ebx, %eax
    ret
```

Let the above program name is "ex2.s". Compile the above program with

gcc –o ex2 ex2.s

Run the same by typing

./ex2

The exit status will become same as factorial value of 5 (execute echo $? command at dollar prompt to see the result).

Example 5

The following example also calculates factorial value of 5. However, we have written a function to calculate factorial value and the same is called from main. This example is used demonstrate how function call in assembly is made.

```
.globl main
main:
    movl $5, %eax
    call fact
    ret
fact:
    movl $1, %ebx
```

```
L1:cmpl $0, %eax
    je L2
    imull    %eax, %ebx
    decl     %eax
    jmp L1
L2:movl %ebx, %eax
    ret
```

Let the above program name as "ex3.s". Compile the above program with

gcc –o ex3 ex3.s

Run the same by typing

./ex3

The exit status will become same as factorial value of 5 (execute echo $? command at dollar prompt to see the result).

Example 6

This example is to explain how space is allocated on the stack

```
.globl main
main:
    call ft
    ret
ft:
    pushl %ebp
    movl %esp, %ebp
    subl $4, %esp
    movl $10, -4(%ebp)
    movl %ebp, %esp
    popl %ebp
    ret
```

Let the above program name is "ex4.s". Compile the above program with

gcc –o ex4 ex4.s

Run the same by typing

./ex4

The exit status will become same as factorial value of 5 (execute echo $? command at dollar prompt to see the result).

Example 7

The following program calls _exit function directly. As explained in second chapter, main is called by _start (libc library function) and it inturn calls exit. However, here, we are calling exit directly by overriding _start function.

```
.text
.extern _exit
.globl _start
_start:
            pushl   $42
    call _exit
```

Let the above program name is "s2.s". Compile the above program with

gcc –o s2 s2.s –nostartfiles

Run the same by typing

./s2
echo $?

Now let us use main instead of _start in the above program and carry out the same experimentation.

```
.text
.globl main
main:
            pushl   $42
    call _exit
```

Let the above program name is "s3.s". Compile the above program with

gcc –o s3 s3.s

Run the same by typing

./s3
echo $?

Now run objdump on both the executable files s2 and s3 and check the difference. The one which uses main contains _start, main and _exit functions, where as the other one did not. Which supports our explanation.

objdump -R s2

```
s2:     file format elf32-i386
```

```
DYNAMIC RELOCATION RECORDS
OFFSET   TYPE              VALUE
08049238 R_386_JUMP_SLOT   _exit
```

objdump -R s3

```
s3:     file format elf32-i386

DYNAMIC RELOCATION RECORDS
OFFSET   TYPE              VALUE
08049530 R_386_GLOB_DAT    __gmon_start__
08049540 R_386_JUMP_SLOT   __libc_start_main
08049544 R_386_JUMP_SLOT   _exit
```

We can find that when we use main, first _start is called and then at the end exit is called.

Example 8

This is another example to support the above. Make sure that it sould be also compiled with –nostartfiles option.

```
.text
.globl _start
_start:
    movl $1, %eax
    movl $42,%ebx
    int $0x80
```

Example 9

This example is used to explain that we can use Intel style assembly instructions also.

```
BITS 32
GLOBAL main
SECTION .text
main:
    mov     eax, 42
    ret
```

To Compile, Run and test:

```
nasm –f elf tiny.asm
gcc –o tiny tiny.o
./tiny
echo $?
```

Example 10

This is another example to show how Intel style of assembly can be used. Unlike previous example, we have directly used _start.

```
BITS 32
EXTERN _exit
GLOBAL _start
SEGMENT .text
_start:
    push   dword  92
    call   _exit
```

To Compile & Run

```
nasm –f elf tiny1.asm
gcc –o tiny1 tiny1.o -nostartfiles
./tiny1
echo $?
```

Example 11

Here, we have incremented eax register value after taking xor of its initial value. That is, after xor statement eax will contain 0 and after inc statement it will contain 1 which is incidentally system call number of exit() system call. Now, we have moved 42 to register bl (we can as well do the same into ebx). Then we have called int 0x80 such that exit() system call is executed.

```
global      _start
section .text
_start:
    xor      eax,eax
    inc      eax
    mov      bl,42
    int      0x80
```

To Compile & Run

```
nasm –f elf tiny2.asm
gcc –o tiny2 tiny2.o -nostartfiles
./tiny2
echo $?
```

6.2.1 The stack Operations

We are sure, we are not attempting to go through this book with out having orientation to data structures, computer organizations, etc., where we except students gets exposed to stacks. However, for the sake of completeness we would like to give few statements on usual stack.

A stack is what is called a Last In First Out data structure or LIFO. Think of it as a stack of plates in a luncheon. The most recent (last) plate pushed on top of the stack is the first one to be removed. This allows us to manage the stack with only one register if needed, namely the stack pointer or SP register.

6.2.2 Programmer's perpective of stack

The stack is a region of memory that is present throughout the entire lifetime of a program. It is where local variables are stored, and it is also how function call arguments are passed. On almost all modern computers, the stack is said to grow down, that is, as elements are pushed on to it, the SP register value is decremented by the size of the element pushed. So the stack starts from a high memory address, and works down to a lower address. This is because another section of memory called the heap grows up, and its handy to have the two of them grow towards each other to fill in a single empty hole in the program address space.

Note: It is easy to become confused when dealing with the stack. Remember that while it may grow down, variables are still addressed sequentially upwards. So an array of char b[4] at esp of 80 will have b[0] at 80 (right at the stack pointer), b[1] above that at 81, b[2] at 82, and b[3] at 83, which is where the stack pointer was before the push. The next push will then place the stack pointer at 76.

6.2.3 Working with the stack

There are two assembly instructions that deal with the stack directly: push and pop. Each take a register or value as an argument. Push will place its argument onto the stack, and then decrement the SP by the size of its argument (4 for pushl, 2 for pushw, 1 for pushb). Pop copies the value on the top of the stack into its argument, then increments SP. pusha and popa push and pop all the registers with one instruction. Because of speed considerations, the value is not touched, just the SP register is changed to point to the next location at the stack. So, SP is always pointing to the top value of the stack and not at invalid memory.

Normal arithmetic expressions can also be used to modify SP to make space for working directly with stack memory with other instructions.

6.2.4 How gcc works with the stack

Right before a function is called, its arguments are pushed onto the stack in reverse order. Then the call instruction pushes the address of the next instruction (i.e. the value of IP after call) onto the stack, and then the CPU begins executing the address of the call by copying that value into the invisible instruction pointer (IP) register. The called function then starts with what is known as the function prolog, which pushes the current base pointer onto the stack, and then copies the current stack pointer to the base pointer, and then subtracts from SP enough space to hold all local variables (and then some!). The base pointer is then used to reference variables and parameters during function execution, since its value is not affected by pushes and pops. Thus, parameters all have fixed positive offsets from the BP, where as local variables all have fixed negative offsets from the BP. At the end of function execution, the base pointer is copied to the stack pointer during ret, and the return address is popped off the stack and placed into the invisible IP register to return to the caller function.

Note: Unless **-fomit-frame-pointer** is specified, gcc always generates code that references local variables by negative offsets from the BP instead of positive offsets from the SP.

6.2.5 Function Parameter Passing and Return Value

The stack can be used for passing parameters to functions. We will follow a convention (which is used by our C compiler) that the value stored by a function in the *eax* register is taken to be the return value of the function. The calling program passes a parameter to the callee by pushing its value on the stack. The following Listing (Example 12) demonstrates this with a simple function called DBL.

Example 12

```
.globl main
main:
    movl $12, %ebx
    pushl %ebx
    call DBL
    addl $4, %esp       //adjust esp to its value before the push
    ret
DBL:
    movl 4(%esp), %eax
    imull %eax, %eax    //compute eax * eax, store result in eax
    ret
```

Read the first line of DBL carefully. The calling function pushes the content of *ebx* on the stack and then executes a *call* instruction. The call will push the return address on the stack. So inside DBL, the parameter is accessible at an offset of four bytes from the top of stack.

6.2.6 How to Run system calls from Assembly

It is possible to directly call Linux system calls from an assembly program. Whenever we want to use system calls in a assemble program we use their equivalent macros which are defined as SYS_<syscall name> i.e. SYS_exit, SYS_close, etc else where in the header files. However, in kernel point of view, for all system calls there exists an integer number. First, this system call number (or its macro name) should go in to %eax (The system call numbers can be found in header files /usr/include/asm/unistd.h, /usr/include/bits/syscall.h which are included in /usr/include/sys/syscall.h). For system calls that have less than six args, the args can go in from %ebx,%ecx,%edx,%esi,%edi in order. The return value of the system call is stored in %eax after its execution.

Advantages of Using system calls from assembly.

- program size becomes the smallest possible size; squeezing the last byte out of the system.
- program becomes the highest possible speed; squeezing cycles out of your favorite benchmark
- we will have full control. We can adapt our program/library to our specific language or memory requirements or whatever

- no pollution by libc code.
- no pollution by C calling conventions (if we are developing our own language or environment)
- static binaries makes our code as independent from libc upgrades or crashes, or from dangling #! path to an interpreter.

Disadvantages of Using system calls from assembly.

- If any other program on our computer uses the libc, then duplicating the libc code will actually wastes memory, not saves it.
- Services redundantly implemented in many static binaries are a waste of memory. But we can make your libc replacement a shared library.
- We cannot benefit from the many functionality's that libc provides besides mere Linux syscalls. Therefore, we might have to reimplement large parts of libc, from printf() to malloc() and gethostbyname. It's redundant with the libc effort, and can be quite boring sometimes.
- Static libraries prevent us to benefit from libc upgrades as well as from libc add-ons such as the zlibc package, that does on-the-fly transparent decompression of gzip-compressed files.
- The few instructions added by the libc can be a ridiculously small speed overhead as compared to the cost of a system call. If speed is a concern, your main problem is in our usage of system calls, not in their wrapper's implementation.
- Using the standard assembly API for system calls is much slower than using the libc API when running in micro-kernel versions of Linux such as L4Linux, that have their own faster calling convention, and pay high convention-translation overhead when using the standard one (L4Linux comes with libc recompiled with their syscall API; of course, we can recompile our code with their API, too).

For example we need to write a assembly program which prints "Hello How are you" message by calling write() system call.

We know that the write() system call requires opened file descriptor, memory address from where data has to be printed and the total number of the byte to be printed. Its prototype is given as: (Richard Steven, venkateshwarlu):

ssize_t write(int fd, const void *buf, size_t count);

In order to call this system call, first we have to move its number to %eax and file descriptor fd to %ebx, buf (address) to %ecx, count to %edx. This is followed by a call to int $0x80 which executes the system call. The return value of the system call is stored in %eax.

Example 13

```
.data
hello:
    .string  "Hello How are you\n"
.text
.globl      main
main:
    movl    $4, %eax
    movl    $1, %ebx
    movl    $hello, %ecx
    movl   $18,%edx
    int    $0x80
    ret
```

Let us assume the above code is stored in a file "write.s". Then by running the following command it can be compiled.

gcc –o write write.s

To run

./write

The above program can be also used using the Intel style as given below.

Example 14

```
BITS 32
SECTION .data
msg db      'Hello How are you'
GLOBAL main
SECTION .text
.text
main:
    mov     eax, 4
    mov     ebx, 1
    mov     ecx,msg
    mov     edx,18
    int     80h

    ret
```

Assuming the file name as "write.asm" the following commands can be used to compile and run.

nasm –f elf write.asm
gcc –o write write.o
./write

Example 15

This program is same as the above program with the exception that length of the string is used in the instructions instead of directly giving the same as literal in the instruction.

```
BITS 32
SECTION .data
msg db      'Hello How are you'
len equ     $ - msg
SECTION .text
global main
```

```
main:
    mov     edx, len
    mov     ecx, msg
    mov     ebx,1
    mov    eax,4
    int    80h

    ret
```

To compile and Run

```
nasm –f elf hello.asm
gcc –o hello hello.o
./hello
```

Example 16

The following file "hello1.agm" works in the some fashion, however directly starts from – start rather than – main as explained earlier.

```
BITS 32
SECTION .data
msg db      'Hello How are you'
len equ     $ - msg
SECTION .text
global _start

_start:
    mov     edx, len
    mov     ecx, msg
    mov     ebx,1
    mov   eax,4
    int   80h

     push  dword 0
    mov   eax,0x1
    int       80h
```

To compile and Run

```
nasm –f elf hello1.asm
gcc –o hello1 hello1.o   -nostartfiles
./hello1
```

Please check the file size differences of files "hello" and "hello1". The file "hello1" will be of smaller size as we have asked not to include any startup files.

Example 17

In this example, system call 64 is called (getpid()) whose return value, i.e PID of the shell is stored in register eax which is moved to register ebx before calling kill() system call whose system call number is 37. First system call number 37 is pushed into eax, and signal number 9 is moved to register ecx and already ebx contains the PID of the process which we wanted to kill. Now, int 0x80 is executed. When we run this program, we will be logged out from the current shell.

```
.data
.text
.globl      main
main:
    movl    $64, %eax
    int     $0x80

    movl    %eax,%ebx
    movl    $37, %eax
    movl    $9, %ecx
    int   $0x80
    ret
```

Example 18

The following code is used to explain how fork() system call and _exit() system call can be used in the assembly program. Please note that after every system call we have to execute int $0x80. This program prints the string two times; i.e from parent process and child process. Refer [Richard Stevens, Ventkateshwarlu) for more details about fork() system call.

```
.data
hello:
    .string  "Hello How are you\n"
.text
.globl      main
main:
    movl    $2, %eax
    int     $0x80

    movl    $4, %eax
    movl    $1, %ebx
    movl    $hello, %ecx
    movl   $18,%edx
    int   $0x80

    movl    $1, %eax
    xorl    %ebx, %ebx
    int     $0x80

    ret
```

Let us assume the above code is stored in a file "forkwrite.s". Then by running the following command it can be compiled.

gcc –o forkwrite forkwrite.s

To run

./forkwrite

Example 19

This program is to explain how read() write() system calls usage in assembly.

```
.data
hello:
    .string  "Hello How are you\n"
.text
.globl      main
main:
    movl    $4, %eax
    movl    $1, %ebx
    movl    $hello, %ecx
    movl   $18,%edx
    int    $0x80

    movl    $3, %eax
    movl    $0, %ebx
    movl    $hello, %ecx
    movl   $8,%edx
    int    $0x80

    movl    $4, %eax
    movl    $1, %ebx
    movl    $hello, %ecx
    movl   $18,%edx
    int    $0x80

    movl    $1, %eax
    xorl    %ebx, %ebx
    int     $0x80

    ret
```

Let us assume the above code is stored in a file "readwrite.s". Then by running the following command it can be compiled.

gcc –o readwrite readwrite.s

To run

./readwrite

Example 20

Similarly, the above code can be written in Intel style in the following manner.

```
BITS 32
SECTION .data
msg db    ' '
GLOBAL main
SECTION .text
.text
main:
    mov     eax, 3
    mov     ebx, 0
    mov     ecx, msg
    mov   edx,1
    int   80h

    mov     eax, 4
    mov     ebx, 1
    mov     ecx, msg
    mov   edx,1
    int   80h

    mov     eax,1        ; the exit syscall number
    mov     ebx,0        ; have an exit code of 0
    int     80h          ; interrupt 80h, the thing that pokes the kernel
                  ; and says, "do this"
```

Assuming the file name as "readwrite.asm" the following commands can be used to compile and run.

nasm –f elf readwrite.asm
gcc –o write readwrite.o
/readwrite

Example 21

The following program when executed works like logout command. Here, first, system call number 64 (getppid()) is executed whose results is stored in %eax. The same is moved to %ebx. Then system call kill() is executed by moving its number 37 to %eax and signal number 9 to %ecx. Please note that already pid of the shell is in %ebx. Thus, when signal 9 (SIGKILL) is sent to the shell it gets killed. Thus, we will be logged out to the current shell. Please mind that when we execute a program, a new process will be created and then executed in it. For this process, Shell is the parent.

```
.data
.text
.globl     main
main:
    movl    $64, %eax    //SIG_getppid() system call number is 64
    int   $0x80

    movl    %eax, %ebx    //returned value of getppid() is moved to %ebx
    movl   $37, %eax   //SIG_kill number  is loaded into %eax
    movl    $9, %ecx    //signal number 9 is loaded into %ecx
    int   $0x80

    ret
```

Calling System Calls with more than 5 Arguments

The same process applies to system calls which have less than five arguments. Just leave the un-used registers unchanged. System calls whose number of arguments are greater than five still expect the system call number to be in %eax, but the arguments are arranged in memory and the pointer to the first argument is stored in %ebx. If you are using the stack, arguments must be pushed onto it backwards, i.e. from the last argument to the first argument. Then the stack pointer should be copied to %ebx.

Example 22

To explain the above situation, the following example which maps a file to the address space of the process using mmap() system call is described.

Using mmap() in C:

```
#include <sys/types.h>
#include <sys/stat.h>
#include <sys/mman.h>
#include <fcntl.h>
#include <unistd.h>

#define STDOUT   1
```

```
void main(void) {
    char file[]="mmap.s";
    char *mappedptr;
    int fd,filelen;

    fd=fopen(file, O_RDONLY);
    filelen=lseek(fd,0,SEEK_END);
    mappedptr=mmap(NULL,filelen,PROT_READ,MAP_SHARED,fd,0);
    write(STDOUT, mappedptr, filelen);
    munmap(mappedptr, filelen);
    close(fd);
}
```

Arrangement of mmap() args in memory:

%esp	%esp+4	%esp+8	%esp+12	%esp+16	%esp+20
00000000	Filelen	00000001	00000001	fd	00000000

ASM Equivalent:

```
fd:
    .long   0
fdlen:
    .long   0
mappedptr:
    .long   0

.text
.globl main
main:
    subl    $24,%esp

    movl    $5,%eax
    movl    32(%esp),%ebx
    xorl    %ecx,%ecx
    int     $0x80

    test    %eax,%eax
    js      exit

    movl    %eax,fd

    movl    %eax,%ebx
    xorl    %ecx,%ecx
    movl    $2,%edx
```

```
	movl	$19,%eax
	int	$0x80

	movl	%eax,fdlen

	xorl	%edx,%edx

	movl	%edx,(%esp)
	movl	%eax,4(%esp)
	movl	$1,8(%esp)
	movl	$1,12(%esp)
	movl	fd,%eax
	movl	%eax,16(%esp)
	movl	%edx,20(%esp)

	movl	$90,%eax
	movl	%esp,%ebx
	int	$0x80

	movl	%eax,mappedptr

	movl	$1,%ebx
	movl	%eax,%ecx
	movl	fdlen,%edx
	movl	$4,%eax
	int	$0x80

	movl	mappedptr,%ebx
	movl	fdlen,%ecx
	movl	$91,%eax
	int	$0x80

	movl	fd,%ebx
	movl	$6,%eax
	int	$0x80
exit:
	movl	$1,%eax
	xorl	%ebx,%ebx
	int	$0x80

	ret
```

6.3 Mixing C and Assembly

As mentioned earlier mixing c and assembly is used for per performance reasons; especially in embedded systems.

The following example shows how a C program can call an assembly language function. The C function is defined in a file called *canssembly.c* and the assembly language function in *DBL.s*.

Example 23

You compile and link the files together by typing

gcc candassembly.c DBL.s.

File candassembly.c

```
#include<stdio.h>
main()
{
    int i = DBL(11);
    printf("%d\n",i);
}
```

File DBL.s

```
.globl DBL
DBL:
    movl 4(%esp), %eax
    addl %eax, %eax
    ret
```

Example 24

Calling A C Function from Assembly

File DBLPRINT.c

```
void DBLPRINT(int I)
{
printf("%d\n",2*I);
}
```

FIle assemblyandc.c

```
.globl main
main:
    movl   $10,    %eax
    pushl  %eax
    call   DBLPRINT
    addl   $4,%esp
    ret
```

To compile

```
gcc assemblyandc.s  DBLPPRINT.c
./a.out
```

6.3.1 GCC Inline Assembly

We can embed assembly instructions in c program itself and it is called as inline assembly. This section on GCC inline asm will only cover the x86 applications. Operand constraints will differ on other processors. Basic inline assembly in gcc is very straightforward. In its basic form it looks like this:

```
__asm__("movl%esp,%eax");
                                        or
ASM("movl       %esp, %eax");
```

We can maintain a group of instructions in an asm block such as:

```
__asm__("     movl       $1,%eax              // SYS_exit
              xor        %ebx,%ebx
              int        $0x80
");
```

Example 25

The following example is used to explain how assembly instructions can be used in a C program. Here, first we have pushed system call number of exit() to eax, 42 into ebx and then we have called int 0x80 such that the system call can be executed. When we run this program without executing the second printf() function, the program exits. We can check the exit status by executing the command **echo $?** after running this program.

```
#include<stdio.h>

 main()
{
printf("Before EXIT\n");

asm(" mov $1, %eax; movl $42, %ebx; int $0x80 ");

printf("After EXIT\n");
}
```

Example 26

In the following example, the above asm statements are kept in a function and then it is called from the main().

```
#include<stdio.h>

void EXIT()
{
```

```
asm(" movl $1, %eax; movl $42, %ebx; int $0x80 ");
}

 main()
{
printf("Before EXIT\n");
EXIT();
printf("After EXIT\n");
}
```

Example 27

This example is just to show that we can use __asm__ instead of asm. More over, here exit status is taken as 0. That the second assembly instruction "xorl %ebx %ebx" makes the ebx value as zero which is considered as the argument for exit() system call.

```
#include<stdio.h>

void EXIT()
{

__asm__(" movl   $1,  %eax;  xor         %ebx,  %ebx; int        $0x80 ");
}

int main()
{
printf("Before EXIT\n");
EXIT();
printf("After EXIT\n");
return 0;
}
```

Example 28

This example is to show that we can write a group of asm blocks also in a C program.

```
#include<stdio.h>

void EXIT()
{

__asm__(" movl   $1,  %eax  ");
__asm__(" movl   $2,      %ebx");
```

```
__asm__(" int     $0x80 ");
}

int main()
{
printf("Before EXIT\n");
EXIT();
printf("After EXIT\n");
return 0;
}
```

6.3.2 Extended inline assembly

The basic format of the extended inline assembly stays much the same with the exception that it extends input arguments and output arguments. Here is the basic format:

```
statements:output_registers:input_registers:clobbered_registers);
```

The output and input fields must consist of an operand constraint string followed by a C expression enclosed in parentheses. The output operand constraints must be preceded by an '=' which indicates that it is an output. There may be multiple outputs, inputs, and modified registers. Each "entry" should be separated by commas (',') and there should be no more than 10 entries total. The operand constraint string may either contain the full register name, or an abbreviation.

Abbreviation	Register
a	%eax/%ax/%al
b	%ebx/%bx/%bl
c	%ecx/%cx/%cl
d	%edx/%dx/%dl
S	%esi/%si
D	%edi/%di
A	Eax and ebx combined 64 bit operand
G	eax,ebx,ecx,edx or variable in memory
I	Constant value(0-31)
q,r	Dynamic register
m	Memory

Let's just jump straight to a nifty example, which we will then explain:

```
asm ("movl %1, %2":: "c"(count),"a" (fill_value), "D" (dest):"%ecx", "%edi" );
```

Let us explore the following part of the above asm inline statement.

```
: "c" (count), "a" (fill_value), "D" (dest)
```

Here we load **ecx** with **count**, **eax** with **fill_value**, and **edi** with **dest**. Here, count, dest, fill_value are C variables. If we use "r" in input or output parts then the GCC will select the registers for these variables according to their availability. Why make GCC do it instead of doing it ourselves? Because GCC, in its register allocating, might be able to arrange for, say, **fill_value** to already be in **eax**. If this is in a loop, it might be able to preserve **eax** through the loop, and save some **movl operations** once per loop.

```
: "%ecx", "%edi" );
```

And here's where we specify to GCC, "we can no longer count on the values we loaded into **ecx** or **edi** to be valid." This doesn't mean they will be reloaded for certain. This is the clobberlist. It really helps when optimizing, when GCC can know exactly what we are doing with the registers before and after. It folds our assembly code into the code it's generates (whose rules for generation look *remarkably* like the above) and then optimizes. It's even smart enough to know that if we tell it to put (x+1) in a register, then if we don't clobber it, and later C code refers to (x+1), and it was able to keep that register free, it will reuse the computation.

Example 29

Here, %0 refers to the register allocated for variable y and %1 to variable x. The assembly instruction moves the value of x to y.

```
#include<stdio.h>

int main(void)
{

int x=10, y;

asm("movl  %1, %0"  :"=r"(y)  :"r"(x));

printf("%d %d\n", x, y);

}
```

Example 30

This example is to show that we use some expressions (such as x+2) while specifying the input instructions in the extended asm format. Here, the value of x+2 is first stored in the register and then "movl %1, %0" is executed.

```
#include<stdio.h>

int main(void)
{

int x=10, y;

asm("movl  %1, %0"  :"=r"(y)  :"r"(x+2));

printf("%d %d\n", x, y);

}
```

Example 31

This example is another example to strengthen the above statements.

```
#include<stdio.h>

int main(void)
{

int x=10, y=9;

asm("movl  %2, %0;  movl %0, %1"  :"=r"(y), "=r"(x)  :"r"(x+2));

printf("%d %d\n", x, y);

}
```

Example 32

This example is another example to strengthen the above statements.

```
#include<stdio.h>

int main(void)
{

int x=10, y=9;
```

```
asm("movl  %2, %0;  movl %0, %1"  :"=r"(y), "=r"(x)  :"r"(x+2));

printf("%d %d\n", x, y);

}
```

Example 33

```
#include<stdio.h>

#define     t3(a1,a2) asm("leal (%0, %0, 2), %0" : "=r" (a2) : "0"  (a1))

int main()
{
 int x=2,y=3;

t3(x,y);

printf("%d %d\n", x, y);
}
```

Example 34

To find bit position using bsrl instruction in inline assembly.

```
#include <stdio.h>
#include <stdlib.h>

int main(int argc, char *argv[])
{
    long max = atoi(argv[1]);
    long number;
    unsigned position;
    volatile unsigned result;

    for (number = 1; number <= max; ; ++number) {
          asm("bsrl %1, %0" : "=r" (position) : "r" (number));
          result = position;
    }
    return 0;
}
```

6.4 How To Create Small Executable Files

Usually if we left everything to the compiler it adds many objects to the executable file. Thus it is better to use means to reduce the executable file size of the programs. There are many ways to deal this problem. We can refer books on compilers and specifically topics or code optimization. One good web page which explains the possible executable file size reduction is: http://www.muppetlabs.com/~breadbox/software/tiny.

1. Use strip command to remove symbol table and other information to executable files. However, with some object files which we want to use with other modules symbol table may be needed. One has to put this in mind.
2. Use –O1, -O2,....,-O6 options with compiler.
3. If we are writing programs using assembly, try to bypass the library's startup code (as explined in some examples) and also the library's shutdown code as well, and go directly to the operating system's shutdown processing such as calling directly system call's etc. If needed, we may use **–nostartfiles** option with gcc compiler. Also, **-nostdlib** option is used to specify that not to use the standard system libraries and startup files when linking. Only the files we specify will be passed to the linker.
4. Use shorter instructions wherever needed. For example instead of writing "mov ebx 42" we can as well write "mov bl 42".
5. Executable files headers may contain information which is some time redundant. This can be eliminated without disturbing the structure.
6. -O2: This takes longer to compile (but not much) and the speed difference is pretty big over -O0 or -O1. -O3 is also available, but it goes nuts with the inlining of functions, and that can blow out our cache pretty well. Give it a try and time it both ways.
7. -m386 and -m486: Pick which machine you are targeting. It'll still work on either one if it's run on the other. Use -m486 for Pentium and up, too.
8. -fomit-frame-pointer: If we will not be debugging or profiling. this option gives gcc another register to play with (ebp), which can make all the difference in tight loops.
9. -funroll-loops. Time the code before and after. It speeds up loops on 486's but won't have as much effect on Pentiums and up. And the extra code size may have cache side effects.
10. -ffast-math: Try this flag if we are doing a lot of floating-point and we don't need accuracy to the last bit (few programs really do, usually scientific programs.) Also causes sqrt() calls to be inlined.
11. -S: This option causes gcc to emit the assembler code it would feed into its assembler into a .s file. Look at this. Find out *exactly* what is being generated.
12. Flags that sometimes help, sometimes don't:
    - -fforce-addr: Force all memory locations to be copied into a register before doing arithmetic on them.
    - -fstrength-reduce: A loop optimizer.
    - -funroll-all-loops: also turns on -fstrength-reduce and -frerun-cse-after-loop. These days, cache coherency is everything, so this option is rarely useful. If we stick to -funroll-loops, we'll get a good compromise.

6.4.1 Coding methodology

1. Try to avoid 16-bit variables in performance-critical code. It takes 1 or more extra cycles on 386/486/P5 (and it's even *worse* on the P6!) to use the 16-bit versions of the registers. Stick to 32-bit int's and 8-bits chars (chars don't slow it down, just shorts. This is because DJGPP runs our code in a 32-bit segment and it must issue a register size override prefix (which stalls the pipeline) to specify that the register width differs from the segment width).

2. If you need to use memcpy, try to give it fixed-length copies to do. This lets GCC convert it to an inline rep movsl, which saves we the overhead of a function call and some other calcs memcpy does. It will stick on extra movsb's and movsw's as necessary; it doesn't have to be longwords. It will not necessarily align the destination in this case.
3. Try to use
   for (i = len; i; i--)
   instead of
   for (i = 0; i < len; i++)
   Otherwise len must either be kept in a register or loaded from memory every time. -fstrength-reduce supposedly would make this unnecessary, but it sometimes produces incorrect code in this version of GCC, so it's by default disabled.
4. Use inline assembly for our critical loops.
5. Alternately, we can use the inline keyword to cause any function to be inlined (as fast as macros) whether we 're doing C++ or C. We have to call it from the same source file to get the inlining, and we can still call it from an external object.

6.5 How To Create Loadable Modules in Assembly

In Linux, device driver's are other Kernel modulus designed as loadable modules.

It is also possible to write kernel modules in assembly. While in general it is not a good idea (it hardly will speedup anything), there may be a need of developing modules in assembly. The process of writing a module itself is not that hard -- a module must have some predefined global function, it may also need to call some external functions from the kernel. Examine kernel source code (that can be built as module).

Example 35

Meanwhile, here's an example of a minimum dumb kernel module (module.asm)

```
section .text

        global init_module
        global cleanup_module
        global kernel_version

        extern printk

init_module:
        push   dword str1
        call   printk
        pop    eax
        xor    eax,eax
        ret

cleanup_module:
        push   dword str2
        call   printk
        pop    eax
        ret
```

```
str1          db     "Hello. Module is Initiated",0xa,0
str2          db     "Cleaning the Module. Done",0xa,0

kernel_version  db     "2.4.8-20",0
```

Modify kernel_version to match yours, and build module with:

```
nasm -f elf -o module.m module.asm
ld -r -o module.o module.m

lsmod|grep module   // to check  this loadable module is  loaded  or not.
insmod –f module.o  //to load this module
dmesg               //check whether you get "Hello Module is Initiated"
lsmod|grep module   // to check  this loadable module is  loaded  or not.
rmmod module        //to remove from kernel
lsmod|grep module   //to check whether module is unloaded or not
```

6.6 A Glimpse of Writing a Bootstrap Program

In the following paragraph, we shall explain with simple examples about how to develop a boot strap program. As usual, this discussion is very much specific to IBM-PC x86 machines.

A typical PC boot procedure starts with a hardware reset to the processor which makes processor to fetch a instruction at 0xFFFFFFF0 (which falls in ROM) and execute the same. This instruction is a jump instruction which transfers the control to POST (Power on self test) of BIOS. After verifying that the HW is functioning properly, the BIOS initializes the interrupt vector, enables interrupts, and then jumps to a primitive bootstrap loader in ROM which in turn loads the image of our disk bootstrap loader and then transfers control to the first instruction in the loaded image.

These are the rules that we must follow while writing bootstrap program. As our objective is show a demonstrative bootstrap loader and it is not purely a book on either assembly or OS, we are directly going to discuss about the bootstrap program to be developed while only summarizing important points [thanks for Mr. Daniel Marjamäki (daniel.marjamaki@home.se) for informal discussions on this topic].

- The BIOS will load our bootstrap to address 07C00h.
  (the segment and offset varies).
- Bootstraps must be compiled as plain binary files.
- The file size for the plain binary file must be 512 bytes.
- The file must end with AA55h.

The following three assembly files :boot.asm", "prog.asm" and "image.asm" are used. Here first a boot loader is loaded and then the program in "prog.asm" is loaded which in turn displays "=====" after booting.

Example 36

```
; boot.ASM
   ; Load a program off the disk and jump to it

         jmp 07C0h:start     ; Goto segment 07C0
```

```
start:
        ; Update the segment registers
        mov ax, cs
        mov ds, ax
        mov es, ax

reset:                  ; Reset the floppy drive
        mov ax, 0         ;
        mov dl, 0         ; Drive=0 (=A)
        int 13h         ;
        jc reset        ; ERROR => reset again

read:
        mov ax, 1000h      ; ES:BX = 1000:0000
        mov es, ax        ;
        mov bx, 0         ;

        mov ah, 2         ; Load disk data to ES:BX
        mov al, 5        ; Load 5 sectors
        mov ch, 0         ; Cylinder=0
        mov cl, 2        ; Sector=2
        mov dh, 0         ; Head=0
        mov dl, 0        ; Drive=0
        int 13h         ; Read!

        jc read         ; ERROR => Try again

        jmp 1000h:0000     ; Jump to the program

times 510-($-$$) db 0    ; Fill the file with 0's
dw 0AA55h
```

This is the program to be loaded after bootstrap program is loaded.

```
; PROG.ASM

        mov ah, 9
        mov al, '='
        mov bx, 7
        mov cx, 10
        int 10h

hang:
        jmp hang
```

This program creates a disk image file that contains both the bootstrap and the small loadable program.

```
; IMAGE.ASM
; Disk image

%include 'boot.asm'
%include 'prog.asm'
```

To compile the bootstrap, use this command:

nasm image.asm -o image.bin

If we want to test the bootstrap, we must first put it on the first sector on a floppy disk.

We can for example use 'dd' or 'rawrite'. When the bootstrap is on the floppy, test it by restarting our computer with the floppy inserted. The computer should hang after giving "=====".

How to write into a floopy:

dd if=image.bin of=/dev/fd0

rawrite image.bin a:

6.7 Debugging a C Program with functions in Assembly

Some tomes, we may ned to debug programs which uses a mixture of c and assembly. In this section we explained the same.

Compile the programs (*candassembly.c, DBL.s* discussed above with -g option.

```
gcc -g candassembly.c DBL.s
gdb -q a.out
```

```
Using host libthread_db library "/lib/tls/libthread_db.so.1".
   (gdb) b DBL
Breakpoint 1 at 0x80483ac: file DBL.s, line 3.
   (gdb) l
        1       #include<stdio.h>
        2       main()
        3       {
        4
        5       int i=DBL(11);
        6       printf("%d\n", i);
        7       }
        8
        (gdb) r
```

```
Starting program: /root/gdb/a.out

Breakpoint 1, DBL () at DBL.s:3

    3           movl  4(%esp),  %eax
Current language:  auto; currently asm
(gdb) info registers
eax         0x10    16
ecx         0x1     1
edx         0x60c19c 6341020
ebx         0x609ff4 6332404
esp         0xfefff79c      0xfefff79c
ebp         0xfefff7c8      0xfefff7c8
esi         0xfefff854      -16779180
edi         0xfefff7e0      -16779296
eip         0x80483ac       0x80483ac
eflags      0x200292 2097810
cs          0x73    115
ss          0x7b    123
ds          0x7b    123
es          0x7b    123
---Type <return> to continue, or q <return> to quit---q
Quit
(gdb) n
4           addl   %eax,   %eax
(gdb) info registers
eax         0xb     11
ecx         0x1     1
edx         0x60c19c 6341020
ebx         0x609ff4 6332404
esp         0xfefff79c      0xfefff79c
ebp         0xfefff7c8      0xfefff7c8
esi         0xfefff854      -16779180
edi         0xfefff7e0      -16779296
eip         0x80483b0       0x80483b0
eflags      0x200392 2098066
cs          0x73    115
ss          0x7b    123
ds          0x7b    123
es          0x7b    123
---Type <return> to continue, or q <return> to quit---q
Quit
(gdb) n
5           ret
(gdb) n
main () at s1.c:6
```

```
6      printf("%d\n", i);
Current language:  auto; currently c
(gdb) n
22
7      }
(gdb) n
0x004fbe33 in __libc_start_main ()
  from /lib/tls/libc.so.6
(gdb) q
```

Here, after starting the gdb, we have set a break point at symbol DBL(function name) which we have defined in the assembly file DBL.s. The gdb changes its mode automatically to assembly when it encounters assembly source code and also it reverses to C mode soon after the control returns from assembly code. We can observe the same in the above screen shot of the gdb session.

6.8 Conclusions

This chapter describes how assembly programming to be done in Linux. Also, it emphasizes how assembly instructions can be intermixed with C and C++ languages. Also, it describes about optimizing the code size of the machine language files by using assembly instructions. How a assembly language can be loaded into Linux kernel is described with a lucid example. A separate section on "How from write small size programs is also included". At the end, a section on bootstrap program explains about how to develop OS's using assembly.

7 Libraries

7.1 Introduction

Use of libraries became natural practice in SW development since early 1970's. Popular mathematical function libraries such as NAG[1], IMSL[2], SAS, SAP etc are in wide use in scientific community since 30 years. Libraries such as NAG, EISPACK, LINPACK (procedures for solving Linear system of Equations), etc., are used for benchmarking of processors both parallel and serial. Statistical Package for Social Sciences (SPSS) is in wide use in psychology, sociology. MATLAB[3] (which is derived from NAG) contains extensive set of functions for matrix operations, boundary value problems, signal processing problems such as Fast Fourier Transform, etc.,. EISPACK contains functions for eigen value problems. All of them contains a set of readymade functions/subroutines (which are often compiled) which can be used (called) by any programmer. Thus, SW development, testing, reusability improves. In the next chapter, we have discussed about lex and yacc libraries that are widely used for compiler, file filter's development.

To give little more strength to our discussion, we want to remind that the **scanf()**, **printf()** statements used in C language for I/O operations are functions of C standard library which is called as **libc**. Also, for example, while using MS Windows we may often get an error message **"So and So DLL file is needed for an application and if we remove the same that application will not run in future"**. Here, DLL indicates dynamic link library. Thus, many current day applications use libraries.

Evidently, there are two types of libraries are available; namingly function libraries and class libraries. Also, libraries can be classified as static and dynamic. After the compilation, linker extracts the machine language codes of the functions used in our program from the respective libraries and attaches to our compiler file in the case of static linking. (See chapter 2) Where as in the case dynamic linking, actual linking is done while the program is running. We shall explain these concepts in detail in the forth coming sections.

A Unix object library is also a group of compiled files combined into a single library file. Note the distinction between a Unix "object file" and the concept of an **object** under object-oriented programming; there is no connection between the two. The term "object" has been used to refer to unlinked compiled code under Unix since long before OOP became widely known. Unix object files are created using the "-c" parameter of the standard C compiler, **cc**, and the HP C++ compiler, **CC**, as well. The standard Unix archiving command, **ar**, is used to combine and maintain these files. The standard naming scheme for these libraries is **libXXX.a**, where **XXX** is a brief descriptive string. For example, the system library of math functions is called **libm.a**. The Athena Widget Library for X Windows is called **libXaw.a**.

By convention, most Unix system libraries are stored in **/usr/lib**. Some libraries may also exist in **/lib** and in **/usr/local/lib**, depending on the version of Unix and the system administrator's needs. In contrast, a developer's application-specific libraries may be placed anywhere on the file system. The files contained in Unix object libraries have been compiled, but have not yet been linked. These object files usually have the extension ".o" to indicate this state. During the final phase of building an application, the C compiler or system linker is used to link against the object library. This makes building an application with an object library considerably faster than compiling the separate routines down from source. Object libraries are useful for other reasons as well. They

---

[1] Numerical Algorithms Group, USA

[2] IMSL Inc, USA

[3] The MathWorks, Inc.,

provide a mechanism for combining multiple related functions. Libraries simplify code re-use, providing ready access to debugged routines. A standard header file is usually provided for each object library to provide prototypes for library functions. This allows the compiler to verify correct function parameter types for each library call.

7.1.1 Shared (Dynamic) vs Static libraries

As discussed earlier, the last stage of building a program is to `link' it; i.e, to join all the pieces of it together and see what is missing. When using a static library, the linker finds the bits that the program modules need, and physically copies them into the executable output file that it generates.

For shared libraries, it doesn't copy the code of functions from libraries, instead it leaves a note in the output saying `when this program is run, it will first have to load this library'. Obviously shared libraries tend to make for smaller executables; they also use less memory and mean that less disk space is used They allow a commonly-used library to be linked such that it can be loaded into memory, and made available to other programs without having to have its compiled object code combined with the executable program. A reference table is placed in the executable instead, which the system dynamic loader, can use to find the shared library functions. Since the shared library is already memory resident, the application loads and runs faster.

The default behavior of Linux is to link shared if it can find the shared libraries, static otherwise. If we are getting static binaries when we want shared, check that the shared library files (*.sa for a.out, *.so for ELF) are where they should be, and are readable or not.

On Linux, static libraries have names like **libname.a**, while shared libraries are called **libname.so.x.y** where x.y is some form of version number. For example, in the shared library **libGL.so.1.2**, the "1" indicates major revision 1 and "2" indicates minor revision. All libraries with the same major revision number should extend same API to programmers of that library – that is, if you can compile your code against all libraries releases whose major release number is "1" without changing your code. Changes in major number indicate a change in the external interface of API. Whereas, the minor number indicates bug fixes.

Shared libraries often also have links pointing to them, which are important, and (on a.out configurations) associated .sa files. The standard libraries come in both shared and static formats.

We can find out what shared libraries a program requires by using ldd (List Dynamic Dependencies) command. For example:

```
ldd /usr/bin/lynx

   libncursesw.so.5 => /usr/lib/libncursesw.so.5 (0x0064d000)
   libssl.so.4 => /lib/libssl.so.4 (0x00d1a000)
   libcrypto.so.4 => /lib/libcrypto.so.4 (0x00ace000)
   libc.so.6 => /lib/tls/libc.so.6 (0x004e7000)
   libz.so.1 => /usr/lib/libz.so.1 (0x0063b000)
   libgssapi_krb5.so.2 => /usr/lib/libgssapi_krb5.so.2 (0x00ab8000)
   libkrb5.so.3 => /usr/lib/libkrb5.so.3 (0x00a2e000)
   libcom_err.so.2 => /lib/libcom_err.so.2 (0x00a11000)
   libk5crypto.so.3 => /usr/lib/libk5crypto.so.3 (0x00a95000)
   libresolv.so.2 => /lib/libresolv.so.2 (0x0075e000)
   libdl.so.2 => /lib/libdl.so.2 (0x00635000)
   /lib/ld-linux.so.2 (0x004ca000)
```

This shows that on my system the WWW browser `lynx' depends on the presence of **libc.so.5** (the C library) and **libncurses.so.1** (used for terminal control). If a program has no dependencies, ldd will say `statically linked' or `statically linked (ELF)'.

Building shared libraries requires system-specific tools, and are not very portable across different Unix platforms. For this reason, using them for non-system level applications is a serious undertaking. The process of building and maintaining shared libraries is more complex, but for frequently used, system-wide applications, the overhead is worth the trouble.

7.1.2 Unix ANSI C Object Library & Header File Organization

Standard Unix libraries, such as the math library **libm.a**, require one or more standard header files (in /usr/include) along with the object files in the library itself.

The header files for ANSI C libraries contain, in general, three categories of items that will need to be public, or visible to user programs. These items are

- Precompiler definitions, including constants and macros
- Standard data structures, such as structs and unions
- Library function prototypes

These elements provide the interface for correctly accessing the object libraries' functions. Precompiler macros, for instance, replace library functions for some simple, frequently used routines; **getc()** and **putc()** are two examples. Common structures provide consistent means of handling data formats that are standard to the Unix operating system. For example, struct **tm** in **time.h** is a complete means of referencing time under Unix.

Function prototypes are an important way to ensure that library functions are being correctly referenced, under ANSI C. The ability of modern compilers to flag errors in function parameters saves an enormous amount of time spent on debugging.

Header files must be well documented to be useful. Standard Unix libraries are documented in the man pages under category #3, User Library Functions. For individual application libraries, the method of documentation usually is comprised of the library specification, combined with consistent and adequate comments in the header files themselves.

The object library code for Unix standard libraries is usually proprietary, and is unavailable to the application developer. This code is considered private in scope, and contains the body code for the functions described in the header file(s) for the library. Since standardized means of accessing the library functions are provided and well documented, there is no need to reference the internal code in these libraries.

7.1.3 Linking An Object Library to an Application

The parameters and syntax that are used to link Unix object libraries to applications have become standardized. With cc or gcc command "-l" option is used to specify each individual object library; "-L" is used to specify the pathnames on which to search for object libraries. We have discussed about this in the chapter on "**C/C++ Compilers**" with lucid example.

In Unix/Linux, library names are normally abbreviated, when specified to the compiler, using the "-l" parameter. This differs from how source and object file names are provided. Since object library names have the format "libXXX.a", the beginning "lib" and the final ".a" are stripped from the library name in the parameter specification.

For example, to link the standard math library **/lib/libm.a** to our program, we need only specify "-lm" in the compile/link command. The compiler uses this information to build the library name, and links it in.

As mentioned previously, the paths to standard system libraries are built into the compiler and do not need to be explicitly stated (in some version of Linux such as Redhat 10, or Fedora this is true). Application specific library pathnames, however, need to be specified using the "-L" parameter, one for each pathname.

The path for each application specific library must be placed prior to the "-l" parameter specifying the library itself. The library path specification need only be given once; the linker will thereafter search the specified path for each subsequent library in the compile/link command.

A complete specification for an example application compile & link, using the Unix math library and our example object library (**libtest.a**, whose creation is explained later), would be

gcc -o test test.c –lm -ltest

Here, we are assuming that library file libtest.a in the directories such as /lib, /usr/lib or /usr/local/lib where linker generally checks for the library files.

For the sake of completeness, it's necessary to mention that this clever arrangement for linked library specification can be ignored, if one uses the entire path and library filename in the "-l" specification. If a single library in a nonstandard location is needed, it can be specified using, for example:

gcc -g -o test test.c -lm /usr/local/lib/libtest.a

If there are several libraries to include, this method can make builds difficult to write. Thus, all the libraries are kept in a directory and linker is designed to check for them in those directories when we specify the library to link in a shorthand notation such as "-lm" in the command line during compilation.

7.2 How to Create a Static Object Library

As stated above, **ar**, the standard Unix archiving command, is routinely used to create Unix object libraries. The resulting file, which ends in ".a", can therefore be referred to as an **archive**; however, the term library is recommended as it is more descriptive for our purposes. Archive files created by **ar** can contain any type of file, including text and executable files; in contrast, object libraries contain only compiled object files.

A minimal set of options available with ar command is described below.

c	create a new library
q	add the named file to the end of the archive
r	replace a named archive/library member
t	print a table of archive contents

The syntax for building a library from a group of object files is

ar r <library file> <list of object files>

Example 1

Consider the following files having one function in each.

File a.c

```
void f()
{
printf("Hello\n");
}
```

File b.c

```
void ff()
{
printf("How are you\n");
}
```

File d.c

```
void fff()
{
printf("My Dear\n");
}
```

First create object files for each of the individual files. That is, execute the following commands.

```
gcc –c  a.c
gcc –c  b.c
gcc –c  d.c
```

Now, to create library, execute the following command(s).

```
ar crs libtest.a  a.o  b.o  d.o
            or
ar cr libtest.a  a.o  b.o  d.o
```

These library files has to be kept in the directories such as /lib, /usr/lib where linker checks for the libraries during the execution of gcc command. We can say that this is commissioning of the library!!.

Note: some versions of Unix require an additional step to prepare an object library, which is building a symbol table. This operation requires the **ranlib** utility. Under some Unix's, including HP-UX, Linux, **ar** builds the symbol table automatically. In the first ar command we have used 's' option to indicate that index table also to be created such that during linking phase, linker's task becomes easy.

Note:The Unix make utility has built-in rules that allow convenient building and maintaining of object libraries. **ar** can update an individual object file "on the fly", without having to rebuild the entire library. For this reason, updating an object library is usually as simple as editing a particular source file and typing "make". The rest is done automatically, with the help of an appropriately written Makefile. This will be discussed later in the chapter on "make".

7.2.1 Finding Out What's Inside an Object Library

The command **ar** has several options, and one of them, the "t" parameter, tells it to print a table of contents for the archive. For our example, typing "**ar t libtest.a**" would provide this result:

```
a.o
b.o
d.o
```

It is possible to list the symbols used by the files inside our library using the Unix **nm** (for "name symbols") command. When one types

nm libXXX.a

each object file within the library is shown, followed by a list of the symbols within the object file.

nm may also be used to examine the symbol tables of individual object files and executable programs. Keep in mind that for this to work, the "-g" parameter of the compiler must be used to include the symbolic information. In addition, if **strip** is used to remove the symbol table from an executable program, **nm** will no longer be able to list it's contents.

nm library name should list all the symbols that library name has references to. It works on both static and shared libraries. Suppose that we want to know where sqrt() is defined: we might execute:

```
nm /usr/lib/libm.so |grep sqrt
0000ab90  W  sqrt
00019940  W sqrtl
0000c7c0  t __csqrtf
```

The `W' stands for `weak', which means that the symbol is defined, but in such a way that It can be overridden by another definition in a different library. A straightforward `normal' definition (such as the one for tcgetpgrp) is marked by a `T'. Similarly, we may see U also, which stands for `undefined' --- it shows that the library uses but does not define it.

7.2.2 Linking with Created Library

All the prototypes of the functions in the library can be kept in a file and preferably give an extension "h". For example, for the above libtest.a library, we have created the file ("**a.h**") as:

```
void f();
void ff();
void fff();
```

Now, write a program which uses the above functions from the library.

Example 2

File mm.c

```
#include<stdio.h>
#include "a.h"
int main()
{
f();
ff();
fff();
}
```

To create executable file:

```
gcc -o aa mm.c libtest.a
```

To run:

```
./aa
```

Now, modify the printf statement in the file "a.c" to "Hello 1" and run the following command.

```
gcc –o aa mm.c a.c libtest.a
./aa
```

Run the program and check up the output. We will get "Hello 1" from the program. Linker tries to extract function definitions from the libraries only when the function definition is not found in any of the source files specified along the command line to the compiler. Thus, the f() is used from the modified file "a.c". Not from the library file libtest.a.

However, if we run the following command we will get an error multiple definition of function 'f'.

```
gcc –o aa mm.c libtest.a a.c
```

If we are able to place "a.h" file in /usr/include (or other directories where linker checks for the directories) and "libtest.a" in "/lib" (or other directories where linker checks for the directories). Then, we can modify the above program "mm.c" to place file "a.h" in between '<' and '>' such that compiler will check for that file in standard directories.

```
gcc –o aa mm.c -ltest
```

If we have kept "a.h" file in some directory say /home/rao and "libtest.a" in /home/xyz, then we can run the following command to compile the above program "mm.c".

```
gcc –o aa mm.c -I /home/rao  -L /home/xyz -ltest
```

The compiler checks for the library file in the given directory with –L option and then checks for standard directories.

7.2.3 Updating an Object Library

What do we do if we need to change just one of the object files within a library? ar makes this straightforward. The same parameter used to build the library, "r", also has the function of replacing an object file in an archive with a new version.

```
ar r libtest.a d.o
```

would remove the existing object file d.**o** from the library, and insert an object file with the same name from the current working directory. At the same time, the library's symbol table is rebuilt to reflect any changes.

7.2.4 Removing and Extracting Object Files from a Library

Occasionally it is useful to remove an object file from a library. This is necessary when one of the internal files' functions are replaced by those in another file, or when an object file must be renamed. ar performs this operation using the "d" parameter. Typing

```
ar d libtest.a d.o
```

would delete the d.**o** object file from the library.

It is unlikely that we will have need to extract an object file from a library, but for completeness' sake, the "x" parameter provides this ability. Typing

```
ar x libtest.a d.o
```

will extract a copy of d.o into the current directory.

Note that the object file will continue to exist inside the library. Also note that if a file already existed with the same name in the current directory, it could be silently overwritten -- unless the user's shell is set to warn of this condition.

7.3 How to Create a Shared Object Library

As mentioned earlier, shared libraries are libraries that are loaded by programs when they start to run. When a shared library is installed properly, all programs that start afterwards automatically use the new shared library. It's actually much more flexible and sophisticated than this, because the approach used by Linux permits us to:

- update libraries and still support programs that want to use older, non-backward-compatible versions of those libraries;
- override specific libraries or even specific functions in a library when executing a particular program.
- do all this while programs are running using existing libraries.

Position Independent Code is used while creating shared object libraries. PIC code differs from traditional code in the method it will perform access to function code and data objects/variables through an indirect accessing table. This table is called the "Global Offset Table" because it contains the addresses of code functions and data objects exported by a shared library.

The dynamic loader modifies the GOT slots to resemble the current memory address for every exported symbol in the library. When the dynamic loader has completed, the GOT contains full absolute addresses for each symbol reference constructed from the load address (PT_LOAD) of the shared library that contains these symbols plus their offset inside this shared library.

7.3.1 Using PIC For Building Shared Libraries

Besides for using position independent executables, the natural reason for using "-fPIC" (position independent code) option with GCC is the use in shared dynamic libraries. This makes the overall footprint of all dynamically linked ELF executables on the system as small as possible, while it also prevents possible code duplication and actively reduces requirements on memory and file system.

A unique characteristic of a typical shared library is that it can be located anywhere in the process memory layout. Because of this, the contents of the shared library are not accessed directly but via clearly exported definitions in symbol tables during building. Today, shared libraries can be easily implemented by incorporating this key advantage of the ELF standard. Making libraries larger, smaller or moving around functions in the library is very easy as long as the symbol table to access the functions does not change.

During building, The linker is only responsible for setting up exported symbols of the library in question. Telling the object code that it needs to be position independent is the task of the preprocessor and the compiler. Here, the role of the Makefiles and the CFLAGS/LDFLAGS feeding the compiler with instructions becomes visible. The preprocessor is adding special definitions ("__PIC__" "__pic__") and the compiler is using "-fPIC" or "-fpic" depending on the data access model. Hopefully, when there is no PIC unaware assembler in the source code, these flags are generating the object code needed for position independence. The object code needs to be generated PIC for successfully opening the doors to position independent relocation of the library, created from the PIC .o relocatable objects.

Relocations in the 'text' segment of shared libraries used by dynamically linked executables

The performance penalty of text relocations is the reason that every shared library object code should be generated with -fPIC or -fpic, depending on the addressing range of the data that is used. Otherwise the library is considered not "clean".

A text relocation is a memory address in the "LOAD READ-EXECUTE" text segment of a shared library where text segment means the segment that contains the program code. Such a nonPIC text segment often contains large amounts of memory addresses that need to be "patched" (manipulated, modified, corrected) with the runtime location of functions and data. This is performed by the dynamic loader (ld.so in glibc) during startup of the dynamically linked executable and invocation of these libraries in the process space. The reason that the dynamic loader needs to spend so much time "patching" memory addresses (relocations) was stated above: a unique characteristic of a typical shared library is that it can be located anywhere in the process memory layout.

So the dynamic loader is the key to the "located anywhere" functionality: it recognizes and reorganizes the memory addresses that need to be refurbished and applies the change to these locations. This means that the dynamic loader will be responsible for relocating the memory address. For example, in a non-PIC compiled **libmpeg3** library there are roughly 6000 memory locations left inside the shared library to point to some 200-300 functions and data referred by the instructions.

7.3.2 Using prelink and LD_BIND_NOW

Using prelink somehow mitigates the performance-intensive relocation process to a one-time operation: the relocation is satisfied and prematurely resolved/patched inside the binaries and the nonPIC shared libraries. This can be reached with using a program like prelink that is working on the actual files and modifying the relocations and GOT slots in the executables and libraries directly, thus saving the dynamic loader a lot of work during actually starting and running the executable. While dealing with executables, note that prelink inserts a "hint" into the PT_LOAD segment of every shared library to make the kernel load it at the expected address.

Bear in mind that not all relocations are resolved at startup time. When LD_BIND_NOW is not used, the lazy binding for libraries somehow tries to minimize the overhead to a more timely fashion by only relocating symbols at their first invocation during program flow. The environment variable LD_BIND_NOW (and the ld switch "-z now") tries to address this problem for slow machines by moving all needed relocations to be done at startup of a binary, invoking much slower startup times but later making the binary run more fluently on slower machines because relocations are satisfied now. But we should be careful and know that using LD_BIND_NOW is not recommended on machines where responsiveness is an issue, clicking on an icon in KDE or GNOME and waiting 20 seconds for evolution to start is sometimes unacceptable by users. Thus, in doubt, use prelink!

7.3.3 More about negative side effects of text relocations in shared libraries

There are two drawbacks of nonPIC shared libraries currently.

There is a moderate security risk on nonPIC libraries containing text relocations. The TEXT pages for shared libraries cannot be marked READONLY by the kernel starting the binary and mapping in ELF segments and libraries.

There is also a memory overhead and performance penalty: data and code cannot be shared amongst processes via COW. COW means "copy on write", this uses the same read-only memory pages for all instances of the same binary and for all processes referring to the same used libraries. Using COW, read-only memory pages for shared libraries and executables need not to be recreated for new processes in their memory until they are about to be changed by the new process, like for patching in text relocations by the dynamic loader, this is all implemented transparently in the virtual memory management of the Linux kernel.

7.3.4 So, why not use -fPIC building as default for all applications?

So why not compile all applications with -fPIC if it has so much advantages? The impact of "-fPIC" on certain architectures like AMD64 can be tolerated due to the true PIC-oriented data and code addressing scheme and is even necessary on several (considered broken) architectures that refuse to build certain applications without -fPIC (errors with nonPIC relocation types on PARISC). There is only one official method to add flags like "-fPIC" to builds: using the flag-o-matic and "append-flags". However, it is not a good idea to enable "-fPIC" in global CFLAGS or create builds that automatically add the "-fPIC" flag independent of the situation and architecture it is applied. There are people referring to a noticeable performance penalty when running executables containing position independent code compared to executables incorporating normally compiled object code.

Normally, the setup of the PIC register takes about three assembler commands per function that is entered and additional overhead of 1-2 assembler commands per accessed symbol (code function or data object). Thus, we have the inverted situation for normal executables that the invocation of the "-fPIC" flag is doing the exact opposite like in shared libraries. Instead of giving us speed for low memory profile by saving memory via COW and making text relocations unnecessary, the additional overhead in the addressing mode is imposing a speed penalty on our executable.

Why does a normal dynamically linked executable (not position independent shared executable) need no text relocations and PIC addressing? Because the kernel (in a normal world) always moves it to the same location in process memory when started, making it unnecessary for the dynamic loader to address any TEXT relocations in the normal executable: because there are none! We have learned that only shared libraries are located at a given, freely chosen, address space in the process memory of the dynamically linked executable. So, in the text segment of a "fixed load location" normal executable there are no TEXT segment relocations because all addresses are at the same location in memory during every invocation of the program. The addressing of data and functions inside the executable are provided via relative and absolute relocations in a common used set of platform-dependent, performance oriented assembler commands.

Direct non-PIC-aware addressing is always cheaper (read: faster) than PIC addressing. For example the RISC (Reduced Instruction Set) architectures sparc, ppc and hppa sometimes use more than one assembler command issuing several more opcodes to do what x86 does with a single variable length assembler command, loading a full 32-Bit address for example. Only the AMD64 seems to support some kind of "emulation" mode where it does not seem to make a difference if PIC or normal addressing is used for referring code functions and data to access.

For normal executables that are dynamically linked to these shared libraries, the executables themselves need not to be using -fPIC for building the object code they consist of. These executables simply do not need the PIC addressing mode for their functions and data and will use the PLT (Process Linkage Table) and the GOT (Global Offset Table) anyway for addressing external data in shared libraries.

7.3.5 Creating shared library

Here, first each source file has to be compiled with –fPIC option. With the help of –shared option with gcc, shared library is created as shown below.

Example 3

```
gcc –c –fPIC a.c
gcc –c –fPIC b.c
gcc –c –fPIC d.c

gcc –shared  -fPIC –o libtest.so a.o b.o d.o
```

We assume the same content for the "mm.c" file and is given as:

```
#include<stdio.h>
#include "a.h"
int main()
{
 f();
ff();
fff();
}
```

```
gcc –o bb mm.c  libtest.so
```

The above command creates executable file "bb", but when we try to execute the same we will get an error message such as:

bb: error while loading shared libraries:libtest.so: can not open shared object file:No such file or directory.

This indicates that the dynamic loader is unable to load the code of the functions used in our program during run time as it is unable to locate the library file.

However, If we run the following command, it creates the executable file "bb" and it runs also.

```
gcc –o bb mm.c ./libtest.so

./bb
```

When we specify ./libtest.a (i.e with location details of the library file) the dynamic loader checks for the shared library in the current working directory. To strengthen our understanding, try to run this program from some other directory. For example, if I assume you are in the directory (EX2) where the file "bb" is located and go back one directory up-wards and try to run the same.

```
cd ..
EX2/bb
```

Now also you will get the same error message as above as dynamic loader is unable to locate the required library file.

Here also, if we keep the header file "a.h" in standard directories such as /usr/include and libtest.so in /lib, then we can include "a.h" file in a normal way (i.e between < and >) in C language programs and also we can inform the compiler to include library in normal manner. That is, the following command can be also used to create the executable file.

```
gcc –o bb mm.c -ltest
```

Usually the gcc compiler uses shared libraries. To support this carry out the following simple exercise. Modify the printf statement of the file "a.c" to have "Hello1" instead of "Hello" and compile the "a.c" file and recreate the shared library libtest.so. That is, run the following commands.

```
gcc –c –fPIC a.c
gcc –shared –fPIC libtest.so a.o b.o d.o
```

Now, move libtest.a and libtest.so to /lib directory. Also, make sure that "a.h" is in /usr/include. If we execute the following commands we can find the function f() is taken from libtest.so (i.e we will get the message "Hello1").

```
gcc –o bb mm.c -ltest
./bb
```

Similarly, if we use static option while compiling the file "mm.c", we will get the message "Hello"; which indicates that static library libtest.a is used for. We can check the size differences of the executable files created with and without static option.

```
gcc -static –o bb mm.c -ltest
./bb
```

Now, modify the file "a.c" such that now "Hello2" is placed in the printf statement. Then, compile the file and re-create the shared library libtest.so. Remember that previous version of the libtest.so is in /lib directory. Now, execute the following commands.

```
gcc -o bb mm.c  libtest.so
./bb
```

We will get "Hello1" not the "Hello2" message. This indicates that the function body f() is taken from the library file libtest.so which is available in /lib directory. Now, copy libtest.so to /lib and run the "bb" program; we will get "Hello2" message.

Now, modify the file "a.c" such that now "Hello3" is placed in the printf statement. Then, compile the file "a.c" and re-create the shared library libtest.so. Now, copy this library file to /usr/include. Remember that previous version of the libtest.so is in /lib directory. Now, execute the following commands.

```
gcc -o bb mm.c  libtest.so
./bb
```

We will get "Hello3" not the "Hello2" message. This indicates that the function body f() is taken from the library file libtest.so which is available in /usr/lib directory. That is, the dynamic linker is first checking in /usr/lib and then /lib for the shared libraries. This may be different in your machine!!!. **On some implementations of dynamic loaders, the latest .so file is used independent of the their locations**.

Now, modify the file "a.c" such that now "Hello4" is placed in the printf statement. Then, compile the file "a.c" and re-create the shared library libtest.so. Remember, previous versions of libtest.so are available in /usr/lib and /lib.

Now, set the value of the environment variable LD_LIBRARY_PATH as the directory in which recent libtest.so is located and export the environment variable. That is run the following commands.

```
LD_LIBRARY_PATH=/root/libraries/EX2
export LD_LIBRARY_PATH
gcc -o bb mm.c  -ltest
./bb
```

We will get "Hello4". This indicates that the function body f() is taken from the library file libtest.so which is available in /root/libraries/EX2 directory. That is, the dynamic linker is first checking in /root/libraries/EX2 and then in /usr/lib, /lib for the shared libraries. This may be different in your machine!!!.

Now, undefined the environment variable and run the above program "bb" (you don't required to recompile it). We will not get "Hello4" message. That is run the following sequence of commands.

```
LD_LIBRARY_PATH=
./bb
```

If one wants to extend the set of directories searched one should add the paths to these directories to the LD_LIBRARY_PATH environment variable.

Also, It should be understood that libraries load in the order in which they were linked, thus for the following command:

gcc mysource.c -lmy1 -lmy2 -lmy3 ...

The dynamic linker loads the libraries in the order libmy1.so, libmy2.so, libmy3.so, etc. If a shared library includes additional library dependencies, those libraries are appended to the end of the library list during loading. For example, if the library libmy2.so depends on an additional library libmy4.so, that library loads after all the other libraries on the link line (in our example after libmy3.so). The load process guarantees that no library is ever loaded more than once with previously loaded copies being used when a library is repeated

7.3.6 soname

Every shared library has a special name called the ``soname''. The soname has the prefix ``lib'', the name of the library, the phrase ``.so'', followed by a period and a version number that is incremented whenever the interface changes (as a special exception, the lowest-level C libraries don't start with ``lib''). A fully-qualified soname includes as a prefix the directory it's in; on a working system a fully-qualified soname is simply a symbolic link to the shared library's ``real name''.

Every shared library also has a ``real name'', which is the filename containing the actual library code. The real name adds to the soname a period, a minor number, another period, and the release number. The last period and release number are optional. The minor number and release number support configuration control by letting we know exactly what version(s) of the library are installed. Note that these numbers might not be the same as the numbers used to describe the library in documentation, although that does make things easier.

In addition, there's the name that the compiler uses when requesting a library, (I'll call it the ``linker name''), which is simply the soname without any version number.

The key to managing shared libraries is the separation of these names. Programs, when they internally list the shared libraries they need, should only list the soname they need. Conversely, when we create a shared library, we only create the library with a specific filename (with more detailed version information). When we install a new version of a library, we install it in one of a few special directories and then run the program ldconfig(8). ldconfig examines the existing files and creates the sonames as symbolic links to the real names, as well as setting up the cache file /etc/ld.so.cache (described in a moment).

ldconfig doesn't set up the linker names; typically this is done during library installation, and the linker name is simply created as a symbolic link to the ``latest'' soname or the latest real name. We would recommend having the linker name be a symbolic link to the soname, since in most cases if we update the library we would like to automatically use it when linking. ldconfig makes no assumptions about what we want programs to link to, so installers must specifically modify symbolic links to update what the linker will use for a library.

Thus, /usr/lib/libreadline.so.3 is a fully-qualified soname, which ldconfig would set to be a symbolic link to some realname like /usr/lib/libreadline.so.3.0. There should also be a linker name, /usr/lib/libreadline.so which could be a symbolic link referring to /usr/lib/libreadline.so.3.

A properly built shared object (in ELF format, which is the format GNU/Linux uses) will have a soname built into it. This is a name that is specified at the library's build-time, to

GCC's link editor (ld), with the -soname option. We can inspect any sensibly-built library's soname like so:

objdump -p /usr/X11R6/lib/libGL.so.1.2 | grep SONAME

The above command displays, the following output.

SONAME libGL.so.1

In this case, libGL.so.1.2's soname is "libGL.so.1". The point of the soname is for the creator of the library to be able to provide version compatibility information to the system. In this case, libGL.so.1.2's soname says that libGL.so.1.2 is compatible with any program that says it needs libGL.so.1.

Programs know what libs they need to link to at runtime -- they know the soname's they want. When an OpenGL program starts up and asks the system for libGL.so.1, the system delivers libGL.so.1.2. (Recall, this is on my system. Our system may (I would hope :) have a more recent version of OpenGL installed.) :

For example, we can also create our sample library and assign a soname for it.

gcc –shared –fPIC –Wl,-soname="libtest.so.1.1" –o libtest.so a.o b.o d.o

Run the following command to check the soname of the created library.

objdump -p libtest.so.1.1 | grep SONAME

We will get result as:

SONAME libtest.so.1.1

7.3.7 ldconfig

With the help of ldconfig command we can configure dynamic linkers to have run time bindings such as:

1. where it has to check for the shared libraries.
2. to cache the most recently used shared libraries (in ld.so.cache), etc.,.

When we run the ldconfig command the following actions takes place.

1. It searches through /lib, /usr/lib and all the directories listed in /etc/ld..so.conf for shared libraries.
2. For all the libraries in the directories listed in ld.so.conf, it takes note of their sonames.
3. It updates /etc/ld.so.cache with this information.

4. Using ld.so.cache it creates symlinks: one pointing from the soname named symlink to the actual lib and the other pointing from the library base name to the actual library.

The following command will display the list of directories and candidate libraries stored in the current cache.

ldconfig -p

The following command can be used to inform the ldconfig about the location of shared libraries.

ldconfig -n directory_with_shared_libraries

The following command will display the list of directories as ldconfig is scanned. Also, cache will be rebuild.

ldconfig -v

We can now check that libtest.so is also scanned by running the following command.

ldconfig –p|grep libtest

It is common that when we install a software it may place it's shared objects in different directories. Once the program is installed, the install script will add the location of the .so files to 'ld.so.conf' and rerun 'ldconfig' to create a fresh 'ld.so.cache'. If we have just installed some new package and it refuse to run, then try adding the subdirectories to 'ld.co.conf' and rerun 'ldconfig'. It just might work!!!.

7.3.8 Loading shared libs at runtime

When we run a program, a series of events happen culminating in the application being loaded into memory as well as any shared objects the program needs which weren't already loaded. Here's a walkthrough of those events:

- We execute the program.
- The OS's dynamic linker, ld.so checks the executable to see which shared libs it needs, thus discovering the sonames of the needed libs.
- With sonames in-hand, ld.so consults ld.so.cache to find out the locations of the shared ib files it needs to load into memory.
- ld.so loads the required libs, and then the program is allowed to execute.

Now, modify the /etc/ld.so.conf such that the directory of the file libtest.so.1.1 is the first entry. Now run ldconfig command such that it updates ld.so.cache. Please make sure that no version of libtest.so file is not seen in /lib or /usr/lib. Now compile out program with of the following commands and run the same as follows.

gcc –o bb mm.c libtest.so

or

gcc –o bb mm.c –L /root/libraries/EX2 -ltest

./bb

Now the dynamic linker will check in the directory /root/libraries/EX2 for the library. Also, to get some more support, run the following command and verify its result.

```
ldd bb
```

Result is:

```
libtest.so.1.1 => /root/libraries/EX2/libtest.so.1.1 (0xf6fde000)
libc.so.6 => /lib/tls/libc.so.6 (0x004e7000)
/lib/ld-linux.so.2 (0x004ca000)
```

Run the following commands and check that what libraries are loaded during the run time.

```
export LD_DEBUG=files
./bb
export LD_DEBUG=libs
./bb
```

Please make sure that this LD_DEBUG to be undefined (execute "LD_DEBUG=" command at the shell prompt); otherwise for every program or command which we start this LD_DEBUG effect will be seen.

Sometimes useful information can be obtained by studying the (huge) output generated by setting the LD_DEBUG environment variable to the value bindings before starting your program.

```
export LD_DEBUG=bindings
./bb
```

The above command gives verbose output. For terseness reasons, only few lines from the same is displayed here. We can find that which file is binded to which library and when it takes place, i.e when which function is called, this binding is taking place.

```
initialize program: ./bb
transferring control: ./bb
binding file ./bb to /root/libraries/EX2/libtest.so.1.1: normal symbol `f'
binding file /root/libraries/EX2/libtest.so.1.1 to /lib/tls/libc.so.6: normal symbol `printf' [GLIBC_2.0]
binding file ./bb to /root/libraries/EX2/libtest.so.1.1: normal symbol `ff'
binding file ./bb to /root/libraries/EX2/libtest.so.1.1: normal symbol `fff'
calling fini: /root/libraries/EX2/libtest.so.1.1 [0]
```

If we want to just override a few functions in a library, but keep the rest of the library, we can enter the names of overriding libraries (.o files) in /etc/ld.so.preload; these ``preloading'' libraries will take precedence over the standard set. This preloading file is typically used for emergency patches; a distribution usually won't include such a file when delivered.

For example, modify the file "a.c" to have "Hello 6" in its printf statement then run the following commands.

```
gcc -c -fPIC a.c
gcc -shared -fPIC -o aa.o a.o
```

Create an entry in the file /etc/ld.so.preload with the file "aa.o" path (say /root/libraries/EX2/aa.o) then run the above program "bb". Now you will get "Hello 6". Please note that in the libtest.so file the function f() is having different printf statement.

The same can be achieved by setting LD_PRELOAD environment variable like the following.

```
export LD_PRELOAD=/root/libraries/EX2/aa.o
./bb
```

On Linux we can even invoke the program loader directly and pass it arguments. For example, the following will use the given PATH instead of the content of the environment variable LD_LIBRARY_PATH, and run the given executable:

```
/lib/ld-linux.so.2 --library-path /root/libraries/EX2 bb
```

Please check whether LD_PRELOAD or /etc/ld.so.preload are defined. Otherwise, result will be different.

A few points worth noting regarding shared libraries.

Don't strip the resulting library, and don't use the compiler option -fomit-frame-pointer unless we really have to. The resulting library will work, but these actions make debuggers mostly useless.

Use -fPIC or -fpic to generate code. Whether to use -fPIC or -fpic to generate code is target-dependent. The -fPIC choice always works, but may produce larger code than -fpic (mnemonic to remember this is that PIC is in a larger case, so it may produce larger amounts of code). Using -fpic option usually generates smaller and faster code, but will have platform-dependent limitations, such as the number of globally visible symbols or the size of the code. The linker will tell you whether it fits when we create the shared library. When in doubt, choose -fPIC, because it always works.

In some cases, the call to gcc to create the object file will also need to include the option ``-Wl,-export-dynamic'', when there are 'reverse dependencies', i.e., a DL library has unresolved symbols that by convention must be defined in the programs that intend to load these libraries. For ``reverse dependencies'' to work, the master program must make its symbols dynamically available.

During development, there's the potential problem of modifying a library that's also used by many other programs -- and we don't want the other programs to use the ``developmental'' library, only a particular application that we are testing against it. One link option we might use is ld's ``rpath'' option, which specifies the runtime library search path of that particular program being compiled. From gcc, we can invoke the rpath option by specifying it this way:

-Wl,-rpath,$(DEFAULT_LIB_INSTALL_PATH)

If we use this option when building the library client program, we don't need to bother with LD_LIBRARY_PATH (described next) other than to ensure it's not conflicting, or using other techniques to hide the library.

7.4 Dynamically Loaded (DL) Libraries

Dynamically loaded (DL) libraries are libraries that are loaded at times other than during the startup of a program. They're particularly useful for implementing plugins or modules, because they permit waiting to load the plugin until it's needed. For example, the Pluggable Authentication Modules (PAM) system uses DL libraries to permit administrators to configure and reconfigure authentication. They're also useful for implementing interpreters that wish to occasionally compile their code into machine code and use the compiled version for efficiency purposes, all without stopping. For example, this approach can be useful in implementing a just-in-time compiler or multi-user dungeon (MUD).

In Linux, DL libraries aren't actually special from the point-of-view of their format; they are built as standard object files or standard shared libraries as discussed above. The main difference is that the libraries aren't automatically loaded at program link time or start-up; instead, there is an API for opening a library, looking up symbols, handling errors, and closing the library. C users will need to include the header file <dlfcn.h> to use this API.

The interface used by Linux is essentially the same as that used in Solaris, which we will call the ``dlopen()'' API. However, this same interface is not supported by all platforms.

7.4.1 dlopen()

The dlopen(3) function opens a library and prepares it for use. In C, its prototype is:

```
void * dlopen(const char *filename, int flag);
```

If filename begins with ``/'' (i.e., it's an absolute path), dlopen() will just try to use it (it won't search for a library). Otherwise, dlopen() will search for the library in the following order:

A colon-separated list of directories in the user's LD_LIBRARY_PATH environment variable.

The list of libraries specified in /etc/ld.so.cache (which is generated from /etc/ld.so.conf).

/lib, followed by /usr/lib. Note the order here; this is the reverse of the order used by the old a.out loader. The old a.out loader, when loading a program, first searched /usr/lib, then /lib (see the man page ld.so(8)). This shouldn't normally matter, since a library should only be in one or the other directory (never both), and different libraries with the same name are a disaster waiting to happen.

In dlopen(), the value of flag must be either RTLD_LAZY, meaning ``resolve undefined symbols as code from the dynamic library is executed'', or RTLD_NOW, meaning ``resolve all undefined symbols before dlopen() returns and fail if this cannot be done''. RTLD_GLOBAL may be optionally or'ed with either value in flag, meaning that the external symbols defined in the library will be made available to subsequently loaded libraries. While we are debugging, we will probably want to use RTLD_NOW; using

RTLD_LAZY can create inscrutable errors if there are unresolved references. Using RTLD_NOW makes opening the library take slightly longer (but it speeds up lookups later); if this causes a user interface problem you can switch to RTLD_LAZY later.

If the libraries depend on each other (e.g., X depends on Y), then first we need to load those things on which others are dependent (in this example, load Y first, and then X).

The return value of dlopen() is a ``handle'' that should be considered an opaque value to be used by the other DL library routines. dlopen() will return NULL if the attempt to load does not succeed, and we need to check for this. If the same library is loaded more than once with dlopen(), the same file handle is returned.

7.4.2 dlerror()

Errors can be reported by calling dlerror(), which returns a string describing the error from the last call to dlopen(), dlsym(), or dlclose(). One oddity is that after calling dlerror(), future calls to dlerror() will return NULL until another error has been encountered.

7.4.3 dlsym()

There's no point in loading a DL library if we can't use it. Thus we have to know how to use it in our program. The main routine for using a DL library is dlsym(3), which looks up the value of a symbol in a given (opened) library. This function is defined as:

```
void * dlsym(void *handle, char *symbol);
```

the handle is the value returned from dlopen, and symbol is a NIL-terminated string. If we can avoid it, don't store the result of dlsym() into a void* pointer, because then we will have to cast it each time we use it (and we will give less information to other people trying to maintain the program).

dlsym() will return a NULL result if the symbol wasn't found. If we know that the symbol could never have the value of NULL or zero, that may be fine, but there's a potential ambiguity otherwise: if we got a NULL, does that mean there is no such symbol, or that NULL is the value of the symbol? The standard solution is to call dlerror() first (to clear any error condition that may have existed), then call dlsym() to request a symbol, then call dlerror() again to see if an error occurred. A code snippet would look like this:

```
dlerror(); /* clear error code */
s = (actual_type) dlsym(handle, symbol_being_searched_for);
if ((err = dlerror()) != NULL) {
 /* handle error, the symbol wasn't found */
} else {
 /* symbol found, its value is in s */
}
```

7.4.4 dlclose()

The converse of dlopen() is dlclose(), which closes a DL library. The dl library maintains link counts for dynamic file handles, so a dynamic library is not actually deallocated until dlclose has been called on it as many times as dlopen has succeeded on it. Thus, it's not a problem for the same program to load the same library multiple times.

Example 4

Here's an example from the man page of dlopen(3). This example loads the math library and prints the cosine of 2.0, and it checks for errors at every step (recommended):

```
#include <stdlib.h>
#include <stdio.h>
#include <dlfcn.h>

int main(int argc, char **argv) {
   void *handle;
   double (*cosine)(double);
   char *error;

   handle = dlopen ("/lib/libm.so.6", RTLD_LAZY);
   if (!handle) {
      fputs (dlerror(), stderr);
      exit(1);
   }

   cosine = dlsym(handle, "cos");
   if ((error = dlerror()) != NULL)  {
      fputs(error, stderr);
      exit(1);
   }

   printf ("%f\n", (*cosine)(2.0));
   dlclose(handle);
}
```

If this program were in a file named "foo.c", you would build the program with the following command:

```
gcc -o foo foo.c -ldl
```

Example 5

In the same manner, we have loaded the function f() from the library libtest.so with the following example.

```
#include <stdlib.h>
#include <stdio.h>
#include <dlfcn.h>

int main(int argc, char **argv) {
   void *handle;
   void (*example)();
```

```
        char *error;

        handle = dlopen ("libtest.so", RTLD_LAZY);
        if (!handle) {
           fputs (dlerror(), stderr);
           exit(1);
        }

        example= dlsym(handle, "f");
        if ((error = dlerror()) != NULL)  {
           fputs(error, stderr);
           exit(1);
        }

         (*example)();
        dlclose(handle);
    }
```

7.5 Unix C++ Class Library & Header Organization

Unix C++ class library header files contain, primarily, C++ class definitions. These class definitions have various public definitions needed by applications developers. Some of these elements are

- Public Member Function Prototypes
- Inline Member Function Definitions
- Virtual Member Function Definitions
- Public Enumerated Type Definitions

With the exception of small inline member function definitions, the majority of the member functions are defined in the separately compiled object library code. Since the standard C++ header files use full OOP data hiding, there is no question of access to class library internal variables. Use of the well-defined standard class library interfaces is therefore required.

Many C++ class library functions use the ANSI C library functions internally. Since C++ is "downwardly compatible" with ANSI C, it makes sense to use the predefined and well-tested functions in the standard libraries, when the need arises. For this reason several of the C++ class library headers include, within themselves, ANSI C standard Unix library headers.

7.5.1 C++ Class Libraries

When C++ Class Libraries are built for Unix systems, object libraries are how they are stored. Our HP-UX standard C++ class library is stored as **/usr/lib/libC.a**. This library contains object modules that contain the **iostream** and **fstream** classes, among others. This library is linked to a C++ program by default, much as **/lib/libc.a** (the standard C library) is linked to an ANSI C program whenever one is compiled.

For example, the **iostream** class library header is **/usr/include/c++/3.3.4/iostream.h**. This path is searched automatically when the header file is included between "<" and ">" brackets in the **#include** precompiler statement; therefore

```
#include <iostream.h>
```

is all that's required for the compiler to find the header file.

Header files for application-specific C++ class libraries may be placed anywhere on the file system; if this is done, the "-I" parameter will be needed to specify the path to the include files.

Note that while header files are not directly related to the concept of a Unix object library, in practice, it is difficult to discuss one without referring to the other. Header files are essential in that they provide the information necessary to interface with an object library.

7.6 Libtool: An Automatic Library Development Tool

If a source code package developer wanted to take advantage of the power of shared libraries, he needed to write custom support code for each platform on which his package ran. He also had to design a configuration interface so that the package installer could choose what sort of libraries were built.

GNU Libtool simplifies the developer's job by encapsulating both the platform-specific dependencies, and the user interface, in a single script. GNU Libtool is designed so that the complete functionality of each host type is available via a generic interface, but nasty quirks are hidden from the programmer.

GNU Libtool's consistent interface is reassuring... users don't need to read obscure documentation in order to have their favorite source package build shared libraries. They just run our package configure script (or equivalent), and libtool does all the dirty work.

7.6.1 Motivation for writing libtool

Since early 1995, several different GNU developers have recognized the importance of having shared library support for their packages. The primary motivation for such a change is to encourage modularity and reuse of code (both conceptually and physically) in GNU programs.

Such a demand means that the way libraries are built in GNU packages needs to be general, to allow for any library type the package installer might want. The problem is compounded by the absence of a standard procedure for creating shared libraries on different platforms.

The following sections outline the major issues facing shared library support in GNU, and how shared library support could be standardized with libtool.

The following specifications were used in developing and evaluating this system:

1. The system must be as elegant as possible.
2. The system must be fully integrated with the GNU Autoconf and Automake utilities, so that it will be easy for GNU maintainers to use. However, the system must not require these tools, so that it can be used by non-GNU packages.
3. Portability to other (non-GNU) architectures and tools is desirable.

7.6.2 Implementation issues

The following issues need to be addressed in any reusable shared library system, specifically libtool:

1. The package installer should be able to control what sort of libraries are built.

2. It can be tricky to run dynamically linked programs whose libraries have not yet been installed. LD_LIBRARY_PATH must be set properly (if it is supported), or programs fail to run.
3. The system must operate consistently even on hosts which don't support shared libraries.
4. The commands required to build shared libraries may differ wildly from host to host. These need to be determined at configure time in a consistent way.
5. It is not always obvious with which suffix a shared library should be installed. This makes it difficult for `Makefile' rules, since they generally assume that file names are the same from host to host.
6. The system needs a simple library version number abstraction, so that shared libraries can be upgraded in place. The programmer should be informed how to design the interfaces to the library to maximize binary compatibility.
7. The install `Makefile' target should warn the package installer to set the proper environment variables (LD_LIBRARY_PATH or equivalent), or run ldconfig.

7.6.3 Other implementations

Even before libtool was developed, many free software packages built and installed their own shared libraries. At first, these packages were examined to avoid reinventing existing features.

Now it is clear that none of these packages have documented the details of shared library systems that libtool requires. So, other packages have been more or less abandoned as influences.

7.6.4 A postmortem analysis of other implementations

In all fairness, each of the implementations that were examined do the job that they were intended to do, for a number of different host systems. However, none of these solutions seem to function well as a generalized, reusable component.

Most were too complex to use (much less modify) without understanding exactly what the implementation does, and they were generally not documented.

The main difficulty is that different vendors have different views of what libraries are, and none of the packages which were examined seemed to be confident enough to settle on a single paradigm that just *works*.

Ideally, libtool would be a standard that would be implemented as series of extensions and modifications to existing library systems to make them work consistently. However, it is not an easy task to convince operating system developers to mend their evil ways, and people want to build shared libraries right now, even on buggy, broken, confused operating systems.

For this reason, libtool was designed as an independent shell script. It isolates the problems and inconsistencies in library building that plague `Makefile' writers by wrapping the compiler suite on different platforms with a consistent, powerful interface.

With luck, libtool will be useful to and used by the GNU community, and that the lessons that were learned in writing it will be taken up by designers of future library systems.

7.6.5 Creating object files

As explained earlier, for most library systems, creating object files that become part of a static library is as simple as creating object files that are linked to form an executable:

Shared libraries, however, may only be built from *position-independent code* (PIC). So, special flags must be passed to the compiler to tell it to generate PIC rather than the standard position-dependent code.

Since this is a library implementation detail, libtool hides the complexity of PIC compiler flags by using separate library object files (which end in `.lo' instead of `.o'). On systems without shared libraries (or without special PIC compiler flags), these library object files are identical to "standard" object files.

To create library object files for `foo.c' and `hello.c', simply invoke libtool with the standard compilation command as arguments

```
libtool --mode=compile gcc -g -O -c a.c
gcc -g -O -c a.c
echo timestamp > a.lo
libtool --mode=compile gcc -g -O -c b.c
gcc -g -O -c b.c
echo timestamp > b.lo
libtool --mode=compile gcc -g -O -c d.c
gcc -g -O -c d.c
echo timestamp > d.lo
```

Note that libtool creates two files for each invocation. The `.lo' file is a library object, which may be built into a shared library, and the `.o' file is a standard object file.

On shared library systems, libtool automatically inserts the PIC generation flags into the compilation command, so that the library object and the standard object differ:

```
libtool --mode=compile gcc -g -O -c a.c
gcc -g -O -c –fPIC -DPIC a.c
mv -f a.o a.lo
gcc -g -O -c a.c >/dev/null 2>&1
libtool --mode=compile gcc -g -O -c b.c
gcc -g -O -c –fPIC –DPIC b.c
mv -f b.o b.lo
gcc -g -O -c b.c >/dev/null 2>&1
libtool --mode=compile gcc -g -O -c d.c
gcc -g -O -c –fPIC –DPIC d.c
mv -f d.o d.lo
gcc -g -O -c d.c >/dev/null 2>&1
```

Notice that the second run of GCC has its output discarded. This is done so that compiler warnings aren't annoyingly duplicated.

7.6.6 Linking libraries

Again, the libtool library name differs from the standard name (it has a `.la' suffix instead of a `.a' suffix). The arguments to libtool are the same ones we would use to produce an executable named `libhello.la' with your compiler

```
libtool --mode=link gcc -g -O -o libhello.la a.lo b.lo d.lo

mkdir .libs
ar cru .libs/libhello.a a.o b.o d.o
ranlib .libs/libhello.a
creating libhello.la
```

The same can be used with the shared library option.

We can identify that the libtool just ran an obscure ld command to create a shared library, as well as the static library.

Note how libtool creates extra files in the `.libs' subdirectory, rather than the current directory. This feature is to make it easier to clean up the build directory, and to help ensure that other programs fail horribly if we accidentally forget to use libtool when we should.

7.6.7 Linking executables

If we choose at this point to *install* the library (put it in a permanent location) before linking executables against it, then we don't need to use libtool to do the linking. Simply use the appropriate `-L' and `-l' flags to specify the library's location.

Some system linkers insist on encoding the full directory name of each shared library in the resulting executable. Libtool has to work around this disfeature by special magic to ensure that only permanent directory names are put into installed executables.

The importance of this bug must not be overlooked: it won't cause programs to crash in obvious ways. It creates a security hole, and possibly even worse, if we are modifying the library source code after we have installed the package, we will change the behavior of the installed programs!

So, if we want to link programs against the library before we install it, we must use libtool to do the linking.

Here's the way of linking against an uninstalled library:

```
libtool --mode=link gcc -g -O -o bb mm.c libhello.la
gcc -g -O –o bb mm.c ./.libs/libhello.a
```

That looks too simple to be true. All libtool did was transform `libhello.la' to `./.libs/libhello.a'

Now assume `libhello.la' had already been installed, and we want to link a new program with it. We could figure out where it lives by yourself, then run:

```
gcc -g -O -o test mm.c -L/usr/local/lib –lhello
```

However, unless `/usr/local/lib' is in the standard library search path, we won't be able to run test.

Notice that the executable, test or mm, was actually created in the `.libs' subdirectory. Then, a wrapper script was created in the current directory.

7.6.8 Installing libraries

Normally, installing libraries on a non-libtool system is quite straightforward... just copy them into place

Libtool installation is quite simple, as well. Just use the install or cp command that we normally would

```
libtool --mode=install cp libhello.la /usr/local/lib/libhello.la
cp libhello.la /usr/local/lib/libhello.la
cp .libs/libhello.a /usr/local/lib/libhello.a
ranlib /usr/local/lib/libhello.a
```

Note that the libtool library `libhello.la' is also installed, to help libtool with uninstallation

Here is the shared library example:

```
libtool --mode=install install -c libhello.la /usr/local/lib/libhello.la
install -c .libs/libhello.so.0.0 /usr/local/lib/libhello.so.0.0
install -c libhello.la /usr/local/lib/libhello.la
install -c .libs/libhello.a /usr/local/lib/libhello.a
 ranlib /usr/local/lib/libhello.a
```

It is safe to specify the `-s' (strip symbols) flag if we use a BSD-compatible install program when installing libraries. Libtool will either ignore the `-s' flag, or will run a program that will strip only debugging and compiler symbols from the library.

Once the libraries have been put in place, there may be some additional configuration that we need to do before using them. First, we must make sure that where the library is installed actually agrees with the `-rpath' flag we used to build it.

Then, running `**libtool -n --mode=finish *libdir***' can give us further hints on what to do

```
libtool -n --mode=finish /usr/local/lib
PATH="$PATH:/sbin" ldconfig -m /usr/local/lib
----------------------------------------------------------------------
Libraries have been installed in:
   /usr/local/lib

To link against installed libraries in a given directory, LIBDIR,
 you must use the `-LLIBDIR' flag during linking.

 You will also need to do one of the following:
   - add LIBDIR to the `LD_LIBRARY_PATH' environment variable
     during execution
   - add LIBDIR to the `LD_RUN_PATH' environment variable
     during linking
   - use the `-RLIBDIR' linker flag

See any operating system documentation about shared libraries for
More information, such as the ld and ld.so manual pages.
----------------------------------------------------------------------
```

After we have completed these steps, we can go on to begin using the installed libraries. We may also install any executables that depend on libraries we created.

7.6.9 Installing executables

If we have you used libtool to link any executables against uninstalled libtool, we need to use libtool to install the executables after the libraries have been installed. So, for our example, we would run:

libtool install -c bb /usr/local/bin/bb
Install -c bb /usr/local/bin/bb

On shared library systems, libtool just ignores the wrapper script and installs the correct binary:

```
libtool install -c bb /usr/local/bin/bb
install -c .libs/bb /usr/local/bin/bb
```

7.7 The command prelink

This command prelink can be used to prelink shared libraries and binaries to speed up their startup time. This command modifies ELF shared libraries and binaries such that the time they need for their relocation at startup time will be reduced dramatically and in addition run-time memory consumption decreases. If after prelinking, dependent libraries changes, then normal relocation takes place. This command first gathers information about the shared libraries on which a ELF binary depends and assigns a unique virtual address space for each library such that when the dynamic linker attempts to load such a library, unless its allocated virtual address space is occupied, it will loaded into the selected virtual slot during relinking stage.

If we want to prelink an executable file then simply execute the following command.

prelink -vm executablefilename

7.8 Conclusions

This chapter explains about how shared and static libraries are created in Linux system. All the concepts are dealt in a step-by-step fashion. Also, at the end, libtool is explored to automate library development activity.

8 Lex and Yacc

8.1 Introduction

First phase in the compiler development is tokenization. That is, the input or source program is decomposed into tokens which are also known as lexeme's (thus this phase is also called as lexical analysis). Each language will be having its own lexical rules. Only after extracting the tokens, syntactical analysis is carried out to test the validity of the expression in terms of that language specific grammatical rules. After this, actual transformation to machine language (via assembly language in the case of C language) takes place.

In the past, Lex library is widely used for lexical analysis. However, in the recent years, under Free Software Foundation license, Flex (fast lexical analyzer) is distributed along with Gnu compiler package which can be effectively used for lexical analysis purpose. In compiler construction terminology these SW's which are used for lexical analysis are called as scanners.

In addition to scanner development, Lex/Flex is also used for some other applications in system administration where text processing is needed.

8.2 Lex Specification File

In essence, while using lex or flex we have to first create a specification file (used to specify the tokenization rules, i.e regular expressions to represent the tokens of the language and also C code, called as rules) and has to be presented to **lex** command which generates a C language file known as **lex.yy.c** (in which yylex() and other functions given in Table 8.2 are defined) which when compiled with gcc (with –lfl option) we get an executable file which does the required tokenization.

The flex input or specification file consists of three sections namingly definitions, rules and user code.

```
%{

 %}

definitions

%%
rules
%%

user code
```

8.2.1 The Definitions Section

The *definitions* section contains declarations of simple *name* definitions to simplify the scanner specification, and declarations of *start conditions*, which are explained in a later section.

Name definitions have the form:

Name definition

The "name" is a word beginning with a letter or an underscore ('_') followed by zero or more letters, digits, '_', or '-' (dash). The definition is taken to begin at the first non-white-space character following the name and continuing to the end of the line. The definition can subsequently be referred to using "{name}", which will expand to "(definition)". For example,

```
DIGIT   [0-9]
ID      [a-z][a-z0-9]*
```

defines "DIGIT" to be a regular expression which matches a single digit, and "ID" to be a regular expression which matches a letter followed by zero-or-more letters-or-digits. A subsequent reference to

```
{DIGIT}+"."{DIGIT}*
```

is identical to

```
([0-9])+"."([0-9])*
```

and matches one-or-more digits followed by a '.' followed by zero-or-more digits.

8.2.2 The Rules Section

The *rules* section of the flex input contains a series of rules of the form:

pattern action

where the pattern must be unindented and the action must begin on the same line.

See below for a further description of patterns and actions.

8.2.3 The User Code Section

The user code section is simply copied to `lex.yy.c' verbatim. It is used for companion routines which call or are called by the scanner. The presence of this section is optional; if it is missing, the second `%%' in the input file may be skipped, too.

In the definitions and rules sections, any *indented* text or text enclosed in `%{' and `%}' is copied verbatim to the output (with the `%{` and '%}' removed). The `%{`, and '%}'' must appear unindented on lines by themselves.

In the rules section, any indented or %{ } text appearing before the first rule may be used to declare variables which are local to the scanning routine and (after the declarations) code which is to be executed whenever the scanning routine is entered. Other indented or %{} text in the rule section is still copied to the output, but its meaning is not well-defined and it may well cause compile-time errors (this feature is present for POSIX compliance; see below for other such features).

In the definitions section (but not in the rules section), an unindented comment (i.e., a line beginning with "/*") is also copied verbatim to the output up to the next "*/".

8.2.4 Patterns

The patterns in the input are written using an extended set of regular expressions. These are:

`x'

match the character `x'

`.'

any character (byte) except newline

`[xyz]'

a "character class"; in this case, the pattern matches either an `x', a `y', or a `z'

`[abj-oZ]'

a "character class" with a range in it; matches an `a', a `b', any letter from `j' through `o', or a `Z'

`[^A-Z]'

a "negated character class", i.e., any character but those in the class. In this case, any character EXCEPT an uppercase letter.

`[^A-Z\n]'

any character EXCEPT an uppercase letter or a newline

`*r**'

zero or more *r*'s, where *r* is any regular expression

`*r*+'

one or more *r*'s

`*r*?'

zero or one *r*'s (that is, "an optional *r*")

`*r*{2,5}'

anywhere from two to five *r*'s

`*r*{2,}'

two or more *r*'s

`*r*{4}'

exactly 4 *r*'s

`{*name*}'

the expansion of the "*name*" definition (see above)

`"[xyz]\"foo"'

the literal string: `[xyz]"foo'

`*x*'

if *x* is an `a', `b', `f', `n', `r', `t', or `v', then the ANSI-C interpretation of \*x*. Otherwise, a literal `*x*' (used to escape operators such as `*')

`\0'

a NUL character (ASCII code 0)

`\123'

the character with octal value 123

`\x2a'

the character with hexadecimal value 2a

`(*r*)'

match an *r*; parentheses are used to override precedence (see below)

`*rs*'

the regular expression *r* followed by the regular expression *s*; called "concatenation"

`*r*|*s*'

either an *r* or an *s*

`*r*/*s*'

an *r* but only if it is followed by an *s*. The text matched by *s* is included when determining whether this rule is the *longest match*, but is then returned to the input before the action is executed. So the action only sees the text matched by *r*. This type of pattern is called *trailing context*. (There are some combinations of `*r*/*s*' that flex cannot match correctly; see notes in the Deficiencies / Bugs section below regarding "dangerous trailing context".)

`^*r*'

an *r*, but only at the beginning of a line (i.e., which just starting to scan, or right after a newline has been scanned).

`*r*$'

an *r*, but only at the end of a line (i.e., just before a newline). Equivalent to "*r*/\n". Note that flex's notion of "newline" is exactly whatever the C compiler used to compile flex interprets '\n' as; in particular, on some DOS systems you must either filter out \r's in the input yourself, or explicitly use *r*/\r\n for "r$".

`<*s*>*r*'

an *r*, but only in start condition *s* (see below for discussion of start conditions) <*s1*,*s2*,*s3*>*r* same, but in any of start conditions *s1*, *s2*, or *s3*

`<*>*r*'

an *r* in any start condition, even an exclusive one.

`<<EOF>>'

an end-of-file

`<*s1*,*s2*><<EOF>>'

an end-of-file when in start condition *s1* or *s2*

Note that inside of a character class, all regular expression operators lose their special meaning except escape ('\') and the character class operators, '-', ']', and, at the beginning of the class, '^'.

The regular expressions listed above are grouped according to precedence, from highest precedence at the top to lowest at the bottom. Those grouped together have equal precedence. For example,

```
foo|bar*
is the same as
(foo)|(ba(r*))
```

since the '*' operator has higher precedence than concatenation, and concatenation higher than alternation ('|'). This pattern therefore matches *either* the string "foo" *or* the string "ba" followed by zero-or-more r's. To match "foo" or zero-or-more "bar"'s, use:

```
foo|(bar)*
and to match zero-or-more "foo"'s-or-"bar"'s:
(foo|bar)*
```

In addition to characters and ranges of characters, character classes can also contain character class *expressions*. These are expressions enclosed inside `[': and `:'] delimiters (which themselves must appear between the '[' and ']' of the character class; other elements may occur inside the character class, too). The valid expressions are:

```
[:alnum:] [:alpha:] [:blank:]
[:cntrl:] [:digit:] [:graph:]
[:lower:] [:print:] [:punct:]
[:space:] [:upper:] [:xdigit:]
```

These expressions all designate a set of characters equivalent to the corresponding standard C `isXXX' function. For example, `[:alnum:]' designates those characters for which `isalnum()' returns true - i.e., any alphabetic or numeric. Some systems don't provide `isblank()', so flex defines `[:blank:]' as a blank or a tab.

For example, the following character classes are all equivalent:

```
[[:alnum:]]
[[:alpha:][:digit:]]
[[:alpha:]0-9]
[a-zA-Z0-9]
```

If our scanner is made to act as case-insensitive by using the `-i' flag, then `[:upper:]' and `[:lower:]' are equivalent to `[:alpha:]'.

Some notes on patterns:

- A negated character class such as the example "[^A-Z]" above *will match a newline* unless "\n" (or an equivalent escape sequence) is one of the characters explicitly present in the negated character class (e.g., "[^A-Z\n]"). This is unlike how many other regular expression tools treat negated character classes, but unfortunately the inconsistency is historically entrenched. Matching newlines means that a pattern like [^"]* can match the entire input unless there's another quote in the input.

- A rule can have at most one instance of trailing context (the '/' operator or the '$' operator). The start condition, '^', and "<<EOF>>" patterns can only occur at the beginning of a pattern, and, as well as with '/' and '$', cannot be grouped inside parentheses. A '^' which does not occur at the beginning of a rule or a '$' which does not occur at the end of a rule loses its special properties and is treated as a normal character. The following are illegal:

```
foo/bar$
<sc1>foo<sc2>bar
```

Note that the first of these, can be written "foo/bar\n". The following will result in '$' or '^' being treated as a normal character:

```
foo|(bar$)
foo|^bar
```

If what's wanted is a "foo" or a bar-followed-by-a-newline, the following could be used (the special '|' action is explained below):

```
foo     |
bar$    /* action goes here */
```

A similar trick will work for matching a foo or a bar-at-the-beginning-of-a-line.

8.2.5 How the input is matched

When the generated scanner is run, it analyzes its input looking for strings which match any of its patterns. If it finds more than one match, it takes the one matching the most text (for trailing context rules, this includes the length of the trailing part, even though it will then be returned to the input). If it finds two or more matches of the same length, the rule listed first in the flex input file is chosen.

Once the match is determined which satisfying one of the regular expression or rule, the text corresponding to the match (called the *token*) is made available in the global character pointer **yytext (see Table 8.1 for other lex specific variables)**, and its length in the global integer yyleng. The *action* corresponding to the matched pattern is then executed (a more detailed description of actions follows), and then the remaining input is scanned for another match.

If no match is found, then the *default rule* is executed: the next character in the input is considered matched and copied to the standard output. Thus, the simplest legal flex input is: (see Example 1).

```
%%
```

which generates a scanner that simply copies its input (one character at a time) to its output.

Note that yytext can be defined in two different ways: either as a character *pointer* or as a character *array*. We can control which definition flex uses by including one of the special directives `%pointer' or `%array' in the first (definitions) section of our flex input. The default is `%pointer', unless we use the `-l' lex compatibility option, in which case yytext will be an array. The advantage of using `%pointer' is substantially faster scanning and no buffer overflow when matching very large tokens (unless you run out of dynamic memory). The disadvantage is that we are restricted in how our actions can modify yytext (see the next section), and calls to the `unput()' function destroys the present contents of yytext, which can be a considerable porting headache when moving between different lex versions.

The advantage of `%array' is that we can then modify yytext to our heart's content, and calls to `unput()' do not destroy yytext (see below). Furthermore, existing lex programs sometimes access yytext externally using declarations of the form:

```
extern char yytext[];
```

This definition is erroneous when used with `%pointer', but correct for `%array'.

`%array' defines yytext to be an array of YYLMAX characters, which defaults to a fairly large value. We can change the size by simply #define'ing YYLMAX to a different value in the first section of our flex input. As mentioned above, with `%pointer' yytext grows dynamically to accommodate large tokens. While this means our `%pointer' scanner can accommodate very large tokens (such as matching entire blocks of comments), bear in mind that each time the scanner must resize yytext it also must rescan the entire token from the beginning, so matching such tokens can prove slow. yytext presently does *not* dynamically grow if a call to `unput()' results in too much text being pushed back; instead, a run-time error results.

Actions

Each pattern in a rule has a corresponding action, which can be any arbitrary C statement. The pattern ends at the first non-escaped whitespace character; the remainder of the line is its action. If the action is empty, then when the pattern is matched the input token is simply discarded.

Table 8.1 Lex variables.

yyin	Of the type FILE*. This points to the current file being parsed by the lexer.
Yyout	Of the type FILE*. This points to the location where the output of the lexer will be written. By default, both yyin and yyout point to standard input and output.
yytext	The text of the matched pattern is stored in this variable (char*).
yyleng	Gives the length of the matched pattern.
yylineno	Provides current line number information. (May or may not be supported by the lexer.)

Table 8.2 Lex functions.

yylex()	The function that starts the analysis. It is automatically generated by Lex.
yywrap()	This function is called when end of file (or input) is encountered. If this function returns 1, the parsing stops. So, this can be used to parse multiple files. Code can be written in the third section, which will allow multiple files to be parsed. The strategy is to make yyin file pointer (see the preceding Table 8.1) point to a different file until all the files are parsed. At the end, yywrap() can return 1 to indicate end of parsing.
yyless(int n)	This function can be used to push back all but first 'n' characters of the read token.
yymore()	This function tells the lexer to append the next token to the current token.

Example 1

This Lex specification file contains no patterns and no actions. Thus, any string matches and default action, i.e printing takes place.

```
%{
%}
%%
%%
main()
{
yylex();
return 0;
}
```

Let the lex specification file as ex1.lex. Then, run the following sequence of commands.

lex ex1.lex (creates lex.yy.c)

gcc -o ex1 lex.yy.c -lfl

To Use the generated program.

./ex1 < filename

This displays the content of the file "filename".

Even this ex1 program can take standard input. That is, we can simply type its name along the command line.

```
./ex1
dd
ds
dads
^d
```

We can also make this program "ex1" to take input till we type a specified string with the help of "**Here the document (<<)**" facility. That is:

```
./ex1 <<END
dsdsa asdd
asdkads asdk
asdkd asd
asdsd
adsd sdd
END
```

This also simply displays what ever we have typed on the screen again.

Example 2

A lex program which adds line numbers to the given file and displays the same onto the standard output. Here, we are defining line as any sequence of characters terminated with new line. The action is to print the value of lineno variable and the line which is read.

```
%{
/*

*/

int lineno=1;
%}

line        .*\n

%%
{line}      {       printf("%5d     %s",lineno++,yytext); }
%%
main()
{
yylex();
return 0;
}
```

If we assume this file name is "ex2.lex", at the command prompt we have to execute the following commands to use lex.

lex ex2.lex (creates lex.yy.c)

gcc -o ex2 lex.yy.c -lfl

To use the program.

./ex < filename

This displays the content of the file "filename" along with line numbers.

This "ex2" program takes standard input also. Try the following at the command prompt.

```
./ex1
dd
ds
dads
^d
```

Also try the following at the command prompt.

```
./ex2 <<END
dsdsa asdd
asdkads asdk
asdkd asd
asdsd
adsd sdd
END
```

Example 3

This is also a lex specification program which adds line numbers to the given file and displays the same onto standard output. Only difference is that main() is not included unlike previous example. However, automatically main() is added by the lex.

```
%{
/*

*/

int lineno=1;
%}

line        .*\n
```

```
%%
{line}      {       printf("%5d     %s",lineno++,yytext); }
%%
```

Try at the command prompt the following commands assuming the file name is ex3.c.

lex ex3.lex (creates lex.yy.c)

gcc -o ex3 lex.yy.c -lfl

./ex3 < filename

Example 4

This is a lex specification program which adds line numbers to the given file and displays the same onto standard output. However, it explains about the use of external variable yyin (see Table 8.1). The resultant program takes filename to be tokenized as command line argument unlike previous programs ex1, ex2 and ex3.

```
%{
/*

*/

int lineno=1;
%}

line        .*\n

%%
{line}      {       printf("%5d     %s",lineno++,yytext); }
%%
main(int argc, char*argv[])
{
extern FILE *yyin;
yyin=fopen(argv[1],"r");
yylex();
return 0;
}
```

If we assume this file name is "ex4.lex", we have to execute the following commands to use lex.

```
lex   ex4.lex        (creates lex.yy.c)

gcc -o ex4  lex.yy.c  -lfl
```

How to Use the program.

```
./ex4  filename
./ex4  < filename
```

Both the commands displays the file "filename" content on the screen along with the line numbers.

Also, try the following at the command prompt and note the differences with the above programs.

```
./ex4
dd
ds
dads
^d

./ex4 <<END
dsdsa asdd
asdkads asdk
asdkd asd
asdsd
adsd sdd
END
```

Example 5

This specification program is an attempt to emulate od (octal dump) command. Here, for every character its octal value is printed. However, newline character is also printed in octal fashion.

```
%{

%}

character   .
newline             \n

%%
```

```
{character}          {        printf("%o ",yytext[0]); }
{newline} {          printf("%o ", '\n');}
%%
main(int argc, char*argv[])
{
extern FILE *yyin;
yyin=fopen(argv[1],"r");
yylex();
printf("\n");
return 0;
}
```

Let the specification file be "ex5.lex". Run the following commands.

lex ex5.lex
gcc –o ex5 lex.yy.c –lfl
./ex5 filename

Compare the result with the following command.

od -t oC filename

Example 6
This program is an attempt to extract only comments from a C program and display the same on standard output. Here, we have defined C language comment as a regular expression and action os specified as to display nothing when comment is encountered.

```
%{

%}

comment              V\*.*\*V

%%
{comment}            ECHO;
%%
main(int argc, char*argv[])
{
extern FILE *yyin;
yyin=fopen(argv[1],"r");
yylex();
printf("\n");
return 0;
}
```

Let the above specification file be "ex6.lex". Run the following commands.

```
lex ex6.lex
gcc –o ex6 lex.yy.c –lfl
./ex6  filename.c
```

Example 7

This lex specification program is an attempt to replace all nonnull sequences of white spaces by a single blank character. Here, pattern 'ws" is specified as a series of spaces of tab characters and action is specified as return or print a single space. Any other string is returned as it is.

```
%{
%}
ws [ \t]

%%
{ws}+      {printf(" "); }
.   {printf("%s",yytext);}

%%
main(int argc, char*argv[])
{
extern FILE *yyin;
yyin=fopen(argv[1],"r");
yylex();
printf("\n");
return 0;
}
```

Let the above specification file be "ex7.lex". Run the following commands.

```
lex ex7.lex
gcc –o ex7 lex.yy.c –lfl
./ex7  filename
```

Example 8

This specification program replaces all the occurrences of "rama" with "RAMA" and "sita" with "SITA". This example is used from explain that we can use a string as a direct pattern in the specification file.

```
%{
%}

%%
```

```
"rama"      {printf("RAMA");}

"sita"      {printf("SITA"); }
%%
main(int argc, char*argv[])
{
extern FILE *yyin;
yyin=fopen(argv[1],"r");
yylex();
printf("\n");
return 0;
}
```

Let the above specification file be "ex8.lex". Run the following commands.

```
lex ex8.lex
gcc -o ex8 lex.yy.c -lfl
./ex8  filename
```

Example 9

This lex specification program is used to count all occurrences of "rama" and "sita" in a given file.

```
%{
int count=0;

%}

%%
"rama"      {count++;}

"sita"      {count++; }
.  ;
%%
main(int argc, char*argv[])
{
extern FILE *yyin;
yyin=fopen(argv[1],"r");
yylex();
printf("No of Occurrences=%d\n",count);
return 0;
}
```

Let the above specification file be "ex9.lex". Run the following commands.

```
lex ex9.lex
gcc –o ex9 lex.yy.c –lfl
./ex9  filename
```

Example 10

This lex specification program is used from generate a C program which removes all the occurrences of "sita" and "rama" in the given file.

```
%{
%}

%%
"rama"
"sita"
.   ECHO;

%%
```

Let the above specification file be "ex10.lex". Run the following commands.

```
lex ex10.lex
gcc –o ex10 lex.yy.c –lfl
./ex10< filename
```

Example 11

This lex specification program is used to count and print the number of pages, lines, words and characters in a given file.

```
%{

int lines=0,words=0,characters=0,pages=0;

%}
%START   InWord
NewLine    [\n]
WhiteSpace          [\t ]
NewPage             [\f]
```

```
%%

{NewPage}          {BEGIN 0; characters++;pages++;}
{NewLine} {BEGIN 0; characters++;lines++;}
{WhiteSpace}       {BEGIN 0; characters++;}
<InWord>.characters++;
.   {BEGIN InWord; characters++; words++;}
%%
int main()
{
yylex();
printf("%d %d %d %d\n",lines,words,characters,pages);
}
```

Let the above specification file be "ex11.lex". Run the following commands.

lex ex11.lex
gcc –o ex11 lex.yy.c –lfl
./ex11 filename

Example 12

This lex specification program also can be used to find no of lines, words and characters in a given file. Here, yyleng indicates the length of the string yytext.

```
%{

int lines=0,words=0,characters=0;

%}
word        [^ \t\n]+
eol\n
%%
{word}      {words++;characters+=yyleng;}
{eol}       {characters++;lines++;}
.   { characters++; }
%%
int main()
{
yylex();
printf("%d %d %d \n",lines,words,characters);
}
```

Let the above specification file be "ex12.lex". Run the following commands.

```
lex ex12.lex
gcc -o ex12 lex.yy.c -lfl
./ex12  filename
```

Example 13

This lex specification program is to replace all the occurrences of the word "username" with users login name.

```
%{
%}

%%
username  printf("%s",getlogin() );
%%
main(int argc, char*argv[])
{
extern FILE *yyin;
yyin=fopen(argv[1],"r");
yylex();
printf("\n");
return 0;
}
```

Let the above specification file be "ex13.lex". Run the following commands.

```
lex ex13.lex
gcc -o ex13 lex.yy.c -lfl
./ex13  filename
```

Example 14

This lex specification program is to extract all html tags in the given file.

```
%{
%}

%%
"<"[^>]*>          {printf("%s\n", yytext); }
.  ;
%%
main(int argc, char*argv[])
{
extern FILE *yyin;
```

```
yyin=fopen(argv[1],"r");
yylex();
printf("\n");
return 0;
}
```

Let the above specification file be “ex14.lex”. Run the following commands.

```
lex ex14.lex
gcc –o ex14 lex.yy.c –lfl
./ex14  filename.html
```

Example 15

This lex specification program is from generate a program which simulates cat command to create files. While giving input first "start" word has from be typed and at the end "end" word has from be typed.

```
%{
%}

%%
"start"       ;
"end"        exit(-1);
.   ECHO ;
%%
main(int argc, char*argv[])
{
extern FILE *yyin;
yyout=fopen(argv[1],"w");
yylex();
printf("\n");
return 0;
}
```

Let the above specification file be “ex15.lex”. Run the following commands.

```
lex ex15.lex
gcc –o ex15 lex.yy.c –lfl
./ex15  filename
```

Example 16

This lex specification program is to eliminate multiple spaces and tabs and replace with a single space and remove empty lines. Here, yytext is processed in our actions.

```
%{

#include<stdlib.h>
#include<stdio.h>
int emptyline=0;
%}

SPACES    [ \t]
eol\n

%%
{SPACES}+  {printf(" "); }
\n|.               {
     char c=yytext[0];
    if(!isspace(c))  {
                        emptyline=1;
                        putchar(c);
                        }
    if(c=='\n')
             {
             if(emptyline)putchar(c);
             emptyline=0;
             }
         }
%%
main(int argc, char*argv[])
{
extern FILE *yyin;
yyin=fopen(argv[1],"r");
yylex();
printf("\n");
return 0;
}
```

Example 17

This lex specification program is to display only C comments in a given C file. Here, whenever "/*" pattern is encountered in the input, we have written code to process next characters in the input till we encounter the pattern "*/". Whenever, "/*" pattern is encountered the C code will be executed. Here, we have used lex specific function (see Table 8.2)input() is used to read characters from the lex input buffer and print them till it encounters "*/" pattern.

```
%{
%}

%%
"/*"          {char c;
   int done=0;
   ECHO;
   do
   {
   while((c=input())!='*') putchar(c);
   putchar(c);
   while((c=input())=='*') putchar(c);
   putchar(c);
   if(c=='/') done=1;
   }         while(!done);
   }

.  ;
\n ;
%%
main(int argc, char*argv[])
{
extern FILE *yyin;
yyin=fopen(argv[1],"r");
yylex();
printf("\n");
return 0;
}
```

Example 18

This lex specification file is to display a file's content by replacing ":" with \t

```
%{

%}

%%
":" {printf("\t");}

\n|.          ECHO ;
```

```
%%
main(int argc, char*argv[])
{
extern FILE *yyin;
yyin=fopen(argv[1],"r");
yylex();
printf("\n");
return 0;
}
```

Let the above specification file be "ex18.lex". Run the following commands.

```
lex ex18.lex
gcc -o ex18  lex.yy.c -lfl
./ex18  /etc/passwd
```

REJECT directs the scanner to proceed on to the "second best" rule which matched the input (or a prefix of the input). The rule is chosen as described above in "How the Input is Matched", and yytext and yyleng set up appropriately. It may either be one which matched as much text as the originally chosen rule but came later in the flex input file, or one which matched less text

Example 19

For example, to count all instance of she and he, including the instances of he that are included in she, use the following action:

```
%{
int s=0;
%}

%%
she          {s++; REJECT;}
he           {s++}
\n           |
.            ;

%%
main(int argc, char*argv[])
{
extern FILE *yyin;
yyin=fopen(argv[1],"r");
yylex();
printf("No of ocurrences of he including in he in she=%d\n",s);
return 0;
}
```

After counting the occurrences of she, the **lex** command rejects the input string and then counts the occurrences of he. Because he does not include she, a **REJECT** action is not necessary on he.

Example 20

The following lex specification file is used to generate a C program which counts number of words in a file other than the word "incl".

```
%{
int nw=0;
%}
%%
incl                    nw--; REJECT;
[^ \t\n]+  nw++;
%%
main(int argc, char*argv[])
{
extern FILE *yyin;
yyin=fopen(argv[1],"r");
yylex();
printf("No of words other than the word incl=%d\n",nw);
return 0;
}
```

Example 21

The following lex specification program generates a C program which takes a string "abcd" and prints the following output. From terminate the program enter ^d.

```
abcd
abc
ab
a
%{
%}
%%
a|ab|abc|abcd      printf("%s\n",yytext);REJECT
.|\n

%%
main(int argc, char*argv[])
{
extern FILE *yyin;
yyin=fopen(argv[1],"r");
yylex();
return 0;
}
```

Example 22

The following lex specification file generates a C program which extract http, ftp or telnet tags from the given file.

```
%{
%}
%%
(ftp|http|telnet):\/\/[^ \n<>"]*
.|\n
%%
main(int argc, char*argv[])
{
extern FILE *yyin;
yyin=fopen(argv[1],"r");
yylex();
return 0;
}
```

The above program is supposed extract URL's with capitol letters such as HTTP, FTP or TELENT then we tell flex to build a case-insensitive lexer using the **"-i"** option.

Example 23

The following lex program generates a C program which takes standard input as output of Unix date and gives either of the following messages

```
Good Morning
Good Afternoon
Good Evening
        %{
        %}
%%
Morning         [ ](00|01|02|03|04|05|06|07|08|09|10|11)[:]
Afternoon       [ ](12|13|14|15|16|17)[:]
Evening         [ ](18|19|20|21|22|23)[:]

%%
{Morning}        printf("Good Morning ");
{Afternoon}      printf("Good Afternoon ");
{Evening}        printf("Good Evening ");
;
```

If we assume that executable file name of the generated C program is "greet" then we can run the following command from see the output.

date | greet

BEGIN followed by the name of a start condition places the scanner in the corresponding start condition .

Example 24

The `yymore()' tells the scanner that the next time it matches a rule, the corresponding token should be *appended* onto the current value of yytext rather than replacing it. First, `yymore()' depends on the value of yyleng correctly reflecting the size of the current token, so you must not modify yyleng if you are using `yymore()'. Second, the presence of `yymore()' in the scanner's action entails a minor performance penalty in the scanner's matching speed.

Example 25

The yyless(n)' returns all but the first *n* characters of the current token back to the input stream, where they will be rescanned when the scanner looks for the next match. yytext and yyleng are adjusted appropriately (e.g., yyleng will now be equal to *n*). An argument of 0 to yyless will cause the entire current input string to be scanned again. Unless you've changed how the scanner will subsequently process its input (using BEGIN, for example), this will result in an endless loop. Note that yyless is a macro and can only be used in the flex input file, not from other source files.

Example 26

The following lex specification file is used to generate scanner program for a toy Pascal-like language which extracts integers type of numbers, float type of numbers, key words such as if, procedure etc.

```
%{
#include <math.h>
#include<stdlib.h>
 %}

 DIGIT   [0-9]
 ID      [a-z][a-z0-9]*

 %%

 {DIGIT}+   {
        printf( "An integer: %s (%d)\n", yytext,
              atoi( yytext ) );
        }

 {DIGIT}+"."{DIGIT}*       {
        printf( "A float: %s (%g)\n", yytext,
              atof( yytext ) );
        }
```

```
if|then|begin|end|procedure|function       {
        printf( "A keyword: %s\n", yytext );
        }

{ID}        printf( "An identifier: %s\n", yytext );

"+"|"-"|"*"|"/"   printf( "An operator: %s\n", yytext );

"{"[\^{$\;$}}\n]*"}"     /* eat up one-line comments */

[ \t\n]+         /* eat up whitespace */

.          printf( "Unrecognized character: %s\n", yytext );

%%

main( argc, argv )
int argc;
char **argv;
{
++argv, --argc;  /* skip over program name */
if ( argc > 0 )
    yyin = fopen( argv[0], "r" );
else
    yyin = stdin;

yylex();
}
```

Example 27

A lex input file that changes all numbers to hexadecimal in input file while ignoring all others.

```
%{

#include<stdlib.h>
 %}

digit  [0-9]
number {digit}+
%%
{number} { int n = atoi(yytext); printf("%x", n); }
. {;}
 %%
```

```
main(int argc, char*argv[])
{
extern FILE *yyin;
yyin=fopen(argv[1],"r");
yylex();
return 0;
}
```

Example 28

The lex specification file generates a C program which counts number of word with length 1 character, 2 characters vice versa in the given input.

```
%{
int leng[100];

%}
%%
[a-z]+      leng[yyleng]++;
.|\n        ;
%%
main(int argc, char*argv[])
{
extern FILE *yyin;
int i;
for(i=1;i<100;i++) leng[i]=0;
yyin=fopen(argv[1],"r");
yylex();
printf("Word Length Frequency\n");
for(i=1;i<100;i++)
printf("%11d %10d\n",i,leng[i]);
return 0;
}
```

Example 29

```
%{
int leng[100];

%}
%%
[a-z]+      leng[yyleng]++;
.|\n        ;
```

```
%%
int yywrap()
{
int i;
printf("Word Length   Frequency\n");

for(i=1;i<100;i++)
if(leng[i]) printf("%11d %10d\n",i,leng[i]);
return 1;
}
main(int argc, char*argv[])
{
extern FILE *yyin;
int i;
for(i=1;i<100;i++) leng[i]=0;
yyin=fopen(argv[1],"r");
yylex();
return 0;
}
```

Example 30

This lex specification file is used to generate a C program which counts how many times a given alphabet is next to another alphabet in the given input (This frequency table is called as diagram in natural language processing terminology and also in algorithms.

```
%{
#include<stdlib.h>
int F[26][26];

%}
%%
[A-Za-z][A-Za-z] {
    F[toupper(yytext[0])-65][toupper(yytext[1])-65]++;REJECT;
    }
.|\n          ;
%%
main(int argc, char*argv[])
{
extern FILE *yyin;
int i,j;
for(i=0;i<26;i++)
for(j=0;j<26;j++)F[i][j]=0;
```

```
yyin=fopen(argv[1],"r");
yylex();
for(i=0;i<26;i++){
for(j=0;j<26;j++) printf("%d", F[i][j]);
printf("\n");
}
return 0;
}
```

If we give the following input to the program which is created compiling lex.yy.c file generated from the above lex specification file.

ABCDEFGHIJKLMNOPQRSTUVWXYZabcdefghijklmnopqrstuvwxyz

Result is:

```
02000000000000000000000000
00200000000000000000000000
00020000000000000000000000
00002000000000000000000000
00000200000000000000000000
00000020000000000000000000
00000002000000000000000000
00000000200000000000000000
00000000020000000000000000
00000000002000000000000000
00000000000200000000000000
00000000000020000000000000
00000000000002000000000000
00000000000000200000000000
00000000000000020000000000
00000000000000002000000000
00000000000000000200000000
00000000000000000020000000
00000000000000000002000000
00000000000000000000200000
00000000000000000000020000
00000000000000000000002000
00000000000000000000000200
00000000000000000000000020
00000000000000000000000002
10000000000000000000000000
```

Example 31

In the C program generated by the lex specification file, when yylex() finished with the first file, it calls yywrap(), which opens the next file, and yylex() continues. When yywrap() has exhausted all the command line arguments, it returns 1, and yylex() returns with value 0 (but we don't use the return value).

Like previous examples, this also extracts URL's from the given files whose names are given along the command line to the above program.

```
%{
#include <stdio.h>
#include <errno.h>
int file_num;
int file_num_max;
char **files;
extern int errno;
%}
%%
(ftp|http):\/\/[^ \n<>"]*     printf("%s\n",yytext);
.|\n                          ;
%%
int main(int argc, char *argv[]) {
   file_num=1;
   file_num_max = argc;
   files = argv;
   if ( argc > 1 ) {
         if ( (yyin = fopen(argv[file_num],"r")) == 0 ) {
                   perror(argv[file_num]);
                   exit(1);
         }
   }
   while( yylex() )
         ;
   return 0;
}

int yywrap() {
   fclose(yyin);
   if ( ++file_num < file_num_max ) {
         if ( (yyin = fopen(files[file_num],"r")) == 0 ) {
                   perror(files[file_num]);
                   exit(1);
         }
         return 0;
   } else {
         return 1;
   }
}
```

Start Conditions

Also, flex provides a mechanism for conditionally activating rules. Any rule whose pattern is prefixed with "<sc>" will only be active when the scanner is in the start condition named "sc". For example,

```
<STRING>[^"]*      {                    }
```

will be active only match is found when the scanner is in the "STRING" start condition. Also, if we want same action to be done for a given regular expression under different states, we may have to enter all the states names like the following manner

```
<STRING, ERROR, WARNING>"\*" ;
```

where STRING, ERROR, and WARNING are different states.

Example 32

This example is used to remove C comments from the file. It uses states facility available in the lex. Initially, lex is assumed to be in INITIAL state and when "/*" pattern is found it will be changing to COMMENT state. When it is in COMMENT state then pattern "*/" puts the lex in again INITIAL state. When it is in COMMENT state, whatever it encounters it will be eaten whereas if it is in INITIAL state simply the same is displayed.

```
%{
%}

%s COMMENT

%%
<INITIAL>"//".*          ;
<INITIAL>"/*"            BEGIN COMMENT;
<INITIAL>.               ECHO;
<INITIAL>[\n]            ECHO;
<COMMENT>"*/"            BEGIN INITIAL;
<COMMENT>.               ;
<COMMENT>[\n]            ;
%%

main() {
  yylex();
}
```

Example 33

The following lex specification file is used to generate a C program which is used to generate a html file from a data file.

The input format is that of a textual spreadsheet. Each spreadsheet entry is numbered using an alphabetical character (indicating the row) and an integer (indicating the column). To make the task easier, we can assume several things. First there will not be more than 26 columns. Second, that the entries will be ordered in the obvious way, i.e. A1, followed by B1, ... then A2, followed by B2, etc. Third, there will only be one entry per line and that all entries exist in the file. Finally, we are going to assume that there are no spreadsheet equations.

An example input might be

```
A0 = "Name"
B0 = "SSN"
C0 = "HW1"
D0 = "HW2"
A1 = "Scott Smith"
B1 = "123-44-5678"
C1 = 82
D1 = 44.2
A2 = "Sam Sneed"
B2 = "999-88-7777"
C2 = 92
D2 = 84
```

For output, we what to generate the appropriate HTML table. In html, tables are surrounded by <table> ... </table>. Each row of the table is surrounded by <tr> ... </tr> and each entry in a row by <td> ... </td>. For the above input we would want to output:

```
<table>
<tr>
<td> Name </td>
<td> SSN </td>
<td> HW1 </td>
<td> HW2 </td>
</tr>
<tr>
<td> Scott Smith </td>
<td> 123-44-5678 </td>
<td> 82 </td>
<td> 44.2 </td>
</tr>
<tr>
<td> Sam Sneed </td>
<td> 999-88-7777 </td>
<td> 92 </td>
<td> 84 </td>
</tr>
</table>
```

When viewed with a viewer, this looks like:

Name	SSN	HW1	HW2
Scott Smith	123-44-5678	82	44.2
Sam Sneed	999-88-7777	92	84

Lex specification for the conversion

```
%%
^A0                {printf("<table>\n<tr>\n");}
^A[0-9]*  {printf("</tr>\n<tr>\n");}
^[B-Z][0-9]*       ;
[0-9]*             {printf("<td> "); ECHO; printf(" </td>\n");}
[0-9]*"."[0-9]*    {printf("<td> "); ECHO; printf(" </td>\n");}
\"[^"]*\"  {printf("<td>   ");   yytext[yyleng-1]   =   '   ';   printf("%s
</td>\n",yytext+1);}
= ;
[ \n]              ;
.   ECHO;
%%

main() {
  printf("<html>\n");
  yylex();
  printf("</tr>\n</table>\n</html>\n");
}
```

Example 34

The following specification file is for the opposite purpose. That is, given html languages <table> specification such the following it has to extract only field's information.

Sample Input:

```
<table>
<tr>
<td> Name </td>
<td> SSN </td>
<td> HW1 </td>
<td> HW2 </td>
</tr>
<tr>
<td> Scott Smith </td>
```

```
<td> 123-44-5678 </td>
<td> 82 </td>
<td> 44.2 </td>
</tr>
<tr>
<td> Sam Sneed </td>
<td> 999-88-7777 </td>
<td> 92 </td>
<td> 84 </td>
</tr>
</table>
```

Sample output:

Name SSN HW1 HW2 Scott Smith 123-44-5678 82 44.2 Sam Sneed 999-88-7777 92 84

```
Lex Specification File
%{
%}

%s  TABL REC DATA

%%
<INITIAL>"<table>"              BEGIN TABL;
<TABL>"<\/table>"               BEGIN INITIAL;
<TABL><tr>        BEGIN REC;
<REC><\/tr>       BEGIN TABL;
<REC><td>         BEGIN DATA;
<DATA><\/td>      BEGIN REC;
<DATA>.           ECHO;
<DATA>[ \t\n]               ;
<REC>[ \t\n]      ;
<TABL>[ \t\n]     ;
%%

main() {
  yylex();
}
```

Example 35

The above specification file can be also written as the following by combining last three state conditions.

```
%{
%}

%s  TABL REC DATA

%%
<INITIAL>"<table>"                BEGIN TABL;
<TABL>"<\/table>"                 BEGIN INITIAL;
<TABL><tr>          BEGIN REC;
<REC><\/tr>         BEGIN TABL;
<REC><td>           BEGIN DATA;
<DATA><\/td>        BEGIN REC;
<DATA>.             ECHO;
<DATA,REC,TABL>[ \t\n];
%%

main() {
  yylex();
}
```

Example 36

This example is used to explain yymore() and other pattern usage. Run the program by giving input like BOMBAYB.

```
%{
  int flag=0;
%}

%%
B[^B]*      { if (flag == 0) {
              flag = 1;
              yymore();
            }
            else    {
              flag = 0;
    printf("%s", yytext);
              printf("%d\n",yyleng);
             }
            }
%%
```

```
int main()
{
yylex();
}
```

8.3 Yacc - A Parser Generator

Normally, syntax analysis is employed to validate or check the syntax of any program. SW systems which are used for this purpose are referred as parsers. It *is* also possible to create a simple parser using Lex alone by making extensive use of the user-defined states (i.e. start-conditions). However, such a parser quickly becomes un-maintainable, as the number of user-defined states tends to explode.

Once our input file syntax contains complex structures, such as "balanced" brackets, or contains elements which are context-sensitive, compiler-compilers such as **yacc (yet another compiler compiler)** is best available alternative. "Context-sensitive" in this case means that a word or symbol can have different interpretations, depending on *where* it appears in the input language. For example in C, the '*' character is used for both multiplication, and to specify indirection (i.e. to dereference a pointer to a piece of memory). That is, it's meaning is "context-sensitive".

Yacc provides a general tool for imposing structure on the input to a computer program. That is, yacc user prepares a specification of the input process (grammar rules) as explained in detail in the following sections. Then, when yacc command is used with this specification file as input, it generates a C language program which checks the grammar (specified in the **.y** file) in the given input file. This generated C language program in turn calls lexical analyzer, probably generated by using Lex command, to pick up the basic items (called tokens) and test their syntactical validity according to the specified grammatical rules. Thus, both lex and yacc commands are used while writing compilers. For detailed discussion on compilers one can refer [Aho, 1985].

To summarize, the steps involved in developing compilers (parsers) using Yacc and Lex are:

- Write the grammar in a .y file (also specify the actions here that are to be taken in C).
- Write a lexical analyzer to process input and pass tokens to the parser whenever it is needed. This can be done using Lex command as explained in previous section. That is, we may prepare Lex specification file also.
- Write error handling routines (like yyerror()).
- Run yacc command on .y file such that it gives **y.tab.c** file and **y.tab.h** file.
- Run lex command on lex specification file such that it gives **lex.yy.c** file.
- Compile code produced by Yacc and lex as well as any other relevant source files.
- Test the resulting executable file by giving sample input file.

8.3.1 The Yacc Specification Rules

Like lex, **yacc** has it's own specification language. A yacc specification is structured along the same lines as a Lex specification. By convention, a Yacc file has the suffix .y. The Yacc compiler is invoked from the compile line as **yacc -dv file.y**

```
%{
  /* C declarations and includes */
%}
  /* Yacc token and type declarations */
%%
  /* Yacc Specification
```

```
    in the form of grammar rules like this:
  */
  symbol   :  symbols tokens
              { $$ = my_c_code($1); }
           ;
%%
  /* C language program (the rest) */
```

The Yacc Specification rules are the place where we "glue" the various tokens together that lex has conveniently provided to us.

Each grammar rule defines a symbol in terms of:

- other symbols
- tokens (or terminal symbols) which come from the lexer.

Each rule can have an associated action, which is executed *after* all the component symbols of the rule have been parsed. Actions are basically C-program statements surrounded by curly braces.

Terminal and non-terminal symbols

Terminal symbol: Represents a class of syntactically equivalent tokens. Terminal symbols are of three types:

Named token: These are defined via the %token identifier. By convention, these are all upper case.

Character token: A character constant written in the same format as in C. For example, + is a character token.

Literal string token: is written like a C string constant. For example, "<;>" is a literal string token.

The lexer returns named tokens.

Non-terminal symbol: Is a symbol that is a group of non-terminal and terminal symbols. By convention, these are all lower case.

For example, in English one of the valid form of a sentence is the one having subject, verb and object.

Sentence: Subject Verb Object

Similarly, in US style, date is represented as:

Date: Month / Day / Year

Here, Date can be termed as Non-terminal and Month, '/', Day, and Year can be termed as terminals (i.e they are not further decomposable). In Yacc specification, the same rule can be specified as:

```
Date:  MONTH '/' DAY '/' YEAR { /*actions */}
```

Actual values for MONTH, DAY and YEAR are returned from the lexical analyzer by tokenizing the given input.

Similarly, Context-free grammar production such as:

p->AbC

will have equivalent Yacc Rule as:

p : A b C { /* actions */}

The general style for coding the rules is to have all Terminals in upper-case and all non-terminals in lower-case (Surprise!!. Exactly opposite to Automata Theory or compiler construction books notation's).

Also, we can use few Yacc specific declarations which begins with a %sign in yacc specification file such as:

1. **%union** It defines the Stack type for the Parser. It is a union of various datas/structures/ objects.
2. **%token** These are the terminals returned by the yylex function to the yacc. A token can also have type associated with it for good type checking and syntax directed translation. A type of a token can be specified as %token <stack member> tokenName.
3. **%type** The type of a non-terminal symbol in the Grammar rule can be specified with this.
   The format is %type <stack member> non-terminal.
4. **%noassoc** Specifies that there is no associativity of a terminal symbol.
5. **%left** Specifies the left associativity of a Terminal Symbol
6. **%right** Specifies the right assocoativity of a Terminal Symbol.
7. **%start** Specifies the L.H.S non-terminal symbol of a production rule which should be taken as the starting point of the grammar rules.
8. **%prec** Changes the precedence level associated with a particular rule to that of the following token name or literal.

Let us discuss about how to write a parser to recognize US style date.

File date.y

```
%token NUMBER SLASH NL
%%

   date   :
   |NUMBER SLASH NUMBER SLASH NUMBER NL {printf("OK"); }
   ;
%%
void yyerror(char *s)
{
 printf("Error\n");
}
```

File date.lex

```
%{
#include"y.tab.h"
%}

%%
[0-9]+              return NUMBER;
"\/"                return SLASH;
'\n'        return NL;
```

Run the following command.

yacc -dv date.y

This command generates the files y.tab.c, y.tab.h and y.output.

File y.tab.h contains:

```
#ifndef YYERRCODE
#define YYERRCODE 256
#endif

#define NUMBER 257
#define SLASH 258
#define NL 259
```

The file y.tab.c contains the C code for the parser which recognizes the given grammatical rules (here it is date format) in a given input file.

Also, run the following commands to generate the final parser.

lex date.lex

gcc -o DATE y.tab.c lex.yy.c -ly -lfl

Run the program DATE and enter interactively a string other than of the format 12/31/1998 and observe the error message. Otherwise, it displays the message OK.

As mentioned earlier, Yacc uses symbolic tokens. In the above Yacc specification file we have declared symbolic Tokens such as NUMBER, NL, and SLASH using %token declaration. When we run Yacc command on this specification file it generates the file y.tab.h (an example is shown above) in which for all these token a number assigned starting from 257.

Also, observe that these symbolic tokens are used in lex specification file, in which when a regular expression match occurs, yylex() returns this symbolic token. That is, the lexical analyzer, yylex() generated by lex command takes responsibility of reading input stream and recognizing low level structures (regular expressions) historically called as terminal symbols and communicates these tokens to the parser which in turn recognizes the nonterminals, i.e grammatical structures.

Tokens also will have assigned values during the scanning process and the same is assigned to variable yylval which is defined internally by Yacc.

Example 37

This example is to develop parser which recognizes strings of form $a^n b^n$, where n>=1.

Yacc Specification File (ab.y)

```
%token A B
%%
start: anbn '\n' {return 0;}
anbn :  A B
    | A anbn B
    ;
%%
#include"lex.yy.c"
```

Lex Specification File (ab.lex)

```
%%
a    return(A);
b    return(B);
.    return(yytext[0]);
\n   return('\n');
```

To create parser which recognizes strings of for $a^n b^n$, run the following commands

lex ab.lex
yacc –dv ab.y
gcc –o anbn y.tab.c lex.yy.c -ly –lfl

Run the resulting program (anbn) and check by giving pattern such as:

aabb or aaaabbbb.

If we do not give matching input it gives error message "Syntax Error". Otherwise it displays nothing.

Example 38

The following is a little modified version of the above program with error checking and better user interface when match occurs.

Yacc Specification File (ab1.y)

```
%token A B
%%
```

```
start: anbn '\n' { printf("  is in anbn\n");                return 0; }
anbn:  A B
    | A anbn B
    ;
%%
#include "lex.yy.c"

yyerror(s)
char *s;
{
  printf("%s, it is not in anbn\n", s);
}
```

Lex Specification File(ab1.lex)

```
%%
a     return(A);
b     return(B);
.     return(yytext[0]);
\n    return('\n');
```

To create parser, run the following commands

lex ab1.lex
yacc –dv ab1.y
gcc –o anbn1 y.tab.c lex.yy.c -ly –lfl

Run the resulting program (anbn1) and check by giving pattern such as:

aa bb   or aaaabbbb

Example 39
This example is also to explain simple yacc example.

Yacc Specification File(two.y)

```
%token DING DONG BELL
%%
rhyme      :      sound place
    ;
sound      :      DING DONG
    ;

place      :      BELL
```

```
    ;
%%
#include "lex.yy.c"
```

Lex Specification File (two.lex)

```
%%
"ding"      return (DING);
"dong"      return (DONG);
"bell"      return (BELL);
```

To create parser which accepts "ding dong bell", run the following commands

```
lex  two.lex
yacc -dv two.y
gcc -o two y.tab.c  lex.yy.c  -ly -lfl
```

After creating parser if we give input "ding dong bell" it accepts otherwise rejects, i.e it gives an error message "Syntax Error".

Example 40

This Yacc specification and lex specification program's are for testing balanced parentheses.

Yacc Specification File (bp.y)

```
%{
#include <ctype.h>
#include <stdio.h>
#include "y.tab.h"
extern int yydebug;
%}
%token     OPEN    CLOSE
%%
lines       : s '\n' {printf("OK\n"); }
    ;
s   :
    | OPEN s CLOSE  s
        ;
%%
```

```
void yyerror(char * s)
{
  fprintf (stderr, "%s\n", s);
}

int yywrap(){return 1; }
int main(void) {
yydebug=1;
return yyparse();}
```

Lex Specification File (bp.lex)

```
%{
#include"y.tab.h"
%}

%%
[ \t]     { /* skip blanks and tabs */ }
"(" return OPEN;
")" return CLOSE;
\n|.      { return yytext[0]; }
```

To create parser which accepts strings having balanced parentheses, run the following commands

lex bp.lex
yacc –dv bp.y
gcc –o bp y.tab.c lex.yy.c -ly –lfl

Test the generated parser (bp) by giving the following input.

(()) or (()(()()))

Example 41

The following Yacc and Lex specification files are used to generate parser which recognizes arithmetic expressions involving + and -.

Yacc Specification File (ath.y)

```
%{
%}

%token NAME NUMBER EQUL PLUS MINUS

%%
```

```
Stmt  :  NAME EQUL exp
      | exp
      ;

exp   :  NUMBER PLUS NUMBER
      | NUMBER MINUS NUMBER
      | NUMBER MINUS exp
      | NUMBER PLUS exp
      ;

%%

void yyerror(char * s)
{

  printf ( "%s\n", s);

}
int yywrap(){return 1;}

int main(void) {return yyparse();}
```

Lex Specification File (ath.lex)

```
%{
#include"y.tab.h"
%}

%%
[a-zA-Z\_][a-zA-Z\_0-9]*  return NAME;
[0-9]+       return NUMBER;
"+"          return PLUS;
"-" return MINUS;
"="          return EQUL;
```

To create parser which accepts arithmetic expressions with +, - operators, run the following commands

lex ath.lex
yacc –dv ath.y
gcc –o ath y.tab.c lex.yy.c -ly –lfl

Run the command "ath" and enter the following expressions

1 + 2 + 3 - 2 or 1 - 2 - 3 - 5 + 4

Example 42

This Yacc and Lex specification files can be used to generate a tiny language which can be used (simulation only!!) to control a thermostat. It accepts commands such as "on", "off" etc.

Yacc Specification File (thermo.y)

```
%{
#include <stdio.h>
#include <string.h>
void yyerror(const char *str)
{
      fprintf(stderr,"error: %s\n",str);
}
int yywrap()
{
      return 1;
}

main()
{
      yyparse();
}

%}

%token NUMBER TOKHEAT STATE TOKTARGET TOKTEMPERATURE
%%
commands :
    | commands command
            ;

command:
      heat_switch
      |
      target_set
      ;

heat_switch:
      TOKHEAT STATE
      {
            printf("\tHeat turned on or off\n");
```

```
        }
        ;

target_set:
        TOKTARGET TOKTEMPERATURE NUMBER
        {
                printf("\tTemperature set\n");
        }
        ;
```

Lex Specification File (thermo.lex)

```
%{
#include <stdio.h>
#include "y.tab.h"
%}
%%
 [0-9]+              return NUMBER;
heat                 return TOKHEAT;
on|off               return STATE;
target               return TOKTARGET;
temperature          return TOKTEMPERATURE;
\n                   /* ignore end of line */;
[ \t]+               /* ignore whitespace */;
%%
```

To create parser which accepts the above language, run the following commands

lex thermo.lex
yacc –dv thermo.y
gcc –o thermo y.tab.c lex.yy.c -ly –lfl

Example 43

The following Yacc and Lex specification files are used to recognize addresses which are in a specific format only.

Yacc Specification File (add.y)

```
%{
#include <stdio.h>
void yyerror(const char *str)
{

        fprintf(stderr,"error: %s\n",str);
}
```

```
int yywrap()
{
      return 1;
}

%}

%token CAPSTRING CAPLETTER NUMBER STATE ZIPPLUSFOUR COMMA
HASH DOT NEWLINE DOORNO

%%

sentence: firstline secondline thirdline { printf("Have a valid address.\n"); }
       ;

firstline: firstname surname NEWLINE
        | firstname middlename surname NEWLINE
        ;

secondline: DOORNO street NEWLINE
         | DOORNO street HASH NUMBER NEWLINE
         ;

thirdline: city STATE COMMA zip NEWLINE
        ;

firstname: CAPSTRING ;

middlename: CAPLETTER DOT ;

surname: CAPSTRING ;

street: CAPSTRING
      | CAPSTRING street
      ;

city: CAPSTRING
   | CAPSTRING city
   ;

zip: ZIPPLUSFOUR
  ;

%%
```

```
int main( void ) {

    yyparse();
return 0;
}
```

Lex Specification File (add.lex)

```
%{
#include "y.tab.h"
%}
%%
 [\t ]+              /* ignore whitespace */;
 [A-Z][a-z]+          { return CAPSTRING; };
 [A-Z][A-Z]          {return STATE; }
 [A-Z]               {return CAPLETTER; }
 [0-9]+              {return NUMBER; }
 [0-9]+-[0-9]+-[0-9]+      {return DOORNO; }
 PIN-[0-9][0-9][0-9][0-9][0-9][0-9]                  {return ZIPPLUSFOUR; }

\,  {return COMMA; }

#  {return HASH; }

\.  {return DOT; }

\n  {return NEWLINE; }

%%
```

To create parser which accepts addresses, run the following commands

```
lex  add.lex
yacc –dv add.y
gcc –o add y.tab.c  lex.yy.c  -ly –lfl
```

Sample input which is accepted by the parser developed is:

Ravi Teja
12-33-33 First Street
Visakhapatnam AP, PIN-121212

8.3.2 Use of Pseudovariables

While writing actions for each grammar rule, we can make use of pseudovariables supported by the Yacc. As mentioned earlier, when a grammar rule is matched, every symbol in the rule will have a value which is returned by yylex(). Usually, this is assumed to be integer unless redefined by the user. These values are maintained as a separate stack known as value stack in addition to parse stack which maintains the symbols.

The variable $$ represents the value of nonterminal and $1, $2, .. as the values of symbols on the right hand side of the nonterminal(rule). Thus, in the following example,

```
expr        : expr PLUS term        { $$ = $1 + $3; }
```

$$ refers to expression value and $1 and $3 refers to both the operands. That is sum of these operands are assigned to the expression.

In order to tell YACC about the new type of yylval, we add this line to the header of our YACC grammar:

```
#define YYSTYPE char *
extern YYSTYPE yylval;
```

Also, we can use the %union in yacc file such that we can declare that yylval to be a union of an integer, a string pointer, and a character.

```
%union { int integer_value; char *string_value; char op_value; }
```

Now, we can declare both terminals and nonterminals as either integer or char type using the following manner.

```
%token <int> OPRND1
%token<char> OPR1
%token<integer> exp
```

Run the Yacc command and check how the union is declared in the y.tab.h file.

Example 44

This Yacc specification file used to develop calculator which accepts single digit operands. Also, here we are not using any lexical specification file. The necessary lexical analysis program (yylex()) is written directly.

Yacc specification File (calc.y)

```
%{
#include<stdio.h>
#include<stdlib.h>
%}

%token PLUS MINUS MUL DIV NEWLINE RPAR LPAR
%token NUMBER
```

```
/* grammar rules & actions section */

%%

/* These two rules are for reading expressions from the keyboard */

lines       : lines line
    |
    ;
line        : expr NEWLINE                    { printf("%d\n> ", $1); }
    | NEWLINE                 { printf ("> "); }
    ;

/* Grammar rules for integer expressions evaluation */

expr        : expr PLUS term          { $$ = $1 + $3; }
    | expr MINUS term         { $$ = $1 - $3; }
    | term                    { $$ = $1; } /* default action */
    ;
term        : term MUL factor         { $$ = $1 * $3; }
    | term DIV factor         { if ($3 == 0)
                        yyerror("divide by zero");
                      else
                        $$ = $1 / $3;
                    }
    | factor            { $$ = $1; } /* default action */
    ;
factor      : LPAR expr RPAR          { $$ = $2; }
    | NUMBER                { $$ = $1; } /* default action */
    ;

%%

yylex() {
      /* My lexer */
    int c;
     do {
     c=getchar();
     switch (c) {
          case '0': case '1': case '2': case '3': case '4': case '5': case '6':
       case '7': case '8': case '9':
          yylval= c - '0';
          return NUMBER;
       case '+':  return PLUS;
```

```
        case '-':  return MINUS;
        case '*':  return MUL;
        case '/':  return DIV;
        case '(':  return LPAR;
        case ')':  return RPAR;
        case '\n':  return NEWLINE;
         }
    } while (c!= EOF);

    return(EOF);
}

main() {
    printf("> ");
    yyparse();
}
```

To generate the calculator program (executable file), run the following commands.

```
yacc –dv calc.y
gcc –o calc y.tab.c –ly
```

Example 45

This Yacc and Lex specification programs are used to generate a calculator which is flexible than the previous one. It accepts, integer and float type arguments.

Yacc Specification File (calculator.y)

```
%{
#include <stdio.h>
%}

%union{ double   real; /* real value */
        int   integer; /* integer value */
      }

%token <real> REAL
%token <integer> INTEGER
%token PLUS MINUS TIMES DIVIDE LP RP NL

%type <real> rexpr
%type <integer> iexpr

%left PLUS MINUS
%left TIMES DIVIDE
```

```
%left UMINUS

%%

lines: /* nothing */
     | lines line
     ;

line:  NL
     | iexpr NL
      { printf("%d) %d\n", lineno, $1);}
     | rexpr NL
      { printf("%d) %15.8lf\n", lineno, $1);}
     ;

iexpr: INTEGER
     | iexpr PLUS iexpr
      { $$ = $1 + $3;}
     | iexpr MINUS iexpr
      { $$ = $1 - $3;}
     | iexpr TIMES iexpr
      { $$ = $1 * $3;}
     | iexpr DIVIDE iexpr
      { if($3) $$ = $1 / $3;
        else { fprintf(stderr, "divide by zero\n");
             yyerror();
          }
      }
     | MINUS iexpr %prec UMINUS
      { $$ = - $2;}
     | LP iexpr RP
      { $$ = $2;}
     ;

rexpr: REAL
     | rexpr PLUS rexpr
      { $$ = $1 + $3;}
     | rexpr MINUS rexpr
      { $$ = $1 - $3;}
     | rexpr TIMES rexpr
      { $$ = $1 * $3;}
     | rexpr DIVIDE rexpr
      { if($3) $$ = $1 / $3;
        else { fprintf(stderr, "divide by zero\n");
```

```
                yyerror();
            }
        }
      | MINUS rexpr %prec UMINUS
        { $$ = - $2;}
      | LP rexpr RP
        { $$ = $2;}
      | iexpr PLUS rexpr
        { $$ = (double)$1 + $3;}
      | iexpr MINUS rexpr
        { $$ = (double)$1 - $3;}
      | iexpr TIMES rexpr
        { $$ = (double)$1 * $3;}
      | iexpr DIVIDE rexpr
        { if($3) $$ = (double)$1 / $3;
          else { fprintf(stderr, "divide by zero\n");
                yyerror();
            }
        }
      | rexpr PLUS iexpr
        { $$ = $1 + (double)$3;}
      | rexpr MINUS iexpr
        { $$ = $1 - (double)$3;}
      | rexpr TIMES iexpr
        { $$ = $1 * (double)$3;}
      | rexpr DIVIDE iexpr
        { if($3) $$ = $1 / (double)$3;
          else { fprintf(stderr, "divide by zero\n");
                yyerror();
            }
        }
      ;

%%
#include "lex.yy.c"
int lineno;
```

Lex Specification File (calculator.lex)

```
integer     [0-9]+
dreal       ([0-9]*\.[0-9]+)
ereal       ([0-9]*\.[0-9]+[Ee][+-]?[0-9]+)
real        {dreal}|{ereal}
nl          \n
```

```
%%
[ \t]       ;
{integer}   { sscanf(yytext, "%d", &yylval.integer);
             return INTEGER;
            }
{real}       { sscanf(yytext, "%lf", &yylval.real);
             return REAL;
            }
\+          { return PLUS;}
\-          { return MINUS;}
\*          { return TIMES;}
V           { return DIVIDE;}
\(          { return LP;}
\)          { return RP;}

{nl}         { extern int lineno; lineno++;
             return NL;
            }
.           { return yytext[0]; }
```

To create parser which accepts arithmetic expressions with +, - operators, run the following commands

```
lex  calculator.lex
yacc –dv calculator.y
gcc –o calculator y.tab.c  lex.yy.c  -ly –lfl
```

Example 46

The following Yacc and Lex specification files are used to generate a program which identify the number of words in the given input file.

Yacc Specification File (words.y)

```
%{
#include<stdlib.h>
#include<string.h>
int yylex();
#include "words.h"
int nwords=0;
#define MAXWORDS 100
char * words[MAXWORDS];
%}
```

```
%token WORD
%%
text        : ;
    | text WORD; {
            if($2<0) printf("New Word\n");
            else  printf("Matched\n");
    }
%%

int find_word(char *x)
{
int i;

for(i=0;i<nwords;i++) if(strcmp(x,words[i])==0) return i;

words[nwords++]=strdup(x);
return -1;
}

int main()
{
yyparse();
printf("No of Words=%d\n", nwords);
}

void yyerror(char *a)
{
}

int yywrap()
{
return 1;
}
```

Lex Specification File (words.lex)

```
%{
#include "y.tab.h"
int find_word(char *);
extern int yylval;
%}
```

```
%%

[a-zA-Z]+  {yylval=find_word(yytext); return WORD;}
.|\n        ;
%%
```

To create parser which counts the number of words in a given file, run the following commands

```
lex words.lex
yacc -dv words.y
gcc -o words y.tab.c lex.yy.c -ly -lfl
```

Tracing the execution of a Yacc generated parser can be done by including the following lines to the Yacc specification file and while compiling give -DYYDEBUG option.

```
extern in yydebug;
yydebug=1;
```

8.4 Conclusions

This chapter discusses about the use of Lex and Yacc libraries for developing lexical analysis programs (compilers), file processing utilities and parsers. Many examples are given to explain each concept of lex and yacc library.

9 Unix Memory Management

9.1 Introduction

Unix operating system uses virtual memory management. To allow a program to access more memory than might be physically installed in the machine, most modern operating systems including all Unix variants employs this concept. Virtual memory works by the operating system (in tight cooperation with the CPU) by mapping virtual addresses used by a process, into physical addresses. When a process allocates a new block of memory, the operating system assigns this block to some section (called 'page') of physical memory, using a virtual memory translation table. Each access to a memory location by the process is translated to access to the matching physical memory page. In order to avoid slowing down the program, this translation is done directly by the CPU.

9.1.1 Memory Protection

The operating system uses a translation table to map virtual memory to physical memory. Taking this a further step, the system can use a different translation table for each process, thereby giving each process its own address space. This means that the same virtual memory address used by two different processes, will be mapped into two different physical memory addresses. This means that one process cannot access the contents of the memory used by the other process, and thus one process corrupting its memory won't interfere with the contents of the memory of any other process in the system. This feature is known as "memory protection", and is used now by most operating systems (including all Unix variants).

9.2 Run-time Management Of Virtual Memory

Some of the virtual memory sections might be mapped to no physical memory page. When a process tries to access a memory cell in such a section, the CPU identifies a page fault, and invokes an operating system routine that needs to handle this fault. Most operating systems use this feature to store part of the virtual memory sections on disk, rather than in RAM, thereby allowing the program to use an address space larger than the physical RAM of the machine. When a page fault occurs, the operating system loads the contents of the faulted virtual memory section from the disk, copies it into a free physical memory page, and updates the virtual memory translation table so the CPU will know to map the virtual memory section to the new physical RAM page.

During the search for a free page, it might be that no free page is found. In such case, the operating system takes the contents of a busy physical memory page, copies it to the hard disk, and uses this memory page to load the data of the desired virtual memory section. The virtual memory section that was previously mapped to this physical memory page, is now marked as paged out.

As we can see from this, the algorithm used to decide which memory page should be taken when there are no free pages, has to be efficient. With a bad algorithm, a process that accesses two virtual memory sections alternately, might cause the system to keep paging these sections in and out. Since access to the disk is much slower than access to RAM, this will slow down the system tremendously. A common algorithm used to find candidates for paging out is called LRU - Least Recently Used. In this algorithm, the memory page that was used least recently, is the page that will have its contents paged out. This algorithm works well due to the locality principle - if a process accessed a given memory page, it is likely to access this same page or one near it on the next instruction.

9.2.1 Signals: SIGSEGV & SIGBUS

We saw that some virtual memory sections aren't mapped to physical memory. While some of them were simply paged out, others were never allocated by the process. When a process runs, its virtual memory table is small. As it allocates more memory pages, the table grows. However, if the process tries to access a virtual memory address of a section it hasn't allocated yet, the operating system has no where to bring this page from. The designers of the Unix system decided that this situation indicates a program bug, and thus instead of making an automatic allocation of a memory page in such a case, they chose to send a signal to the process. This signal is a SEGV signal (or SIGSEGV), and its default signal handler prints out a "Segmentation violation - core dumped" message, and dumps the memory image of the process into a file named 'core' in the process's current directory (see example in chapter on signals).

Another way to cause a 'segmentation violation' is trying to access an illegal location of virtual memory. Because many invalid pointer problems occur with very low pointer values, the operating system does not allow a process to allocate a memory page for the virtual memory section beginning with the virtual address '0'. This is what causes programs to receive a SEGV signal when trying to de-reference a NULL pointer (NULL on _most_ machine architectures is defined as '0').

Example 1

```
#include<stdio.h>
int main()
{
char *s;
s=(char *)0;
printf("%c\n", *s);
return 0;
}
```

The above program gives run time error "segment violation" as memory location 0 is not accessible. When you say " ***s**", the hardware sees that you want to read memory location zero. It checks with the operating system, which says "I haven't allocated the page containing location zero for you". Thus, this results in a segmentation violation.

Example 2

```
#include<stdio.h>
int main()
{
int x;

scanf("%d", x);

}
```

The above program compiles but gives run time error "segment violation". In this program, we are calling scanf function with x as argument whose value is undefined and we are asking scanf to read an integer from keyboard and store the same in the memory pointed by the value of this variable x. If that memory is not allocated to our program we get this error. By chance if that value refers to an allocated memory then we will not be getting any such error.

What about a BUS (or SIGBUS) signal? this signal is sent to a program that tries to access a non-aligned pointer. For instance, on many machine architectures, access to 'long' (4 byte) numbers must be done using a memory address that divides by 4. Trying to access such an entity using an address that does not abide by this rule will cause the CPU to emit a trap. The operating system's kernel catches this trap, and then sends a BUS signal to the program. The default signal handler for this signal emits a "Bus error - core dumped" message, and dumps the memory contents to a 'core' file, much like the handler for the SEGV signal does.

9.2.2 Load On Demand

As we have seen, the efficiency of virtual memory is based on the locality principle. The same principle can be used when loading programs into memory. There is no point in loading all the executable file during application startup. Large parts of the code are likely not to be ever executed during the process's lifetime. Furthermore, loading all of the code at once will mean it will take more time until the process can start running.

Thus, what Unix systems do, is just allocate the page table entries, and mark the pages as "load on demand". When the process tries to access a virtual memory cell in a page that wasn't loaded yet, a page fault will occur, causing the operating system to load the contents of this specific page into memory. The code part of shared libraries is treated in a similar manner.

This feature, together with some properties of file management could explain the following phenomena: if you have a process executing program file 'foo', and you then compile a new version of 'foo' and copy it on top of the original 'foo' file - the process is likely to crash very quickly. The reason for this is that the process is likely to access a virtual memory cell of a page whose contents were not loaded yet. This will cause the system to load the page from the *new* binary file - which is most likely different from the original binary file. Thus, the program will be executing a random machine instruction, instead of the machine instruction it was supposed to perform, most likely resulting a process crash.

Example 3

```
#include<stdio.h>
void main()
{
 while(1);
}
```

Let this file name be "a.c", the following sequence of commands are executed at the command prompt.

```
gcc -o a a.c
./a&
gcc –o a a.c
```

In the first command, we have compiled a.c and created an executable file "a". The second command starts this program in background. In the third command we are trying to recompile the same program 'a.c". This may give raise to an error message **"text file busy"** on some Unix systems. The reason is as explained above.

In order to avoid the above scenario, there are several options. First One is killing all processes currently executing the program's binary, before updating it. A better method is to rename the old binary file to a new name (e.g. foo.old) and then copy the new binary to 'foo'. This will work, because the name of a file is relevant only when a process tries to open it. After the file was opened, the process accesses it via its disk location (I-node number) - which is different for the old and the new files. Actually, we may even erase the old binary file without renaming it - the file will be removed from the directory, but not from the disk. It will be removed from disk only when all processes keeping it open (e.g. processes executing this binary program file) will close it (or exit). Note that this is NOT true if the binary file is accessed via NFS, only if it is accessed on a local file system. NFS file accesses always use the file name, whether for open operations or for read operations.

9.2.3 Read-Only Memory

Some of the virtual memory space used by a process does not ever need to change during the process's life. This fact can be used to optimize handling of such memory pages by the paging code of the operating system. For example, executable memory pages are read-only pages, and are marked so by the system. Trying to write into them would fail, and generate a CPU trap which will be caught by the operating system, that will send a SEGV signal to the process.

When the system needs to page out read-only code pages of this sort, it doesn't even have to page them out to disk - it already has a copy of them inside the binary executable (or the shared library) they were taken from. Thus, paging these pages out just requires marking them as free.

The process can mark other memory pages as read-only too (see the man page for the mmap() system call, for example). This could be useful to make sure no part of the code tries to modify the contents of that memory - useful for trapping down some bugs.

9.2.4 Shared Memory

Another feature supported by Unix systems is shared memory. Using this feature, virtual memory sections of different processes are marked as shared, and thus point to the same physical memory pages. When one process changes the contents of this memory, the other processes immediately see the new contents. Of course this means that access to this shared memory should be synchronized among the processes sharing it, using some locking mechanism.

Writable memory pages can be shared by processes using various system APIs, such as the System-V shared memory API (see the man page of shmget() and shmat() for details) or using the mmap() system call. Note that a page may be shared between more than 2 processes, and some of these processes might only require read-only access to these shared memory pages.

Read-only shared memory is easier to manage. One place where sharing read-only memory pages comes in very handy is sharing of executable code coming from program binary files and from shared libraries. The system automatically takes care of that - if a process tries to execute a program that is already loaded to memory due to being executed by another process, the memory pages holding the binary code will be mapped to the virtual address space of the new process, and thus overall memory usage of the system would not increase (other than the memory needed to hold the translation table for the new process - this table is not shared between processes). Note that dynamic data won't be shared by processes in this manner, since it is stored to writable memory pages. This is, ofcourse, the expected behavior - you wouldn't want one process changing a variable's contents, affecting another process running the same program, would you?.

9.2.5 Memory Managers

Memory managers are software libraries that perform memory allocation and de-allocation on behalf of the program. Every programming language comes with a runtime environment that includes at least one memory manager. Since the programming languages we deal with tend to be general purpose, the memory manager is also general purpose - it does not assume anything about the pattern of allocations, sizes of memory chunks allocated and the likes. Therefore, it is possible to find an allocation pattern that will cause a given memory allocation to perform poorly. Thus, having an idea regarding how a memory manager works could allow us to write programs that make more efficient use of memory, in terms of speed and of overall memory usage.

9.2.6 Memory Alignment

One property of all memory managers is that they return memory chunks which are aligned best for the architecture of the machine on which they are run. Alignment means that the memory chunks returned to the user begin on an address that divides by the size of a word for the CPU they are running on. This size is often of 4 bytes (for 32 bit architectures) or 8 bytes (for 64 bit architectures). Further, the size of returned chunks is also kept to a multiple of the word size. This ensures that the returned memory blocks can be used to store the largest data type the machine supports (e.g. a long integer).

The price of this mechanism is that often memory is wasted. For example, suppose that we have a machine with a word size of 4 bytes. Further, suppose that we want to store a string whose length is 5 bytes (including the terminating null character, if we're referring to a C language string). The memory manager will give me a memory chunk whose size is 8 bytes (2 words). We use 5 bytes, and 3 are wasted. Thus, general-purpose memory managers cause a lot of memory waste for programs that allocate many small memory chunks. We will discuss methods of overcoming this problem when we discuss specialized memory managers. We will also see how this affects issues with pointers and memory smearing (memory contents corrupting).

Because of the same reason, on most of the systems the following program prints complete string even if its size is declared as 4 bytes.

Example 4

```
#include<stdio.h>
void main()
{
char x[4]="Ramya";
 printf("%s\n",x);
}
```

We have claimed that the memory manager begins with one chunk on its list of free memory chunks. This chunk has to be taken from some place - this is the role of the operating system's virtual memory manager. As we remember, the memory the process accesses is actually virtual memory. Also, most virtual memory sections are not mapped anywhere. This is done for efficiency - when a process's virtual address space is of a size of several giga-bytes, it will be wasteful to allocate a map to handle this amount of virtual memory, especially since most processes use a much smaller amount of memory.

The way the operating system handles this situation is by not allocating any memory for the process, unless it asks for it. Of course, the program's binary and shared library sizes can be known in advance, but memory used to store data is of an arbitrary size. When the process requires more memory to store data pages, it uses the brk() system call (or sbrk()) to ask the system to enlarge its allocated address space. The system then adds entries to the translation map for this process, and the pages themselves will be then mapped into physical memory when they are accessed.

As the program runs, and memory is allocated from the heap using **malloc()**, the heap grows. To figure out the boundary of the heap, we must use **brk()** or **sbrk()**. Both are system calls, and you can read their man pages.

```
caddr_t sbrk(int incr);
```

A **caddr_t** is a "c address pointer". It is the same as a **(char *)** or a **(void *)**.

This specifies for the operating system to give **incr** more bytes to the heap. It returns a pointer to the end of the heap before **sbrk()** was called. Thus, the new end of the heap after an **sbrk()** call is at address

```
sbrk(incr) + incr;
```

If we call **sbrk(0)**, then it returns the current end of the heap.

Now, **malloc()** (and the related programs **realloc()** and **calloc()**) all call **sbrk()** to get the memory to allocate in the heap. They are the only routines that call **sbrk()**. Thus, the only way that we can get memory in the heap is through **malloc()** or **sbrk()**. However, we should use **malloc()**, as it is more efficient.

Actually, the system call interface is hardly ever used by programmers. The memory manager of the runtime environment of our programming language is the one that uses this interface. Thus, whenever it runs out of free memory chunks on its list, it'll call the brk() system call to allocate more memory pages, and add the new block to its chunks list. The amount of memory it will ask the system to allocate can vary. Asking for too small sizes will cause many calls to brk(), which is time consuming. Allocating a too large block will take time for the system to update the virtual translation map for the process.

Note: there is usually no system call that can be used to return unused memory back to the operating system. when you free memory, the memory manager cannot return this memory back to the operating system. If this freed memory is never used again, it will eventually be paged out to disk - but won't be freed until the process exits. Thus, the amount of virtual memory used by a process always increases - never decreases.

Note 2: the above rule has an exception - shared memory, and *mmap()*-ed memory. Shared memory is counted as part of the memory space used by the process. Thus, when the process attached to a shared memory chunk, its 'accounted' virtual address space size is increased by the amount of space in the shared memory page. When the process releases a shared memory chunk, the process's 'accounted' virtual address space size is decreased. The same goes for memory mapped using the *mmap()* system call.

Memory Manager's Interaction With Program's Code

As we have seen, the memory manager keeps its own data structures in the address space of the process for which it works. This means that if the process overwrites memory out of bounds (e.g. referencing a location right before an array it has allocated using the manager) - the data structures of the memory manager itself may be corrupted. This would explain cases where a program we write crashes, and the stack shows it was in a middle of a call to the memory manager's functions.

Note that these kinds of bugs are not always easy to track - the memory corruption might have occurred in a completely different part of the code, and just looking at the functions on the stack and the code they execute often won't help locating the cause of the problem.

The cause of such a problem could be that our program had overwritten a location that had stored the size of a chunk, and thus when it was freed, the memory manager overtook a larger chunk than had originally been allocated. The manager later allocated parts of this chunk for other purposes, and thus we get the same chunk of memory used by different parts of our code for different purposes. Or a bug in our code might cause the list of free memory chunks to be corrupted, causing one of its pointers to contain an invalid value (e.g. pointing outside the process's address space).

9.3 C Runtime Memory Management

The C programming language and its runtime environment serve as the basic language used on Unix systems. The runtime environment defines not only how memory is allocated and freed, but also how the process's different pieces of information are layered out in memory. Also, being a language that works on a low level, it allows the programmer a lot of control on how memory is used. This means a lot of power - together with responsibility.

9.3.1 Program Memory Segments

A C program is layered out in memory in several separate segments - code segment, stack segment and data segment. These segments are layered out inside the virtual address space of the process.

The code segment holds the executable code of the program (both coming from the program's binary itself, and any shared libraries it loads). All memory pages of the code segment are marked as read-only, and are shared with any other process using the same program file and/or shared library files.

Note: not all pages are shared in this way, due to 'relocation' issues. These are cases when a part of the program needs to know the address of another part, but the exact address will only be known at run-time. This address might be different for different processes (since they load a different set of shared libraries, for example), and thus cannot be written in a shared page. The dynamic loader (which is responsible for handling such situations, among other things) uses "indirect jumps" - it stores non-shared pages that contain these varied addresses in them, and the program's code is compiled in a way that it will read the addresses from these non-shared pages. If this was not done, complete pages of executable code will need to be copied, just to change one or two locations holding such addresses.

The stack segment is used to hold the contents of the stack of the process. The stack size is defined at process startup, and cannot be increased while the process runs. For a multi-threaded process, several stacks will exist in the stack segment.

The data segment occupies the space from the stack segment, to the last address allocated by the process using the brk() system call. This segment can grow as the process runs and needs more virtual memory.

Example 5

```
#include <stdio.h>

        extern end;
        extern etext;

        int I;

        main(int argc, char **argv)
        {
```

```
    int i;
    int *ii;

    printf("&etext = 0x%lx\n", &etext);
    printf("&end   = 0x%lx\n", &end);

    printf("\n");
    ii = (int *) malloc(sizeof(int));

    printf("main   = 0x%lx\n", main);
    printf("&I     = 0x%lx\n", &I);
    printf("&i     = 0x%lx\n", &i);
    printf("&argc  = 0x%lx\n", &argc);
    printf("&ii    = 0x%lx\n", &ii);
    printf("ii     = 0x%lx\n", ii);

}
```

&etext and &end.

These are two external variables that are defined as follows:

extern etext;

extern end;

Note that they are typeless. We never use just "**etext**" and "**end**". Instead, we use their addresses - these variables point to the end of the text and globals (data) segments respectively.

When we run the above program it prints out the addresses of **etext** and **end**. Then it also prints out 6 values:

- **main** is a pointer to the first instruction of the **main()** procedure. This is simply a location in the code segment, which should be familiar to we from the assembler lectures.
- **I** is a global variable. Thus **&I** should be an address in the globals segment.
- **i** is a local variable. Thus **&i** should be an address in the stack.
- **argc** is an argument to **main()**. Thus, **&argc** should be an address in the stack.
- **ii** is another local variable. Thus, **&ii** should be an address in the stack. However, **ii** is a pointer to memory that has been **malloc**'d. Thus, **ii** should be an address in the heap.

When we run **testaddr1**, we get something like the following:

```
&etext = 0x80484d7
&end   = 0x8049674

main   = 0x804835c
&I     = 0x8049670
&i     = 0xbfffe5c4
&argc  = 0xbfffe5d0
&ii    = 0xbfffe5c0
ii     = 0x80496c8
```

So, what this says is that the code segment is upto 0x80484d7. The globals segment goes upto 0x8049674.

Run the following program to check which range of addresses are meaningful (i.e which don't give any segment violation error) and which are not meaningful. This is done by taking a HEX address from the user and trying to read and write into it. If the location is not accessible then we may get SIGSEGV error and some times if the location is read only type (such as code area) then during writing we will get error. Run this program and play it by giving different addresses.

Example 6

```
#include <stdio.h>

        extern end;
        extern etext;

        main()
        {
          char *s;
          char c;

          printf("&etext = 0x%lx\n", &etext);
          printf("&end    = 0x%lx\n", &end);

          printf("\n");

          printf("Enter memory location in hex (start with 0x): ");
          fflush(stdout);

          scanf("0x%x", &s);

          printf("Reading 0x%x:  ", s);
          fflush(stdout);
          c = *s;
          printf("%d\n", c);
          printf("Writing %d back to  0x%x:  ", c, s);
          fflush(stdout);
          *s = c;
          printf("ok\n");
        }
```

When we give address is 0x862121 we will get the following result and segment violation.

```
&etext = 0x804855b
&end   = 0x804973c
```

Enter memory location in hex (start with 0x): Reading 0x862121:

When the first **malloc()** is called, a call to **sbrk()** is made to get a new chunk of memory. To support this, run the following program and see the values of &end and sbrk(0) values.

Example 7

```
#include <stdio.h>

        extern end;
        extern etext;

        main()
        {
         char *s;
         char c;

         printf("&etext = 0x%lx\n", &etext);
         printf("&end   = 0x%lx\n", &end);
         printf("sbrk(0)= 0x%lx\n", sbrk(0));
         printf("&c     = 0x%lx\n", &c);

         printf("\n");

         printf("Enter memory location in hex (start with 0x): ");
         fflush(stdout);

         scanf("0x%x", &s);

         printf("Reading 0x%x:  ", s);
         fflush(stdout);
         c = *s;
         printf("%d\n", c);
         printf("Writing %d back to  0x%x:  ", c, s);
         fflush(stdout);
         *s = c;
         printf("ok\n");
        }
```

Results of the above program supports the above statement. That is before malloc() call sbrk(0) value is same as &end.

```
&etext = 0x80485c3
&end   = 0x80497e0
sbrk(0)= 0x80497e0
&c     = 0xbfffdcc3
```

Enter memory location in hex (start with 0x): Reading 0x812121:

Now, run the following program in which malloc() is called before printing values and we can find that the &end and sbrk(0) values as different.

Example 8

```
#include <stdio.h>

        extern end;
        extern etext;

        main()
        {
         char *s;
         char c;
         char *buf;

         buf = (char *) malloc(1000);

         printf("&etext = 0x%lx\n", &etext);
         printf("&end   = 0x%lx\n", &end);
         printf("sbrk(0)= 0x%lx\n", sbrk(0));
         printf("&c     = 0x%lx\n", &c);

         printf("\n");

         printf("Enter memory location in hex (start with 0x): ");
         fflush(stdout);

         scanf("0x%x", &s);

         printf("Reading 0x%x:  ", s);
         fflush(stdout);
         c = *s;
         printf("%d\n", c);
         printf("Writing %d back to  0x%x:  ", c, s);
         fflush(stdout);
         *s = c;
         printf("ok\n");
        }
```

Results of the above program

```
&etext = 0x8048607
```

```
&end    = 0x8049824
sbrk(0)= 0x804b000
&c     = 0xbfffe7c3
```

Enter memory location in hex (start with 0x): Reading 0x8612121:

The function malloc keeps a big buffer of memory in the heap and carves it up and doles it out whenever the user calls **malloc()**. If there is not enough room in the buffer for what the user desires, then **sbrk()** is called to get heap storage for a big enough buffer.

Malloc really maintain a linked list of free memory. When **malloc()** is called, it looks on its list for a piece of memory that is big enough. If it finds one, then it removes that memory from the linked list and returns it to the user. When **free()** is called, the memory is put back on the linked list. Now, to be efficient, if there is a chunk of memory on the free list that much bigger than what is requested, then it breaks up that chunk into two chunks -- one which is the size of the request (padded to a multiple of 8), and the remainder. The remainder is put on the free list and the one the size of the request is returned to the user. This is the standard way that you view **malloc** -- it manages a free list of memory. **Malloc()** takes memory from the free list and gives it to the user, and **free()** gives memory back to the free list.

When the first **malloc()** is called, we call **sbrk()** to get a new chunk of memory for the free list. This memory is split up so that some is returned to the user, and the rest goes back onto the free list. Similarly, nodes of the free lists are also coalesced. The link may maintain the address of previous and next lists in addition to the size of the chunk which we may call as book keeping.

Example 9

```
#include <stdio.h>
#include <sys/types.h>

main()
{
 int *i1, *i2, *i3;

 printf("sbrk(0) before malloc(4): 0x%x\n", sbrk(0));
 i1 = (int *) malloc(4);
 printf("sbrk(0) after `i1 = (int *) malloc(4)': 0x%x\n", sbrk(0));
 i2 = (int *) malloc(4);
 printf("sbrk(0) after `i2 = (int *) malloc(4)': 0x%x\n", sbrk(0));
 printf("i1 = 0x%x, i2 = 0x%x, sbrk(0)-i2 = %d\n", i1, i2,
          (char *) sbrk(0)- (char *) i2);
 i3 = (int *) malloc(8164);
 printf("sbrk(0) after `i3 = (int *) malloc(8164)': 0x%x\n", sbrk(0));
 printf("i3 = 0x%x\n", i3);

}
```

```
Results of the above program  are as follows.
sbrk(0) before malloc(4): 0x804978c
sbrk(0) after `i1 = (int *) malloc(4)': 0x804b000
sbrk(0) after `i2 = (int *) malloc(4)': 0x804b000
i1 = 0x80497e0, i2 = 0x80497f0, sbrk(0)-i2 = 6160
sbrk(0) after `i3 = (int *) malloc(8164)': 0x804c000
i3 = 0x8049800
```

This corroborates of our statements such as

1. malloc() calls sbrk() first time and gets a chunk of free memory. Also, after both malloc() calls also sbrk(0) value did not change. Which supports the above discussion of free list.
2. Also, check the addresses of i1 and i2 which are differed by 16 bytes. Though we have asked for 4 bytes, malloc() allocated 16 bytes. That is remaining memory book keeping information and empty bytes as explained earlier.
3. When we try to allocate memory of 8192 bytes again sbrk(0) values is changed. Which indicates that sbrk() is called again to accommodate the required memory request.

To support the second statement given above, run the following program and check the results.

Example 10

```
#include<stdio.h>
int main()
{
int *s; char *p; int i;
s=(int *)malloc(sizeof(int));
scanf("%d", s);
printf("%d\n",*s);
p=(char *)s;
for(i=0;i<8;i++)
printf("%c\n",  *(p+i));
return 0;
}
```

Here, first memory (4 bytes) is allocated for an integer and its address is assigned to "s" and the same address is assigned to a character pointer "p" through typecasting. Then, by running a for loop eight elements (characters) are printed. Though actually, we should be in a position to access only 4 bytes, we are able to access some of the next bytes also. This supports that malloc() allocates memory more than what we have asked for. Ofcourse, the next location may contain book keeping information of the chunk. Refer for dope vectors in principles of programming language books.

9.3.2 The Stack And Local Variables

The stack is used by the process to store the chain of functions which are currently in the middle of execution. Each function call causes the process to add an execution frame to the top of the stack. This execution frame would contain the contents of CPU registers as they were before the function call was made, the return address (i.e. where in the code this function was invoked, so we can return there when the function returns), the parameters passed to the function and all local variables of the function. Thus, when we have function 'main' calling function 'a' which calls function 'b', we will have 3 frames on the stack.

The 'allocation' of a stack frame does not require performing real memory allocation - as the space for the stack was reserved during process startup. Instead, this is done by merely marking a part of the stack as containing the frame, and copying data to that frame. Note that local variables are "allocated" by simply advancing the stack pointer beyond their location on the stack, so allocating local variables takes a fixed amount of time, no matter their size. When a function returns - its stack frame is freed by simply modifying the stack pointer to point below its frame.

The local variables are not initialized - they just contain the values that were accidentally placed in the memory locations these variables occupy. We may consider a situation in which a function was called, its variables used and given some values. Later the function returned, and its frame was released. Then, another function was called. the stack frame of this new function is located in the same place in memory as the frame of the former function, so the new function's local variables will get the values that were left there by the local variables of the former function. This can explain why the values of un-intialized local variables are often neither 0, nor look like total garbage.

Since all local variables are stored in consecutive memory on the stack, if we take a pointer to such a variable, and later on write right above or right below this pointer, we'll be modifying the contents of another local variable, or even that of the function's return address, if we're "lucky". For example, consider the following code:

```
int foo()
{
   int numbers[2];
   int j;

   j = 2;
   printf("j - %d\n", j);
   numbers[2] = 3;
   printf("j - %d\n", j);
}
```

During execution of this function, we first assign 2 to 'j', and thus the first print command will show "j - 2". Then, we try to assign a value to 'numbers[2]'. However, the 'numbers' array only has 2 cells - 0 and 1. Writing into subscript '2' of this array will cause us to write just beyond the array (which is fully located on the stack). The variable 'j' just happens to be stored in that location in memory, and thus, the value '3' will be actually assigned to 'j'. Our second print command will thus show "j - 3". Note that this assumes that the variables are stored in memory in the same order as they were declared inside the function's code. With some compilers, this might not be the case, and the out-of-range assignment might overwrite a different variable, or a part of the stack that does not hold variables, leading to other unexpected results.

Note: local variables (as well as function parameters) might be stored in registers, rather than on the stack. This could be either because we used the 'register' keyword when declaring these variables, or because the compiler's optimization chose to place a variable in a register. Ofcourse, such variables cannot be over-written by stack overflows.

Now, lets break the stack. This can be done by writing a program that allocates too much stack memory. One such program is in given below performs infinite recursion, and at each recursive step it allocates 10000 bytes of stack memory in the variable **iptr**. When you run this, we'll see that we get a segmentation violation when the recursive call is made. Often when we have infinite recursion and overflow the stack, we get "illegal instruction" instead of Segmentation fault.

Example 11

```
#include <stdio.h>

         extern end;
         extern etext;

         main()
         {
          char c;
          char iptr[100000];

          printf("&c     = 0x%lx, iptr = 0x%x  ...  ", &c, iptr);
          fflush(stdout);
          c = iptr[0];
          printf("ok\n");
          main();
         }
```

The second way to break the stack is to simply allocate too much local memory. E.g. look at the following program. It tries to allocate 10M of memory in the stack.

Example 12

```
#include <stdio.h>

         extern end;
         extern etext;

         a()
         {
          char c;
          char iptr[10000000];

          printf("&c     = 0x%lx, iptr = 0x%x  ...  ", &c, iptr);
```

```
  fflush(stdout);
  c = iptr[0];
  printf("ok\n");
}

main()
{
  printf("Calling a\n");
  a();
}
```

Also, recursive function calls may lead to stack overflow. Normally, tail recursion is employed to alleviate this problem.

See the following program to show stack information.

Example 13

```
#include <stdio.h>

a(int j, int *k)
{
  char **s;
  char *s2;
  int i;

  s = (char **) &s;

  printf("a: &i = 0x%x, &j = 0x%x, &k = 0x%x\n", &i, &j, &k);

  for (i = 0; i < 10; i++) {
    s++;
    s2 = (char *) s;
    printf("0x%x : %15d 0x%-8x\n", s, *s, *s);
  }
}

b(int j)
{
  int i;

  j++;
  i = j+15;

  printf("b: &i = 0x%x, &j = 0x%x\n", &i, &j);

  a(49, &j);
```

```
}

main()
{
 int i;

 i = 333;

 b(i);
}
```

If we run the above program we may get the results which displays the details of the stack frames.

```
b: &i = 0xbffff624, &j = 0xbffff630
a: &i = 0xbffff5fc, &j = 0xbffff610, &k = 0xbffff614
0xbffff608 :    -1073744344 0xbffff628
0xbffff60c :     134513603 0x80483c3
0xbffff610 :            49 0x31
0xbffff614 :    -1073744336 0xbffff630
0xbffff618 :    -1073744336 0xbffff630
0xbffff61c :     134513318 0x80482a6
0xbffff620 :    1108545272 0x42130ef8
0xbffff624 :           349 0x15d
0xbffff628 :    -1073744312 0xbffff648
0xbffff62c :     134513642 0x80483ea
```

This example also explains the status of the stack.

Example 14

```
#include<stdio.h>
safechar(char c)
{
 if (c >= 'a' && c <= 'z') return(c);
 if (c >= 'A' && c <= 'Z') return(c);
 if (c >= '0' && c <= '9') return(c);
 if (c == ' ') return(c);
 if (c == '.') return(c);
 if (c == '-') return(c);
 if (c == ',') return(c);
 if (c == '(') return(c);
 if (c == ')') return(c);
```

```
  if (c == '[') return(c);
  if (c == ']') return(c);
  if (c == '{') return(c);
  if (c == '}') return(c);
  return '@';
}
main(int argc, char **argv, char **envp)
{
  char **s;
  char *s2;
  int i, top;

  if (argc < 2) {
    fprintf(stderr, "usage: printstack nentries (& other junk if you want)\n");
    exit(1);
  }

  top = atoi(argv[1]);

  printf("&s = 0x%x\n", &s);
  printf("&argc = 0x%x\n", &argc);
  printf("&argv = 0x%x\n", &argv);
  printf("&envp = 0x%x\n", &envp);
  printf("\n");

  s = (char **) &s;
  for (i = 0; i < top; i++) {
    s++;
    s2 = (char *) s;
    printf("0x%x : %15d 0x%-8x %2c %2c %2c %2c\n", s, *s, *s,
safechar(s2[0]),
           safechar(s2[1]), safechar(s2[2]), safechar(s2[3]));
  }
}
```

Results of the above program is as follows.

```
&s = 0xbfffe044
&argc = 0xbfffe050
&argv = 0xbfffe054
&envp = 0xbfffe058

0xbfffe048 :    -1073749912 0xbfffe068  h  @  @  @
0xbfffe04c :     1107383668 0x42015574  t  U  @  B
```

9.3.3 Free()

When we want to free a memory chunk previously allocated by malloc(), we use the free function. This function accepts a char pointer to a previously allocated memory chunk, and frees it - that is, adds it to the list of free memory chunks, that may be re-allocated. Several notes about free():

- The size of the chunk was stored by malloc() previously in its memory map, and that is how free() knows how many bytes to free.
- The freed memory is not being cleared or erased in any manner. This is why accessing memory that was just freed often does not cause a crash - any data in it is still the same as before calling free().
- The free() function cannot nullify pointers to the given memory chunk that might still exist in our program. After we call free(), it is up to us (the programmers) not to try and Dereference pointers that still point to that memory chunk. Such pointers are known as 'dangling pointers' - they point to memory that was already freed, and thus they should NOT be dereferenced again, unless they are assigned the address of a different (not-freed) memory chunk.

As we can see, free() only *marks* the memory chunk as free - there is no enforcement of this freeing operation. Accessing memory chunks that were previously freed is the cause of many memory errors for novices and experienced programmers. A good practice is that always nullify a pointer that was just freed, as in:

```
char* p = malloc(10);
strcpy(p, "hello");
printf("%s\n", p);
free(p);
p = NULL;
```

One might ask - what if i accidentally free a memory chunk twice? this kind of bug could occur, for example, if we free a data point but don't nullify it, and during cleanup later, we see its not NULL, and try to free it again.

To understand what this kind of error might cause, we should remember how the memory manager normally works. Often, it stores the size of the allocated chunk right before the chunk itself in memory. If we freed the memory, this memory chunk might have been allocated again by another malloc() request, and thus this double-free will actually free the wrong memory chunk - causing us to have a dangling pointer somewhere else in our application. Such bugs tend to show themselves much later than the place in the code where they occurred. Sometimes we don't see them at all, but they still lurk around, waiting for an opportunity to rear their ugly heads.

Another problem that might occur, is that this double-free will be done after the freed chunk was merged together with neighboring free chunks to form a larger free chunk, and then the larger chunk was re-allocated. In such a case, when we try to free() our chunk for the 2nd time, we'll actually free only part of the memory chunk that the application is currently using. This will cause even more unexpected problems.

Example 15

The following example sets the end of the data segment to a pointer variable. Whenever, we try to store some thing in that location segment violation occurs which makes the signal handler to run which in turn calls sbrk(256) to increase the data segment size.

```
#include<unistd.h>
#include<signal.h>

void catcher(int signo)
{
   char *cp2;
   printf("%d Occurred", signo);
   cp2 = sbrk(256);
   printf("Current brk value = %d\n",(int)cp2);
   sleep(5);
   signal(SIGSEGV, catcher);
}

int main()
{
   char *old, *cp;
   void catcher();
   old = sbrk(0);
   cp = old;
   signal(SIGSEGV, catcher);
   for(;;)
    *cp++ = 1;
}
```

realloc()

The function prototype is given as:

Void * realloc(void *oldaddress, int size)

This function takes two arguments, one pointer to already allocated memory and size of the new memory required. It not only allocates the memory (new memory) but also copies the content of the old memory. If the required size of the new memory is smaller than the existing one it will not allocates new memory.

Example 16

```
#include<stdio.h>
int main()
{
char  *p, *q;

p=(char *) malloc(10);
scanf("%s", p);
```

```
printf("%s\n", p);
q=realloc(p,20);

printf("%s\n", q);

}
```

calloc()

This function also works similar to malloc() with the exception that it initializes allocated memory also.

9.3.6 Displaing Memory Details

The following command displays the available physical memory.

grep MemTotal /proc/meminfo

The following command displays the available swap memory.

grep SwapTotal /proc/meminfo

9.4 Electric Fence Library For Testing Memory Errors

Electric Fence helps us to detect two common programming bugs: software that overruns the boundaries of a malloc() memory allocation, and software that touches a memory allocation that has been released by free(). Unlike other malloc() debuggers, Electric Fence will detect read accesses as well as writes, and it will pinpoint the exact instruction that causes an error.

Electric Fence uses the virtual memory hardware of our computer to place an inaccessible memory page immediately after (or before, at the user option) each memory allocation. When software reads or writes this inaccessible page, the hardware issues a segmentation fault, stopping the program at the offending instruction. It is then trivial to find the erroneous statement using your favorite debugger. In a similar manner, memory that has been released by free() is made inaccessible, and any code that touches it will get a segmentation fault.

Simply linking our application with libefence.a will allow us to detect most, but not all, malloc buffer overruns and accesses of free memory.

Electric Fence (EF) is a library which can be linked to our program. EF will cause a segmentation fault on the exact line of the wrong instruction, so by tracking the program with a debugger, we can get to the root of the problem. Place an inaccessible memory page after (or before, by using the correct option) each area allocated by our program, and EF will cause an immediate error when the program goes out of the bounds.

For Electric Fence, we need to recompile the program, including the reference library. For example, consider the following program (postr.c).

Example 17

```
#include <stdio.h>
/* Example of Post-Read */
int main(void)
{
  char *foo;
  foo = (char *) malloc(10);
  memset(foo,0x20,sizeof(foo));
  foo[0] = 'e';
  foo[1] = 'x';
  foo[2] = 'a';
  /* The string is not null terminated */
  printf("%s\n",foo);
  free(foo);
  return(0);
}
```

Compile this using the following command.

gcc -g -o postr postr.c -lefence

Indeed the -g option is used to include the debugging information in the executable. This is needed because EF will cause a segmentation fault exactly at the buggy line, so we will need to walk through the code to find the exact line causing the problem. This is the output of the executable:

Electric Fence 2.0.5 Copyright (C) 1987-1995 Bruce Perens. exa

EF didn't find any problem in the code, so no errors were generated.

We can compile the program with out -lefence option and then execute the resulting executable file with "ef" command. For example:

gcc -f -o postr postr.c
ef ./postr

EF has four different switches, which can be enabled by setting one of these environment variables: EF_ALIGNMENT, EF_PROTECT_BELOW, EF_PROTECT_FREE or EF_ALLOW_MALLOC_0.

EF_ALIGNMENT sets the alignment for each memory allocation done by malloc (or calloc and realloc). By default, this size is set to sizeof(int), because this is usually the alignment required by the CPU. This could be a problem when we allocate a size that is not a multiple of the word size. Since the inaccessible page must be set to word-aligned address, we have a hole after the allocated memory to the inaccessible page. We can fix this by setting the environment variable to 0; in this way, we will be able to find a single-byte overrun. This will force malloc to return a non-aligned address, but this is not a problem in most cases. In some cases (when we have an odd-size allocation for an object that must be word-aligned), we will get a bus error (SIGBUS).

EF will usually place the inaccessible page after each memory allocation. By setting EF_PROTECT_BELOW to 1, it will place this page before the allocation, so we can check for under-runs.

EF allows we to allocate freed memory. If we think our program is touching free memory, set EF_PROTECT_FREE to 1. EF will not reallocate any freed memory, and any access will be detected.

A malloc call with zero bytes is considered an error. If we need to use such a call, we can tell EF to ignore this error by making EF_ALLOW_MALLOC_0 non-zero.

EF_ALIGNMENT is set to 0 in order to see if the postr error would be detected, but again EF did not see it.

Example 18

```
#include <stdio.h>
#include <string.h>
/* Example of Pre-Read */
int main(void)
{
  char *foo;
  foo = (char *) malloc(10);
  strcpy(foo,"hello");
  foo--;
  /* printf access before allocated area */
  printf("%s\n",foo);
  free(foo);
  return(0);
}
```

If we link the EF library without specifying any switch, Electric Fence returns only an error regarding the freeing of a non-malloc returned value:

```
Electric Fence 2.0.5 Copyright (C) 1987-1995 Bruce Perens.
ElectricFence Aborting: free(400b3ff3): address not from malloc().
```

Illegal Instruction (core dumped)

Then, try to set the protect below switch:

```
EF_PROTECT_BELOW=1
export EF_PROTECT_BELOW
```

With this variable, EF caused a segmentation fault. With gdb, we tracked down the program to the printf where the segmentation fault occurred.

Example 19

```
#include <stdio.h>
#include <string.h>
/* Example of Post-Write */
int main(void)
{
  char *foo;
  foo = (char *) malloc(10);
  /* strcpy write beyond the allocated area */
  strcpy(foo,"1234567890100");
  printf("%s\n",foo);
  free(foo);
  return(0);
}
```

Again, the first run (without any switch) of Electric Fence did not report any error. Then we set EF_ALIGNMENT to 0, and the strcpy caused a core dump.

Example 20

```
#include <stdio.h>
#include <string.h>
/* Example of Pre-Write */
int main(void)
{
  char *foo;
  foo = (char *) malloc(10);
  foo--;
  /* strcpy access before allocated area */
  strcpy(foo,"123456789");
  printf("%s\n",foo);
  free(foo);
  return(0);
}
```

When we didn't set a switch, Electric Fence detected only the wrong free, but with EF_PROTECT_BELOW set, it also found the pre-write.

Un-initialized Pointer

Electric Fence did not detect this error. When we run the program, we will get a core dump whether we use EF or not.

Example 21

```
#include<stdio.h>

int main()
{
 char *a,*b;

free(a);
 b=(char*) malloc(10);

free(b);

}
```

gcc -g -o a1a a1a.c -lefence
./a1a

```
ElectricFence Aborting: free() called before first malloc().
Illegal instruction
```

Example 22

```
#include<stdio.h>

int main()
{
 char *a,*b;

 b=(char*) malloc(10);

free(b);

free(a);
}
```

gcc -g -o a1 a1b.c -lefence
./a1

```
 Electric Fence 2.2.0 Copyright (C) 1987-1999 Bruce Perens <bruce@perens.com>

ElectricFence Aborting: free(4dfc80): address not from malloc().
Illegal instruction
```

Example 23

Similarly, the following program if executed after linking with EF library it will not give any error. However, if we set EF_ALIGNMENT as 1 and export this variable and execute then we will get error on line 7.

```
#include<stdio.h>

int main()
{
 char *b=(char *) malloc(17);

 b[19]='A';

return 0;
}
```

Example 24

However, similar type of error on the common arrays other than dynamic arrays are not be reported by the EF. Check with the following program

```
#include<stdio.h>

int main()
{
 char b[10]="ram";

 b[10]='A';
return 0;
}
```

Example 25

File a10.c

```
/* for memory leak*/

#include <stdlib.h>
#include <stdio.h>

int main(void)
{
  char *ptr1;
  char *ptr2;
  ptr1 = malloc(512);
  ptr2 = malloc(512);
```

```
  ptr2 = ptr1;
  free(ptr2);
   ptr1[0]='A'; ptr1[1]='\0';
}
```

gcc -g -o a1 a10.c –lefence

gdb –q a1

```
GNU gdb Red Hat Linux (6.1post-1.20040607.41rh)
This GDB was configured as "i386-redhat-linux-gnu"...Using host libthread_db
library "/lib/tls/libthread_db.so.1".

(gdb) b 15
Breakpoint 1 at 0x80484d0: file a10.c, line 15.
(gdb) b 16
Breakpoint 2 at 0x80484de: file a10.c, line 16.
(gdb) r
Starting program: /root/memory/a1

 Electric Fence 2.2.0 Copyright (C) 1987-1999 Bruce Perens
<bruce@perens.com>

Breakpoint 1, main () at a10.c:15
15       free(ptr2);
(gdb) n

Breakpoint 2, main () at a10.c:16
16        ptr1[0]='A'; ptr1[1]='\0';
(gdb) n

Program received signal SIGSEGV, Segmentation fault.
0x080484e1 in main () at a10.c:16
16        ptr1[0]='A'; ptr1[1]='\0';
(gdb) n

Program terminated with signal SIGSEGV, Segmentation fault.
The program no longer exists.
(gdb) q
```

Example 26

File a11.c

```
#include <stdlib.h>
#include <stdio.h>

int main(void)
{
  char *ptr1;
  char *ptr2;
  char *chptr;
  int i = 1;
  ptr1 = malloc(512);
  ptr2 = malloc(512);
  chptr = (char *)malloc(512);
  for (i; i <= 512; i++) {
    chptr[i] = 'S';
  }
  ptr2 = ptr1;
  free(ptr2);
  free(ptr1);
  free(chptr);
}
```

gcc -g -o a1 a11.c –lefence

gdb -q a1

GNU gdb Red Hat Linux (6.1post-1.20040607.41rh)

Copyright 2004 Free Software Foundation, Inc.

GDB is free software, covered by the GNU General Public License, and you are welcome to change it and/or distribute copies of it under certain conditions.

Type "show copying" to see the conditions.

There is absolutely no warranty for GDB. Type "show warranty" for details.

This GDB was configured as "i386-redhat-linux-gnu"...Using host libthread_db library "/lib/tls/libthread_db.so.1".

(gdb) **b 16**

Breakpoint 1 at 0x80484fd: file a11.c, line 16.

```
(gdb) r
Starting program: /root/memory/a1

 Electric Fence 2.2.0 Copyright (C) 1987-1999 Bruce Perens
<bruce@perens.com>

Program received signal SIGSEGV, Segmentation fault.
0x080484f3 in main () at a11.c:14
14 chptr[i] = 'S';
(gdb) print i
$1 = 512
(gdb) q
```

The program is running. Exit anyway? (y or n) y

INSTRUCTIONS FOR DEBUGGING YOUR PROGRAM

- Link with libefence.a as explained above.
- Run your program in a debugger and fix any overruns or accesses to free memory.
- Quit the debugger.
- Set EF_PROTECT_BELOW = 1 in the shell environment.
- Repeat step 2, this time repairing underruns if they occur.
- Quit the debugger.
- Read the restrictions in the section on WORD-ALIGNMENT AND OVERRUN DETECTION. See if we can set EF_ALIGNMENT to 0 and repeat step 2. Sometimes this will be too much work, or there will be problems with library routines for which we don't have the source, that will prevent we from doing this.

Exercise

Check whether EF can find out mistakes in the following program or not.

```
#include <stdlib.h>
char *alloc_two ()
{
      char *tmp = malloc(1024*10);
       // Create a memory leak
      return malloc(1024*20);
}
char *alloc_one ()
{
      return malloc (1024);
}
int
```

```
main ()
{
        char *mem1 = alloc_two ();
        char *mem2 = alloc_one ();
        free (mem1);
        return 0;
}
```

9.5 Conclusions

This chapter explains about general memory management in Unix system, specifically with C language programs. It also, emphasizes the general memory errors and how they occur is explained with simple examples which users can be simulated instantaneously. A popular library, Electric Fence is explained in detail. How the same can be used to find dynamic memory related errors is explained with illustrative examples.

10 Memory Mapping Files

10.1 Memory Mapping

Memory mapping is a file access technique that works very well under UNIX. Under Windows, it only makes sense in read-only applications, and even there, the "local copy" option (covered in a topic below) makes more sense. So it is for all practical purposes only of interest under UNIX. The concept is to map a disk file onto a processes memory address space, such that it can be accessed via memory operations rather than disk operations, that is the file is treated as an extension of virtual memory: Conceptually, the mapped file is simply another swap file mapped to a range of memory The file doesn't have to fit entirely in memory, because the demand paging system (otherwise associated with virtual memory) takes care of swapping pages in and out of memory as needed.

It may appear that this is hardly different that ordinary disk caching, in which frequently accessed disk blocks are held in memory to minimize physical disk accesses. However, there is significant performance difference between accessing a cached disk record via a disk service call and accessing a memory record. Disk service calls require a context switch from user to supervisor mode, even if the data is in cache, whereas memory access calls do not. Such context switches are relatively expensive operations, being perhaps hundreds of times slower than ordinary instructions. So even though reading a disk record from cache and reading the equivalent data directory from memory may both appear to be "lightning fast", the difference can become significant when you have a lot of little disk accesses.

If memory mapping is so wonderful, one might ask why we don't just use it all the time. The answer would be that it can cause memory to be used inefficiently, which can have an adverse impact on the system performance. The recommendation would be to only use memory mapping with reasonably small files that are heavily accessed in specific programs. Good candidates would be any custom (non-ISAM) index files, or any small file whose records are accessed multiple times in a particular program. (ISAM files are not generally good candidates except perhaps in certain individual programs and when the files are not too large, because there is no convenient way to map the index without the data).

10.2 Reading Large Files With File Mapping

Mapping a large file into memory (rather than performing a number of sequential read operations on that file) can significantly enhance I/O performance. Reading a file into a buffer can directly incur up to three I/O operations:

- paging out enough modified pages to allow for the allocation of the read buffer
- reading bytes from the file into the buffer
- later, paging out the buffer memory

Additionally, any pages paged out will likely need to be paged in again.

As mentioned earlier, mapping a file, on the other hand causes the file to be treated as an extension of virtual memory: Conceptually, the mapped file is simply another swap file mapped to a range of memory. Thus, reading from the file can incur only two I/O operations directly: paging in the desired section of the file and paging out any modified pages needed to make room for the page in memory.

The pages of a file are maintained in a shareable state in memory. If the system runs low on memory, the pages are purged, but no I/O operation is incurred; if the data is referenced again, it is paged in again from the file.

Additionally, our code is often smaller with file mapping, because the file is accessed through a pointer, like all random-access memory, and **no file system calls need to be used**.

However, the worst candidates examples are large files that are accessed sequentially or sporadically, with little repetitive access to the same records. For example, it would be a bad idea to memory map a customer master file probably in the customer maintenance program. Such a program is not likely to be disk-bound, and the amount of memory spent mapping the file would be better spent on other uses, like ordinary disk caching

Memory mapping can be used when we want to read and write to and from files so that the information is shared between processes. Think of it in this way: two processes both open the same file and both read and write from it, thus sharing the information. The problem is, sometimes it's a pain to do all those fseek()s and stuff to get around. However, with the help of memory mapping we can just map a section of the file into memory, and get a pointer to it and simply use pointer arithmetic to get (and set) data in the file. Ofcourse, If we have multiple processes manipulating the data in the same file concurrently, we could be in for troubles. We might have to lock the file or use semaphores to regulate access to the file while a process messes with it.

In some applications, any time when they start the same calculations or table initializations (data structures) has to be carried out before starting actual service. In order to improve the response time of such a programs we can use memory mapping. We can make this application program to do all necessary calculations when it is started first time and store the same in a file. Next time on wards when this program is started, simply it memory map this file and uses the calculated tables and data structures in it. Thus, the response time becomes better.

Memory mapping must be activated within individual programs, and applies only to files opened after the memory mapping option is turned on, so in addition to identifying heavily accessed files, we would need to identify specific programs that were disk-bound in order to benefit from it.

It is safe and acceptable to allow a mixture of simultaneous memory-mapped and traditional I/O to any given file under UNIX.

10.2.1 Local Copies (Read-Only Access Under Windows)

Networked Windows environments are quite efficient at serving up entire files over the network from a fileserver (as in word processing applications), but they are relatively slow at serving up record-level operations. Here, the disk operation overhead is much higher than in the UNIX world because of the need for machine-to-machine communication. Loading a file from the server may require only a couple of units of machine-to-machine communication, but reading the file via thousands of individual record operations (which is typical of AMOS-style report programs) requires thousands of units of machine-to-machine communications. This overhead typically becomes the limiting factor in Windows installations of A-Shell.

Memory mapping doesn't really help here, since it doesn't eliminate the need for machine-to-machine communication, and in any case, it only works properly for read-only situations anyway. If we can limit ourselves to read-only access to a file in a particular program, then a better solution is to request that A-Shell give you a local copy of the file. In this case, when the file is opened, A-Shell copies the entire file (in one big transfer operation) from the server to the local workstation and then references the local copy until the file is closed (after which the local copy is deleted). This technique can significantly speed up report programs, or any other program that performs many read operations from a file, by eliminating that machine-to-machine communication overhead. As a side effect, it also reduces network traffic and the load on the fileserver, thus potentially speeding up other programs running across the network.

10.2.2 Memory Mapping of File

As mentioned earlier, before mapping a file to memory, we need to get a file descriptor for it by using the open() system call:

```
int fd;

fd = open("mapdemofile", O_RDWR);
```

In this example, we've opened the file for read/write access. We can open it in whatever mode we want, but it has to match the mode specified in the *prot* parameter to the mmap() call, below.

To memory map a file, we use the mmap() system call, which is defined as follows:

void *mmap(void ****addr*, size_t** ***len*****, int** ***prot*****, int** ***flags*****,**
int ***fildes*****, off_t** ***off*****);**

addr

This is the address we want the file mapped into. The best way to use this is to set it to (caddr_t)0 and let the OS choose it for us. If we tell it to use an address the OS doesn't like (for instance, if it's not a multiple of the virtual memory page size), it'll give us an error.

len

This parameter is the length of the data we want to map into memory. This can be any length we want. (Aside: if *len* not a multiple of the virtual memory page size, we will get a blocksize that is rounded up to that size. The extra bytes will be 0, and any changes we make to them will not modify the file.)

prot

The "protection" argument allows us to specify what kind of access this process has to the memory mapped region. This can be a bitwise-ORd mixture of the following values: PROT_READ, PROT_WRITE, and PROT_EXEC, for read, write, and execute permissions, respectively. The value specified here must be equivalent to the mode specified in the open() system call that is used to get the file descriptor.

flags

There are just miscellaneous flags that can be set for the system call. We want to set it to MAP_SHARED if we are planning to share our changes to the file with other processes, or MAP_PRIVATE otherwise. If we set it to the latter, our process will get a copy of the mapped region, so any changes you make to it will not be reflected in the original file--thus, other processes will not be able to see them. We won't talk about MAP_PRIVATE here at all, since it doesn't have much to do with IPC.

fildes

This is where you put that file descriptor we opened earlier.

off

This is the offset in the file that we want to start mapping from. A restriction: this **must** be a multiple of the virtual memory page size. This page size can be obtained with a call to getpagesize().

The function mmap() returns -1 on error, and sets errno. Otherwise, it returns a pointer to the start of the mapped data.

We shall discuss a short demo that maps the second "page" of a file into memory. First we'll open() it to get the file descriptor, then we'll use getpagesize() to get the size of a virtual memory page and use this value for both the *len* and the *off*. In this way, we'll start mapping at the second page, and map for one page's length. (On my Linux box, the page size is 4K.)

```
#include <unistd.h>
#include <sys/types.h>
#include <sys/mman.h>

int fd, pagesize;
char *data;

fd = fopen("foo", O_RDONLY);
pagesize = getpagesize();
data = mmap((caddr_t)0, pagesize, PROT_READ, MAP_SHARED, fd,
pagesize);
```

Once this code stretch has run, we can access the first byte of the mapped section of file using data[0]. Notice there's a lot of type conversion going on here. For instance, mmap() returns caddr_t, but we treat it as a char*. Well, the fact is that caddr_t usually is defined to be a char*, so everything's fine.

Also notice that we've mapped the file PROT_READ so we have read-only access. Any attempt to write to the data (data[0] = 'B', for example) will cause a segmentation violation. Open the file O_RDWR with *prot* set to PROT_READ|PROT_WRITE if we want read-write access to the data.

10.2.3 Unmapping the file

There is, of course, a munmap() function to un-memory map a file:

int munmap(caddr_t *addr*, size_t *len*);

This simply unmaps the region pointed to by *addr* (returned from mmap()) with length *len* (same as the *len* passed to mmap()). munmap() returns -1 on error and sets the errno variable.

Once we have unmapped a file, any attempt to access the data through the old pointer will result in a segmentation fault.

The following program maps its own source program to memory and prints the byte that's found at whatever offset we specify on the command line.

The program restricts the offsets we can specify to the range 0 through the file length. The file length is obtained through a call to stat(). It returns a structure full of file info, one field of which is the size in bytes.

Example 1

Here is the source for mmapdemo.c

```
#include <stdio.h>
#include <stdlib.h>
#include <fcntl.h>
#include <unistd.h>
#include <sys/types.h>
#include <sys/mman.h>
#include <sys/stat.h>
#include <errno.h>

int main(int argc, char *argv[])
{
   int fd, offset;
   char *data;
   struct stat sbuf;

   if (argc != 2) {
      fprintf(stderr, "usage: mmapdemo offset\n");
      exit(1);
   }

   if ((fd = open("mmapdemo.c", O_RDONLY)) == -1) {
      perror("open");
      exit(1);
   }

   if (stat("mmapdemo.c", &sbuf) == -1) {
      perror("stat");
      exit(1);
   }

   offset = atoi(argv[1]);
   if (offset < 0 || offset > sbuf.st_size-1) {
```

```
        fprintf(stderr, "mmapdemo: offset must be in the range 0-%d\n", \
                                              sbuf.st_size-1);
        exit(1);
    }

    if ((data = mmap((caddr_t)0, sbuf.st_size, PROT_READ, MAP_SHARED, \
                                  fd, 0)) == (caddr_t)(-1)) {
        perror("mmap");
        exit(1);
    }

    printf("byte at offset %d is '%c'\n", offset, data[offset]);

    return 0;
}
```

Run it with some command like:

mmapdemo 30

```
byte at offset 30 is 'e'
```

A memory mapped region will be inherited by a child process across a fork (since its part of the parent's address space), but for the same reason is not inherited by the new program across an exec. A memory mapped region is automatically unmapped when the process terminates or by calling munmap directly.

Execute the above program by simply inserting a instruction **fork() before last printf() statement.** We shall get the same byte information two times such as:

```
byte at offset 30 is 'e'
byte at offset 30 is 'e'
```

Example 2

In this example, We define a RECORD structure and then create NRECORDS each recording their number. These are appended to the file records.dat. Then, this file is memory mapped and a specified record is simply changed by accessing the same as if it is an array.

```
#include <unistd.h>
#include <stdio.h>
#include <sys/mman.h>
#include <fcntl.h>

typedef struct {
    int integer;
```

```
    char string[24];
} RECORD;

#define NRECORDS (100)

int main()
{
    RECORD record, *mapped;
    int i, f;
    FILE *fp;

    fp = fopen("records.dat","w+");
    for(i=0; i<NRECORDS; i++) {
        record.integer = i;
        sprintf(record.string,"RECORD-%d",i);
        fwrite(&record,sizeof(record),1,fp);
    }
    fclose(fp);

/*  We now change the integer value of record 43 to 143
    and write this to the 43rd record's string.  */

    fp = fopen("records.dat","r+");
    fseek(fp,43*sizeof(record),SEEK_SET);
    fread(&record,sizeof(record),1,fp);

    record.integer = 143;
    sprintf(record.string,"RECORD-%d",record.integer);

    fseek(fp,43*sizeof(record),SEEK_SET);
    fwrite(&record,sizeof(record),1,fp);
    fclose(fp);

/*  We now map the records into memory
    and access the 43rd record in order to change the integer to 243
    (and update the record string), again using memory mapping.  */

    f = open("records.dat",O_RDWR);

    mapped = (RECORD *)mmap(0, NRECORDS*sizeof(record),
                      PROT_READ|PROT_WRITE, MAP_SHARED, f, 0);

    mapped[43].integer = 243;
    sprintf(mapped[43].string,"RECORD-%d",mapped[43].integer);
```

```
    msync((void *)mapped, NRECORDS*sizeof(record), MS_ASYNC);

    /* this system call immediately writes the file information into disk */

    munmap((void *)mapped, NRECORDS*sizeof(record));

    close(f);

    exit(0);
}
```

Example 3

The following functions can be used to memory map a file and related operations.

```
void ProcessFile( char * inPathName )
{
    size_t  dataLength;
    void *  dataPtr;

    if( MapFile( inPathName, &dataPtr, &dataLength ) == 0 )
    {
        //
        // process the data and unmap the file
        //

        // ...

        munmap( dataPtr, dataLength );
    }
}

//
// MapFile
// Return the contents of the specified file as a read-only pointer.
//
// Enter:  inPathName is a "/"-delimited pathname
//
// Exit:   outDataPtra      pointer to the mapped memory region
//         outDataLength    size of the mapped memory region
//         return value     either an errno error condition
//                          or zero for success
//
```

```
int MapFile( char * inPathName, void ** outDataPtr, size_t * outDataLength )
{
   int        outError;
   int        fileDescriptor;
   struct stat statInfo;

   // Return safe values on error.
   outError       = 0;
   *outDataPtr     = NULL;
   *outDataLength  = 0;

   //
   // Open the file.
   //
   fileDescriptor = open( inPathName, O_RDONLY, 0 );
   if( fileDescriptor < 0 )
   {
     outError = errno;
   }
   else
   {
      //
      // We now know the file exists. Retrieve the file size.
      //
      if( fstat( fileDescriptor, &statInfo ) != 0 )
      {
         outError = errno;
      }
      else
      {
         //
         // Map the file into a read-only memory region.
         //

         *outDataPtr = mmap( NULL,
                        statInfo.st_size,
                        PROT_READ,
                        0,
                        fileDescriptor,
                        0);
```

```
            if( *outDataPtr == MAP_FAILED )
            {
               outError = errno;
            }
            else
            {
               //
               // On success, return the size of the mapped file.
               //
               *outDataLength = statInfo.st_size;
            }
         }

         //
         // Now close the file.The kernel doesn't use our file descriptor.
         //
         close( fileDescriptor );
      }

      return outError;
   }
```

Example 4

The following program is used to explain about the possible error which we get when we try to access the memory mapped file.

```
#include <stdio.h>
#include <unistd.h>
#include <sys/mman.h>
#include <sys/stat.h>
#include <fcntl.h>
#include <ctype.h>
#include <errno.h>
#include <stdlib.h>

static int alloc_size;
static char *memory;

void sighandle(int signo)
{
printf("Memory Accessed\n");
```

```
mprotect(memory, alloc_size, PROT_READ|PROT_WRITE);
}

int main()
{
int fd;
struct sigaction sa;

memset(&sa,0, sizeof(struct sigaction));

sa.sa_handler=sighandler;
sigaction(SIGSEGV,&sa, NULL);

alloc_size=getpagesize();

fd=open("/dev/zero", O_RDONLY);
memory=mmap(NULL, alloc_size, PROT_WRITE, MAP_PRIVATE, fd, 0);
close(fd);

memory[0]=0;
mprotect(memory, alloc_size, PROT_NONE);

memory[0]=0;
munmap(memory, alloc_size);
return (0);
}
```

Example 5

The following program has the following command line interface.

Proganame <file> [perm] [shared/private] [size]

Whatever filename we will give along the command line is memory mapped and the same is accessed like a character array and each character will be displayed on the screen such that 80 characters are printed in one line. Whenever it encounters a non printable character it prints '*'.

```
#include <stdio.h>
#include <unistd.h>
#include <sys/mman.h>
#include <sys/stat.h>
#include <fcntl.h>
#include <ctype.h>
#include <errno.h>
#include <stdlib.h>
```

```
#define BUFSIZE (1024-1)

static char *program_name;

void print_useage(void)
{
  fprintf(stdout, "usage: ");
  fprintf(stdout,     "%s     <file>     [perm]     [shared/private]     [size]\n",
program_name);
}

void printdata(int len, const char *data)
{
   int i;

   for(i=0; i<len; i++)
   {
      if(isprint(data[i]))
      {
        putchar(data[i]);
      }
      else
      {
        putchar('*');
      }
      if(len % 79 == 79)
      {
        putchar('\n');
      }
   }
   putchar('\n');
}

int main(int argc, char **argv)
{
  struct stat statbuf;
  int fd;
  char *mmfilename;
  char *mmdata;
  size_t len;
  int mmmode = 0;
  int mmflags = 0;
  char buf[BUFSIZE+1];
```

```
buf[BUFSIZE] = '\0';
program_name = argv[0];

if(argc > 1)
{
  mmfilename = argv[1];
}
else
{
  print_useage();
  exit(1);
}

if(argc > 2)
{
  if(strcmp("w", argv[2]) == 0 || strcmp("write", argv[2]) == 0)
  {
    mmmode |= PROT_WRITE;
  }
  else if(strcmp("r", argv[2]) == 0 || strcmp("read", argv[2]) == 0)
  {
    mmmode |= PROT_READ;
  }
  else if(strcmp("rw", argv[2]) == 0 || strcmp("read/write", argv[2]) == 0)
  {
    mmmode |= PROT_READ | PROT_WRITE;
  }
  else
  {
    fprintf(stderr, "unkown permissions `%s'\n", argv[4]);
    exit(1);
  }
}
else
{
  mmmode |= PROT_READ;
}

if(argc > 3)
{
  if(strcmp("shared", argv[3]) == 0)
  {
    mmflags |= MAP_SHARED;
  }
```

```
  else if(strcmp("private", argv[3]) == 0)
  {
   mmflags |= MAP_PRIVATE;
  }
  else
  {
   fprintf(stderr, "unknown permissions `%s'\n", argv[4]);
   exit(1);
  }
 }
 else
 {
  mmflags |= MAP_PRIVATE;
 }

 if((fd=open(mmfilename, O_RDWR | O_CREAT, 0666)) == -1)
 {
  perror(mmfilename);
  exit(errno);
 }

 if(fstat(fd, &statbuf) != 0)
 {
  perror("stat");
  exit(errno);
 }

 if(argc > 4)
 {
   len = atoi(argv[4]);
 }
 else
 {
   len = statbuf.st_size;
 }

 if((mmdata=mmap(NULL, len, mmmode, mmflags, fd, 0)) == NULL)
 {
  perror("mmap");
  exit(errno);
 }

 printf("mmap()'d %d bytes at addr 0x%08X\n", len, (unsigned
int)mmdata);
```

```
  while(fgets(buf, BUFSIZE, stdin) != NULL)
  {
   printdata(len, mmdata);
  }
  munmap(mmdata, len);

  return 0;
}
```

Example 6

This Program creates duplicate copy of a file by using the mmap function. Identify time requirement for this program. Write another program which uses fgetc(), fputc() and compare its time requirements with this.

```
#include<unistd.h>
#include<sys/mman.h>
#include<sys/types.h>
#include<sys/stat.h>
#include<fcntl.h>

int main(int n, char **a)
{
   int fd1,fd2;
   size_t size, i=0;
   char *src, *dest;
   struct stat X;
   if(n != 3)
   {
    printf("Usage: %s SRC DEST\n",a[0]);
    return -1;
   }
   if((fd1 = open(a[1],O_RDONLY)) < 0)
   {
    perror("Open for read");
    return -1;
   }
   if((fd2 = open(a[2],O_RDWR|O_CREAT,S_IRWXU)) < 0)
   {
    perror("Open for write");
    return -1;
   }
   fstat(fd1, &X);
```

```
    size = X.st_size;
    src =
(char*)mmap(NULL,size,PROT_READ,MAP_FILE|MAP_SHARED,fd1,0);

    lseek(fd2, size-1, SEEK_SET);
    if (write(fd2, " ", 1) != 1)
    {
        perror("write");
        return -1;
    }

    dest =
(char*)mmap(NULL,size,PROT_WRITE,MAP_FILE|MAP_SHARED,fd2,0);
    while(i < size)
    {
    dest[i] = src[i];
    i++;
    }
    munmap(src, size);
    munmap(dest, size);
    return 0;
}
```

10.3 Conclusions

In this chapter, we have explained about memory mapping of files. We have emphasized when the same can be used for improving an applications performance. Easy examples are included.

11 GNU Debugger

11.1 Introduction

Debugging is very vital in identifying bugs and fixing them. GNU Debugger mainly concerned with debugging of program's of some languages that run under Linux operating system. This debugger consists of gdb command and commands that run with gdb shell. The gdb command concerns with what is to be debugged and shell commands with how it is to be debugged.

11.1.1 Bugs And Debugging

A bug is an error. Debugging means detecting the bugs. Bugs occur at specification or design or coding times. If a program is incorrectly specified, inevitably fail to perform as required. Bugs that occur at design time lead to incorrect results. Bugs that occur at coding time are detected and removing using many methods. These methods include debuggers and some system defined functions and displays messages at runtime.

Normally, We debug program's by including printf statements in the code as and when require. Apart from this, there are three types of debugging methods that are usually employed. They are :

- First, we can do debugging using constants defined by # define. (see chapter 2)
- Second, debugging can be done by system defined macros. Macros and their description is as follows:

Macro	Description
LINE	A decimal constant representing the current line number.
FILE	A string representing the current file name.
DATE	A string of the form "Mmm:dd:yyyy", the current date.
TIME	A string of the form "hh:mm:ss", the current time.

- Third is the debugger provided and used with Linux. They are gdb, sdb and dbx. There are front ends for gdb (such as xxgdb, tgdb, ddd)which makes it more user friendly.

11.2 Debugging Using gdb

GDB, a short name of gnu debugger is a free software protected by GNU General Public License (GPL). GDB allows user to see what is happening when a program is getting executed.

GDB can do the following things.

- Start our program, specifying anything that might affect its behavior.
- Make our program stop on specified conditions.
- Examine what has happened, when our program has stopped.
- Change things in our program, so that we can experiment with correcting effects of one bug and learn about others.

GDB can be also used to debug Fortran programs if Fortran compiler is loaded. GDB is invoked with a shell command gdb. Once started, it reads commands from the terminal until we press quit command.

We can run gdb command without options. But in general we run it as follows.

gdb program

Here program is the name of the executable file to be debugged.

In order to run a file using gdb, the program must be compiled with –g option. This option makes debugging information attached to original executable file. If we want to know more details about gdb, we can run the same with -help option as shown below.

gdb -help

This command displays the following output.

This is the GNU debugger. Usage:

```
gdb [options] [executable-file [core-file or process-id]]
gdb [options] --args executable-file [inferior-arguments ...]
```

Options:

--args	Arguments after executable-file are passed to inferior
--[no]async	Enable (disable) asynchronous version of CLI
-b BAUDRATE	Set serial port baud rate used for remote debugging.
--batch	Exit after processing options.
--cd=DIR	Change current directory to DIR.
--command=FILE	Execute GDB commands from FILE.
--core=COREFILE	Analyze the core dump COREFILE.
--pid=PID	Attach to running process PID.
--dbx	DBX compatibility mode.
--directory=DIR	Search for source files in DIR.
--epoch	Output information used by epoch emacs-GDB interface.
--exec=EXECFILE	Use EXECFILE as the executable.

--fullname Output information used by emacs-GDB interface.

--help Print this message.

--interpreter=INTERP

Select a specific interpreter / user interface

--interpreter=INTERP

Select a specific interpreter / user interface

--mapped Use mapped symbol files if supported on this system.

--nw Do not use a window interface.

--nx Do not read .gdbinit file.

--quiet Do not print version number on startup.

--readnow Fully read symbol files on first access.

--se=FILE Use FILE as symbol file and executable file.

--symbols=SYMFILE Read symbols from SYMFILE.

--tty=TTY Use TTY for input/output by the program being debugged.

--version Print version information and then exit.

-w Use a window interface.

--write Set writing into executable and core files.

--xdb XDB compatibility mode.

Example 1

Let us consider a simple program (ex1.c) and see how we can debug using gdb.

```
#include<stdio.h>
int main()
{
 printf("Hello How are you?\n");
return 23;
}
```

First compile the same using -g option. That is, execute the following command.

gcc -g ex1.c

In order to debug the resultant executable file, execute the following command which gives many details before displaying gdb prompt (i.e (gdb))

gcc a.out

GNU gdb Red Hat Linux (5.3post-0.20021129.18rh)

Copyright 2003 Free Software Foundation, Inc.
GDB is free software, covered by the GNU General Public License, and you are welcome to change it and/or distribute copies of it under certain conditions.
Type "show copying" to see the conditions.
There is absolutely no warranty for GDB. Type "show warranty" for details.
This GDB was configured as "i386-redhat-linux-gnu"...
(gdb) **r**

Starting program: /root/nav/a.out
Hello How are You?
Program exited with code 023.
(gdb) **q**

If we want to start gdb and do not interested to see all the starting messages then we can start gdb with **-q option** such as:

gdb -q a.out

(gdb) **r**

Starting program: /root/a.out

Hello How are You?

Program exited with code 023.

(gdb) **q**

11.2.1 Commands which can be used at gdb prompt

Break:

Break command is used to set a breakpoint at any line of a file or any function such that program execution stops when break point is encountered. One can see the values of registers, variables at that time.

Synopsis:

Break [file :] function

Here file is name of file and function is the name of function where breakpoint is needed. If we want a break point at a line. The execution stops just before that instruction. If we give a break point for a function, the execution stops at the first statement of function.

Run: Run command is used to run the program being debugged. If we type this command while program is being debugged then we are asked if we want to do it from the beginning.

Synopsis:

Run [arglist]

Arglist is the list of command line arguments. It is optional. The short form of run is 'r'

Back Trace:

Back trace command is used for displaying program stack. This display the runtime stack of program.

Synopsis:

bt:

This command enables us to know the functions and their information that are currently active. bt is short form of back t race.

Print:

Print command is used to display the values of variables and expressions at the moment of program.

Synopsis:

Print Expr:

Expression might be a single variable or an expression in general. If we give name of variable proceeded by '&' symbol for expr then the address where the value is stored displayed. The short form of print is p.

Continue:

Continue command continues the execution of a program from a break point until the next break pointy or end of the program.

Synopsis:

Continue:

Continue helps in flow of program from break point to break point enabling the programmers detect the points where bug is present. Short form of continue is C.

Next:

Next command is used to executed the next line of program being debugged. It step-over any function calls in the line.

Synopsis:

Next:

This command steps over any function calls in the line it treats the line with function call as a single instruction. Short form is in.

Step:

Step command is same as next except that it steps into any function that occurs in the line.

Synopsis:

Step command is same as next except that it steps into any function that occurs in the line.

Synopsis:

Step:

This command helps in tracking even the functions that occur in the line thus making the process of debugging a file much more clearer than with next.

Edit:

Edit helps in finding the line of program where execution was stopped.

Synopsis:

Edit [file :] function

List:

List command types the text of program in the vicinity where it is presently stopped. Function is name of function and file is name of file.

Help:

Help command shows information about command name.

Help [name]

Here name of command is optional. If it is not given, then the information about gdb commands is displayed.

Quit:

This is used for exiting from gdb.

Synopsis:

Quit

Short from of quite is q.

Example 2

Consider another example (ex2.c) which takes command line arguments.

```
#include<stdio.h>
int main(int N, char *a[])
{
  int i;
 for(i=0;i<N;i++)
 printf("%s\n". a[i]);
return 23;
}
```

Compile the above program with –g option and then start gdb. That is:

```
gcc -g ex2.c

gdb -q a.out
(gdb)r Ram Rao 123
Starting program: /root/a.out Ram Rao 123
/root/a.out
Ram
Rao
123

Program exited with code 04
(gdb)q
```

If we want, we can write all the commands which we want to give to gdb in a file and then ask gdb to use them while debugging our program. For example, let the file "abc" contains the following gdb commands.

```
break 2
break 3
r Ram Rao 123
next
next
next
next
next
next
next
next
next
next
q
```

Now, start gdb as follows:

```
gdb -q a.out -x abc
```

Example 3

Some other gdb commands are explained using the following example. In the following output of a gdb session, we can see (bold underlined ones) how gdb commands can be used while debugging a program.

Line No. Program Text

```
# include <stdioh>
int isprime (int x)
{
int i;
for (i=2; i <=x/2; i++)
if (x % i = = 0)
return 0;
return 1;
}
int main ( )
{
int I, x;
for (I=1; I< = 3; I ++)
{
printf ("Enter a number")
scanf ("%d",&x);
if (! isprime (x) )
printf ("not a prime number\n")
else
printf (" a prime number")
}
return 0;
}
```

Now the commands are executed for this program gdbex.c at the command prompt.

gcc –g gdbex.c

gdb –q a.out

(gdb) **r**

Starting program: /root/a.out.

Enter a number **23**

It is a prime number.

Enter a number **44**

Not a prime number

Enter a number **31**

A prime number

Program is exited with code 060

Here the program is executed until end as it has no break points.

Now we keep breakpoints

(gdb) **break 18**

Breakpoint 1 at OX80483 Fe: file gdbex.c line 18.

Here a breakpoint at; line 18 is created with number 1.

Now turn the program.

(gdb) r

Starting program: /root/a.out

Enter a number **23**

It is a prime

Enter a number **44**

Break point/main ( ) at gdbex.c: 18

18 printf ("not a prime")'

Here it is observed that execution of program stopped at line 18.

We can print the values of variable currently as follows:

(gdb) **print x**

$ 1 = 44

(gdb) **print &x**

$ 2 = (int *) OXFFF ecb 4

Here address of x is displayed

(gdb) **print I**

$ 3 = 2

(gdb) **print &I**

$ 4 = (int *)) OXbFFF ecbo

In for requires a special mention.

Info command gives information of files when it is being debugged. The information consists of addresses, registers, args, breakpoints, catch points, files functions, local variables, macros, memory and procedures

(gdb) **info locals**

x = 44

i = 2

The above gave information about local variables in the program.

```
(gdb) info registers
eax         0X0         0
ecx         0X0         0
edx         0X0         0
ebx         0X42130a14      1708544020
esp         0XFFFecbo       0XbFFFecb0
ebp         0XbFFFecb8      0XbFFFecb8
esi 0X40015360      1073828704
edc         0X80484sc       134513756
eip 0X80483fe       0X80483fe
e flags     0X243   582
es  0X236   35
ss  0X2b    43
es  0x2b    43
es  0X2b    43
Fs  0X0     0
Gs  0X33    51
```

The above gave information about values of registers.

(gdb) **info args**
no arguments
this is regarding command line arguments
(gdb) **info functions**
All defined Functions
File gdbex .c
int isprime (int)
Non-debugging symbols
0X08048254 – init
0X0804827C – scanf
the above gave info about functions
(gdb) **info breakpoints**

Num	Type		Disp	Enb	AddressWhat
1	breakpoint	la	y	0X080483Fe	in main at gdbex.C;8

breakpoint already hit 1 time.
The above gave information about breakpoints currently active.
(gdb) **info files**
This gives information about files are follows:
Name of targets and file being debugged.
Unix child process.
Using the running image of child process 2077.............
Local execfile
'/root/a-out', fitype ELF32-i386

```
    entry point; 0X80482ac.
    ..........
    ..........
(gdb) info proc
process 2077
cmdline = a.out
cmd = /root
exe = /a.out.
(gdb) list
13 for (I = 1, I <=3, I + +)
14 {
15 printf ("Enter a number");
16 scanf ("%d", &x)
17 if (!isprime (x))
18 printf ("not a prime number");
19 else
21 }
22 }
Back tracing at this stage is as follows:
(gdb) bt
# 0 main ( ) at gdbex. C: 18
# 1.0X4215574 in_libc_start_main ( )
    from lib/tls/.libc. so.6
(gdb) break 5
break point 2 at 0X8048362: File of gdbex.c lines
(gdb) c
continuing
not a prime number
enter a number 7
'breakpoint 2, is pime(x=7) at gdbex.c:5
5 For (i=2; i<=x/2; i ++)
(gdb) info locals
i = 1108544020
  contains garbage as it is not get initialized
(gdb) step
6 if (x % ==0)
(gdb) info locals
i = 2
i is initialized.
(gdb) c
continuing
is a prime number
program exited with code 0260
This ends the program
```

(gdb) **delete 1**
(gdb) **delete**
Delete all breakpoints? 1 y or n 2 y
The first deletes deletes a specific
Breakpoint named 1 and second deletes all breakpoints.
(gdb) **break 16**
breakpoint 3 at 0X80483 ds: file gdbex.c, line 10.
(gdb) **step 2**
    isprime (x = 23) at gdbex.c:5
    5 For (i =, i<=x/2, i ++)
this step made 2 steps forward (one into the function is prime)
(gdb) **c**
continuing
it is prime
break point 3, main ( ) at gdbex.c: 16
16 scan F ("%d", & x);
(gdb) **step**
enter a number 56
17 (Fcl, isprime (x))
(gdb) **next**
18 printf ("not a prime");
her it is observed that next stepper over function is prime in line 17.
(gdb) **c**
enter a number 33
not a prime
program exited with code. 060.
(gdb) **break isprime**
break point 1 at 0X6; File gdbex.c, line 5
(gdb) **r**
starting program: /root/a.out
enter a number 54
breakpoint 1, is prime (x=54) at gdbex.c.5
5 for (i =2; i <=x/2; i ++)
here break point is given for a function
(gdb) **break main**
breakpoint 2 at 0X8048369: File gdbex.c, line 13
(gdb) **r**
starting program: /root/a.out
breakpoint 2 main ( ) at gdbex.c:13
13 For (i =1; i <=3; i ++)
(gb) **break 5**
breakpoint 5, at 0X8048362: File gdbex.c Line 5.
(gdb) **delete**
delete all breakpoints/y orn) y

```
(gdb) break 5
breakpoint 1, at 0X8048362: File gdbex.c, line 5
(gdb) r
starting program: /root/a.out
enter a number 34
breakpoint, is prime (x=34) at gdbex.c:5
for (i =2; i <=x/2; i ++)
(gdb) bt
# 0 is prime (x=34) at gdbex..c: 5
# 1 0X0804887 in main ( ) at gdbex.c:17
#2 42015574 in lib_start_main ( )
From /lib/tls/libc.so.6.
```

Example 4

The following program is also taken to explain about how gdb can be used for debugging programs. The example gdb-example.c, is listed below. It is a simple, yet buggy program that we will run under gdb.

```
#include "stdio.h"

void
print_scrambled(char *message)
{
  int i = 3;
  do {
    printf("%c", (*message)+i);
  } while (*++message);
  printf("\n");
}

int
main()
{
  char * bad_message = NULL;
  char * good_message = "Hello, world.";

  print_scrambled(good_message);
  print_scrambled(bad_message);
}
```

gcc -g gdb-example.c -o gdb-example

The backtrace command produces a list of the function calls, which is known as either a backtrace or a stack trace.

Reading backtraces is fairly straightforward. The data associated with each function call in the list is known as a stack frame. The outermost frame is the initial function that our program started in, and is printed at the bottom of the list. Each frame is given a number (0, 1, 2, etc.). Following the frame number is an associated memory address, which is almost entirely useless and which we can ignore. Then each frame contains the name of the function that was called, its arguments, the name of the file where the function appears, and line number. So, the stack trace for our program says that at line 20 of gdb-example.c in function main, the print_scrambled function was called--and that the program got to line eight of gdb-example.c inside the print_scrambled function.

Getting more information

Getting a backtrace may provide enough information, but it is sometimes helpful to get more information, such as the values of arguments or local variables. Another convenience provided by gdb is listing a small segment of the code around where the program is currently stopped so we can see which statements have been executed and which ones are about to be. The following gdb session demonstrates how to do these things as well as how to switch to previous stack frames using the up command.

gdb -q gdb-example

```
This GDB was configured as "i386-redhat-linux-gnu"...Using host libthread_db library "/lib/tls/libthread_db.so.1".
(gdb) run
Starting program: /home/newren/examples/gdb-example
Program received signal SIGSEGV, Segmentation fault.
0x0804835b in print_scrambled (message=0x0) at gdb-example.c:8
8         printf("%c", (*message)+i);
(gdb) backtrace
#0  0x0804835b in print_scrambled (message=0x0) at gdb-example.c:8
#1  0x080483c3 in main () at gdb-example.c:20
(gdb) list
3     void
4     print_scrambled(char *message)
5     {
6       int i = 3;
7       do {
8         printf("%c", (*message)+i);
9       } while (*++message);
10      printf("\n");
11    }
12
(gdb) info locals
i = 3
```

```
(gdb) info args
message = 0x0
(gdb) up
#1  0x080483c3 in main () at gdb-example.c:20
20        print_scrambled(bad_message);
(gdb) list
15      {
16        char * bad_message = NULL;
17        char * good_message = "Hello, world.";
18
19        print_scrambled(good_message);
20        print_scrambled(bad_message);
21      }
(gdb) info locals
bad_message = 0x0
good_message = 0x80484a1 "Hello, world."
(gdb) info args
No arguments.
(gdb) quit
The program is running.  Exit anyway? (y or n) y
```

From the gdb output, it is fairly clear that the list, info locals, and info args commands get information about the currently selected stack frame. Besides using the up command to choose a previous frame, we can also use the down command to choose a later one or use the frame command (with a numeric argument) to choose which stack frame to switch to.

Walking through the program

The gdb can also allow we to walk through the program while it is running so that we can trace its steps carefully. The following gdb session illustrates this, using the break, print, next, and step commands.

Example 5

```
gdb -q gdb-example
This GDB was configured as "i386-redhat-linux-gnu"...Using host libthread_db library "/lib/tls/libthread_db.so.1".
(gdb) break main
Breakpoint 1 at 0x804839c: file gdb-example.c, line 16.
(gdb) run
Starting program: /home/newren/examples/gdb-example
Breakpoint 1, main () at gdb-example.c:16
16        char * bad_message = NULL;
```

```
(gdb) print bad_message
$1 = 0x8048410 "U\211%G%@VS"
(gdb) next
17      char * good_message = "Hello, world.";
(gdb) print bad_message
$2 = 0x0
(gdb) next
19      print_scrambled(good_message);
(gdb) next
Khoor/#zruog$
20      print_scrambled(bad_message);
(gdb) step
print_scrambled (message=0x0) at gdb-example.c:6
6       int i = 3;
(gdb) step
8         printf("%c", (*message)+i);
(gdb) step
Program received signal SIGSEGV, Segmentation fault.
0x0804835b in print_scrambled (message=0x0) at gdb-example.c:8
8         printf("%c", (*message)+i);
(gdb) print (*message)+i
Cannot access memory at address 0x0
(gdb) quit
The program is running.  Exit anyway? (y or n) y
```

The break command sets a breakpoint--a location in the program where gdb should stop when it gets to there. Breakpoints can be set at the beginning of a function or at specific lines in program file. There are many things that can be done with breakpoints, such as making them conditional or temporary. In this example, a common and simple usage case was shown that made had gdb to stop at the beginning of the main function.

The next and step commands were used to make gdb to move forward in the program. For statements that do not involve functions, the next and step commands are identical and merely make gdb execute one statement. For statements that involve a function, however, the two commands are different. next tells gdb to execute the entire function, while step tells gdb to move inside the function.

The print command displays the value of variables or expressions. In the example, the bad_message variable was shown both before and after it was initialized. Later in the example, gdb responded that it could not display the expression (*message)+i because a pointer (the message variable) had a NULL (meaning invalid) value. In fact, this is the bug in this program--print_scrambled does not check to see whether its argument contains a valid value.

More on setting breakpoints

We can set break points on any line, function, and library function.

Example 6

The example below demonstrates setting breakpoints at a specific line number and in a function in a library used by the program.

```
gdb -q gdb-example
This GDB was configured as "i386-redhat-linux-gnu"...Using host libthread_db library "/lib/tls/libthread_db.so.1".
(gdb) break gdb-example.c:19
Breakpoint 1 at 0x80483d2: file gdb-example.c, line 19.
(gdb) break printf
Function "printf" not defined.
Make breakpoint pending on future shared library load? (y or [n]) y

Breakpoint 2 (printf) pending.
(gdb) run
Starting program: /data/home/newren/floss-development/developing-with-gnome/examples/debugging/gdb/gdb-example
Breakpoint 1, main () at gdb-example.c:19
19      print_scrambled(good_message);
(gdb) where
#0  main () at gdb-example.c:19
(gdb) cont
Continuing.

Breakpoint 3, 0x004692a6 in printf () from /lib/tls/libc.so.6
(gdb) where
#0  0x004692a6 in printf () from /lib/tls/libc.so.6
#1  0x08048394 in print_scrambled (message=0x80484c9 "Hello, world.")
    at gdb-example.c:8
#2  0x080483dd in main () at gdb-example.c:19
(gdb) cont
Continuing.

Breakpoint 3, 0x004692a6 in printf () from /lib/tls/libc.so.6
(gdb) where
#0  0x004692a6 in printf () from /lib/tls/libc.so.6
#1  0x08048394 in print_scrambled (message=0x80484ca "ello, world.")
    at gdb-example.c:8
#2  0x080483dd in main () at gdb-example.c:19
(gdb) delete 3
(gdb) cont
```

```
Continuing.
Khoor/#zruog1

Program received signal SIGSEGV, Segmentation fault.
0x08048383 in print_scrambled (message=0x0) at gdb-example.c:8
8         printf("%c", (*message)+i);
(gdb) quit
The program is running.  Exit anyway? (y or n) y
```

The cont command (shorthand form of "continue") just instructs gdb to continue running until it either hits another breakpoint or the program ends. There where command is identical to the backtrace command (it is merely an alias). The delete command removes a breakpoint, given the number of the breakpoint (the command "info breakpoints" can come in handy in connection with delete).

Segment Violations

What is a segmentation fault?

When our program runs, it has access to certain portions of memory. First, we have local variables in each of our functions; these are stored in the stack frame. Second, we may have some memory, allocated during runtime (using either malloc, in C, or new, in C++), stored on the heap (we may also hear it called the "free store"). Our program is only allowed to touch memory that belongs to it -- the memory previously mentioned. Any access outside that area will cause a segmentation fault. Segmentation faults are commonly referred to as segment faults (Also refer chapter on Memory management).

The following common mistakes that lead to segmentation faults

- dereferencing NULL
- dereferencing an uninitialized pointer
- dereferencing a pointer that has been freed (or deleted, in C++) or that has gone out of scope (in the case of arrays declared in functions)
- writing off the end of an array.
- a recursive function that uses all of the stack space. On some systems, this will cause a "stack overflow" report, and on others, it will merely appear as another type of segmentation fault.

The strategy for debugging all of these problems is the same: load the core file into GDB, do a backtrace, move into the scope of our code, and list the lines of code that caused the segmentation fault.

Example 7

Here is an example session to demonstrate segment violation.

```
#include<stdio.h>
    void foo()
    {
      char *x = 0;
      *x = 3;
    }
```

```
int main()
{
  foo();
 return 0;
 }
```

```
gcc -g –o example example.c
./example
```

The above program if executed gives segment violation as it is trying to store 3 at address 0. Some times, core dumped message also appears and a file named core with extension as process's PID is seen in the current working directory. If in our configuration file such as /etc/profile core file size is mentioned as zero then core file will not be created. Thus, if we want to create core file for analyzing our program crash then we can run the following command at shell prompt and then run our program, say example.

```
ulimit  -S –c 100000
./example
```

Now to debug your program along with core file(refer also bug-buddy[15]), run the following command.

```
gdb -q  example  corefilename
```

This just loads the program called example along with the core file which contains all the information needed by GDB to reconstruct the state of execution when the invalid operation caused a segmentation fault.

Once we've loaded up gdb, we get the following:

Program terminated with signal 11, Segmentation fault.

Some information about loading symbols

```
#0  0x0804838c in foo() () at example.c p:4
4         *x = 3;
```

So, execution stopped inside the function called foo() on line 4, which happened to be the assignment of the number 3 to the location pointed to by x.

Simply printing the value of the pointer can often lead to the solution. In this case:

```
(gdb) print x
$1 = 0x0
```

[15] A command bug-buddy is available in Fedora releases which can be used for bug reporting graphically.

Printing out x reveals that it points to memory address 0x0 (the 0x indicates that the value following it is in hexadecimal, traditional for printing memory addresses). The address 0x0 is invalid -- in fact, it's NULL. If we dereference a pointer that stores the location 0x0 then we'll definitely get a segmentation fault, just as we did.

If we'd gotten something more complicated, such as execution crashing inside a system call or library function (perhaps because we passed an uninitialized pointer to fgets), we'd need to figure out where we called the library function and what might have happened to cause a segment fault within it. Here's an example from another debugging session.

Example 8

File t.c

```
#include<stdio.h>
#include<string.h>
    void foo()
    {
      char *x = 0;
      strcpy(x,"Hello");
    }

    int main()
    {
      foo();
     return 0;
     }
```

```
gcc -g –o example1 t.c
./example 1

#0  0x40194f93 in strcpy () from /lib/tls/libc.so.6
(gdb)
```

This time, the segment fault occurred because of something inside strcpy. Does this mean the library function did something wrong?. It means that we probably passed a bad value to the function. To debug this, we need to see what we passed into strcpy.

So let's see what function call we made that led to the segment fault.

```
(gdb) backtrace
#0  0x40194f93 in strcpy () from /lib/tls/libc.so.6
#1  0x080483c9 in foo() () at t.:6
#2  0x080483e3 in main () at t.:11
(gdb)
```

Backtrace lists the function calls that had been made at the time the program crashed. Each function is directly above the function that called it. So foo was called by main in this case. The numbers on the side (#0, #1, #2) also indicate the order of calls, from most recent to longest ago.

To move from viewing the state within each function (encapsulated in the idea of a stack frame), we can use the up and down commands. Right now, we know we're in the strcat stack frame, which contains all of the local variables of strcat, because it's the top function on the stack. We want to move "up" (toward the higher numbers); this is the opposite of how the stack is printed.

```
(gdb) up
#1  0x080483c9 in foo() () at t.c :6
6         strcpy(x, "Hello");
(gdb)
```

This helps a little -- we know that we have a variable called x and a constant string. We should probably lookup the strcat function at this point to make sure that we got the order of arguments correct. Since we did, the problem must be with x.

```
(gdb) print x
$1 = 0x0
```

There it is again: a NULL pointer. The strcpy function must be derefencing a NULL pointer that we gave it, and even though it's a library function, it doesn't do anything magical.

Example 9

The following example also gives segment violation because of the above reasons.

```
#include <stdio.h>

int main (int argc, char **argv)
{
   int i;

   printf ("Hello, world!\n");

   /* print first characters of command-line arguments */
   for (i=0; i<=argc; i++) {
      printf ("%c", argv[i][0]);
   }
   printf ("\n");

   return 0;
}
```

```
./a.out rao rama
Hello, world!
```

```
Segmentation fault (core dumped)
ls -l core.*
-rw------- 1 root root 1818624 Apr 29 12:04 core.4969

gdb -q a.out core.4969

Using host libthread_db library "/lib/tls/libthread_db.so.1".
Core was generated by `./a.out rao rama'.
Program terminated with signal 11, Segmentation fault.
Reading symbols from /lib/tls/libc.so.6...done.
Loaded symbols for /lib/tls/libc.so.6
Reading symbols from /lib/ld-linux.so.2...done.
Loaded symbols for /lib/ld-linux.so.2
#0  0x080483b6 in main (argc=3,
   argv=0xfee4f394) at a4.c:11
11              printf ("%c", argv[i][0]);
(gdb) print i
$1 = 3
(gdb) print argv[i]
$2 = 0x0
 (gdb) q
```

As we did not give third argument along the command line, when i value is 3 the argv[i] is observed to be zero. Thus we are getting segment violation.

Another common mistake is not checking the return from malloc to make sure that the system isn't out of memory. In addition, another common mistake is to assume that a function that calls malloc doesn't return NULL even though it returns the result of malloc. Note that in C++, when we call new, it will throw an exception, bad_alloc, if sufficient memory cannot be allocated. Our code should be prepared to handle this situation cleanly, and if we choose to catch the exception and return NULL inside a function that ordinarily returns a new'ed pointer, this advice still holds.

```
char *create_memory()
{
   char *x = malloc(10);
   if(x == NULL)
   {
      return NULL;
   }
   strcpy(x, "a string");
   return x;
}

void use_memory()
{
   char *new_memory = create_memory();
   new_memory[0] = 'A'; /* make it a capital letter */
}
```

We did a good thing by checking to make sure that malloc succeeds before using the memory in create_memory, but we don't check to make sure that create_memory returns a valid pointer!. This is a bug that won't catch we until we run our code on a real system unless we explicitly test our code in low memory situations.

Dereferencing an Uninitialized Pointer

Figuring out whether or not a pointer has been initialized is a bit harder than figuring out whether a pointer is NULL. The best way to avoid using an uninitialized pointer is to set your pointers to NULL when you declare them (or immediately initialize them). That way, if we do use a pointer that hasn't had memory allocated for it, we will immediately be able to tell.

If we don't set our pointers to NULL when we declare them, then we will have a much harder time of it (remember that non-static variables aren't automatically initialized to anything in C or C++). We might need to figure out if 0x4025e800 is valid memory. One way we can get a sense of this in GDB is by printing out the addresses stored in other pointers we have allocated. If they're fairly close together, we have probably correctly allocated memory. Of course, there's no guarantee that this rule of thumb will hold on all systems.

In some cases, our debugger can tell us that an address is invalid based on the value stored in the pointer. For instance, in the following example, GDB indicates that the char* x, which is set to point to the memory address "30", is not accessible.

```
(gdb) print x
$1 = 0x1e <out of bounds>
(gdb) print *x
Cannot access memory at address 0x1e
```

Generally, though, the best way to handle such a situation is just to avoid having to rely on memory's being close together or obviously invalid. Set our variables to NULL from the beginning.

Dereferencing Free'd Memory

This is another tricky bug to find because we're working with memory addresses that look valid. The best way to handle such a situation is again preventative: set our pointer to point to NULL as soon as we've freed it. That way, if we do try to use it later, then we'll have another "dereferencing NULL" bug, which should be much easier to track.

Another form of this bug is the problem of dealing with memory that has gone out of scope. If we declare a local array such as

```
char *return_buffer()
{
   char x[10];
   strncpy(x, "a string", sizeof(x));
   return x;
}
```

then the array, x, will no longer be valid once the function returns. This is a really tricky bug to find because once again the memory address will look valid when we print it out in GDB. In fact, our code might even work sometimes (or just display weird behavior by printing whatever happens to be on the stack in the location that used to be the memory of the array x). Generally, the way we'll know if we have this kind of bug is that we'll get garbage when we print out the variable even though we know that it's initialized. Watch out for the pointers returned from functions. If that pointer is causing us trouble, check the function and look for whether the pointer is pointing to a local variable in the function. Note that it is perfectly fine to return a pointer to memory allocated in the function using new or malloc, but not to return a pointer to a statically declared array (e.g., char x[10]).

Writing off the end of the array

Generally, if we're writing off the bounds of an array, then the line that caused the segment fault in the first place should be an array access. (There are a few times when this won't actually be the case -- notably, if the fact that we wrote off an array causes the stack to be smashed -- basically, overwriting the pointer that stores where to return after the function completes.)

Of course, sometimes, we won't actually cause a segment fault writing off the end of the array. Instead, we might just notice that some of our variable values are changing periodically and unexpectedly. This is a tough bug to crack; one option is to set up our debugger to watch a variable for changes and run our program until the variable's value changes. Your debugger will break on that instruction, and we can poke around to figure out if that behavior is unexpected.

```
(gdb) watch [variable name]
Hardware watchpoint 1: [variable name]
(gdb) continue
...
Hardware watchpoint 1: [variable name]

Old value = [value1]
New value = [value2]
```

This approach can get tricky when we're dealing with a lot of dynamically allocated memory and it's not entirely clear what we should watch. To simplify things, use simple test cases, keep working with the same inputs, and turn off randomized seeds if we're using random numbers!

Stack Overflows

A stack overflow isn't the same type of pointer-related problem as the others. In this case, we don't need to have a single explicit pointer in our program; we just need a recursive function without a base case. Nevertheless, this is a tutorial about segmentation faults, and on some systems, a stack overflow will be reported as a segmentation fault. (This makes sense because running out of memory on the stack will violate memory segmentation.)

To diagnose a stack overflow in GDB, typically we just need to do a backtrace:

Explanation of Normal Recursion and Tail recursion in GDB Way

In this section, we would like to demonstrate the conceptual difference between normal recursion (also called as straight or self recursion) and tail recursion. For this purpose, we have used two versions of the functions to calculate factorial value of an integer. See, programs fact1.c and fact2.c.

As we have mentioned earlier that whenever we call a function a activation record (or stack frame) is created and memory for arguments and local variables of that function are allocated in it. The memory needed for this is used from stack part of the program.

This is true even with recursive functions. That is, for each function call of a recursive function a stack frame is created in the direct recursion. Where as in the case of tail recursive realizations of recursive functions one stack frame is used for all recursive calls. Thus, stack utilization will be better. However, in some compilers this will not become practical unless we enable optimization flags during compilation.

In order to explain these concepts, fact1.c is compiled with –g and dubugged with gdb. Similarly, fact2.c (tail recursive version) is also compiled with –g option and debugged with gdb. In addition, fact2.c is compiled with –g and –O6 options and debugged with gdb. We have specified break point after line 6 and input is given as 4 in all experiments. In each experiment, we have asked gdb to print stack frame details using bt command. We can find that no of stack frames with third experiment are always less. Please look at the starting addresses of stack frames!! Also, we can find from the following experiment how during rewinding stage of recursive function calls number of stack frames reduces. The following output is captured using "script" facility of the Linux system.

We can also recompile fact1.c with –g and –O6 and debug and carry the same experiment. We may find that same number of stack frames is used here also. This supports that writing a function a tail recursive fashion is important and also the compiler has to identify the same during optimizations.

Example 10

File fact1.c

```
#include <stdio.h>
int fact(int n)
    {
    if(n==0) return 1;
    else
    return (n * fact(n-1) );
    }

int main ()
{
    int N;
    printf("Enter a Integer\n");
    scanf("%d", &N);

    printf("Factorial Value=%d\n", fact(N) );
    return 0;
}
```

```
gcc -g  fact1.c

gdb -q a.out
Using host libthread_db library "/lib/tls/libthread_db.so.1".
(gdb) break 6
Breakpoint 1 at 0x80483b1: file fact1.c, line 6.(gdb) r
Starting program: /root/gdb/a.out
Enter a Integer
4

Breakpoint 1, fact (n=4) at fact1.c:6
6           return (n * fact(n-1) );
(gdb) n

Breakpoint 1, fact (n=3) at fact1.c:6
6           return (n * fact(n-1) );
(gdb) n

Breakpoint 1, fact (n=2) at fact1.c:6
6           return (n * fact(n-1) );
(gdb) n

Breakpoint 1, fact (n=1) at fact1.c:6
6           return (n * fact(n-1) );
(gdb) bt
#0  fact (n=1) at fact1.c:6
#1  0x080483be in fact (n=2) at fact1.c:6
#2  0x080483be in fact (n=3) at fact1.c:6
#3  0x080483be in fact (n=4) at fact1.c:6
#4  0x08048418 in main () at fact1.c:15
(gdb) n
7           }
(gdb) bt
#0  fact (n=1) at fact1.c:7
#1  0x080483be in fact (n=2) at fact1.c:6
#2  0x080483be in fact (n=3) at fact1.c:6
#3  0x080483be in fact (n=4) at fact1.c:6
#4  0x08048418 in main () at fact1.c:15
(gdb) n
7           }
(gdb) bt
#0  fact (n=2) at fact1.c:7
#1  0x080483be in fact (n=3) at fact1.c:6
#2  0x080483be in fact (n=4) at fact1.c:6
```

```
#3  0x08048418 in main () at fact1.c:15
(gdb) n
7               }
(gdb) bt
#0  fact (n=3) at fact1.c:7
#1  0x080483be in fact (n=4) at fact1.c:6
#2  0x08048418 in main () at fact1.c:15
(gdb) n
7               }
(gdb) bt
#0  fact (n=4) at fact1.c:7
#1  0x08048418 in main () at fact1.c:15
(gdb) n
Factorial Value=24
main () at fact1.c:16
16              return 0;
(gdb) bt
#0  main () at fact1.c:16
(gdb) n
17          }
(gdb) n
0x004fbe33 in __libc_start_main ()
  from /lib/tls/libc.so.6
(gdb) n
Single stepping until exit from function __libc_start_main,
which has no line number information.

Program exited normally.
(gdb) q
```

Example 11

File fact 2.c

```
#include <stdio.h>
int fact(int n, int a)
    {
    if(n==0) return a;
    else
    return (fact(n-1,a*n) );
    }

 int main ()
```

```
{
    int N;
    printf("Enter a Integer\n");
    scanf("%d", &N);

    printf("Factorial Value=%d\n", fact(N,1) );
    return 0;
}
```

gcc -g fact2.c

gdb -q a.out

```
Using host libthread_db library "/lib/tls/libthread_db.so.1".
(gdb) break 6
Breakpoint 1 at 0x80483b0: file fact2.c, line 6.(gdb) r
Starting program: /root/gdb/a.out
Enter a Integer
4

Breakpoint 1, fact (n=4, a=1) at fact2.c:6
6           return (fact(n-1,a*n) );
(gdb) n

Breakpoint 1, fact (n=3, a=4) at fact2.c:6
6           return (fact(n-1,a*n) );
(gdb) n

Breakpoint 1, fact (n=2, a=12) at fact2.c:6
6           return (fact(n-1,a*n) );
(gdb) n

Breakpoint 1, fact (n=1, a=24) at fact2.c:6
6           return (fact(n-1,a*n) );
(gdb) bt
#0  fact (n=1, a=24) at fact2.c:6
#1  0x080483c5 in fact (n=2, a=12) at fact2.c:6
#2  0x080483c5 in fact (n=3, a=4) at fact2.c:6
#3  0x080483c5 in fact (n=4, a=1) at fact2.c:6
#4  0x0804841d in main () at fact2.c:15
(gdb) n
7           }
```

```
(gdb) bt
#0  fact (n=1, a=24) at fact2.c:7
#1  0x080483c5 in fact (n=2, a=12) at fact2.c:6
#2  0x080483c5 in fact (n=3, a=4) at fact2.c:6
#3  0x080483c5 in fact (n=4, a=1) at fact2.c:6
#4  0x0804841d in main () at fact2.c:15
(gdb) n
7           }
(gdb) bt
#0  fact (n=2, a=12) at fact2.c:7
#1  0x080483c5 in fact (n=3, a=4) at fact2.c:6
#2  0x080483c5 in fact (n=4, a=1) at fact2.c:6
#3  0x0804841d in main () at fact2.c:15
(gdb) n
7           }
(gdb) bt
#0  fact (n=3, a=4) at fact2.c:7
#1  0x080483c5 in fact (n=4, a=1) at fact2.c:6
#2  0x0804841d in main () at fact2.c:15
(gdb) n
7           }
(gdb) bt
#0  fact (n=4, a=1) at fact2.c:7
#1  0x0804841d in main () at fact2.c:15
(gdb) n
Factorial Value=24
main () at fact2.c:16
16          return 0;
(gdb) bt
#0  main () at fact2.c:16
(gdb) n
17        }
(gdb) n
0x004fbe33 in __libc_start_main ()
  from /lib/tls/libc.so.6
(gdb) n
Single stepping until exit from function __libc_start_main,
which has no line number information.
Program exited normally.
(gdb) q
```

```
gcc -g -O6 fact2.c

gdb -q a.out
Using host libthread_db library "/lib/tls/libthread_db.so.1".
(gdb) break 6
Breakpoint 1 at 0x80483dc: file fact2.c, line 6.(gdb) r
Starting program: /root/gdb/a.out
Enter a Integer
4

Breakpoint 1, fact (n=3, a=4) at fact2.c:6
6           return (fact(n-1,a*n) );
(gdb) n
4           if(n==0) return a;
(gdb) n

Breakpoint 1, fact (n=2, a=12) at fact2.c:6
6           return (fact(n-1,a*n) );
(gdb) n
4           if(n==0) return a;
(gdb) bt
#0  fact (n=1, a=24) at fact2.c:4
#1  0x08048438 in main () at fact2.c:4
(gdb) n

Breakpoint 1, fact (n=1, a=24) at fact2.c:6
6           return (fact(n-1,a*n) );
(gdb) bt
#0  fact (n=1, a=24) at fact2.c:6
#1  0x08048438 in main () at fact2.c:4
(gdb) n
4           if(n==0) return a;
(gdb) bt
#0  fact (n=0, a=24) at fact2.c:4
#1  0x08048438 in main () at fact2.c:4
(gdb) n
7           }
(gdb) bt
#0  fact (n=0, a=24) at fact2.c:7
#1  0x08048438 in main () at fact2.c:4
(gdb) n
main () at fact2.c:3
3           {
(gdb) bt
```

```
#0  main () at fact2.c:3
(gdb) n
4           if(n==0) return a;
(gdb) n
3           {
(gdb) n
Factorial Value=24
17        }
(gdb) n
0x004fbe33 in __libc_start_main ()
  from /lib/tls/libc.so.6
(gdb) n
Single stepping until exit from function __libc_start_main,
which has no line number information.

Program exited normally.
(gdb) q
exit
```

Attaching To an Already Running Process

We want to debug a program that cannot be launched from the command line. This may be because the program is launched from some system daemon (such as a CGI program on the web). Or perhaps the program takes very long time to run its initialization code, and starting it with a debugger attached to it will cause this startup time to be much longer. There are also other reasons, but hopefully we got the point. In order to debug a running program, we will launch the debugger in this way:

gdb debug_me 9561

Here we assume that "debug_me" is the name of the program in execution, and 9561 is the process id (PID) of it.

What happens is that gdb first tries looking for a "core" file named "9561" (we'll see what core files are in the next section), and when it won't find it, it'll assume the supplied number is a process ID, and try to attach to it. If there process executes exactly the same program whose path we gave to gdb (not a copy of the file. it must be the exact same file that the process runs), it'll attach to the program, pause its execution, and will let us continue debugging it as if we started the program from inside the debugger. Doing a "where" right when we get gdb's prompt will show us the stack trace of the process, and we can continue from there. Once we exit the debugger, It will detach itself from the process, and the process will continue execution from where we left it.

In order to demonstrate this, we are using the following program which displays natural numbers from 0 onwards such that one number will be printed for every 5 seconds.

Example 12

File a7.c

```
#include<stdio.h>
int N=0;
void f()
{
printf("%d\n",N++);
}

void ff()
{
f();
sleep(5);
}

int main()
{
while(1)
ff();
return 0;
}
```

```
gcc -g a7.c
./a.out &
[1] 5167
0
```

The abve program "a.out" is made as background process. It's PID is given as 5167. Now run :

```
gdb –q  a.out 5167
1
2
Using host libthread_db library "/lib/tls/libthread_db.so.1".
Attaching to program: /root/gdb/a.out, process 5167
Reading symbols from /lib/tls/libc.so.6...done.
Loaded symbols for /lib/tls/libc.so.6
Reading symbols from /lib/ld-linux.so.2...done.
Loaded symbols for /lib/ld-linux.so.2
0x004ca7a2 in _dl_sysinfo_int80 ()
   from /lib/ld-linux.so.2
(gdb) r
```

```
The program being debugged has been started already.
Start it from the beginning? (y or n) n
Program not restarted.
(gdb) bt
#0  0x004ca7a2 in _dl_sysinfo_int80 ()
   from /lib/ld-linux.so.2
#1  0x00570110 in __nanosleep_nocancel ()
   from /lib/tls/libc.so.6
#2  0x0056ff33 in sleep ()
   from /lib/tls/libc.so.6
#3  0x080483d5 in ff () at a7.c:11
#4  0x080483fb in main () at a7.c:17
(gdb) n
Single stepping until exit from function _dl_sysinfo_int80,
which has no line number information.
0x00570110 in __nanosleep_nocancel ()
   from /lib/tls/libc.so.6
(gdb) n
Single stepping until exit from function __nanosleep_nocancel,
which has no line number information.
0x0056ff33 in sleep () from /lib/tls/libc.so.6
(gdb) n
Single stepping until exit from function sleep,
which has no line number information.
ff () at a7.c:12
12      }
(gdb) n
0x080483fb in main () at a7.c:17
17      ff();
(gdb) n
3
4
5
6
7
q
8
9
10
(press ^C)
Program received signal SIGINT, Interrupt.
```

```
0x004ca7a2 in _dl_sysinfo_int80 ()
   from /lib/ld-linux.so.2
(gdb) q
The program is running.  Quit anyway (and detach it)? (y or n) y
Detaching from program: /root/gdb/a.out, process 5167
11
12
13
```

Now run ps command.

```
  PID TTY          TIME CMD
 5145 pts/3    00:00:00 bash
 5167 pts/3    00:00:00 a.out
 5171 pts/3    00:00:00 ps
14
15
16
```

We can see from the above experiment that "a.out" printed 1 and 2 before starting gdb to debug it. During debugging we have got numbers 3 to 13. After exiting gdb also we found "a.out" is running from ps commands output.

11.3 An Introduction to Kdbg

KDbg is a front-end for gdb, but not the debugger itself. It communicates with gdb, by sending commands to it and receiving the output, such as variable values. The menu commands and mouse clicks are translated into gdb commands, and the output of gdb is translated into visible information. KDbg can do no more than gdb can. For example, if we have a gdb that does not supports debugging of threaded programs, KDbg can not.

Either we can start kdbg by simply typing its name at the $ prompt when we are in a X terminal or we can as well select the same from Applications -> Programming -> Debugger (a spider like Icon!!). We will get a screen similar to Figure 11.1.

Before we test our program with kdbg, we have to compile the program with -g option.

First, check File|Global Options and if needed adjust as we like.

To debug a program, choose File|Executable from the menu. If we have debugged the program earlier, we can choose it from File|Recent Executables. The program is loaded.

For example, the example 4 is compiled with -g option and resulting executable file is selected for debugging (see Figure 11.1). Note that its source file is displayed automatically in the display window. Source lines are prepended with '+' symbols. When we click on this '+', we will see there assembly code of that instruction (see Figure 11.2). We can set breakpoints on this assembly code also. Also, by clicking before '+' symbol we can insert break point on any line. The same can be done through breakpoint menu also. If we want to debug a core dump, we must first load the executable that produced the core dump, then choose File|Core Dump from the menu. Now KDbg goes to the point in the program that caused the core dump.

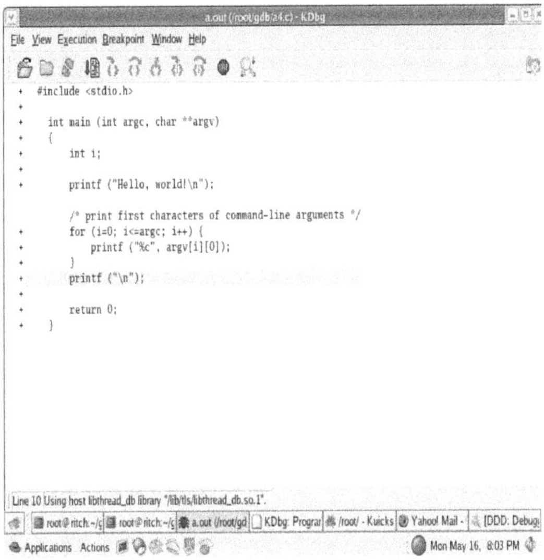

a.out (/root/gdb/a4.c) - KDbg

File View Execution Breakpoint Window Help

```
#include <stdio.h>

int main (int argc, char **argv)
{
    int i;

    printf ("Hello, world!\n");

    /* print first characters of command-line arguments */
    for (i=0; i<=argc; i++) {
        printf ("%c", argv[i][0]);
    }
    printf ("\n");

    return 0;
}
```

Line 10 Using host libthread_db library "/lib/tls/libthread_db.so.1".

Applications Actions Mon May 16, 8:03 PM

We can now set breakpoints, using the Breakpoint menu, the right mouse button menu, or the breakpoint window.

We can also choose program specific settings that apply only to the currently loaded executable using File|Settings, in the Program Settings dialog.

Now run the program by selecting Execution|Run. The program now executes as usual until it either exits, hits a breakpoint or watchpoint, or receives a signal.

We can run the program with arguments, set a working directory, or set environment variables. To do this, choose Execution|Arguments and specify our options in the Program Arguments dialog (before we start the program).

We can also attach to a program that is currently running. To do this, first load the executable file like above. Then choose Execution|Attach. Specify the process number and click OK. The running program is halted (not terminated), and the current point of execution is displayed in the source window.

When the program stops at a breakpoint, watchpoint, or due to a signal, the source code window displays the line where the program stopped. It is very common that the program stops due to a signal (usually a SIGSEGV, segmentation violation) in a function that is not part of the program, that we have written. In this case we investigate the stack window and look for a function that we have written (start at the top of the list) and click on it. This will bring we to a location that we can start our search for the real bug.

In the menu Execution, we find the commands that we need to run the program, step through code, and to interrupt the program (Break) while it is running. The important commands (Run and all kinds of Step) are bound to function keys. For efficient debugging it is strongly recommend that we get used to using them.

From the Breakpoint menu, we find options to set, clear, disable, and enable permanent and temporary breakpoints. We can display a list of breakpoints in the breakpoints window. We can also set a breakpoint by clicking at the left end of the source line (using the left mouse button), and we can enable and disable a breakpoint by clicking it using the middle mouse button.

a.out (/root/gdb/a4.c) - KDbg

File View Execution Breakpoint Window Help

```
+  #include <stdio.h>
+
+    int main (int argc, char **argv)
+    {
+        int i;
+
+        printf ("Hello, world!\n");

        /* print first characters of command-line arguments */
+        for (i=0; i<=argc; i++) {
-            printf ("%c", argv[i][0]);
   0x80483a3 sub    $0x8,%esp
   0x80483a6 mov    0xfffffffc(%ebp),%eax
   0x80483a9 lea    0x0(,%eax,4),%edx
   0x80483b0 mov    0xc(%ebp),%eax
   0x80483b3 mov    (%edx,%eax,1),%eax
   0x80483b6 movsbl (%eax),%eax
   0x80483b9 push   %eax
   0x80483ba push   $0x80484d7
   0x80483bf call   0x80482b0 <_init+56>
   0x80483c4 add    $0x10,%esp
+        }
+        printf ("\n");
+
+        return 0;
+    }
```

active Line 11 Program received signal SIGSEGV, Segmentation fault.

The gearwheel in the toolbar indicates whether gdb is working, in which case it rotates. It rotates fast while KDbg wouldn't accept execution commands, and it rotates slowly while KDbg retrieves the values of variable.

KDbg displays information and accepts commands in number of different windows. In the menu View we find commands to show and hide these windows. They are docking windows, which means that we can drag them around and arrange them in any manner we like.

- The source code window
- The local variables window
- The stack window
- The watched expressions window
- The breakpoint list
- The output window
- The register dump window
- The memory dump window
- The threads window

Please remember that the KDbg's works for libraries that are linked dynamically to the program.

11.4 Debugging with DDD

DDD is another graphical front-end for GDB and other command-line Debuggers and is more powerful than Kdbg.

DDD can do four main kinds of things to help we catch bugs in the act:

- Start our program, specifying anything that might affect its behavior.
- Make our program stop on specified conditions.
- Examine what has happened, when our program has stopped.
- Change things in our program, so we can experiment with correcting the effects of one bug and go on to learn about another.

As usual, first, we must compile our C programs with \`-g' flag to use DDD. We can invoke DDD by the following manner from the command prompt.

ddd executablefilename

we can run DDD and then load executable file from the menu. A DDD window shown in Fig. 11.3 will appear along with the source code window, gdb window and execution window.

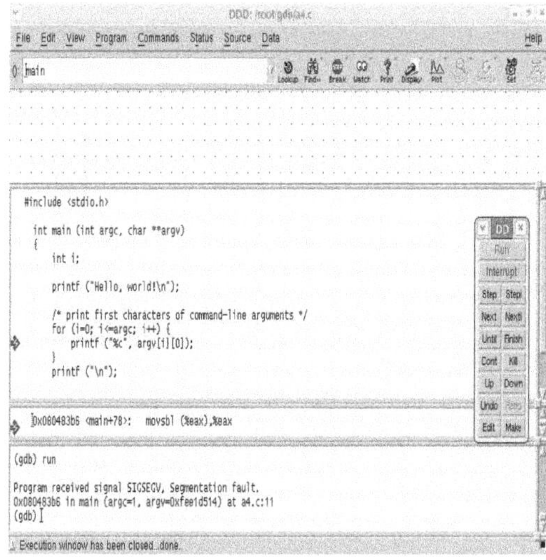

Figure. 11.3 DDD window.

If we want to debug a program which generated a core file, the following command can be used at the prompt.

ddd executablefilename corefilename

If we want to debug a running program then we can run the following at the command prompt.

ddd executablefilename PIDoftherunningprocess

To place a "Breakpoints, Click on the blank space left to the initialization of line. Now, click on \`Break' to create a breakpoint at the location in \`()'. We see a little red stop sign appear in line.

The next thing to do is to actually "execute" the program, such that we can examine its behavior. Select \`Program => Run' to execute the program; the \`Run Program' dialog appears.

In \`Run with Arguments', we can now enter arguments for the program.

Execution stops after a few moments as the breakpoint is reached. This is reported in the debugger console.

We can now examine the variable values. To examine a simple variable, we can simply move the mouse pointer on its name and leave it there. After a second, a small window with the variable value pops up. If a local variable `a' is not yet initialized; we'll probably see `0x0' or some other invalid pointer value.

To execute the current line, click on the `Next' button on the command tool. The arrow advances to the following line. Now, point again on a variable to see that the value has changed or not. It is also possible to see values of an array either by element by element or a whole.

Persistent Sessions

If we want to interrupt our current DDD session, we can save the entire the entire DDD state as "session" on disk and resume later.

Saving Sessions

To save a session, select `File => Save Session As'. We will be asked for a symbolic session name SESSION.

If our program is running, or if we have opened a core file, DDD can also include a core file in the session such that the debuggee data will be restored when re-opening it. To get a core file, DDD typically must "kill" the debuggee. Including a core dump is necessary for restoring memory contents and the current execution position. To include a core dump, enable `Include Core Dump'.

After clicking on `Save', the session is saved in `~/.ddd/sessions/SESSION'.

Here's a list of the items whose state is saved in a session:

- The state of the debugged program, as a core file.
- All breakpoints and watchpoints
- All signal settings.
- All displays
- All DDD options.
- All debugger settings.
- All user-defined buttons.
- All user-defined commands.
- The positions and sizes of DDD windows.
- The command history.

Resuming Sessions

To resume a previously saved session, select `File => Open Session' and choose a session name from the list. After clicking on `Open', the entire DDD state will be restored from the given session.

The session named `[None]' is the "default session" which is active when starting DDD. To save options for default sessions, choose the default session before exiting DDD.

If a the restored session includes a core dump, the program being debugged will be in the same state at the time the session was saved; in particular, we can examine the program data. However, we will not be able to resume program execution since the process and its environment (open files, resources, etc.) no longer exist. However, we can restart the program, re-using the restored breakpoints and data displays.

Remote Debugging

We can have each of DDD, the inferior debugger, and the debugged program run on different machines.

The DDD Windows

DDD is composed of three main windows. From top to bottom, we have:

- The "Data Window" shows the current data of the debugged program.
- The "Source Window" shows the current source code of the debugged program.
- The "Debugger Console" accepts debugger commands and shows debugger messages.

Besides these three main windows, there are some other optional windows:

- The "Command Tool" offers buttons for frequently used commands. It is usually placed on the source window.
- The "Machine Code Window" shows the current machine code. It is usually placed beneath the current source.
- The "Execution Window" shows the input and output of the debugged program.

Opening Core Dumps

To open a core dump for the program, select `File => Open Core Dump'. Click on `Open' to open the core dump. Before `Open Core Dump', we should first use `File => Open Program' to specify the program that generated the core dump and to load its symbol table.

Setting Breakpoints by Location

If the source line is visible, click with mouse button 1 on the left of the source line and then on the `Break' button.

As a faster alternative, we can simply press mouse button 3 on the left of the source line and select the `Set Breakpoint' item from the line popup menu.

As an even faster alternative, we can simply double-click on the left of the source line to set a breakpoint.

As yet another alternative, we can select `Source => Breakpoints'. Click on the `Break' button and enter the location.

Breakpoints are indicated by a plain stop sign, or as `#N', where N is the breakpoint number. A greyed out stop sign (or `_N_') indicates a disabled breakpoint. A stop sign with a question mark (or `?N?') indicates a conditional breakpoint or a breakpoint with an ignore count set.

If we set a breakpoint by mistake, use `Edit => Undo' to delete it again.

Setting Breakpoints by Name

If the function name is visible, click with mouse button 1 on the function name. The function name is then copied to the argument field. Click on the `Break' button to set a breakpoint there.

As a shorter alternative, we can simply press mouse button 3 on the function name and select the `Break at' item from the popup menu.

As yet another alternative, we can click on `Break...' from the Breakpoint editor (invoked through `Source => Breakpoints') and enter the function name.

Setting Regexp Breakpoints

Using GDB, we can also set a breakpoint on all functions that match a given string. `Break => Set Breakpoints at Regexp ()' sets a breakpoint on all functions whose name matches the _regular expression_ given in `()'.

Deleting Breakpoints

To delete a visible breakpoint, click with mouse button 1 on the breakpoint. The breakpoint location is copied to the argument field. Click on the `Clear' button to delete all breakpoints there.

If the function name is visible, click with mouse button 1 on the function name. The function name is copied to the argument field. Click on the `Clear' button to clear all breakpoints there.

As a faster alternative, we can simply press mouse button 3 on the breakpoint and select the `Delete Breakpoint' item from the popup menu.

Temporary Breakpoints

A "temporary breakpoint" is immediately deleted as soon as it is reached.

To set a temporary breakpoint, press mouse button 3 on the left of the source line and select the `Set Temporary Breakpoint' item from the popup menu.

As a faster alternative, we can simply double-click on the left of the source line while holding <Ctrl>.

Temporary breakpoints are convenient to make the program continue up to a specific location: just set the temporary breakpoint at this location and continue execution.

The `Continue Until Here' item from the popup menu sets a temporary breakpoint on the left of the source line and immediately continues execution. Execution stops when the temporary breakpoint is reached.

We can also Edit Breakpoint Properties.

Breakpoint Conditions

The simplest sort of breakpoint breaks every time our program reaches a specified place. We can also specify a "condition" for a breakpoint. A condition is just a Boolean expression in our programming language. A breakpoint with a condition evaluates the expression each time our program reaches it, and our program stops only if the condition is true.

This is the converse of using assertions for program validation; in that situation, we want to stop when the assertion is violated-that is, when the condition is false. In C, if we want to test an assertion expressed by the condition ASSERTION, we should set the condition `!ASSERTION' on the appropriate breakpoint.

Break conditions can have side effects, and may even call functions in our program. This can be useful, for example, to activate functions that log program progress, or to use our own print functions to format special data structures. The effects are completely predictable unless there is another enabled breakpoint at the same address. (In that case, DDD might see the other breakpoint first and stop our program without checking the condition of this one.)

Breakpoint Ignore Counts

A special case of a breakpoint condition is to stop only when the breakpoint has been reached a certain number of times. This is so useful that there is a special way to do it, using the "ignore count" of the breakpoint. Every breakpoint has an ignore count, which is an integer. Most of the time, the ignore count is zero, and therefore has no effect.

But if our program reaches a breakpoint whose ignore count is positive, then instead of stopping, it just decrements the ignore count by one and continues. As a result, if the ignore count value is N, the breakpoint does not stop the next N times our program reaches it.

In the field `Ignore Count' of the `Breakpoint Properties' panel, we can specify the breakpoint ignore count.

If a breakpoint has a positive ignore count and a condition, the condition is not checked. Once the ignore count reaches zero, DDD resumes checking the condition.

Watchpoints

We can make the program stop as soon as some variable value changes, or when some variable is read or written. This is called "setting a watchpoint on a variable".

Watchpoints have much in common with breakpoints: in particular, we can enable and disable them. We can also set conditions, ignore counts, and commands to be executed when a watched variable changes its value.

Please note: on architectures without special watchpoint support, watchpoints currently make the program execute two orders of magnitude more slowly. This is so because the inferior debugger must interrupt the program after each machine instruction in order to examine whether the watched value has changed. However, this delay can be well worth it to catch errors when we have no clue what part of our program is the culprit.

Setting Watchpoints

If the variable name is visible, click with _mouse button 1_ on the variable name. The variable name is copied to the argument field. Otherwise, enter the variable name in the argument field. Click on the `Watch' button to set a watchpoint there.

Editing Watchpoint Properties

To change the properties of a watchpoint, enter the name of the watched variable in the argument field. Click and hold _mouse button 1_ on the `Watch' button and select `Watchpoint Properties'.

The Watchpoint Properties panel has the same functionality as the Breakpoint Properties panel. As an additional feature, we can click on `Print' to see the current value of a watched variable.

Editing all Watchpoints

To view and edit all watchpoints at once, select `Data => Watchpoints'. This will popup the "Watchpoint Editor" which displays the state of all watchpoints.

The Watchpoint Editor has the same functionality as the Breakpoint Editor. As an additional feature, we can click on `Print' to see the current value of a watched variable.

Deleting Watchpoints

To delete a watchpoint, enter the name of the watched variable in the argument field and click the `Unwatch' button.

Interrupting

If the program is already running, we can interrupt it any time by clicking the `Interrupt' button or typing <ESC> in a DDD window. Using GDB, this is equivalent to sending a `SIGINT' (Interrupt) signal.

`Interrupt' and <ESC> also interrupt a running debugger command, such as printing data.

Running the Program

We may start the debugged program with its arguments, if any, in an environment of your choice. We may redirect our program's input and output, debug an already running process, or kill a child process.

Starting Program Execution

To start execution of the debugged program, select `Program => Run'. We will then be prompted for the arguments to pass to your program. We can either select from a list of previously used arguments or enter own arguments in the text field. Afterwards, press the `Run' button to start execution with the selected arguments.

To run our program again, with the same arguments, select `Program => Run Again' or press the `Run' button on the command tool. We may also enter `run', followed by arguments at the debugger prompt instead.

When we click on `Run', our program begins to execute immediately. *Note Stopping::, for a discussion of how to arrange for your program to stop. Once our program has stopped, we may call functions in our program to examine data.

If the modification time of symbol file has changed since the last time GDB read its symbols, GDB discards its symbol table, and reads it again. When it does this, GDB and DDD try to retain our current debugger state, such as breakpoints.

Using the Execution Window

By default, input and output of our program go to the debugger console. As an alternative, DDD can also invoke an "execution window", where the program terminal input and output is shown.

To activate the execution window, select `Program => Run in Execution Window'.

Using the execution window has an important side effect: The output of our program no longer gets intermixed with the output of the inferior debugger. This makes it far easier for DDD to parse the debugger output correctly.

The execution window is opened automatically as soon as we start the debugged program. While the execution window is active, DDD redirects the standard input, output, and error streams of our program to the execution window.

Program Stops

After the program has been started, it runs until one of the following happens:

- A breakpoint is reached
- A watched value changes
- The program is interrupted
- A signal is received
- Execution completes.

DDD shows the current program status in the debugger console. The current execution position is highlighted by an arrow.

If `Edit => Preferences => General => Uniconify When Ready' is set, DDD automatically discontinues itself when the program stops. This way, we can iconify DDD during a lengthy computation and have it uniconify as soon as the program stops.

Continuing

To resume execution, at the current execution position, click on the `Continue' button. Any breakpoints set at the current execution position are bypassed.

Stepping one Line

To execute just one source line, click on the `Step' button. The program is executed until control reaches a different source line, which may be in a different function. Then, the program is stopped and control returns to DDD.

Continuing to the Next Line

To continue to the next line in the current function, click on the `Next' button. This is similar to `Step', but any function calls appearing within the line of code are executed without stopping.

Execution stops when control reaches a different line of code at the original stack level that was executing we you clicked on `Next'.

Continuing Until Here

To continue running until a specific location is reached, use the `Continue Until Here' facility from the line popup menu.

Continuing Until a Greater Line is Reached

To continue until a greater line in the current function is reached, click on the `Until' button. This is useful to avoid single stepping through a loop more than once.

`Until' is like `Next', except that when `Until' encounters a jump, it automatically continues execution until the program counter is greater than the address of the jump.

This means that when we reach the end of a loop after single stepping though it, `until' makes our program continue execution until it exits the loop. In contrast, clicking on `Next' at the end of a loop simply steps back to the beginning of the loop, which forces us to step through the next iteration.

`Until' always stops our program if it attempts to exit the current stack frame.

'Until' works by means of single instruction stepping, and hence is slower than continuing until a breakpoint is reached.

Continuing Until Function Returns

To continue running until the current function returns, use the `Finish' button. The returned value (if any) is printed.

Continuing at a Different Address

Ordinarily, when we continue our program, we do so at the place where it stopped. We can instead continue at an address of our own choosing.

The most common occasion to use this feature is to back up—perhaps with more breakpoints set-over a portion of a program that has already executed, in order to examine its execution in more detail.

To set the execution position to the current location, use `Set Execution Position' from the breakpoint popup menu. This item is also accessible by pressing and holding the `Break/Clear' button.

As a quicker alternative, we can also press _mouse button 1 on the arrow and drag it to a different location.

Moving the execution position does not change the current stack frame, or the stack pointer, or the contents of any memory location or any register other than the program counter.

Some inferior debuggers (notably GDB) allow us to set the new execution position into a different function from the one currently executing. This may lead to bizarre results if the two functions expect different patterns of arguments or of local variables. For this reason, moving the execution position requests confirmation if the specified line is not in the function currently executing.

After moving the execution position, click on `Continue' to resume execution.

Examining the Stack

When our program has stopped, the first thing we need to know is where it stopped and how it got there.

Each time our program performs a function call, information about the call is generated. That information includes the location of the call in our program, the arguments of the call, and the local variables of the function being called. The information is saved in a block of data called a "stack frame". The stack frames are allocated in a region of memory called the "call stack".

When our program stops, the DDD commands for examining the stack allow us to see all of this information.

One of the stack frames is "selected" by DDD and many DDD commands refer implicitly to the selected frame. In particular, whenever we ask DDD for the value of a variable in our program, the value is found in the selected frame. There are special DDD commands to select whichever frame we are interested in.

Stack Frames

The call stack is divided up into contiguous pieces called "stack frames", or "frames" for short; each frame is the data associated with one call to one function. The frame contains the arguments given to the function, the function's local variables, and the address at which the function is executing.

When our program is started, the stack has only one frame, that of the function `main'. This is called the "initial" frame or the "outermost" frame. Each time a function is called, a new frame is made. Each time a function returns, the frame for that function invocation is eliminated. If a function is recursive, there can be many frames for the same function. The frame for the function in which execution is actually occurring is called the "innermost" frame. This is the most recently created of all the stack frames that still exist.

Inside our program, stack frames are identified by their addresses. A stack frame consists of many bytes, each of which has its own address; each kind of computer has a convention for choosing one byte whose address serves as the address of the frame. Usually this address is kept in a register called the "frame pointer register" while execution is going on in that frame.

GDB assigns numbers to all existing stack frames, starting with zero for the innermost frame, one for the frame that called it, and so on upward. These numbers do not really exist in our program; they are assigned by GDB to give us a way of designating stack frames in GDB commands.

Backtraces

DDD provides a "backtrace window" showing a summary of how our program got where it is. It shows one line per frame, for many frames, starting with the currently executing frame (frame zero), followed by its caller (frame one), and on up the stack.

To enable the backtrace window, select `Status => Backtrace'.

Using GDB, each line in the backtrace shows the frame number and the function name. The program counter value is also shown--unless we use the GDB command `set print address off'. The backtrace also shows the source file name and line number, as well as the arguments to the function. The program counter value is omitted if it is at the beginning of the code for that line number.

Selecting a Frame

Most commands for examining the stack and other data in our program work on whichever stack frame is selected at the moment. Here are the commands for selecting a stack frame.

In the backtrace window, you can _select_ an arbitrary frame to move from one stack frame to another. Just click on the desired frame.

The `Up' button selects the function that called the current one--that is, it moves one frame up.

The `Down' button selects the function that was called by the current one--that is, it moves one frame down.

We can also directly type the `up' and `down' commands at the debugger prompt. Typing <Ctrl+Up> and <Ctrl+Down>, respectively, will also move us through the stack.

`Up' and `Down' actions can be undone via `Edit => Undo'.

"Undoing" Program Execution

If we take a look at the `Edit => Undo' menu item after an execution command, you'll find that DDD offers us to undo execution commands just as other commands. Does this mean that DDD allows us to go backwards in time, undoing program execution as well as undoing any side-effects of our program?

DDD cannot undo what our program did. (After a little bit of thought, we'll find that this would be impossible in general.) However, DDD can do something different: it can show _previously recorded states_ of our program.

After "undoing" an execution command (via `Edit => Undo', or the `Undo' button), the execution position moves back to the earlier position and displayed variables take their earlier values. Our program state is in fact unchanged, but DDD gives us a _view_ on the earlier state as recorded by DDD.

In this so-called "historic mode", most normal DDD commands that would query further information from the program are disabled, since the debugger cannot be queried for the earlier state. However, we can examine the current execution position, or the displayed variables. Using `Undo' and `Redo', we can move back and forward in time to examine how our program got into the present state.

To know that we are operating in historic mode, the execution arrow gets a dashed-line appearance (indicating a past position); variable displays also come with dashed lines. Furthermore, the status line informs us that we are seeing an earlier program state.

Here's how historic mode works: each time our program stops, DDD collects the current execution position and the values of displayed variables. Backtrace, thread, and register information is also collected if the corresponding dialogs are open. When "undoing" an execution command, DDD updates its view from this collected state instead of querying the program.

If we want to collect this information without interrupting our program--within a loop, for instance--we can place a breakpoint with an associated `cont' command (*note Breakpoint Commands::). When the breakpoint is hit, DDD will stop, collect the data, and execute the `cont' command, resuming execution. Using a later `Undo', we can step back and look at every single loop iteration.

To leave historic mode, we can use `Redo' until we are back in the current program state. However, any DDD command that refers to program state will also leave historic mode immediately by applying to the current program state instead. For instance, `Up' leaves historic mode immediately and selects an alternate frame in the restored current program state.

If we want to see the history of a specific variable, as recorded during program stops, we can enter the DDD command

graph history NAME

This returns a list of all previously recorded values of the variable NAME, using array syntax. Note that NAME must have been displayed at earlier program stops in order to record values.

Examining Threads

In some operating systems, a single program may have more than one _thread_ of execution. The precise semantics of threads differ from one operating system to another, but in general the threads of a single program are akin to multiple processes--except that they share one address space (that is, they can all examine and modify the same variables). On the other hand, each thread has its own registers and execution stack, and perhaps private memory.

For debugging purposes, DDD lets us to display the list of threads currently active in our program and lets us to select the _current thread_--the thread which is the focus of debugging. DDD shows all program information from the perspective of the current thread.

To view all currently active threads in our program, select `Status=> Threads'. The current thread is highlighted. Select any thread to make it the current thread.

Handling Signals

A signal is an asynchronous event that can happen in a program. The operating system defines the possible kinds of signals, and gives each kind a name and a number. For example, in UNIX, `SIGINT' is the signal a program gets when you type an interrupt; `SIGSEGV' is the signal a program gets from referencing a place in memory far away from all the areas in use; `SIGALRM' occurs when the alarm clock timer goes off (which happens only if our program has requested an alarm).

Some signals, including `SIGALRM', are a normal part of the functioning of our program. Others, such as `SIGSEGV' (explained in chapter on memory management) (kill our program immediately) if the program has not specified in advance some other way to handle the signal. `SIGINT' does not indicate an error in our program, but it is normally fatal so it can carry out the purpose of the interrupt: to kill the program.

GDB has the ability to detect any occurrence of a signal in our program. We can tell GDB in advance what to do for each kind of signal.

Normally, DDD is set up to ignore non-erroneous signals like `SIGALRM' (so as not to interfere with their role in the functioning of your program) but to stop our program immediately whenever an error signal happens. In DDD, we can view and edit these settings via `Status => Signals'.

`Status => Signals' pops up a panel showing all the kinds of signals and how GDB has been told to handle each one. The settings available for each signal are:

`Stop'

If set, GDB should stop our program when this signal happens. This also implies `Print' being set.

`Print'

If set, GDB should print a message when this signal happens.

If unset, GDB should not mention the occurrence of the signal at all. This also implies `Stop' being unset.

`Pass'

If set, GDB should allow our program to see this signal; our program can handle the signal, or else it may terminate if the signal is fatal and not handled.

If unset, GDB should not allow our program to see this signal.

The entry `All Signals' is special. Changing a setting here affects _all signals at once_--except those used by the debugger, typically `SIGTRAP' and `SIGINT'.

To undo any changes, use `Edit => Undo'. The `Reset' button restores the saved settings.

When a signal stops our program, the signal is not visible until we continue. Our program sees the signal then, if `Pass' is in effect for the signal in question _at that time_. In other words, after GDB reports a signal, we can change the `Pass' setting in `Status =>

Signals' to control whether our program sees that signal when we continue.

We can also cause our program to see a signal it normally would not see, or to give it any signal at any time. The `Send' button will resume execution where our program stopped, but immediately give it the signal shown.

On the other hand, we can also prevent our program from seeing a signal. For example, if our program stopped due to some sort of memory reference error, we might store correct values into the erroneous variables and continue, hoping to see more execution; but our program would probably terminate immediately as a result of the fatal signal once it saw the signal. To prevent this, we can resume execution using `Commands => Continue Without Signal'.

Signal settings are not saved across DDD invocations, since changed signal settings are normally useful within specific projects only. Instead, signal settings are saved with the current session, using `File => Save Session As'.

Killing the Program

We can kill the process of the debugged program at any time using the `Kill' button.

Killing the process is useful if we wish to debug a core dump instead of a running process. GDB ignores any core dump file while our program is running.

The `Kill' button is also useful if we wish to recompile and relink our program, since on many systems it is impossible to modify an executable file while it is running in a process. In this case, when we next click on `Run', GDB notices that the file has changed, and reads the symbol table again (while trying to preserve our current debugger state).

Examining Data

DDD provides several means to examine data.

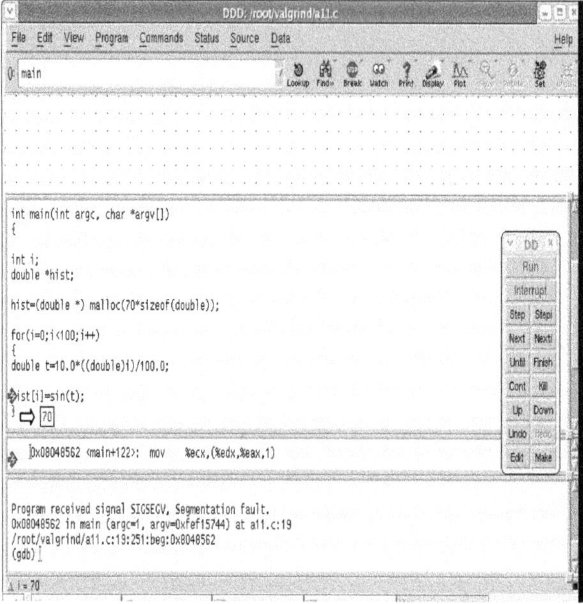

Figure. 11.4 DDD window to examine the data.

The quickest way to examine variables is to move the pointer on an occurrence in the source text. The value is displayed in the source line; after a second, a popup window (called "value tip") shows the variable value. This is useful for quick examination of several simple values.

If we want to refer to variable values at a later time, we can "print" the value in the debugger console. This allows for displaying and examining larger data structures.

If we want to examine complex data structures, we can "display" them graphically in the data window. Displays remain effective until we delete them; they are updated each time the program stops. This is useful for large dynamic structures.

If we want to examine arrays of numeric values, we can "plot" them graphically in a separate plot window. The plot is updated each time the program stops. This is useful for large numeric arrays.

Showing Simple Values using Value Tips

To display the value of a simple variable, move the mouse pointer on its name. After a second, a small window (called "value tip") pops up showing the value of the variable pointed at. The window disappears as soon as we move the mouse pointer away from the variable. The value is also shown in the status line (see Figure 11.4).

We can disable value tips via `Edit => Preferences => General => Automatic display of variable values as popup tips'.

We can disable displaying variable values in the status line via `Edit => Preferences => General => Automatic display of variable values in the status line'.

We can turn off value tips via `Edit => Preferences => General => Automatic Display of Variable Values'.

Printing Simple Values in the Debugger Console

The variable value can also be printed in the debugger console, making it available for future operations. To print a variable value, select the desired variable by clicking _mouse button 1_ on its name. The variable name is copied to the argument field. By clicking the `Print' button, the value is printed in the debugger console. The printed value is also shown in the status line.

As a shorter alternative, we can simply press mouse button 3 on the variable name and select the `Print' item from the popup menu.

Entering Plotting Commands

Via `File => Command', we can enter Gnuplot commands directly. Each command entered at the `gnuplot>' prompt is passed to Gnuplot, followed by a Gnuplot `replot' command to update the view. This is useful for advanced Gnuplot tasks.

Here's a simple example. The Gnuplot command

```
set xrange [XMIN:XMAX]
```

sets the horizontal range that will be displayed to XMIN...XMAX. To plot only the elements 10 to 20, enter:

```
gnuplot> set xrange [10:20]
gnuplot> _
```

After each command entered, DDD adds a `replot' command, such that the plot is updated automatically.

Exporting Plot Data

If we want some external program to process the plot data (a stand-alone Gnuplot program or the `xmgr' program, for instance), we can save the plot data in a file, using `File => Save Data As'. This pops up a dialog that lets us to choose a data file to save the plotted data in.

The generated file starts with a few comment lines. The actual data follows in X/Y or X/Y/Z format. It is the same file as processed by Gnuplot.

Examining Memory

Using GDB or DBX, we can examine memory in any of several formats, independently of our program's data types. The item `Data => Memory' pops up a panel where we can choose the format to be shown.

There are two ways to examine the values:

We can dump the memory in the debugger console (using `Print'). If we repeat the resulting `x' command by pressing <Return> in the debugger console, the following area of memory is shown.

We can also display the memory dump in the data window (using `Display'). If we choose to display the values, the values will be updated automatically each time the program stop.

Machine-Level Debugging

Sometimes, it is desirable to examine a program not only at the source level, but also at the machine level. DDD provides special machine code and register windows for this task.

Examining Registers

DDD provides a register window showing the machine register values after each program stop. To enable the register window, select `Status => Registers'.

By selecting one of the registers, its name is copied to the argument field. We can use it as value for `Display', for instance, to have its value displayed in the data window.

Changing the Program

DDD offers some basic facilities to edit and recompile the source code, as well as patching executables and core files.

Editing Source Code

In DDD itself, we cannot change the source file currently displayed. Instead, DDD allows us to invoke a text editor. To invoke a text editor for the current source file, select the `Edit' button or `Source => Edit Source'.

Recompiling

To recompile the source code using `make', we can select `File => Make'. This pops up a dialog where we can enter a _Make Target_--typically the name of the executable. Clicking on the `Make' button invokes the `make' program with the given target.

The `Make' button on the command tool re-invokes `make' with the most recently given arguments.

Patching

Using GDB, we can open our program's executable code (and the core file) for both reading and writing. This allows alterations to machine code, such that we can intentionally patch our program's binary. For example, we might want to turn on internal debugging flags, or even to make emergency repairs.

Note that depending on our operating system, special preparation steps, such as setting permissions, may be needed before we can change executable files.

To patch the binary, enable `Edit => GDB Settings => Writing into executable and core files'. This makes GDB open executable and core files for both reading and writing. If we have already loaded a file, we must load it again (using `Edit => Open File' or `Edit => Open Core'), for your new setting to take effect.

Be sure to turn off `Writing into executable and core files' as soon as possible, to prevent accidental alterations to machine code.

11.5 Conclusions

This chapter deals with debugging C programs. How gdb can be used for debugging C programs is explained with many lucid examples. Many common errors such as memory segment violation, use of uninitialized variables, stack overflow problem, etc., are explained and simulated through concept oriented examples. Also, GUI oriented front end tools kdbg and DDD are also explored to make reader to find out bugs in the code in an easy manner.

12 GCOV: A Coverage Testing Tool

12.1 Introduction

A common need for certain projects is to ensure that each statement in a particular function has been executed at some point during the development cycle. For obvious reasons this is best done at the "unit" level (e.g. on a subset of the code, usually wrapped within drivers).

Often, Software developers use coverage testing in concert with testsuites, to make sure software is actually good enough for a release. Testsuites can verify that a program works as expected; a coverage program tests to see how much of the program is exercised by the testsuite. Developers can then determine what kinds of test cases need to be added to the testsuites to create both better testing and a better final product.

12.2 gcov

The program **gcov** is a test coverage program which can be used with GCC to analyze programs to help to create more efficient, faster running code and to discover untested parts of our programs. In some cases it is appropriate to identify dead or obsolete code.

We can use **gcov** as a profiling tool to help discover where our optimization efforts will best affect our code and this can be used along with the other profiling tool, **gprof**, to assess which parts of our code use the greatest amount of computing time.

Profiling tools help us to analyze our code's performance. Using a profiler such as **gcov** or **gprof**, we can find out some basic performance statistics, such as:

- how often each line of code executes
- what lines of code are actually executed
- how much computing time each section of code uses

Once we know these things about how our code works when compiled, we can look at each module to see which modules should be optimized. Also, gcov helps us to determine where (which part of the code) to be optimized. Note that the gcov can not find logical errors!!.

If we plan to use gcov, we have to compile our code without optimization as the optimization involves combining some lines of code into one function, thus it may not give us as much information as we need to look for `hot spots' where the code is using a great deal of computer time. As gcov accumulates statistics by line (at the lowest resolution), it works best with a programming style that places only one statement on each line. If we use complicated macros that expand to loops or to other control structures, the statistics are less helpful---they only report on the line where the macro call appears. If our complex macros behave like functions, we can replace them with inline functions to solve this problem.

gcov creates a logfile called **sourcefile. gcov** which indicates how many times each line of a source file sourcefile.c has executed. We can use these logfiles along with gprof to aid in fine-tuning the performance of your programs. gprof gives timing information which we can use along with the information we get from gcov.

gcov works only on code compiled with GCC. It is not compatible with any other profiling or test coverage mechanism as of now.

The following options can be used with gcov command.

-b
--branch-probabilities

Write branch frequencies to the output file, and write branch summary info to the standard output. This option allows us to see how often each branch in our program was taken.

-c
--branch-counts

Write branch frequencies as the number of branches taken, rather than the percentage of branches taken.

-l
--long-file-names

Create long file names for included source files. For example, if the header file x.h contains code, and was included in the file a.c, then running gcov on the file a.c will produce an output file called a.c##x.h. gcov instead of x.h.gcov. This can be useful if x.h is included in multiple source files.

-f
--function-summaries

Output summaries for each function in addition to the file level summary.

-o directory|file
--object-directory directory
--object-file file

Specify either the directory containing the gcov data files, or the object path name. If a file is specified here, the data files are named after that file, without its extension. If this option is not supplied, it defaults to the current directory.

gcov should be run with the current directory as the same as that when we invoke the compiler. Otherwise it will not be able to locate the source files. gcov produces files called **filename.gcov** in the current directory. These contain the coverage information of the source file they correspond to. One .gcov file is produced for each source file containing code, which was compiled to produce the data files. The .gcov files contain the ':' separated fields along with program source code. The format is

<execution_count>:<line_number>:<source line text>

Additional block information may succeed each line, when requested by command line option. The execution_count is - for lines containing no code and ##### for lines which were never executed. Some lines of information at the start have line_number of zero.

When printing percentages, 0% and 100% are only printed when the values are exactly 0% and 100% respectively. Other values which would conventionally be rounded to 0% or 100% are instead printed as the nearest non-boundary value.

When using gcov, we must first compile our program with two special GCC options namingly **-fprofile-arcs -ftest-coverage**. This tells the compiler to generate additional information needed by gcov (basically a flow graph of the program) and also includes additional code in the object files for generating the extra profiling information needed by gcov. These additional files are placed in the directory where the object file is located.

Running the program will cause profile output to be generated. For each source file compiled with -fprofile-arcs, an accompanying .da file will be placed in the object file directory.

Example 1

Running gcov with our program's source file names as arguments will now produce a listing of the code along with frequency of execution for each line. For example, if our program is called tmp.c, this is what we see when we use the basic gcov facility:

```
gcc -fprofile-arcs -ftest-coverage tmp.c
./a.out
gcov tmp.c
```

```
90.00% of 10 source lines executed in file tmp.c
Creating tmp.c.gcov.
```

The file **tmp.c.gcov** contains output from gcov. Here is a sample:

```
      -:    0:Source:tmp.c
      -:    0:Object:tmp.bb
      -:    1:#include <stdio.h>
      -:    2:
      -:    3:int main (void)
      1:    4:{
      1:    5:  int i, total;
      -:    6:
      1:    7:  total = 0;
      -:    8:
     11:    9:  for (i = 0; i < 10; i++)
     10:   10:    total += i;
      -:   11:
      1:   12:  if (total != 45)
  #####:   13:    printf ("Failure\n");
      -:   14:  else
      1:   15:    printf ("Success\n");
      1:   16:  return 0;
      1:   17:}
```

When you use the -b option, output looks like this:

```
$ gcov -b tmp.c
90.00% of 10 source lines executed in file tmp.c
80.00% of 5 branches executed in file tmp.c
80.00% of 5 branches taken at least once in file tmp.c
50.00% of 2 calls executed in file tmp.c
Creating tmp.c.gcov.
```

Here is content of the resulting **tmp.c.gcov** file:

```
        -:    0:Source:tmp.c
        -:    0:Object:tmp.bb
        -:    1:#include <stdio.h>
        -:    2:
        -:    3:int main (void)
        1:    4:{
        1:    5:  int i, total;
        -:    6:
        1:    7:  total = 0;
        -:    8:
       11:    9:  for (i = 0; i < 10; i++)
branch  0: taken 90%
branch  1: taken 100%
branch  2: taken 100%
       10:   10:    total += i;
        -:   11:
        1:   12:  if (total != 45)
branch  0: taken 100%
    #####:   13:    printf ("Failure\n");
call    0: never executed
branch  1: never executed
        -:   14:  else
        1:   15:    printf ("Success\n");
call    0: returns 100%
        1:   16:  return 0;
        1:   17:}
```

For each basic block, a line is printed after the last line of the basic block describing the branch or call that ends the basic block. There can be multiple branches and calls listed for a single source line if there are multiple basic blocks that end on that line. In this case, the branches and calls are each given a number. There is no simple way to map these branches and calls back to source constructs. In general, though, the lowest numbered branch or call will correspond to the leftmost construct on the source line.

For a branch, if it was executed at least once, then a percentage indicating the number of times the branch was taken divided by the number of times the branch was executed will be printed. Otherwise, the message ``never executed'' is printed.

For a call, if it was executed at least once, then a percentage indicating the number of times the call returned divided by the number of times the call was executed will be printed. This will usually be 100%, but may be less for functions call "exit" or "longjmp", and thus may not return every time they are called.

The execution counts are cumulative. If the example program were executed again without removing the .da file, the count for the number of times each line in the source was executed would be added to the results of the previous run(s). This is potentially useful in several ways. For example, it could be used to accumulate data over a number of program runs as part of a test verification suite, or to provide more accurate long-term information over a large number of program runs.

The data in the .da files is saved immediately before the program exits. For each source file compiled with -fprofile-arcs, the profiling code first attempts to read in an existing .da file; if the file doesn't match the executable (differing number of basic block counts) it will ignore the contents of the file. It then adds in the new execution counts and finally writes the data to the file.

Using gcov with GCC Optimization

If we plan to use gcov to help optimize our code, we must first compile our program with two special GCC options: -fprofile-arcs -ftest-coverage. Aside from that, we can use any other GCC options; but if we want to prove that every single line in our program was executed, we should not compile with optimization at the same time. On some machines the optimizer can eliminate some simple code lines by combining them with other lines. For example, code like this:

```
if (a != b)
  c = 1;
else
  c = 0;
```

can be compiled into one instruction on some machines. In this case, there is no way for gcov to calculate separate execution counts for each line because there isn't separate code for each line. Hence the gcov output looks like this if we compiled the program with optimization:

```
100:  12:if (a != b)
100:  13:  c = 1;
100:  14:else
100:  15:  c = 0;
```

The output shows that this block of code, combined by optimization, executed 100 times. In one sense this result is correct, because there was only one instruction representing all four of these lines. However, the output does not indicate how many times the result was 0 and how many times the result was 1.

Example 2

```
#include<stdio.h>
int main()
{
int i,j,k,m1,m2,n1,n2,a[10][10], b[10][10], c[10][10];
scanf("%d%d%d%d", &m1,&n1,&m2,&n2);
if(n1!=m2)
{
printf("Matrix Multiplication is not possible\n");
exit(-1);
}
printf("Enter Data for 1st Matrix\n");
for(i=0;i<m1;i++)
for(j=0;j<n1;j++)scanf("%d", &a[i][j]);
printf("Enter Data for 2nd Matrix\n");
for(i=0;i<m2;i++)
for(j=0;j<n2;j++)scanf("%d", &b[i][j]);
for(i=0;i<m1;i++)
for(j=0;j<n2;j++)
{
 c[i][j]=0;
for(k=0;k<n1;k++)
c[i][j]+=a[i][k]*b[k][j];
}
for(i=0;i<m1;i++)
{
for(j=0;j<n2;j++)
printf("%d", c[i][j]);
printf("\n");
}
exit(0);
}
```

Assume the above C program name is a1.c. Run the following commands to experiment gcov on this program.

```
gcc –fprofile-arcs –ftest-coverage –o a1 a1.c
./a1
```

(Give the first and second matrix size's and followed by the actual data of the matrices).

gcov a1.c

cat a1.c.gcov will produce the following result.

```
    -:    0:Source:a1.c
    -:    0:Graph:a1.gcno
    -:    0:Data:a1.gcda
    -:    0:Runs:2
    -:    0:Programs:1
    -:    1:#include<stdio.h>
    -:    2:int main()
function main called 2 returned 0% blocks executed 100%
    2:    3:{
    2:    4:int i,j,k,m1,m2,n1,n2,a[10][10], b[10][10], c[10][10];
    2:    5:scanf("%d%d%d%d", &m1,&n1,&m2,&n2);
    2:    6:if(n1!=m2)
    -:    7:{
    1:    8:printf("Matrix Multiplication is not possible\n");
    1:    9:exit(-1);
    -:   10:}
    1:   11:printf("Enter Data for 1st Matrix\n");
    3:   12:for(i=0;i<m1;i++)
    2:   13:for(j=0;j<n1;j++)scanf("%d", &a[i][j]);
    1:   14:printf("Enter Data for 2nd Matrix\n");
    4:   15:for(i=0;i<m2;i++)
    3:   16:for(j=0;j<n2;j++)scanf("%d", &b[i][j]);
    3:   17:for(i=0;i<m1;i++)
    6:   18:for(j=0;j<n2;j++)
    -:   19:{
    4:   20: c[i][j]=0;
   16:   21:for(k=0;k<n1;k++)
   12:   22:c[i][j]+=a[i][k]*b[k][j];
    -:   23:}
    3:   24:for(i=0;i<m1;i++)
    -:   25:{
    6:   26:for(j=0;j<n2;j++)
    4:   27:printf("%d", c[i][j]);
    2:   28:printf("\n");
    -:   29:}
    1:   30:exit(0);
    -:   31:}
    -:   32:
```

While running the above a1 program, we gave size of the matrices as 2x3 and 3x2. Thus, the line is reported to be executing 12 times (=2x3x2) and is as expected. Thus, with the help of gcov we can identify how many times a statement(s) is executed in each run. It is common that some portions of the programs are executed some times while some other portions of the programs are executed some other times based on input or calculated parameters. In order to know fuller details of the statements and their frequency of execution for a given input we can use gcov.

For, run the same program a1 and give matrix sizes as 2x3 and 4x3. The program terminates as matrix sizes are not matching. Now, run the following commands.

```
./a.out
gcov a1.c
cat a1.c.gcov
```

```
        -:    0:Source:a1.c
        -:    0:Graph:a1.gcno
        -:    0:Data:a1.gcda
        -:    0:Runs:1
        -:    0:Programs:1
        -:    1:#include<stdio.h>
        -:    2:int main()
function main called 1 returned 0% blocks executed 11%
        1:    3:{
        1:    4:int i,j,k,m1,m2,n1,n2,a[10][10], b[10][10], c[10][10];
        1:    5:scanf("%d%d%d%d", &m1,&n1,&m2,&n2);
        1:    6:if(n1!=m2)
        -:    7:{
        1:    8:printf("Matrix Multiplication is not possible\n");
        1:    9:exit(-1);
        -:   10:}
    #####:   11:printf("Enter Data for 1st Matrix\n");
    #####:   12:for(i=0;i<m1;i++)
    #####:   13:for(j=0;j<n1;j++)scanf("%d", &a[i][j]);
    #####:   14:printf("Enter Data for 2nd Matrix\n");
    #####:   15:for(i=0;i<m2;i++)
    #####:   16:for(j=0;j<n2;j++)scanf("%d", &b[i][j]);
    #####:   17:for(i=0;i<m1;i++)
    #####:   18:for(j=0;j<n2;j++)
        -:   19:{
    #####:   20: c[i][j]=0;
    #####:   21:for(k=0;k<n1;k++)
    #####:   22:c[i][j]+=a[i][k]*b[k][j];
        -:   23:}
```

```
#####:   24:for(i=0;i<m1;i++)
    -:   25:{
#####:   26:for(j=0;j<n2;j++)
#####:   27:printf("%d", c[i][j]);
#####:   28:printf("\n");
    -:   29:}
#####:   30:exit(0);
    -:   31:}
    -:   32:
```

From the above execution and outputs of gcov file, we can find that the code lines started with ##### are the ones not executed.

Example 3 [16]

Compile the file sample.c shown below using the following command.

gcc -fprofile-arcs -ftest-coverage -g sample.c -o sample

File: sample.c

```
#include <stdlib.h>
#include <stdio.h>

int main(argc, argv)
int argc;
char **argv;
{
 int x, y;
 int arraysize;
 int **array;
 if (argc != 2) {
  printf("Usage: %s Enter arraysize value \n",argv[0]);
  exit(-1);
 } else {
  arraysize = atoi (argv[1]);
  if (arraysize <= 0) {
   printf("Array size must be larger than 0 \n");
   exit(-1);
  }
 }
```

[16] Steve best http://www.linux-mag.com/2003-07/compile_01.html

```
array = (int **) malloc (arraysize*sizeof (int *));

 printf("Creating an %d by %d array \n", arraysize, arraysize);

 if (array == NULL) {
   printf("Malloc failed for array size %d \n", arraysize);
   exit(-1);
 }
 for (x=0; x < arraysize; x++) {
   array[x] = (int *) malloc (arraysize*sizeof (int));
   if (array[x] == NULL) {
     printf("Failed malloc for array size %d \n", arraysize);
     exit(-1);
   }
 }
 exit(0);
}
```

Now we're ready to see how much coverage each test case provides. Run the sample application with input of 1000.

```
./sample 1000
```

The application displays "Creating an 1000 by 1000 array," and creates a new file called sample.da. Next, run gcov on the source code.

```
gcov sample.c
```

gcov emits "69.23 % of 26 source lines executed in file sample.c." This gcov command also creates the file sample.c.gcov, shown in Listing Two. In the listing, a ###### marker indicates that the associated line of source code hasn't been executed.

Listing Two: sample.c.gcov after running the application with input 1000

```
#include <stdlib.h>
#include <stdio.h>

int main(argc, argv)
  int argc;
  char **argv;
  1   {
  1     int x, y;
int arraysize;
```

```
int **array;
  1     if (argc != 2) {
######      printf("Usage: %s Enter arraysize value \n",argv[0]);
######      exit(-1);

  1     }
        else {
  1       arraysize = atoi (argv[1]);
  1       if (arraysize <= 0) {
######        printf("Array size must be larger than 0 \n");
######        exit(-1);
  1       }
  1     }
  1     array = (int **) malloc (arraysize*sizeof (int *));

  1     printf("Creating an %d by %d array \n", arraysize, arraysize);

  1     if (array == NULL) {
######      printf("Malloc failed for array size %d \n", arraysize);
######      exit(-1);
  1     }
1001      for (x=0; x < arraysize; x++) {
1000        array[x] = (int *) malloc (arraysize*sizeof (int));
1000        if (array[x] == NULL) {
######          printf("Failed malloc for array size %d \n", arraysize);
######          exit(-1);
1000        }
1000      }
  1       exit(0);
}
```

Next, run the sample program with no input.

./sample

The application displays "Usage: ./sample Enter arraysize value." Next, run gcov again.

gcov sample.c

76.92 % of 26 source lines executed in sample.c

Now run the sample program with the parameter 0.

./sample 0

The application should display "Array size must be larger than 0" message. Again, run gcov.

gcov sample.c

84.62 % of 26 source lines executed in sample.c

Now comes the interesting part of testing this program. There are two malloc() error conditions; both must be tested to get 100% coverage of this code. Let's use the gdb debugger to simulate the malloc() failures. Let's set a break point and then jump to the error condition.

gdb ./sample

The list command displays the line numbers for the source.

```
(gdb) list
12  int **array;
13  if (argc != 2) {
```

Use the break command to set a break point on line number 13.

```
(gdb) break 13
```

Then start the program with run.

```
(gdb) run
(gdb) list 30

36  if (array[x] == NULL)
37     printf("Failed malloc for array size %d \n", arraysize);

(gdb) jump 31
```

Malloc failed for array size

```
(gdb) quit
```

Once again, run gcov.

gcov sample.c

92.31 % of 26 source lines executed in file sample.c

One more test to run. Follow the steps shown above to set a break point on line 13. Run the program with run and then jump to line 37.

```
gdb ./sample
(gdb) break 13
(gdb) run

(gdb) list 30

36  if (array[x] == NULL)
37  printf("Failed malloc for array size %d \n", arraysize);

(gdb) jump 37
Failed malloc for array size

(gdb) quit
```

Finally, run gcov one last time.

gcov sample.c

100 % of 26 source lines executed in file sample.c

Listing Three shows no lines flagged with #####, so all lines of this program have been executed. The number before each line of code tells how many times it was executed.

Listing Three: sample.c.gcov after the five tests

```
#include <stdlib.h>
#include <stdio.h>

int main(argc, argv)
  int argc;
  char **argv;
  3  {
  3     int x, y;
 int arraysize;
 int **array;
  3     if (argc != 2) {
  1         printf("Usage: %s Enter arraysize value \n",argv[0]);
  1        exit(-1);
```

```
        2    }
        else {
        2       arraysize = atoi (argv[1]);
        2       if (arraysize <= 0) {
        1         printf("Array size must be larger than 0 \n");
        1         exit(-1);
        1       }
        1    }
        1    array = (int **) malloc (arraysize*sizeof (int *));

        1    printf("Creating an %d by %d array \n", arraysize, arraysize);

        1    if (array == NULL) {
        1      printf("Malloc failed for array size %d \n", arraysize);
        1      exit(-1);
        1    }
     1001      for (x=0; x < arraysize; x++) {
     1000        array[x] = (int *) malloc (arraysize*sizeof (int));
     1000        if (array[x] == NULL) {
        1         printf("Failed malloc for array size %d \n", arraysize);
        1         exit(-1);
     1000        }
     1000      }
        1     exit(0);
      }
```

12.3 Conclusions

In this chapter, we have explained about **gcov,** a test coverage program which can be used with GCC to analyze programs to help to create more efficient, faster running code and to discover untested parts of our programs. Also, we have emphasized how it can be used to identify dead or obsolete code in the programs.

13 Profiling

13.1 Indtroduction

Profiling allows us to know where our program is spending more time and which function call's the other functions. Profiling information can show which parts of the program are slower than the expected; and might be the best candidates for rewriting the code to make our program to execute faster. It can also tell us which functions are being called more than the expected number of times such that bug fix can be done for them.

Since the profiler uses information collected during the actual execution of our program, it can be used on programs that are too complex to analyze by reading the source.

13.2 Design Aims of a Profiler

As an important of a programmers artillery a profiler should avoid getting in the way of the human analyst. This leads to a number of design parameters every profiler should aim at.

Unobtrusive

A profiler should not require a significant expenditure (time) of developer effort. The need for recompiles, preprocessors, special modifications to the tool chain etc., should be avoided, as they are inconvenient to the developer. An ideal solution should allow profiling at will, without needing any changes in the source.

Accurate

The data and reports generated by the profiler system should aim towards accuracy. Inaccurate data runs the risk of miss-informing the developer of the true situation, leading to vast of efforts and additional maintainability problems.

Complete

Profilers should aim towards a complete data set. If a system component or facet is not represented in the results, the developer may not be aware of its impact on the system as a whole.

General

Profilers should avoid special-purpose techniques where possible.

Fast

If the profiling method is too slow, it will impinge on the developer's development time. Slow profilers often can't be used in realistic environments, which make collecting meaningful data as hazardous and prone to error.

13.3 Instrumentation Methods.

Commonly, the target application must include some *instrumentation* to enable the profiling mechanisms to operate.

Some techniques are :

Simulation

A simulator can easily collect detailed data as part of the simulation run. Such techniques tend to be very obtrusive and slow, so are best used when the level of detail is critical.

Source-level instrumentation

Source-level instrumentation involves altering the source code that eventually becomes the application by inserting profiling code. This can happen semi-automatically via a pre-processor, or may require a programmer to add explicit calls to some profiling API.

Compile-time instrumentation

The compiler itself can be used to insert profiling code. This has the advantage above source-level instrumentation of being more convenient, but of course requires the source code to be recompiled, which is not always practicable.

Offline binary instrumentation

Binary images that contain the text sections for shared libraries or applications can be rewritten to add instrumentation. This technique is complex to implement, but is relatively unobtrusive unless system-wide performance data is needed.

Online binary instrumentation

Mapped binary images are re-written to add profiling instrumentation. To some degree, just-in-time compiling environments are in of this class of techniques.

13.4 About GPROF system call.

Command **gprof** produces an execution profile of C, Pascal or Fortran 77 programs. The effect of called routines is incorportated in the profile of each caller. The profile data is taken from the call graph profile file (**gmon.out**) which is created by programs that are compiled with the '-pg' option of 'cc' , "gcc", and 'f77'. The "-pq" option with cc or gcc commands links in versions of the library routines that are compiled for profiling.

"Gprof" reads the given object file and establishes the relation between its symbol table and the call graph profile from gmon.out

Steps in Profiling:

- Compile and link program with profiling enabled. That is, source has to be compiled with "-pg" option. **Please make sure that the C program which you are profiling to have at least one function!!.**

```
gcc –pg -o executable_filename file.c
```

- Execute program to generate a profile data file.

```
./executable_filename
```

- Run GPROF to analyze data

```
gprof executable_filename
```

"Gprof" calculates the amount of the time spent in each routine and these times are propagated along the edges of the call graph. Cycles are discovered, and calls into a cycle are made to share the time of the cycle. "gprof" gives several forms of outputs from the analysis such as:

1. **Flat profile**:

   It shows how much time the program spent in each function and how many times the functions were called. This is useful to know which function consumed more time.

2. **Call graph:**

   It shows for each function, which functions called it which other functions it called, and how many times. Also, we will be getting an estimate of how much time was spent in subroutines of each function. This can suggest places where we might try to eliminate function calls that use a lot of time.

3. **Annotated Source:**

   This listing is a copy of programs source code, labeled with the number of times each line of program was executed.

   As mentioned above, once the program is compiled for profiling, we must run it in order to generate the information that gprof needs. Simply run the program as usual, using the normal arguments, file names, etc. The program should run normally, producing the same output as usual. It will, however, run somewhat slower than normal because of the time spent collecting and the writing the profile data.

   The way we run the program--the arguments and input that we give it—may have a dramatic effect on what the profile information shows. The profile data will describe the parts of the program that were activated for the particular input we use. For example, if the first command given to our program is to quit, the profile data will show the time used in initialization and in cleanup, but not much else.

   Program will write the profile data into a file called `gmon.out' just before exiting. If there is already a file called `gmon.out', its contents are overwritten. There is currently no way to tell the program to write the profile data under a different name, but we can rename the file afterward if we are concerned that it may be overwritten.

   In order to write the `gmon.out' file properly, our program must exit normally: by returning from main or by calling exit. Calling the low-level function _exit does not write the profile data, and neither does abnormal termination due to an unhandled signal.

   The `gmon.out' file is written in the program's current working directory when it exits. This means that if our program calls chdir, the `gmon.out' file will be left in the last directory our program chdir'd to. If we don't have permission to write in this directory, the file is not written. We may get a confusing error message if this happens.

Example 1

```
#include<stdio.h>

int f(int x)
{
```

```
    int val;
    val=x;
    if(x!=1);
    val=val*fact(x-1);
    return val;
}

int main ()
 {
    int a;
    printf("Enter a number ::");
    scanf("%d",&a);
    printf("\nFactorial value of %d is %d \n", a, f(a));
    return 0;
 }
```

Compile the program using:

gcc -pg fact.c

As mentioned above, to make the program ready for profiling, use '-pg' option in addition to usual compiling options.

Execute the program by typing

./a.out

(We gave input as 12)

After running the program, the profiler writes the profile data in a file called 'gmon.out'.

This file is created in the current working directory.

Now run gprof command. It's format is as follows.

gprof [executable-file [profile -data-files...]] [>out file]

Example:

gprof a.out

gives the following output.

```
Flat profile:

Each sample counts as 0.01 seconds.
     no time accumulated
   %   cumulative  self     self   total
  time    seconds   seconds   calls   Ts/call   Ts/call   name
  0.00    0.00      0.00      1       0.00      0.00      f
```

% time	the percentage of the total running time of the program used by this function.
cumulative seconds	a running sum of the number of seconds accounted for by this function and those listed above it.
self seconds	the number of seconds accounted for by this function alone. This is the major sort for this listing.
calls	the number of times this function was invoked, if this function is profiled, else blank.
self ms/call	the average number of milliseconds spent in this function per call, if this function is profiled, else blank.
total ms/call	the average number of milliseconds spent in this function and its descendents per call, if this function is profiled, else blank.
name	the name of the function. This is the minor sort for this listing. The index shows the location of the function in the gprof listing. If the index is in parenthesis it shows where it would appear in the gprof listing if it were to be printed.

Call graph (explanation follows)

granularity: each sample hit covers 4 byte(s) no time propagated

index	% time	self	children	called	name
				11	f [1]
		0.00	0.00	1/1	main [8]
[1]	0.0	0.00	0.00	1+11	f [1]
				11	f [1]

This table describes the call tree of the program, and was sorted by the total amount of time spent in each function and its children.

Each entry in this table consists of several lines. The line with the index number at the left hand margin lists the current function. The lines above it list the functions that called this function, and the lines below it list the functions this one called.

This line lists:

Index — A unique number given to each element of the table.

Index numbers are sorted numerically. The index number is printed next to every function name so it is easier to look up where the function in the table.

% time — This is the percentage of the `total' time that was spent in this function and its children. Note that due to different viewpoints, functions excluded by options, etc, these numbers will NOT add up to 100%.

Self — This is the total amount of time spent in this function.

children — This is the total amount of time propagated into this function by its children.

called — This is the number of times the function was called. If the function called itself recursively, the number only includes non-recursive calls, and is followed by a `+' and the number of recursive calls.

name — The name of the current function. The index number is printed after it. If the function is a member of a cycle, the cycle number is printed between the function's name and the index number.

For the function's parents, the fields have the following meanings:

Self — This is the amount of time that was propagated directly from the function into this parent.

Children — This is the amount of time that was propagated from the function's children into this parent.

called — This is the number of times this parent called the function `/' the total number of times the function was called. Recursive calls to the function are not included in the number after the `/'.

name — This is the name of the parent. The parent's index number is printed after it. If the parent is a member of a cycle, the cycle number is printed between the name and the index number.

If the parents of the function cannot be determined, the word `<spontaneous>' is printed in the `name' field, and all the other fields are blank.

For the function's children, the fields have the following meanings:

self — This is the amount of time that was propagated directly from the child into the function.

children This is the amount of time that was propagated from the child's children to the function.

called This is the number of times the function called this child `/' the total number of times the child was called. Recursive calls by the child are not listed in the number after the `/'.

name This is the name of the child. The child's index number is printed after it. If the child is a member of a cycle, the cycle number is printed between the name and the index number.

If there are any cycles (circles) in the call graph, there is an entry for the cycle-as-a-whole. This entry shows who called the cycle (as parents) and the members of the cycle (as children.) The `+' recursive calls entry shows the number of function calls that were internal to the cycle, and the calls entry for each member shows, for that member, how many times it was called from other members of the cycle.

Options for 'gprof' command

There are

- Output Options : Controlling 'gprof's ouput style.
- Analysis Options : Controlling how 'gprof' analysis its data.
- Miscellaneous Options
- Deprecated Options.

OUTPUT OPTIONS:

1. -A[SYMSPEC]
   --annotated-source[=SYMSPEC]

Causes to print annotated source code.

Note:

What are 'SYNSPEC'?

These are symbol specifications.

Some Symbol specifications are.

1. 'main.c' Selects every thing in file 'main.c'. If no .c or.extension then gives it as 'filename:'

2. 'main' selects all functions named 'main'. If- - function name contains dot then- -- ': function name'

3.'main.c:main' Selects function 'main' in file 'main.c'

4.'main.c:134' Selects line 134 in file 'main.c'

2.'-b'

'—brief'

Doesn't prints the verbose blurbs.

3.'C[SYMSPEC]'

'—exec-counts[=SYMSPEC]'

Prints a tally of functions and the no. of times each was called.

4. '-i'

Display the summary information about profile data file.

gporf p5 –i

File 'gmon.out' (Version) contains:

1 histogram record

0 call-graph record

0 basic-block count records.

5. 'J[SYMSPEC]'

Causes not to print annotated source code.

6. '-p[SYMSPEC]'

To print only flat profile. If symspec is specified print flat- - profile only for matching symbols.

7.'-q[SYMSPEC]'

To print only call-graph analysis.

8.'-T'

Causes gprof to print its out put in 'traditional' BSD style.

9.'—function_ordering'

Causes to print a suggested function ordering for the program based on profiling data.this option may suggest to improve paging tlb and cache behavior for the program on the systems which supports arbitrary ordering of function in an executable.

Example 2

```
#include<stdio.h>
fun(int x)
    {
     printf(":%d time",x+1);
    }
```

```
        fun1(int y)
        {
         printf("totally %d times ",y*3);
        }

int     main()
        {
         int i;
          for(i=0;i<10;i++)
          {
           printf("\nHello Hello Hello");
           fun(i); fun(i+1);
          }
return 0;
    }
```

Assuming that the above program name as "sirm.c" and run the folloing commands.

gcc –o tmp sirm.c

./tmp

gprof tmp –function_ordering gives the following results.

```
fun
fun1
-init
-start
-gmon_start-
call_gmon_start
```

SOME ANALYSIS OPTIONS.

1. '-a'

   '—no_static'

   Suppresses the printing of statically declared functions.

2. '-D'

   '—ignore_non_functions'

   Ignores symbols which are not known to functions. This option will give more accurate profile data on systems where it is supported.

3. '-I'

   '—min_count=NOM'

   Symbols that are executed less than NUM times are suppressed.

SOME MESCELLANIOUS OPTIONS OF GPROF COMMAND.

1. '-d[NUM]'

   '—debug[=NUM]'

   Specifies debugging options. If NUM is not specified enabled all debugging.

Debugging `gprof':

If `gprof' was compiled with debugging enabled, the `-d' option triggers debugging output (to stdout) which can be helpful in Understanding its operation. The debugging number specified is interpreted as a sum of the following options:

2 - Topological sort

   Monitor depth-first numbering of symbols during call graph analysis

4 - Cycles

   Shows symbols as they are identified as cycle heads

16 - Tallying

   As the call graph arcs are read, show each arc and how the total calls to each function are tallied

32 - Call graph arc sorting

   Details sorting individual parents/children within each call graph entry

64 - Reading histogram and call graph records

   Shows address ranges of histograms as they are read, and each call graph arc

128 - Symbol table

   Reading, classifying, and sorting the symbol table from the object file. For line-by-line profiling (`-l' option), also shows line numbers being assigned to memory addresses.

256 - Static call graph

   Trace operation of `-c' option

512 - Symbol table and arc table lookups

1024 - Call graph propagation

   Shows how function times are propagated along the call

For example the following command

gcov -d executable_filenmae

gives the following result.

```
[main] debug-level=0xffffffff
[core_sym_class] called.0 is of class b
[core_sym_class] __CTOR_LIST__ is of class d
[core_sym_class] __DTOR_LIST__ is of class d
[core_sym_class] __EH_FRAME_BEGIN__ is of class r
[core_sym_class] __JCR_LIST__ is of class d
[core_sym_class] p.0 is of class d
..
...
...
[core_create_function_syms] rejecting: 0x0
[core_create_function_syms] rejecting: 0x0
[core_create_function_syms] rejecting: 0x0
...
..
..
[core_create_function_syms] 0 call_gmon_start 0x8048410
[core_create_function_syms] rejecting: 0x0 crtstuff.c
[core_sym_class] __CTOR_LIST__ is of class d
[core_create_function_syms] rejecting: 0x0 __CTOR_LIST__
..
....
[symtab_finalize] 0x8048314-0x80483ab  _init
[symtab_finalize] 0x80483ac-0x80483cf  _start
[symtab_finalize] 0x80483d0-0x804840f  __gmon_start__
[symtab_finalize] 0x8048410-0x8048433  call_gmon_start

root@localhost sirm]# gcc  tmp -d 2
[main] debug-level=0x3
...
..
root@localhost sirm]# gcc  tmp -d 4
[main] debug-level=0x5
 Flat profile:
  ..
...
Call graph:
..
..
```

Note that only one function can be specified with each -e, -E, -f or -F option. To specify more than one function, use multiple options. For example, this command:

gprof -e boring -f foo -f bar myprogram > gprof.output

lists in the call graph all functions that were reached from either foo or bar and were not reachable from boring.

Profiling with the fork and exec Subroutines

Profiling using the gprof command is problematic if our program runs the fork or exec subroutine on multiple, concurrent processes. Profiling is an attribute of the environment of each process, so if we are profiling a process that forks a new process, the child is also profiled. However, both processes write a gmon.out file in the directory from which we run the parent process, overwriting one of them.

If we must use the gprof command, one way around this problem is to call the chdir subroutine to change the current directory of the child process. Then, when the child process exits, its gmon.out file is written to the new directory. The following example demonstrates this method:

```
#include<stdio.h>
int sub1(pid)
int pid;
{
int i;
printf("I'm the parent, child pid is %i.\n",pid);
}
int sub2()
{
printf("I'm the child.\n");
}
int main()
{
int i, pid;
static char path[]="./test2";
pid=fork();
/* fork a child process */
if(pid==0) {
/* Ok, this is the child process */
   chdir (path);
/* create new home directory so gmon.out isn't clobbered! */
   for (i=0; i<30; i++) sub2();
  /* 30 calls to sub2 in child profile */
   }
else
/* Parent process... leave gmon.out in current directory */
   for (i=0;i<10; i++) sub1(pid);
  /* 10 calls to sub1 in parent profile */
}
```

Processes that run the exec subroutine do not inherit profiling. However, the program executed by the exec subroutine should be profiled if it was compiled with the -pg option. As with the preceding forker.c example, if both the parent and the program run by the exec subroutine program are profiled, one overwrites the other's gmon.out file unless we use the chdir subroutine in one of them.

Profiling with the gprof command can cause programs to page excessively since the -pg option dedicates pinned real-memory buffer space equal to one-half the size of our program's text. Excessive paging does not affect the data generated by profiling, since profiled programs do not generate ticks when waiting on I/O, only when using the CPU.

It is also possible some modules to be made escaped from profiling by compiling them separately without -pg option. If we compile only some of the modules of the program with `-pg', we can still profile the program, but we won't get complete information about the modules that were compiled without `-pg'. The only information we get for the functions in those modules is the total time spent in them; there is no record of how many times they were called, or from where. This will not affect the flat profile (except that the calls field for the functions will be blank), but will greatly reduce the usefulness of the call graph.

13.5 KERNAL PROFILING

Kernel profiling is a mechanism that allows us to determine where the operating system is spending its time during operation. It consists of commands that control the profiling process and commands that generate reports. The system profiler samples the program counter on every clock interrupt and increments the counter corresponding to the kernel function shown by that value of the program counter.

When enabled, the system profiler initializes the sampling mechanism with the addresses of kernel functions. During initialization, any dynamically loadable kernel modules that are present in memory are locked in place. Likewise, any modules that are later loaded are locked in place if profiling is enabled.

If kernel profiling is enabled (by means of external commands or system calls), the clock interrupt handler invokes interrupt handler of the profiler driver, which determines weather the processor mode at the time of interrupt was user or kernel.

If mode is user: The profiler increments count for user execution.

If mode is kernel: It increments internal counter corresponding to program counter.

For Example:

If a program counter values are sampled over 10 clock interrupts is

110, 330, 145, address from userspace, 125, 140, 130, 320, address from user space, 104.

And if some sample address of kernel algorithms are

Algorithm	address	count
Bread	100	5
Brada	150	0
Bwrite	200	0
Brelse	300	2
Getblk	400	2
User	----	2

So we can guess that 20% of time system spends in user address space and 50% of time it spends in dealing with 'bread' algorithm.

Users can profile execution of process at user level using 'profil' system call.

About profil system call:

Format of profil is **profil(buff,bufsize,offset, scale)**

Where buff = address of user space is an array

Buff size = size of the array

Offset = Virtual address of user routine

Scale = A factor that maps user virtual address into memory.

This routine provides a means to find out in what areas program spends most of time,. the argument of 'buff' prints the 'buffsize' bytes of code. Every virtual 10 milliseconds the users programs counter is examined, 'offset' is subtracted and the result is multiplied by scale and divided by 65,536.If the resulting value is less than 'buff size' then the corresponding entry in 'buff' is incremented. If 'buff' is null, profiling is disabled.

Kernel treats scale as fixed point binary fraction with binary point at the extreme left.

0xffff: gives one to one mapping of program counter to words in 'buff'

0x7fff: pairs of program address into a single buff word

0x3ff : Groups of 4 program words into a single word.

Example 4

Example program illustrating about profil system call.

```
#include<signal.h>
#include<unistd.h>
#include<stdio.h>
#include<stdlib.h>
 short int buffer[4096];
main()
{
  int offset,endof,scale,eff,gee,text;
   signal(SIGINT,theend);
   endof=(int)theend;
   offset=(int) main;
   text=(endof-offset+sizeof(int)-1)/sizeof(int);
   scale=0x1555;
   printf("offset %d endof %d text %d\n",offset, endof, text);
   eff=(int) f;
   gee=(int) g;
   printf("f %d g %d fdiff %d gdiff %d \n", eff, gee, eff-offset, gee-offset);
   profil(buffer,sizeof(int)*text,offset,scale);
   sleep(5);
   for(;;)
   {
     f();
     g();
```

```
  }
}

void f()
   {
     printf("f\n");
   }
void g()
   {
     printf("g\n");
   }
void theend()
  {
    int i;
    printf("sai\n");
    //sleep(10);
    for(i=0;i<4096;i++)
     if(buffer[i])
       printf("buf[%d]=%d\n",i,buffer[i]);
    exit(0);
  }
```

gcc –o app sirm.c
./app

```
offset 134513806   endof 134513704   text 1073741799
f:134513656   g:134513680   fdiff:-150  gdiff :-126
f
g
f
g
..
..
```

It specifies

Offset: offset of main program

F : offset of function f()

G : offset of function g()

Fdiff: difference of offsets from f() to main()

Gdiff: difference of offsets from g() to main()

Endof: offset of function endof()

Text: specifies last value in buffer area.

Note.

After running the program on our machine for 10 seconds, buffer area mapped by process allocated by processor for the functions f() ,g() and endof().

Buffer[0]=f()'s address
Buffer[12]=g()'s address
Buffer[22]=g()'s address
Buffer[231]=endoff()'s address

In the following chapter we have dealt with Valgrind[1] which can be used to find memory errors, cache performance.

13.6 Conclusions

In this chapter, we dealt with Profiling (gprof), which allows us to know where our program is spending more time and which function call's the other functions. Profiling information can show which parts of the program are slower than the expected; and might be the best candidates for rewriting the code to make our program to execute faster. It can also tell us which functions are being called more than the expected number of times such that bug fix can be done for them. Also, we have explained kernel level profiling in a lucid manner.

[1] Valgrind.com

14 Valgrind and Alleyoop

14. 1 Introduction

Valgrind is a flexible system for debugging and profiling Linux-x86 executables. The system consists of a core, which provides a synthetic x86 CPU in software, and a series of tools, each of which performs some kind of debugging, profiling, or similar task.

A number of useful tools are supplied as standard. In summary, they are:

Memcheck detects memory-management problems in your programs. All reads and writes of memory are checked, and calls to malloc/new/free/delete are intercepted. As a result, Memcheck can detect the following problems:

- Use of uninitialised memory
- Reading/writing memory after it has been free'd
- Reading/writing off the end of malloc'd blocks
- Reading/writing inappropriate areas on the stack
- Memory leaks -- where pointers to malloc'd blocks are lost forever
- Mismatched use of malloc/new/new [] vs free/delete/delete []
- Overlapping src and dst pointers in memcpy() and related functions
- Some misuses of the POSIX pthreads API

Problems like these can be difficult to find by other means, often lying undetected for long periods, then causing occasional, difficult-to-diagnose crashes.

Addrcheck is a lightweight version of Memcheck. It is identical to Memcheck except for the single detail that it does not do any uninitialised-value checks. All of the other checks -- primarily the fine-grained address checking -- are still done. The downside of this is that we don't catch the uninitialised-value errors that Memcheck can find.

But the upside is significant: programs run about twice as fast as they do on Memcheck, and a lot less memory is used. It still finds reads/writes of freed memory, memory off the end of blocks and in other invalid places, bugs which we really want to find before release!

Cachegrind is a cache profiler. It performs detailed simulation of the I1, D1 and L2 caches in our CPU and so can accurately pinpoint the sources of cache misses in your code. If we desire, it will show the number of cache misses, memory references and instructions accruing to each line of source code, with per-function, per-module and whole-program summaries. If we ask really nicely it will even show counts for each individual x86 instruction.

Cachegrind auto-detects our machine's cache configuration using the CPUID instruction, and so needs no further configuration info, in most cases.

Cachegrind is nicely complemented by Josef Weidendorfer's amazing KCacheGrind visualisation tool (http://kcachegrind.sourceforge.net), a KDE application which presents these profiling results in a graphical and easier-to-understand form.

Helgrind finds data races in multithreaded programs. Helgrind looks for memory locations which are accessed by more than one (POSIX p-)thread, but for which no consistently used (pthread_mutex_)lock can be found. Such locations are indicative of missing synchronization between threads, and could cause hard-to-find timing-dependent problems.

Helgrind ("Hell's Gate", in Norse mythology) implements the so-called "Eraser" data-race-detection algorithm, along with various refinements (thread-segment lifetimes) which reduce the number of false errors it reports. It is as yet somewhat of an experimental tool.

A number of minor tools (corecheck, lackey and Nulgrind) are also supplied. These aren't particularly useful -- they exist to illustrate how to create simple tools and to help the valgrind developers in various ways.

Valgrind is closely tied to details of the CPU, operating system and to a less extent, compiler and basic C libraries. Thus it is designed to work on a widely used platform: Linux on x86s.

14.2 Using and understanding the Valgrind core

Valgrind is designed to be as non-intrusive as possible. It works directly with existing executables. We don't need to recompile, relink, or otherwise modify, the program to be checked. Simply put valgrind --tool=tool_name at the start of the command line normally used to run the program. For example, if want to run the command ls -l using the heavyweight memory-checking tool Memcheck, issue the command:

valgrind --tool=memcheck ls -l

Regardless of which tool is in use, Valgrind takes control of your program before it starts. Debugging information is read from the executable and associated libraries, so that error messages and other outputs can be phrased in terms of source code locations (if that is appropriate)

Our program is then run on a synthetic x86 CPU provided by the Valgrind core. As new code is executed for the first time, the core hands the code to the selected tool. The tool adds its own instrumentation code to this and hands the result back to the core, which coordinates the continued execution of this instrumented code.

The amount of instrumentation code added varies widely between tools. At one end of the scale, Memcheck adds code to check every memory access and every value computed, increasing the size of the code at least 12 times, and making it run 25-50 times slower than natively. At the other end of the spectrum, the ultra-trivial "none" tool (a.k.a. Nulgrind) adds no instrumentation at all and causes in total "only" about a 4 times slowdown.

Valgrind simulates every single instruction our program executes. Because of this, the active tool checks, or profiles, not only the code in our application but also in all supporting dynamically-linked (.so-format) libraries, including the GNU C library, the X client libraries, Qt, if we work with KDE, and so on.

If we're using one of the error-detection tools, Valgrind will often detect errors in libraries, for example the GNU C or X11 libraries, which we have to use. We might not be interested in these errors, since we probably have to control over that code. Therefore, Valgrind allows we to selectively suppress errors, by recording them in a suppressions file which is read when Valgrind starts up. The build mechanism attempts to select suppressions which give reasonable behavior for the libc and XFree86 versions detected on our machine. To make it easier to write suppressions, we can use the --gen-suppressions=yes option which tells Valgrind to print out a suppression for each error that appears, which we can then copy into a suppressions file.

Different error-checking tools report different kinds of errors. The suppression mechanism therefore allows us to say which tool or tool(s) each suppression applies to.

14.2.1 Getting started

First consider whether it might be beneficial to recompile our application and supporting libraries with debugging info enabled (the -g flag). Without debugging info, the best Valgrind tools will be able to do is guess which function a particular piece of code belongs to, which makes both error messages and profiling output nearly useless. With -g, we'll hopefully get messages which point directly to the relevant source code lines.

Another flag we might like to consider, if we are working with C++, is -fno-inline. That makes it easier to see the function-call chain, which can help reduce confusion when navigating around large C++ apps. For whatever it's worth, debugging OpenOffice.org with Memcheck is a bit easier when using this flag.

We don't have to do this, but doing so helps Valgrind produce more accurate and less confusing error reports. Chances are we are set up like this already, if we intended to debug your program with GNU gdb, or some other debugger.

This paragraph applies only if we plan to use Memcheck: On rare occasions, optimization levels at -O2 and above have been observed to generate code which fools Memcheck into wrongly reporting uninitialised value errors. We have looked in detail into fixing this, and unfortunately the result is that doing so would give a further significant slowdown in what is already a slow tool. So the best solution is to turn off optimization altogether. Since this often makes things unmanageably slow, a plausible compromise is to use -O. This gets us the majority of the benefits of higher optimization levels whilst keeping relatively small the chances of false complaints from Memcheck. All other tools (as far as we know) are unaffected by optimization level.

Valgrind understands both the older "stabs" debugging format, used by gcc versions prior to 3.1, and the newer DWARF2 format used by gcc 3.1 and later. We continue to refine and debug our debug-info readers, although the majority of effort will naturally enough go into the newer DWARF2 reader.

When we are ready to roll, just run our application as we would normally, but place valgrind --tool=tool_name in front of our usual command-line invocation. Note that we should run the real (machine-code) executable here. If our application is started by, for example, a shell or perl script, we need to modify it to invoke Valgrind on the real executables. Running such scripts directly under Valgrind will result in getting error reports pertaining to /bin/sh, /usr/bin/perl, or whatever interpreter you're using. This may not be what we want and can be confusing. We can force the issue by giving the flag --trace-children=yes, but confusion is still likely.

Valgrind tools write a commentary, a stream of text, detailing error reports and other significant events. All lines in the commentary have following form:

```
==12345== some-message-from-Valgrind
```

The 12345 is the process ID. This scheme makes it easy to distinguish program output from Valgrind commentary, and also easy to differentiate commentaries from different processes which have become merged together, for whatever reason.

By default, Valgrind tools write only essential messages to the commentary, so as to avoid flooding us with information of secondary importance. If we want more information about what is happening, re-run, passing the -v flag to Valgrind.

We can direct the commentary to three different places:

The default: send it to a file descriptor, which is by default 2 (stderr). So, if we give the core no options, it will write commentary to the standard error stream. If we want to send it to some other file descriptor, for example number 9, you can specify --log-fd=9.

A less intrusive option is to write the commentary to a file, which we specify by --log-file=filename. Note carefully that the commentary is not written to the file we specify, but instead to one called filename.pid12345, if for example the pid of the traced process is 12345. This is helpful when valgrinding a whole tree of processes at once, since it means that each process writes to its own logfile, rather than the result being jumbled up in one big logfile.

The least intrusive option is to send the commentary to a network socket. The socket is specified as an IP address and port number pair, like this: --log-socket=192.168.0.1:12345 if you want to send the output to host IP 192.168.0.1 port 12345 (I have no idea if 12345 is a port of pre-existing significance). We can also omit the port number: --log-socket=192.168.0.1, in which case a default port of 1500 is used. This default is defined by the constant VG_CLO_DEFAULT_LOGPORT in the sources.

A simple listener program, valgrind-listener is available, which accepts connections on the specified port and copies whatever it is sent to stdout. This is useful for remote debugging!.

Here is an important point about the relationship between the commentary and profiling output from tools. The commentary contains a mix of messages from the Valgrind core and the selected tool. If the tool reports errors, it will report them to the commentary. However, if the tool does profiling, the profile data will be written to a file of some kind, depending on the tool, and independent of what --log-* options are in force. The commentary is intended to be a low-bandwidth, human-readable channel. Profiling data, on the other hand, is usually voluminous and not meaningful without further processing, which is why we have chosen this arrangement.

14.2.2 Reporting of errors

When one of the error-checking tools (Memcheck, Addrcheck, Helgrind) detects something bad happening in the program, an error message is written to the commentary. For example:

```
==25832== Invalid read of size 4
==25832== at 0x8048724: BandMatrix::ReSize(int, int, int) (bogon.cpp:45)
==25832== by 0x80487AF: main (bogon.cpp:66)
==25832== by 0x40371E5E: __libc_start_main (libc-start.c:129)
==25832== by 0x80485D1: (within /home/sewardj/newmat10/bogon)
==25832== Address 0xBFFFF74C is not stack'd, malloc'd or free'd
```

This message says that the program did an illegal 4-byte read of address 0xBFFFF74C, which, as far as Memcheck can tell, is not a valid stack address, nor corresponds to any currently malloc'd or free'd blocks. The read is happening at line 45 of bogon.cpp, called from line 66 of the same file, etc. For errors associated with an identified malloc'd/free'd block, for example reading free'd memory, Valgrind reports not only the location where the error happened, but also where the associated block was malloc'd/free'd.

Valgrind remembers all error reports. When an error is detected, it is compared against old reports, to see if it is a duplicate. If so, the error is noted, but no further commentary is emitted. This avoids us being swamped with bazillions of duplicate error reports.

If we want to know how many times each error occurred, run with the -v option. When execution finishes, all the reports are printed out, along with, and sorted by, their occurrence counts. This makes it easy to see which errors have occurred most frequently.

Errors are reported before the associated operation actually happens. If we are using a tool (Memcheck, Addrcheck) which does address checking, and our program attempts to read from address zero, the tool will emit a message to this effect, and the program will then duly die with a segmentation fault.

In general, we should try and fix errors in the order that they are reported. Not doing so can be confusing. For example, a program which copies uninitialised values to several memory locations, and later uses them, will generate several error messages, when run on Memcheck. The first such error message may well give the most direct clue to the root cause of the problem.

The process of detecting duplicate errors is quite an expensive one and can become a significant performance overhead if your program generates huge quantities of errors. To avoid serious problems here, Valgrind will simply stop collecting errors after 300 different errors have been seen, or 30000 errors in total have been seen. In this situation we might as well stop our program and fix it, because Valgrind won't tell us anything else useful after this. Note that the 300/30000 limits apply after suppressed errors are removed. These limits are defined in vg_include.h and can be increased if necessary.

To avoid this cutoff you can use the --error-limit=no flag. Then Valgrind will always show errors, regardless of how many there are. Use this flag carefully, since it may have a dire effect on performance.

14.2.3 Suppressing errors

The error-checking tools detect numerous problems in the base libraries, such as the GNU C library, and the XFree86 client libraries, which come pre-installed on your GNU/Linux system. We can't easily fix these, but we don't want to see these errors (and yes, there are many!) So Valgrind reads a list of errors to suppress at startup. A default suppression file is cooked up by the ./configure script when the system is built.

We can modify and add to the suppressions file at our leisure, or, better, write our own. Multiple suppression files are allowed. This is useful if part of our project contains errors we can't or don't want to fix, yet we don't want to continuously be reminded of them.

Note: By far the easiest way to add suppressions is to use the --gen-suppressions=yes flag described in this section.

Each error to be suppressed is described very specifically, to minimize the possibility that a suppression-directive inadvertently suppresses a bunch of similar errors which you did want to see. The suppression mechanism is designed to allow precise yet flexible specification of errors to suppress.

If we use the -v flag, at the end of execution, Valgrind prints out one line for each used suppression, giving its name and the number of times it got used. Here's the suppressions used by a run of valgrind --tool=memcheck ls -l:

```
--27579-- supp: 1 socketcall.connect(serv_addr)/__libc_connect/__nscd_getgrgid_r
--27579-- supp: 1 socketcall.connect(serv_addr)/__libc_connect/__nscd_getpwuid_r
--27579-- supp: 6 strrchr/_dl_map_object_from_fd/_dl_map_object
```

Multiple suppressions files are allowed. By default, Valgrind uses $PREFIX/lib/valgrind/default.supp. We can ask to add suppressions from another file, by specifying --suppressions=/path/to/file.supp.

If we want to understand more about suppressions, look at an existing suppressions file whilst reading the following documentation. The file glibc-2.2.supp, in the source distribution, provides some good examples.

Each suppression has the following components:

First line: its name. This merely gives a handy name to the suppression, by which it is referred to in the summary of used suppressions printed out when a program finishes. It's not important what the name is; any identifying string will do.

Second line: name of the tool(s) that the suppression is for (if more than one, comma-separated), and the name of the suppression itself, separated by a colon, eg:

```
tool_name1,tool_name2:suppression_name
```

(Nb: no spaces are allowed).

Recall that Valgrind-2.0.X is a modular system, in which different instrumentation tools can observe your program whilst it is running. Since different tools detect different kinds of errors, it is necessary to say which tool(s) the suppression is meaningful to.

Tools will complain, at startup, if a tool does not understand any suppression directed to it. Tools ignore suppressions which are not directed to them. As a result, it is quite practical to put suppressions for all tools into the same suppression file.

Valgrind's core can detect certain PThreads API errors, for which this line reads:

```
core:PThread
```

Next line: a small number of suppression types have extra information after the second line (eg. the Param suppression for Memcheck)

Remaining lines: This is the calling context for the error -- the chain of function calls hat led to it. There can be up to four of these lines.

Locations may be either names of shared objects/executables or wildcards matching function names. They begin obj: and fun: respectively. Function and object names to match against may use the wildcard characters * and ?.

Important note: C++ function names must be mangled. If we are writing suppressions by hand, use the --demangle=no option to get the mangled names in our error messages.

Finally, the entire suppression must be between curly braces. Each brace must be the irst character on its own line.

A suppression only suppresses an error when the error matches all the details in the suppression. Here's an example:

```
{
  __gconv_transform_ascii_internal/__mbrtowc/mbtowc
  Memcheck:Value4
  fun:__gconv_transform_ascii_internal
  fun:__mbr*toc
  fun:mbtowc
}
```

What is means is: for Memcheck only, suppress a use-of-uninitialised-value error, when the data size is 4, when it occurs in the function __gconv_transform_ascii_internal, when that is called from any function of name matching __mbr*toc, when that is called from mbtowc. It doesn't apply under any other circumstances. The string by which this suppression is identified to the user is

__gconv_transform_ascii_internal/__mbrtowc/mbtowc.

Another example, again for the Memcheck tool:

```
{
libX11.so.6.2/libX11.so.6.2/libXaw.so.7.0
Memcheck:Value4
obj:/usr/X11R6/lib/libX11.so.6.2
obj:/usr/X11R6/lib/libX11.so.6.2
obj:/usr/X11R6/lib/libXaw.so.7.0
}
```

Suppress any size 4 uninitialised-value error which occurs anywhere in libX11.so.6.2, when called from anywhere in the same library, when called from anywhere in libXaw.so.7.0. The inexact specification of locations is regrettable, but is about all you can hope for, given that the X11 libraries shipped with Red Hat 7.2 have had their symbol tables removed.

14.3 Command-line flags for the Valgrind core

As mentioned above, Valgrind's core accepts a common set of flags. The tools also accept tool-specific flags, which are documented separately for each tool. We invoke Valgrind like this:

```
valgrind --tool=tool_name [options-for-Valgrind] your-prog [options for your-prog]
```

Valgrind's default settings succeed in giving reasonable behavior in most cases. We group the available options by rough categories.

Tool-selection option

The single most important option.

--tool=name

Run the Valgrind tool called name, e.g. Memcheck, Addrcheck, Cachegrind, etc.

14.3.1 Basic Options

These options work with all tools.

--help

Show help for all options, both for the core and for the selected tool.

--help-debug

Same as --help, but also lists debugging options which usually are only of use to developers.

--version

Show the version number of the Valgrind core. Tools can have their own version numbers. There is a scheme in place to ensure that tools only execute when the core version is one they are known to work with. This was done to minimize the chances of strange problems arising from tool-vs-core version incompatibilities.

-v --verbose

Be more verbose. Gives extra information on various aspects of your program, such as: the shared objects loaded, the suppressions used, the progress of the instrumentation and execution engines, and warnings about unusual behavior. Repeating the flag increases the verbosity level.

-q --quiet

Run silently, and only print error messages. Useful if you are running regression tests or have some other automated test machinery.

--trace-children=no [default]

--trace-children=yes

When enabled, Valgrind will trace into child processes. This is confusing and often not what you want, so is disabled by default.

Note that the name of this option is slightly misleading. It actually controls whether programs started with exec() are run under Valgrind's control. If our program calls fork(), both the parent and the child will run under Valgrind's control.

--log-fd=<number> [default: 2, stderr]

Specifies that Valgrind should send all of its messages to the specified file descriptor. The default, 2, is the standard error channel (stderr). Note that this may interfere with the client's own use of stderr.

--log-file=<filename>

Specifies that Valgrind should send all of its messages to the specified file. In fact, the file name used is created by concatenating the text filename, ".pid" and the process ID, so as to create a file per process. The specified file name may not be the empty string.

--log-socket=<ip-address:port-number>

Specifies that Valgrind should send all of its messages to the specified port at the specified IP address. The port may be omitted, in which case port 1500 is used. If a connection cannot be made to the specified socket, Valgrind falls back to writing output to the standard error (stderr). This option is intended to be used in conjunction with the valgrind-listener program. For further details, see section 2.3.

--time-stamp=no [default]

--time-stamp=yes

Specifies that valgrind should output a timestamp before each message that it outputs.

14.3.2 Error-related options

These options are used by all tools that can report errors, e.g. Memcheck, but not Cachegrind.

--demangle=no

--demangle=yes [default]

Disable/enable automatic demangling (decoding) of C++ names. Enabled by default. When enabled, Valgrind will attempt to translate encoded C++ procedure names back to something approaching the original. The demangler handles symbols mangled by g++ versions 2.X and 3.X.

An important fact about demangling is that function names mentioned in suppressions files should be in their mangled form. Valgrind does not demangle function names when searching for applicable suppressions, because to do otherwise would make suppressions file contents dependent on the state of Valgrind's demangling machinery, and would also be slow and pointless.

```
--num-callers=<number> [default=4]
```

By default, Valgrind shows four levels of function call names to help us to identify program locations. We can change that number with this option. This can help in determining the program's location in deeply-nested call chains. Note that errors are commoned up using only the top three function locations (the place in the current function, and that of its two immediate callers). So this doesn't affect the total number of errors reported.

The maximum value for this is 50. Note that higher settings will make Valgrind run a bit more slowly and take a bit more memory, but can be useful when working with programs with deeply-nested call chains.

```
--error-limit=yes [default]
--error-limit=no
```

When enabled, Valgrind stops reporting errors after 30000 in total, or 300 different ones, have been seen. This is to stop the error tracking machinery from becoming a huge performance overhead in programs with many errors.

```
--show-below-main=yes
--show-below-main=no [default]
```

By default, stack traces for errors do not show any functions that appear beneath main(); most of the time it's uninteresting C library stuff. If this option is enabled, these entries below main() will be shown.

```
--suppressions=<filename> [default: $PREFIX/lib/valgrind/default.supp]
```

Specifies an extra file from which to read descriptions of errors to suppress. We may use as many extra suppressions files as you like.

```
--gen-suppressions=no [default]
--gen-suppressions=yes
```

When enabled, Valgrind will pause after every error shown, and print the line ---- Print suppression ? --- [Return/N/n/Y/y/C/c] ----

The prompt's behavior is the same as for the --db-attach option.

If we choose to, Valgrind will print out a suppression for this error. We can then cut and paste it into a suppression file if we don't want to hear about the error in the future.

This option is particularly useful with C++ programs, as it prints out the suppressions with mangled names, as required.

Note that the suppressions printed are as specific as possible. We may want to common up similar ones, eg. by adding wildcards to function names. Also, sometimes two different errors are suppressed by the same suppression, in which case Valgrind will output the suppression more than once, but we only need to have one copy in our suppression file (but having more than one won't cause problems). Also, the suppression name is given as <insert a suppression name here>; the name doesn't really matter, it's only used with the -v option which prints out all used suppression records.

--track-fds=no [default]

--track-fds=yes

When enabled, Valgrind will print out a list of open file descriptors on exit. Along with each file descriptor, Valgrind prints out a stack backtrace of where the file was opened and any details relating to the file descriptor such as the file name or socket details.

--db-attach=no [default]

--db-attach=yes

When enabled, Valgrind will pause after every error shown, and print the line

---- Attach to debugger ? --- [Return/N/n/Y/y/C/c] ----

Pressing Ret, or N Ret or n Ret, causes Valgrind not to start a debugger for this error.

Y Ret or y Ret causes Valgrind to start a debugger, for the program at this point. When we have finished with the debugger, quit from it, and the program will continue. Trying to continue from inside the debugger doesn't work.

C Ret or c Ret causes Valgrind not to start a debugger, and not to ask again.

--db-attach=yes conflicts with --trace-children=yes. We can't use them together. Valgrind refuses to start up in this situation. 1 May 2002: this is a historical relic which could be easily fixed if it gets in your way. Mail me and complain if this is a problem for us.

--db-command=<command> [default: gdb -nw %f %p]

This specifies how Valgrind will invoke the debugger. By default it will use whatever GDB is detected at build time, which is usually /usr/bin/gdb. Using this command, we can specify some alternative command to invoke the debugger you want to use.

The command string given can include one or instances of the %p and %f expansions. Each instance of %p expands to the PID of the process to be debugged and each instance of %f expands to the path to the executable for the process to be debugged.

--input-fd=<number> [default=0, stdin]

When using --db-attach=yes and --gen-suppressions=yes, Valgrind will stop so as to read keyboard input from us, when each error occurs. By default it reads from the standard input (stdin), which is problematic for programs which close stdin. This option allows us to specify an alternative file descriptor from which to read input.

malloc()-related options

For tools that use their own version of malloc() (e.g. Memcheck and Addrcheck), the following options apply.

--alignment=<number> [default: 8]

By default Valgrind's malloc, realloc, etc, return 4-byte aligned addresses. These are suitable for any accesses on x86 processors. Some programs might however assume that malloc et al return 8- or more aligned memory. The supplied value must be between 4 and 4096 inclusive, and must be a power of two.

--sloppy-malloc=no [default]

--sloppy-malloc=yes

When enabled, all requests for malloc/calloc are rounded up to a multiple of 4 bytes. For example, a request for 17 bytes of space would result in a 20-byte area being made available. This works around bugs in sloppy libraries which assume that they can safely rely on malloc/calloc requests being rounded up in this fashion. Without the workaround, these libraries tend to generate large numbers of errors when they access the ends of these areas.

14.3.3 Rare options

These options apply to all tools, as they affect certain obscure workings of the Valgrind core. Most people won't need to use these.

--run-libc-freeres=yes [default]

--run-libc-freeres=no

--signal-polltime=<time> [default=50]

How often to poll for signals (in milliseconds). Only applies for older kernels that need signal routing.

```
--lowlat-signals=no [default]
--lowlat-signals=yes
```

Improve wake-up latency when a thread receives a signal.

```
--lowlat-syscalls=no [default]
--lowlat-syscalls=yes
```

Improve wake-up latency when a thread's syscall completes.

There are also some options for debugging Valgrind itself. We shouldn't need to use them in the normal run of things. Nevertheless:

```
--single-step=no [default]
--single-step=yes
```

When enabled, each x86 instruction is translated separately into instrumented code. When disabled, translation is done on a per-basic-block basis, giving much better translations.

```
--optimise=no
--optimise=yes [default]
```

When enabled, various improvements are applied to the intermediate code, mainly aimed at allowing the simulated CPU's registers to be cached in the real CPU's registers over several simulated instructions.

```
--profile=no
--profile=yes [default]
```

When enabled, does crude internal profiling of Valgrind itself. This is not for profiling your programs. Rather it is to allow the developers to assess where Valgrind is spending its time. The tools must be built for profiling for this to work.

```
--trace-syscalls=no [default]
--trace-syscalls=yes
```

Enable/disable tracing of system call intercepts.

```
--trace-signals=no [default]
--trace-signals=yes
```

Enable/disable tracing of signal handling.

--trace-sched=no [default]

--trace-sched=yes

Enable/disable tracing of thread scheduling events.

--trace-pthread=none [default]

--trace-pthread=some

--trace-pthread=all

Specifies amount of trace detail for pthread-related events.

--trace-symtab=no [default]

--trace-symtab=yes

14.3.4 Setting default options

Note that Valgrind also reads options from three places:

The file ~/.valgrindrc

The environment variable $VALGRIND_OPTS

The file ./.valgrindrc

These are processed in the given order, before the command-line options. Options processed later override those processed earlier; for example, options in ./.valgrindrc will take precedence over those in ~/.valgrindrc. The first two are particularly useful for setting the default tool to use.

Any tool-specific options put in $VALGRIND_OPTS or the .valgrindrc files should be prefixed with the tool name and a colon. For example, if we want Memcheck to always do leak checking, we can put the following entry in ~/.valgrindrc:

--memcheck:leak-check=yes

This will be ignored if any tool other than Memcheck is run. Without the memcheck: part, this will cause problems if we select other tools that don't understand --leak-check=yes.

14.3.5 The Client Request mechanism

Valgrind has a trapdoor mechanism via which the client program can pass all manner of requests and queries to Valgrind and the current tool. Internally, this is used extensively to make malloc, free, signals, threads, etc, work, although you don't see that.

For our convenience, a subset of these so-called client requests is provided to allow us to tell Valgrind facts about the behavior of our program, and conversely to make queries. In particular, our program can tell Valgrind about changes in memory range permissions that Valgrind would not otherwise know about, and so allows clients to get Valgrind to do arbitrary custom checks.

Clients need to include a header file to make this work. Which header file depends on which client requests us to use. Some client requests are handled by the core, and are defined in the header file valgrind.h. Tool-specific header files are named after the tool, e.g. memcheck.h. All header files can be found in the include directory of wherever Valgrind was installed.

The macros in these header files have the magical property that they generate code in-line which Valgrind can spot. However, the code does nothing when not run on Valgrind, so we are not forced to run our program on Valgrind just because we use the macros in this file. Also, we are not required to link our program with any extra supporting libraries.

Here is a brief description of the macros available in valgrind.h, which work with more than one tool (see the tool-specific documentation for explanations of the tool-specific macros).

RUNNING_ON_VALGRIND: returns 1 if running on Valgrind, 0 if running on the real CPU.

VALGRIND_DISCARD_TRANSLATIONS: discard translations of code in the specified address range. Useful if we are debugging a JITter or some other dynamic code generation system. After this call, attempts to execute code in the invalidated address range will cause Valgrind to make new translations of that code, which is probably the semantics we want. Note that this is implemented naively, and involves checking all 200191 entries in the translation table to see if any of them overlap the specified address range. So try not to call it often, or performance will nosedive. Note that we can be clever about this: we only need to call it when an area which previously contained code is overwritten with new code. We can choose to write code into fresh memory, and just call this occasionally to discard large chunks of old code all at once.

Warning: minimally tested, especially for tools other than Memcheck.

VALGRIND_COUNT_ERRORS: returns the number of errors found so far by Valgrind. Can be useful in test harness code when combined with the --log-fd=-1 option; this runs Valgrind silently, but the client program can detect when errors occur. Only useful for tools that report errors, e.g. it's useful for Memcheck, but for Cachegrind it will always return zero because Cachegrind doesn't report errors.

VALGRIND_MALLOCLIKE_BLOCK: If our program manages its own memory instead of using the standard malloc()/new/new[], tools that track information about heap blocks will not do nearly as good a job. For example, Memcheck won't detect nearly as many errors, and the error messages won't be as informative. To improve this situation, use this macro just after our custom allocator allocates some new memory. See the comments in valgrind.h for information on how to use it.

VALGRIND_FREELIKE_BLOCK: This should be used in conjunction with VALGRIND_MALLOCLIKE_BLOCK. Again, see memcheck/memcheck.h for information on how to use it.

VALGRIND_CREATE_MEMPOOL: This is similar to VALGRIND_MALLOCLIKE_BLOCK, but is tailored towards code that uses memory pools. See the comments in valgrind.h for information on how to use it.

VALGRIND_DESTROY_MEMPOOL: This should be used in conjunction with VALGRIND_CREATE_MEMPOOL Again, see the comments in valgrind.h for information on how to use it.

VALGRIND_MEMPOOL_ALLOC: This should be used in conjunction with VALGRIND_CREATE_MEMPOOL Again, see the comments in valgrind.h for information on how to use it.

VALGRIND_MEMPOOL_FREE: This should be used in conjunction with VALGRIND_CREATE_MEMPOOL Again, see the comments in valgrind.h for information on how to use it.

VALGRIND_NON_SIMD_CALL[0123]: executes a function of 0, 1, 2 or 3 args in the client program on the real CPU, not the virtual CPU that Valgrind normally runs code on. These are used in various ways internally to Valgrind. They might be useful to client programs. Warning: Only use these if we really know what we are doing.

VALGRIND_PRINTF(format, ...): printf a message to the log file when running under Valgrind. Nothing is output if not running under Valgrind. Returns the number of characters output.

VALGRIND_PRINTF_BACKTRACE(format, ...): printf a message to the log file along with a stack backtrace when running under Valgrind. Nothing is output if not running under Valgrind. Returns the number of characters output.

Note that valgrind.h is included by all the tool-specific header files (such as memcheck.h), so we don't need to include it in our client if we include a tool-specific header.

14.3.6 Support for POSIX Pthreads

Valgrind supports programs which use POSIX pthreads. Getting this to work was technically challenging but it all works well enough for significant threaded applications to work.

14.3.7 Handling of signals

Valgrind provides suitable handling of signals, so, provided we stick to POSIX stuff, we should be ok. Basic sigaction() and sigprocmask() are handled. Signal handlers may return in the normal way or do longjmp(); both should work ok. As specified by POSIX, a signal is blocked in its own handler. Default actions for signals should work as before. Etc, etc.

Under the hood, dealing with signals is a real pain, and Valgrind's simulation leaves much to be desired. If our program does way-strange stuff with signals, bad things may happen. If so, let me know. We don't promise to fix it, but we would at least like to be aware of it.

14.3.8 Limitations

The following list of limitations seems depressingly long. However, most programs actually work fine.

Valgrind will run x86-GNU/Linux ELF dynamically linked binaries, on a kernel 2.4.X or 2.6.X system, subject to the following constraints:

No support for 3DNow instructions. If the translator encounters these, Valgrind will generate a SIGILL when the instruction is executed.

Pthreads support is improving, but there are still significant limitations in that department. See the section above on Pthreads. Note that our program must be dynamically linked against libpthread.so, so that Valgrind can substitute its own implementation at program startup time. If we're statically linked against it, things will fail badly.

Memcheck assumes that the floating point registers are not used as intermediaries in memory-to-memory copies, so it immediately checks definedness of values loaded from memory by floating-point loads. If we want to write code which copies around possibly-uninitialised values, we must ensure these travel through the integer registers, not the FPU.

If our program does its own memory management, rather than using malloc/new/free/delete, it should still work, but Valgrind's error checking won't be so effective.

Valgrind's signal simulation is not as robust as it could be. Basic POSIX-compliant sigaction and sigprocmask functionality is supplied, but it's conceivable that things could go badly awry if we do weird things with signals.

x86 instructions, and system calls, have been implemented on demand. So it's possible, although unlikely, that a program will fall over with a message to that effect. If this happens, please report ALL the details printed out, so we can try and implement the missing feature.

x86 floating point works correctly, but floating-point code may run even more slowly than integer code, due to my simplistic approach to FPU emulation.

Memory consumption of our program is majorly increased whilst running under Valgrind. This is due to the large amount of administrative information maintained behind the scenes. Another cause is that Valgrind dynamically translates the original executable. Translated, instrumented code is 14-16 times larger than the original (!) so we can easily end up with 30+ MB of translations when running (eg) a web browser.

Valgrind can handle dynamically-generated code just fine. However, if we regenerate code over the top of old code (i.e. at the same memory addresses) Valgrind will not realize the code has changed, and will run its old translations, which will be out-of-date. We need to use the VALGRIND_DISCARD_TRANSLATIONS client request in that case.

14.3.9 Programs which are known not to work are:

emacs starts up but immediately concludes it is out of memory and aborts as Emacs has it's own memory-management scheme

14.4 Background Behind Valrind

Valgrind is compiled into a shared object, valgrind.so. The shell script valgrind sets the LD_PRELOAD environment variable to point to valgrind.so. This causes the .so to be loaded as an extra library to any subsequently executed dynamically-linked ELF binary, viz, the program we want to debug.

The dynamic linker allows each .so in the process image to have an initialization function which is run before main(). It also allows each .so to have a finalization function run after main() exits.

When valgrind.so's initialization function is called by the dynamic linker, the synthetic CPU to starts up. The real CPU remains locked in valgrind.so for the entire rest of the program, but the synthetic CPU returns from the initialization function. Startup of the program now continues as usual -- the dynamic linker calls all the other .so's initialization routines, and eventually runs main(). This all runs on the synthetic CPU, not the real one, but the client program cannot tell the difference.

Eventually main() exits, so the synthetic CPU calls valgrind.so's finalization function. Valgrind detects this, and uses it as its cue to exit. It prints summaries of all errors detected, possibly checks for memory leaks, and then exits the finalization routine, but now on the real CPU. The synthetic CPU has now lost control -- permanently -- so the program exits back to the OS on the real CPU, just as it would have done anyway.

On entry, Valgrind switches stacks, so it runs on its own stack. On exit, it switches back. This means that the client program continues to run on its own stack, so we can switch back and forth between running it on the simulated and real CPUs without difficulty. This was an important design decision, because it makes it easy (well, significantly less difficult) to debug the synthetic CPU.

14.4.1 The translation/instrumentation engine

Valgrind does not directly run any of the original program's code. Only instrumented translations are run. Valgrind maintains a translation table, which allows it to find the translation quickly for any branch target (code address). If no translation has yet been made, the translator - a just-in-time translator - is summoned. This makes an instrumented translation, which is added to the collection of translations. Subsequent jumps to that address will use this translation.

Valgrind no longer directly supports detection of self-modifying code. Such checking is expensive, and in practice (fortunately) almost no applications need it. However, to help people who are debugging dynamic code generation systems, there is a Client Request (basically a macro you can put in your program) which directs Valgrind to discard translations in a given address range. So Valgrind can still work in this situation provided the client tells it when code has become out-of-date and needs to be retranslated.

The JITter translates basic blocks -- blocks of straight-line-code -- as single entities. To minimize the considerable difficulties of dealing with the x86 instruction set, x86 instructions are first translated to a RISC-like intermediate code, similar to sparc code, but with an infinite number of virtual integer registers. Initially each instruction is translated separately, and there is no attempt at instrumentation.

The intermediate code is improved, mostly so as to try and cache the simulated machine's registers in the real machine's registers over several simulated instructions. This is often very effective. Also, we try to remove redundant updates of the simulated machine's condition-code register.

The intermediate code is then instrumented, giving more intermediate code. There are a few extra intermediate-code operations to support instrumentation; it is all refreshingly simple. After instrumentation there is a cleanup pass to remove redundant value checks.

This gives instrumented intermediate code which mentions arbitrary numbers of virtual registers. A linear-scan register allocator is used to assign real registers and possibly generate spill code. All of this is still phrased in terms of the intermediate code. This machinery is inspired by the work of Reuben Thomas (Mite).

Then, and only then, is the final x86 code emitted. The intermediate code is carefully designed so that x86 code can be generated from it without need for spare registers or other inconveniences.

The translations are managed using a traditional LRU-based caching scheme. The translation cache has a default size of about 14MB.

14.4.2 Tracking the status of memory

Each byte in the process' address space has nine bits associated with it: one A bit and eight V bits. The A and V bits for each byte are stored using a sparse array, which flexibly and efficiently covers arbitrary parts of the 32-bit address space without imposing significant space or performance overheads for the parts of the address space never visited. The scheme used, and speedup hacks, are described in detail at the top of the source file vg_memory.c, so we should read that for the gory details.

System calls

All system calls are intercepted. The memory status map is consulted before and updated after each call. It's all rather tiresome. See coregrind/vg_syscalls.c for details.

Signals

All system calls to sigaction() and sigprocmask() are intercepted. If the client program is trying to set a signal handler, Valgrind makes a note of the handler address and which signal it is for. Valgrind then arranges for the same signal to be delivered to its own handler.

When such a signal arrives, Valgrind's own handler catches it, and notes the fact. At a convenient safe point in execution, Valgrind builds a signal delivery frame on the client's stack and runs its handler. If the handler longjmp()s, there is nothing more to be said. If the handler returns, Valgrind notices this, zaps the delivery frame, and carries on where it left off before delivering the signal.

The purpose of this nonsense is that setting signal handlers essentially amounts to giving callback addresses to the Linux kernel. We can't allow this to happen, because if it did, signal handlers would run on the real CPU, not the simulated one. This means the checking machinery would not operate during the handler run, and, worse, memory permissions maps would not be updated, which could cause spurious error reports once the handler had returned.

An even worse thing would happen if the signal handler longjmp'd rather than returned: Valgrind would completely lose control of the client program.

We can't allow the client to install signal handlers directly. Instead, Valgrind must catch, on behalf of the client, any signal the client asks to catch, and must delivery it to the client on the simulated CPU, not the real one. This involves considerable gruesome fakery; see vg_signals.c for details.

14.5 MemCheck

14.5.1 An example run

This is the log for a run of a small program using Memcheck The program is in fact correct, and the reported error is as the result of a potentially serious code generation bug in GNU g++ (snapshot 20010527).

```
~/Valgrind-6/valgrind -v ./bogon
==25832== Valgrind 0.10, a memory error detector for x86 RedHat 7.1.
==25832== Copyright (C) 2000-2001, and GNU GPL'd, by Julian Seward.
==25832== Startup, with flags:
==25832== --suppressions=/home/sewardj/Valgrind/redhat71.supp
==25832== reading syms from /lib/ld-linux.so.2
==25832== reading syms from /lib/libc.so.6
==25832== reading syms from /mnt/pima/jrs/Inst/lib/libgcc_s.so.0
==25832== reading syms from /lib/libm.so.6
==25832== reading syms from /mnt/pima/jrs/Inst/lib/libstdc++.so.3
==25832== reading syms from /home/sewardj/Valgrind/valgrind.so
==25832== reading syms from /proc/self/exe
==25832== loaded 5950 symbols, 142333 line number locations
==25832==
==25832== Invalid read of size 4
==25832== at 0x8048724: _ZN10BandMatrix6ReSizeEiii (bogon.cpp:45)
==25832== by 0x80487AF: main (bogon.cpp:66)
==25832== by 0x40371E5E: __libc_start_main (libc-start.c:129)
==25832== by 0x80485D1: (within /home/sewardj/newmat10/bogon)
==25832== Address 0xBFFFF74C is not stack'd, malloc'd or free'd
==25832==
==25832== ERROR SUMMARY: 1 errors from 1 contexts (suppressed: 0 from 0)
==25832== malloc/free: in use at exit: 0 bytes in 0 blocks.
==25832== malloc/free: 0 allocs, 0 frees, 0 bytes allocated.
==25832== For a detailed leak analysis, rerun with: --leak-check=yes
==25832==
==25832== exiting, did 1881 basic blocks, 0 misses.
==25832== 223 translations, 3626 bytes in, 56801 bytes out.
```

The GCC folks fixed this about a week before gcc-3.0 shipped.

Memcheck: a heavyweight memory checker

To use this tool, we may specify --tool=memcheck on the Valgrind command line. However, this is the default tool. Thus, we do not required required to specify.

14.5. 2 Kinds of bugs that memcheck can find

All reads and writes of memory are checked, and calls to malloc/new/free/delete are intercepted. As a result, memcheck can detect the following problems:

- Use of uninitialised memory
- Reading/writing memory after it has been free'd
- Reading/writing off the end of malloc'd blocks
- Reading/writing inappropriate areas on the stack
- Memory leaks -- where pointers to malloc'd blocks are lost forever
- Mismatched use of malloc/new/new [] vs free/delete/delete []
- Overlapping src and dst pointers in memcpy() and related functions
- Some misuses of the POSIX pthreads API

Command-line flags specific to memcheck

```
--leak-check=no [default]
--leak-check=yes
```

When enabled, search for memory leaks when the client program finishes. A memory leak means a malloc'd block, which has not yet been free'd, but to which no pointer can be found. Such a block can never be free'd by the program, since no pointer to it exists. Leak checking is disabled by default because it tends to generate dozens of error messages.

```
--show-reachable=no [default]
--show-reachable=yes
```

When disabled, the memory leak detector only shows blocks for which it cannot find a pointer to at all, or it can only find a pointer to the middle of. These blocks are prime candidates for memory leaks. When enabled, the leak detector also reports on blocks which it could find a pointer to. Your program could, at least in principle, have freed such blocks before exit. Contrast this to blocks for which no pointer, or only an interior pointer could be found: they are more likely to indicate memory leaks, because we do not actually have a pointer to the start of the block which we can hand to free, even if we wanted to.

```
--leak-resolution=low [default]
--leak-resolution=med
--leak-resolution=high
```

When doing leak checking, determines how willing Memcheck is to consider different backtraces to be the same. When set to low, the default, only the first two entries need match. When med, four entries have to match. When high, all entries need to match.

For hardcore leak debugging, we probably want to use --leak-resolution=high together with --num-callers=40 or some such large number. Note however that this can give an overwhelming amount of information, which is why the defaults are 4 callers and low-resolution matching.

--freelist-vol=<number> [default: 1000000]

When the client program releases memory using free (in C) or delete (C++), that memory is not immediately made available for re-allocation. Instead it is marked inaccessible and placed in a queue of freed blocks. The purpose is to delay the point at which freed-up memory comes back into circulation. This increases the chance that Memcheck will be able to detect invalid accesses to blocks for some significant period of time after they have been freed.

This flag specifies the maximum total size, in bytes, of the blocks in the queue. The default value is one million bytes. Increasing this increases the total amount of memory used by Memcheck but may detect invalid uses of freed blocks which would otherwise go undetected.

--partial-loads-ok=yes [the default]

--partial-loads-ok=no

Controls how Memcheck handles word (4-byte) loads from addresses for which some bytes are addressable and others are not. When yes (the default), such loads do not elicit an address error. Instead, the loaded V bytes corresponding to the illegal addresses indicate undefined, and those corresponding to legal addresses are loaded from shadow memory, as usual.

When no, loads from partially invalid addresses are treated the same as loads from completely invalid addresses: an illegal-address error is issued, and the resulting V bytes indicate valid data.

--cleanup=no

--cleanup=yes [default]

This is a flag to help debug valgrind itself. It is of no use to end-users. When enabled, various improvements are applied to the post-instrumented intermediate code, aimed at removing redundant value checks.

14.5.3 Explanation of error messages from Memcheck

Despite considerable sophistication under the hood, Memcheck can only really detect two kinds of errors, use of illegal addresses, and use of undefined values. Nevertheless, this is enough to help us to discover all sorts of memory-management nasties in our code. This section presents a quick summary of what error messages mean. The precise behavior of the error-checking machinery is described in this section.

Illegal read / Illegal write errors

For example:

```
Invalid read of size 4
        at 0x40F6BBCC: (within /usr/lib/libpng.so.2.1.0.9)
        by 0x40F6B804: (within /usr/lib/libpng.so.2.1.0.9)
        by 0x40B07FF4: read_png_image__FP8QimageIO (kernel/qpngio.cpp:326)
        by 0x40AC751B: QImageIO::read() (kernel/qimage.cpp:3621)
        Address 0xBFFFF0E0 is not stack'd, malloc'd or free'd
```

This happens when our program reads or writes memory at a place which Memcheck reckons it shouldn't. In this example, the program did a 4-byte read at address 0xBFFFF0E0, somewhere within the system-supplied library libpng.so.2.1.0.9, which was called from somewhere else in the same library, called from line 326 of qpngio.cpp, and so on.

Memcheck tries to establish what the illegal address might relate to, since that's often useful. So, if it points into a block of memory which has already been freed, we'll be informed of this, and also where the block was free'd at. Likewise, if it should turn out to be just off the end of a malloc'd block, a common result of off-by-one-errors in array subscripting, we'll be informed of this fact, and also where the block was malloc'd.

In this example, Memcheck can't identify the address. Actually the address is on the stack, but, for some reason, this is not a valid stack address -- it is below the stack pointer, %esp, and that isn't allowed. In this particular case it's probably caused by gcc generating invalid code, a known bug in various flavors of gcc.

Note that Memcheck only tells us that our program is about to access memory at an illegal address. It can't stop the access from happening. So, if our program makes an access which normally would result in a segmentation fault, our program will still suffer the same fate -- but we will get a message from Memcheck immediately prior to this. In this particular example, reading junk on the stack is non-fatal, and the program stays alive.

14.5.4 Use of uninitialised values

For example:

```
Conditional jump or move depends on uninitialised value(s)
        at 0x402DFA94: _IO_vfprintf (_itoa.h:49)
        by 0x402E8476: _IO_printf (printf.c:36)
        by 0x8048472: main (tests/manuel1.c:8)
        by 0x402A6E5E: __libc_start_main (libc-start.c:129)
```

An uninitialised-value use error is reported when our program uses a value which hasn't been initialised -- in other words, is undefined. Here, the undefined value is used somewhere inside the printf() machinery of the C library. This error was reported when running the following small program:

```
int main()
{
  int x;
  printf ("x = %d\n", x);
}
```

It is important to understand that our program can copy around junk (uninitialised) data to its heart's content. Memcheck observes this and keeps track of the data, but does not complain. A complaint is issued only when our program attempts to make use of uninitialised data. In this example, x is uninitialised. Memcheck observes the value being passed to _IO_printf and thence to _IO_vfprintf, but makes no comment. However, _IO_vfprintf has to examine the value of x so it can turn it into the corresponding ASCII string, and it is at this point that Memcheck complains.

Sources of uninitialised data tend to be:

Local variables in procedures which have not been initialised, as in the example above.

The contents of malloc'd blocks, before we write something there. In C++, the new operator is a wrapper round malloc, so if we create an object with new, its fields will be uninitialised until we (or the constructor) fill them in, which is only Right and Proper.

14.5.6 Illegal frees

For example:

```
Invalid free()
        at 0x4004FFDF: free (vg_clientmalloc.c:577)
        by 0x80484C7: main (tests/doublefree.c:10)
        by 0x402A6E5E: __libc_start_main (libc-start.c:129)
        by 0x80483B1: (within tests/doublefree)
        Address 0x3807F7B4 is 0 bytes inside a block of size 177 free'd
        at 0x4004FFDF: free (vg_clientmalloc.c:577)
        by 0x80484C7: main (tests/doublefree.c:10)
        by 0x402A6E5E: __libc_start_main (libc-start.c:129)
        by 0x80483B1: (within tests/doublefree)
```

Memcheck keeps track of the blocks allocated by our program with malloc/new, so it can know exactly whether or not the argument to free/delete is legitimate or not. Here, this test program has freed the same block twice. As with the illegal read/write errors, Memcheck attempts to make sense of the address free'd. If, as here, the address is one which has previously been freed, we will be told that -- making duplicate frees of the same block easy to spot.

When a block is freed with an inappropriate deallocation function

In the following example, a block allocated with new[] has wrongly been deallocated with free:

```
Mismatched free() / delete / delete []
      at 0x40043249: free (vg_clientfuncs.c:171)
      by 0x4102BB4E: QGArray::~QGArray(void) (tools/qgarray.cpp:149)
      by 0x4C261C41: PptDoc::~PptDoc(void) (include/qmemarray.h:60)
      by 0x4C261F0E: PptXml::~PptXml(void) (pptxml.cc:44)
      Address 0x4BB292A8 is 0 bytes inside a block of size 64 alloc'd
      at 0x4004318C: __builtin_vec_new (vg_clientfuncs.c:152)
      by 0x4C21BC15: KLaola::readSBStream(int) const (klaola.cc:314)
      by 0x4C21C155: KLaola::stream(KLaola::OLENode const *) (klaola.cc:416)
      by 0x4C21788F: OLEFilter::convert(QCString const &) (olefilter.cc:272)
```

In C++ it's important to deallocate memory in a way compatible with how it was allocated. The deal is:

- If allocated with malloc, calloc, realloc, valloc or memalign, you must deallocate with free.
- If allocated with new[], you must deallocate with delete[].
- If allocated with new, you must deallocate with delete.

14.5.7 Passing system call parameters with inadequate read/write permissions

Memcheck checks all parameters to system calls. If a system call needs to read from a buffer provided by our program, Memcheck checks that the entire buffer is addressable and has valid data, i.e., it is readable. And if the system call needs to write to a user-supplied buffer, Memcheck checks that the buffer is addressable. After the system call, Memcheck updates its administrative information to precisely reflect any changes in memory permissions caused by the system call.

Example 1

Here's an example of a system call with an invalid parameter:

```
#include <stdlib.h>
#include <unistd.h>
int main( void )
{
  char* arr = malloc(10);
  (void) write( 1 /* stdout */, arr, 10 );
  return 0;
}
```

We get this complaint ...

```
Syscall param write(buf) contains uninitialised or unadvisable byte(s)
        at 0x4035E072: __libc_write
        by 0x402A6E5E: __libc_start_main (libc-start.c:129)
        by 0x80483B1: (within tests/badwrite)
        by <bogus frame pointer> ???
        Address 0x3807E6D0 is 0 bytes inside a block of size 10 alloc'd
        at 0x4004FEE6: malloc (ut_clientmalloc.c:539)
        by 0x80484A0: main (tests/badwrite.c:6)
        by 0x402A6E5E: __libc_start_main (libc-start.c:129)
        by 0x80483B1: (within tests/badwrite)
```

... because the program has tried to write uninitialised junk from the malloc'd block to the standard output.

14.5.8 Overlapping source and destination blocks

The following C library functions copy some data from one memory block to another (or something similar): memcpy(), strcpy(), strncpy(), strcat(), strncat(). The blocks pointed to by their src and dst pointers aren't allowed to overlap. Memcheck checks for this.

For example:

```
==27492== Source and destination overlap in memcpy(0xbffff294, 0xbffff280, 21)
==27492== at 0x40026CDC: memcpy (mc_replace_strmem.c:71)
==27492== by 0x804865A: main (overlap.c:40)
==27492== by 0x40246335: __libc_start_main (../sysdeps/generic/libc-start.c:129)
==27492== by 0x8048470:
                (within /auto/homes/njn25/grind/head6/memcheck/tests/overlap)
==27492==
```

We don't want the two blocks to overlap because one of them could get partially trashed by the copying.

14.5.9 Writing suppressions files

The basic suppression format was described in this section.

The suppression (2nd) line should have the form:

Memcheck:suppression_type

Or, since some of the suppressions are shared with Addrcheck:

Memcheck, Addrcheck:suppression_type

The Memcheck suppression types are as follows: Value1, Value2, Value4, Value8, Value16, meaning an uninitialised-value error when using a value of 1, 2, 4, 8 or 16 bytes. Or Cond (or its old name, Value0), meaning use of an uninitialised CPU condition code. Or: Addr1, Addr2, Addr4, Addr8, Addr16, meaning an invalid address during a memory access of 1, 2, 4, 8 or 16 bytes respectively. Or Param, meaning an invalid system call parameter error. Or Free, meaning an invalid or mismatching free. Overlap, meaning a src/dst overlap in memcpy() or a similar function. Last but not least, you can suppress leak reports with Leak. Leak suppression was added in valgrind-1.9.3, I believe.

The extra information line: for Param errors, is the name of the offending system call parameter. No other error kinds have this extra line.

The first line of the calling context: for Value and Addr errors, it is either the name of the function in which the error occurred, or, failing that, the full path of the .so file or executable containing the error location. For Free errors, is the name of the function doing the freeing (eg, free, __builtin_vec_delete, etc). For Overlap errors, is the name of the function with the overlapping arguments (eg. memcpy(), strcpy(), etc).

Lastly, there's the rest of the calling context.

14.5.10 Details of Memcheck's checking machinery

Read this section if we want to know, in detail, exactly what and how Memcheck is checking.

Valid-value (V) bits

It is simplest to think of Memcheck implementing a synthetic Intel x86 CPU which is identical to a real CPU, except for one crucial detail. Every bit (literally) of data processed, stored and handled by the real CPU has, in the synthetic CPU, an associated "valid-value" bit, which says whether or not the accompanying bit has a legitimate value. In the discussions which follow, this bit is referred to as the V (valid-value) bit.

Each byte in the system therefore has a 8 V bits which follow it wherever it goes. For example, when the CPU loads a word-size item (4 bytes) from memory, it also loads the corresponding 32 V bits from a bitmap which stores the V bits for the process' entire address space. If the CPU should later write the whole or some part of that value to memory at a different address, the relevant V bits will be stored back in the V-bit bitmap.

In short, each bit in the system has an associated V bit, which follows it around everywhere, even inside the CPU. Yes, the CPU's (integer and %eflags) registers have their own V bit vectors.

Copying values around does not cause Memcheck to check for, or report on, errors. However, when a value is used in a way which might conceivably affect the outcome of your program's computation, the associated V bits are immediately checked. If any of these indicate that the value is undefined, an error is reported.

Here's an (admittedly nonsensical) example:

```
int i, j;
int a[10], b[10];
for (i = 0; i < 10; i++) {
  j = a[i];
  b[i] = j;
}
```

Memcheck emits no complaints about this, since it merely copies uninitialised values from a[] into b[], and doesn't use them in any way. However, if the loop is changed to

```
for (i = 0; i < 10; i++) {
  j += a[i];
}
if (j == 77)
   printf("hello there\n");
```

then Valgrind will complain, at the if, that the condition depends on uninitialised values. Note that it doesn't complain at the `j += a[i];`, since at that point the undefinedness is not "observable". It's only when a decision has to be made as to whether or not to do the printf -- an observable action of our program -- that Memcheck complains.

Most low level operations, such as adds, cause Memcheck to use the V bits for the operands to calculate the V bits for the result. Even if the result is partially or wholly undefined, it does not complain.

Checks on definedness only occur in two places: when a value is used to generate a memory address, and where control flow decision needs to be made. Also, when a system call is detected, valgrind checks definedness of parameters as required.

If a check should detect undefinedness, an error message is issued. The resulting value is subsequently regarded as well-defined. To do otherwise would give long chains of error messages. In effect, we say that undefined values are non-infectious.

This sounds overcomplicated. Why not just check all reads from memory, and complain if an undefined value is loaded into a CPU register? Well, that doesn't work well, because perfectly legitimate C programs routinely copy uninitialised values around in memory, and we don't want endless complaints about that. Here's the canonical example. Consider a struct like this:

```
struct S { int x; char c; };
struct S s1, s2;
s1.x = 42;
s1.c = 'z';
s2 = s1;
```

The question to ask is: how large is struct S, in bytes? An int is 4 bytes and a char one byte, so perhaps a struct S occupies 5 bytes? Wrong. All (non-toy) compilers we know of will round the size of struct S up to a whole number of words, in this case 8 bytes. Not doing this forces compilers to generate truly appalling code for subscripting arrays of struct S's.

So, s1 occupies 8 bytes, yet only 5 of them will be initialised. For the assignment s2 = s1, gcc generates code to copy all 8 bytes wholesale into s2 without regard for their meaning. If Memcheck simply checked values as they came out of memory, it would yelp every time a structure assignment like this happened. So the more complicated semantics described above is necessary. This allows gcc to copy s1 into s2 any way it likes, and a warning will only be emitted if the uninitialised values are later used.

One final twist to this story. The above scheme allows garbage to pass through the CPU's integer registers without complaint. It does this by giving the integer registers V tags, passing these around in the expected way. This complicated and computationally expensive to do, but is necessary. Memcheck is more simplistic about floating-point loads and stores. In particular, V bits for data read as a result of floating-point loads are checked at the load instruction. So if our program uses the floating-point registers to do memory-to-memory copies, we will get complaints about uninitialised values.

Valid-address (A) bits

Notice that the previous subsection describes how the validity of values is established and maintained without having to say whether the program does or does not have the right to access any particular memory location. We now consider the latter issue.

As described above, every bit in memory or in the CPU has an associated valid-value (V) bit. In addition, all bytes in memory, but not in the CPU, have an associated valid-address (A) bit. This indicates whether or not the program can legitimately read or write that location. It does not give any indication of the validity or the data at that location -- that's the job of the V bits -- only whether or not the location may be accessed.

Every time our program reads or writes memory, Memcheck checks the A bits associated with the address. If any of them indicate an invalid address, an error is emitted. Note that the reads and writes themselves do not change the A bits, only consult them.

So how do the A bits get set/cleared? Like this:

When the program starts, all the global data areas are marked as accessible.

When the program does malloc/new, the A bits for the exactly the area allocated, and not a byte more, are marked as accessible. Upon freeing the area the A bits are changed to indicate inaccessibility.

When the stack pointer register (%esp) moves up or down, A bits are set. The rule is that the area from %esp up to the base of the stack is marked as accessible, and below %esp is inaccessible. (If that sounds illogical, bear in mind that the stack grows down, not up, on almost all Unix systems, including GNU/Linux.) Tracking %esp like this has the useful side-effect that the section of stack used by a function for local variables etc is automatically marked accessible on function entry and inaccessible on exit.

When doing system calls, A bits are changed appropriately. For example, mmap() magically makes files appear in the process's address space, so the A bits must be updated if mmap() succeeds.

Optionally, our program can tell Valgrind about such changes explicitly, using the client request mechanism described above.

14.5.11 Putting it all together

Memcheck's checking machinery can be summarized as follows:

Each byte in memory has 8 associated V (valid-value) bits, saying whether or not the byte has a defined value, and a single A (valid-address) bit, saying whether or not the program currently has the right to read/write that address.

When memory is read or written, the relevant A bits are consulted. If they indicate an invalid address, Valgrind emits an Invalid read or Invalid write error.

When memory is read into the CPU's integer registers, the relevant V bits are fetched from memory and stored in the simulated CPU. They are not consulted.

When an integer register is written out to memory, the V bits for that register are written back to memory too.

When memory is read into the CPU's floating point registers, the relevant V bits are read from memory and they are immediately checked. If any are invalid, an uninitialised value error is emitted. This precludes using the floating-point registers to copy possibly-uninitialised memory, but simplifies Valgrind in that it does not have to track the validity status of the floating-point registers.

As a result, when a floating-point register is written to memory, the associated V bits are set to indicate a valid value.

When values in integer CPU registers are used to generate a memory address, or to determine the outcome of a conditional branch, the V bits for those values are checked, and an error emitted if any of them are undefined.

When values in integer CPU registers are used for any other purpose, Valgrind computes the V bits for the result, but does not check them.

One the V bits for a value in the CPU have been checked, they are then set to indicate validity. This avoids long chains of errors.

When values are loaded from memory, valgrind checks the A bits for that location and issues an illegal-address warning if needed. In that case, the V bits loaded are forced to indicate Valid, despite the location being invalid.

This apparently strange choice reduces the amount of confusing information presented to the user. It avoids the unpleasant phenomenon in which memory is read from a place which is both unaddressable and contains invalid values, and, as a result, we get not only an invalid-address (read/write) error, but also a potentially large set of uninitialised-value errors, one for every time the value is used.

There is a hazy boundary case to do with multi-byte loads from addresses which are partially valid and partially invalid. See details of the flag --partial-loads-ok for details.

Memcheck intercepts calls to malloc, calloc, realloc, valloc, memalign, free, new and delete. The behavior you get is:

malloc/new: the returned memory is marked as addressable but not having valid values. This means you have to write on it before you can read it.

calloc: returned memory is marked both addressable and valid, since calloc() clears the area to zero.

realloc: if the new size is larger than the old, the new section is addressable but invalid, as with malloc.

If the new size is smaller, the dropped-off section is marked as unaddressable. We may only pass to realloc a pointer previously issued to you by malloc/calloc/realloc.

free/delete: we may only pass to free a pointer previously issued to we by malloc/calloc/realloc, or the value NULL. Otherwise, Valgrind complains. If the pointer is indeed valid, Valgrind marks the entire area it points at as unaddressable, and places the block in the freed-blocks-queue. The aim is to defer as long as possible reallocation of this block. Until that happens, all attempts to access it will elicit an invalid-address error, as you would hope.

14.5.12 Memory leak detection

Memcheck keeps track of all memory blocks issued in response to calls to malloc/calloc/realloc/new. So when the program exits, it knows which blocks are still outstanding -- have not been returned, in other words. Ideally, we want your program to have no blocks still in use at exit. But many programs do.

For each such block, Memcheck scans the entire address space of the process, looking for pointers to the block. One of three situations may result:

A pointer to the start of the block is found. This usually indicates programming sloppiness; since the block is still pointed at, the programmer could, at least in principle, free'd it before program exit.

A pointer to the interior of the block is found. The pointer might originally have pointed to the start and have been moved along, or it might be entirely unrelated. Memcheck deems such a block as "dubious", that is, possibly leaked, because it's unclear whether or not a pointer to it still exists.

The worst outcome is that no pointer to the block can be found. The block is classified as "leaked", because the programmer could not possibly have free'd it at program exit, since no pointer to it exists. This might be a symptom of having lost the pointer at some earlier point in the program.

Memcheck reports summaries about leaked and dubious blocks. For each such block, it will also tell you where the block was allocated. This should help you figure out why the pointer to it has been lost. In general, we should attempt to ensure our programs do not have any leaked or dubious blocks at exit.

The precise area of memory in which Memcheck searches for pointers is: all naturally-aligned 4-byte words for which all A bits indicate addressability and all V bits indicated that the stored value is actually valid.

14.5.13 Client Requests

The following client requests are defined in memcheck.h. They also work for Addrcheck. See memcheck.h for exact details of their arguments.

VALGRIND_MAKE_NOACCESS, VALGRIND_MAKE_WRITABLE and VALGRIND _ MAKE _ READABLE. These mark address ranges as completely inaccessible, accessible but containing undefined data, and accessible and containing defined data, respectively. Subsequent errors may have their faulting addresses described in terms of these blocks. Returns a "block handle". Returns zero when not run on Valgrind.

VALGRIND_DISCARD: At some point we may want Valgrind to stop reporting errors in terms of the blocks defined by the previous three macros. To do this, the above macros return a small-integer "block handle". We can pass this block handle to VALGRIND_DISCARD. After doing so, Valgrind will no longer be able to relate addressing errors to the user-defined block associated with the handle. The permissions settings associated with the handle remain in place; this just affects how errors are reported, not whether they are reported. Returns 1 for an invalid handle and 0 for a valid handle (although passing invalid handles is harmless). Always returns 0 when not run on Valgrind.

VALGRIND_CHECK_WRITABLE and VALGRIND_CHECK_READABLE: check immediately whether or not the given address range has the relevant property, and if not, print an error message. Also, for the convenience of the client, returns zero if the relevant property holds; otherwise, the returned value is the address of the first byte for which the property is not true. Always returns 0 when not run on Valgrind.

VALGRIND_CHECK_DEFINED: a quick and easy way to find out whether Valgrind thinks a particular variable (lvalue, to be precise) is addressable and defined. Prints an error message if not. Returns no value.

VALGRIND_DO_LEAK_CHECK: run the memory leak detector right now. Returns no value.

VALGRIND_COUNT_LEAKS: fills in the four arguments with the number of bytes of memory found by the previous leak check to be leaked, dubious, reachable and suppressed. Again, useful in test harness code, after calling VALGRIND_DO_LEAK_CHECK.

VALGRIND_GET_VBITS and VALGRIND_SET_VBITS: allow us to get and set the V (validity) bits for an address range. We should probably only set V bits that we have got with VALGRIND_GET_VBITS. Only for those who really know what they are doing.

Example 2

```
#include <stdlib.h>
char *alloc_two ()
{
      char *tmp = malloc(1024*10);
      return malloc(1024*20);
}
char *alloc_one ()
{
      return malloc (1024);
}
int
main ()
{
      char *mem1 = alloc_two ();
      char *mem2 = alloc_one ();
      free (mem1);
      return 0;
}
```

gcc -g a0.c
valgrind --tool=memcheck --leak-check=yes a.out

```
==4795== ERROR SUMMARY: 0 errors from 0 contexts (suppressed: 13 from 1)
==4795== malloc/free: in use at exit: 11264 bytes in 2 blocks.
==4795== malloc/free: 3 allocs, 1 frees, 31744 bytes allocated.
==4795==
==4795== 1024 bytes in 1 blocks are definitely lost in loss record 1 of 2
==4795== by 0x80483E5: alloc_one (a0.c:10)
==4795== by 0x8048413: main (a0.c:16)
==4795==
==4795==
==4795==10240 bytes in 1 blocks are definitely lost in loss record 2 of 2
==4795== by 0x80483BA: alloc_two (a0.c:4)
==4795== by 0x804840B: main (a0.c:15)
==4795==
==4795== LEAK SUMMARY:
==4795== definitely lost: 11264 bytes in 2 blocks.
==4795== possibly lost:   0 bytes in 0 blocks.
==4795== still reachable: 0 bytes in 0 blocks.
==4795== suppressed: 0 bytes in 0 blocks.
==4795==Reachable blocks (those to which a pointer was found) are not shown.
```

The output shows that some memory which is allocated but not freed. Incidentally, if we check the source, we can find that the memory pointed by mem2 is not freed. Thus, we are getting this error.

Example 3

```
#include <stdlib.h>
#include <stdio.h>

int main(void)
{
  char *ptr1;
  char *ptr2;

  ptr1 = malloc(512);
  ptr2 = malloc(512);

  ptr2 = ptr1;
  free(ptr2);
   ptr1[0]='A'; ptr1[1]='\0';
}
```

gcc -g a10.c

valgrind --tool=memcheck --leak-check=yes a.out 2>>result

```
==4811== Invalid write of size 1
==4811== at 0x8048401: main (a10.c:16)
==4811== Address 0x1B92B028 is 0 bytes inside a block of size 512 free'd
==4811== at 0x1B904FB1: free (vg_replace_malloc.c:153)
==4811== by 0x80483FA: main (a10.c:15)
==4811==
==4811==Invalid write of size 1
==4811== at 0x8048408: main (a10.c:16)
==4811== Address 0x1B92B029 is 1 bytes inside a block of size 512 free'd
==4811== at 0x1B904FB1: free (vg_replace_malloc.c:153)
==4811== by 0x80483FA: main (a10.c:15)
==4811==
==4811== ERROR SUMMARY: 2 errors from 2 contexts (suppressed: 13 from 1)
==4811== malloc/free: in use at exit: 512 bytes in 1 blocks.
==4811== malloc/free: 2 allocs, 1 frees, 1024 bytes allocated.
==4811== 512 bytes in 1 blocks are definitely lost in loss record 1 of 1
```

```
==4811==  at 0x1B904A90: malloc (vg_replace_malloc.c:131)
==4811==  by 0x80483E3: main (a10.c:12)
==4811==
==4811==  LEAK SUMMARY:
==4811==definitely lost: 512 bytes in 1 blocks.
==4811== possibly lost:   0 bytes in 0 blocks.
==4811== still reachable: 0 bytes in 0 blocks.
==4811== suppressed: 0 bytes in 0 blocks.
==4811== Reachable blocks (those to which a pointer was found) are not shown.
==4811== To see them, rerun with: --show-reachable=yes
```

In this example also, the output shows that some memory which is allocated but not freed. Also, we are getting an error message indicating invalid write. This is acceptable as in our program really we are trying access 0'th and 1'st element after freeing the array pointed by ptr1 pointer.

```
gcc -g a10.c  -lefence
valgrind --tool=memcheck --leak-check=yes a.out 2>>result
```

```
Electric Fence 2.2.0 Copyright (C) 1987-1999 Bruce Perens <bruce@perens.com>
==4818== Invalid write of size 1
==4818== at 0x80484ED: main (a10.c:16)
==4818== Address 0x1B931E00 is not stack'd, malloc'd or (recently) free'd
==4818==
==4818== Process terminating with default action of signal 11 (SIGSEGV)
==4818== Bad permissions for mapped region at address 0x1B931E00
==4818== at 0x80484ED: main (a10.c:16)
==4818==
==4818== ERROR SUMMARY: 1 errors from 1 contexts (suppressed: 15 from 1)
==4818== malloc/free: in use at exit: 0 bytes in 0 blocks.
==4818== malloc/free: 0 allocs, 0 frees, 0 bytes allocated.
==4818== For counts of detected errors, rerun with: -v
==4818== No malloc'd blocks -- no leaks are possible.
```

From the above output, we can observe that when we compile the program after linking Electric Fence library and run valgrind, the same write operation is giving Segment violation error.

Example 4

```
#include<stdio.h>

int main()
{
 char *a,*b;

free(a);
 b=(char*) malloc(10);

free(b);

}
```

gcc -g a1a.c

valgrind --tool=memcheck --leak-check=yes a.out 2>>result

```
==4827==Conditional jump or move depends on uninitialised value(s)
==4827==  at 0x1B904F62: free (vg_replace_malloc.c:153)
==4827==  by 0x80483CE: main (a1a.c:7)
==4827==
==4827==Invalid free() / delete / delete[]
==4827== at 0x1B904FB1: free (vg_replace_malloc.c:153)
==4827== by 0x80483CE: main (a1a.c:7)
==4827== Address 0x1B8F9C80 is not stack'd, malloc'd or (recently) free'd
==4827==
==4827== ERROR SUMMARY: 2 errors from 2 contexts (suppressed: 13 from 1)
==4827== malloc/free: in use at exit: 0 bytes in 0 blocks.
==4827== malloc/free: 1 allocs, 2 frees, 10 bytes allocated.
==4827== For counts of detected errors, rerun with: -v
==4827== No malloc'd blocks -- no leaks are possible.
```

gcc -g a1a.c -lefence

valgrind --tool=memcheck --leak-check=yes a.out 2>>result

```
==4834== Conditional jump or move depends on uninitialised value(s)
==4834== at 0x1B92A2DC: free (in /usr/lib/libefence.so.0.0)
==4834== by 0x80484BA: main (a1a.c:7)
```

ElectricFence Aborting: free() called before first malloc().

--4834-- adding signal 4 to pending set

==4834==

==4834== ERROR SUMMARY: 1 errors from 1 contexts (suppressed: 15 from 1)

==4834== malloc/free: in use at exit: 0 bytes in 0 blocks.

==4834== malloc/free: 0 allocs, 0 frees, 0 bytes allocated.

==4834== For counts of detected errors, rerun with: -v

==4834== No malloc'd blocks -- no leaks are possible.

In this example, we are trying to free memory which is not at all allocated. That is, the value of pointer variable "a" is not initialised and still used in free. Thus, we are getting error message use of uninitialised variable. The same results is observed when thee program is linked with Electric Fence library.

Example 5

```
#include<stdio.h>

int main()
{
int X;

scanf("%d", X);

free(&X);

return 0;
}
```

gcc -g a1.c

valgrind --tool=memcheck --leak-check=yes a.out 2>>result

==4844==Use of uninitialised value of size 4

==4844== at 0x530F4F: _IO_vfscanf_internal (in /lib/tls/libc-2.3.3.so)

==4844== by 0x537305: scanf (in /lib/tls/libc-2.3.3.so)

==4844== by 0x80483CF: main (a1.c:7)

==4844==

==4844==Process terminating with default action of signal 11 (SIGSEGV)

==4844== Bad permissions for mapped region at address 0x1B8F9C80

```
==4844== at 0x530F4F: _IO_vfscanf_internal (in /lib/tls/libc-2.3.3.so)
==4844== by 0x537305: scanf (in /lib/tls/libc-2.3.3.so)
==4844== by 0x80483CF: main (a1.c:7)
==4844==
==4844== ERROR SUMMARY: 1 errors from 1 contexts (suppressed: 13 from 1)
==4844== malloc/free: in use at exit: 0 bytes in 0 blocks.
==4844== malloc/free: 0 allocs, 0 frees, 0 bytes allocated.
==4844== For counts of detected errors, rerun with: -v
==4844== No malloc'd blocks -- no leaks are possible.
```

In this example also, our program is trying to use un-initialised variable and also it is trying to access memory referred by it. Thus, we are getting the above errors.

Example 6

```
#include<stdio.h>

int main()
{
 char *b=(char *) malloc(17);

 b[19]='A';

}
```

gcc -g a1d.c

valgrind --tool=memcheck --leak-check=yes a.out 2>>result

```
==4860== Invalid write of size 1
==4860==  at 0x80483A6: main (a1d.c:7)
==4860== Address 0x1B92B03B is 2 bytes after a block of size 17 alloc'd
==4860==   at 0x1B904A90: malloc (vg_replace_malloc.c:131)
==4860==   by 0x8048399: main (a1d.c:5)
==4860==
==4860==   ERROR SUMMARY: 1 errors from 1 contexts (suppressed: 13 from 1)
==4860==   malloc/free: in use at exit: 17 bytes in 1 blocks.
==4860==   malloc/free: 1 allocs, 0 frees, 17 bytes allocated.
==4860==   For counts of detected errors, rerun with: -v
==4860==   searching for pointers to 1 not-freed blocks.
==4860==   checked 1500576 bytes.
```

```
==4860==
==4860==
==4860==  17 bytes in 1 blocks are definitely lost in loss record 1 of 1
==4860==  at 0x1B904A90: malloc (vg_replace_malloc.c:131)
==4860==  by 0x8048399: main (a1d.c:5)
==4860==
==4860==  LEAK SUMMARY:
==4860==  definitely lost: 17 bytes in 1 blocks.
==4860==  possibly lost:   0 bytes in 0 blocks.
==4860==  still reachable: 0 bytes in 0 blocks.
==4860==  suppressed: 0 bytes in 0 blocks.
==4860==  Reachable blocks (those to which a pointer was found) are not shown.
==4860==  To see them, rerun with: --show-reachable=yes
```

Example 7

```
#include <stdio.h>
#include <string.h>

int main(void)
{
  char *foo;
  foo = (char *) malloc(10);
  strcpy(foo,"hello");
  foo--;
  /* printf access before allocated area */
  printf("%s\n",foo);
  free(foo);
  return(0);
}
```

gcc -g a2.c
valgrind --tool=memcheck --leak-check=yes a.out 2>>result

```
==4876== Invalid read of size 1
==4876==  at 0x54ED7B: strlen (in /lib/tls/libc-2.3.3.so)
==4876==  by 0x52968F: _IO_printf (in /lib/tls/libc-2.3.3.so)
==4876==  by 0x8048463: main (a2.c:11)
==4876==  Address 0x1B92B027 is 1 bytes before a block of size 10 alloc'd
==4876==  at 0x1B904A90: malloc (vg_replace_malloc.c:131)
==4876==  by 0x8048435: main (a2.c:7)
==4876==
```

```
==4876== Invalid free() / delete / delete[]
==4876==  at 0x1B904FB1: free (vg_replace_malloc.c:153)
==4876==  by 0x8048471: main (a2.c:12)
==4876==  Address 0x1B92B027 is 1 bytes before a block of size 10 alloc'd
==4876==  at 0x1B904A90: malloc (vg_replace_malloc.c:131)
==4876==  by 0x8048435: main (a2.c:7)
==4876==
==4876==  ERROR SUMMARY: 2 errors from 2 contexts (suppressed: 13 from 1)
==4876== malloc/free: in use at exit: 10 bytes in 1 blocks.
==4876== malloc/free: 1 allocs, 1 frees, 10 bytes allocated.
==4876== For counts of detected errors, rerun with: -v
==4876== searching for pointers to 1 not-freed blocks.
==4876== checked 1500580 bytes.
==4876==
==4876==
==4876== 10 bytes in 1 blocks are definitely lost in loss record 1 of 1
==4876== at 0x1B904A90: malloc (vg_replace_malloc.c:131)
==4876== by 0x8048435: main (a2.c:7)
==4876==
==4876== LEAK SUMMARY:
==4876== definitely lost: 10 bytes in 1 blocks.
==4876== possibly lost:   0 bytes in 0 blocks.
==4876== still reachable: 0 bytes in 0 blocks.
==4876== suppressed: 0 bytes in 0 blocks.
==4876== Reachable blocks (those to which a pointer was found) are not shown.
==4876== To see them, rerun with: --show-reachable=yes
```

gcc -g a2.c -lefence

valgrind --tool=memcheck --leak-check=yes a.out 2>>result

```
Electric Fence 2.2.0 Copyright (C) 1987-1999 Bruce Perens <bruce@perens.com>
ElectricFence Aborting: free(1b931ff3): address not from malloc().
```

```
--4883-- adding signal 4 to pending set
==4883==
==4883== ERROR SUMMARY: 0 errors from 0 contexts (suppressed: 15 from 1)
==4883== malloc/free: in use at exit: 0 bytes in 0 blocks.
==4883== malloc/free: 0 allocs, 0 frees, 0 bytes allocated.
==4883== For counts of detected errors, rerun with: -v
==4883== No malloc'd blocks -- no leaks are possible.
```

The above error results of valgrind shows that the given program is having the following errors.

1. Memory which is not allocated is being read.
2. Memory which is not allocated is beeing freed.
3. Memory before a dynamically allocated memory is beeing accessed.

Example 8

```
#include <stdio.h>
#include <string.h>

int main(void)
{
  char *foo;
  foo = (char *) malloc(10);
  foo--;
  /* strcpy access before allocated area */
  strcpy(foo,"123456789");
  printf("%s\n",foo);
  free(foo);
  return(0);
}
```

gcc -g a4a.c
valgrind --tool=memcheck --leak-check=yes a.out 2>>result

```
==4893== Invalid write of size 1
==4893==  at 0x1B904434: strcpy (mac_replace_strmem.c:198)
==4893==  by 0x8048450: main (a4a.c:10)
==4893== Address 0x1B92B027 is 1 bytes before a block of size 10 alloc'd
==4893==  at 0x1B904A90: malloc (vg_replace_malloc.c:131)
==4893==  by 0x8048435: main (a4a.c:7)
==4893==
==4893==  Invalid read of size 1
==4893==  at 0x54ED7B: strlen (in /lib/tls/libc-2.3.3.so)
==4893==  by 0x52968F: _IO_printf (in /lib/tls/libc-2.3.3.so)
==4893==  by 0x8048463: main (a4a.c:11)
==4893==  Address 0x1B92B027 is 1 bytes before a block of size 10 alloc'd
==4893==  at 0x1B904A90: malloc (vg_replace_malloc.c:131)
==4893==  by 0x8048435: main (a4a.c:7)
==4893==
==4893==  Invalid read of size 1
```

```
==4893==  at 0x545821: _IO_default_xsputn_internal (in /lib/tls/libc 2.3.3.so)
==4893==  by 0x5447D8: _IO_file_xsputn@@GLIBC_2.1 (in /lib/tls/libc 2.3.3.so)
==4893==  by 0x52452B: _IO_vfprintf_internal (in /lib/tls/libc-2.3.3.so)
==4893==  by 0x52968F: _IO_printf (in /lib/tls/libc-2.3.3.so)
==4893==  Address 0x1B92B027 is 1 bytes before a block of size 10 alloc'd
==4893==  at 0x1B904A90: malloc (vg_replace_malloc.c:131)
==4893==  by 0x8048435: main (a4a.c:7)
==4893==
==4893==  Invalid free() / delete / delete[]
==4893==  at 0x1B904FB1: free (vg_replace_malloc.c:153)
==4893==  by 0x8048471: main (a4a.c:12)
==4893==  Address 0x1B92B027 is 1 bytes before a block of size 10 alloc'd
==4893==  at 0x1B904A90: malloc (vg_replace_malloc.c:131)
==4893==  by 0x8048435: main (a4a.c:7)
==4893==
==4893==  ERROR SUMMARY: 4 errors from 4 contexts (suppressed: 13 from 1)
==4893==  malloc/free: in use at exit: 10 bytes in 1 blocks.
==4893==  malloc/free: 1 allocs, 1 frees, 10 bytes allocated.
==4893==  For counts of detected errors, rerun with: -v
==4893==  searching for pointers to 1 not-freed blocks.
==4893==  checked 1500584 bytes.
==4893==
==4893==
==4893==  10 bytes in 1 blocks are definitely lost in loss record 1 of 1
==4893==   at 0x1B904A90: malloc (vg_replace_malloc.c:131)
==4893==   by 0x8048435: main (a4a.c:7)
==4893==
==4893==   LEAK SUMMARY:
==4893==   definitely lost: 10 bytes in 1 blocks.
==4893==   possibly lost:   0 bytes in 0 blocks.
==4893==   still reachable: 0 bytes in 0 blocks.
==4893==   suppressed: 0 bytes in 0 blocks.
==4893==   Reachable blocks (those to which a pointer was found) are not shown.
==4893==   To see them, rerun with: --show-reachable=yes
```

gcc -g a4a.c -lefence
valgrind --tool=memcheck --leak-check=yes a.out 2>>result

```
Electric Fence 2.2.0 Copyright (C) 1987-1999 Bruce Perens <bruce@perens.com>
ElectricFence Aborting: free(1b931ff3): address not from malloc().
```

--4900-- adding signal 4 to pending set

Example 9

```
#include<stdio.h>
#include<string.h>
char * CHR(int n)
{
return ((char*) malloc(n));
}

int main()
{
char *X;

X=(char *) malloc(10);
strcpy(X,"rama");
printf("%s\n", X);
free(X);
printf("%s\n", X);
return 0;
}
```

gcc -g a4.c
valgrind --tool=memcheck --leak-check=yes a.out

```
==4910==  Invalid read of size 4
==4910==  at 0x54EDA3: strlen (in /lib/tls/libc-2.3.3.so)
==4910==  by 0x52968F: _IO_printf (in /lib/tls/libc-2.3.3.so)
==4910==  by 0x8048495: main (a4.c:16)
==4910==  Address 0x1B92B028 is 0 bytes inside a block of size 10 free'd
==4910==  at 0x1B904FB1: free (vg_replace_malloc.c:153)
==4910==  by 0x8048482: main (a4.c:15)
==4910==
==4910==  Invalid read of size 4
==4910==  at 0x54EDB9: strlen (in /lib/tls/libc-2.3.3.so)
==4910==  by 0x52968F: _IO_printf (in /lib/tls/libc-2.3.3.so)
==4910==  by 0x8048495: main (a4.c:16)
==4910==  Address 0x1B92B02C is 4 bytes inside a block of size 10 free'd
==4910==  at 0x1B904FB1: free (vg_replace_malloc.c:153)
==4910==  by 0x8048482: main (a4.c:15)
==4910==
```

```
==4910==    Invalid read of size 1
==4910==    at 0x544826: _IO_file_xsputn@@GLIBC_2.1 (in /lib/tls/libc 2.3.3.so)
==4910==    by 0x52452B: _IO_vfprintf_internal (in /lib/tls/libc-2.3.3.so)
==4910==    by 0x52968F: _IO_printf (in /lib/tls/libc-2.3.3.so)
==4910==    by 0x8048495: main (a4.c:16)
==4910==    Address 0x1B92B02B is 3 bytes inside a block of size 10 free'd
==4910==    at 0x1B904FB1: free (vg_replace_malloc.c:153)
==4910==    by 0x8048482: main (a4.c:15)
==4910==
==4910==    Invalid read of size 1
==4910==    at 0x544660: _IO_file_xsputn@@GLIBC_2.1 (in /lib/tls/libc 2.3.3.so)
==4910==    by 0x52452B: _IO_vfprintf_internal (in /lib/tls/libc-2.3.3.so)
==4910==    by 0x52968F: _IO_printf (in /lib/tls/libc-2.3.3.so)
==4910==    by 0x8048495: main (a4.c:16)
==4910==    Address 0x1B92B028 is 0 bytes inside a block of size 10 free'd
==4910==    at 0x1B904FB1: free (vg_replace_malloc.c:153)
==4910==    by 0x8048482: main (a4.c:15)
==4910==
==4910==    ERROR SUMMARY: 10 errors from 4 contexts (suppressed: 13 from 1)
==4910==    malloc/free: in use at exit: 0 bytes in 0 blocks.
==4910==    malloc/free: 1 allocs, 1 frees, 10 bytes allocated.
==4910==    For counts of detected errors, rerun with: -v
==4910==    No malloc'd blocks -- no leaks are possible.
```

gcc -g a4.c -lefence
valgrind --tool=memcheck --leak-check=yes a.out

```
Electric Fence 2.2.0 Copyright (C) 1987-1999 Bruce Perens <bruce@perens.com>
==4917==    Invalid read of size 4
==4917==    at 0x54EDA3: strlen (in /lib/tls/libc-2.3.3.so)
==4917==    by 0x52968F: _IO_printf (in /lib/tls/libc-2.3.3.so)
==4917==    by 0x8048581: main (a4.c:16)
==4917==    Address 0x1B931FF4 is not stack'd, malloc'd or (recently) free'd
==4917==
==4917==    Process terminating with default action of signal 11 (SIGSEGV)
==4917==    Bad permissions for mapped region at address 0x1B931FF4
==4917==    at 0x54EDA3: strlen (in /lib/tls/libc-2.3.3.so)
==4917==    by 0x52968F: _IO_printf (in /lib/tls/libc-2.3.3.so)
==4917==    by 0x8048581: main (a4.c:16)
==4917==
==4917==    ERROR SUMMARY: 1 errors from 1 contexts (suppressed: 15 from 1)
==4917==    malloc/free: in use at exit: 0 bytes in 0 blocks.
==4917==    malloc/free: 0 allocs, 0 frees, 0 bytes allocated.
==4917==    For counts of detected errors, rerun with: -v
==4917==    No malloc'd blocks -- no leaks are possible.
```

Example 10

```
#include <stdio.h>
int main(void)
{
  char *ptr = NULL;
  *ptr = 10;
  return(0);
}
```

gcc -g a5a.c
valgrind --tool=memcheck --leak-check=yes a.out

```
==4926== Invalid write of size 1
==4926==  at 0x8048366: main (a5a.c:5)
==4926==  Address 0x0 is not stack'd, malloc'd or (recently) free'd
==4926==
==4926== Process terminating with default action of signal 11 (SIGSEGV)
==4926==  Access not within mapped region at address 0x0
==4926==  at 0x8048366: main (a5a.c:5)
==4926==
==4926==  ERROR SUMMARY: 1 errors from 1 contexts (suppressed: 13 from 1)
==4926==  malloc/free: in use at exit: 0 bytes in 0 blocks.
==4926==  malloc/free: 0 allocs, 0 frees, 0 bytes allocated.
==4926==  For counts of detected errors, rerun with: -v
==4926==  No malloc'd blocks -- no leaks are possible.
```

gcc -g a5a.c -lefence
valgrind --tool=memcheck --leak-check=yes a.out

```
==4933==  Invalid write of size 1
==4933==  at 0x8048452: main (a5a.c:5)
==4933==  Address 0x0 is not stack'd, malloc'd or (recently) free'd
==4933==
==4933==  Process terminating with default action of signal 11 (SIGSEGV)
==4933==  Access not within mapped region at address 0x0
==4933==  at 0x8048452: main (a5a.c:5)
==4933==
==4933==  ERROR SUMMARY: 1 errors from 1 contexts (suppressed: 15 from 1)
==4933==  malloc/free: in use at exit: 0 bytes in 0 blocks.
==4933==  malloc/free: 0 allocs, 0 frees, 0 bytes allocated.
==4933==  For counts of detected errors, rerun with: -v
==4933==  No malloc'd blocks -- no leaks are possible.
```

Example 11

```
#include <stdlib.h>
#include <stdio.h>
int
main (int argc, char **argv)
{
        char    *msg = malloc (4);
         // Allocate 4 bytes
        strcpy (msg, "hello Linux users");
         // Overflow the allocated memory
        printf ("%s\n", msg);
        free (msg);
         // Free the allocated memory
        strcpy (msg, "hello again");
         // Write to freed memory
        printf ("%s\n", msg);
        free (msg);
         // Free the freed memory
        realloc (msg, 2);
         // Reallocate freed memory
        strcpy (msg, "hello there");
         // Writing to erroneous memory
        printf ("%s\n", msg);
        return 0;
}
```

gcc -g a7a.c
valgrind --tool=memcheck --leak-check=yes a.out

```
==4942==  Invalid write of size 1
==4942==  at 0x1B904434: strcpy (mac_replace_strmem.c:198)
==4942==  by 0x8048483: main (a7a.c:8)
==4942==  Address 0x1B92B02C is 0 bytes after a block of size 4 alloc'd
==4942==  at 0x1B904A90: malloc (vg_replace_malloc.c:131)
==4942==  by 0x804846D: main (a7a.c:6)
==4942==
==4942==  Invalid write of size 1
```

```
==4942==  at 0x1B904440: strcpy (mac_replace_strmem.c:199)
==4942==  by 0x8048483: main (a7a.c:8)
==4942==  Address 0x1B92B039 is 13 bytes after a block of size 4 alloc'd
==4942==  at 0x1B904A90: malloc (vg_replace_malloc.c:131)
==4942==  by 0x804846D: main (a7a.c:6)
==4942==
==4942==  Invalid read of size 4
==4942==  at 0x54EDB9: strlen (in /lib/tls/libc-2.3.3.so)
==4942==  by 0x52968F: _IO_printf (in /lib/tls/libc-2.3.3.so)
==4942==  by 0x8048496: main (a7a.c:10)
==4942==  Address 0x1B92B02C is 0 bytes after a block of size 4 alloc'd
==4942==  at 0x1B904A90: malloc (vg_replace_malloc.c:131)
==4942==  by 0x804846D: main (a7a.c:6)
==4942==
==4942==  Invalid read of size 4
==4942==  at 0x54EDD0: strlen (in /lib/tls/libc-2.3.3.so)
==4942==  by 0x52968F: _IO_printf (in /lib/tls/libc-2.3.3.so)
==4942==  by 0x8048496: main (a7a.c:10)
==4942==  Address 0x1B92B030 is 4 bytes after a block of size 4 alloc'd
==4942==  at 0x1B904A90: malloc (vg_replace_malloc.c:131)
==4942==  by 0x804846D: main (a7a.c:6)
==4942==
==4942==  Invalid read of size 4
==4942==  at 0x54EDE7: strlen (in /lib/tls/libc-2.3.3.so)
==4942==  by 0x52968F: _IO_printf (in /lib/tls/libc-2.3.3.so)
==4942==  by 0x8048496: main (a7a.c:10)
==4942==  Address 0x1B92B034 is 8 bytes after a block of size 4 alloc'd
==4942==  at 0x1B904A90: malloc (vg_replace_malloc.c:131)
==4942==  by 0x804846D: main (a7a.c:6)
==4942==
==4942==  Invalid read of size 4
==4942==  at 0x54EDA3: strlen (in /lib/tls/libc-2.3.3.so)
==4942==  by 0x52968F: _IO_printf (in /lib/tls/libc-2.3.3.so)
==4942==  by 0x8048496: main (a7a.c:10)
==4942==  Address 0x1B92B038 is 12 bytes after a block of size 4 alloc'd
==4942==  at 0x1B904A90: malloc (vg_replace_malloc.c:131)
==4942==  by 0x804846D: main (a7a.c:6)
==4942==
==4942==  Invalid read of size 1
==4942==  at 0x545821: _IO_default_xsputn_internal (in /lib/tls/libc-2.3.3.so)
==4942==  by 0x5447D8: _IO_file_xsputn@@GLIBC_2.1 (in /lib/tls/libc-2.3.3.so)
```

```
==4942==  by 0x52452B: _IO_vfprintf_internal (in /lib/tls/libc-2.3.3.so)
==4942==  by 0x52968F: _IO_printf (in /lib/tls/libc-2.3.3.so)
==4942==  Address 0x1B92B02C is 0 bytes after a block of size 4 alloc'd
==4942==  at 0x1B904A90: malloc (vg_replace_malloc.c:131)
==4942==  by 0x804846D: main (a7a.c:6)
==4942==
==4942==  Invalid write of size 1
==4942==  at 0x1B904434: strcpy (mac_replace_strmem.c:198)
==4942==  by 0x80484B7: main (a7a.c:13)
==4942==  Address 0x1B92B028 is 0 bytes inside a block of size 4 free'd
==4942==  at 0x1B904FB1: free (vg_replace_malloc.c:153)
==4942==  by 0x80484A4: main (a7a.c:11)
==4942==
==4942==  Invalid write of size 1
==4942==  at 0x1B904440: strcpy (mac_replace_strmem.c:199)
==4942==  by 0x80484B7: main (a7a.c:13)
==4942==  Address 0x1B92B033 is 7 bytes after a block of size 4 free'd
==4942==  at 0x1B904FB1: free (vg_replace_malloc.c:153)
==4942==  by 0x80484A4: main (a7a.c:11)
==4942==
==4942==  Invalid read of size 4
==4942==  at 0x54EDA3: strlen (in /lib/tls/libc-2.3.3.so)
==4942==  by 0x52968F: _IO_printf (in /lib/tls/libc-2.3.3.so)
==4942==  by 0x80484CA: main (a7a.c:15)
==4942==  Address 0x1B92B028 is 0 bytes inside a block of size 4 free'd
==4942==  at 0x1B904FB1: free (vg_replace_malloc.c:153)
==4942==  by 0x80484A4: main (a7a.c:11)
==4942==
==4942==  Invalid read of size 4
==4942==  at 0x54EDB9: strlen (in /lib/tls/libc-2.3.3.so)
==4942==  by 0x52968F: _IO_printf (in /lib/tls/libc-2.3.3.so)
==4942==  by 0x80484CA: main (a7a.c:15)
==4942==  Address 0x1B92B02C is 0 bytes after a block of size 4 free'd
==4942==  at 0x1B904FB1: free (vg_replace_malloc.c:153)
==4942==  by 0x80484A4: main (a7a.c:11)
==4942==
==4942==  Invalid read of size 4
==4942==  at 0x54EDD0: strlen (in /lib/tls/libc-2.3.3.so)
==4942==  by 0x52968F: _IO_printf (in /lib/tls/libc-2.3.3.so)
==4942==  by 0x80484CA: main (a7a.c:15)
==4942==  Address 0x1B92B030 is 4 bytes after a block of size 4 free'd
```

```
==4942==    at 0x1B904FB1: free (vg_replace_malloc.c:153)
==4942==    by 0x80484A4: main (a7a.c:11)
==4942==
==4942== Invalid read of size 1
==4942==    at 0x544826: _IO_file_xsputn@@GLIBC_2.1 (in /lib/tls/libc-2.3.3.so)
==4942==    by 0x52452B: _IO_vfprintf_internal (in /lib/tls/libc-2.3.3.so)
==4942==    by 0x52968F: _IO_printf (in /lib/tls/libc-2.3.3.so)
==4942==    by 0x80484CA: main (a7a.c:15)
==4942==  Address 0x1B92B032 is 6 bytes after a block of size 4 free'd
==4942==    at 0x1B904FB1: free (vg_replace_malloc.c:153)
==4942==    by 0x80484A4: main (a7a.c:11)
==4942==
==4942== Invalid read of size 1
==4942==    at 0x544660: _IO_file_xsputn@@GLIBC_2.1 (in /lib/tls/libc-2.3.3.so)
==4942==    by 0x52452B: _IO_vfprintf_internal (in /lib/tls/libc-2.3.3.so)
==4942==    by 0x52968F: _IO_printf (in /lib/tls/libc-2.3.3.so)
==4942==    by 0x80484CA: main (a7a.c:15)
==4942==  Address 0x1B92B028 is 0 bytes inside a block of size 4 free'd
==4942==    at 0x1B904FB1: free (vg_replace_malloc.c:153)
==4942==    by 0x80484A4: main (a7a.c:11)
==4942==
==4942== Invalid free() / delete / delete[]
==4942==    at 0x1B904FB1: free (vg_replace_malloc.c:153)
==4942==    by 0x80484D8: main (a7a.c:16)
==4942==  Address 0x1B92B028 is 0 bytes inside a block of size 4 free'd
==4942==    at 0x1B904FB1: free (vg_replace_malloc.c:153)
==4942==    by 0x80484A4: main (a7a.c:11)
==4942==
==4942== Invalid free() / delete / delete[]
==4942==    at 0x1B9054FA: realloc (vg_replace_malloc.c:197)
==4942==    by 0x80484E8: main (a7a.c:18)
==4942==  Address 0x1B92B028 is 0 bytes inside a block of size 4 free'd
==4942==    at 0x1B904FB1: free (vg_replace_malloc.c:153)
==4942==    by 0x80484A4: main (a7a.c:11)
==4942==
==4942== Invalid write of size 1
==4942==    at 0x1B904434: strcpy (mac_replace_strmem.c:198)
==4942==    by 0x80484FB: main (a7a.c:20)
```

```
==4942==  Address 0x1B92B028 is 0 bytes inside a block of size 4 free'd
==4942==  at 0x1B904FB1: free (vg_replace_malloc.c:153)
==4942==  by 0x80484A4: main (a7a.c:11)
==4942==
==4942==  Invalid write of size 1
==4942==  at 0x1B904440: strcpy (mac_replace_strmem.c:199)
==4942==  by 0x80484FB: main (a7a.c:20)
==4942==  Address 0x1B92B033 is 7 bytes after a block of size 4 free'd
==4942==  at 0x1B904FB1: free (vg_replace_malloc.c:153)
==4942==  by 0x80484A4: main (a7a.c:11)
==4942==
==4942==  Invalid read of size 4
==4942==  at 0x54EDA3: strlen (in /lib/tls/libc-2.3.3.so)
==4942==  by 0x52968F: _IO_printf (in /lib/tls/libc-2.3.3.so)
==4942==  by 0x804850E: main (a7a.c:22)
==4942==  Address 0x1B92B028 is 0 bytes inside a block of size 4 free'd
==4942==  at 0x1B904FB1: free (vg_replace_malloc.c:153)
==4942==   by 0x80484A4: main (a7a.c:11)
==4942==
==4942==  Invalid read of size 4
==4942==  at 0x54EDB9: strlen (in /lib/tls/libc-2.3.3.so)
==4942==  by 0x52968F: _IO_printf (in /lib/tls/libc-2.3.3.so)
==4942==  by 0x804850E: main (a7a.c:22)
==4942==  Address 0x1B92B02C is 0 bytes after a block of size 4 free'd
==4942==  at 0x1B904FB1: free (vg_replace_malloc.c:153)
==4942==  by 0x80484A4: main (a7a.c:11)
==4942==
==4942==  Invalid read of size 4
==4942==  at 0x54EDD0: strlen (in /lib/tls/libc-2.3.3.so)
==4942==  by 0x52968F: _IO_printf (in /lib/tls/libc-2.3.3.so)
==4942==  by 0x804850E: main (a7a.c:22)
==4942==  Address 0x1B92B030 is 4 bytes after a block of size 4 free'd
==4942==  at 0x1B904FB1: free (vg_replace_malloc.c:153)
==4942==  by 0x80484A4: main (a7a.c:11)
==4942==
==4942==  Invalid read of size 1
==4942==  at 0x544826: _IO_file_xsputn@@GLIBC_2.1 (in /lib/tls/libc-2.3.3.so)
==4942==  by 0x52452B: _IO_vfprintf_internal (in /lib/tls/libc-2.3.3.so)
```

```
==4942==   by 0x52968F: _IO_printf (in /lib/tls/libc-2.3.3.so)
==4942==   by 0x804850E: main (a7a.c:22)
==4942==   Address 0x1B92B032 is 6 bytes after a block of size 4 free'd
==4942==   at 0x1B904FB1: free (vg_replace_malloc.c:153)
==4942==   by 0x80484A4: main (a7a.c:11)
==4942==
==4942==   Invalid read of size 1
==4942==   at 0x544660: _IO_file_xsputn@@GLIBC_2.1 (in /lib/tls/libc-2.3.3.so)
==4942==   by 0x52452B: _IO_vfprintf_internal (in /lib/tls/libc-2.3.3.so)
==4942==   by 0x52968F: _IO_printf (in /lib/tls/libc-2.3.3.so)
==4942==   by 0x804850E: main (a7a.c:22)
==4942==   Address 0x1B92B028 is 0 bytes inside a block of size 4 free'd
==4942==   at 0x1B904FB1: free (vg_replace_malloc.c:153)
==4942==   by 0x80484A4: main (a7a.c:11)
==4942==
==4942==   ERROR SUMMARY: 107 errors from 23 contexts (suppressed: 13 from 1)
==4942==   malloc/free: in use at exit: 0 bytes in 0 blocks.
==4942==   malloc/free: 2 allocs, 3 frees, 6 bytes allocated.
==4942==   For counts of detected errors, rerun with: -v
==4942==   No malloc'd blocks -- no leaks are possible.
```

gcc -g a7a.c -lefence
valgrind --tool=memcheck --leak-check=yes a.out

```
   Electric Fence 2.2.0 Copyright (C) 1987-1999 Bruce Perens <bruce@perens.com>

==4949==   Invalid write of size 1
==4949==   at 0x1B904434: strcpy (mac_replace_strmem.c:198)
==4949==   by 0x80485A7: main (a7a.c:8)
==4949==   Address 0x1B932000 is not stack'd, malloc'd or (recently) free'd
==4949==
==4949==   Process terminating with default action of signal 11 (SIGSEGV)
==4949==   Bad permissions for mapped region at address 0x1B932000
==4949==   at 0x1B904434: strcpy (mac_replace_strmem.c:198)
==4949==   by 0x80485A7: main (a7a.c:8)
==4949==
==4949==   ERROR SUMMARY: 1 errors from 1 contexts (suppressed: 15 from 1)
==4949==   malloc/free: in use at exit: 0 bytes in 0 blocks.
==4949==   malloc/free: 0 allocs, 0 frees, 0 bytes allocated.
==4949==   For counts of detected errors, rerun with: -v
==4949==   No malloc'd blocks -- no leaks are possible.
```

Example 12

```
#include<stdio.h>
#include<string.h>
int main()
{
int i;
char *p=(char*) malloc(1);

for(i=0;i<1024;i++)
{
p[i]='N';
printf("%d\n",i);
}
p[i]='\0';
printf("%s",p);
return 0;
}
```

gcc -g a7.c
valgrind --tool=memcheck --leak-check=yes a.out

```
==4958== Invalid write of size 1
==4958== at 0x80483EA: main (a7.c:10)
==4958== Address 0x1B92B029 is 0 bytes after a block of size 1 alloc'd
==4958== at 0x1B904A90: malloc (vg_replace_malloc.c:131)
==4958== by 0x80483CD: main (a7.c:6)
==4958==
==4958== Invalid write of size 1
==4958== at 0x804840D: main (a7.c:13)
==4958== Address 0x1B92B428 is not stack'd, malloc'd or (recently) free'd
==4958==
==4958== Invalid read of size 4
==4958== at 0x54EDB9: strlen (in /lib/tls/libc-2.3.3.so)
==4958== by 0x52968F: _IO_printf (in /lib/tls/libc-2.3.3.so)
==4958== by 0x804841F: main (a7.c:14)
==4958== Address 0x1B92B02C is 3 bytes after a block of size 1 alloc'd
==4958== at 0x1B904A90: malloc (vg_replace_malloc.c:131)
==4958== by 0x80483CD: main (a7.c:6)
==4958==
==4958== Invalid read of size 4
```

```
==4958==    at 0x54EDD0: strlen (in /lib/tls/libc-2.3.3.so)
==4958==    by 0x52968F: _IO_printf (in /lib/tls/libc-2.3.3.so)
==4958==    by 0x804841F: main (a7.c:14)
==4958==    Address 0x1B92B030 is 7 bytes after a block of size 1 alloc'd
==4958==    at 0x1B904A90: malloc (vg_replace_malloc.c:131)
==4958==    by 0x80483CD: main (a7.c:6)
==4958==
==4958==    Invalid read of size 4
==4958==    at 0x54EDE7: strlen (in /lib/tls/libc-2.3.3.so)
==4958==    by 0x52968F: _IO_printf (in /lib/tls/libc-2.3.3.so)
==4958==    by 0x804841F: main (a7.c:14)
==4958==    Address 0x1B92B034 is 11 bytes after a block of size 1 alloc'd
==4958==    at 0x1B904A90: malloc (vg_replace_malloc.c:131)
==4958==    by 0x80483CD: main (a7.c:6)
==4958==
==4958==    Invalid read of size 4
==4958==    at 0x54EDA3: strlen (in /lib/tls/libc-2.3.3.so)
==4958==    by 0x52968F: _IO_printf (in /lib/tls/libc-2.3.3.so)
==4958==    by 0x804841F: main (a7.c:14)
==4958==    Address 0x1B92B038 is 15 bytes after a block of size 1 alloc'd
==4958==    at 0x1B904A90: malloc (vg_replace_malloc.c:131)
==4958==    by 0x80483CD: main (a7.c:6)
==4958==
==4958==    Invalid read of size 1
==4958==    at 0x544826: _IO_file_xsputn@@GLIBC_2.1 (in /lib/tls/libc-2.3.3.so)
==4958==    by 0x52452B: _IO_vfprintf_internal (in /lib/tls/libc-2.3.3.so)
==4958==    by 0x52968F: _IO_printf (in /lib/tls/libc-2.3.3.so)
==4958==    by 0x804841F: main (a7.c:14)
==4958==    Address 0x1B92B427 is not stack'd, malloc'd or (recently) free'd
==4958==
==4958==    Invalid read of size 4
==4958==    at 0x55001C: mempcpy (in /lib/tls/libc-2.3.3.so)
==4958==    by 0x52452B: _IO_vfprintf_internal (in /lib/tls/libc-2.3.3.so)
==4958==    by 0x52968F: _IO_printf (in /lib/tls/libc-2.3.3.so)
==4958==    by 0x804841F: main (a7.c:14)
==4958==    Address 0x1B92B02C is 3 bytes after a block of size 1 alloc'd
==4958==    at 0x1B904A90: malloc (vg_replace_malloc.c:131)
==4958==    by 0x80483CD: main (a7.c:6)
==4958==
==4958==    Syscall param write(buf) contains uninitialised or unaddressable byte(s)
==4958==    at 0x59D573: __write_nocancel (in /lib/tls/libc-2.3.3.so)
```

```
==4958==    by 0x54302A: _IO_do_write@@GLIBC_2.1 (in /lib/tls/libc-2.3.3.so)
==4958==    by 0x543AB7: _IO_file_overflow@@GLIBC_2.1 (in /lib/tls/libc-2.3.3.so)
==4958==    by 0x545F5A: _IO_flush_all_lockp (in /lib/tls/libc-2.3.3.so)
==4958==    Address 0x1B908001 is not stack'd, malloc'd or (recently) free'd
==4958==
==4958==    ERROR SUMMARY: 2559 errors from 9 contexts (suppressed: 13 from 1)
==4958==    malloc/free: in use at exit: 1 bytes in 1 blocks.
==4958==    malloc/free: 1 allocs, 0 frees, 1 bytes allocated.
==4958==    For counts of detected errors, rerun with: -v
==4958==    searching for pointers to 1 not-freed blocks.
==4958==    checked 1500576 bytes.
==4958==
==4958==
==4958==    1 bytes in 1 blocks are definitely lost in loss record 1 of 1
==4958==    at 0x1B904A90: malloc (vg_replace_malloc.c:131)
==4958==    by 0x80483CD: main (a7.c:6)
==4958==
==4958==    LEAK SUMMARY:
==4958==    definitely lost: 1 bytes in 1 blocks.
==4958==    possibly lost:   0 bytes in 0 blocks.
==4958==    still reachable: 0 bytes in 0 blocks.
==4958==    suppressed: 0 bytes in 0 blocks.
==4958==    Reachable blocks (those to which a pointer was found) are not shown.
==4958==    To see them, rerun with: --show-reachable=yes
```

gcc -g a7.c -lefence
valgrind --tool=memcheck --leak-check=yes a.out

```
Electric Fence 2.2.0 Copyright (C) 1987-1999 Bruce Perens <bruce@perens.com>

==4965==    Invalid write of size 1
==4965==    at 0x80484D6: main (a7.c:10)
==4965==    Address 0x1B932000 is not stack'd, malloc'd or (recently) free'd
==4965==
==4965==    Process terminating with default action of signal 11 (SIGSEGV)
==4965==    Bad permissions for mapped region at address 0x1B932000
==4965==    at 0x80484D6: main (a7.c:10)
==4965==
==4965==    ERROR SUMMARY: 1 errors from 1 contexts (suppressed: 15 from 1)
==4965==    malloc/free: in use at exit: 0 bytes in 0 blocks.
==4965==    malloc/free: 0 allocs, 0 frees, 0 bytes allocated.
==4965==    For counts of detected errors, rerun with: -v
==4965==    No malloc'd blocks -- no leaks are possible.
```

Example 13

```
#include <stdlib.h>
int main()
{
    float *p, *a;
    p = malloc(10*sizeof(float));
    a = malloc(10*sizeof(float));
    a[3] = p[3];
    free(a);
    free(p);
    return 0;
}
```

gcc -g v10.c

valgrind --tool=memcheck --leak-check=yes a.out

```
==4974== ERROR SUMMARY: 0 errors from 0 contexts (suppressed: 13 from 1)
==4974== malloc/free: in use at exit: 0 bytes in 0 blocks.
==4974== malloc/free: 2 allocs, 2 frees, 80 bytes allocated.
==4974== For counts of detected errors, rerun with: -v
==4974== No malloc'd blocks -- no leaks are possible.
```

Example 14

```
#include <stdlib.h>
int main()
{
    int *p, i,j;
    p = malloc(5*sizeof(int));
    j = p[5];
    if (p[5] == 1)
        i = p[5]+1;
    free(p);
    return 0;
}
```

gcc -g v11.c

valgrind --tool=memcheck --leak-check=yes a.out

```
==4990== Invalid read of size 4
==4990== at 0x80483DA: main (v11.c:6)
==4990== Address 0x1B92B03C is 0 bytes after a block of size 20 alloc'd
==4990== at 0x1B904A90: malloc (vg_replace_malloc.c:131)
==4990== by 0x80483CD: main (v11.c:5)
==4990==
==4990== Invalid read of size 4
==4990== at 0x80483E5: main (v11.c:7)
==4990== Address 0x1B92B03C is 0 bytes after a block of size 20 alloc'd
==4990== at 0x1B904A90: malloc (vg_replace_malloc.c:131)
==4990== by 0x80483CD: main (v11.c:5)
==4990==
==4990== ERROR SUMMARY: 2 errors from 2 contexts (suppressed: 13 from 1)
==4990== malloc/free: in use at exit: 0 bytes in 0 blocks.
==4990== malloc/free: 1 allocs, 1 frees, 20 bytes allocated.
==4990== For counts of detected errors, rerun with: -v
==4990== No malloc'd blocks -- no leaks are possible.
```

gcc -g v11.c -lefence

valgrind --tool=memcheck --leak-check=yes a.out

```
Electric Fence 2.2.0 Copyright (C) 1987-1999 Bruce Perens <bruce@perens.com>

==4997== Invalid read of size 4
==4997== at 0x80484C6: main (v11.c:6)
==4997== Address 0x1B932000 is not stack'd, malloc'd or (recently) free'd
==4997==
==4997== Process terminating with default action of signal 11 (SIGSEGV)
==4997== Bad permissions for mapped region at address 0x1B932000
==4997== at 0x80484C6: main (v11.c:6)
==4997==
==4997== ERROR SUMMARY: 1 errors from 1 contexts (suppressed: 15 from 1)
==4997== malloc/free: in use at exit: 0 bytes in 0 blocks.
==4997== malloc/free: 0 allocs, 0 frees, 0 bytes allocated.
==4997== For counts of detected errors, rerun with: -v
==4997== No malloc'd blocks -- no leaks are possible.
```

Example 15

```
#include <stdlib.h>
#include <unistd.h>
int main()
{
        int *p;
        p = malloc(10);
        read(0, p, 100);        /* Error: unaddressable bytes */
        free(p);
        return 0;
}
```

gcc -g v12.c
valgrind --tool=memcheck --leak-check=yes a.out

```
==5006==  Syscall param read(buf) contains unaddressable byte(s)
==5006==  at 0x59D4F3: __read_nocancel (in /lib/tls/libc-2.3.3.so)
==5006==  by 0x4FBE32: __libc_start_main (in /lib/tls/libc-2.3.3.so)
==5006==  by 0x8048350: (within /root/valgrind/bookexamples/a.out)
==5006==  Address 0x1B92B032 is 0 bytes after a block of size 10 alloc'd
==5006==  at 0x1B904A90: malloc (vg_replace_malloc.c:131)
==5006==  by 0x80483FD: main (v12.c:6)
==5006==
==5006==  ERROR SUMMARY: 1 errors from 1 contexts (suppressed: 13 from 1)
==5006==  malloc/free: in use at exit: 0 bytes in 0 blocks.
==5006==  malloc/free: 1 allocs, 1 frees, 10 bytes allocated.
==5006==  For counts of detected errors, rerun with: -v
==5006==  No malloc'd blocks -- no leaks are possible.
```

Example 16

```
#include <malloc.h>
int main()
{
    char *x = malloc(100);
/* or, in C++, "char *x = new char[100] */
   return 0;
}
```

gcc -g v1.c
valgrind --tool=memcheck --leak-check=yes a.out

```
==5022== 100 bytes in 1 blocks are definitely lost in loss record 1 of 1
==5022==  at 0x1B904A90: malloc (vg_replace_malloc.c:131)
==5022==  by 0x8048399: main (v1.c:4)
==5022==
==5022==  LEAK SUMMARY:
==5022==  definitely lost: 100 bytes in 1 blocks.
==5022==  possibly lost:   0 bytes in 0 blocks.
==5022==  still reachable: 0 bytes in 0 blocks.
==5022==  suppressed: 0 bytes in 0 blocks.
==5022==  Reachable blocks (those to which a pointer was found) are not shown.
==5022==  To see them, rerun with: --show-reachable=yes
```

Example 17

```
#include <stdio.h>

int main()
{
   char *x=malloc(10);
   x[10] = 'a';
   return 0;
}
```

gcc -g v2.c
valgrind --tool=memcheck --leak-check=yes a.out

```
==5038==  Invalid write of size 1
==5038==  at 0x80483A6: main (v2.c:6)
==5038==  Address 0x1B92B032 is 0 bytes after a block of size 10 alloc'd
==5038==  at 0x1B904A90: malloc (vg_replace_malloc.c:131)
==5038==  by 0x8048399: main (v2.c:5)
==5038==
==5038==  ERROR SUMMARY: 1 errors from 1 contexts (suppressed: 13 from 1)
==5038==  malloc/free: in use at exit: 10 bytes in 1 blocks.
==5038==  malloc/free: 1 allocs, 0 frees, 10 bytes allocated.
==5038==  For counts of detected errors, rerun with: -v
==5038==  searching for pointers to 1 not-freed blocks.
==5038==  checked 1500576 bytes.
```

```
==5038==
==5038==
==5038==  10 bytes in 1 blocks are definitely lost in loss record 1 of 1
==5038==  at 0x1B904A90: malloc (vg_replace_malloc.c:131)
==5038==  by 0x8048399: main (v2.c:5)
==5038==
==5038==  LEAK SUMMARY:
==5038==  definitely lost: 10 bytes in 1 blocks.
==5038==  possibly lost:   0 bytes in 0 blocks.
==5038==  still reachable: 0 bytes in 0 blocks.
==5038==  suppressed: 0 bytes in 0 blocks.
==5038==  Reachable blocks (those to which a pointer was found) are not shown.
==5038==  To see them, rerun with: --show-reachable=yes
```

Example 18

```
#include <stdio.h>

int main()
{
   int x;
   if(x == 0)
   {
      printf("X is zero");
/* replace with cout and include
iostream for C++ */
   }
   return 0;
}
```

gcc -g v3.c
valgrind --tool=memcheck --leak-check=yes a.out

```
==5054==  Conditional jump or move depends on uninitialised value(s)
==5054==  at 0x8048394: main (v3.c:6)
==5054==
==5054==  ERROR SUMMARY: 1 errors from 1 contexts (suppressed: 13 from 1)
==5054==  malloc/free: in use at exit: 0 bytes in 0 blocks.
==5054==  malloc/free: 0 allocs, 0 frees, 0 bytes allocated.
==5054==  For counts of detected errors, rerun with: -v
==5054==  No malloc'd blocks -- no leaks are possible.
```

Example 19

```
#include <stdio.h>

int foo(int x)
{
   if(x < 10)
   {
      printf("x is less than 10\n");
   }
}

int main()
{
   int y;
   foo(y);
}
```

gcc -g v4.c
valgrind --tool=memcheck --leak-check=yes a.out

```
==5070==  Conditional jump or move depends on uninitialised value(s)
==5070==  at 0x804837E: foo (v4.c:5)
==5070==  by 0x80483B8: main (v4.c:14)
==5070==
==5070==  ERROR SUMMARY: 1 errors from 1 contexts (suppressed: 13 from 1)
==5070==  malloc/free: in use at exit: 0 bytes in 0 blocks.
==5070==  malloc/free: 0 allocs, 0 frees, 0 bytes allocated.
==5070==  For counts of detected errors, rerun with: -v
==5070==  No malloc'd blocks -- no leaks are possible.
```

Example 20

```
#include <malloc.h>
int main()
{
    char *x = malloc(10);
    x[10]='A';
   printf("%d\n", x[10]);
    free(x);
   printf("%d\n", x[1]);
    return 0;
}
```

gcc -g v5.c
valgrind --tool=memcheck --leak-check=yes a.out

```
==5086==  Invalid write of size 1
==5086==  at 0x804840E: main (v5.c:5)
==5086==  Address 0x1B92B032 is 0 bytes after a block of size 10 alloc'd
==5086==  at 0x1B904A90: malloc (vg_replace_malloc.c:131)
==5086==  by 0x8048401: main (v5.c:4)
==5086==
==5086==  Invalid read of size 1
==5086==  at 0x804841A: main (v5.c:6)
==5086==  Address 0x1B92B032 is 0 bytes after a block of size 10 alloc'd
==5086==  at 0x1B904A90: malloc (vg_replace_malloc.c:131)
==5086==  by 0x8048401: main (v5.c:4)
==5086==
==5086==  Invalid read of size 1
==5086==  at 0x8048440: main (v5.c:8)
==5086==  Address 0x1B92B029 is 1 bytes inside a block of size 10 free'd
==5086==  at 0x1B904FB1: free (vg_replace_malloc.c:153)
==5086==  by 0x8048435: main (v5.c:7)
==5086==
==5086==  ERROR SUMMARY: 3 errors from 3 contexts (suppressed: 13 from 1)
==5086==  malloc/free: in use at exit: 0 bytes in 0 blocks.
==5086==  malloc/free: 1 allocs, 1 frees, 10 bytes allocated.
==5086==  For counts of detected errors, rerun with: -v
==5086==  No malloc'd blocks -- no leaks are possible.
```

gcc -g v5.c -lefence
valgrind --tool=memcheck --leak-check=yes a.out

Electric Fence 2.2.0 Copyright (C) 1987-1999 Bruce Perens <bruce@perens.com>

```
==5093==  Invalid read of size 1
==5093==  at 0x804852C: main (v5.c:8)
==5093==  Address 0x1B931FF5 is not stack'd, malloc'd or (recently) free'd
==5093==
==5093==  Process terminating with default action of signal 11 (SIGSEGV)
==5093==  Bad permissions for mapped region at address 0x1B931FF5
==5093==  at 0x804852C: main (v5.c:8)
```

```
==5093==
==5093==  ERROR SUMMARY: 1 errors from 1 contexts (suppressed: 15 from 1)
==5093==  malloc/free: in use at exit: 0 bytes in 0 blocks.
==5093==  malloc/free: 0 allocs, 0 frees, 0 bytes allocated.
==5093==  For counts of detected errors, rerun with: -v
==5093==  No malloc'd blocks -- no leaks are possible.
```

Example 21

```
#include <stdlib.h>
#include <unistd.h>
int main()
{
        int *p;
        p = malloc(10);
        read(0, p, 100);        /* Error: unaddressable bytes */
        free(p);
        return 0;
}
```

gcc -g v7.c
valgrind --tool=memcheck --leak-check=yes a.out

```
==5116==  Syscall param read(buf) contains unaddressable byte(s)
==5116==  at 0x59D4F3: __read_nocancel (in /lib/tls/libc-2.3.3.so)
==5116==  by 0x4FBE32: __libc_start_main (in /lib/tls/libc-2.3.3.so)
==5116==  by 0x8048350: (within /root/valgrind/bookexamples/a.out)
==5116==  Address 0x1B92B032 is 0 bytes after a block of size 10 alloc'd
==5116==  at 0x1B904A90: malloc (vg_replace_malloc.c:131)
==5116==  by 0x80483FD: main (v7.c:6)
==5116==
==5116==  ERROR SUMMARY: 1 errors from 1 contexts (suppressed: 13 from 1)
==5116==  malloc/free: in use at exit: 0 bytes in 0 blocks.
==5116==  malloc/free: 1 allocs, 1 frees, 10 bytes allocated.
==5116==  For counts of detected errors, rerun with: -v
==5116==  No malloc'd blocks -- no leaks are possible.
```

14.6 Cachegrind: a cache-miss profiler

To use this tool, we must specify **--tool=cachegrind** on the Valgrind command line.

Detailed technical documentation on how Cachegrind works is available here. If we want to know how to use it, we only need to read this page.

14.6.1 Cache profiling

Cachegrind is a tool for doing cache simulations and annotating our source line-by-line with the number of cache misses. In particular, it records:

L1 instruction cache reads and misses;

L1 data cache reads and read misses, writes and write misses;

L2 unified cache reads and read misses, writes and writes misses.

On a modern x86 machine, an L1 miss will typically cost around 10 cycles, and an L2 miss can cost as much as 200 cycles. Detailed cache profiling can be very useful for improving the performance of your program.

Also, since one instruction cache read is performed per instruction executed, we can find out how many instructions are executed per line, which can be useful for traditional profiling and test coverage.

14.6.2 Overview

First, as for normal Valgrind use, we probably want to compile with debugging info (the -g flag). But by contrast with normal Valgrind use, we probably do want to turn optimization on, since we should profile our program as it will be normally run. The two steps are:

Run our program with valgrind --tool=cachegrind in front of the normal command line invocation. When the program finishes, Cachegrind will print summary cache statistics. It also collects line-by-line information in a file cachegrind.out.pid, where pid is the program's process id.

This step should be done every time we want to collect information about a new program, a changed program, or about the same program with different input.

Generate a function-by-function summary, and possibly annotate source files, using the supplied cg_annotate program. Source files to annotate can be specified manually, or manually on the command line, or "interesting" source files can be annotated automatically with the --auto=yes option. We can annotate C/C++ files or assembly language files equally easily.

This step can be performed as many times as we like for each Step 2. We may want to do multiple annotations showing different information each time.

14.6.3 Cache simulation specifics

Cachegrind uses a simulation for a machine with a split L1 cache and a unified L2 cache. This configuration is used for all (modern) x86-based machines we are aware of. Old Cyrix CPUs had a unified I and D L1 cache, but they are ancient history now.

The more specific characteristics of the simulation are as follows.

Write-allocate: when a write miss occurs, the block written to is brought into the D1 cache. Most modern caches have this property.

Bit-selection hash function: the line(s) in the cache to which a memory block maps is chosen by the middle bits M--(M+N-1) of the byte address, where:

- line size = 2^M bytes
- (cache size / line size) = 2^N bytes

Inclusive L2 cache: the L2 cache replicates all the entries of the L1 cache. This is standard on Pentium chips, but AMD Athlons use an exclusive L2 cache that only holds blocks evicted from L1. Ditto AMD Durons and most modern VIAs.

The cache configuration simulated (cache size, associatavity and line size) is determined automatically using the CPUID instruction. If we have an old machine that (a) doesn't support the CPUID instruction, or (b) supports it in an early incarnation that doesn't give any cache information, then Cachegrind will fall back to using a default configuration (that of a model 3/4 Athlon). Cachegrind will tell we if this happens. We can manually specify one, two or all three levels (I1/D1/L2) of the cache from the command line using the --I1, --D1 and --L2 options.

Other noteworthy behavior:

References that straddle two cache lines are treated as follows:

- If both blocks hit --> counted as one hit
- If one block hits, the other misses --> counted as one miss
- If both blocks miss --> counted as one miss (not two)

Instructions that modify a memory location (eg. inc and dec) are counted as doing just a read, i.e. a single data reference. This may seem strange, but since the write can never cause a miss (the read guarantees the block is in the cache) it's not very interesting.

Thus it measures not the number of times the data cache is accessed, but the number of times a data cache miss could occur.

If we are interested in simulating a cache with different properties, it is not particularly hard to write our own cache simulator, or to modify the existing ones in vg_cachesim_I1.c, vg_cachesim_D1.c, vg_cachesim_L2.c and vg_cachesim_gen.c. We'd be interested to hear from anyone who does.

14.6.4 Profiling programs

To gather cache profiling information about the program ls -l, invoke Cachegrind like this:

```
valgrind --tool=cachegrind ls -l
```

The program will execute (slowly). Upon completion, summary statistics that look like this will be printed:

```
==31751== I   refs:      27,742,716
==31751== I1  misses:           276
==31751== L2  misses:           275
==31751== I1  miss rate:        0.0%
==31751== L2i miss rate:        0.0%
==31751==
==31751== D   refs:      15,430,290  (10,955,517 rd + 4,474,773 wr)
==31751== D1  misses:        41,185  (    21,905 rd +    19,280 wr)
==31751== L2  misses:        23,085  (     3,987 rd +    19,098 wr)
==31751== D1  miss rate:        0.2% (       0.1%   +       0.4%)
==31751== L2d miss rate:        0.1% (       0.0%   +       0.4%)
==31751==
==31751== L2 misses:         23,360  (     4,262 rd +    19,098 wr)
==31751== L2 miss rate:         0.0% (       0.0%   +       0.4%)
```

Cache accesses for instruction fetches are summarized first, giving the number of fetches made (this is the number of instructions executed, which can be useful to know in its own right), the number of I1 misses, and the number of L2 instruction (L2i) misses.

Cache accesses for data follow. The information is similar to that of the instruction fetches, except that the values are also shown split between reads and writes (note each row's rd and wr values add up to the row's total).

Combined instruction and data figures for the L2 cache follow that.

4.6.5 Output file

As well as printing summary information, Cachegrind also writes line-by-line cache profiling information to a file named cachegrind.out.pid. This file is human-readable, but is best interpreted by the accompanying program cg_annotate, described in the next section.

Things to note about the cachegrind.out.pid file:

It is written every time Cachegrind is run, and will overwrite any existing cachegrind.out.pid in the current directory (but that won't happen very often because it takes some time for process ids to be recycled).

It can be huge: ls -l generates a file of about 350KB. Browsing a few files and web pages with a Konqueror built with full debugging information generates a file of around 15 MB.

14.6.6 Cachegrind options

Cache-simulation specific options are:

* --I1=<size>,<associativity>,<line_size>

--D1=<size>,<associativity>,<line_size>

--L2=<size>,<associativity>,<line_size>

Manually specifies the I1/D1/L2 cache configuration, where size and line_size are measured in bytes. The three items must be comma-separated, but with no spaces, eg:

valgrind --tool=cachegrind --I1=65535,2,64

We can specify one, two or three of the I1/D1/L2 caches. Any level not manually specified will be simulated using the configuration found in the normal way (via the CPUID instruction, or failing that, via defaults).

Annotating C/C++ programs

Before using cg_annotate, it is worth widening our window to be at least 120-characters wide if possible, as the output lines can be quite long.

To get a function-by-function summary, run cg_annotate --pid in a directory containing a cachegrind.out.pid file. The --pid is required so that cg_annotate knows which log file to use when several are present.

The output looks like this:

```
--------------------------------------------------------------------------------
I1 cache:              65536 B, 64 B, 2-way associative
D1 cache:              65536 B, 64 B, 2-way associative
L2 cache:              262144 B, 64 B, 8-way associative
Command:               concord vg_to_ucode.c
Events recorded:       Ir I1mr I2mr Dr D1mr D2mr Dw D1mw D2mw
Events shown:          Ir I1mr I2mr Dr D1mr D2mr Dw D1mw D2mw
Event sort order:      Ir I1mr I2mr Dr D1mr D2mr Dw D1mw D2mw
Threshold:             99%
Chosen for annotation:
Auto-annotation:       on
--------------------------------------------------------------------------------
Ir       I1mr I2mr Dr        D1mr   D2mr  Dw       D1mw   D2mw
--------------------------------------------------------------------------------
27,742,716  276  275 10,955,517 21,905 3,987 4,474,773 19,280 19,098  PROGRAM
TOTALS


--------------------------------------------------------------------------------
Ir       I1mr I2mr Dr        D1mr  D2mr  Dw        D1mw   D2mw   file:function
--------------------------------------------------------------------------------
8,821,482   5   5 2,242,702 1,621    73 1,794,230    0     0  getc.c:_IO_getc
5,222,023   4   4 2,276,334    16    12   875,959    1     1  concord.c:get_word
2,649,248   2   2 1,344,810 7,326 1,385         .    .     .  vg_main.c:strcmp
2,521,927   2   2   591,215     0     0   179,398    0     0  concord.c:hash
2,242,740   2   2 1,046,612   568    22   448,548    0     0  ctype.c:tolower
1,496,937   4   4   630,874 9,000 1,400   279,388    0     0  concord.c:insert
  897,991  51  51   897,831    95    30        62    1     1  ???:???
  598,068       1       1      299,034        0         0       149,517         0         0
../sysdeps/generic/lockfile.c:__flockfile
  598,068       0       0      299,034        0         0       149,517         0         0
../sysdeps/generic/lockfile.c:__funlockfile
  598,024   4   4   213,580    35    16   149,506    0     0  vg_clientmalloc.c:malloc
  446,587        1         1        215,973  2,167       430        129,948  14,057  13,957
concord.c:add_existing
  341,760       2       2      128,160        0         0       128,160         0         0
vg_clientmalloc.c:vg_trap_here_WRAPPER
  320,782   4   4   150,711   276     0    56,027   53    53  concord.c:init_hash_table
  298,998   1   1   106,785     0     0    64,071    1     1  concord.c:create
  149,518   0   0   149,516     0     0         1    0     0  ???:tolower@@GLIBC_2.0
  149,518   0   0   149,516     0     0         1    0     0  ???:fgetc@@GLIBC_2.0
   95,983   4   4    38,031     0     0    34,409 3,152 3,150  concord.c:new_word_node
   85,440   0   0    42,720     0     0    21,360    0     0
```

vg_clientmalloc.c:vg_bogus_epilogue

First up is a summary of the annotation options:

I1 cache, D1 cache, L2 cache: cache configuration. So we know the configuration with which these results were obtained.

Command: the command line invocation of the program under examination.

Events recorded: event abbreviations are:

- Ir : I cache reads (ie. instructions executed)
- I1mr: I1 cache read misses
- I2mr: L2 cache instruction read misses
- Dr : D cache reads (ie. memory reads)
- D1mr: D1 cache read misses
- D2mr: L2 cache data read misses
- Dw : D cache writes (ie. memory writes)
- D1mw: D1 cache write misses
- D2mw: L2 cache data write misses

Note that D1 total accesses is given by D1mr + D1mw, and that L2 total accesses is given by I2mr + D2mr + D2mw.

Events shown: the events shown (a subset of events gathered). This can be adjusted with the --show option.

Event sort order: the sort order in which functions are shown. For example, in this case the functions are sorted from highest Ir counts to lowest. If two functions have identical Ir counts, they will then be sorted by I1mr counts, and so on. This order can be adjusted with the --sort option.

Note that this dictates the order the functions appear. It is not the order in which the columns appear; that is dictated by the "events shown" line (and can be changed with the --show option).

Threshold: cg_annotate by default omits functions that cause very low numbers of misses to avoid drowning you in information. In this case, cg_annotate shows summaries the functions that account for 99% of the Ir counts; Ir is chosen as the threshold event since it is the primary sort event. The threshold can be adjusted with the --threshold option.

Chosen for annotation: names of files specified manually for annotation; in this case none.

Auto-annotation: whether auto-annotation was requested via the --auto=yes option. In this case no.

Then follows summary statistics for the whole program. These are similar to the summary provided when running valgrind --tool=cachegrind.

Then follows function-by-function statistics. Each function is identified by a file_name:function_name pair. If a column contains only a dot it means the function never performs that event (eg. the third row shows that strcmp() contains no instructions that write to memory). The name ??? is used if the the file name and/or function name could not be determined from debugging information. If most of the entries have the form ???:??? the program probably wasn't compiled with -g. If any code was invalidated (either due to self-modifying code or unloading of shared objects) its counts are aggregated into a single cost center written as (discarded):(discarded).

It is worth noting that functions will come from three types of source files:

From the profiled program (concord.c in this example).

From libraries (eg. getc.c)

From Valgrind's implementation of some libc functions (eg. vg_clientmalloc.c:malloc).

These are recognizable because the filename begins with vg_, and is probably one of vg_main.c, vg_clientmalloc.c or vg_mylibc.c.

There are two ways to annotate source files -- by choosing them manually, or with the --auto=yes option. To do it manually, just specify the filenames as arguments to cg_annotate. For example, the output from running cg_annotate concord.c for our example produces the same output as above followed by an annotated version of concord.c, a section of which looks like:

--User-annotated source: concord.c

Ir	I1mr	I2mr	Dr	D1mr	D2mr	Dw	D1mw	D2mw	file:function
8,821,482	5	5	2,242,	702 1,	621	73 1,	794,2300	0	getc.c:_ IO_getc
5,222,023	4	4	2,276,334	16	12	875,959	1	1	concord.c: get_word
2,649,248	2	2	1,344,810	7,326	1,385	.	.	.	vg_main.c :strcmp
2,521,927	2	2	591,215	0	0	179,398	0	0	concord.c: hash
2,242,740	2	2	1,046,612	568	22	448,548	0	0	ctype.c: tolower
1,496,937	4	4	630,874	9,000	1,400	279,388	0	0	concord.c: insert
897,991	51	51	897,831	95	30	62	1	1	???:???
598,068	1	1	299,034	0	0	149,517	0	0	../sysdeps/ generic/lock filec:_flockfile
598,068	0	0	299,034	0	0	149,517	0	0	../sysdeps/ generic/lock file.c:_funlockfile
598,024	4	4	213,580	35	16	149,506	0	0	vg_client malloc. c:malloc
446,587	1	1	215,973	2,167	430	129,948	14,057	13,957	concord.c: add_existing
341,760	2	2	128,160	0	0	128,160	0	0	vg_client\ malloc. c:vg _trap_here_ WRAPPER
320,782	4	4	150,711	276	0	56,027	53	53	concord.c: init_hash_ table
298,998	1	1	106,785	0	0	64,071	1	1	concord.c :create
149,518	0	0	149,516	0	0	1	0	0	???:tolower @@GLIBC _2.0
149,518	0	0	149,516	0	0	1	0	0	???:fgetc @@GLIBC_ 2.0
95,983	4	4	38,031	0	0	34,409	3,152	3,150	concord. c:new_word _node
85,440	0	0	42,720	0	0	21,360	0	0	}

(Although column widths are automatically minimized, a wide terminal is clearly useful.)

Each source file is clearly marked (User-annotated source) as having been chosen manually for annotation. If the file was found in one of the directories specified with the -I/--include option, the directory and file are both given.

Each line is annotated with its event counts. Events not applicable for a line are represented by a `.'; this is useful for distinguishing between an event which cannot happen, and one which can but did not.

Sometimes only a small section of a source file is executed. To minimize uninteresting output, Valgrind only shows annotated lines and lines within a small distance of annotated lines. Gaps are marked with the line numbers so we know which part of a file the shown code comes from, eg:

```
(figures and code for line 704)
-- line 704 ----------------------------------------
-- line 878 ----------------------------------------
(figures and code for line 878)
```

The amount of context to show around annotated lines is controlled by the --context option.

To get automatic annotation, run cg_annotate --auto=yes. cg_annotate will automatically annotate every source file it can find that is mentioned in the function-by-function summary. Therefore, the files chosen for auto-annotation are affected by the --sort and --threshold options. Each source file is clearly marked (Auto-annotated source) as being chosen automatically. Any files that could not be found are mentioned at the end of the output, eg:

```
------------------------------------------------------------------------------
The following files chosen for auto-annotation could not be found:
------------------------------------------------------------------------------

        getc.c
        ctype.c
        ../sysdeps/generic/lockfile.c
```

This is quite common for library files, since libraries are usually compiled with debugging information, but the source files are often not present on a system. If a file is chosen for annotation both manually and automatically, it is marked as User-annotated source. Use the -I/--include option to tell Valgrind where to look for source files if the filenames found from the debugging information aren't specific enough. Beware that cg_annotate can take some time to digest large cachegrind.out.pid files, e.g. 30 seconds or more. Also beware that auto-annotation can produce a lot of output if our program is large!

14.6.7 Annotating assembler programs

Valgrind can annotate assembler programs too, or annotate the assembler generated for your C program. Sometimes this is useful for understanding what is really happening when an interesting line of C code is translated into multiple instructions.

To do this, we just need to assemble your .s files with assembler-level debug information. gcc doesn't do this, but you can use the GNU assembler with the --gstabs option to generate object files with this information, eg:

```
as --gstabs foo.s
```

We can then profile and annotate source files in the same way as for C/C++ programs.

cg_annotate options

```
--pid
```

Indicates which cachegrind.out.pid file to read. Not actually an option -- it is required.

```
-h, --help
```

```
-v, --version
```

Help and version, as usual.

```
--sort=A,B,C [default: order in cachegrind.out.pid]
```

Specifies the events upon which the sorting of the function-by-function entries will be based. Useful if you want to concentrate on eg. I cache misses (--sort=I1mr,I2mr), or D cache misses (--sort=D1mr,D2mr), or L2 misses (--sort=D2mr,I2mr).

```
--show=A,B,C [default: all, using order in cachegrind.out.pid]
```

Specifies which events to show (and the column order). Default is to use all present in the cachegrind.out.pid file (and use the order in the file).

```
--threshold=X [default: 99%]
```

Sets the threshold for the function-by-function summary. Functions are shown that account for more than X% of the primary sort event. If auto-annotating, also affects which files are annotated. Note: thresholds can be set for more than one of the events by appending any events for the --sort option with a colon and a number (no spaces, though). E.g. if we want to see the functions that cover 99% of L2 read misses and 99% of L2 write misses, use this option:

```
--sort=D2mr:99,D2mw:99
```

```
--auto=no [default]
--auto=yes
```

When enabled, automatically annotates every file that is mentioned in the function-by-function summary that can be found. Also gives a list of those that couldn't be found.

```
--context=N [default: 8]
```

Print N lines of context before and after each annotated line. Avoids printing large sections of source files that were not executed. Use a large number (eg. 10,000) to show all source lines.

-I=<dir>, --include=<dir> [default: empty string]

Adds a directory to the list in which to search for files. Multiple -I/--include options can be given to add multiple directories.

14.6.8 Accuracy

Valgrind's cache profiling has a number of shortcomings:

It doesn't account for kernel activity -- the effect of system calls on the cache contents is ignored.

It doesn't account for other process activity (although this is probably desirable when considering a single program).

It doesn't account for virtual-to-physical address mappings; hence the entire simulation is not a true representation of what's happening in the cache.

It doesn't account for cache misses not visible at the instruction level, eg. those arising from TLB misses, or speculative execution.

Valgrind's custom threads implementation will schedule threads differently to the standard one. This could warp the results for threaded programs.

The instructions bts, btr and btc will incorrectly be counted as doing a data read if both the arguments are registers, eg:

```
btsl %eax, %edx
```

This should only happen rarely.

FPU instructions with data sizes of 28 and 108 bytes (e.g. fsave) are treated as though they only access 16 bytes. These instructions seem to be rare so hopefully this won't affect accuracy much.

Another thing worth nothing is that results are very sensitive. Changing the size of the valgrind.so file, the size of the program being profiled, or even the length of its name can perturb the results. Variations will be small, but don't expect perfectly repeatable results if your program changes at all.

While these factors mean you shouldn't trust the results to be super-accurate, hopefully they should be close enough to be useful.

Example 22

The following example is used to demonstrate how Cache utilization can be found with the help of Valgrind. Also, the following experiments shows the difference of cache performance on the physical organization of the data, i.e on row major order storage or array and column major order. For more details on row and column major order storage, reader are advised to refer Data Structures or algorithms books such as [Sahini, Corman].

```
#include<stdio.h>
#include<string.h>

#define N 4096*2
int main()
{
 int a[N][N],i,j;

for(i=0;i<N;i++)
for(j=0;j<N;j++)a[j][i]=i;
return 0;
}
```

valgrind --tool=cachegrind ./a.out

```
==4261== Cachegrind, an I1/D1/L2 cache profiler for x86-linux.
--4261--    Simulating a 16 KB cache with 32 B lines

==4261== I   refs:      14,034,791
==4261== I1  misses:           918
==4261== L2i misses:           513
==4261== I1  miss rate:        0.0%
==4261== L2i miss rate:        0.0%
==4261==
==4261== D   refs:       7,647,641  (6,367,252 rd + 1,280,389 wr)
==4261== D1  misses:     1,266,435  (145 rd + 1,266,290 wr)
==4261== L2d misses:     1,266,435  (145 rd + 1,266,290 wr)
==4261== D1  miss rate:       16.5% (0.0%  + 98.8%  )
==4261== L2d miss rate:       16.5% ( 0.0% + 98.8%  )
==4261==
==4261== L2 refs:        1,267,353  (1,063 rd + 1,266,290 wr)
==4261== L2 misses:      1,266,948  (658 rd + 1,266,290 wr)
==4261== L2 miss rate:         5.8% (0.0%   +     98.8%  )
```

Now we have changed the statement as a[i][j]=i in the above program and then compiled.

gcc -g a8.c

valgrind --tool=cachegrind ./a.out

```
==4272== Cachegrind, an I1/D1/L2 cache profiler for x86-linux.
--4272--         Simulating a 16 KB cache with 32 B lines

==4272== I   refs:      738,371,470
==4272== I1  misses:            983
==4272== L2i misses:            557
==4272== I1  miss rate:         0.0%
==4272== L2i miss rate:         0.0%
==4272==
==4272== D   refs:      402,737,489  (335,605,960 rd + 67,131,529 wr)
==4272== D1  misses:      4,194,677  (240 rd + 4,194,437 wr)
==4272== L2d misses:      4,194,677  (240 rd + 4,194,437 wr)
==4272== D1  miss rate:         1.0% (0.0% + 6.2%  )
==4272== L2d miss rate:         1.0% (0.0%    +      6.2%  )
==4272==
==4272== L2 refs:         4,195,660  (1,223 rd +  4,194,437 wr)
==4272== L2 misses:        4,195,234  (797 rd +4,194,437 wr)
==4272== L2 miss rate:          0.3% (0.0% + 6.2%  )
```

We can find that miss rates of first experiment (i.e when we access elements column by column) is more than the second experiment. This is expected as the array is stored in row major order and we are referring elements in column by column fashion.

Example 23

We did create a Fortran program (see below) for the above C program to test how it performs as Fortran uses column major order storage.

```
INTEGER*4 M(8192,8192)

do 1 j=1,8192
do 1 i=1,8192
1   M(i,j)=i
stop
end
```

g77 a.F

valgrind --tool=cachegrind ./a.out

```
==4526== Cachegrind, an I1/D1/L2 cache profiler for x86-linux.
--4526--        Simulating a 16 KB cache with 32 B lines
==4526== I   refs:      805,669,562
==4526== I1  misses:          1,183
==4526== L2i misses:            685
==4526== I1  miss rate:         0.0%
==4526== L2i miss rate:         0.0%
==4526==
==4526== D   refs:      469,953,999  (402,792,510 rd + 67,161,489 wr)
==4526== D1  misses:      4,195,073  (        537 rd +  4,194,536 wr)
==4526== L2d misses:      4,195,073  (        537 rd +  4,194,536 wr)
==4526== D1  miss rate:         0.8% (        0.0%   +        6.2%  )
==4526== L2d miss rate:         0.8% (        0.0%   +        6.2%  )
==4526==
==4526== L2 refs:         4,196,256  (      1,720 rd +  4,194,536 wr)
==4526== L2 misses:       4,195,758  (      1,222 rd +  4,194,536 wr)
==4526== L2 miss rate:          0.3% (        0.0%   +        6.2%  )
```

14.7 Kinds of bugs that Addrcheck can find

Addrcheck is a simplified version of the Memcheck tool described in Section 3. It is identical in every way to Memcheck, except for one important detail: it does not do the undefined-value checks that Memcheck does. This means Addrcheck is about twice as fast as Memcheck, and uses less memory. Addrcheck can detect the following errors:

- Reading/writing memory after it has been free'd
- Reading/writing off the end of malloc'd blocks
- Reading/writing inappropriate areas on the stack
- Memory leaks -- where pointers to malloc'd blocks are lost forever
- Mismatched use of malloc/new/new [] vs free/delete/delete []
- Overlapping src and dst pointers in memcpy() and related functions
- Some misuses of the POSIX pthreads API

The result is that Addrcheck's leak checker may "discover" pointers to blocks that Memcheck would not. So it is possible that Memcheck could (correctly) conclude that a block is leaked, yet Addrcheck would not conclude that.

Addrcheck is, therefore, a fine-grained address checker. All it really does is check each memory reference to say whether or not that location may validly be addressed. Addrcheck has a memory overhead of one bit per byte of used address space. In contrast, Memcheck has an overhead of nine bits per byte.

error messages from Addrcheck do not distinguish reads from writes. So it will say, for example, "Invalid memory access of size 4", whereas Memcheck would have said whether the access is a read or a write.

Addrcheck is quite pleasant to use. It's faster than Memcheck, and the lack of valid-value checks has another side effect: the errors it does report are relatively easy to track down, compared to the tedious and often confusing search sometimes needed to find the cause of uninitialised-value errors reported by Memcheck.

To use this tool, we must specify --tool=addrcheck on the Valgrind command line.

14.8 Helgrind: a data-race detector

To use this tool, we must specify --tool=helgrind on the Valgrind command line.

Helgrind is a Valgrind tool for detecting data races in C and C++ programs that use the Pthreads library.

Basically what Helgrind does is to look for memory locations which are accessed by more than one thread. For each such location, Helgrind records which of the program's (pthread_mutex_)locks were held by the accessing thread at the time of the access. The hope is to discover that there is indeed at least one lock which is used by all threads to protect that location. If no such lock can be found, then there is (apparently) no consistent locking strategy being applied for that location, and so a possible data race might result.

Helgrind also allows for "thread segment lifetimes". If the execution of two threads cannot overlap -- for example, if your main thread waits on another thread with a pthread_join() operation -- they can both access the same variable without holding a lock.

14.9 Massif: a heap profiler

To use this tool, you must specify --tool=massif on the Valgrind command line.

Massif is a heap profiler, i.e. it measures how much heap memory programs use. In particular, it can give you information about:

- Heap blocks;
- Heap administration blocks;
- Stack sizes.

Heap profiling is useful to help you reduce the amount of memory our program uses. On modern machines with virtual memory, this provides the following benefits:

It can speed up our program -- a smaller program will interact better with our machine's caches, avoid paging, and so on.

If our program uses lots of memory, it will reduce the chance that it exhausts our machine's swap space.

Also, there are certain space leaks that aren't detected by traditional leak-checkers, such as Memcheck's. That's because the memory isn't ever actually lost -- a pointer remains to it -- but it's not in use. Programs that have leaks like this can unnecessarily increase the amount of memory they are using over time.

Everybody knows how useful time profilers are for speeding up programs. They are particularly useful because people are notoriously bad at predicting where are the bottlenecks in their programs.

But the story is different for heap profilers. Some programming languages, particularly lazy functional languages like Haskell, have quite sophisticated heap profilers. But there are few tools as powerful for profiling C and C++ programs.

Why is this? Maybe it's because C and C++ programmers must think that they know where the memory is being allocated. After all, we can see all the calls to malloc() and new and new[], right? But, in a big program, do we really know which heap allocations are being executed, how many times, and how large each allocation is? Can we give even a vague estimate of the memory footprint for our program? Do we know this for all the libraries our program uses? What about administration bytes required by the heap allocator to track heap blocks -- have you thought about them? What about the stack? If we are unsure about any of these things, maybe we should think about heap profiling.

Massif can tell we these things.

Or maybe it's because it's relatively easy to add basic heap profiling functionality into a program, to tell we how many bytes we have allocated for certain objects, or similar. But this information might only be simple like total counts for the whole program's execution. What about space usage at different points in the program's execution, for example? And re-implementing heap profiling code for each project is a pain.

Massif can save you this effort.

First off, as for normal Valgrind use, we probably want to compile with debugging info (the -g flag). But, as opposed to Memcheck, we probably do want to turn optimization on, since we should profile our program as it will be normally run.

Then, run our program with valgrind --tool=massif in front of the normal command line invocation. When the program finishes, Massif will print summary space statistics. It also creates a graph representing the program's heap usage in a file called massif.pid.ps, which can be read by any PostScript viewer, such as Ghostview.

It also puts detailed information about heap consumption in a file massif.pid.txt (text format) or massif.pid.html (HTML format), where pid is the program's process id.

Basic Results of Profiling

To gather heap profiling information about the program prog, type:

```
valgrind --tool=massif prog
```

The program will execute (slowly). Upon completion, summary statistics that look like this will be printed:

```
==27519== Total spacetime:  2,258,106 ms.B
==27519== heap:              24.0%
==27519== heap admin:        2.2%
==27519== stack(s):          73.7%
```

All measurements are done in spacetime, i.e. space (in bytes) multiplied by time (in milliseconds). Note that because Massif slows a program down a lot, the actual spacetime figure is fairly meaningless; it's the relative values that are interesting.

Which entries we see in the breakdown depends on the command line options given. The above example measures all the possible parts of memory:

Heap: number of words allocated on the heap, via malloc(), new and new[].

Heap admin: each heap block allocated requires some administration data, which lets the allocator track certain things about the block. It is easy to forget about this, and if your program allocates lots of small blocks, it can add up. This value is an estimate of the space required for this administration data.

Stack(s): the spacetime used by the programs' stack(s). (Threaded programs can have multiple stacks.) This includes signal handler stacks.

Spacetime Graphs

As well as printing summary information, Massif also creates a file representing a spacetime graph, massif.pid.hp. It will produce a file called massif.pid.ps, which can be viewed in a PostScript viewer.

Massif uses a program called hp2ps to convert the raw data into the PostScript graph. It's distributed with Massif, but came originally from the Glasgow Haskell Compiler. We shouldn't need to worry about this at all. However, if the graph creation fails for any reason, Massif tell you, and will leave behind a file named massif.pid.hp, containing the raw heap profiling data.

Here's an example graph:

spacetime graph

The graph is broken into several bands. Most bands represent a single line of your program that does some heap allocation; each such band represents all the allocations and de-allocations done from that line. Up to twenty bands are shown; less significant allocation sites are merged into "other" and/or "OTHER" bands. The accompanying text/HTML file produced by Massif has more detail about these heap allocation bands. Then there are single bands for the stack(s) and heap admin bytes.

7.6 Details of Heap Allocations

The text/HTML file contains information to help interpret the heap bands of the graph. It also contains a lot of extra information about heap allocations that you don't see in the graph.

Here's part of the information that accompanies the above graph.

== 0 ===========================

Heap allocation functions accounted for 50.8% of measured spacetime

Called from:

* 22.1%: 0x401767D0: _nl_intern_locale_data (in /lib/i686/libc-2.3.2.so)
* 8.6%: 0x4017C393: read_alias_file (in /lib/i686/libc-2.3.2.so)
* (several entries omitted)
* and 6 other insignificant places

The first part shows the total spacetime due to heap allocations, and the places in the program where most memory was allocated (nb: if this program had been compiled with -g, actual line numbers would be given). These places are sorted, from most significant to least, and correspond to the bands seen in the graph. Insignificant sites (accounting for less than 0.5% of total spacetime) are omitted.

That alone can be useful, but often isn't enough. What if one of these functions was called from several different places in the program? Which one of these is responsible for most of the memory used? For _nl_intern_locale_data(), this question is answered by clicking on the 22.1% link, which takes us to the following part of the file.

```
== 1 ===========================
Context accounted for 22.1% of measured spacetime
0x401767D0: _nl_intern_locale_data (in /lib/i686/libc-2.3.2.so)
```

Called from:

```
* 22.1%: 0x40176F95: _nl_load_locale_from_archive (in /lib/i686/libc-2.3.2.so)
```

At this level, we can see all the places from which _nl_load_locale_from_archive() was called such that it allocated memory at 0x401767D0. (We can click on the top 22.1% link to go back to the parent entry.) At this level, we have moved beyond the information presented in the graph. In this case, it is only called from one place. We can again follow the link for more detail, moving to the following part of the file.

```
== 2 ===========================
Context accounted for 22.1% of measured spacetime
  0x401767D0: _nl_intern_locale_data (in /lib/i686/libc-2.3.2.so)
  0x40176F95: _nl_load_locale_from_archive (in /lib/i686/libc-2.3.2.so)
```

Called from:

```
* 22.1%: 0x40176184: _nl_find_locale (in /lib/i686/libc-2.3.2.so)
```

In this way we can dig deeper into the call stack, to work out exactly what sequence of calls led to some memory being allocated. At this point, with a call depth of 3, the information runs out (thus the address of the child entry, 0x40176184, isn't a link). We could rerun the program with a greater --depth value if we wanted more information.

Sometimes you will get a code location like this:

```
* 30.8% : 0xFFFFFFFF: ???
```

The code address isn't really 0xFFFFFFFF -- that's impossible. This is what Massif does when it can't work out what the real code address is.

Massif produces this information in a plain text file by default, or HTML with the --format=html option. The plain text version obviously doesn't have the links, but a similar effect can be achieved by searching on the code addresses. (In Vim, the '*' and '#' searches are ideal for this.)

7.7 Massif options

Massif-specific options are:

```
--heap=no
--heap=yes [default]
```

When enabled, profile heap usage in detail. Without it, the massif.pid.txt or massif.pid.html will be very short.

--heap-admin=n [default: 8]

The number of admin bytes per block to use. This can only be an estimate of the average, since it may vary. The allocator used by glibc requires somewhere between 4--15 bytes per block, depending on various factors. It also requires admin space for freed blocks, although Massif does not count this.

--stacks=no

--stacks=yes [default]

When enabled, include stack(s) in the profile. Threaded programs can have multiple stacks.

--depth=n [default: 3]

Depth of call chains to present in the detailed heap information. Increasing it will give more information, but Massif will run the program more slowly, using more memory, and produce a bigger .txt/.hp file.

--alloc-fn=name

Specify a function that allocates memory. This is useful for functions that are wrappers to malloc(), which can fill up the context information uselessly (and give very uninformative bands on the graph). Functions specified will be ignored in contexts, i.e. treated as though they were malloc(). This option can be specified multiple times on the command line, to name multiple functions.

--format=text [default]

--format=html

Produce the detailed heap information in text or HTML format. The file suffix used will be either .txt or .html.

14.10 Alleyoop: A front end for Valgrind

This is a front end for Valgrind. As of now it supports memcheck, addresscheck and cachecheck from its GUI. To run Alleyoop, execute the following command at a shell prompt (See Figure 14.1 for the Alleyoop's Main Windows).

alleyoop

This will start the main user interface. At this point we will likely wish to click on the "Run" toolbar button (or use the shortcut keys: Control+R) which will prompt us to enter the name of a program to debug and any command-line arguments we wish to pass. Beware that environment variables in the command-line entered in the prompt will NOT be expanded.

An easier way to do this (in my opinion, anyway) is to specify the program on the command-line:

alleyoop ./a.out -v --arg1=foo aout.in

The example above will initialize Alleyoop to run the command:

./a.out -v --arg1=foo aout.in

when you click on the Run toolbar button.

Command-line Arguments and Environment Variables:

-I, --include

These arguments allow you to specify a single source path for Alleyoop to scan when you request it to load a source preview or launch an editor. We may use these as many times as you like.

-R, --recursive

These arguments, like -I or --include, allow us to specify a source path to Alleyoop. The difference is that -R and --recursive will also add all subdirectories of the path specified to Alleyoop's internal list of source paths.

ALLEYOOP_INCLUDE_PATH

Also for our convenience, there exists an environment variable, ALLEYOOP_INCLUDE_PATH, that Alleyoop will also use for this purpose. Like the PATH and LD_LIBRARY_PATH environment variables, directory names are delimited using the colon (:) character.

Note: paths passed to Alleyoop via the command-line arguments take precedence over any specified in the environment variable under the assumption that the user will have likely set ALLEYOOP_INCLUDE_PATH for all the core libraries that the programs he/she is interested in debugging while using the command-line arguments for source paths limited to the program itself.

--tool

This command-line argument allows us to specify which Valgrind tool we want to use by default for this particular "Alleyoop Debug Session". An example usage might be:

alleyoop --tool=addrcheck

-h, --help

-v, --version

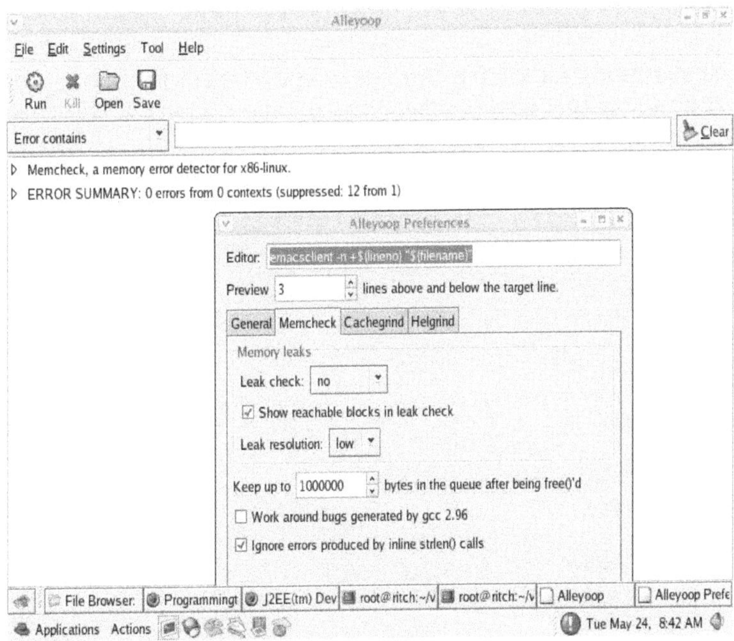

Figure 14.1 Alleyoop main window.

The first thing we are likely to notice is a big white rectangular area right below the toolbar/searchbar. This is the most important user interface element because this is where the errors will be reported (see Figure 14.2).

Once we hit that Run button in the toolbar, messages will start to appear. We should immediately notice that each line of text will have a side-ways triangle next to it. When we click on one of these triangles, the error message will expand to present us with more information. Generally, this information will consist of at least 1 call-chain[1]. When multiple call-chains appear, they will be separated by a singleton line giving further information about the error. Usually, call chains after the first will be used to provide us with clues as to where memory involved in the error was allocated or freed.

Each line of a call-chain (A call-chain is the first few parent stack frames leading up to the Error) will normally have a side-ways triangle next to it as well. Expanding a call-chain tree node will, presuming Alleyoop can find the source file, load a preview of the source code involved in the error (you can configure the number of lines of context you wish to see in the preview, by default the number of context lines are 2 lines above and below the line with the error).

There are several operations that we can do with a call-chain node:

1. Double-clicking a call-chain node with the left mouse button will launch your preferred editor on the source file containing the error (using the command-line you configured in the Preferences dialog).
2. Right-clicking a call-chain node will popup a context menu allowing us to:

(a) Cut/Copy: Selecting either of these items will copy the current error condition into your clipboard buffer in the format used by Valgrind.

(b) Suppress[2]: This item will open a suppression editor dialog pre-filled with the currently selected call-chain information. The suppression editor (see Figure 14.2) will also default the Suppression-Type and System-call values if it can.

(c) Edit in ...: These items all launch the editor specified in the menu name on the source file containing the error (similar to double-clicking a call-chain node as explained above).

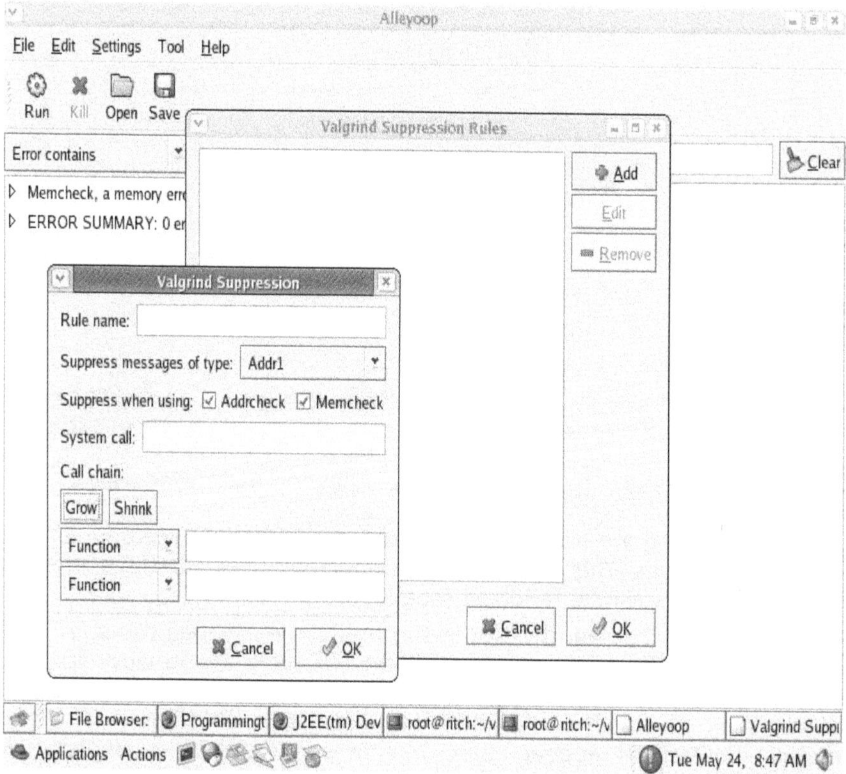

Figure 14.2 Error window: suppression editor.

Note: The GNU/Emacs item is special - it first tries to use `emacsclient -n +${lineno} "${filename}"`. Failing that, it falls back to launching a new emacs editor.

Using the Search Bar:

Like suppressions, the Search Bar (located just below the toolbar) can be a valuable tool in limiting the errors you see to those that you care about seeing.

Unlike suppressions, however, they:

1) do not act like as a blacklist (instead, they act more as a whitelist).

2) are not permanently applied - clearing the search will restore the full error log.

You are currently able to search using the following criteria:

Error contains: This option can be used to search for substrings in the error summary (top level node for each error).

Function contains: Search for errors with a particular function in the call-chain.

Object contains: Search for errors with a particular shared library (or other object) in a call-chain.

Source filename contains: Search for errors where a function in the call-chain is in a particular source file.

14.11 Conclusions

This chapter deals with a versatile tool valgrind, which can be used to find out memory leaks, memory violations, null pointer assignment problems, etc., in the code. Also, how the same can be used for analyzing cache performance with a program and how to improve the same is also dealt. How other tools available with valgrind can be used is explained. Also, alleyoop (which is in alpha release) a GUI based front end to valgrind is also dealt.

15 Make

15.1 Introduction

Make is most commonly used in Linux/Unix for automating SW system compiling and development. Compiling a program made of one source file is easy compared to the ones which is made of many sources. It is not uncommon a SW system to have multiple source files; and a function in one source file may be calling another function in another file. Thus, when a program (file) is modified or rebuilt, make helps in saving the memory space and reducing SW compilation time by re-compiling only those files which depends on the modified file.

As mentioned above, the purpose of make utility is to determine automatically which pieces of a large program need to be recompiled, and issue the commands to recompile them. This is done based on time stamps of the files in SW system and the specification file (also called as makefile) which contains dependencies among the source files. We can use make with any programming language whose compiler can be run with a shell command. Make is not limited to programs. We can use it to describe any task where some files must be updated automatically from others whenever the other one changes.

The make command has a lot of built in knowledge such as how a object file is to be created from a C/C++ source, how a C file to be generated from lex/yacc specification files, etc.,. However, we must provide a file that tells make how our application is constructed and this file is called the make file whose name can be makefile or Makefile (or any other thing).

The make file most often resides in the same directory as the other source files for the project. We can have many different make files on the same machine at any one time for different SW systems. The combination of the make command and a make file provides a very powerful tool for SW projects.

15.2 SYNTAX OF MAKEFILES

A makefile consists of a set of dependencies and rules. A dependency has a target (a file to be created) and a set of source files upon which it is dependent. The rules describe how to create the target from the dependent file.

The make file is read by the make command, which determines the target file or files on which make command to be executed and then compares the dates and times of the source files to decide which rules need to be invoked to construct the target. Also, the make command uses the makefile to determine the order in which the targets have to be made and the correct sequence of rules to invoke.

15.2.1 Options and parameters to make:

Example 1

For example consider the following files:

File a.c

```
void f()
{
printf("Hello\n");
}
```

File b.c

```
void ff()
{
printf("How are you?\n");
}
```

File a.h

```
void f();
void ff();
```

File main.c

```
#include<stdio.h>
#include"a.h"

int main()
{

f();
ff();

return 0;
}
```

For the above examples, the following file "makefile" is written which indicates the dependencies among the files.

```
myapp: main.o. a.o b.o
        gcc  -o myapp main.o  a.o  b.o
main o: main.c.   a.h
   gcc -c   main.c
a.o: a. c
   gcc   -c a.c
b.o: b.c
   gcc  -c b.c
```

15.2.2 Dependencies

In the above example, the main.o is affected by changes to main.c and a.h, and it needs to be recreated by recompiling man.c if either of the two files changes.

Similarly, the final target file (executable) "myapp" depends on main.o, a.o and b.o; which in turn have their dependencies mentioned above.

In a makefile, we rite these rules by writing the name of the target, a colon, spaces or tabs and then a space or tab separated list of files that are used to create the target file. The dependency list for our example is

```
myapp: main o  a.o b.o
main.o: main.c   a.h
a.o: a.c
b.o: b.c
```

We can see quite easily that, if b.c changes, then we need to recompile b.c to get b.o and also we need to rebuild myapp.

15.2.3 Rules

The second part of the makefile specifies the rules that describe how to create a target. In our example, what command should be used after the make command has determined that a.o needs rebuilding.

A very strange and unfortunate syntax of makefile's: the difference between a space and tab. All rules must be on line that start with a tab; a space won't do.

Run the make command by typing simply **make** at the command prompt. We will get the following messages on the screen.

```
gcc –c main.c
gcc –c a.c
gcc –c b
gcc –o myapp main.o a.o b.o
```

Now, you can run the program "myapp" by simply typing the following at command prompt.

```
./myapp
```

We can invoke the make command with the -f option along with make file name if it is different from default make file name's such as makefile or Makefile.

If we invoke the above example in a directory containing no source code files, we get this make error message.

```
make: * * * no rule to make target 'main.c', needed by 'main.o' stop.
```

Also, the above makefile can be modified as shown below as make command can employ it's own target generation rules.

```
myapp: main.o. a.o b.o
        gcc -o myapp main.o a.o b.o
main o: main.c. a.h
a.o: a. c
b.o: b.c
```

Run the above makefile (modified) by typing **make** command at the command prompt. We get the following messages on the screen.

```
cc -o a.o a.c
cc -o b.o b.c
cc -o main main.c
gcc -o myapp main.o a.o b.o
```

Further, we can modify the makefile to have the following lines only (Test it) as make command has inherent mechanism to know how a.o and b.o can be generated, i.e it assumes that a.o can be generated from a.c and b.o from b.c. Thus, it uses it's default object file creation command "cc -o".

```
myapp: main.o. a.o b.o
        gcc -o myapp main.o a.o b.o
main o: main.c. a.h
```

For example, if a.c file is modified then when we run make command, we find the following messages indicating that a.o is recreated and myapp also recreated.

```
gcc -c a.c
gcc -o myapp main.o a.o b.o
```

In order to simulate the above without really changing a.c file, we can run "touch a.c" command followed by make. As a.c file time stamp is changing, the program "myapp" is recreated.

Also, we can ask make to create the required target only. For example, the following commands are acceptable.

```
make myapp          //to create myapp program
make a.o            //to create object file a.o
make main.o         //to create object file main.o
```

15.2.4 Options to be used with make command

-C Dir

Change to directory dir before reading the makefile's or doing anything else. If multiple -c options are specified. Each is interpreted relative to the previous one. –c/ -c etc is equivalent – c/etc.

For example let us take the above mentioned example whose files are in x directory and also in y directory . Suppose that if the object files of x were removed then when we give a command

make –C y –f mkfile
make –c dkp – f mkfil

The files in the DPK directory will be taken and thus we get an output as

```
make : Entering directory '/home/ ravi / dpk'
make :'myapp' is upto date
make : Leaving directory 'home/ravi/dpk'
```

-d

print debugging information in addition to normal processing. The debugging information says which files are being considered for remaking which file-times are being compared and with what results, which files actually need to be remade, which implicit rules are considered and which are applied .... every-thing.

Example: make -d -f makefile

- e

Give variables taken from the environment precedence over variables from makefile's.

```
make -e -f makefile
make : 'myapp' is upto date
```

-f file

Use file as a makefile

For using the –f option we must first create makefile's with the required rules.

- i

Ignore all errors in commands executed to remake files

```
make -i -f makefile
myapp is upto date
```

-I dir

Specifies a directory dir to search for included make files. If several – I options are used to specify several directories. The directories are searched in the order specified.

Unlike the arguments to other flags of make, directories given with –I flags may come directly after the flag : Idir is allowed , as well as –I dir. This syntax is allowed for compatibility with the (pre processors flag of gcc).

-j jobs

Specifies the number of job (commands) to run simultaneously.

-k

Continues as much as possible often an error. While the target that failed, and those that depend on it. Can not be remade, the other dependencies of these targets can be processed all the same.

Let us consider the file b.c is modified as follows. Note that semicolon is missing with the printf() function.

```
void ff ( )
{
   printf ("How are you?")
}
```

make –k –f makefile

```
cc -c 3.c
b.c: 4: parse error at end of input
make: * * * [b.0] error 1
make: Target 'myapp' not remade because of errors.
```

As the error we made is not ignorable the makefile is now updated.

- **n**

This options prints the commands that would be executed (but are not executed really) them.

make –n -f makefile

```
gcc -c -o a.o a.c
gcc -c b.c -o b.o
```

Do not remake the file file, even if it is older then its dependencies, and do not remake anything on account of changes in file. Initially the file is treated as very old and its rules are ignored.

-p

print the database (rules and variables values) that results from reading the make files; I then execute as usual or as otherwise specified. This also prints the version information given by the –v switch.

make -p -f makefile

- **q**

"Question mode" Do not run any commands, or print anything; just return an exit status that is zero if the specified target already exists (up to date). Non zero otherwise.

-r

eliminate use of the built-in implicit rules. Also clear out the default list of suffix rules.

-s

silent operation do not print the commands as they are executed.

make –s – f makefile

- **S** (capital)

cancel the effect of the – k option. This is never necessary except in a recursive make where – k might be inherited from the top-level make via MAKE FLAGS or if you set – k in MAKEFLAGS in the env.

make –s -f makefile

make: myap is upto date.

- **t**

Touch files (mark them up to date without really charging them) instead of running their commands this is used to pretend that the commands were done, in order to fool future invocations of make.

- v

Print the version of the make program plus a copyright, a list of authors and a notice that

make –v

GNU make version 3.791 by Richard Stalman and Roland McGrath

Built for 1686-pc-linux – gnu

Copyright © 1988. 89, 90, 91, 92, 93, 94, 95 , 96, 97, 98, 99, 2000

Free software foundation, Inc.

This is free software, see the source for copying conditions.

There is no warranty: not even for MERCHANTABILITY or FITNESS FOR A PARTICULAR PURPOSE.

-w

print a message containing the working directory before and often other processing. This may be useful for tracking down errors from complicated rest of recursive make commands.

make –w –f makefile

```
make: Entering directory '/home/ravi/dpk'
make. makefile: No such file or directory
make: * * * NO rule to make target 'mkfile'. Stop.
Make. Leaving directory '/home/ravi/dpk'
```

- **W** (capital)

- w file

retend that the target file has just been modified. When used with the –n flag. This Shows us what would happen if we were to modify that file, without – n. It is almost the same as running a touch command on the given file before running make. Except that the modification time is changed only in the imagination of make.

make –w -f makefile

```
make. Nothing to be done for makefile
```

15.2.5 Little More Generalised makefile

Whatever we have explained till now explains only a fraction of what make can do really. Make has extensive set of facilities and structure with the help of which we can write efficient, re-usable make scripts quickly.

A typical makefile may contain lines of the following types:

- Variable Definitions - these lines define values for variables. For example:

```
CFLAGS = -O6 –g -Wall
SRCS = main.c file1.c file2.c
CC = gcc
```

- Dependency Rules - these lines define under what conditions a given file (or a type of file) needs to be re-compiled, and how to compile it. For example:

```
main.o: main.c
	gcc -g -Wall -c main.c
```

Note that each line in the commands list must begin with a TAB character. "make" is quite picky about the makefile's syntax.

- Comments - Any line beginning with a "#" sign, or any line that contains only white-space.

For example, our example makefile can be modified as a structured one as:

```
CFLAGS = -g  -O6  -Wall // these options use is discussed earlier
SRCS =  main.c  a.c  b.c
CC = gcc

myapp:a.o b.o m.o
   gcc –o myapp m.o a.o b.o
main.o:main.c a.h

clean: /bin/rm -f  main.o a.o b.o
```

The above program can be invoked as usual to create myapp. We can execute "make clean" to remove all object files created during the process of make file's execution.

When make is invoked, it first evaluates all variable assignments, from top to bottom, and when it encounters a rule "A" whose target matches the given target (or the first rule, if no target was supplied), it tries to evaluate this rule. First, it tries to recursively handle the dependencies that appear in the rule. If a given dependency has no matching rule, but there is a file in the disk with this name, the dependency is assumed to be up-to-date. After all the dependencies were checked, and any of them required handling, or refers to a file newer than the target, the command list for rule "A" is executed, one command at a time.

When we try to compile the same source code with different compilers, or on different platforms, we write makefile's with little more flexible manner. Lets see the same makefile, but this time with the introduction of variables:

```
# use "gcc" to compile source files.
CC = gcc

# the linker is also "gcc". It might be something else with other compilers.
LD = gcc

# Compiler flags go here.
CFLAGS = -g  O6  -Wall

LDFLAGS =

# use this command to erase files.
RM = /bin/rm -f

# list of generated object files.
OBJS = main.o file1.o file2.o
```

```
# program executable file name.
PROG = myapp
# top-level rule, to compile everything.

all: $(PROG)

# rule to link the program
$(PROG): $(OBJS)
	$(LD) $(LDFLAGS) $(OBJS) -o $(PROG)

# rule for file "main.o".
main.o: main.c a.h
	$(CC) $(CFLAGS) -c main.c

# rule for file "a.o".
a.o: a.c
	$(CC) $(CFLAGS) -c a.c

# rule for file "b.o".
b.o: b.c
	$(CC) $(CFLAGS) -c b.c

# rule for cleaning re-compilable files.
clean:
	$(RM) $(PROG) $(OBJS)
```

To use one rule for all source files as all can be compiled in the same way, we may follow the following approach.

```
# linking rule
$(PROG): $(OBJS)
	$(LD) $(LDFLAGS) $(OBJS) -o $(PROG)

# now comes a meta-rule for compiling any "C" source file.
%.o: %.c
	$(CC) $(CFLAGS) -c $<
```

Here, meta-rule indicates the following:

1. The "%" character is a wildcard, that matches any part of a file's name. If we mention "%" several times in a rule, they all must match the same value, for a given rule invocation. Thus, our rule here means "A file with a '.o' suffix is dependent on a file with the same name, but a '.c' suffix".
2. The "$<" string refers to the dependency list that was matched by the rule (in our case - the full name of the source file). There are other similar strings, such as "$@" which refers to the full target name, or "$*", that refers the part that was matched by the "%" character.

Main crunch in writing make files is identifying dependencies. It is advised that programmers interested in this issue read about the compiler's "-M" flag (discussed in previous chapter on compiling), and read the manual page of "makedepend" carefully.

15.3 Conclusions

This chapter explains about how make utility can be used for SW development. Simple and lucid examples are given such that a new entrant can also understand how to use make for SW development.

16 Revision Control System

16.1 Introduction

Software development is an incremental process involving updating of source files and testing their functionality and reverting back to previous version of the same if not behaving as expected by us. Thus, we may often find need to have the content of file(s) of a specified date and time. Revision control system's (RCS) will come to rescue us for this type of situations. RCS stores the differences of versions of a file. Files can be restored without regard to the system manager. RCS software maintains two fundamental commands " ci "(check in) –to check in the file and " co "(check out) – to check out the file.

RCS is a file management tool designed to aid development of text files (programs, documents, almost any printable file) under UNIX. RCS meets an important need in managing large projects. It allows to automate many of the tasks involved in co-ordinating a team of people who are editing and using files. These tasks include maintaining all versions of a file in a recoverable form, preventing several people from modifying the same code simultaneously, helping people to merge two different development tracks into a single version, ensuring that a single program is not undergoing multiple simultaneous versions and maintaining logs for versions and other changes.

By using RCS, we can restore files without regard with the system manager. RCS won't protect from disk crash, but they can protect from many cases of accidental file deletion (or) corruption. This tool is developed to manage multiperson development projects, ensuring that only one person has write access to a file at one time and making it possible to go back to any previous versions of a file. They are handy for any user who has important files that change frequently.

16.1.1 Creation of a file under RCS management :

- Create a subdirectory called RCS in the directory where we keep the code (or) other text files we want to protect.
- It is not essential, but a good idea to add the characters id somewhere in the file we want to place under RCS. Out this in a comment filed i.e. use /*id*/ in a C program and # id in a shell script.
- Place the file under revision control . This is done by typing :

```
# ci  filename
```

and to retrieve the file, use the following command:

```
# co filename
```

- Basic Operations

The two fundamental commands for using RCS are ci and co. These command ci – "check in" and co- "checkout" are the one's that RCS software maintains.

RCS creates a separate RCS file for every file under its management. This file stores a description of the file, the entire change log, the current version of the file, list of users who are allowed to access the file, the file's date and time and list of changes that lets RCS reproduce any obsolete version of the file at will. On many system, by default, RCS is in the strict-access mode. This mode has two important features :

- No one is allowed to check in a file without locking it first.
- No one can modify a file unless that user (person) checked it out locked.

The first version of a file under RCS control is given number 1.1 Succeeding versions that descend linearly this file are numbered 1.2, 1.3 etc.

RCS gives the first "branch" beginning at version 1.3, the number 1.3.1. It numbers the second branch beginning at this point 1.3.2 etc. The first version along the first branch is 1.3.1.1 and the second is 1.3.1.2 etc.

The tool "rcsmerge' exists to help us to merge versions from different branches of development and the tool "rcsdiff" is used to find out the differences between the two files and to create a new version that incorporates the modifications to both files.

RCS stores the differences between version of a file.

NAME

rcs – change RCS file attributes

SYNOPSIS

rcs options file ....

DESCRIPTION

rcs creates new RCS files (or) changes attributes of existing ones. An RCS file contains multiple revisions of text, an access list, a change log, descriptive text, and some control attributes. Pathnames matching an RCS suffix denote RCS files, all other denote working files.

OPTIONS

-i : create and initialise a new RCS file, but do not deposit any revision. If the RCS file has no path prefix, try to place it first into the subdirectory ./ RCS and then into the current directory. If the RCS file already exists , print an error message.

For example with the following commands a.c file is created and the same is deposited to rcs system.

```
touch a.c.

rcs –i  a.c
   RCS file : a.c,v
   Enter description, terminated with a single :'(or)
end of file.

Note : This is NOT the log message !

>> This is a rcs file of a.c.
   >>.
```

Check the content of the file created by running vi command on it.

vi a.c,v

```
Head ;
Access;
Symbols;
Locks, strict;
Comment @ * @;
Desc
@ this is a rcs file of a.c.
@
```

-a logins : Append the login names appearing in the comma-separated list logins to the access list of the RCS file.

For example to give access to priya, we can run the following command.s

rcs –apriya a.c

```
RCS file : a.c,v
done
```

Now check the content of file a.c,v by running vi command on it and we can see that the user name is seen in the Access list.

vi a.c,v

```
Head ;
Access;
priya
Symbols;
Locks, strict;
Comment @ * @;
Desc
@ this is a rcs file of a.c.
@
```

-A oldfile : Append the access list of old file to the access list of the RCS file.

For example create another file, say b.c and run the following command to access list.

```
rcs –i  b.c
   RCS file : b.c,v
   Enter description, terminated with a single '.'(or)
end of file.

   Note : This is NOT the log message !
   >> temporary file
   >>.
   done
```

Now we can assign access to user dolly for this file "b.c".

```
rcs   - adolly   b.c

   RCS file : b.c,v
   done
```

Now when we run the following command then user names who has permissions for b.c will be added to a.c file.

```
rcs   -Ab.c.    a.c

   RCS file : a.c,v
   done
```

Now, see the content of file a.c,v.

```
vi a.c,v
   head ;
   access;
   priya;
   dolly;
   symbols;
   locks, strict;
   comment @ * @;
   desc
   @ this is a rcs file of a.c.
   @
```

- e [logins] :   Erase the login names appearing in the comma-separated list logins from the access list of the RCS file. If logins are omitted, erase the access list.

Now to remove dolly from acess list of a file we can use –e option as below.

```
rcs  - edolly  a.c

RCS file : a.c,v
done

vi a.c,v
head ;
access;
   priya;
symbols;
locks, strict;
comment @ * @;
desc
@ this is a rcs file of a.c.
@
```

- b [rev] : set the default branch to rev. If rev is omitted, eh default branch is reset to the highest branch on the trunk. If rev begins with a period, then the default branch is prepended to it. If rev is a branch number followed by a period, then the latest revision on that branch is used.

The following command sets the 1.1 as the revision of the file a.c.

```
rcs  -b1.1  a.c
   RCS file : a.c,v
   done
```

Run vi command to check the same in the revision file.

```
vi a.c,v
   head  1.1 ;
   branch 1.1.1;
access;
   priya;
   symbols;
   locks, strict;
   comment @ * @;
   desc
   @ this is a rcs file of a.c.
   @
```

- C string: Set the comment leader to string. An res –i without –c guesses the comment leader from the suffix of the working file name.

res -cDIE a.c

Res file: a.c, V

Done

Now, check the a.c,v file output by opening the same using vi command.

vi a.c,V

=> the string "DIE" overwrites over the comment string.

Comment @ DIE @

- l [rev]: Look the revision with number rev. If a branch is given, lock the latest revision on that branch. If rev is omitted, lock the latest revision on the default branch locking prevents overlapping changes.

The following command lock the file with the given revision.

rcs -l1.1 a.c

RCS file: RCS/a.c,V

1.1 locked

done

vi a.c,v

=> The 'lock' file is modified as

lock

root 1.1; strict;

- Rev: msg: Replace revision rev's with log message.

rcs –m1.1: FORV al.c

RCS file: a.c, v

Done

vi a1.c,v

Also, we can create create a RCS file using ci command. For example,

touch a1.c

ci a1.c

```
RCS/a.c, v   a.c
Enter description, terminated with single'.' (or) end of file.
> > This is a1 file
> >  initial revision 1.1
done
```

vi a1.c,v

```
head;l
access;
symbols;
locks, strict;
comment @ * @;
1.1
data 2004.08.07.02..10.16; author root;
State Exp;
Branches ;
Next;
Desc
@ this is a1 file
@
1.1
log
@ initial revision
@
```

vi a1.c,v

```
=> The log message is modified as 'FOR U',
   log
   @ FOR U
   @
```

- n name [: [rev]]: Associate the symbolic name with the branch (or) revision rev. Delete the symbolic name, if both: and rev are omitted, print an error message if name is already associated with another No. A rcs –n name: RCS/A associates name with the current latest revision of all the named RCS files.

For example,

rcs -nAng:1.1 a1.c
RCS file: a1.c,v
Done

vi a1.c,v

The symbol field is modified as
Symbols
Ang: 1.1 ;

- N name [: [rev]]: act like -n, except override any previous assignment of name.

rcs -Ngel:1.1 a1.c
RCS file: a1.c,v
Done

vi a1.c, v
=> the symbol field is mofided as
symbols
gel: 1.1;

-O range: Delete the revision given by range. A range consisting of a single revision no. means that revision. A range consisting of a branch no. means the latest revision on that branch. A range of the form rev1: rev2 means revisions rev1 to rev2 on the same branch: rev means from the beginning of the branch containing rev upto and including rev and rev: means from revision rev to the end of the branch containing rev.

To create new revision 1.2 and 1.3 of a1.c,v file

co -l a1.c

RCS/a1.c,v a1.c
Revision 1.1 (locked)
Done

vi a1.c
=> Update the a1.c file

ci a1.c

RCS/a1.c,v a1.c
New revision 1.2; previous : 1.1
Done

co -l a1.c

```
RCS/a1.c,v  a1.c
Revision 1.2 (locked)
Done
```

vi a1.c

```
=> Update the a1.c file
   RCS/a1.c,v  a1.c
   New revision 1.3; previous: 1.2
   Done
```

To delete revisions from a file (say revisions 1.2 and 1.3) run the following command with –o option.

rcs -o1.2:1.3 a1.c

```
RCS file: a1.c,
Deleting revision: 1.3
Deleting revision: 1.2
Done
```

vi a1.c,v

```
head 1.1;
access ;
  |
  |
@
```

-q: Run quietly, do not print diagnostics

- : Run interactively, even if the standard input is not a terminal.

-

- s State (:[rev]: Set the state attribute of the revision rev to state. If rev is a branch no., assume the latest revision on that branch. If rev is omitted, assume the latest revision on the default branch. A useful set of states is Exp. (experimental) stab (stable) and Rel (released). By default ci(1) sets the state of a revision to Exp.

rcs -sExp:1.1 a1.c

```
RCS file: a1.c,v
   Done
```

vi a1,c,v

The state file is modified as

Date - - - - - - - state Exp;

rcs -sstab: 1.1 a1.c

RCS file: a1. c,v

Done

vi a.c,v ,,_

The state field is modified as

Date - - - - - - - - - - -state stab;

- t [file]: Write descriptive text from the contents of the named file into the RCS file, deleting the existing text. If the file is omitted obtain the text from standard input, terminated by end-of-file (or) by a line containing. By itself.

vi D.C

This is Linux world

rcs -tD.C a1.c

RCS file: a1.c, v

Done

vi a1.c, v

head 1.1:

|

|

|

desc

@ this is Linux word

@

-t – string: Write descriptive text from the string into the RCS file, deleting the existing text.

rcs -t"GNU" a1.c

RCS file: a1.c, V

Done

vi a1.c,v

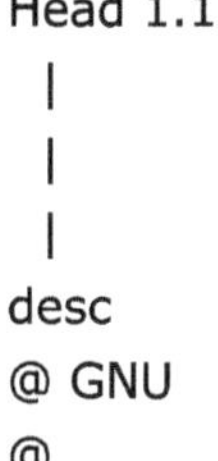

-T: Preserves the modification time on the RCS file unless a revision is removed. This option can suppress extensive re-compilation caused by a make (1) dependency of some copy of the working file.

On the RCS file

-V: Prints RCS's version numbers

rcs –V a1.c

RCS version 5.7

-Vn : Emulate RCS version n.

- X suffixes: Use suffices to characterise RCS files.

-Z zone: Use zone as the default time zone. This option has no effect; it is present for compatibility with other RCS commands.

-K Subset: set the default key word substitution to subset. The affect of key substitution is described in co (1). Giving an explicit –k option to co, rcs diff and rcs merge overrides this default.

- u [rev]: Unlock the revision with number rev. If a branch is given, unlock the latest revision on that branch. If rev is omitted, remove the latest lock held by the caller. Normally only the locker of a revision can unlock it.

- L: Set locking to strict. Strict locking means that the owner of an RCS file is not exempt from locking for check in. * This option should be used for files that are shared.

- U: Set locking to non –strict. Non-strict locking means that the owner of a file need not lock a revision for check in. * This option should not be used for files that are shared.

- M: Do not send mail when breaking somebody else's lock. This options meant for programs that warn users by other uses.

- u [rev]:

touch gel..c
ci gel.c

```
RCS/gel.c,v gel.c
    Enter description terminated with single '.' (or) end-of-file.
    Note: This is not the log message !
    > > this
    > >
    initial revision 1.1
    done
    initial revision 1.1
    done
```

rcs -l1.1 gel.c

```
RCS file: RCS/gel.c,v
1. 1 (locked)
done
```

rcs – u1.1 gel.c

```
RCS file: gel. C, V
1.1 unlocked
done.
```

16.1.2 ci-Check in command :

ci is one of the fundamental command used by the RCS. When a file is check in , RCS deletes source file and creates (or) modifies a file called source, v where source is the name of the original and, v is an extension that indicates an RCS file.

To do a simple check in, use the following command :

ci filename

This creates a new RCS version of your file. If the file is not currently managed by RCS, this command places the file under RCS management, gives it the version no. 1.1 , and prompt for a description of the file. If the file is already being managed by RCS, this command will assign the next higher version number in the sequence (1.2 follows 1.1) and will prompt for a description of the changes have made since the last check in.

The following example shows what happens when checking a version 1.4 of a file called my test.

ci mytest

Mytest, v ··········▶ my test

New revision 1.4; previous revision : 1.3

Enter log message :

(terminate with ^D (or) single '.')

The prompt >> indicates that RCS is waiting for a line of text

RCS warns if a checking a file has not been modified since it was check out. We can force it to check the file in by typing y response to its warning message:

ci mytest

Mytest, v ··········▶ my test

New revision : 1.8; previous revision : 1.7

File mytest is unchanged with respect to revision 1.7

Checking anyway? [ny] (n) : y

Used by itself, the command ci deletes the working version of the file

If you want to retain a read-only version of the file,

Enter the command :

ci –u filename

in this case, a copy of filename for reference is retained. The ci command may refer to let check in a file, printing the message:

ci error ; no lock set by your name.

This can only occur under two circumstances :

1. If you did not lock the file upon checkout in the strict-access mode.
2. If someone locked the file after you checked it out in open-access mode.

If you want to do a checking, followed immediately by a checkout. We may want to install a version reflecting the current state of your program (possible as a back up), then continue editing immediately. other than using two operations, RCS lets us to perform both with the command

ci – l filename

This updates the RCS file and gives a lock with a fresh copy of working file, allowing to edit continue immediately.

NAME

ci-checkin RCS revisions

SYNOPSIS

ci[options] file..........

DESCRIPTION

ci stores new revisions into RCS files. Each pathname matching an RCS suffix is taken to be RCS file. All others are assumed to be working files containing new revisions. Ci deposits the contents of each working file into the corresponding RCS file. For ci to work, the caller's login must be on the access list, except if the accesslist is empty (or) the caller is the superuser (or) the owner of the file. To append a new revision to an existing branch, the top revision on that branch must be locked by the caller, otherwise, only a new branch can be created. This restriction is not enforced for the owner of the file if non-strict locking is used. A lock held by someone else can be broken with the RCS command.

Unless if option is given, ci checks whether the revision to be deposited differs from the preceding one. Ordinary ci removes the working file and nay lock ci - l keeps and ci -u removes any lock and then they both generate a new working file much as if co –l (or) co-u had been applied to the preceding revision.

When reverting, any –n and –s options apply to the preceding revision. For each revision deposited, ci prompts for a log message. The log message should summarize the change and must be terminated by end of the file (or) by a line containing by itself. If RCS file does not exist, ci creates it and deposits the contents of the working file as the initial revision (default number : 1.1). The access list is initialised to empty. Instead of the log message, ci requests descriptive text.

The number rev of the deposited revision can be given an of the options –f, -I, -I, -j, -k, -l, -m, -q, - r (or) –u. *rev can be symbolic, numeric (or) mixed. Symbols names in rev must already be defined. If rev is $, ci determines the revision no form keyboard values in the working file.

If rev begins with a period, then the default branch is prepended to it. If rev is a branch no. followed by a . Then the latest revision on that branch is used.

If rev is a revision no, it must be higher than the latest one on the branch to which rev belongs, (or) must start a new branch.

If rev is a branch rather than a revision no, the new revision is appended to that branch. The level number is obtained by incrementing the tip revision no. If the caller locked a non-tip revision, a new branch is started at that revision by incrementing the highest branch no. at that revision. The default initial branch and level no's are 1.

If rev is omitted and the caller has no lock, but owns the file and locking is not set to strict , then the revision is appended to the default branch.

Options

-mmsg : uses the string msg as the logmessage for all revisions checked in.

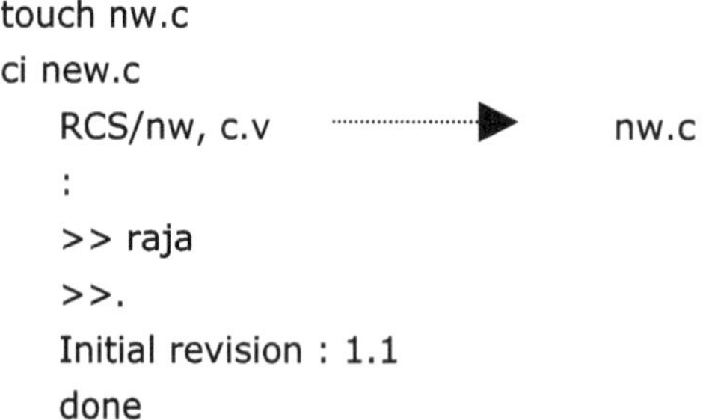

co -l nw.c

RCS / nw.c,v ⟶ nw.c
Revision 1.1 (locked)
done
vi nw.c

ci -mnaveen nw.c

RCS/nw.c.v ⟶ nw.c
new revision : 1.2; previous revision : 1.1
done

vi nw.c.v

The log message is changed to Naveen

- name :assign the symbolic name to the number of the checked-in revision

co -l nw.c

RCS/nw.c,v ⟶ nw.c
new revision : 1.2 , previous revision :1.1
done

vi nw.c,v

The log message is changed to Naveen

- n name : assign the symbolic name to the number of the checked-in revision.

co -l nw.c

RCS / nw.c, v ⟶ nw.c
revision 1.2
done
vi nw.c
ci -nrp nw.c

vi nw.c,v

symbolic name is changed to rp.

- s state : set the state of checked-in revision to the identifier state. The default state is exp.

co -l nw.c

ci -sExp nw.c

vi nw.c, v

state is exp.

-t file : write descriptive text from the contents of the named file into the RC5 file, deleting the existing text.

co -l nw.c

co -t gel.c nw.c

vi nw.c,v

text is changed to raj.

-t -string:write descriptive text from the string into the RCS file

co -l nw.c

ci -t"raja" nw.c

vi nw.c,v

text is changed to raja.

-wlogin : uses login or the author field of the deposited revision.

-v : Print RCS'5 version number.

-x suffixes : specifies the suffices for RCS files. A non-empty suffix matches any pathname ending in the suffix.

-z zone : specifies the date output format in keyword substitution and specifies the default time zone for date in the –date option.

-q [rev] : quiet mode, diagnostic output is not printed.

-M [rev] : set the modification time on any new working file to be the date of the retrieved revision.

-d [date] : uses date for the checkin date and time

-I [rev] : interactive mode, the user is prompted and questioned even if the standard input is not a terminal.

-I [rev] : interactive mode, the user is prompted and questioned even if the standard input is not a terminal.

-f [rev] : forces a deposit; the new revision is deposited even it is not different from the preceding one.

touch s5.c

ci ss.c

```
RCS / ss.c, v  ........►  ss.c
.
.
.
.
>> pittichi
>>.
initial revision : 1.1
done
```

co -l ss.c

vi ss.c

ci ss.c

RCS / ss.cn, ⟶ ss.c

.

.

.

.

new revision ; 1.2; previous revision : 1.2; previous revision : 1.1

done

co -l ss.c

ci -f1.4 ss.c

RCS / ss.cn, ⟶ ss.c,v

.

.

.

.

new revision 1.4; previous revision : 1.2;

.

.

.

done

-k [rev]	:	searches the working file for keyword values to determine its revision number, creation date, state and author, assign these values to the deposited revision, rather than computing them locally
-j [rev]	:	just checkin and do not initialise; report an error if the RCS file does not already exist .
-l [rev]	:	works like –r, except it performs an additional co –l for the deposited revision.
-u [rev]	:	works like –l, except that the deposited revision is not locked. The –l , bare – r and –u options are mutually exclusive and silently override each other for example, is –u -r is equipment to ci – r because –r overrides –u.
-rrev	:	checkin revision rev.
-r	:	with other RCS commands, a bare – r option specifies the most recent revision on the default branch, but with ci, a bare –r option re-established the default behaviour of releasing a lock and removing the working file.

16.1.3 CO-CHECK OUT COMMAND

Co-check out command can be used recover or restore file of any date or version.

Syntax of the co command.

co [options] file ...

co retrieves a revision from each RCS file and stores it into the corresponding working file. Revisions of an RCS file can be checked out locked or unlocked. Lock-ing a revision prevents overlapping updates. A revision checked out for reading or processing (e.g., compiling) need not be locked. A revision checked out for editing and later checkin must normally blocked. Checkout with locking fails if the revision to be checked out is currently locked by another user. (A lock can be broken with rcs(1).) Checkout with locking also requires the caller to be on the access list of the RCS file, unless he is the owner of the file or the superuser, or the access list is empty. Checkout without locking is not subject to accesslist restrictions, and is not affected by the presence of locks.

A revision or branch number can be attached to any of the options -f, -I, -l, -M, -p, -q, -r, or -u. The options -d (date), -s (state), and -w (author) retrieve from a single branch, the selected branch, which is either specified by one of -f, ..., -u, or the default branch. A co command applied to an RCS file with no revisions creates a zero length working file.

OPTIONS

-r[rev]

retrieves the latest revision whose number is less than or equal to rev. If rev indicates a branch rather than a revision, the latest revision on that branch is retrieved. If rev is omitted, the latest revision on the default branch option of is retrieved. If rev is $, co determines the revision number from keyword values in the working file. Otherwise, a revision is composed of one or more numeric or symbolic fields separated by periods. If rev begins with a period, then the default branch (normally the trunk) is prepended to it. If rev is a branch number followed by a period, then the latest revision on that branch is used.

-l[rev]

same as -r, except that it also locks the retrieved revision for the caller.

-u[rev]

same as -r, except that it unlocks the retrieved revision if it was locked by the caller. If rev is omitted, -u retrieves the revision locked by the caller, if there is one; otherwise, it retrieves the latest revision on the default branch.

-f[rev]

forces the overwriting of the working file; useful in connection with -q. .

-kkv

Generate keyword strings using the default form, e.g. $Revision: 5.13 $ for the Revision keyword. A locker's name is inserted in the value of the Header, Id, and Locker keyword strings only as a file is being locked, i.e. by ci -l and co -l. This is the default.

-kkvl

Like -kkv, except that a locker's name is always inserted if the given revision is currently locked.

-kk

Generate only keyword names in keyword strings; omit their values For example, for the evision keyword, generate the string $Revision$ instead of Revision: 5.13 $. This option is useful to ignore differences due to keyword substitution when comparing different revisions of a file. Log messages are inserted after Log keywords even f -kk is specified, since this tends to be more useful when merging changes.

-ko

Generate the old keyword string, present in the working file just before it was checked in. For example, for the Revision keyword, generate the string $Revision: 1.1 $ instead of $Revision: 5.13 $ if that is how the string appeared when the file was checked in. This can be useful for file formats that cannot tolerate any changes to substring's that happen to take the form of keyword strings.

-kb

Generate a binary image of the old keyword string. This acts like -ko, except it performs all working file input and output in binary mode. This makes little difference on Posix and Unix hosts, but on DOS-like hosts one should use rcs -i -kb to initialize an RCS file intended to be used for binary files.

-kv

Generate only keyword values for keyword strings. For example, for the Revision keyword, generate the string 5.13 instead of $Revision: 5.13 $. This can help generate files in programming languages where it is hard to strip keyword delimiters like $Revision: $ from a string.

-p[rev]

prints the retrieved revision on the standard output rather than storing it in the working file. This option is useful when co is part of a pipe.

-q[rev]

quiet mode; diagnostics are not printed.

-I[rev]

interactive mode; the user is prompted and questioned even if the standard input is not a terminal.

-M[rev]

Set the modification time on the new working file to be the date of the retrieved revision.

-sstate

retrieves the latest revision on the selected branch whose state is set to state.

-T

Preserve the modification time on the RCS file even if the RCS file changes because a lock is added or removed. This option can suppress extensive recompilation caused by a make dependency of some other copy of the working file on the RCS file.

-w[login]

retrieves the latest revision on the selected branch which was checked in by the user with login name login. For each pair, co joins revisions rev1 and rev3 with respect torev2. This means that all changes that transform rev2 into rev1are applied to a copy of rev3. This is particularly useful ifrev1 and rev3 are the ends of two branches that have rev2 as a common ancestor. If rev1<rev2<rev3 on the same branch, joining generates a new revision which is like rev3, but with all changes that lead from rev1 to rev2 undone. If changes fromrev2 to rev1 overlap with changes from rev2 to rev3, For the initial pair, rev2 can be omitted.

-V Print RCS's version number.

-Vn Emulate RCS version n, where n can be 3, 4, or 5. This can be useful when interchanging RCS files with others who are running older versions of RCS.

-xsuffixes

Use suffixes to characterize RCS files.

16.2 Conclusions

SW management is explained and how RCS can be used under Linux to manage the code development in a SW project. Few illustrative examples are included to let students to practice.

17 SW Distribution Tools

17. 1 Tar Command

Tar files are a type of archive (either compressed or not) files in the Unix/Linux OS's. This is much like a .zip file in Windows. SW (either source distributions or binary distributions) are often released as tar archives for Unix/Linux systems. Thus, while installing new SW's (either free ware, shareware or commercial ones) tar command is the a way to get the actual source code of a program, compile the source (if needed) and install it on your machine.

Now for installing .tar files, first thing we need to do is go to the console and change directory as the one in which downloaded archive files are stored. For example, if we downloaded the file 'newfile.tar' and saved it to /downloads, in the console we will type "cd /downloads" then hit 'enter'. Now we are in the directory that the file is stored in. Next, we need to unpack or 'untar' the file. That is,

tar -xvf newfile.tar

If the file is a .tar.gz do run the following command at the dollar prompt.

tar -zxvf newfile.tar.gz

This will create a directory in the /downloads directory called 'newfile'. Next change directories to the 'newfile' directory by typing 'cd newfile'. (Notice we didnt include the / in front of the dir name. This is because downloads (which is the current directory) is the parent directory for the 'newfile' directory. If we want to change to a directory not in the current directory path, we would have to include the /.) In the 'newfile' directory, we will have a number of files which are extracted from the archive. Often, README file will be seen in the extracted files which may contain the details about the package and how to deal with it. Also, we may find files such as INSTALL, README, CONFIG, etc. These files will tell we exactly how to configure and install this package. For the most of the SW distributions, once we are in the newfile directory, we can type 'make', then 'make install' followed by 'make clean' to install the program. Be careful though, some programs require us to change settings before we install the program.

After downloading the tarball from our trusted software archive site, change to the appropriate top-level directory and untar the archive by typing commands (as root, if necessary) as in the following example:

tar -zxvpf cardgame.tar.gz

The above command will extract all files from the example ``cardgame.tar.gz'' compressed archive. The ``z'' option tells tar that the archive is compressed with gzip (so omit this option if your tarball is not compressed); the ``x'' option tells tar to extract all files from the archive. The ``v'' option is for verbose, listing all filenames to the display as they are extracted. The ``p'' option maintains the original and permissions the files had as the archive was created. Finally, the ``f'' option tells tar that the very next argument is the file name. Don't forget that options to tar are cAsE-sEnSiTiVe.

Once the tarball has been installed into the appropriate directory, we will almost certainly find a ``README'' or a ``INSTALL'' file included with the newly installed files, with further instructions on how to prepare the software package for use. Likely, we will need to enter commands similar to the following example:

```
./configure
make
make install
```

The above commands would configure the software to ensure our system has the necessary functionality and libraries to successfully compile the package, compile all source files into executable binaries, and then install the binaries and any supporting files into the appropriate locations. The actual procedures we will need to follow may, of course, vary between various software packages, so we should read any included documentation thoroughly.

This command is used to join a group of files and prepare a archive file.

tar -cvf a.tar directoryname(s)orfilename(s)

This command creates a archive file a.tar by joining the given files or files in the given directories.

tar -cvZf a.tZ directoryname(s)orfilename(s)

This command creates compressed tar archive.

tar -cvzf a.tgz directoryname(s)orfilename(s)

This command creates gzipped tar archive.

tar -xvf a.tar

This command extracts all files from the archive.

tar -xvZf a.tZ

This command extracts all files from the compressed archive.

tar -xvzf a.tgz

This command extracts all files from the gzipped archive.

tar -xvf a.tar fileordirectoryname

This extracts the given file or directory from the archive.

tar -xvZf a.tZ fileordirectoryname

This extracts the given file or directory from the archive.

tar -xvzf a.tgz fileordirectoryname

This extracts the given file or directory from the archive.

17.2 Redhat Packet Manager(RPM)[1]

The Red Hat distribution of Linux, including kernel, libraries, and applications are provided as RPM files. An RPM file, also known as a "package" is a way of distributing software so that it can be easily installed, upgraded, queried, and deleted. RPM files contain information on the package's name, version, other file dependency information (if applicable), platform (such as Intel or Alpha, etc.), as well as default file install locations.

The RPM utility was first developed by Red Hat and provided as an Open Source product as is common in the Linux community. Other developers picked it up and added extra functionality. The RPM method of packaging files has become popular and is used not only on Red Hat's but on some other distributions as well.

Popular Linux applications are almost always released as RPM files, usually in fairly short order. However, in the Unix world the defacto-standard for package distribution continues to be by way of so-called "tarballs". Tarballs are simply files that are readable with the ``tar'' utility. Installing from tar is usually significantly more tedious than using RPM. So why would people choose to do so? Unfortunately, sometimes it takes a few weeks for developers to get the latest version of a package converted to RPM.

To query a package, use "**rpm -q pkg-name**" (eg. ``rpm -q pine''). RPM will either tell you what version of the package is already installed, or that the package is not installed. Assuming the package is installed already, and is an earlier version than the update package you downloaded (which it should be), then we should be able to apply the update with "**rpm -Uvh pkg-name**". If all goes well, the package will be automatically installed and immediately ready for use. If not, RPM will give we a pretty good reason (for example, perhaps a supporting package needs to be upgraded first etc.,.).

If, on the other hand, the package is not yet installed, and we decide what we wish to install it, type ``rpm -ivh pkg-name''. If there are any supporting packages that are required, RPM will tell us.

In order to freshen up a package (i.e to install those files which are later versions of already installed packages in out system. To do this operation we have to execute "**rpm –Fvh pkg-name**".

To delete a installed package, we can use "**rpm –e packagename**".

To test a developed package whether it is having all expected files or not, we can use –test option with rpm command. That is, we can run "**rpm - -test packagename**".

If we want, we can exclude any files from the installation with the help of option "**- - excludepath PATH**".

We don't have to compile anything to install any packages. First cd downloads(assume we have downloaded the file to a dir called downloads). Once in that directory, type **rpm -ihf newfile.rpm.** The **rpm -e newfile.rpm** will uninstall the complete program if needed. No need to search for all the files it installed to remove individually. Also **rpm -Uhv --force newfile.rpm**. The --force is a command that (but we can't guess) forces the install even if errors exist.

The way to install a package from source is to specify the ``rebuild'' switch to the RPM utility. For example:

[1] ftp://ftp.redhat.com/redhat/updates

rpm -ivh --rebuild foo.src.rpm

The above command would configure and compile the ``foo'' package, producing a binary RPM file in the ``/usr/src/redhat/RPMS/i386/'' directory (assuming you are using Linux on the Intel platform). We can then install the package as you normally would.

Finally, if we are having problems getting a source package to compile (perhaps we need to modify a makefile, or change a configuration option, etc.) we can use the following steps to compile the source, build a new binary package, and then install from the binary package:

rpm -ivh foo.src.rpm

cd /usr/src/redhat/SPECS

pico -w foo.spec

Make whatever changes we feel are needed to the .spec ' file, and then type:

rpm -ba foo.spec

This will rebuild the package using whatever changes we have made to the ".spec'' file. As above, the resultant binary RPM file will be located in /usr/src/redhat/RPMS/i386/'', and can be installed as we normally would.

After installing a SW package by executing the following command we can check whether any files related to that package are modified since installation.

rpm –V package-name

RPM packages includes built-in information about other components such as libraries etc., that are needed for the package to run. Whenever, we try to install the packages if the required libraries are not available then the installation fails. Same is true in the case of package removal. That is, when we try to un-install any packages which are using some libraries and these libraries are further used by some other packages then the un-install command fails.

In order to know the package release numbers etc., the –q option can be uses such as:

rpm –q package-name

Also, to know about the package version, from which web site it is downloaded, etc., -qi option can be used. For example run the same on samba package.

rpm –qi samba

The above command displays the following output.

Name : samba Relocations: (not relocatable)

Version : 3.0.8 Vendor: Red Hat, Inc.

Release : 0.pre1.3 Build Date: Wed 20 Oct 2004 01:10:51 AM IST

Install Date: Mon 02 Aug 2004 10:15:11 AM IST Build Host: bugs.build.redhat.com

Group : System Environment/Daemons Source RPM: samba-3.0.8-0.pre1.3.src.rpm

Size : 24519856 License: GNU GPL Version 2

Signature : DSA/SHA1, Wed 20 Oct 2004 11:19:07 PM IST, Key ID b44269d04f2a6fd2

Packager : Red Hat, Inc. <http://bugzilla.redhat.com/bugzilla>

URL : http://www.samba.org/

Summary : The Samba SMB server.

Description :

Samba is the protocol by which a lot of PC-related machines share
files, printers, and other information (such as lists of available
files and printers). The Windows NT, OS/2, and Linux operating systems
support this natively, and add-on packages can enable the same thing
for DOS, Windows, VMS, UNIX of all kinds, MVS, and more. This package
provides an SMB server that can be used to provide network services to
SMB (sometimes called "Lan Manager") clients. Samba uses NetBIOS over
TCP/IP (NetBT) protocols and does NOT need the NetBEUI (Microsoft Raw
NetBIOS frame) protocol.

RPM uses scripts for installing, configuring, upgrading and un-installing the packages. For example –scripts option with the rpm command displays the script files used in that package. For example,

rpm –q - - scripts samba

Some packages contains special scripts called as trigger scripts which are invoked during installation if certain conditions are met. These are used to upgrade the packages and works based on the previously installed components. For example the following will display the trigger scripts used in the sendmail package.

rpm –q - -trigger sendmail

In order to know which configuration files are used, we can use the following command.

rpm –qc package-name

In order to know which documentation files are used, we can use the following command.

rpm –qd package-name

To see changelog entries of an RPM package we can use –changelog option as:

rpm –changelog samba

Every rpm package consists of header, signature and the actual files which are to be installed from the package. Each of them are marked with tags. When we query an rpm package with the above mentioned options the content of the above tags are accesses. For example, "- -querytags" option with rpm command displays all of these tags.

It is possible that some times rpm database can break (which can be identified by system handing while installing packages). We can rebuild the rpm database by removing the previous databases from /var/lib/rpm/__db.* and then running the following command.

rpm –v --rebuilddb

If we want, we can start package management tool from the GUI. That is, select **Applications** tab in the main tool bar and then select **System Settings** and then select **Add/remove applications**.

17.2.1 File Roller

In KDE or GNOME tool kit, we have an archive manager known as File Roller with the help of which we can create archives, extract files from archives. It works similar to WinZip or WinZipExpress of Windows world. With the help of this utility, we can manage archives of different types such as .arj, .ear, .jar, .lzh, .rar, tar, compressed tar, gzipped tar, tar compressed with bzip, tar compressed with lzop, .war, .zip and .zoo.

17.3 PAX

This is another facility available in Linux. With the help of pax command, we can read and write file archives and copy directory hierarchies. It supports tar archives, cpio archives of various releases. It is POSIX compliant.

```
pax -w -f /tmp/a.pax .
```

Copies the contents of the current directory to the file /tmp/a.pax. By default, pax uses tar as default archive format.

```
pax -v -f /tmp/a.pax
```

Gives the verbose table of contents of archive file /tmp/a.pax.

```
pax -r -f /tmp/a.pax
pax -r</tmp/a.pax
```

These commands extracts all the files from pax archive.

```
pax –r –f /tmp/a.pax  a4
```

The above command extract file a4 from the pax archive a.pax of /tmp directory.

The following command creates a tar archive file by joing the files a1, a2, a3, and a4.

```
tar -cvf a.tar a1 a2 a3 a4

rm -f a1 a2 a3 a4
ls -al a[0-9]
```

Now, when we run the pax command, files a1, a2, a3 and a4 are extracted from a.tar file.

```
pax -r -f a.tar
```

The following two commands adds (appends) a new file to archive aa.pax.

touch a5

pax -w -a -f aa.pax a5

The above command can be used to add files to tar archive also.

The following command creates cpio archive by joining files a1,a2,a3,a4 and a5.

pax -x cpio -w -f aa.cpio a1 a2 a3 a4 a5

We can give names of the files to be archived from standard input also. For example, type the following command at the dollar prompt and go on enter file names such as a1, a2, a3, etc., and at the end press ^d. All the files will be archived in the specified file.

pax -w -f aaa.pax

a1

a2

a3

a4

^d

mkdir newdir cd olddir pax -rw . newdir

This sequence of commands will copy the entire olddir directory hierarchy to newdir.

pax –r –s ',^//*usr//* ,,' -f a.pax

Reads the archive a.pax, with all files rooted in /usr into the archive extracted relative to the current directory

.

pax -rw -i . dest_dir

Can be used to interactively select the files to copy from the current directory to dest_dir.

pax -r -pe -U root -G bin -f a.pax

Extract all files from the archive a.pax which are owned by root with group bin and preserve all file permissions.

```
pax -r -w -v -Y -Z home /backup
```

Update (and list) only those files in the destination directory /backup which are older (less recent inode change or file modification times) than files with the same name found in the source file tree home.

17.4 SW Patching

Normally SW products are supplied either as binary distribution or source distribution. In source distribution, all the source program files are supplied to the customer and the customer is required to compile on his target machine to get binary or executable code of the SW. Moreover, it is common that SW systems are released in an incremental fashion. When a new release is made, a patch file (difference file) is prepared by comparing with the previous release files. This can downloaded by the customer who is having previous release and by applying the SW patching he can get recent version of the SW source which he can compile to get updated version of SW running on his machine.

Example:

diff p1 p2>p3

Here p3 can be called as patch file.

patch p1 <p3 will change the content of the file p1 as p2.

patch p2 <p3 will change the p2 file content as p1.

Note in some Linux installations, patch file name can be specified with out standard input indirection operator. That is,

patch p1 p3 (here p3 is patch file)

If we have two directories with their own tree structures and files then with the help of the following command we can create the difference between them.

```
diff -ruN olddir newdir >tree.diff
```

If we want to patch olddir with this difference information, we can execute the following command.

```
patch -p0 –u<tree.diff
```

We can replace 0 with 1 to patch the second directory.

17.5 Conclusions

In this chapter, we have discussed about SW archiving tools such as tar, PAX, cpio, rpm are explained in a lucid way. Also, SW patching is explained with easy examples.

Aknowledgement of Sources from Where Materials Have Been Taken and Used in this book

http://jan.netcomp.monash.edu.au/ssw/intro/generic.html

http://jan.netcomp.monash.edu.au/OS/|1 2.html

http://jan.netcomp.monash.edu.au/OS/|1 2..html

http://infocom.cqu.edu.au./Archives/Units/1998/Autumn/85321 Systems Administration/Old Stuff/1996

Website/85321/85321 1996/docs/study-guide/chap3/chpter3.html

http://jan,netcomp.monash,edu.au/OS/|1 2.html

http://www.telenoveia-

world.com~spade/linux/LDP/abs/html/textproc.html,http://infocom,cqu.edu.au/Archives/Units/1998/Autumn/85321 Systems Administration/Old Stuff/1996 Website/85321/study-guide/chap3/chapter3.htm l

http://www.kevinboone.com/boot.html
http://www.telenovela-world.com/~spade/linux/LDP/abs/html/why-shell.html

http://www.aboutdebian.com/install3.htm

http://www.aboutdebian.com/install3.htm
http://www.aboutdebian.com/install3.htm

http://stanton-finely.net/fedora core 4 installation notes nocs.html

http://staton/finely.net/fedora core 4 installation notes nocs.html

http://www.kplug.org/apache tutorial

http://www.kplug.org/apache tutorial

http://www.sendmail.org/email-explained.html

http://www.rettesoft.hu/download/kerio/MailServer 5.5/MailServer 5.5 manual/kmss55-en-v1.pdf

http://www.cups.org/doc-1.1/overview.html

http://www.cups.org/doc-1.1/sam.html

http://www.cups.org/doc-1.1/sam.html

http://www.netfilter.org/projects/iptables

http://www.informatik.uni-hamburg.de/SVS/teaching/ws2004-05/netzsicherheit/Exercises part b.htm

http://www.squid-cache.org

http://www.blue.net.au/support/linux/setup squid proxy.html

http://infocom.cqu.edu.au/Archives/Units/1998/Autumn/85321 Systems Administration/Old Stuff/1996

Websites/85321/study-guide/textbook/chap6.html

http://infocom.cqu.edu.au/Archives/Units/1998/Autumn/85321 Systems Administration/Old Stuff/1996

Websites/85321/study-guide/textbook/chap6.html

http://infocom.cqu.edu.au/Archives/Units/1998/Autumn/85321 Systems Administration/Old Stuff/1996 Websites/85321/study-guide/textbook/chap6.html

http://infocom.cqu.edu.au/Archives/Units/1998/Autumn/85321 Systems Administration/Old Stuff/1996 Websites/85321/study-guide/textbook/chap6.html

http://www.infocom.cqc.edu.au/Archives/Units/aut2000/85321/Resources/Study Guide/Chapter 10

http://www.infocom.cqc.edu.au/Archives/Units/aut2000/85321/Resources/Study Guide/Chapter 10

http://www.infocom.cqc.edu.au/Archives/Units/aut2000/85321/Resources/Study Guide/Chapter 12

http://www.-128.ibm.com/developerworks/library/pa-migrate2

http://www.infocom.cqc.edu.au/Units/aut2000/85321/Resources/Study Guide/Chapter 14

http://www.infocom.cqc.edu.au/Units/aut2000/85321/Resources/Study Guide/Chapter 14

http://www.infocom.cqc.edu.au/Units/aut2000/85321/Resources/Study Guide/Chapter 14

http://www.infocom.cqc.edu.au/Units/aut2000/85321/Resources/Study Guide/Chapter 15

http://www.infocom.cqc.edu.au/Units/aut2000/85321/Resources/Study Guide/Chapter 15

http://www.infocom.cqc.edu.au/Units/aut2000/85321/Resources/Study Guide/Chapter 15

http://www.infocom.cqc.edu.au/Units/aut99/85321/Resources/Print Resources/Textbook/chap 16

http://www.infocom.cqc.edu.au/Units/aut99/85321/Resources/Print Resources/Textbook/chap 16

http://users.actcom.co.il/~choo/lupg/tutorials/c-on-unix/c-on-unix.html

http://users.actcom.co.il/~choo/lupg/tutorials/c-on-unix/c-on-unix.html

http://users.actcom.co.il/~choo/lupg/tutorials/c-on-unix/c-on-unix.html

http://linuxgazette.net/issue84/hawk.html

http://users.actom.co.il/~choo/lupg/tutorials/c-on-unix./c-on-unix.html

http://users.actom.co.il/~choo/lupg/tutorials/c-on-unix./c-on-unix.html

http://www.gnome.org/~newren/tutorials/dveloping-with-gnome/html/ch03.html

http://www.enterprise networksandservers.com/monthly/art.php/1685

http://konst .org.ua/articles/en/linuxcom.gnutools.html

http://dinosaur.compiler5tools.net/flex.

http://www.network-theory.co.uk/docs/pytut/tut 6.html

http://www.iu.hio.no/~mark/unix/unix.html

http://www.rubyist.net/~slagell/ruby/

http://www.faqs.org/docs/Linux-HOWTO/Xwindow-Overview-HOWTO.html

http://www.gtk.org/tutorial

http://www.inf.ethz.ch/personal/biere/projects/ccmalloc

http://ww.gnu.org/software/checker/checker.html

http://dickey.his.com/dbmalloc.html

http://www.cs.bris.ac.uk/~mm7323/DbMalloc/

http://quoru.tamu.edu/jon/gnu/

http://dmalloc.com/.

http://www.andreasen.org/LeakTreacer/

http://www.bell-labs.com/org/11356/libsafe.html

http://www.cs.vu.nl/~veldema/mcheck/mcheck.html

ftp://ftp.x.org/pub/R6.4/xc/util/memprof/

http://www.bss.lu/Memdebug/Memdebug.html

http://people.redhat.com/otaylor/memproff/

http://www.link-data.com/sourcecode.html

http://www.cbmamiga.demon.co.uk/mpatrol/

http://fscked.org/proj/njamd.shtml

http://www3.hmc.edu/~neldredge/yamd/

www.microsoft.com

www.gnu.org

www.msn.com

www.ntfs.com

www.linuxaseembly.com

http://www.linkdata.se/sourcecode.html

ftp://ftp.perens.com/pub/ElectricFence

http://www.gnu.org/software/ddd

http://ald.sourceforge.net

Websites of Interest

ccmalloc: http://www.inf.ethz.ch/personal/biere/projects/ccmalloc/
Checker: http://www.gnu.org/software/checker/checker.html
dbmalloc: http://dickey.his.com/dbmalloc/dbmalloc.html
DbMalloc: http://www.cs.bris.ac.uk/~mm7323/DbMalloc/
debauch: http://quorum.tamu.edu/jon/gnu/
dmalloc: http://dmalloc.com/
LeakTracer: http://www.andreasen.org/LeakTracer/
libsafe: http://www.bell-labs.com/org/11356/libsafe.html
MCheck: http://www.cs.vu.nl/~rveldema/mcheck/mcheck.html
Memleak (Part of X11R6.4): ftp://ftp.x.org/pub/R6.4/xc/util/memleak/
Memdebug: http://www.bss.lu/Memdebug/Memdebug.html
MemProf: http://people.redhat.com/otaylor/memprof/
Memwatch: http://www.link-data.com/sourcecode.html
mpatrol: http://www.cbmamiga.demon.co.uk/mpatrol/
NJAMD: http://fscked.org/proj/njamd.shtml
YAMD: http://www3.hmc.edu/~neldredge/yamd/
www.microsoft.com
www.gnu.org
www.msn.com
www.ntfs.com
linuxassembly.com

References

1. N.B. Venakteswarlu, Advanced Unix Programming, BS Publications, Hyderabad, 2005.
2. B.W. Kernigham and R. Pike, The Unix Programming Environment, Prentice Hall India, New Delhi, 1994.
3. S. Prata, Advanced Unix-A programmer's Guide, SAMS, New Delhi, 1986.
4. G.Nutt, Operating Systems Projects Using Windows NT, Pergamon, 1999.
5. Microsoft A Unix Migration guide, Prentice Hall India, New Delhi, 2004.
6. Aho, Sethi and Ullman,Compilers: Principles, Techniques and Tools, Addison-Wesley Pub. Co., Nov, 1985
7. Chris Drake and K. Brown, Panic! Unix System Crash Dump Analysis handbook, PH,2003.
8. Ellis Horiwitz and Sartaj Sahini,Computer Algorithms, Galgotia Publ, New Delhi 1992.
9. T.H. Cormen, C.E. Leiserson, and R.L. Reivest, Introduction to Algorithms, PHI, New Delhi, 1990.
10. Richard L. Petersen, LINUX fifth edition, The Complete Reference, TMH .
11. Shelley Powers, Jerry Peek, Timo Reilly, Mike loukides UNIX power tools.
12. Michael K. Johnson, Erik W. Troan, Linux Application DevelopmentAddison-Wesley, Hardcover, 2nd edition, Published November 2004, 702 pages, ISBN 0321219147.
13. Phillip G. Ezolt, Optimizing Linux Performance: A Hands-on Guide to Linux(R) Performance,

    Prentice Hall, March 2005.
14. Peter Abel, IBM PC Assembly language and Programming, Pearson, New Delhi, 2002.
15. Sivarama P.D, Fundamentals of Computer Organization and Design, Springer International, New Delhi, 2003.
16. Lewis, DW, Fundamentals of Embedded Software where C and assembly meet, Pearson, New Delhi, 2002.
17. Stuart Bennett, Real Time computer control: An introduction, Pearson, New Delhi, 2003.
18. Steven Holzner, C with Assembly Language, BPB, 1990.
19. Detection of Dynamic Memory Errors,David Evans, MIT laboratory for Computer Science report(NSF-9115797-CCR), evs@larch.lcs.mit.edu.
20. Davide Evans and David Larochelle, Improoving Security Using Extensible lightweight static analysis, IEEE Software, Jan/Feb, 2002.

21. Robert Mecklenburg, Managing Projects with GNU Make, 3E; Addison-Wesley.
22. Robert Love, Linux Kernel Development, Addison Wesley,
23. Chris Drake, Kimberley Brown, PANIC! UNIX System Crash Dump Analysis Handbook , www.amazon.com.
24. Cesare Pizzi, Memory Access Error Checkers, 1999, Linux Journal.
25. Ronald F. Guilmette, Compiling and Linking Under the Hood, February 2002, Linux Magazine.
26. Benjamin Chelf, Building the Perfect Executable, March 2002 Linux Magazine.
27. Benjamin Chelf, Building and Using Shared Libraries April 2002 Linux Magazine.
28. Benjamin Chelf, Linux and Executables, May 2002, Linux Magazine.
29. Jeffrey Stedfast, Alleyoop:A GUI front end for Valgrind, <fejj@ximian.com>.
30. Patrick Alken, ald:a The Assembly Language Debugger, http://ald.sourceforge.net
31. Mike Heffner, BFBtester: Brute Force Binary Tester, <mheffner@vt.edu> http://bfbtester.sourceforge.net
32. Data Display Debugger <http://www.gnu.org/software/ddd/>
33. The GNU Debugger <http://sources.redhat.com/gdb/>
34. Electric Fence <ftp://ftp.perens.com/pub/ElectricFence/>
35. Steve Best, Mastering Linux debugging techniques, IBM devloperWorks Journal, Aug, 2002.
36. Memwatch:a memory leak detection tool. http://www.linkdata.se/sourcecode.html.
37. Filip Rooms, Some Advanced Debuuging techniques in C Under Linux, filip_rooms@hotmail.com.
38. Steve Best, Debugging Memory Problems May 2003, Linux Magazine.
39. Benjamin Chelf, Dynamic MemoryAllocation -- Part II July 2001, Linux Magazine.
40. Benjamin Chelf, Dynamic MemoryAllocation -- Part I June 2001, Linux Magazine.
41. Finding memory Leaks and invalid memory use using Valgrind, Cprogramming.com.

Index

A

B

C

D

E

F

S

T

U

V

W

Y

www.ingramcontent.com/pod-product-compliance
Ingram Content Group UK Ltd.
Pitfield, Milton Keynes, MK11 3LW, UK
UKHW061534190726
13845UKWH00005B/103